Lecture Notes in Computer Science 8524

Commenced Publication in 1973
Founding and Former Series Editors:
Gerhard Goos, Juris Hartmanis, and Jan van Leeuwen

T0212219

Panayiotis Zaphiris   Andri Ioannou (Eds.)

Learning and Collaboration Technologies

Technology-Rich Environments for Learning and Collaboration

First International Conference, LCT 2014
Held as Part of HCI International 2014
Heraklion, Crete, Greece, June 22-27, 2014
Proceedings, Part II

 Springer

Volume Editors

Panayiotis Zaphiris
Andri Ioannou
Cyprus University of Technology
Department of Multimedia and Graphic Arts
Lemesos, Cyprus
E-mail: {panayiotis.zaphiris; andri.i.ioannou}@cut.ac.cy

ISSN 0302-9743   e-ISSN 1611-3349
ISBN 978-3-319-07484-9   e-ISBN 978-3-319-07485-6
DOI 10.1007/978-3-319-07485-6
Springer Cham Heidelberg New York Dordrecht London

Library of Congress Control Number: 2014939302

LNCS Sublibrary: SL 3 – Information Systems and Application,
incl. Internet/Web and HCI

Typesetting: Camera-ready by author, data conversion by Scientific Publishing Services, Chennai, India

Printed on acid-free paper

Springer is part of Springer Science+Business Media (www.springer.com)

Foreword

The 16th International Conference on Human–Computer Interaction, HCI International 2014, was held in Heraklion, Crete, Greece, during June 22–27, 2014, incorporating 14 conferences/thematic areas:

Thematic areas:

- Human–Computer Interaction
- Human Interface and the Management of Information

Affiliated conferences:

- 11th International Conference on Engineering Psychology and Cognitive Ergonomics
- 8th International Conference on Universal Access in Human–Computer Interaction
- 6th International Conference on Virtual, Augmented and Mixed Reality
- 6th International Conference on Cross-Cultural Design
- 6th International Conference on Social Computing and Social Media
- 8th International Conference on Augmented Cognition
- 5th International Conference on Digital Human Modeling and Applications in Health, Safety, Ergonomics and Risk Management
- Third International Conference on Design, User Experience and Usability
- Second International Conference on Distributed, Ambient and Pervasive Interactions
- Second International Conference on Human Aspects of Information Security, Privacy and Trust
- First International Conference on HCI in Business
- First International Conference on Learning and Collaboration Technologies

A total of 4,766 individuals from academia, research institutes, industry, and governmental agencies from 78 countries submitted contributions, and 1,476 papers and 225 posters were included in the proceedings. These papers address the latest research and development efforts and highlight the human aspects of design and use of computing systems. The papers thoroughly cover the entire field of human–computer interaction, addressing major advances in knowledge and effective use of computers in a variety of application areas.

This volume, edited by Panayiotis Zaphiris and Andri Ioannou, contains papers focusing on the thematic area of learning and collaboration technologies, addressing the following major topics:

- Virtual and augmented learning environments
- Mobile and ubiquitous learning

- Technology@school
- Collaboration, learning and training

The remaining volumes of the HCI International 2014 proceedings are:

- Volume 17, LNCS 8526, Virtual, Augmented and Mixed Reality: Applications of Virtual and Augmented Reality (Part II), edited by Randall Shumaker and Stephanie Lackey
- Volume 18, LNCS 8527, HCI in Business, edited by Fiona Fui-Hoon Nah
- Volume 19, LNCS 8528, Cross-Cultural Design, edited by P.L. Patrick Rau
- Volume 20, LNCS 8529, Digital Human Modeling and Applications in Health, Safety, Ergonomics and Risk Management, edited by Vincent G. Duffy
- Volume 21, LNCS 8530, Distributed, Ambient, and Pervasive Interactions, edited by Norbert Streitz and Panos Markopoulos
- Volume 22, LNCS 8531, Social Computing and Social Media, edited by Gabriele Meiselwitz
- Volume 23, LNAI 8532, Engineering Psychology and Cognitive Ergonomics, edited by Don Harris
- Volume 24, LNCS 8533, Human Aspects of Information Security, Privacy and Trust, edited by Theo Tryfonas and Ioannis Askoxylakis
- Volume 25, LNAI 8534, Foundations of Augmented Cognition, edited by Dylan D. Schmorrow and Cali M. Fidopiastis
- Volume 26, CCIS 434, HCI International 2014 Posters Proceedings (Part I), edited by Constantine Stephanidis
- Volume 27, CCIS 435, HCI International 2014 Posters Proceedings (Part II), edited by Constantine Stephanidis

I would like to thank the Program Chairs and the members of the Program Boards of all affiliated conferences and thematic areas, listed below, for their contribution to the highest scientific quality and the overall success of the HCI International 2014 Conference.

This conference could not have been possible without the continuous support and advice of the founding chair and conference scientific advisor, Prof. Gavriel Salvendy, as well as the dedicated work and outstanding efforts of the communications chair and editor of *HCI International News*, Dr. Abbas Moallem.

I would also like to thank for their contribution towards the smooth organization of the HCI International 2014 Conference the members of the Human–Computer Interaction Laboratory of ICS-FORTH, and in particular George Paparoulis, Maria Pitsoulaki, Maria Bouhli, and George Kapnas.

April 2014   Constantine Stephanidis
                                        General Chair, HCI International 2014

Organization

Human–Computer Interaction

Program Chair: Masaaki Kurosu, Japan

Jose Abdelnour-Nocera, UK
Sebastiano Bagnara, Italy
Simone Barbosa, Brazil
Adriana Betiol, Brazil
Simone Borsci, UK
Henry Duh, Australia
Xiaowen Fang, USA
Vicki Hanson, UK
Wonil Hwang, Korea
Minna Isomursu, Finland
Yong Gu Ji, Korea
Anirudha Joshi, India
Esther Jun, USA
Kyungdoh Kim, Korea

Heidi Krömker, Germany
Chen Ling, USA
Chang S. Nam, USA
Naoko Okuizumi, Japan
Philippe Palanque, France
Ling Rothrock, USA
Naoki Sakakibara, Japan
Dominique Scapin, France
Guangfeng Song, USA
Sanjay Tripathi, India
Chui Yin Wong, Malaysia
Toshiki Yamaoka, Japan
Kazuhiko Yamazaki, Japan
Ryoji Yoshitake, Japan

Human Interface and the Management of Information

Program Chair: Sakae Yamamoto, Japan

Alan Chan, Hong Kong
Denis A. Coelho, Portugal
Linda Elliott, USA
Shin'ichi Fukuzumi, Japan
Michitaka Hirose, Japan
Makoto Itoh, Japan
Yen-Yu Kang, Taiwan
Koji Kimita, Japan
Daiji Kobayashi, Japan

Hiroyuki Miki, Japan
Hirohiko Mori, Japan
Shogo Nishida, Japan
Robert Proctor, USA
Youngho Rhee, Korea
Ryosuke Saga, Japan
Katsunori Shimohara, Japan
Kim-Phuong Vu, USA
Tomio Watanabe, Japan

Engineering Psychology and Cognitive Ergonomics

Program Chair: Don Harris, UK

Guy Andre Boy, USA
Shan Fu, P.R. China
Hung-Sying Jing, Taiwan
Wen-Chin Li, Taiwan
Mark Neerincx, The Netherlands
Jan Noyes, UK
Paul Salmon, Australia

Axel Schulte, Germany
Siraj Shaikh, UK
Sarah Sharples, UK
Anthony Smoker, UK
Neville Stanton, UK
Alex Stedmon, UK
Andrew Thatcher, South Africa

Universal Access in Human–Computer Interaction

**Program Chairs: Constantine Stephanidis, Greece,
and Margherita Antona, Greece**

Julio Abascal, Spain
Gisela Susanne Bahr, USA
João Barroso, Portugal
Margrit Betke, USA
Anthony Brooks, Denmark
Christian Bühler, Germany
Stefan Carmien, Spain
Hua Dong, P.R. China
Carlos Duarte, Portugal
Pier Luigi Emiliani, Italy
Qin Gao, P.R. China
Andrina Granić, Croatia
Andreas Holzinger, Austria
Josette Jones, USA
Simeon Keates, UK

Georgios Kouroupetroglou, Greece
Patrick Langdon, UK
Barbara Leporini, Italy
Eugene Loos, The Netherlands
Ana Isabel Paraguay, Brazil
Helen Petrie, UK
Michael Pieper, Germany
Enrico Pontelli, USA
Jaime Sanchez, Chile
Alberto Sanna, Italy
Anthony Savidis, Greece
Christian Stary, Austria
Hirotada Ueda, Japan
Gerhard Weber, Germany
Harald Weber, Germany

Virtual, Augmented and Mixed Reality

**Program Chairs: Randall Shumaker, USA,
and Stephanie Lackey, USA**

Roland Blach, Germany
Sheryl Brahnam, USA
Juan Cendan, USA
Jessie Chen, USA
Panagiotis D. Kaklis, UK

Hirokazu Kato, Japan
Denis Laurendeau, Canada
Fotis Liarokapis, UK
Michael Macedonia, USA
Gordon Mair, UK

Jose San Martin, Spain
Tabitha Peck, USA
Christian Sandor, Australia

Christopher Stapleton, USA
Gregory Welch, USA

Cross-Cultural Design

Program Chair: P.L. Patrick Rau, P.R. China

Yee-Yin Choong, USA
Paul Fu, USA
Zhiyong Fu, P.R. China
Pin-Chao Liao, P.R. China
Dyi-Yih Michael Lin, Taiwan
Rungtai Lin, Taiwan
Ta-Ping (Robert) Lu, Taiwan
Liang Ma, P.R. China
Alexander Mädche, Germany

Sheau-Farn Max Liang, Taiwan
Katsuhiko Ogawa, Japan
Tom Plocher, USA
Huatong Sun, USA
Emil Tso, P.R. China
Hsiu-Ping Yueh, Taiwan
Liang (Leon) Zeng, USA
Jia Zhou, P.R. China

Online Communities and Social Media

Program Chair: Gabriele Meiselwitz, USA

Leonelo Almeida, Brazil
Chee Siang Ang, UK
Aneesha Bakharia, Australia
Ania Bobrowicz, UK
James Braman, USA
Farzin Deravi, UK
Carsten Kleiner, Germany
Niki Lambropoulos, Greece
Soo Ling Lim, UK

Anthony Norcio, USA
Portia Pusey, USA
Panote Siriaraya, UK
Stefan Stieglitz, Germany
Giovanni Vincenti, USA
Yuanqiong (Kathy) Wang, USA
June Wei, USA
Brian Wentz, USA

Augmented Cognition

Program Chairs: Dylan D. Schmorrow, USA, and Cali M. Fidopiastis, USA

Ahmed Abdelkhalek, USA
Robert Atkinson, USA
Monique Beaudoin, USA
John Blitch, USA
Alenka Brown, USA

Rosario Cannavò, Italy
Joseph Cohn, USA
Andrew J. Cowell, USA
Martha Crosby, USA
Wai-Tat Fu, USA

Digital Human Modeling and Applications in Health, Safety, Ergonomics and Risk Management

Program Chair: Vincent G. Duffy, USA

Design, User Experience, and Usability

Program Chair: Aaron Marcus, USA

Distributed, Ambient and Pervasive Interactions

Program Chairs: Norbert Streitz, Germany, and Panos Markopoulos, The Netherlands

Juan Carlos Augusto, UK
Jose Bravo, Spain
Adrian Cheok, UK
Boris de Ruyter, The Netherlands
Anind Dey, USA
Dimitris Grammenos, Greece
Nuno Guimaraes, Portugal
Achilles Kameas, Greece
Javed Vassilis Khan, The Netherlands
Shin'ichi Konomi, Japan
Carsten Magerkurth, Switzerland

Ingrid Mulder, The Netherlands
Anton Nijholt, The Netherlands
Fabio Paternó, Italy
Carsten Röcker, Germany
Teresa Romao, Portugal
Albert Ali Salah, Turkey
Manfred Tscheligi, Austria
Reiner Wichert, Germany
Woontack Woo, Korea
Xenophon Zabulis, Greece

Human Aspects of Information Security, Privacy and Trust

Program Chairs: Theo Tryfonas, UK, and Ioannis Askoxylakis, Greece

Claudio Agostino Ardagna, Italy
Zinaida Benenson, Germany
Daniele Catteddu, Italy
Raoul Chiesa, Italy
Bryan Cline, USA
Sadie Creese, UK
Jorge Cuellar, Germany
Marc Dacier, USA
Dieter Gollmann, Germany
Kirstie Hawkey, Canada
Jaap-Henk Hoepman, The Netherlands
Cagatay Karabat, Turkey
Angelos Keromytis, USA
Ayako Komatsu, Japan
Ronald Leenes, The Netherlands
Javier Lopez, Spain
Steve Marsh, Canada

Gregorio Martinez, Spain
Emilio Mordini, Italy
Yuko Murayama, Japan
Masakatsu Nishigaki, Japan
Aljosa Pasic, Spain
Milan Petković, The Netherlands
Joachim Posegga, Germany
Jean-Jacques Quisquater, Belgium
Damien Sauveron, France
George Spanoudakis, UK
Kerry-Lynn Thomson, South Africa
Julien Touzeau, France
Theo Tryfonas, UK
João Vilela, Portugal
Claire Vishik, UK
Melanie Volkamer, Germany

HCI in Business

Program Chair: Fiona Fui-Hoon Nah, USA

Andreas Auinger, Austria
Michel Avital, Denmark
Traci Carte, USA
Hock Chuan Chan, Singapore
Constantinos Coursaris, USA
Soussan Djamasbi, USA
Brenda Eschenbrenner, USA
Nobuyuki Fukawa, USA
Khaled Hassanein, Canada
Milena Head, Canada
Susanna (Shuk Ying) Ho, Australia
Jack Zhenhui Jiang, Singapore
Jinwoo Kim, Korea
Zoonky Lee, Korea
Honglei Li, UK
Nicholas Lockwood, USA
Eleanor T. Loiacono, USA
Mei Lu, USA

Scott McCoy, USA
Brian Mennecke, USA
Robin Poston, USA
Lingyun Qiu, P.R. China
Rene Riedl, Austria
Matti Rossi, Finland
April Savoy, USA
Shu Schiller, USA
Hong Sheng, USA
Choon Ling Sia, Hong Kong
Chee-Wee Tan, Denmark
Chuan Hoo Tan, Hong Kong
Noam Tractinsky, Israel
Horst Treiblmaier, Austria
Virpi Tuunainen, Finland
Dezhi Wu, USA
I-Chin Wu, Taiwan

Learning and Collaboration Technologies

Program Chairs: Panayiotis Zaphiris, Cyprus, and Andri Ioannou, Cyprus

Ruthi Aladjem, Israel
Abdulaziz Aldaej, UK
John M. Carroll, USA
Maka Eradze, Estonia
Mikhail Fominykh, Norway
Denis Gillet, Switzerland
Mustafa Murat Inceoglu, Turkey
Pernilla Josefsson, Sweden
Marie Joubert, UK
Sauli Kiviranta, Finland
Tomaž Klobučar, Slovenia
Elena Kyza, Cyprus
Maarten de Laat, The Netherlands
David Lamas, Estonia

Edmund Laugasson, Estonia
Ana Loureiro, Portugal
Katherine Maillet, France
Nadia Pantidi, UK
Antigoni Parmaxi, Cyprus
Borzoo Pourabdollahian, Italy
Janet C. Read, UK
Christophe Reffay, France
Nicos Souleles, Cyprus
Ana Luísa Torres, Portugal
Stefan Trausan-Matu, Romania
Aimilia Tzanavari, Cyprus
Johnny Yuen, Hong Kong
Carmen Zahn, Switzerland

External Reviewers

Ilia Adami, Greece
Iosif Klironomos, Greece
Maria Korozi, Greece
Vassilis Kouroumalis, Greece

Asterios Leonidis, Greece
George Margetis, Greece
Stavroula Ntoa, Greece
Nikolaos Partarakis, Greece

HCI International 2015

The 15th International Conference on Human–Computer Interaction, HCI International 2015, will be held jointly with the affiliated conferences in Los Angeles, CA, USA, in the Westin Bonaventure Hotel, August 2–7, 2015. It will cover a broad spectrum of themes related to HCI, including theoretical issues, methods, tools, processes, and case studies in HCI design, as well as novel interaction techniques, interfaces, and applications. The proceedings will be published by Springer. More information will be available on the conference website:
http://www.hcii2015.org/

General Chair
Professor Constantine Stephanidis
University of Crete and ICS-FORTH
Heraklion, Crete, Greece
E-mail: cs@ics.forth.gr

Table of Contents – Part II

Virtual and Augmented Learning Environments

Mobile and Ubiquitous Learning

Technology@School

Collaboration, Learning and Training

Table of Contents – Part I

Design of Learning Technologies

Novel Approaches in eLearning

Student Modeling and Learning Behaviour

Supporting Problem-Based, Inquiry-Based, Project Based and Blended Learning

Virtual and Augmented Learning Environments

The Effect of Split Attention in Surgical Education

Erol Özçelik[1], Nergiz Ercil Cagiltay[2], Gokhan Sengul[1],
Emre Tuner[2], and Bulent Unal[3]

[1] Atilim University Computer Engineering Department, Kızılcaşar Mahallesi, 06836 İncek
Gölbaşı – Ankara, Turkey
[2] Atilim University Software Engineering Department, Kızılcaşar Mahallesi, 06836 İncek
Gölbaşı – Ankara, Turkey
[3] Atilim University, Department of Industrial Product Design, Kızılcaşar Mahallesi, 06836
İncek Gölbaşı – Ankara, Turkey
eozcelik@atilim.edu.tr

Abstract. Surgical education through simulation is an important area to improve the level of education and to decrease the risks, ethical considerations and cost of the educational environments. In the literature there are several studies conducted to better understand the effect of these simulation environments on learning. However among those studies the human-computer interaction point of view is very limited. Surgeons need to look at radiological images such as magnetic resonance images (MRI) to be sure about the location of the patient's tumor during a surgical operation. Thus, they go back and forth between physically separated places (e.g. the operating table and light screen display for MRI volume sets). This study is conducted to investigate the effect of presenting different information sources in close proximity on human performance in surgical education. For this purpose, we have developed a surgical education simulation scenario which is controlled by a haptic interface. To better understand the effect of split attention in surgical education, an experimental study is conducted with 27 subjects. The descriptive results of study show that even the integrated group performed the tasks with a higher accuracy level (by traveling less distance, entering less wrong directions and hitting less walls), the results are not statistically significant. Accordingly, even there are some evidences about the effect of split attention on surgical simulation environments, the results of this study need to be validated by controlling students' skill levels on controlling the haptic devices and 2D/3D space perception skills. The results of this study may guide the system developers to better design the HCI interface of their designs especially for the area of surgical simulation.

1 Introduction

The Cognitive Theory of Multimedia Learning (Mayer, 2011) suggests that when information sources are presented far from each other rather than close to each other, performance of users decreases. It is suggested that searching for information consumes limited resources in the mind and consequently fewer cognitive resources will be available for the current task (Kalyuga, Chandler, & Sweller, 1999). As a

P. Zaphiris and A. Ioannou (Eds.): LCT 2014, Part II, LNCS 8524, pp. 3–10, 2014.

result, unnecessarily splitting of attention between information sources causes cognitive load that interferes with task performance (van Merrinboer & Sweller, 2005). In light of these theoretical suggestions, the goal of this study is to investigate the effect of spatial distance of different information sources on human performance in surgical education. For this purpose, we have developed a surgical education simulation scenario which is controlled by a haptic interface. To better understand the effect of split attention in surgical education, an experimental study is conducted. In this study, learners use the haptic simulator in order to navigate to a goal place that is presented either in the same screen or in a screen that is apart to the simulator's screen. Half of the learners complete the tasks in an integrated environment and the rest complete the tasks in a split environment. Performance is measured in terms of accuracy and task completion time. The study is conducted by 27 participants who have the same background and having no previous training on the surgical operation. The data is collected by the computer simulation measurements that are automatically recorded by the simulation system on the performance and behaviors of the trainee while using the simulator individually. We believe that this study will guide the user interface designers for surgical education simulation systems to better design and guide trainees.

2   Research Methodology

In this study, to better understand the effect of split attention in surgical education, first a surgical simulation environment that is controlled by a haptic device is developed. This simulation is basically developed for endoscopic surgery purposes. In this type of surgery operations, natural body cavities are used as entry points of the operations. In these kind of operations surgeons use a special type of camera namely endoscope, reach the operation location and complete the operation by the help of special surgical equipment. Although these kinds of surgeries have their advantages, they come with certain problems. One of the major problems is that endoscopic view is two-dimensional, not three-dimensional. In that concern, lack of depth perception can cause serious injuries and even cause patient deaths if not handled carefully in the training period. Surgeon has to operate without having the three-dimensional view and has to gain critical hand-eye coordination skills (Cotin, Delingette & Ayache, 2000). Additionally, surgeons are required to perform the operations causing minimal damage to the surgical area. Hence the accuracy of the surgeon during the operation is important. The surgical simulation tool is designed and developed according to these requirements. Below the details of the research study is provided.

3   Participants

The participants of the study were 27 undergraduate students of Atilim University who were taking Computer Games and Simulation course. They participated in the experiment for extra course credit. The participants ages were ranging from 20 to 26 years old ($M = 23.67$, $SD = 1.49$). The majority (70 %) of the participants were male.

4   Endoscopic Surgery Simulation Tool (ESST)

The endoscopic surgery simulation tool that is developed for this study is developed based on a three dimensional (3D) model of a simulated environment containing different branches of vessel like holes as seen in Figure 1. The designed model has 2 branches of vessel like holes (Figure 1).

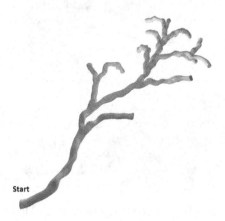

Fig. 1. ESST Model Branches

The participants are able to move inside the 3D model starting from the "Start" point as shown in Figure 1. Figure 1 shows the structure of the 3D Model used for ESST and Figure 2 shows the 3D view of the model while the users move inside the model. This view is prepared to simulate an endoscopic view of the surgical operations.

Fig. 2. ESST Model 3D View

The participants can move inside the 3D modeled environment by using a special haptic device which provides more senses about the simulated environment. As seen in Figure 3, the haptic device is used as an endoscope (a tool having a camera showing the surgical environment in two-dimensional view).

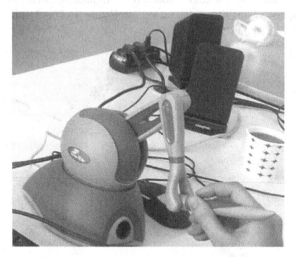

Fig. 3. The Haptic interface of the ESST Model

The ESST is prepared by distributing 10 green balls in 10 branches of the model as seen in Figure 4. Hence, the ESST model designed as containing 10 target nodes as numbered in Figure 4.

Fig. 4. The Target nodes in ESST Model

Additional to the ESST, a map is prepared for the experimental design showing the structure of the model and the locations of each target in three different perspectives: top, right and left views of the model map as seen in Figure 5.

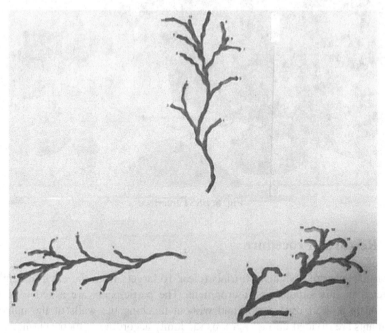

Fig. 5. ESST Model Maps

The participants are asked to find each target and clear it from the environment starting from the start point of the mode (Figure 1) and following the related path as shown in the model map (Figure 5). The participants are asked to clear the targets in an ordered way as shown in the ESST model map (Figure 5). In other words, the participants are asked to start from the starting point of the model view and first clear target 1 by following the first right branch of the model. Immediately after the participant clears target 1, the participants is replaced to the start point and asked to clear target 2 by following the path from the start point of the ESST model map. Immediately after clearing target 10, the experiment ends. The participants are also able to see the target number on the model screen that is aimed to be cleared in the current time period. Hence the participants are required to analyze the ESST model map in order to better understand the path to be followed in order to clear the identified target. During this process they are also asked to complete all task in minimum time period by traveling minimum path. Additionally they are also requested not to hit the walls and move in gentle steps. This design is prepared according to the requirements of endoscopic surgery environments. Accordingly, as seen in Figure 6, the haptic interface is also designed as sensible as in the endoscopic surgery environments. The system recorded time spent for completing each task (task completion time), the distance traveled during completing each trial (traveled path distance), number of entrance of wrong paths during completing each task (wrong direction count) and number of hits to the walls (hits to the walls).

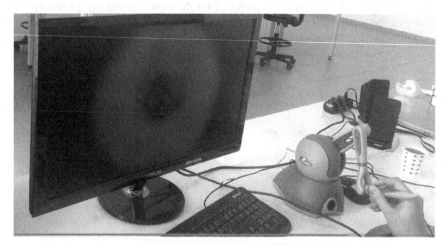

Fig. 6. ESST Interface

5   Research Procedure

The participants are assigned 10 trials (clear 10 targets from the environment) to be completed in this simulation environment. The participants are asked to complete each trial in a short time period and without touching the walls of the model. The participants are divided into two groups randomly according to their entrance order to the laboratory. The integrated group performs the tasks in the simulation environment where the ESST Model Map is placed next to the computer monitor , very close to the simulation screen (Figure 7).

Fig. 7. Group 1: ESST Model Map Placed Next to ESST Screen (Integrated Group)

As seen from Figure 8, the participants in the split group are asked to perform the tasks, but the ESST Model Map is placed away from the ESST screen.

Fig. 8. Group 2: ESST Model Map Placed Away from the ESST Screen (Split Group)

Each participant is given 2 tries in order to better understand the environment and the usage of the haptic device in the training phase. The mentioned dependent variables are recorded automatically by the simulation tool.

6   Results

An independent samples t-test was run to examine the effect of group on task completion time. The results showed that the effect of group was not significant, $t(25) = .15$, $p = .88$. The effect of group on distance of the traveled path was not significant, $t(25) = .23$, $p = .07$. No significant effect of group was found on number of wrong directions followed, $t(25) = .15$, $p = .88$ and on number of hits to the walls, $t(25) = .69$, $p = .50$. The non-significant results of statistical analysis may be due to high variance observed in the dependent variables (see Table 1) and to diverse skills of the participants.

Table 1. The dependent variables with respect to the group

Group	Task competition time		Traveled path distance		Wrong direction count		Hits to the walls	
	M	*SD*	*M*	*SD*	*M*	*SD*	*M*	*SD*
Integrated Group	49.47	20.27	3902.22	7228.78	1.47	0.63	135.32	51.79
Split Group	50.98	30.89	14406.68	30081.80	1.51	0.66	150.49	62.41

7   Discussions and Conclusion

In this study, the effect of split attention on human performance in an environment which reflects the endoscopic surgery simulation environments. In this environment a haptic device is used for representing an endoscopic view. The results of this study show that even the integrated group performed the tasks with a higher accuracy (by traveling less distance, entering less wrong directions and less hitting the walls), the results are not statistically significant. We believe that the main reason for this non-significant result is the high standard deviations. In other words, there was a big deviation among the performance of each participant. In this study all participants were having the same background. However, in this study the skill levels of each participant need to be considered as well. In this environment participants had to operate without having the three-dimensional view and had to gain critical hand-eye coordination skills as in endoscopic surgery operation environments (Cotin, Delingette & Ayache, 2000). Additionally, their 2D/3D space perception (Greco et al., 2010) was another important skill affecting their performance. Finally their ability to control the haptic device was another factor affecting their performance. We believe that the participants who have gained these skills in their earlier experiences with game environments may outperform the others which in turn caused the variance in the standard deviation values. For example playing games by using joystick or similar devices may be an affective factor for better skills on haptic control. In this study we did not collect this democratic information from the participants. Hence by controlling the participants' skill levels for controlling the haptic device and for cognitive processes of 2D/3D space perception skills, this variation in the standard deviations may be eliminated.

Acknowledgement. This study is conducted for improving the scenario designs of the educational materials which are developed for neurosurgery education project (ECE: Tubitak 1001, Project No: 112K287) purposes. The authors would like to thank the support of TÜBİTAK 1001 program for realizing the ECE project.

References

1. Cotin, S., Delingette, H., Ayache, N.: A hybrid elastic model for real-time cutting, deformations, and force feedback for surgery training and simulation. The Visual Computer 16, 437–452 (2000)
2. Greco, E.F., Regehr, G., Okrainec, A.: Identifying and Classifying Problem Areas in Laparoscopic Skills Acquisition: Can Simulators Help? Academic Medicine 85(10), S5–S8 (2010)
3. Kalyuga, S., Chandler, P., Sweller, J.: Managing split-attention and redundancy in multimedia instruction. Applied Cognitive Psychology 13, 351–371 (1999)
4. Mayer, R.E.: Multimedia learning. University Press, Cambridge (2001)
5. Van Merrienboer, J.J., Sweller, J.: Cognitive load theory and complex learning: Recent developments and future directions. Educational Psychology Review 17(2), 147–177 (2005)

Supporting Learning with 3D Interactive Applications in Early Years

Antonia Cascales Martínez[1], María-José Martínez-Segura[1], Maria Laguna-Segovia[2], David C. Pérez-López[3] and Manuel Contero[3]

[1] Universidad de Murcia, Avda. Teniente Flomesta 5, 30003 Murcia, Spain
antonia.cascales@um.es
[2] Universidad de Alicante, Cra. San Vicente del Raspeig s/n,
03690 San Vicente del Raspeig, Spain
isabel.laguna@ua.es
[3] Instituto de Investigación en Bioingeniería y Tecnología Orientada al Ser Humano (I3BH), Universitat Politècnica de València, Camino de Vera s/n, 46022 Valencia, Spain
{dapelo,mcontero}@i3bh.es

Abstract. Early years education is an key element for the introduction of children in the education system. In order to improve this process, the aim of this study was to explore how guided interaction with 3D apps can fit into a preschool setting, how it can help children learn through playing and how it can improve their learning outcomes. A study was conducted with six classes of 87 students aged between 3 years to 6 years, over a 12-week period. Children used 10 inch Android tablets with a series of apps developed by our research team, about houses of the world, the skeleton & five senses and, animals. A quasi-experimental design based on a nonequivalent groups pretest and posttest design revealed that an active behavior and better learning outcomes are obtained by children participating in the experimental group.

Keywords: augmented reality, preschool, knowledge.

1 Introduction

Learning through playing and child-initiated activity is central to preschool education for children aged between 3 and 5. In this context, 3D interactive applications (apps) used on digital tablets can provide better support for mobility and collaborative use. They are easy to integrate into game activities and they also are funny. This range of technologies also increases pupils' confidence, supports learning in all the curricular areas, is more affordable for preschoolers and gives children the opportunity to work on competences and knowledge that they may develop in their life

3D apps as an educational tool can help the students to develop their own aptitude to learn by increasing self-esteem and confidence. They also have potential for promoting pleasure in learning by enhancing engagement, motivation and the desire to learn. Therefore, when students' activities are supported by guided interaction there is a potential to promote the three main areas of learning according to the Spanish legislation: "Knowledge of self and personal autonomy", "Social, physical and natural environments", and "Languages".

P. Zaphiris and A. Ioannou (Eds.): LCT 2014, Part II, LNCS 8524, pp. 11–22, 2014.

2   Related Work

Children's learning with ICT goes beyond developing skills such as using a mouse or developing hand–eye coordination. When their encounters with ICT are supported by guided interaction there is a big potential to promote learning [1]. To maximize the learning benefits of ICT and 3D apps it is required a responsive, reflective and pedagogical response, encouraging pleasure and engagement as well as operational skills. Guided interaction as a mean to creating opportunities for supported learning with 3D interactive applications in early years is at the core of this research.

Progressive reduction in the cost of tablet devices is opening an opportunity to explore the introduction of more natural interfaces for the design of learning applications. Multitouch interaction has changed the way technology is adopted in classrooms for all ages [2]. Nowadays children are exposed to it on mobile phones and tablets at a very early age. Tablets portability is a great advantage to promote cooperation and collaboration though sharing activities that are very interesting from an educational point of view [3, 4, 5].

Couse and Chen [6] studied the use of tablet computers in early education by analyzing preschool children's ease in adapting to tablet technology and its effectiveness in engaging them to draw. The study found significant differences in level of tablet use between sessions, and engagement increased with age. Participant teachers stated high child interest and children quickly developed ease with the stylus for drawing.

According to Kearney [7], educational apps should been designed to include aspects that are relevant to the child's development: social experiences, expressive tools and control; so they can help children in their motor-skill and cognitive development.

Rankothge et al. [8] conducted a study on the introduction of a technology assisted tool for the learning skills development in early childhood. The final outcome was a Tablet PC based application to help the children in their learning experience at early ages. The developed tool improved the writing and speaking skills of the participant children in an entertainment based way.

Sandvik et al. [9] concluded that tablets devices were able to raise kindergarten children language and literacy skills through interaction with an image repository. It was tested that children developed the ability to pick up elements from the real-world contexts and connect them to technology.

Priyankara et al. [10] investigated how to support self-learning of preschoolers. They developed a tablet learning tool that facilitates self-learning of preschool kids. Their app allowed kids to develop cognitive and psychomotor skills such as drawing, writing, recognition of numbers, basic shapes and colors and logical thinking.

Other authors such as Zanchi et al. [11] have used tablet games to support preschool math learning, while Meyer [12] focused on the design of learning material for preschool teaching and learning through the example of a game-based platform for learning English.

3   Case Study

This paper shows the use of 3D interactive applications on tablets in an early years classroom as a tool to support the development of technological skills in a creative environment; environment which is rich in literacy and knowledge opportunities in the three main areas of learning: "Knowledge of self and personal autonomy", "Social, physical and natural environments", and "Languages". The pilot project illustrates how a three-phase process can result in the development of: (1) emergent literacy, (2) digital access preschool learners and (3) basic knowledge concepts of three main areas of learning (Fig. 1).

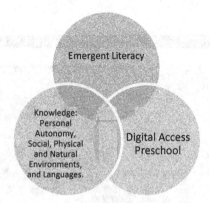

Fig. 1. The pilot project development context

The study was conducted on six groups of eighty seven preschoolers. All groups belonged to the second cycle of pre-primary education, according to the Spanish education system, but they were not the same age. The experiment was performed on a 12-week period. During this period, the students were introduced to the lessons of the skeleton & five senses, animals and houses of the world by using 3D apps on tablets.

Students were expected to acquire both general information about the studied topics and the three main areas of learning: "Knowledge of self and personal autonomy", "Social, physical and natural environments", and "Languages".

This experience has been developed using 10 inch low cost Android tablets as the hardware platform. The 3D interactive applications provide two kinds of activities, "Lesson" and "Exercises". In "Lesson" mode the contents allows the user to observe the scene; there is no more interaction than exploring 3D models from different points of view while listening to the corresponding audio. In "Exercises" mode two games are proposed: "Association", where the user has to associate concepts, and "Composition", where students are asked to compose an object using different elements.

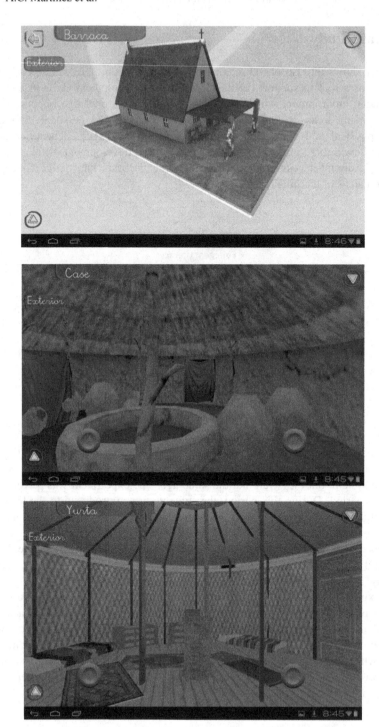

Fig. 2. Different screenshots of the "houses of world" 3D interactive app

Finally, in this research two versions of the didactic units were created, the difference between them was that the "experimental unit" provided the 3D interactive applications described above while de "control unit" provided traditional contents. In this way, both groups have the same educational curriculum content. Therefore, the independent variable of this research was the presence of 3D apps on tablets as a didactic tool. During the pilot study, teachers developed ways of actively guiding and extending children's learning through questioning, modeling, praising and acting as a supportive presence.

3.1   Research Questions

The aim of this study were to explore how guided interaction of 3D Interactive Applications can fit into a preschool culture of child, how it can help them to learn through playing and how it can improve their learning outcomes, without losing sight of children's' many other responsibilities in the classroom. The research questions were:

1. Is there any difference in the students' learning results depending on which of the two proposed teaching scenarios they used?
2. Are there any differences among the three main curricular areas depending on which of the two proposed teaching scenarios are used?
3. Are there any difficulties or barriers that compromise the acceptability of 3D interactive applications on tablets in learning environments depending on kind of worked topics?

3.2   Procedure

The experiment followed a quasi-experimental design based on a nonequivalent group pretest-posttest [14]. Under this schema, one group (the experimental group) received the intervention (3D interactive applications) while the other group (the control group) does not use 3D apps. Therefore, not all the students participated in both learning scenarios. However, that research takes into account the main principles of applied ethics: profit maximization, fairness, confidentiality, autonomy and non-maleficence [15] [16].

3.3   Participants

The pilot study was conducted with six classes of 87 students aged between 3 years to 6 years, over a 12-week period. The sample consisted of: two groups of three-years-old, with 24 students; two groups of four-years-old, with 30 students; and two groups of five-years-old, with 33 students (Table 1). Initial conditions for all groups were not similar: each group was composed by a different number of children. In addition, its relationship with the ICT was very different. None of the groups had studied the topics previously. A text document was provided to students and their parents outlining the purpose of the research and their right to withdraw at any moment. Informed consent was obtained for every participant.

Table 1. Demographic subject information   grouped by age

| | Control Group | | | Experimental Group | | |
| | Gender | | | Gender | | |
Age Group	N	M	F	N	M	F
3 to 4 years old	12	7	5	12	6	6
4 to 5 years old	15	8	7	15	7	8
5 to 6 years old	16	11	5	17	10	7
Total	**43**	26	17	**44**	23	21

3.4   Instrument

The assessment of the didactic units for each of the groups was performed by the participant teachers that completed an evaluative categorical scale for each of the participating students. This scale consisted of different items corresponding to the specific learning outcomes conforming to each of the three main learning areas. Each item was checked according the next categories: A (Achieved), IP (In process) and NA (Not Achieved).

In each area different items were evaluated, all of them were adapted to the age of the students. In the first area, the items were related to their possibilities of action and identity. While in the area number three, the items are more related to the acquisition of reading and writing ability, language and the visual arts. Items valued in the area number two are specific to the studied topics.

3.5   Treatment Plan and Analysis of Information

Once the information collection was done, we proceeded to its analysis using SPSS program (v. 19). The nature of the variables has led us to apply different statistical techniques to achieve the main research goals, that is: direct reading of each of the variables (calculating frequencies and percentages), grouping variables (contingency tables, calculating frequencies and percentages), and performing nonparametric tests comparing several independent samples (Mann-Whitney U test taking a critical level $\alpha=.05$)

To measure the internal consistency of students' categorical estimation scale a Cronbach alpha coefficient was calculated, yielding a value of .976, indicating that the instrument has high internal consistency. To consider the internal reliability of statements concerning the same construct as satisfactory, Cronbach alpha should be greater than 0.7 [3]. Construct validity was obtained from a content validity.

4   Results

Following are the results for each of the specific raised issues.

4.1   Research Question 1

Is there any difference in the students' learning results depending on which of the two proposed teaching scenarios they used?

Table 2. Three curricular areas descriptive statistics for both gorups

Areas	Control Group			Experimental Group		
	N	M	SD	N	M	SD
Knowledge of self and personal autonomy	43	1.70	0.67	44	2.66	0.48
Social, physical and natural environments	43	1.88	0.70	44	2.77	0.42
Languages	43	1.93	0.70	44	2.82	0.39
Total		1.84	0.58		2.75	0.35

Table 2 shows total descriptive statistics used to describe learning results in two teaching scenarios, using tablets o not using tablets. For all curricular areas, the mean scores corresponding at using tablets (M =2.75, SD = 0.35) are higher than those of not using tablets (M = 1.84, SD = 0.58). Whereas all mean scores not using tablets are below 2, while all mean scores using tablets are above 2. The highest differences among mean scores were yielded by "Knowledge of self and personal autonomy" area (M_c = 1.70, M_e = 2.66, M_e-M_c = 0.96). The lowest difference was produced by the "Social, physical and natural environments area" (M_c =1.88, M_e = 2.77, M_e-M_c = 0.89), and "Languages" area (M_c = 1.93, M_e = 2.82, M_e-M_c = 0.89).

For each of the three areas a Mann-Whitney U test was conducted to evaluate the hypothesis that control group students would score lower than experimental group students on the three curricular areas. The results of all the tests were in the expected direction and significant Uarea1 = 297, parea1 < .001, rarea1 = 0.63; Uarea2 = 326, parea2 < .001, rarea2 = 0.62; Uarea3 = 322, parea3 < .001, rarea3 = 0.63.

Table 3. Mann-Whitney U test

	Area 1	Area 2	Area 3
U	297	326	322
p	<.001	<.001	<.001
r	0.63	0.62	0.63

4.2   Research Question 2

Are there any differences among the three main curricular areas depending on which of the two proposed teaching scenarios are used?

Table 4. Curricular areas descriptive statistics for both groups and grouped by student age

3 to 4 years old	Control Group			Experimental Group		
	N	M	SD	N	M	SD
Knowledge of self and personal autonomy	12	1.58	0.67	12	2.58	0.51
Social, physical and natural environments	12	1.75	0.62	12	2.67	0.49
Languages	12	1.92	0.79	12	2.75	0.45
4 to 5 years old	**Control Group**			**Experimental Group**		
	N	M	SD	N	M	SD
Knowledge of self and personal autonomy	15	1.53	0.52	15	2.67	0.49
Social, physical and natural environments	15	1.73	0.59	15	2.80	0.41
Languages	15	1.73	0.46	15	2.87	0.35
5 to 6 years old	**Control Group**			**Experimental Group**		
	N	M	SD	N	M	SD
Knowledge of self and personal autonomy	16	1.94	0.77	17	2.71	0.47
Social, physical and natural environments	16	2.13	0.80	17	2.82	0.39
Languages	16	2.13	0.81	17	2.82	0.39

Table 4 shows the mean scores and standard deviations for each of the areas that compose the curriculum for levels. The highest mean score corresponds in all cases to experimental groups which could mean that the 3D apps learning scenario is better than the other scenario. Mean scores and standard deviations for the different levels are aligned with the results obtained in our own previous studies about supporting learning with 3D interactive applications [17]. The mean scores were higher in all cases. Regarding curricular areas, the highest differences among mean scores were yielded by "Knowledge of self and personal autonomy" area, 3 to 4 years old (M_c = 1.58, M_e = 2.58, M_e-M_c = 1.00), 4 to 5 years old (M_c =1.53, M_e = 2.67, M_e-M_c = 1.14) and 5 to 6 years old (M_c =1.94, M_e = 2.71, M_e-M_c = 0.77). It is high at the level of 4 to 5 years old and 5 to 6 years old and it is identical in the areas "Social, physical and natural environments" and "Languages" for the control group.

None of scores in the experimental group showed a mean value lower than 2.58, thus, these students outperformed the result by the traditional way of teaching the course and they were slightly more motivated when 3D apps were used.

Once again, a Mann-Whitney U test was conducted to evaluate the hypothesis that control group students would score lower than experimental group students on the three curricular areas. The results of all the tests were in the expected direction and significant as can be seen in Table 5.

Table 5. Mann-Whitney U test

	3 to 4 years old			4 to 5 years old			5 to 6 years old		
	Area 1	Area 2	Area 3	Area 1	Area 2	Area 3	Area 1	Area 2	Area 3
U	21.0	22.0	30.0	20.0	22.5	11.0	61.5	69.0	69.0
p	.002	.002	.008	<.001	<.001	<.001	.003	.006	.006
r	0.91	0.90	0.77	1.06	1.04	1.19	0.73	0.69	0.69

4.3   Research Question 3

Are there any difficulties or barriers that compromise the acceptability of 3D interactive applications on tablets in learning environments depending on kind of worked topics?

Experimental group seems to reflect a higher improvement regarding to control group. Table 6 shows the descriptive statistics of the scores obtained by all students in the three topics for the experimental and control groups. An improvement in the final score can be observed when this system is applied to support learning with 3D interactive applications.

Table 6. Learning outcomes in three studied topics (descriptive statistics)

Topics	Control Group			Experimental Group		
	N	M	SD	N	M	SD
Skeleton & five senses	43	1.84	0.58	44	2.75	0.35
Animals	43	1.92	0.56	44	2.68	0.34
Houses of the world	43	2.02	0.54	44	2.80	0.27
Total		1.92	0.54		2.74	0.29

For each of the three topics a Mann-Whitney U test was performed to evaluate the hypothesis that control group students would score lower than experimental group students on the three topics. The results of all the tests were in the expected direction and significant $U_{topic1} = 188$, $p_{topic1} < .001$, $r_{topic1} = 1.02$; $U_{topic2} = 250$, $p_{topic2} < .001$, $r_{topic2} = 0.92$; $U_{topic3} = 196.5$, $p_{topic3} < .001$, $r_{topic3} = 0.99$.

Table 7. Mann-Whitney U test

	Skeleton & five senses	Animals	Houses of the world
U	188	250	196.5
p	<.001	<.001	<.001
r	1.02	0.92	0.99

Table 8. Descriptive statistics in each didactic unit for control and experimental groups, gruoped by student age

3 to 4 years old	Control Group			Experimental Group		
	N	M	SD	N	M	SD
Skeleton & five senses	12	1.75	0.62	12	2.67	0.38
Animals	12	1.86	0.64	12	2.58	0.38
Houses of the world	12	2.03	0.69	12	2.78	0.36
4 to 5 years old	Control Group			Experimental Group		
	N	M	SD	N	M	SD
Skeleton & five senses	15	1.67	0.43	15	2.78	0.35
Animals	15	1.80	0.39	15	2.73	0.29
Houses of the world	15	1.89	0.45	15	2.73	0.26
5 to 6 years old	Control Group			Experimental Group		
	N	M	SD	N	M	SD
Skeleton & five senses	16	2.06	0.62	17	2.78	0.35
Animals	16	2.08	0.63	17	2.71	0.35
Houses of the world	16	2.13	0.52	17	2.86	0.21

Table 8 shows the mean scores and standard deviations for each of the topics for control and experimental groups according students' age. It shows that students who used the 3D apps achieved significantly better academic outcomes than those who did not use it. Moreover, the results of this study indicate that the use of the 3D interactive applications on tablets has important effects on the students' academic outcome. The students who used this system obtained better final grades.

Once again, for each of the three topics and for each of the three age groups a Mann-Whitney U test was performed to evaluate the hypothesis that control group students would score lower than experimental group students on the three topics. The results of all the tests were in the expected direction and significant, as can be seen in Table 9.

Table 9. Mann-Whitney *U* test

	3 to 4 years old			4 to 5 years old			5 to 6 years old		
	Topic1	Topic2	Topic3	Topic1	Topic2	Topic3	Topic1	Topic2	Topic3
U	12,5	24,5	23,5	6,00	6,00	12,0	46,5	54,0	29,0
p	<.001	.005	.003	<.001	<.001	<.001	.001	.002	<.001
r	1.03	0.81	0.85	1.18	1.16	1.10	0.85	0.76	1.00

5 Discussion and Conclusions

After analyzing the results obtained in this study, we observed that several of the issues addressed in the theoretical framework of the research are confirmed by the results presented above.

Data analysis reveals that active behavior is promoted on the children by using 3D interactive applications, moreover, students learn more when they are using the 3D apps and they get learning goals quicker if they used these applications. 3D Interactive Applications also promotes communication skills, promoting all kinds of interactions in the classroom between teacher and students, students and students, students and families, families and families and teachers and teachers. Finally, all study participants considered that the use of 3D apps is a good tool in the teaching-learning process.

Finally, although these are encouraging results, it is advisable to deploy similar research studies in extended periods of time to diminish the novelty effect that can be acting as a disturbing factor. It could be also useful to determine those other types of learning activities where 3D interactive applications on tablets can provide greater benefits than traditional methods.

Acknowledgements. The Spanish Ministry Economy and Competitiveness partially supported this work (Project ref. TIN2010-21296-C02-01). The authors are deeply grateful to professors and students that gently collaborated on this research study.

References

1. Plowman, L., Stephen, C.: Children, Play and Computers in Preschool Education. British Journal of Educational Technology 36(2), 145–157 (2005)
2. Tootell, H., Plumb, M., Hadfield, C., Dawson, L.: Gestural Interface Technology in early childhood education: A framework for fully-engaged communication. In: Proceedings of the Annual Hawaii International Conference on System Sciences, art. no. 6479836, pp. 13–20 (2013)
3. Marco, J., Cerezo, E.: Bringing Tabletop Technologies to Kindergarten Children. In: HCI 2009 International Conference on Human-Computer Interaction–Celebrating People and Technology, pp. 103–111. Springer, Heidelberg (2009)
4. Heft, T.M., Swaminathan, S.: Using Computers in Early Childhood Classrooms: Teachers' Attitudes, Skills and Practices. Journal of Early Childhood Research 6(4), 169–188 (2006)
5. Wang, X.C., Ching, C.C.: Social Construction of Computer Experience in a First-Grade Classroom: Social Processes and Mediating Artifacts. Early Education and Development 14(3), 335–361 (2003)
6. Couse, L.J., Chen, D.W.: A Tablet Computer for Young Children? Exploring Its Viability for Early Childhood Education. Journal of Research on Technology in Education 43(1), 75–98 (2012)
7. Kearney, J.: Educating Young Children - Learning and Teaching in the Early Childhood Years. Early Childhood Teachers' Association (ECTA Inc.) 3(18) (2012)

8. Rankothge, W.H., Sendanayake, S.V., Sudarshana, R.G.P., Balasooriya, B.G.G.H., Alahapperuma, D.R., Mallawarachchi, Y.: Technology Assisted Tool for Learning Skills Development in Early Childhood. In: Proc. of 2012 International Conference on Advances in ICT for Emerging Regions (ICTer), pp. 165–168 (2012)
9. Sandvik, M., Smørdal, O., Østerud, S.: Exploring iPads in Practitioners' Repertoires for Language Learning and Literacy Practices In Kindergarten. Nordic Journal of Digital Literacy 3(7), 204–221 (2012)
10. Priyankara, K.W.T.G.T., Mahawaththa, D.C., Nawinna, D.P., Jayasundara, J.M.A., Tharuka, K.D.N., Rajapaksha, S.K.: Android Based e-Learning Solution for Early Childhood Education in Sri Lanka. In: Proceedings of the 8th International Conference on Computer Science & Education (ICCSE), pp. 715–718 (2013)
11. Zanchi, C., Presser, A.L., Vahey, P.: Next Generation Preschool Math Demo: Tablet Games for Preschool Classrooms. In: Proceedings of the 12th International Conference on Interaction Design and Children, IDC 2013, pp. 527–530 (2013)
12. Meyer, B.: Game-based Language Learning for Pre-School Children: A Design Perspective. Electronic Journal of e-Learning 11(1), 39–48 (2013)
13. Straub, D.W.: Validating Instruments in MIS Research. MIS Quarterly 13(2), 147–169 (1989)
14. Cook, T.D., Campbell, D.T., Day, A.: Quasi-experimentation: Design and Analysis Issues for Field Settings, pp. 19–21. Houghton Mifflin, Boston (1979)
15. Buendía, L., Y Berrocal, E.: La Ética de la Investigación Educativa. Ágora Digital 1 (2011)
16. Tojar, J., Serrano, J.: Ética e Investigación Educativa. RELIEVE 6(2) (2000)
17. Cascales, A., Laguna, I., Pérez-López, D., Perona, P., Contero, M.: 3D Interactive Applications on Tablets for Preschoolers: Exploring the Human Skeleton and the Senses. In: Hernández-Leo, D., Ley, T., Klamma, R., Harrer, A. (eds.) EC-TEL 2013. LNCS, vol. 8095, pp. 71–83. Springer, Heidelberg (2013)

Interrelation between Pedagogical Design
and Learning Interaction Patterns
in different Virtual Learning Environments

Maka Eradze and Mart Laanpere

Tallinn University, Narva rd. 25, 10120 Tallinn, Estonia
{maka.eradze,mart.laanpere}@tlu.ee

Abstract. Different virtual learning environments offer different affordances and pedagogical design for learning interactions which results in difference learning interaction patterns. With the emergence of a new era in VLE (virtual learning environments) a new set of affordances is needed to support the appropriate learning interactions. We argue that there is a strong interrelation between the pedagogical design and learning interaction patterns in a given VLE which is influenced by the affordances of that VLE. In order to create a set of affordances that support learning interactions within the DLE, there is a need of analysis of already existing learning interaction affordances across different platforms.

1 Introduction

Different virtual learning environments offer different affordances and pedagogical design for learning interactions, which results in difference learning interaction patterns. With the emergence of a new era in VLE (virtual learning environments) a new set of affordances is needed to support the appropriate learning interactions.

We argue that there is a strong interrelation between the pedagogical design and learning interaction patterns in a given VLE, which is influenced by the affordances of that VLE. In order to create a set of affordances that support learning interactions within the DLE, there is a need of analysis of already existing learning interaction affordances across different platforms.

In this paper we examine the pedagogical designs and learning interaction patterns in VLEs like EduFeedr, Massive Open Online Courses platforms Coursera, Udacity, traditional LMSs and explore their interrelation patterns with pedagogical design of each course. The typology of the pedagogical design and interaction patterns will be based on the Communities of Inquiry [1,2,3,4].

Teaching is a design profession, today more than before. We define pedagogical design in line with Romizsowski [5] as systematic choice and use of procedures, methods, prescriptions, and devices in order to bring about effective, efficient, and productive learning. In addition to European tradition of didactic design based on heuristic guidelines, there exist several formalised and prescriptive instructional design models (e.g. [26,27,28]). As we are interested in actual pedagogical design models implemented by teachers who do not have any training or guidelines in the

P. Zaphiris and A. Ioannou (Eds.): LCT 2014, Part II, LNCS 8524, pp. 23–32, 2014.

domain of instructional design, we use IMS Learning Design for representing differences of pedagogical designs in online courses.

2   Interaction Patterns

According to Wagner's definition interaction is "Reciprocal events that require at least two objects and two actions. Interactions occur when these objects and events mutually influence each other" [6]. Interaction has a specific function and value in education for it creates a big portion of the learning ambience.

Holmberg [7] introduced the notion of "guided didactic discussion", where the student-teacher interaction is mainly text-based and a teacher is guiding the student through the learning process with the help of didactic discussion. This notion is very much related to the Moore's Theory of Transactional distance [8] - transactional distance is where he differentiates between a dialogue and interaction "dialogue" being loaded with the sense of meaningful interaction. As Anderson notes, interactions are too many including human and inanimate [3]. Distance education theorists have broken the concept down to mainly based on the roles of the human and inanimate actors.

Moore's theory of Three Types of Interaction [9] includes learner-content, learner-instructor, learner-content and is the first systematic approach to defining the typologies of interactions in distance education. For Moore the first type of interaction - learner-content is connected to the Holmberg's notion of *internal didactic conversation* and is the defining characteristic for the education, while the learner-instructor is a four-stage support of the learner 1. Designing the content including maintaining motivation, self-direction 2. Making presentations - from students or teachers themselves. 3. Practice and apply acquired competences. 4. Counseling and encouragement of learners according their levels of progress. The third type of interaction – learner-learner for Moore was a new dimension in the distance education and he indicates on its importance but also stresses its dependence on circumstances – like age of the, experience and the level of "inner autonomy".

One part of "indirect" impacts of the interactions is covered by Sutton [10] that introduced the notion of vicarious interaction defined as what "takes place when a student actively processes both sides of a direct interaction between two other students or between another student and the instructor".

Anderson has expanded Moore's three dyads of interaction - learner-content, learner-teacher and learner-learner to include content-teacher, content-content and teacher-teacher interactions [4]. Anderson's model is learning-centred and also takes into account material resources. The main idea of the Equivalency theorem is that in order the learning to take place, one of the interactions shall be at a high level. Other dyads of interaction can add value and increase the quality of learning but it must also estimate the costs of resources for these types of interactions.

Learning interactions have been regarded in the context of Technology-Enhanced Learning as an important unit of analysis and they have been studied by the community of educational researchers from various perspectives [4, 11]. Most of the research is based on the data collected through learner-reported surveys [11,12, 13] educational data mining techniques [14,15], qualitative text analysis [16] or social network analysis [17]. In our study, we will use content analysis technique and count interaction pattern frequencies and map them to Conole's *Learning Activity Taxonomy* [18]. Conole's taxonomy contains six types of tasks:

- **assimilative tasks**, e.g. reading, viewing or listening;
- **information handling**, e.g. gathering and classifying resources from the Web or manipulating data;
- **adaptive**, e.g. engaging learners in using modelling or simulation software;
- **communicative**, e.g. engaging learners in debate or group discussions;
- **productive**, e.g. actively constructing an artefact such as a written essay, production of a new piece of software or creation of a video clip;
- **experiential**, e.g. practicing skills in a particular real-life context, engaging in live role-play or undertaking an investigation offline.

3   Beyond Counting the Frequencies of Interactions

Within the model of the communities of inquiry different types of interactions are crucial for the learning [1,9,19]. But still interaction is different from presence, interaction does not guarantee the presence itself, these interactions are the building blocks towards the presences in the communities of inquiry. Interaction alone is not enough for the purposes of inquiry and cognitive presence. Therefore the model of the community of inquiry consists of the three core elements that go beyond the social exchanges [3] Understanding the interaction nature of interaction is not simple - though interaction does not always lead to social presence [20] it is the interaction that mostly affects social and cognitive engagement of the students in an online course.

The model of this Community of Inquiry assumes that learning occurs within the Community through the interaction of three core elements [1] CoI model core elements are three presences: Cognitive presence, Social presence and Teacher presence and each of the presences contain hierarchies.

Fig. 1. From Garisson et al [1]

Cognitive presence is the basic element for success of educational experience [1]. It had been conceptualized as "practical inquiry" and has four stages of development:

1. Triggering event – experience resulting in a feeling of unease puzzlement.
2. Exploration - search for information, knowledge alternatives that might help to make sense of the situation or problem
3. Integration – this phase integrates information and knowledge into a coherent idea
4. Resolution – resolution of a problem or issue

Practical inquiry is the variation of *Cognitive Presence* and it's presented as a holistic, phased model that starts with *triggering event* that is later followed by: *exploration, integration* and *resolution* phases. For the authors of the framework, cognitive presence is not a stand-alone process internalized in one's mind only and it is an interaction of personal and shared worlds.

The second core element of CoI is *Social Presence,* which again represents a phased process:
1. Emotional expression – establishment of emotional ambience with the help of emoticons, symbols, humor or self-disclosure
2. Open communication – exchange, mutual awareness, and recognition between the messages that facilitate the process of shaping the learning activities of each participant.
3. Group cohesion - group commitment, sense of togetherness, belonging.

Social presence creates a supportive context for building understanding and ease of communication, thus maintaining the educational community.

Teacher presence is the connecting element of the CoI model [1]. For the authors of the CoI model both – cognitive and teaching presence depend on the presence of the teacher, especially in the VLE. If the educational experience fails, then it is the lack of teacher presence is to blame. Teacher presence can be assessed based/through on the instructional design. Teacher presence consists of:

1. Instructional management – is about setting curriculum, designing methods and assessment means, effective use of the medium.
2. Building understanding – it aims at the construction of collaborative community and academic integrity through sharing meaning, seeking understanding.
3. Direct instruction - it's the ultimate teaching responsibility through the presentation of content, questions and proactively guiding and summarizing the discussion.

4   Three Types of Interaction and CoI model

Swan views Moore's theory of three types of interaction and CoI model as connected concepts, whereas each of the types of interactions correspond to each of the presences.

1. Teaching presence - teacher-learner interaction.
2. Cognitive presence – learner-content
3. Social presence – learner-learner

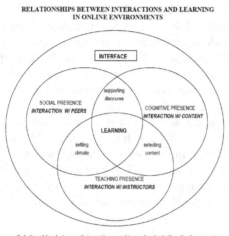

RELATIONSHIPS BETWEEN INTERACTIONS AND LEARNING
IN ONLINE ENVIRONMENTS

Relationships between Interactions and Learning in Online Environments
(Adapted from Rourke, et al.'s (2001) Community of Inquiry Model)

Fig. 2. From Swan [21]

Swan [22] assessed the three types of interaction in the asynchronous online course based on a student-reported survey student satisfaction and perceived learning: her findings for *learner-content* interaction support Moore's theory of interaction and CoI model. "student who reported higher levels of activity in courses also reported higher level of satisfaction and higher levels of learning from them". *Learner-teacher* interactions – her research reports the importance of teacher-student interactions, students with no adequate access to the instructor have less satisfaction and lower perceived learning. *Learner-learner* interactions – are also very important and are in line with Moore and CoI model. Swan's research also tackles the issue of the course design factors and their relation to the interaction patterns – according to the findings, course designers are more influenced by the online environment constraints, than by their affordances. She defines six aspects of course design that affect interactivity in the courses:

1. Frequency of interaction with the instructor
2. Whether there existed any gaps.
3. Frequency of interaction among classmates.
4. Required student participation in course discussions.
5. The authenticity of that discussion
6. Average length of discussion responses.

These factors were correlated to the student perception variables and the findings show that *Learner-content* interaction is influenced by consistency among course modules but no significant correlation was found between course design factors and student perceptions, though Swan also refers to the affordances and constraints of the VLE. No significant results were found for *Learner-teacher* interaction. In *Learner-learner* interaction, strong correlation was found between students' perceptions of their interactions with peers and the actual frequency of interactions between students.

Though the CoI model had been regarded as holistic model for assessing the effectiveness of teaching/learning processes in online communities, much studies concentrate on one of the presences. As we consider that the types of interactions within the CoI model shall be assessed in relation with each other as they are interconnected concepts and necessary for the successful learning. We counted the publications on the official CoI website at coi.athabascau.ca having in mind that the papers listed here are regarded as the most influential: CoI papers – 28, Cognitive presence – 22, Social presence – 10, Teaching presence – 14. Although there is high number of CoI papers listed on the website, altogether much more research is concentrated on assessing single aspect of CoI model (46 publications). We think that, In order to evaluate the existing interaction patterns in different VLEs and get the complete picture, we considered assessing all three core presences in different environments.

5   Methodology

The study used content analysis based on the coding template, which is was validated by several studies [1,2,23,24]. The coding template is directly based on the phased presences in Communities of Inquiry.

Based on the review of several similar studies [1,2,23,24] with the same coding template, we chose the whole message as a unit of analysis. Some of the messages contained two codes from two presences (social and cognitive). Two coders (the authors) coded text consolidated in Coding Analysis Toolkit[1] and coded independently. Coding scheme was developed and discussed. Initial reliability was established. Ethical considerations were followed, the discussion forum messages had been anonymised. In the discussion on results we did not disclose any information about the participants or the names of the sample courses.

---

[1] http://cat.ucsur.pitt.edu

Table 1. Coding template based on CoI approach

Element	Category	Indicators
Cognitive Presence	1.Triggering Event	Sense of puzzlement
	2. Exploration	Information exchange
	3. Integration	Connecting ideas
	4. Resolution	Applying new ideas
Social Presence	5.Emotional Expression	Expression of emotions, use of humor, self-disclosure
	6.Open communication	Continuing a thread, quoting from others
	7. Group Cohesion	Encouraging collaboration
Teaching Presence	8. Instructional management	Defining & initiating discussion topics
	9. Building Understanding	Sharing personal meaning
	10. Direct Instruction	Focusing discussion

6   Sampling

We chose 4 different platforms and 1 course from each to analyse. These courses were chosen from a larger set of courses (a convenience sample, accessible for authors), which we considered as typical for four different virtual learning environments: Coursera, eDX, Moodle and EduFeedr. As the whole dataset for these four courses was too large for analysis, we decided to analyse only the learning resources, assignments and interactions from the 4th week of each course. General discussion topics that were not directly connected to the weekly thematic discussion, where also included in the sample based on the timeframe of that week.

Course 1 (MOOC in Coursera): The course was mostly a video-driven. The videos contained in themselves some interactive quizzes. The platform affordances included discussion forums and wikis. Wikis were not used at all and discussion forums were used separately from the instructional design. The discussions were organized according to study weeks and also contained some general discussions, technical forums. Threads emerged on the bases of the learner interest; they were never used as a part of the assignment and never teacher-led. Teacher presence and facilitation was present in almost every thread. The task for week 4 was information handling.

Course 2 (MOOC in EdX): The course affordances include embedded forums within the video lectures, interactive assignments, discussion topic was also given in every thematic unit (study week) and were organized within the thematic unit. The discussion was triggered by the teacher and given particular question to answer to. The instruction never participated in the discussions besides giving the direct assignment. The task for week 4 was adaptive.

Course 3: The platform was one of the mostly used LMS: Moodle. The difficulty we faced was with choosing a course that used discussions (being a part of instructional design or as a stand-alone). The teacher, giving a task to discuss, initiated the discussion. Teacher never participated in the discussion; neither were any continuity in the threads – only one post per participant and no single case of uptake [25] was shown. The task for week 4 was assimilative.

Course 4. A course that made use of blog-based personal learning environments together with aggregator called Edufeedr[2]. Weekly assignments and learning resources were available in the teacher's blog, each student reflected on his/her learning experiences in a personal blog, which was then commented by teacher. The course was assignment-driven, discussion between students took place rarely. The task for week 4 was combination of assimilative and productive.

7   Results and Discussion

Distribution of interaction events by CoI categories shows significant differences between four courses (see Table 2 below). While in two MOOCs the interactions indicating the social presence were clearly dominating and learners themselves often triggered content-related discussions, Moodle course induced mainly exploration and integration events. EduFeedr course distinguished with strong teacher presence, but also with integration and resolution events. Those differences can be partly attributed to pedagogical design, especially in case of Course 3 and Course 4. Domination of open communication in Coursera and EdX courses occured in spite (not due to) the pedagogical design. We also strongly believe that differences in interaction patterns was influenced by the number of learners and affordances of virtual learning environment.

Table 2. Comparison of four courses regarding to interaction types

	Coursera	EdX	Moodle	Edufeedr
1. Triggering event	17.24%	10.76%	0%	0%
2. Exploration	7.95%	17.59%	51.16%	1.33%
3. Integration	10.51%	13.12%	34.88%	28%
4. Resolution	6.72%	6.82%	0%	20%
5. Emotional expression	4.52%	5.51%	0%	4%
6. Open communication	38.63%	28.61%	0%	13.33%
7. Group cohesion	.37%	1.84%	0%	0%
8. Instructional management	4.77%	6.82%	9.3%	5.33%
9. Building understanding	4.03%	1.05%	0%	18.67%
10. Direct instruction	4.16%	4.72%	4.65%	9.33%
0. Other	1.1%	3.41%	0%	0%

---

[2] http://www.edufeedr.net

8   Conclusion

While our small sample of courses and focus on the activities of a single week in each course does not allow generalizations, we have demonstrated the method for analyzing interrelations between pedagogical design and learning activity patterns in Web-based learning environments. In order to achieve reliable results, the similar study has to be conducted on a larger scale.

References

1. Garrison, D.R., Anderson, T., Archer, W.: Critical inquiry in a text-based environment: Computer conferencing in higher education. The Internet and Higher Education 2(2-3), 87–105 (2000)
2. Garrison, D.R., Anderson, T., Archer, W.: Critical thinking, cognitive presence, and computer conferencing in distance education. The American Journal of Distance Education 15(1), 7–23 (2001)
3. Anderson, T.: Modes of interaction in distance education: Recent developments and research questions. In: Moore, M. (ed.) Handbook of Distance Education, pp. 129–144. Erlbaum, Mahwah (2003)
4. Anderson, T.: Getting the mix right again: An updated and theoretical rationale for interaction. International Review of Research in Open and Distance Learning 4(2) (2003a)
5. Romiszowski, A.J.: Designing Instructional Systems: Decision Making in Course Planning and CurriculumDesign. Psychology Press (January 1, 1984)
6. Wagner, E.D.: In support of a functional definition of interaction. The American Journal of Distance Education 8(2), 6–26 (1994)
7. Holmberg, B.: Theory and practice of distance education. Routledge, London (1989)
8. Moore, M.: Theory of transactional distance. In: Keegan, D. (ed.) Theoretical Principles of Distance Education, pp. 22–38. Routledge, London (1993)
9. Moore, M.G.: Three types of interaction. American Journal of Distance Education 3(2), 1–6 (1989)
10. Sutton, L.A.: The Principle of Vicarious Interaction in Computer-Mediated Communications. International Journal of Educational Telecommunications 7(3), 223–242 (2001)
11. Garrison, D.R.: Facilitating Cognitive Presence in Online Learning: Interaction Is Not Enough. The American Journal of Distance Education 19(3), 133–148 (2005)
12. Miyazoe, T., Anderson, T.: Empirical Research on Learners' Perceptions: Interaction Equivalency Theorem in Blended Learning European Journal of Open. Distance and E-Learning, n1 (2010)
13. Miyazoe, T., Anderson, T.: The interaction equivalency theorem. Journal of Interactive Online Learning (JIOL) 9(2), 94–104 (2010a)
14. Tang, T., McCalla, G.: Smart recommendation for an evolving elearning system: architecture and experiment. International Journal on E-Learning 4(1), 105–129 (2005)
15. Zaiane, O.: Web usage mining for a better web-based learning environment. In: Proceedings of Conference on Advanced Technology for Education, pp. 60–64 (2001)
16. Muirhead, B.: Enhancing Social Interaction in Computer-Mediated Distance Education. Educational Technology & Society - ETS 3(4) (2000)

17. Dawson, S., Bakharia, A., Lockyer, L., Heathcote, E.: 'Seeing' networks: visualising and evaluating student learning networks – report. Education 3(2), 1–6 (2011), http://www.olt.gov.au/system/files/resources/Cg9_994_Lockyer_Report_2011.pdf (retrieved January 31, 2013)

18. Conole, G.: Describing learning activities: tools and resources to guide practice. In: Beetham, H., Sharpe, R. (eds.) Rethinking Pedagogy for a Digital Age, pp. 81–91 (2007)

19. Anderson, T., Garrison, D.R.: Learning in a networked world: New roles and responsibilities. In: Gibson, C. (ed.) Distance Learners in Higher Education, pp. 97–112. Atwood Publishing, Madison (1998)

20. Picciano, A.G.: Beyond Student Perceptions: Issues of Interaction, Presence, and Performance in an Online Course (2002)

21. Swan, K.: Relationships Between Interactions and Learning In Online Environments, http://sloanconsortium.org/publications/books/pdf/interactions.pdf

22. Karen Swan, K.: Virtual interaction: Design factors affecting student satisfaction and perceived learning in asynchronous online courses. Distance Education 22(2), 306–331 (2001)

23. Rourke, L., Anderson, T., Garrison, D.R., Archer, W.: Assessing social presence in asynchronous, text-based computer conferencing. Journal of Distance Education 14(3), 51–70 (2001)

24. Anderson, T., Rourke, L., Garrison, D.R., Archer, W.: Assessing Teaching presence in a Computer Conference Environment. JALN 5(2) (2001)

25. Suthers, D.D., Rosen, D.: A Unified Framework for Multi-level Analysis of Distributed Learning. In: Proceedings of the First International Conference on Learning Analytics & Knowledge, Banff, Alberta, pp. 64–74. ACM, New York (2010)

26. Dick, W., Carey, L., Carey, J.O.: The systematic design of instruction, 6th edn. Allyn and Bacon, New York (2005)

27. Mayer, R.H.: Designing instruction for constructivist learning. In: Reigeluth, C.M. (ed.) A New Paradigm of Instructional Theory, vol. II, pp. 141–159. Lawrence Erlbaum Associates, Mahwah (1999)

28. Merrill, M.D.: Component display theory. In: Reigeluth, C.M. (ed.) Instructional–Design Theories and Models: An Overview? of Their Current Status, pp. 279–333. Lawrence Erlbaum Associates, Hillsdale (1983)

BIZZY – A Social Game for Entrepreneurship Education

Benjamim Fonseca[1,2], Ramiro Gonçalves[1,2], Ricardo Rodrigues Nunes[1],
Mário Sérgio Teixeira[1,3], Hugo Paredes[1,2], Leonel Morgado[2,4], and Paulo Martins[1,2]

[1] Universidade de Trás-os-Montes e Alto Douro (UTAD), Vila Real, Portugal
{benjaf,ramiro,rrnunes,mariosergio,hparedes,pmartins}@utad.pt
[2] INESC TEC - INESC Technology and Science, Porto, Portugal
[3] CETRAD, Vila Real, Portugal
[4] Universidade Aberta, Lisboa, Portugal
leonel.morgado@uab.pt

Abstract. Entrepreneurship education is increasingly being promoted, driven by a wide consensus in modern societies concerning its benefits in fostering the development of several professional and personal attitudes and skills, such as business expertise, creativity, risk assessment or responsibility. In this context, several authorities have been actively developing policies and activities to empower entrepreneurship culture in young people. Serious Games are recognized as having an important role and potential in education and social networks emerged in the last decade as the platform preferred by many people to socialize, play games or conduct professional activities. This paper presents a proposal for BIZZY, a serious game to be developed and implemented as a Facebook application, to enable young people in the range 12-18 years old to learn entrepreneurial skills progressively, by guiding them to develop a business project from the early idea to the business plan.

Keywords: computers in education, entrepreneurship, technology enhanced learning, serious games, social networks, facebook.

1   Introduction

In 2012 Global Entrepreneurship Monitor Study about Portugal [1] this country recorded a rate of Early-Stage Entrepreneurial Activity of 7.7 %. Among 69 countries involved in GEM 2012 study, this value is only the 44th highest, although it is the 7th highest among the 24 participant innovation oriented economies.

In this study, 38 interviews were also carried out by national experts on entrepreneurship, having these considered that "national culture is few oriented to entrepreneurship and that exists in society, a lack of stimulus to individual success" [1]. These experts also "believe that education and training in the country tend to be partially insufficient" and "evaluate very unfavorably the primary and secondary levels of the education system for their ability to promote entrepreneurial activity", although have "a very positive opinion of higher education in business and management" [1].

P. Zaphiris and A. Ioannou (Eds.): LCT 2014, Part II, LNCS 8524, pp. 33–41, 2014.

Games have been adopted exponentially by successive generations over the last 3 decades. More recently, besides the proliferation of console games, mobile and web-based games have also improved hugely, due to their high availability and a distribution model based in advertisement and free access to users.

The emergence of social networks such as Facebook and Twitter, changed the way teenagers and young adults interact, often preferring social network platforms to socialize, share their media and to play games available for free and fully integrated with the social network.

Facebook is nowadays the most used online social network, with a total number of 1.19 billion active users in September 2013, with a 727 million daily average [2], being teenagers and young adults a significant part of them. Facebook is therefore also an attractive media to conduct learning initiatives, taking advantage of the addiction of the vast community of young people and the possibility of conducting game-like activities.

The widespread use of social networking by young people studying at 3rd cycle and secondary education can be harnessed to encourage alternative learning processes, in particular for the acquisition of entrepreneurship skills. A serious game in the field of entrepreneurship that can be developed for social networking, with fun activities and collaborative tools, can be an innovative teaching tool that motivates young people to learning processes about business and personal development of entrepreneurial skills.

UTAD has accumulated experience in developing this type of serious game for entrepreneurship, thanks to its participation in the European project PLAYER - Play and Learn The Young Entrepreneur (Project ID: ENTR/CIP/09/E/N02S001; Grant Agreement No. 216) where was the institution responsible for the development of a set implemented as an application for Facebook. This game tried to motivate and educate young people to become entrepreneurs capable, supporting the gradual acquisition of entrepreneurial skills through the development of a business idea, along all its stages, to draw up a business plan. Integrating Facebook allowed them to develop their ideas in an environment which they were accustomed and allowed them to go getting feedback from friends and other players.BIZZY is a new serious game for motivating and educating young people to become capable entrepreneurs, and it resulted from previous work developed under the PLAYER project [3]. The game is intended to integrate with Facebook to benefit from a wide community of young people and enable them to develop their ideas inside a well-known environment and provides the ability to follow the required steps while playing and getting feedback from friends, competitors and experts.

The rest of the paper is organized as follows: section 2 presents some recent literature review concerning entrepreneurship education; in section 3 we describe the PLAYER project in which experience and results the BIZZY game was inspired; section 4 presents the BIZZY proposal, outlining its main concepts and innovations introduced; finally, some final remarks are presented in section 5.

2   Entrepreneurship Education

Policy-makers generally consider new venture formation relation with economic growth and technological progress [4] and some studies find those positive effects [5].

Because it can make a significant contribution to this new venture formation, with the development of entrepreneurial attitudes and skills, a wide range of entrepreneurship education efforts has been initiated [6].

Martin, McNally, and Kay [7] did a meta-analysis that suggests a positive association between EE and entrepreneurship-related human capital assets (as knowledge, skills, positive perceptions of entrepreneurship or intentions to become an entrepreneur) and entrepreneurship outcomes (as new venture creation or entrepreneurial performance).

Some research suggests that who had received entrepreneurship education have higher intentions or are more likely to start a business or are more successful in opportunity identification tasks [8-10], compared with those who have not received that type of education.

Because of that, over the past decade, entrepreneurship education (EE) is booming worldwide, not only at the university level, but also in primary and secondary schools, where more and more initiatives and interventions are emerging [11].

Aiming to increase the number of entrepreneurs in Europe, the European Commission developed a plan of action based on 3 pillars, one of which involves developing entrepreneurial education and training to support the growth and business. This pillar is supported in a number of studies suggest that "between 15% to 20% of students participating in an entrepreneurship program in secondary education later create his own company, being this number 3 to 5 times higher than for the general population" [12].

The young people who benefit from an entrepreneurial learning develop knowledge about business and a set of skills and attitudes that include creativity, initiative, tenacity, teamwork, understanding of risk and a sense of responsibility that are part of an entrepreneurial mindset [12].

This action plan also recommends that entrepreneurial education follow models of learning with practical experiences and enabling the sharing of experiences with entrepreneurs in the real world.

One entrepreneurial educations method that is used in some schools is "serious games", that allows students with a different environment to practice entrepreneurship, being a playful approach for serious results [13].

For Fayolle [12] the use of internet-based and computer-based technologies could be valuable teaching methods to use in entrepreneurship education.

Gaming aligns learning, play, and participations while exposing students to real challenges in a virtual world, with the expectation of fun [13].

3   Previous Work – The PLAYER Project

The PLAYER project [3] was aimed to foster entrepreneurial skills and behaviors in young people using a serious game approach. The project was implemented by an European consortium that promoted an international competition of business ideas.

The competition was implemented through the PLAYER game, which allowed young players to present and develop their business ideas, describing it with the help of multimedia content, other user's participation and game features that enabled the incremental consolidation of the business concepts and plans. The game was available to the general public of youngsters outside educational environment throughout Europe as well as to high school and university students of the seven countries involved in the consortium of the project.

The game was divided into 4 stages of growing difficulty, gradually introducing entrepreneurial concepts, and aims to leave participants better prepared to start their own business. In the first two stages, participants create their own profile and compile a portfolio that seeks to explain the idea at a conceptual level, using multimedia documents alone. It's also possible to compile an additional portfolio which will not be publicly exhibited, where sensitive critical points of a user's strategy may be revealed to a jury of professionals, or simply use it to include links to additional web documents. Portraying market conditions, the user is faced with uncertainty of the number and the score of votes he/she will attract. This is the phase where lobbying and networking takes place to introduce general public with the business idea.

While the user waits for his portfolio to be voted by other users, he may entertain himself by voting on other portfolios or exploring business strategies and gauging their success with the Sink-or-Swim sub-game. In this sub-game, as one fits together pieces to describe one's strategy, and connects them with verbs that may indicate one's mindset, the whole conceptual map will float or drown in a waving water animation to indicate the likelihood of the company's success.

PLAYER is about easing the users out of what they think they know about business, and making users aware of what they still need to learn and seek out in self-directed study. Sink-or-Swim is about emphasizing the interrelatedness and long-term consequences of difficult choices that users must make about the way they want to do business. Sink-or-Swim is meant to impress upon users that an idea for a business is made up of definite choices, that making one choice might make other options unobtainable, and that each choice carries risks to the way a business proposes to operate. Risks incurred in one choice need to be mitigated by other choices. A business plan presented to investors can therefore be bold and aggressive while safeguarding return of investment, knowing its limits, and catering to a well-defined market.

Soon thereafter a funding quiz must be taken to assess the level of investment required to start their company up, the user's self-confidence and attitude towards risk. Based on it, a recommendation will be made saying which type of investor to contact, or, eventually, advising the user to rethink his answers. This is to represent financial consultations that would happen in this phase in real life situation. An Executive Summary is then compiled based on information provided in the previous stages, and displayed for the user to complete it with more details on his SWOT analysis and submit it for evaluation by a jury of experts. The left side of Figure 1 shows an example of the Sink-or-Swim game and the right side shows the page seen by the user when reaching the end of the Executive Summary stage.

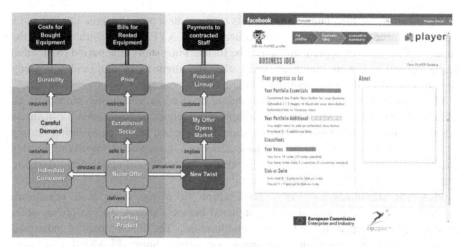

Fig. 1. - Sink-or-Swim game and PLAYER navigation page [3]

While waiting for evaluation, a user may try to get the jury's attention faster by completing weekly challenges, proving he/she is more skilful or more eager to get the attention of evaluators. The user then continues to the last stage, which will require downloading a Business Plan Tool, completing a formal business plan, and uploading it for review. Keeping in mind the 15 to 30 years old target users' age and their inexperience with sometimes complicated business details required in business plans, the game offers them a thorough guidance in the form of Business Plan Tool.

The game had 2706 users registered during the contest period, who completed Stage 1 by just filling their profile. Half of the contestants had secondary or post-secondary school, while the number of users with at least post-graduate education corresponded to 36% of the total respondents. These results show that the contest reached mostly the target population of 15-30 years old

The users that started using effectively the application by giving a name to the business idea were 2009, a 26% drop over registered users. Among these, 1446 created business portfolios and only 128 submitted it for voting, completing Stage 2 (5% of the initial users). These portfolios received votes from 368 users, meaning that a significant number of the users that didn't submit their portfolios for voting still participated and voted in other users' portfolios. There were a total of 2521 votes, with an average of nearly 20 votes per portfolio (it was required 10 votes from 3 different countries to pass to Stage 3) and an average grading of 6.09 (scale 1-10).

Stage 3 was completed by 43 users, who submitted their executive summaries, and only 21 submitted their Business Plan, thus completing Stage 4 and the competition (0.4% of the total users).

Although the considerable participation did not correspond to a number of completed business plans, the overall impression is positive. The reason for not reaching the expected number of business plans can be that the players needed a tutor, to help them in the writing and implementation of management, the short time period of the competition (six months) was an important constrain while some more tangible awards could be a stimulus for the participants to work to a detailed business plan.

Nonetheless, the high number of entrants to the contest proves people interest and a significant need for entrepreneurial education. PLAYER demonstrated that the concept of business entrepreneurship can be fostered in a short time period (6 months) across several European countries, and gather the attention of thousands of young people, supporting them to rationalize some business concepts.

Player project developed a tool that should be used in a lecturing process as an additional motivator for students to accomplish the requirements needed for business oriented courses. Furthermore, the tool should be applied to the engineering classes that offer wide area of ideas and lack economic background. Working in this direction, the current game could be expanded to further sets of economic, marketing and business management concepts.

PLAYER stimulates creativity (presentation of ideas) more than organized, planned business development (few completed business plans). This confirms other experience with projects related to open communities. The development of individual ideas to concrete opportunities requires mentoring. Some PLAYER's partners experience with this contest is that young students are hardly capable to work on their own. Pupils enjoyed the opportunity to use Facebook as an educational tool but they like to work in groups and they could have some good proficiency if followed by teachers during classes.

Players/learners must see the value to them of the learning and they must strongly believe that they are able to play the game with some challenging goals. In order to make the PLAYER game more attractive to players, the questionnaires and the forms should be made more game-like, providing incentives for players, with instant and transparent achievement scores. Also, explanations why some decisions in the game were proper/improper or why some additional game elements suddenly appeared during the play would improve the serious part of the game – the individual learning process. Player/learner need feedback and dialogue on their process and need time and opportunities for repetition (such us in the Sink-or-Swim game, where player could improve their score following the suggestions provided by the system).

4   The BIZZY Project

As we have previously noted, the major use of social networks by young students can and should be used to encourage alternative learning processes, in particular for the acquisition of skills for entrepreneurship. A serious game in the field of entrepreneurship that can be developed for social networking, with fun activities and collaborative tools, can be an innovative teaching tool that motivates young people to processes of learning about business and personal development of entrepreneurial skills.

Previous work with the PLAYER project allowed us to envisage new directions based on the lessons learned by practice and after a careful SWOT analysis of the project process and outcomes. PLAYER has been an innovative project focused on stimulating creativity and inspired potential young entrepreneurs to reflect on business ideas and its formalization.

According to [3] "Fostering the entrepreneurial spirit of young people through a contest based on a game was pioneering and allowed them to communicate with other competitors, using a social network. Future application should improve this communication aspect. Speaking about entrepreneurship, ideas and businesses should make the players look for the potential realization of their idea".

The BIZZY proposal aims to help developing an entrepreneurial education in young people under 18 years old, improving their business knowledge and skills and entrepreneurial attitudes. The idea is to use a practical approach to teaching and learning that allows the sharing of experiences with others, including guidance from experts and entrepreneurs which could act as mentors from the real world.

This new game will be developed by a multidisciplinary team, covering various scientific fields, encompassing the areas of ICT, Business and Economics.

We propose to create a thus embedded game within the social network facebook, using for that purpose all features of interaction and collaboration.

BIZZY has 4 stages with some innovations comparatively to PLAYER, as described below:

- Evaluation of entrepreneurial skills: this is a new starting step for the game, aiming to assess the player's skills in terms of entrepreneurship, economics and business. This will help to adjust the other game steps according to the player's profile. Moreover, this will help the player to understand his own limitations and capabilities and thus guide him in the inherent learning process;
- Business Idea: involve mentors from the very beginning of the game to have an early validation of the idea, according to predefined criteria. This will still be followed by other players' validation, as was done in PLAYER;
- Business model: improve the sink-or-swim game, combining the original concepts with the CANVAS model [14];
- Business Plan: this was one of the most critical issues in PLAYER, leading to a high dropout rate, due to its complex nature. In this context BIZZY will try to simplify the business plan development, adopting a more game oriented approach, increasing mentoring and providing deeper support through multimedia tutoring materials.

The transition between steps requires overcoming a series of activities and challenges. The most successful players will be awarded with intangible prizes, such as privileged contacts with CEO's, reputed people and experts in the fields of business and entrepreneurship.

PLAYER also exhibited problems related with the overall process. One of them was the short time period of the competition (six months), which will be extended to one year in BIZZY.

In order to disseminate the game to primary and secondary schools nationwide, it is essential to strengthen ties with a number of key partners. Thus, an advisory board will be created for the project, with partners linked to schools and public agencies working in boosting entrepreneurship (representatives of the Ministries of Education and Economics as well as Business associations, municipalities, school principals and Parents and Guardians).

Finally, another crucial partnership for the success of the project will be established with secondary education teachers, particularly in the areas of ICT and Business / Management, and other school staff.

5   Final Remarks

Entrepreneurship is nowadays recognized by various stakeholders as a crucial and critical development factor and authorities worldwide have invested increasing public resources in its promotion, including in entrepreneurship education.

Serious games are increasingly being used as educational resources in several contexts, namely as method for learning entrepreneurship skills and attitudes.

Social networks play a key role in the current world, namely among young people. Facebook has a myriad of users that rely on it daily for social interaction of various natures, including sharing information and thus learning in a less structured way.

This paper presented a proposal for a new entrepreneurship education serious game, named BIZZY, that will be implemented in Facebook with young people in the range 12-18 years old enrolled in the national education system. This game is inspired in a previous approach to this educational concept, developed under the PLAYER project, introducing innovations based on the lessons learned.

Acknowledgements. This work is financed by the ERDF – European Regional Development Fund through the COMPETE Programme (operational programme for competitiveness) and by National Funds through the FCT – Fundação para a Ciência e a Tecnologia (Portuguese Foundation for Science and Technology) within project «FCOMP - 01-0124-FEDER-022701

References

1. Global Entrepreneurship Monitor. GEM Portugal 2012 (2012), http://www.gemconsortium.org/docs/search?doc_cat_id=4&team_id=32&q%20= (accessed in January 2014)
2. Facebook Newsroom – Key Facts – Facebook's latest news, announcements and media resources. Facebook (2014), http://newsroom.fb.com/Key-Facts (accessed January 25, 2014)
3. Fonseca, B., et al.: PLAYER - a European Project and a Game to Foster Entrepreneurship Education for Young People. Journal of Universal Computer Science 18(1), 86–105 (2012)
4. Graevenitza, G., Harhoffa, D., Weberb, R.: The effects of entrepreneurship education. Journal of Economic Behavior & Organization 76, 90–112 (2010)
5. Audretsch, D., Fritsch, M.: Growth regimes over time and space. Regional Studies 36, 113–124 (2002)
6. Kuratko, D.F.: The emergence of entrepreneurship education: development, trends, and challenges. Entrepreneurship Theory and Practice 29(5), 577–598 (2005)
7. Martin, B., McNally, J., Kay, M.: Examining the Formation of Human Capital in Entrepreneurship: A Meta-Analysis of Entrepreneurship Education Outcomes. Journal of Business Venturing 28(2), 211–224 (2013)

8. Kolvereid, L., Moen, Ø.: Entrepreneurship among business graduates: does a major in entrepreneurship make a difference? Journal of European Industrial Training 21(4), 154–160 (1997)

9. Galloway, L., Brown, W.: Entrepreneurship education at university: a driver in the creation of high growth firms? Education and Training. Emerald 44, 398–404 (2002)

10. DeTienne, D.R., Chandler, G.N.: Opportunity identification and its role in the entrepreneurial classroom: a pedagogical approach and empirical test. The Academy of Management Learning and Education 3, 242–257 (2004)

11. Fayolle, A.: Personal views on the future of entrepreneurship education. Entrepreneurship & Regional Development 25(7-8), 692–701 (2013)

12. European Commission: Entrepreneurship Action Plan (2020), http://ec.europa.eu/enterprise/policies/sme/entrepreneurship-2020/index_en.htm (accessed in February 2014)

13. Neck, H.M., Greene, P.G.: Entrepreneurship Education: Known Worlds and New Frontiers. Journal of Small Business Management 49(1), 55–70 (2011)

14. Osterwalder, A., Pigneur, Y.: Business Model Generation: A Handbook for Visionaries, Game Changers, and Challengers. Wiley (2010)

An Approach to Holistic Development of Serious Games and Learning Simulations

Aleshia T. Hayes

University of Central Florida, Synthetic Reality Lab, Orlando Florida
Aleshia.prof@gmail.com

Abstract. This discourse is an argument for a holistic approach to developing learning games and computer mediated experiences through the intersections of the areas of efficacy, effectiveness, and user experience in designing and developing serious games and simulated learning experiences. Some examples are explored in which reasonably effective design approaches could have been improved by a more holistic and iterative approach. The approach includes the integration of learning objectives, outcomes, usability, motivation, experience, ludus, aesthetics, cost and sustainability of the systems based on research within the fields of education, learning theory, game design theory, and simulation. These constructs explain the need for an iterative and holistic approach to designing and developing learning games. Embracing iterative and learning centered design of serious games will perpetuate development of effective educational technology.

Keywords: Educational Technology, Efficacy, Engagement, Serious Games, Evaluation.

1 Introduction

Millions of dollars and countless hours are invested in the development of serious games for education internationally every year. While it is widely accepted that games can be effective and engaging learning tools, there is apprehension about the use of technology. This apprehension appears in the discourse on high level discussions of education in technology, such as when Education Nation Town Hall Talks moderator, Alex Witt, posed a question about the value of technology in the classroom with, "...we don't have a lot of concrete evidence that the billions and billions of dollars that schools are using to try and introduce technology into the classrooms are working. We don't have the evidence so far to say that test scores are being raised, that students will not drop out [10]". In addition to concerns about the potential that certain serious games or simulations may be ineffective, the potential of negative training, in which students learn the wrong thing, must be considered in development of learning systems [12]. In the US Department of Education's National Education Technology Plan, there is an explicit call to begin making more "data driven decisions" about how to acquisition and use of educational technology.

P. Zaphiris and A. Ioannou (Eds.): LCT 2014, Part II, LNCS 8524, pp. 42–49, 2014.
© Springer International Publishing Switzerland 2014

1.1   Gap in the Existing Approach

A gap exists in the comprehensiveness of each of these individual evaluation procedures, as the user experience analysis does not necessarily quantify the effectiveness and efficacy of the specific game or experience being evaluated. In his call for more purposeful game design, Dr. Konstantin Mitgutsch of MIT Singapore writes that "Serious games are mainly assessed in terms of the quality of their content, not in terms of their intention-based design" [17]. This void in assessment of intentionality of design largely explains the apprehension that is arising in public forums about the value of technology in the classroom.

This paper is a call for a holistic iterative approach to design and development as well as assessment and evaluation of serious games and learning environments. For the purposes of this paper, holistic is defined as, relating to or concerned with wholes or with complete systems rather than with the analysis of, treatment of, or dissection into parts [16]. Because of the iterative nature of the design and consumption of games, this discourse aims to inform the processes of assessment (formative and summative), evaluation, and design. While the two terms are often erroneously used interchangeably, assessment and evaluation are referred to as distinct processes. Evaluation relates to placing a summative value judgment on an entity or assigning worth to it [1], whereas, assessment refers to a formative process of improvement that is often diagnostic in nature [1], [15], [17]. Test-driven development resembles this approach, but is still missing elements of the specifications, requirements and objectives necessary in educational technology.

1.2   Partnerships Yield Holistic Design and Assessment

Partnership between designers, educators, developers, testers, funding sources, and consumers will resolve many of the questions of efficacy and effectiveness of serious games and simulations as a shared lexicon creates a productive discourse that contributes to the evolution of educational technology. Professional evaluators of serious games and learning systems (e.g. DOE administrators, school districts, software company employees, and bloggers) have a myriad of constructs to consider when evaluating a system.

Not only do they need to answer multiple questions relating to learning objectives, outcomes, usability, motivation, experience, ludus, aesthetics, cost and sustainability of the systems they evaluate, but they also have to look at the intersection of these variables. Does the system do what it says it will do? How hard is it to learn and use? How fun is it? How much and how often will the children play it? At what level will they learn from this system? How sustainable is the investment into this system? Because these considerations are complex and range multiple disciplines, evaluation is often distilled to the lowest common denominators of fun, learning outcomes, and cost. Because of this, design is often also limited to these superficial factors, in an attempt to satisfice the needs of stakeholders [21].

1.3   Constructing a Holistic Design and Assessment Approach

Design should be objective oriented, assessment, on the other hand, pertains to gaining information, such as the needs or accomplishments of an entity [1]. If designers and developers are creating technology to meet the needs of the clients, it behooves these clients to explicitly determine and express their expectations in a holistic way. While both assessment and evaluation are beneficial to game design and measurement, the distinction is important. Parents deciding whether or not to spend $60 on a learning game may wish to evaluate that game or view the evaluation of a professional evaluator. The funding agency supporting development may request a needs assessment or a formative assessment before providing thousands to fund development of a learning system. That same funding agency may follow up by assessing or evaluating the game at certain checkpoints or upon completion.

2   Elements of the Holistic Approach

Developers and designers often evaluate or assess the learning systems that they develop through some objective measure as determined by their goals and values; typical approaches to collecting metrics on systems include usability analysis, user experience, efficacy, effectiveness measures [6], [22], [23]. Some prevalent ways to evaluate the efficacy and effectiveness of learning tools include performance improvement assessments, blind coder ratings, qualitative and quantitative self-reports of social presence, questionnaires, and ultimately performance tests that measure improvement in desired knowledge, skills, or abilities [3], [4]. This discourse calls for the integration of these approaches with innovations in design approaches and subsequent assessment of systems include the learning objectives, MDA (Mechanics, Dynamics, and Aesthetics) Framework, and Game Flow [5], [18]. While measures are often internally designed or imposed upon the development team by the sponsoring agency, this framework can ensure thorough consistency when comparing similar education tools.

Table 1. Elements of a Holistic Approach to Development, and Evaluation

Construct	Formative or Summative
Learning Objectives	Formative
Learning Outcomes	Summative
Usability	Summative
User Experience	Summative
Motivation	Formative & Summative
Ludus	Formative & Summative
Aesthetics	Formative & Summative
Cost	Formative & Summative
Sustainability	Formative & Summative

2.1   Learning Objectives

Whether learning objectives in the serious games are explicit and didactic, or more discovery or inquiry based, there are too few explicit objectives for any serious game that are based on learning outcomes. "The content of a serious game could be well presented, adequately formulated, "correct" or irrelevant, hard to access or insufficient, and in worst cases, just wrong and biased" [17,4] The Serious Game Design Assessment framework posits an approach that looks at content in terms of whether the game environment and mechanisms reflect the necessary information to adequately transfer, and fidelity. This looks at fidelity in terms of name accuracy, narrative, and rules.

Universal Design for Learning is an example of an approach derived from architectural approach, universal design, that include designing structures to be used by people of varied levels of ability. One instrument that may inform the process of game and simulated environment assessment and usability is a 12-item questionnaire that integrates usability and principles of Universal Design, the (RAPUUD) Rapid Assessment of Product Usability & Universal Design [2]. While this tool is intended for assessment of consumer products, this tool provides a starting point for the underlying concepts to be cross-validated to integrate existing usability techniques with structured universal design for learning (UDL) constructs. The Universal Design for Learning principles that have been accepted by the US Department of Education are:

- Provide multiple and flexible methods of presentation of information and knowledge. Examples include digital books, specialized software and websites, text-to-speech applications, and screen readers.
- Provide multiple and flexible means of expression with alternatives for students to demonstrate what they have learned. Examples include online concept mapping and speech-to-text programs.
- Provide multiple and flexible means of engagement to tap into diverse learners' interests, challenge them appropriately, and motivate them to learn. Examples include choices among different scenarios or content for learning the same competency and opportunities for increased collaboration or scaffolding [9].

2.2   Learning Outcomes

Learning objectives and outcomes can be reciprocally impacted by the universal design for learning. Instructional design principles also inform the development of learning objectives. Learning objectives need to be explicit and measureable. To be more effective, effective learning goals can be broken into tasks and subtasks that each have measurable goals. Similarly, learning outcomes should be measured against appropriate learning objectives. Any analysis of learning outcomes without effective learning objectives will be less potent and potentially inaccurate.

2.3   User Experience

Measurements of user experience conducted by designers are generally positive, indicating user engagement, enjoyment, and preference over other methods of instruction [8], [20]. While this is a valuable finding, which some may rely on to allude to engagement, the often subjective construct of engagement without demonstrated benefits to learning has a diminished generalizable meaning. As Frokjear explains, the correlation between user satisfaction and effectiveness are often negligible and should be looked at separately [12]. Because outcome research results are specific to the samples (or populations from which they were drawn) and the outcomes measured, "it is essential that conclusions from the research be clear as to the population(s) and outcomes for which efficacy is claimed" [11]. Flay goes on to explain that, "Effectiveness trials test whether interventions are effective under 'real-world' conditions or in 'natural' settings. Effectiveness trials may also establish for whom, and under what conditions of delivery, the intervention is effective" [11].

User experience is a general term that often encompasses the perceptions derived through interactions that a user has with a system [22] For the purposes of this discourse, user experience refers to the levels of engagement, presence, ludology, learnability, memorability, and general satisfaction with the interface. The MDA framework addresses much of this in its' synthesized approach to considering of mechanics, dynamics, and aesthetics. Specifically, their objective is to understand and "decompose" the formal process of decision-making during gameplay in order to inform design, criticism, and research (pg. 4).

In the domain of student education, engagement is a construct /that captures the quality of students' participation with learning activities in the classroom, ranging from energized, enthusiastic, focused, emotionally positive interactions with academic tasks to apathetic withdrawal [19]. Skinner et. al. provide an instrument that is effective in measuring a learner's levels of Engagement vs. Disaffection with learning.

2.4   Usability

The International Standards Organization has amalgamated usability as effectiveness, efficiency, and satisfaction in reference to users being able to achieve an intended goal using the specified object in an intended context [22]. Notably, at least one of the intended goal for learning simulations and serious games should be achievement of learning objectives. Usability is often criticized as being simplistic, dichotic and excessively generalized [15]. The use of a single test to determine the viability of a product is often insufficient. Some studies are conducted on as few as five participants and the results are then generalized to the population as a whole [22]. While this approach is very effective for a formative or even summative assessment, the criticisms have arisen from the use of these studies to invalidate systems as having poor usability with limited metrics [15]

These critiques of usability analysis are due to the fact that usability studies were not intended to be holistic assessments or evaluations of systems. Instead they were to look at effectiveness, efficiency, and satisfaction in terms of standards [2]. Additionally, usability standards are generally applied to many products, rather than being designed to measure games specifically. Mitgutsch explains, "investigating their impact becomes incomplete if the games' purpose and their coherence in relation to their design is not identified beforehand. Therefore, we argue that research on the impact of serious games starts with the analysis and evaluation of their qualities in terms of their purpose based formal conceptual design" [17]. The reciprocal relationship between design and assessment this article combines the assessment and design constructs to give a thorough analysis of the elements involved in this undertaking.

2.5   Ludus and Motivation

While there are other motivations to engage with serious games, the key element that distinguishes these tools from other educational technology and even traditional approaches to learning is the motivation that is generated from the ludic nature of the experience [19]. Unfortunately, this essential element is often overlooked in the evaluation, assessment, and even design of serious games. The capacity to immerse oneself in a ludic learning experience is becoming more powerful as the technology advances, with tools such as AR (Augmented Reality), MR (Mixed Reality), VR (Virtual Reality) [4], [6], [8]. But, the capacity to create ludic learning does not guarantee such an experience. Multiple elements of engagement, immersion, participation, and discovery must be integrated in order to make these experiences anything more than pixels on a screen.

2.6   Examples

There are several examples where this has been done well, and far more examples in which the attempts have been abysmal. One of the more successful efforts includes the BrainPop products which integrate usability and user experience in their deployment with the targeted and explicit learning objectives and measures of learning. Another successful effort was the River City Project, which modeled the approach of successful games, World of Warcraft and The Sims to create a learning experience in a MUVE (Multi-user Virtual environment) [8]. Both of these experiences are known to increase understanding and self-efficacy, which may be correlated to higher ratings of user enjoyment, engagement, and satisfaction.

2.7   Iterative Implementation

The synthesis of the different approaches to assessment and evaluation may be daunting if conducted simultaneously. Fortunately, the alternative to an exhaustive study evaluating a system on every possible level is to take the iterative approach. The ADDIE model used in instructional system design allows for an iterative approach [7]. The iterative approach requires careful consideration of the interaction of all of the elements of a learning system in order to avoid making small changes that inadvertently change the entire experience. Further research will reveal if there is a correlation or even causal relationship between the holistic constructs within these learning experiences.

3   Conclusion

Because of the nascent nature of this research, the author's recommendation is to consider the synthesis of these principles as heuristics to guide the assessment and design of serious games and learning simulations, rather than as the basis for a finite algorithmic model. In some cases very few of these considerations need to be conducted, while in other cases, the complexity of the learning system or learning objective may demand a more extensive evaluation. This is not intended to drive the development of a rubric by which to judge a learning system, rather, these ideas can be used to shape a more informed and empowered perspective and the discourse that crosses both game designers and consumers or evaluators of those systems. The heuristics that come from a shared discourse about games can lead to a holistic approach to understanding assessing evaluating and designing serious games and simulations.

References

1. Alkin, M.C.: Evaluation Essentials: From A to Z. Guilford Publications (2010)
2. Asundi, K., Lenker, J.A., Nasarwanji, M., Paquet, V., Feathers, D.: A tool for rapid assessment of product usability and universal design: Development and preliminary psychometric testing. Work 39(2), 141–150 (2011)
3. Bailenson, J.: The Effects of Fully Immersive Virtual Reality on the Learning of Physical Tasks. Paper Presented at The 9th International Workshop on Presence Cleveland, Ohio (2006)
4. Botella, C., Bretón-López, J., Quero, S., Baños, R., García-Palacios, A.: Treating cockroach phobia with augmented reality. Behavior Therapy 41(3), 401–413 (2010)
5. Csikszentmihalyi, M.: Flow: the psychology of optimal experience / Mihaly Csikszentmihalyi (1st Harper Perennial Modern Classics ed.). Harper Perennial, New York (1990)
6. Dede, C.: Immersive Interfaces for Engagement and Learning. Science 323(5910), 66–69 (2009)
7. Dick, W., Carey, L., Carey, J.O.: The systematic design of instruction. Merrill/Pearson, Upper Saddle River, N.J (2009)
8. Dieterle, E.: Neomillennial Learning Styles and River City. Children, Youth and Environments 19(1), 245–278 (2009), http://www.colorado.edu/journals/cye (retrieved (date))
9. DOE (Department of Education). National educational technology plan. Transforming American education: learning powered by technology (2010)
10. Education Nation (Producer). Will Technology Transform Learning? (2012), http://www.educationnation.com/index.cfm?objectid=17C1CAAD-FE84-11E1-9448000C296BA163 (retrieved)

11. Flay, B.: Standards of Evidence (2004), http://www.preventionresearch.org/StandardsofEvidencebook.pdf (retrieved)
12. Frokjaer, E., Hertzum, M., Hornbaek, K.: Measuring Usability: Are Effectiveness, Efficiency, and Satisfaction Really Correlated? (2000)
13. Harteveld, C.: Triadic Game Design Balancing Reality, Meaning and Play (2011), http://site.ebrary.com/id/10452578
14. Hogue, J.R., Brickman, N.S., Pelz, C.A., Markham, S.: Virtual Reality Parachute Simulation Enhancements for Improved Aircrew Emergency Training (2005)
15. Hornbaek, K.: Dogmas in the assessment of usability evaluation methods (English). Behaviour & Information Technology (Print) 29(1), 97–111 (2010)
16. Merriam Webster. Holistic. from Encyclopedia Brittanica (2012), http://www.merriam-webster.com/dictionary/holistic
17. Mitgutsch, K., Alvarado, N.: Purposeful by design?: A serious game design assessment framework. Paper Presented at the Proceedings of the International Conference on the Foundations of Digital Games, Raleigh, North Carolina, http://gambit.mit.edu/readme/academic_papers/fdg2012_submission_82-1.pdf
18. Robin, H., Marc, L., Robert, Z.: MDA: A Formal Approach to Game Design and Game Research (2004), doi:citeulike-article-id:382810
19. Skinner, E.A., Kindermann, T.A., Furrer, C.: A motivational perspective on engagement and disaffection: Conceptualization and assessment of children's behavioral and emotional participation in academic activities in the classroom (2009)
20. Thomas, R.G., William John, N., Delieu, J.M.: Augmented Reality for Anatomical Education. Journal of Visual Communication in Medicine 33(1), 6–15 (2010), doi:10.3109/17453050903557359
21. Tullis, T., Albert, B.: Chapter 10 - Case Studies Measuring the User Experience, pp. 237–287. Morgan Kaufmann, San Francisco (2008a)
22. Tullis, T., Albert, B.: Measuring the user experience: collecting, analyzing, and presenting usability metrics. Elsevier/Morgan Kaufmann, Amsterdam, Boston (2008b)
23. Villalta, M., Gajardo, I., Nussbaum, M., Andreu, J.J., Echeverria, A., Plass, J.L.: Design Guidelines for Classroom Multiplayer Presential Games (CMPG). Computers & Education 57(3), 2039–2053 (2011)

Experiencing Physical and Technical Phenomena in Schools Using Virtual Reality Driving Simulator

Polina Häfner, Victor Häfner, and Jivka Ovtcharova

Karlsruhe Institute of Technology, Karlsruhe 76131, Germany
polina.haefner@kit.edu
http://www.imi.kit.edu/

Abstract. In the time of globalization and technical advances, companies want to remain competitive on national and international markets. This requires a qualified workforce with a corresponding level of education in the STEM fields. This paper presents a didactic methodology for a virtual reality-based workshop which supplements the school curricula of secondary education institutions. A virtual reality driving simulation application is used in order to enhance the students understanding of different physical and technical phenomena as well as to teach technical skills, such as the ability to program virtual reality applications. We observed that this methodology helps to reduce complexity and aid the understanding of the subject. This is due to the three main contributing factors: Immersion, interaction and engagement. The enthusiasm for the virtual reality systems kept the students motivated not only during the teaching units, but it has also inspired them to pursue the STEM careers.

Keywords: serious games, technology enhanced learning, STEM fields, secondary education, virtual learning environment, driving simulation.

1 Introduction

STEM is an acronym that stands for the fields of study science, technology, engineering and mathematics. These are very important fields with regard to technology and workforce development. Their development directly relates to the national economic competitiveness [1]. Graduate numbers in STEM fields have seen an increase in the past few years, but the demand still has not been met by a large margin. The corporate sector is urgently looking for graduates from the faculties of mathematics, computer science, natural sciences and technology, resulting in excellent opportunities for students with degrees related to the aforementioned subjects. To address the STEM skills shortage, ministries of education take measures and launch campaigns to further promote interest in STEM (for example European Schoolnet [2] or the Federal Ministry of Education and Research in Germany [3]).

Looking at contemporary products, for example from electronic or automotive industries, we witness a rapidly growing complexity. Handling this new complexity requires well-prepared engineers, able to investigate and solve engineering

P. Zaphiris and A. Ioannou (Eds.): LCT 2014, Part II, LNCS 8524, pp. 50–61, 2014.

problems efficiently and in interdisciplinary teams. Virtual reality (VR) is a technology that can help in dealing with this complexity present both in the industry itself and in the education. With regard to the latter, it can raise the appeal of STEM subjects and bridge the gap between the theoretical knowledge and its practical application to problems in science and industry.

Sherman and Craig [4] define virtual reality as "... a medium composed of interactive computer simulations that sense the participant's position and actions and replace or augment the feedback to one or more senses, giving the feeling of being mentally immersed or present in the simulation". According to Burdea and Coiffet [5], the three most important properties of VR are the so-called "3 Is": Immersion, interaction and imagination. These are realized through multiple input and output devices, enabling the bidirectional information flow between the user and the virtual world. From the technological point of view, we characterize a virtual environment as immersive, if it provides stereoscopic, real size representations of objects, supports user headtracking and offers intuitive interaction.

Due the advantages it offers, VR is often deployed in fields such as medicine [6], automotive [7], aerospace industries [8] and entertainment [9]. One field of application of virtual environments (VEs) is the educational sector [10]. An example of such an interactive, 3-dimensional virtual learning environment is the virtual campus [11]. It opens new types of interactive, visual-spatial learning and therefore enables users to take advantage of its graphical representation of information.

The entertainment industry advances the VR technologies, resulting in hardware available at lower prices and increased customer acceptance. Stereo TVs or head-mounted displays (HMD) for visual output, such as the Oculus Rift, 3D surround sound systems and interaction devices like Kinect or Leap Motion are now affordable for the end user. These are only moderately immersive, but can serve as an alternative to highly immersive yet expensive environments (like CAVEs) for teaching students the fundamentals of virtual reality or employing virtual reality to teach STEM subjects.

Technological advances are leading to familiarization of young people with this new media. From a young age, they are exposed to modern information technologies such as computers, smart devices and game consoles with different interaction devices, as well as stereo output such as 3D TVs and 3D cinemas, making the integration of new media in the classroom very natural for students.

The purpose of deploying VR technologies in education is not only to make lessons more interesting for the students, but also to help their imaginative faculties. VR simulations enable the learners to employ their theoretical knowledge of a certain subject in order to make decisions and observe the results in a safe, controlled environment. Real-time realistic scenarios can be represented virtually, thus saving the costs of lab equipment, while at the same time gaining knowledge and untderstanding of the subject matter. Another clear advantage of using this technology in education are the fun factor and the high level of engagement.

In this paper, we present a methodology, as well as examples of its application, for teaching and increasing interest in STEM subjects among senior grades students in secondary education through familiarization with an immersive virtual reality car driving simulator. In addition to conventional lessons, students can experience physical phenomena and gain technical skills, such as the ability to program VR applications. The following section gives an overview of related works in the area of VR use in education. It is then followed by our methodology. A detailed description of this projects application in a German school is presented in section 4. The paper is concluded with a look on the future work on applications of virtual reality for training and education.

2   Related Works

Not all benefits of virtual learning environments (VLEs) over traditional educational environments have been explored thus far. With regard to the design of effective virtual learning environments it is important to know which features of virtual reality (VR) support cognitive processing [12,13].

In 2006 a study of primary school students examined two different VLEs in comparison to traditional educational methods [14]. The evaluated virtual learning environments included both a complete interactive one as well as a passive one. The VLEs were designed as virtual playgrounds in a Cave Automatic Virtual Environment (CAVE). The passive VLE employed a virtual robot that guided activities. The results indicated that the complete interactive VLE aids primary school students in problem solving, but does not lead to conceptual changes in their thinking. Surprisingly the passive VLE appeared to support the learners recall and reflection abilities, thus hinting at signs of conceptual change in their minds.

Another study describes a VLE [15] for science, physics and chemistry "Virtual Water" at the final year of secondary education and first year of university and indicates that 3D virtual environments may help students with high spatial aptitude to acquire better conceptual understanding of the subject matter. The main advantages according to Trindade et al. are the ability to visualize situations which cannot be seen otherwise and to immerse the students within these situations. Students reported that the stereoscopic view gave them a more tangible grasp of a solid state structures such as that of ice.

There are numerous examples of VLE considering the STEM subjects. One application is the virtual physics laboratory that allows students to control the test environment (gravity, surface friction and atmospheric drag) as well as the physical properties of objects (coefficients of restitution of elastic bodies). The students can both observe physical phenomena at macroscopic and microscopic levels or control the time [16].

An application for mathematics and geometry classes at the latter grades of secondary school and university encourages experimentation with geometric constructions and facilitates learning with the aid of stereoscopy, thus being more effective learning tool than the traditional CAD package [17]. The three dimensional geometric construction tool called "Construct3D", based on the collaborative augmented reality system "Studierstube", uses a stereoscopic head-mounted display and a two-handed 3D interaction tool.

Serious games are being considered as a new method for teaching content and motivate the students for STEM careers. Serious games allow learners to experience situations that are impossible in the real world for reasons such as safety, cost and time. They are also claimed to have a positive impact on the players' development of various skills [18].

Such applications can be implemented in virtual environments on different immersion levels. Miller et al. created and tested a web-based forensic science game among 700 secondary school students [19]. They observed a positive relationship between the role-playing experience and science career motivation as well as significant gain in knowledge of the subject.

A game-based, semi-virtual learning environment called "SMALLab" is presented from Johnson-Glenberg et. al for teaching geology and physics. It relies on multiple modalities: 3D object tracking, real time graphics and surround-sound used to enhance embodied learning [20].

The first cyber classroom lab in Germany was opened in 2009 at Lifecycle Engineering Solution Center (LESC) of the Karlsruhe Institute of Technology in cooperation with the company Visenso [21,22]. During the last six years at Institute for Information Management in Engineering (IMI), we worked on solutions for holistic, interdisciplinary and multilingual education methodologies for the field of engineering by using the benefits of virtual reality and virtual learning environments. In the next section, we present our methodology for experiencing physical and technical phenomena in schools using a VR driving simulator as learning environment.

3 Methodology

The idea behind the project is to enhance the students understanding of different physical and technical phenomena using a driving simulator as testing environment and to utilize appropriate VR technologies to visualize the effects of those phenomena. The aim of this project is the creation of a virtual reality experiment kit for secondary education institutions containing the required hardware and software components along with all necessary teaching materials (for instance exercise sheets and presentations). Using the VR experiment kit, the students acquire and strengthen their interdisciplinary knowledge in the areas of computer science (visual programming), physics (Newtonian mechanics) and technology (control loops). The following goals were defined for this project:

1. to increase the students interest in science and engineering through creative work and hands-on learning
2. to promote the development of skills required for identifying and solving complex, interdisciplinary problems from STEM fields
3. to create situations that reinforce the connection between thinking, action and intuition

4. to stimulate individual and self-determined learning
5. to strengthen the students imaginative faculties using modern media
6. to create a sustainable inner drive for further education in engineering and science

The learning approach is similar to serious games but supported by virtual reality. The focus lies on STEM topics with lessons on VR technologies, basics of computer graphics programing and 3D content authoring. 3D immersive representations aid the students in absorbing new information with greater ease, as they can perceive it in an adequate manner using multiple senses, thus seeing and hearing simultaneously.

The didactic method used is the so-called sandwich strategy. The teaching unit consists of 90 minutes and is divided in multiple activities with the maximum duration of 20 minutes each. These activities can consist of theoretical explanations in front of the class, presentations, discussions, individual programming sessions and testing of the results with the VR setup. This strategy helps in keeping the students focused and motivated as well as in aiding their understanding of the subject matter.

The labs are designed in a modular manner, so they can be easily reconfigured for students of varying grades and educational backgrounds. The teachers can select the topics in an arbitrary manner depending on their schools curriculum. Each topic comes with a standalone programming exercise. This results in a decrease of programming complexity and fosters the concentration of the students on the problem-setting.

The proposed solution is designed to support conventional science lessons in form of extracurricular activities (further referred to as workshops). Another important aspect of the proposed solution is the possibility of collaborative work, which supports interdisciplinary communication and problem solving. The workshop can be divided in the following four parts: introduction to virtual reality and the authoring tool, teaching units, demonstrations of VR and evaluation.

3.1 Introduction

The first teaching unit starts with an introduction to the project, followed by a presentation about virtual reality, its definition and characteristics. At this point, it is important to differentiate between the perception of virtual reality from the point of view of entertainment media, such as science fiction literature and cinema, and the currently available hardware and software.

The next step is to present the virtual reality development environment that will be used for the exercises. The employed software tool has been chosen for its visual programing paradigm that allows to easily implement behaviours in the virtual world. This decreases the programming difficulty level that the students have to achieve and eliminates the need to learn a programming language.

3.2   Exercises

Each exercise has a typical structure following the sandwich strategy described above. First the topic is introduced, describing the problem with its definition, formula and real life examples. The subject should be selected to be something that the students are already familiar with or have already studied as a part of their curriculum. The suggested approach is to organize a group discussion and ask the students to explain the presented problem in their own terms, meanwhile writing down all suggestions on the black board. The main part is a tutored exercise where each student works on the same assignment. The students are asked to investigate and learn independently the influence of system variables on the exercise outcome.

For example, an exercise from the field of Newtonian mechanics could be conducted by simulating the free parabolic trajectory of a car launched from a ramp (see Fig. 1). The students could be tasked with the creation of a visual script that would allow to alter the cars power output as well as the angle at which it is launched. The students would then conduct the experiment several times, noting down the variation among distances the car traveled depending on the figures entered for the two aforementioned parameters. The recorded distances, as well as the entry parameters, can then be presented in a tabular form and verified with regard to their correspondence to established physical models.

3.3   Experiencing Virtual Reality

The solutions from the exercises are presented at the end of the lesson. The best solution can be deployed on the VR setup to experience it in an immersive environment. The chance to test the results in the driving simulator should keep the students motivated while they are completing the tasks. The first contact with immersive virtual reality environments should be as early as possible, preferably during the first unit. It is important to demonstrate different VR hardware, software and applications at the beginning of the workshop, combining both, theory and practice.

3.4   Evaluation

Both, the success of the workshop and the students' performance can be evaluated by conducting discussions with the participants or through the use of questionnaires. There is a possibility to measure the improvement in knowledge acquisition with written tests, conducted at the beginning and at the end of the workshop.

4   Application

The pilot project Driving Simulator in Virtual Reality - DRIVE was a workshop in schools that expanded their traditional laboratory exercises in order to

Fig. 1. Exercise on the free jump and testing it on the driving simulator

give the students the opportunity to experience physical phenomena in VLEs. The target group included public school students from Baden-Württemberg, Germany, grades nine through twelve. The entirety of the workshop lasted one term. The project covered three topics: control loops, energy and mechanics. A total of 18 teaching units took place, with a duration of 90 minutes each.

4.1   Equipment

The driving simulator was introduced in the classroom as a low cost VR setup, serving as a basis for virtual reality exercises. Originally the driving simulator was developed by students of the Karlsruhe Institute of Technology during a practical course on virtual reality [23]. The hardware used for the stereo visual output consists of powerwall equipped with headtracking. The students at the university built a seat-box with a real car seat and used the gaming controller Logitech G25 as car interface (steering wheel, pedals and gear lever). The software solution contains a 3D model of the car, a racing track, the environment, weather conditions and sound. The most important part of the package was the driving simulation and the physics (e.g. collision detection).

The Einstein Gymnasium has a well-equipped computer lab with internet-connected laptops available to each student (see Fig. 2). These are a necessary prerequisite for any type of programming workshop or IT driven lesson. The virtual reality system had been added to the classroom like the one constructed by the students in the virtual reality practical course, but instead of powerwall HMDs were used. This setup is quite immersive but still low-cost and thus affordable for a school that would want to adopt the project's methodology. The total hardware cost was approximately € 2000, which included a computer, an HMDs, a car seat and a Logitech wheel.

The students had the opportunity to visit the labs at LESC at IMI. The center was established in 2007 as a central platform for the institute's research results, the interdisciplinary exchange of knowledge at KIT and the transfer of technology into practice. The laboratories are equipped with state-of-the-art VR hardware and software. The first lab has a high-end virtual reality environment with a distributed stereoscopic visualization in a three-sided CAVE setup,

Fig. 2. Students working on the programming task

which allows the user to dive into virtual worlds. The second lab consists of a mobile powerwall and contains haptic devices. Both labs have an ART tracking system for headtracking and interaction. Moreover, 3D monitors, HMDs, depth cameras, data gloves and smart devices allow to experiment with low-cost VR environments. A computer pool with powerful workstations is used for 3D content authoring, application development and teaching courses.

4.2 Software

For the DRIVE project the VR authoring tool 3DVIA Virtools from Dassault Systèmes was used. It features a graphical programming interface with functional blocks connected by lines that either represent the workflow or the parameter references. The graphical programing paradigm allows a fast prototyping of logic in a virtual world, without having prerequisites like programming skills or advanced knowledge of computer science. The software comes with a good documentation. During the work with 3DVIA Virtools some drawbacks were noticed. The tool lacks a larger community, this makes it difficult to solve problems through the use of forums or mailing lists. A further problem for the suites future adoption in schools are the high incurred costs for licenses and the end of support in 2014.

4.3 Exercises

The exercises are structured around three main topics. Energy is the first topic where we address the energy management in a car. The second topic introduces control loops, the third some basic Newtonian mechanics. All topics have been chosen to fit the theme of car dynamics simulation. As the students proceed, the exercise grows in complexity providing fewer hints than the previous one. At the same time the amount of basic functions grows with each following exercise as more advanced features are implemented.

Energy. The first exercise addresses the topic fuel consumption. The task is to program in an appropriate consumption rate that varies depending on the use of the throttle. The gas tank and the fuel gauge are modeled at the same time. The students learn the relations between the different variables. For instance they have to model the fuel consumption using a Bèzier curve.

The second exercise implements a visual feedback for the wind resistance. Again a Bèzier curve is used to map two parameters. The last exercise consists of recovering energy from the car brakes when slowing down. A booster meter fills up every time the car slows down using the brakes. Once the meter is filled, a key press releases additional torque on the wheels.

Control Loops. The first exercise in the control loops unit features an automatic car light control. The intensity of the car lights is adjusted, depending on the output of two sensors: the car light sensor and the daylight sensor. The second exercise is an automatic windshield wiper. The third is an extension of the first with an indicator for the lights state. Here, we introduced the concept of RGB colors (see Fig. 3). The final exercise in this unit is centered around the automatic control of the cars sunroof. The automatization works through the use of a rain sensor. Furthermore, the students had an opportunity to implement the ability to control the sunroof directly through a push of a button on the Logitech wheel.

Newtonian mechanics. The Newtonian mechanics unit is the largest of the three and consists of six exercises. It starts with a free jump simulation where a launched car has to cross a trench. The width of the trench is constant, only the height between the two sides of the trench and the engine torque can be adjusted. The speed at the beginning of the jump is recorded. This allows the students to validate the theoretical height for a successful jump.

The second exercise puts the free jump in another setup. Now the car is launched from a ramp, which effectively changes the starting angle of the jump. This exercise also includes loading a 3D model in the scene.

The third exercise focuses on friction, demonstrating the driving behaviour depending on the adjustable friction coefficient of the road. An advanced feature

Fig. 3. 3DVIA Virtools script - programming task

of this exercise is the use of a quad generating function that represents the road surface depending on the friction coefficient.

The fourth exercise builds on the previous one. Now the braking distance has to be computed and displayed depending on the friction coefficient and the speed just before pushing the brake.

The fifth exercise allows to tilt the track in a curve sideways at an angle. The goal of this exercise is to discuss the centrifugal and centripetal forces acting on the car and how this changes when tilting the track in a curve sideways at an angle. The last exercise exemplifies the law of conservation of momentum. The students have to observe and discuss the behaviour of the car when crashing into a static object of a mass lesser, equal or greater than that of the car. The second part consists of crashing into a moving object.

5   Conclusion and Future Works

The enthusiasm for virtual reality system kept the students engaged even through some of the less exciting parts of the exercises, thus suggesting that VR approaches result in superior motivation, retention and intellectual stimulation, as well as a better conceptual understanding of the subject matter.

The methodology has been validated by acquiring feedback from the students. The driving simulator was recognized as a valid and beneficial tool for imparting a better understanding of physical concepts and phenomena. The students were able to discern connections between physical principles and their application in vehicles. Furthermore, by performing the tasks offered by our approach, they were able to better understand the interplay between physics, computer science and technology. Various aspects of the pilot project were of particular interest to the participants of the workshop, resulting in diverse suggestions and heterogeneous feedback. Eleven of the twelve surveyed students would recommend the workshop to a friend. During this project, the students also made minor, voluntarily expansions to the driving simulations program code.

The teachers also considered the project to be a success and not only intended to organize the workshop again at future point in time, but also decided to use the topics from the pilot in the schools regular STEM lessons. Some of the students from the pilot are now studying machine engineering and computer science at the university level.

For future research, we suggest involving more homogeneous groups with regard to the participants age when conducting the workshop. Unfortunately our findings will be non-generalizable without a method for evaluating the impact of virtual reality on learning. This is a good opportunity for further investigation.

Acknowledgements. This project would have been impossible without the support of the Baden-Württemberg Stiftung foundation and my colleagues Jurica Katicic and Johannes Herter, who contributed greatly both to the conception and the realization of the project. The authors would like to thank the teachers and the students from the two partner schools, the Einstein Gymnasium and the Tulla Realschule in Kehl, Germany. A special thanks goes to the university students from the practical course in virtual reality at KIT who created the VR driving simulator.

References

1. National Research Council: Rising above the gathering storm: Energizing and employing america for a brighter economic future (2007)
2. European Schoolnet (2014), http://www.eun.org/ (accessed February 21, 2014)
3. Bildungsministerium für Bildung und Forschung: Perspektive MINT-Berufe: Förderung von Technik und Naturwissenschaft (2014), http://www.bmbf.de/de/mint-foerderung.php (accessed February 21, 2014)
4. Sherman, W.R., Craig, A.B.: Understanding virtual reality: Interface, application, and design. Elsevier (2002)
5. Burdea, G., Coiffet, P.: Virtual reality technology. Presence: Teleoperators and Virtual Environments 12(6), 663–664 (2003)
6. Riener, R., Harders, M.: Introduction to virtual reality in medicine. In: Virtual Reality in Medicine, pp. 1–12. Springer, Heidelberg (2012)
7. Jiang, M.: Virtual reality boosting automotive development. In: Ma, D., Fan, X., Gausemeier, J., Grafe, M. (eds.) Virtual Reality and Augmented Reality in Industry, pp. 171–180. Springer, Heidelberg (2011)
8. Stone, R., Panfilov, P., Shukshunov, V.: Evolution of aerospace simulation: From immersive virtual reality to serious games. In: 2011 5th International Conference on Recent Advances in Space Technologies (RAST), pp. 655–662 (June 2011)
9. Hsu, K.S., et al.: Application of a virtual reality entertainment system with human-machine haptic sensor device. Journal of Applied Sciences 11, 2145–2153 (2011)
10. Sampaio, A., Henriques, P., Martins, O.: Virtual reality technology used in civil engineering education. Open Virtual Reality Journal 2, 18–25 (2010)
11. Zhao, H., Sun, B., Wu, H., Hu, X.: Study on building a 3d interactive virtual learning environment based on opensim platform. In: 2010 International Conference on Audio Language and Image Processing (ICALIP), pp. 1407–1411 (November 2010)
12. Bowman, D.A., Sowndararajan, A., Ragan, E.D., Kopper, R.: Higher levels of immersion improve procedure memorization performance. In: Proceedings of the 15th Joint Virtual Reality Eurographics Conference on Virtual Environments, pp. 121–128. Eurographics Association (2009)
13. Häfner, P., Vinke, C., Häfner, V., Ovtcharova, J., Schotte, W.: The impact of motion in virtual environments on memorization performance. In: 2013 IEEE International Conference on Computational Intelligence and Virtual Environments for Measurement Systems and Applications (CIVEMSA), pp. 104–109 (July 2013)
14. Roussou, M., Oliver, M., Slater, M.: The virtual playground: an educational virtual reality environment for evaluating interactivity and conceptual learning. Virtual Reality 10(3-4), 227–240 (2006)
15. Trindade, J., Fiolhais, C., Almeida, L.: Science learning in virtual environments: a descriptive study. British Journal of Educational Technology 33(4), 471–488 (2002)
16. Bowen Loftin, R., Engleberg, M., Benedetti, R.: Applying virtual reality in education: A prototypical virtual physics laboratory. In: Proceedings of the IEEE 1993 Symposium on Research Frontiers in Virtual Reality, pp. 67–74 (October 1993)

17. Kaufmann, H., Schmalstieg, D., Wagner, M.: Construct3d: A virtual reality application for mathematics and geometry education. Education and Information Technologies 5(4), 263–276 (2000)
18. Susi, T., Johannesson, M., Backlund, P.: Serious games: An overview (2007)
19. Miller, L.M., Chang, C.I., Wang, S., Beier, M.E., Klisch, Y.: Learning and motivational impacts of a multimedia science game. Computers and Education 57(1), 1425–1433 (2011)
20. Johnson-Glenberg, M., Birchfield, D., Savvides, P., Megowan-Romanowicz, C.: Semi-virtual embodied learning-real world stem assessment. In: Annetta, L., Bronack, S. (eds.) Serious Educational Game Assessment, pp. 241–257. Sense Publishers (2011)
21. Zimmermann, M., Wierse, A.: From immersive engineering to selling and teaching. In: Virtual Reality and Augmented Reality in Industry, pp. 191–198. Springer (2011)
22. Ovtcharova, J.: Prof. Dr. Dr.–Ing. Jivka Ovtcharova eröffnet zusammen mit VISENSO das erste C3-Lab (2014), http://www.imi.kit.edu/1521.php (accessed: February 21, 2014)
23. Häfner, P., Häfner, V., Ovtcharova, J.: Teaching methodology for virtual reality practical course in engineering education. Procedia Computer Science 25, 251–260 (2013)

Weaving User Immersive Experiences: Scientific Curiosity and Reasoning with Bodily Feelings Mapping and Evolution

Niki Lambropoulos[1] and Tharrenos Bratitsis[2]

[1] Wire Communications Laboratory, Dept. of Electrical and Computer Engineering,
University of Patras, Greece
26504, Rion-Patras
nlampropoulou@wcl.ee.upatras.gr
[2] Early Childhood Education Department, University of Western Macedonia, Greece
bratitsis@uowm.gr

Abstract. The objective of this paper is to propose a gamification platform called Free2Grow that promotes scientific critical thinking based on User Immersive Experience (iX). Essential condition for effective use of media and methods is to make sure that they trigger and direct youngsters' curiosity, support their reasoning and emotional states, so that the learners are engaged and participate in new idea generation in co-creative writing. Free2Grow main characteristics are as follows: (a) diagnose/feed conative characteristics such as curiosity and reasoning as well as body atlas feelings as subtle ways that drive a youngster's reasoning and resilience; (b) enable gamification architecture; (c) team building and group formation techniques; (d) learners' active engagement in team co-creativity projects that will necessitate and make reference to the knowledge and skills acquired.

Keywords: Gamification, Immersive Experience, critical thinking, curiosity, emotional states, Computer Supported Collaborative Learning Communication, E-research with Communities, Team Based Innovation.

1   Introduction

Nowadays, there are several challenges for initial education such as fostering talent and training; transitioning from school to work; gaining and retaining employment; and introducing new skills: personal, social and learning skills such as initiative, resilience, creativity, team-working, empathy, co-construction and connectedness as well as skills for management, organisation and metacognitive skills which are important for learner-centered, social and lifelong learning. Free2Grow is a novel educational collective intelligence multimodal platform aiming to support, advance and challenge the interplay between reasoning and curiosity and feelings mapping charts by the creative use of gamification and enhancing youngsters' associated competencies for the Semantic Web. In result, based on these conative drives as well

P. Zaphiris and A. Ioannou (Eds.): LCT 2014, Part II, LNCS 8524, pp. 62–71, 2014.

as cognitive, affective and social factors, advanced scientific thinking for technological meaning and implementation in action can help youngsters to unlock their potential.

2   Free2Grow Design

Free2Grow is focused on supporting students' natural curiosity and reasoning as well as feeling recognition and control, individual interests, drives and opening up the space for their reasoning including aligning several aspects of diverse information. These directly affect inductive/deductive reasoning preferences and thus, choices on decisions youngsters make on learning pathways, leading to tailor-made, targeted and constructive learning as well as motivating and engaging in teamwork. Consequently, an attractive and efficient gamification educational system provides customisable control, assessment and guidance for the youngsters to be responsible for their learning. Such functionalities can make thoughts and reasoning obvious in metacognition and challenge the youngsters on their preferred technological subject by providing creative flow conditions for their knowledge utilisation. The new unification learning model enables them to develop volition for technological innovation key competences as well as awareness and sensitivity about specific needs, excitement, enthusiasm and joy found in imaginative and innovative activities.

It is already known that emotions are connected to a range of physiological changes, such as perspiration, raised heartbeat, etc. New research reveals that emotional states are universally associated with certain bodily sensations, regardless of individuals' culture or language. Researchers found statistically discrete areas for each emotion tested, such as happiness, contempt and love that were consistent regardless of respondents' nationality. In science of emotion, consciousness and feeling evolution support the Free2Grow feeling mapping [1] and chart: Shame, guilt, apathy, grief, fear, hatred, tension, anxiety, worry, restlessness, desire, anger, pride, courage, neutrality, relief, willingness, acceptance, reason, gratefulness, friendliness, love, happiness, joy and peace. Emotions are often felt in the body, and somatosensory feedback has been proposed to trigger conscious emotional experiences, allowing the construction of culturally universal categorical somatotopic maps. Perception of these emotion-triggered bodily changes may play a key role in generating consciously felt emotions. Basic emotions, such as anger and fear, caused an increase in sensation in the upper chest area, likely corresponding to increases in pulse and respiration rate. Happiness was the only emotion tested that increased sensation all over the body.

Secondly, Free2Grow is focused on Semantic Web allowing the direct interchange of existing and user-generated data with internal and external software components. The two main aims are achieved by (i) separating Free2Grow architecture in the individual and the small-group level; (ii) facilitating users in creating an initial detailed profile for cognitive, affective, conative and emotional characteristics diagnosis, mapping and guidance aiding the individual to evolve in their personality traits and activities; (iii) providing semantic multimedia identification and real-time context-aware analytics; (iv) supporting learning activities coordination on an individual and small group level by adaptive Computer Supported Collaborative eLearning (CSCeL) scripts (learning scenarios); (v) offering customisation of educational resources and learning networks for building up individual and team learning pathways; (vi) addressing these specific personality characteristics as mediating factors between the perception of feedback, the goal pursued and the responses made; and (vii) developing feedback to challenge and keep youngsters into creative flow via innovative forms of CSCeL assessment based on feed-in -back and -forward system suggestions.

Thirdly, Free2Grow follows level descriptors such as knowledge, skills and competences Lifelong learning; key competencies (knowledge, attitudes and skills) are essential in a knowledge society and guarantee more flexibility in the labour force, allowing it to adapt more quickly to constant changes in an increasingly interconnected world. They are also a major factor in innovation, productivity and competitiveness, contributing to the motivation and satisfaction of workers and the quality of work. Following the EC direction, technological and digital competencies are two of the basic the basic ones. Technology is to improve human capabilities, and then using tool-augmented behaviour and habits to influence the further refinement of the tools, in a continual "co-evolution."

For the third focus, Free2Grow provides the knowledge (educational material), enhances youngsters' cognitive (involving the use of logical, intuitive and creative thinking) and practical skills (involving manual dexterity and the use of methods, materials, tools and instruments) and competencies (indicators for individual responsibility and autonomy).

3   Curiosity, Reasoning and Emotions in Gamification

Free2Grow supports the challenging and creative interplay between the conative drive of curiosity and its counterpart cognitive factor of reasoning with an attractive collective intelligence platform using pictorial/rich media databases to enhance user generated context and the co-creation of open-corpus knowledge and open innovation. Such approach requires detailed descriptions of the ways youngsters acquire knowledge, learn and apply new information on both an individual and small-group level, and use pedagogical pathways and scenarios for learning activities coordination to support their learning curve as learning pathways. The following aptitudes exist in learning [2]: Cognitive aptitudes include (a) intellectual ability constructs, consisting mostly of fluid analytic reasoning ability, visual spatial abilities, crystallized verbal abilities, mathematical abilities, memory space, and mental speed; (b) cognitive and learning styles; and (c) prior knowledge. Affective and Conative aptitudes include (a) motivational constructs such as anxiety, achievement motivation, and interests and (b) volitional or action-control constructs such as self-efficacy.

If the reasoning ability is enhanced by specific reasoning techniques associated with several and diverse individual learning styles and curiosity is supported to create a challenging creative flow, a youngster can be motivated either on his/her own or with peers to creative discovery.

3.1   Cognitive, Affective and Conative Learning Aptitudes – Group Cognition

Cognitive-Learning Aptitudes: Reasoning. Emphasis has been given to different aspects of cognitive personality driving to the cognitive and reasoning styles of an individual. A cognitive style refers to an individual's characteristic and consistent approach to organizing and processing information [3], while see it as a fairly fixed, static and in-built characteristic of an individual and thus mostly unconscious [4]. Thus in most cases cognitive and learning styles are studied together as for example, field independence-dependence [5], holistic-analytic [3], auditory-visual (e.g. sensory preferences of divergent and convergent thinking learners. Consciously using appropriate and most suitable reasoning styles is a skill; reasoning is used to associate one idea to the related idea building cognitive structures and synapses in the brain. Thus, achieving cognitive change in the brain leads to behavioural change, translating a skill to competence. Many educational and knowledge-based systems have been based to different reasoning styles such as deductive, inductive, abductive, analogical, fallacious or gestalt reasoning. Therefore, classification is needed based on what the system does and how it does it.. If appropriate tools are integrated in a Collective Intelligence System, they can facilitate technological concepts, taxonomies, causal relationships, co-occurance relationships, etc. Therefore such system tools can facilitate, support and enhance dynamic generation of problems where new instances can be generated for conceptual change and behaviour to occur.

3.2   Affective/Conative Learning Aptitudes

Cognitive abilities are distinguished from affective/conative abilities (such as anxiety, motivation, emotion, interest and curiosity) [6]. Curiosity is based on other affective learning drives and factors calling it as a passion or appetite for learning. Curiosity is the desire to know, see (knowledge) or experience that motivates exploratory behaviour, and, furthermore, curiosity is activated when there is the feeling of lacking knowledge for a subject of interest [7]. Such information need is substantial and capable of increasing subjective feelings of competence, in our case technological and digital competencies. Therefore curiosity also serves as an intrinsic motivational and activation factor. Intrinsic motivation is an internal state typified by a strong desire to engage and interact with the environment with stimuli. It is reinforced by interest and enjoyment, a willingness to initiate and continue autonomous behaviour, and prompts an individual to engage in activity primarily for its own sake, because the individual perceives the activity as interesting, involving, satisfying or personally challenging. Interest can be reinforced by competence and plays a primary role in intrinsic motivation [8]. Interest is defined as the emotion underlying curiosity, exploration, and attention [9]; also it is the result of "conceptual conflict" or "conflict between mutually discrepant symbolic response-tendencies as thoughts, beliefs attitudes, conceptions" [9]. Such configurations, or "schema-experience mismatches," are inherently attention-getting, causing arousal of autonomic nervous system activity which essentially has an interest provoking function [10]. Interest leads to selective attention of a particular stimulus which in turn produces exploration, investigation and manipulation of the stimulus [11]. He also notes that an "active-cognitive" orientation of joy "tends to be associated with a sense of vigor and with feelings of strength, confidence, and competency".

Curiosity seems to be the attitudinal exemplar for intrinsic motivation. It has been extensively used in gaming as the means to re-enforce repetitive desirable behaviours. If effectance and self-determination are necessary and perhaps sufficient conditions for curiosity, their utilization represents two key strategic objectives vital for the construction of intrinsically motivating persuasive messages (self-determination theory). Curiosity is the conative internal state when subjective uncertainty generates a tendency to engage in exploratory behaviour aiming at solving or mitigating this 'inconvenience'. This discordance has also have been linked to anxiety or even fear as the major instigator of exploratory behaviour. There are two types of curiosity, perceptual and epistemic, based on the degree of specificity and diversity of the subject of exploration [9]. Perceptual curiosity is defined as "the curiosity which leads to increased perception of stimuli", activating uncertainty-relieving perceptions [9], while epistemic curiosity, as "the drive to know" activates quests for knowledge that could be stored in structures of symbolic responses. Two associated types of exploratory behavior are differentiated [9], diversive, motivated by boredom, and specific, motivated by the desire to acquire information about novel stimuli. In this way, curiosity triggers exploration, and thus, it is rewarded for situations which include novelty, surprise, incongruity, and complexity.

3.3   Group Interaction and Cognition

Free2Grow work is anchored in the CSCeL field and the associated group cognition theories. Stressing the importance of group cognition, a new science for small group interaction is proposed [12] anchored in: (a) designing testbeds to support interaction within teams, (b) analyzing how interaction takes place within this setting, (c) describing how the teams achieve their tasks, and (d) the ways small groups blend both Computer Supported Collaborative Learning and Work (CSCL/W): "When small groups engage in cooperative problem solving or collaborative knowledge building, there are distinctive processes of interest at the individual, small-group and community levels of analysis, which interact strongly with each other. The science of group cognition is the study of the processes at the small-group level." In small groups, students act on both individual and group level; they each engage in their own, private individual activities. These also function as group actions, contributing to the on-going problem solving by participating in a socialisation process, through which the students become increasingly skilled, in our project acquire competencies to become members of the community of technologically literate citizens.

3.4   Emotion – Group Emotion

Body Atlas and bodily maps of emotions reveal bodily sensations associated with different emotions using a unique topographical self-report method [1]. Silhouettes of bodies alongside emotional words, stories, movies, or facial expressions can be coloured and associated with the bodily regions whose activity they felt increasing or decreasing while viewing each stimulus. Different emotions were consistently associated with statistically separable bodily sensation maps which were concordant across West European and East Asian samples. Statistical classifiers distinguished emotion-specific activation maps accurately, confirming independence of topographies across emotions.

3.5   Connecting the Nodes: The Zone of Proximal Flow

Creative flow is a crucial source of internal rewards for humans, it is the self-engagement in activities which require skills just above their current level. Thus, exploratory behaviour can be explained by an intrinsic motivation for reaching situations which represent a learning challenge [13]. The Zone of Proximal Flow (ZPF) is the area where flow occurs within the zone of proximal development. In this way learners' interest and engagement counteract the anxiety experienced in the creative flow. However, in order for the learners to experience ZPF for an enhanced learning experience, immersion is required [14]. There are ten factors to promote flow and not all of them need to happen simultaneously to experience flow: 1. Clear goals where the challenge level and skill level should both be high; 2. Concentration and focused attention; 3. Loss of feeling and 4. Distorted sense of time as in immersion; 5. Direct and immediate feedback; 6. Balance between ability level and challenge (the activity is neither too easy nor too difficult); 7. Sense of personal control over the situation or activity. 8. The activity is intrinsically rewarding, so there is an effortlessness of action; 9. Lack of awareness of bodily needs; and 10. Absorption into the activity.

ZPF in combination with bodily mapping [15][16] and feelings evolution can provide a multiple perspective view of individuals' and groups' actions and reactions on specific interactions as for example, a creative argument. As internal processes become apparent the team members may be able to solve discrepancies and build gaps or bridges for further development and thus, forward their own evolutionary process in the innovation game.

In free2Grow, there are two directions in which assessment and feedback provision is made by such systems: explicitly via initial questionnaires and implicitly via identification of users' preferences by the system. The socio-cognitive layer of interaction refers to personality traits, emotion and meta-perception, that is to say, interpretation of how a user perceives another user based on observed feedback.

The user profiles are based on user characteristics from the basis of most Web personalisation systems. Mobilised internet now provides different service delivery channels, especially computers, mobile phones and PDAs, accessing ever-more heterogeneous users groups and user environments. If an explicit user-model represents certain user characteristics, a domain model, which is a set of relationships between knowledge elements in the information space, is capable of modifying some visible or functional part of the system based on the information maintained in the user-model. Results from the implementation of such systems related to their effectiveness suggest a positive correlation with academic performance. The most recent research is directed towards a unified model of cognition and emotion. Models integrating emotion and cognition generally do not fully specify why cognition needs emotion and conversely why emotion needs cognition for example, appraisal values direct the participants' emotional states.

There is no research on the actual interplay between the conative drive of curiosity and the cognitive factor of reasoning as well as emotions for a challenging non-linear zone of proximal creative flow in gamification. Dynamic scripting has been used to generate creative behaviour in gaming. Dynamic scripting [17] is a reinforcement learning method for automatically acquiring effective scripts for games and adapts to a number of tactics and learned effective counter-tactics achieving evolutionary learning as well as tactics. Such applied evolutionary learning aids youngsters' metacognitive skills by customising developmental and effective sequences and Free2Grow evaluation of the degree for "novelty," "surprise," "complexity," and "challenge". Free2Grow scripts manage and diminish the occurrence of such mismatch by emerging recommendations on both levels as well as on individual and team basis presenting both students' and groups' projects for individual and small-group presentation and assessment.

4   Interaction Analysis in LAK

Computer-based Interaction Analysis (IA) can be defined as the automatic or semi-automatic processes that aim at understanding the computer mediated activity, drawing on data obtained from the participants' activities. This understanding can serve in supporting the human or artificial actors to take part in the control of the activity, contributing to awareness, self-assessment or even regulation and self-regulation.

Although IA is part of Learning Analytics, the unique implementation in a Collective Intelligence Platform requires a separate view. The IA research field focuses mainly in collaborative activities occurring within a learning context. An IA process consists in recording, filtering and processing data regarding system usage and user activity variables, in order to produce the analysis indicators. These indicators (presented usually in a visual format) may concern: a) the process or the 'quality' of the considered 'cognitive system' within the learning activity; b) the features or the quality of the interaction product; and c) the mode, the process or the quality of the collaboration, when acting in the frame of a social context formed through the technology based learning environment [18].

The core aim is to offer the means directly to the human actors, so as to be aware of and regulate their behaviour, either as individuals or as cognitive groups. The corresponding IA tools support the users in three major levels: awareness, metacognition and evaluation, aiming at optimizing the learning activity through: a) refined participation by the students through reflection, self- and group-assessment and self- and group- regulation, and b) better activity design, regulation, coordination and evaluation by the teachers. It is highlighted in the literature that students often face difficulties in understanding the goals of a collaborative learning activities and project their actions on a higher -group level activity- thus being able to understand the impact of their actions on the overall activity. IA tools facilitate this understanding and thus the application of metacognitive knowledge by the students upon their actions, enhancing the quality of collaboration and group well-being [19].

5   Immersive Experience for Team Projects

Immersive eXperience (iX) [20], as with User Experience (UX), is the creation of immediate, deeply immersive, meaningful and memorable learning experience. Thus, it is appropriate, satisfying, successful, and related to humane values, also directed towards the specific learning objectives for each course or session. User eXperience (UX) is a person's perceptions responses resulting from use and/or anticipated use of a product, system or service.

iX is focused on supporting learners' natural curiosity and reasoning, individual interests, drives and opening up the space for their reasoning including aligning several aspects of diverse information. These factors can be explicit such as cognitive, learning, social and pedagogical, and implicit such as metacognitive, affective and conative such as curiosity. Curiosity is the desire to know, based on knowledge or experience that motivates exploratory behaviour; furthermore, curiosity is activated when there is the feeling of lacking knowledge for a subject of interest. Such needed information is substantial and capable of increasing subjective feelings of competence, in our case technological and digital competencies. Therefore curiosity also serves as an intrinsic motivational and activation factor. Intrinsic motivation is an internal state typified by a strong desire to engage and interact with the environment with stimuli. It is reinforced by interest and enjoyment, a willingness to initiate and continue autonomous behaviour, and prompts an individual to engage in activity primarily for its own sake, because the individual perceives the activity as interesting, involving, satisfying or personally challenging. Also the feelings mapping and evolution on both an individual and group level work on identifying the level of contribution and engagement in both levels. There are specific immersive factors, conditions and associated iX Design attributes that enable and enhance the user's engagement and activity on platforms that require such actions and evolutionary mapping.

These directly affect inductive/deductive reasoning preferences and thus, choices on directions learners make on learning pathways, leading to tailor-made, targeted and constructive anywhere-anytime learning as well as motivating and engaging in teamwork. Consequently, an attractive and efficient 3D iX environment provides customisable control and immediate feedback. Such functionalities can challenge the learners by providing creative flow conditions with enhanced awareness and sensitivity about specific needs, excitement, enthusiasm and joy found in imaginative and innovative activities.

6   Conclusions and Future Work

This paper proposes a combined approach of critical thinking and emotions mapping towards individual and group creativity and innovation. Gamification is the suggested technical approach on and platform called Free2Grow. On Free2Grow youngsters and not only can create their profiles with characteristics related to critical thinking such as curiosity and reasoning as we as bodily feelings mapping and evolution so the system can detect the exact stage and aid in team building and group formation. The semantic multimedia identification and real-time context-aware and interaction analytics support activities convergence towards the team project aims as well coordination on an individual and small group level. Such adaptive approach customizes the educational resources and learning also helping the individual to transform his/her specific personality characteristics in an evolutionary way. As the individual evolves in time, ideas, feelings and thoughts are translated into actions, collaborative activities and learning. If a system can shed light into our internal processes and initial intentions then as human beings, we may be aided to unfold our potential and creativity towards the targets we have chosen ourselves.

References

1. Gull, G.: The Intent of Business: Organizing for a More Sustainable Future. Palgrave Macmillan, Basingstoke (2013)
2. Snow, R.E., Swanson, J.: Instructional Psychology: Aptitude, Adaptation, and Assessment. Annual Review of Psychology 43, 583–626 (1992)
3. Tennant, M.: Psychology and adult learning. Routledge, London (1988)
4. Riding, R.J., Glass, A., Douglas, G.: Individual differences in thinking: cognitive and neurophysiological perspectives. Educational Psychology 13(3-4), 267–279 (1993)
5. Witkin, H.A., Moore, C.A., Goodenough, D.R., Cox, P.W.: Field-dependent and field-independent cognitive styles and their educational implications. Review of Educational Research 47(1), 1–64 (1977)
6. Harrison, S.H., Sluss, D.M., Ashforth, B.E.: Curiosity adapted the cat: The role of trait curiosity in newcomer adaptation. Journal of Applied Psychology 96, 211–220 (2011)
7. Litman, J.: Curiosity and the pleasures of learning: Wanting and liking new information. Cognition and Emotion 19(6), 793–814 (2005)
8. Miller, W.R., Rollnick, S.: Motivational interviewing: Preparing people for change, 2nd edn. Guilford Press, New York (2002)
9. Berlyne, D.E.: Curiosity and exploration. Science 153(731), 25 (1966)
10. Reeve, J.: The intrinsic-enjoyment distinction in intrinsic motivation. Motivation and Emotion 13(2), 83–103 (1989)
11. Izard, C.E.: Human Emotions. Plenum Press, New York (1977)
12. Khine, M.S., Saleh, I.M. (eds.): New science of learning: Computers, cognition and collaboration in education, pp. 23–44. Springer, New York (2010)
13. Csikszentmihalyi, M.: Creativity: Flow and the Psychology of Discovery and Invention. Harper Perennial, New York (1996)

14. Lambropoulos, N., Mystakides, S.: Learning Experience+ within 3D Immersive Virtual Environments. In: The Proceedings of the Federated Conference on Computer Science and Information Systems, FedCSIS 2012, September 9-12, pp. 857–862 (2012), http://fedcsis.org/

15. Nummenmaa, L., Glerean, E., Hari, R., Hietanen, J.K.: Bodily maps of emotions. Proceedings of the National Academy of Sciences of the United States of America (in press), http://www.pnas.org/content/early/2013/12/26/1321664111

16. Nummenmaa, L., Smirnov, D., Lahnakoski, J., Glerean, E., Jääskeläinen, I.P., Sams, M., Hari, R.: Mental action simulation synchronizes action - observation circuits across individuals. The Journal of Neuroscience (in press)

17. Spronck, P., Ponsen, M., Sprinkhuizen-Kuyper, I., Postma, E.: Adaptive game AI with dynamic scripting. Machine Learning 63(3), 217–248 (2006)

18. Bratitsis, T., Dimitracopoulou, A.: Interaction Analysis as a multi-support approach of social computing for learning, in the "Collaborative Era": Lessons learned by using the DIAS system. Paper Presented at the 8th IEEE International Conference on Advanced Learning Technologies (2008)

19. Bratitsis, T.: Future Early Childhood Educators Evaluate Their Performance in Web 2.0 Based Collaborative Learning Activities and Corresponding Interaction Analysis Tools. In: Proceedings of the International Conference on Information Communication Technologies in Education, ICICTE 2012, Rhodes, Greece, July 5-7, pp. 487–497 (2012)

20. Lambropoulos, N., Reinhardt, P., Mystakidis, Σ., Tolis, Δ., Danis, Σ., Gourdin, A.: Immersive Worlds for Learning eXperience+: Engaging users in the zone of proximal flow in Second Life. In: EADTU Conference, Paphos, Cyprus, September 27-28 (2012), http://www.eadtu.eu/

HaptiChem: Haptic and Visual Support in Interactions with the Microscopic World

Elisa Magnanelli[1], Gianluca Brero[1], Rosa Virginia Espinoza Garnier[1],
Giacomo Mazzoletti[2], Alessandro Maria Rizzi[2], and Sara Comai[2]

[1] Politecnico di Torino,
Corso Duca degli Abruzzi, 24, 10129 Torino, Italy
[2] Politecnico di Milano,
Piazza Leonardo Da Vinci, 32, 20133 Milano, Italy
sara.comai@polimi.it,
{gianluca.brero,rosa.garnier,elisa.magnanelli,
giacomo.mazzoletti,alessandro.rizzi}@asp-poli.it

Abstract. Haptic technologies provide physical sensations in the interaction with a computing system, by exploiting the human sense of touch and by applying forces, vibrations, or motions to the user hands or body. Considering their features, they can be a useful tool in life-science teaching, especially when molecules are involved. For this purpose, a framework composed of an haptic device and a visual interface for molecular exploration has been developed to simulate molecular and intermolecular interactions . Furthermore, this work evaluates the visual and haptic tool for molecular exploration in a didactic context, performing tests and interviews with students. The final aim is to properly develop the features of the tool, in order to make it suitable for the introduction in chemistry education. Preliminary results show positive and effective responses and learning gains from the tasks. It has also been noticed that the use of such an innovative instrument raises the interest of students in the learning process, which is one of the main benefits of the haptic device.

Keywords: Haptics, Intermolecular Interaction, Life-Science Education.

1   Introduction

Currently, life-science teaching makes a wide use of visual representations, especially when molecules are involved. Indeed, due to the miniscule size of molecular level, these aids represent an abstract knowledge that can be difficult for students to grasp. Visual perception is usually superior if compared to touch: first of all, it is rapid, while touch involves sensory exploration over time and space. However, visual representation does not provide an immediate method to improve comprehension of how molecules interact with each other. In this context, the haptic technology enables users to apply and feel forces, which would otherwise not be possible. Haptics can be extremely useful in several educational topics where forces play a fundamental role, like in the case of molecular interactions.

P. Zaphiris and A. Ioannou (Eds.): LCT 2014, Part II, LNCS 8524, pp. 72–82, 2014.

A study by Bivall et al. [1] recognized the beneficial effect of using an haptic device in the solution of protein-ligand docking problems, while Schönborn et al. [2] demonstrated that when protein-ligand recognition tasks are accomplished using a visual-haptic support, less errors occur and that the conceptual understanding improves, with respect to the case where just the visual channel was used. Sourina et al. [3] proposed a visual haptic-based biomolecular docking system, developed for research in helix-helix docking typically occurring in drug design, and proposed its application in e-learning. In Sauer et al. [4] work, a Phantom haptic device was used to interact with atoms and to build molecules in a 3D virtual world populated by hydrogen, carbon, and oxygen atoms. The user could feel the strength of molecular bonding, properties of full and partially-full valence shells in bonding, and see how these properties affect the geometric structure of the molecule.

Given these premises, in a previous work, a virtual environment for the exploration of the space around molecules has been developed [5], and the usability of the tool has been assessed [6]. After a further extension of the tool in order to include the simulation of the interaction between two molecules, the tool has been tested in order to evaluate the impact of its use in a chemistry learning context, and results are addressed in the present work.

The paper is organized into two main parts: in the first one, the framework and its Graphical User Interface (GUI) is presented. Some possible applications of the system are also mentioned. The second part outlines the tests and experiences carried out together with students, and the benefits that our project can give to the didactic field are highlighted. We conclude by presenting the current state of the project and possible future developments.

2   The System

Fig. 1 sketches the architecture of the main components of our system. The framework consists of a visual interface showing a 3D representation of a molecule. It is possible to set different modes of 3D molecular rendering among the ones that are typically used in chemistry teaching [7]: some are based on the geometrical structure (e.g., ball-n-stick), while others depend on the involved chemical elements (e.g., covalent or Van der Waals spacefill). The space around the molecule can be explored with the Sensable Phantom Omni haptic device [8] (Fig. 2). The haptic probe can be associated with two different kinds of objects:

- a point charge: with this mode, the user can explore the electrostatic field of the molecule [9]. The entity and the nature of the charge (positive or negative) can be set by the user;
- a molecule: in this case, the user can experience the interactions between the two molecules, as the probing molecule moves in 3D space around the fixed molecule. Both the fixed and the probing molecules can be chosen from a repository of molecules.

In order to simulate the aforementioned phenomena, two different typologies of information are needed:

- Geometrical molecular data to determine how the atoms are located in the 3D space. This information must be provided as input, and for this purpose Protein Data Bank (PDB) files [10] are used;
- Electrostatic field data, that determines the intensity of the forces, and that is calculated from the geometrical information through the General Atomic and Molecular Electronic Structure System (GAMESS [11]) whose output is elaborated by a second tool (wxMacMolPlt) and returns the molecular electrostatic potential (MEP) of the molecule. MEP values are arranged as a grid of voxels around the molecule up to a certain threshold distance in space [9].

A zero MEP value is assumed for the points outside the grid. This is a realistic assumption because molecular interactions are short-range, and they rapidly decrease as the intermolecular distance increases [12]. Since the intensity of the returned forces is naturally very weak (nanoscale), forces are rescaled according to the range of force intensities the Phantom can transmit [12]. In order to solve the problems related to the discontinuous nature of the MEP grid, the force is computed as a linear interpolation in positions between the grid points [9].

To simulate the molecule-molecule interaction, which represents a novel element of this work, the probing molecule is modeled as an aggregate of concentrated charges [13]. Each charge interacts according to its position in the MEP of the fixed molecule. The resulting force is calculated as a sum of the single forces (e.g. Fig. 3 shows a water molecule with its three single forces). To reproduce the nuclear repulsion between atoms of different molecules, the maximum repulsive force that the device can generate is applied when the distance between the atoms reaches the critical limit.

The user can also manipulate the fixed molecule in the 3D space, by rotating, translating or zooming it. In the charge-molecule example in Fig. 4, the Van der Waals representation has been chosen and the surfaces of the atoms are colored according to the electrostatic field associated to these points. The color scale to be used can be set by the user through the bar shown on the right-hand side of the virtual environment. Moreover, other auxiliary visual information is shown; for example, the plot of the electrostatic field along the direction connecting the probe position and the center of the molecule (shown in the rectangle in the bottom-right-hand side of the interface). This information can be useful in the determining the direction and magnitude of the interaction, helping in the understanding of the binding mechanism. In this way, the student receives information on the bonding process through two information channels: the haptic one and the graphical one.

Tests regarding real-time performances have decreed that the molecule size that our tool can support ranges up to 264-308 atoms. This range allows the exploration of all the cases a student may face during high school/basic university courses.

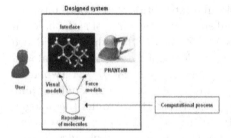

Fig. 1. Architecture of the system

Fig. 2. HaptiChem framework

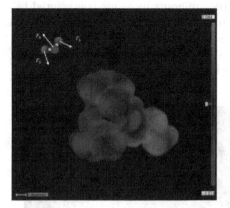

Fig. 3. Ball and stick modality: water-burane interaction

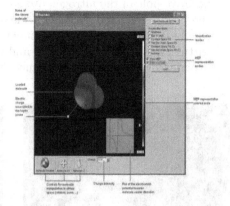

Fig. 4. Screen-shot of the tool: positive charge-water molecule interaction

3   Possible Scenarios for Educational Activities

Some examples of didactic activities that can be performed with the molecule-charge interaction mode have been presented in a previous work of ours [5].

Therefore, we now focus on some possible examples on the molecule-molecule interaction.

- **Hydrogen bonding:** Because of the different electronegativity of the oxygen and the hydrogen, the molecule of water is a permanent dipole. In particular, oxygen represents the negative pole of the molecule while the hydrogens represent the positive ones [14]. This feature is responsible for the hydrogen bonding between water molecules, where the partially positive hydrogen atoms are attracted by the partially negative oxygen ones of other water molecules. This phenomenon can be easily felt with the tool (Fig. 7), since the attractive force reproduced by the haptic device guides the probing molecule towards the bonding site.

– **Halogen bonding:** Another intermolecular interaction that is both interesting for chemistry research activities and supported by our tool is the halogen bonding. A halogen bond $R - X \bullet\bullet\bullet Y - Z$ occurs when there is evidence of a net attractive interaction between an electrophilic region on a halogen atom X belonging to a molecule or a molecular fragment $R - X$ (where R can be another atom, including X, or a group of atoms) and a nucleophilic region of a molecule, or molecular fragment, $Y - Z$ [15]. Around the halogen atoms the potential is expected to be all negative. However, some recent studies based on quantum-mechanics showed that in some molecules there is a region at the edge of the halogen atoms that has a positive potential [16]. This phenomenon can be reproduced by the tool, as in the case of the hydrogen bonding. Fig. 10 shows the interaction between an ammonia molecule (NH_3) and the trifluorine-iodio-methane (CF_3I). It can be noticed that the negative pole of the nitrogen atom of the ammonia molecule is attracted by the positive charged surface on the iodine. Since chemistry aspects are not the main topic in the present paper, we redirect the reader to our website (http://www.haptichem.com/), and we dedicate the rest of the paper to the experiences and the test performed with students.

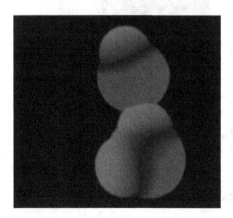

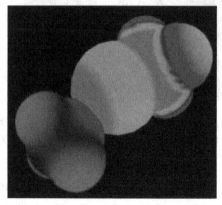

Fig. 5. Hydrogen bonding: Water-Water interaction

Fig. 6. Halogen bonding: Ammonia-TetraFluoroIodioMethane interaction

4   Evaluation of the Tool

The tool has been tested in an informal way by different kinds of users (students, teachers, researchers, but also non-experts) in different occasions (ICCE-ECRICE Conference in Rome[1], MeetMeTonight 2012 night in Milan) and using different molecules stored in the repository. All the users who tested the tool recognized the possibility of combining the typical visualization of chemical data

---

[1] http://www.iccecrice2012.org/

with the rendering of interactions between molecules provided by the haptic device. Students greatly appreciated the novelty represented by the introduction of such a tool in the current teaching activities, in order to make concepts more understandable. Teachers and researchers appreciated the improved awareness of the simulated phenomena they usually explain or deal with theoretically.

Therefore, in this work we perform a more systematic investigation with students at Politecnico di Milano, with the aim of defining the impact of the haptic device in chemistry learning. More in detail, we want to verify what the haptic technology adds to the visual rendering, when molecular interactions are simulated. The initial target population consists of engineering students (bachelor level) enrolled in a chemistry course, which is a part of the Electronic Engineering program at Politecnico di Milano. The course contents give the fundamental basis necessary to the interpretation of chemical phenomena. In particular, one of the topics of the course is organic chemistry, and the theory provides the background to determine how functional groups produce a certain electronic distribution, and how they affect molecular interactions. Therefore, after a canonical lesson given by the professor of the course, the haptic device is presented. Thereafter, a group of students takes part in the test. The test population in the study is 19 students, subdivided into two groups and accomplishing different tasks. There are 9 participants in the group A: 2 females and 7 males, in average 19,3 year old; and 10 participants in the group B: 1 female and 9 males, in average 19,2 year old.

Group A students use the haptic device for molecular exploration. The general aim is to observe how students behave in the virtual environment. Students are asked to express impressions and comments during the experience, the final purpose being the identification of strengths and weaknesses of the tool. Group B is asked to accomplish two tasks, and to fill in a questionnaire. The first task can be performed only using the visualization tool, while the second task is accomplished using a tool combining the visual and haptic rendering; the purpose being to highlight the improvements that the haptic device adds in the comprehension of molecular phenomena. The tasks involve the individuation of the critical points and of the parts of the molecule that take part in bindings. Molecules that are explored are Acetic Acid and Ammonia.

Two surveys are performed in the study: a survey before the test, and a final survey as a summary of the experience. The questions in the first survey are meant for statistical purposes and gather students' basic information, such as age, gender, previous knowledge on haptics, usual studying materials. Through the analysis of the two surveys and the test results, we hope to isolate the effects due to the use of the haptic device, and to highlight the learning potential of the tool.

5   Preliminary Result Analysis

Results from the preliminary survey show that the approach in learning chemistry is quite traditional, since all the participants indicate that during their studies they mainly use books (hard copy) and computer for reading lecture notes, while just two participants use a multimedia application for improving the comprehension of chemical phenomena (Fig. 7). This fact means that there is a great potential for the expansion of the technology in this field.

Afterwards, the participants are asked to provide some information about their prior knowledge, that they have to evaluate on a scale from 1 (I do not know it at all) to 5 (I know it very well). In the figures, the abscissa indicates the number of students that express a given preference. Some specifics are shown in Fig. 8: it appears clearly that their prior knowledge about the haptic technology is very limited, while the majority of the students considers its knowledge about molecular interactions intermediate.

After the preliminary survey, the two groups are involved in two different kinds of experience. The test performed by students in Group A is meant to gather the impressions that users have the first time they use the haptic device, to highlight the strengths and the weaknesses of the tool. The most significant comments that help in understanding how to improve the tool are:

– The plot of the MEP along the direction connecting the probe position and the center of the molecule aids in understanding which direction to move to find the stability points. It would be worthy to make it a default property of the interface. However, some students have troubles in the interpretation of the plot at first; the main difficulty is that the y-axis moves with respect to the MEP minimum as the position of the probe changes.
– Even though it is possible to rotate the fixed molecule, it would be interesting to be able to turn it while using the haptic device, in order to further exploit the attraction force.
– The feeling of repulsion is, somehow, more difficult than attraction to be perceived with the haptic device. In this context, the MEP plot gives important additional information about repulsion, and it helps in understanding when the repulsion is present.
– Only one student (out of 9 in the group) tries independently to switch from one molecular representation to another; all the others simply use the log-scale mode that is already set at the beginning of their experience. A more clear and attractive way to select the 3D representation mode would improve the experience, since different molecular features can be understood with the different rendering modes.
– While moving in the 3D space around the molecule, several students end up with the exploring probe "behind" the molecule, and they do not menage to get back "in front" of the molecule without help. This fact is probably due to a difficulty in properly perceiving the visual representation of the depth.

We notice that, during the experience, most of the students are more focused on the haptic rendering than on the visual one. Even so, visualization is a fundamental aspect to integrate the haptic information.

Participants in group B are asked to solve two tasks initially using only the tool for the visual representation, and then using the haptic rendering as well. The two tasks involve some aspect of the molecular polarity, and the individuation

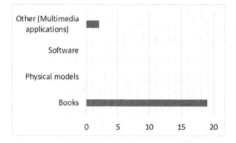

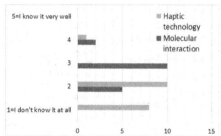

Fig. 7. Kinds of support used for studying in chemistry

Fig. 8. Prior specific knowledge

of the points of the molecule that are critical in the bonding process. Figs. 9
and 10 show a summary of the experience. The majority of the students find it
useful to integrate the visual representation with the haptic rendering, for the
comprehension of molecular properties. Thanks to the haptic device, the tasks
are accomplished in a more precise way, and sometimes their accomplishment
is possible only when the tool is used. An improvement concerning the learning
time is also noticed.

The final survey is aimed gather an overview of the opinions of the students
regarding the tool, and to understand if the device is considered a valid help in
basic chemistry education. The students express a very clear positive response
to this new type of teaching, as more than 85% of the students included in
the study consider the tool capable of generating improvements in chemistry
education (Fig. 11). In general, the level of complexity of the tool is considered
appropriate for the course contents and activity objectives (Fig. 12).

When students are asked to recognize the improvements in their knowledge
concerning different aspects related to the basic chemistry course, mainly two
aspects are highlighted: electrostatic distribution around the molecules, and the
spatial understanding of the molecular structure (Fig. 13), which are the main
aspects of focus of the experience. Nevertheless, some of other minor aspects
that are individuated by the students can represent a valid suggestion for the
application of the tool in the explanation of phenomena that have not been
considered so far.

According to the students, the haptic-based tool has the potential to improve
the understanding of the molecular phenomena (Fig 14), as well as to increase
the spacial ability of the user in a molecular environment (Fig 15). Fig. 16 summarizes the results provided by students when asked to figure out and evaluate
specific aspects of the haptic-based tool. Once more, the students recognize the
awareness in the molecular perception provided by the haptic device, and most
of the students agree that the learning gain due to the experience would not
have been the same without the inclusion of the tool. On the other hand, they
generally show to be skeptical on the usefulness of introducing sounds as an
additional channel for providing information.

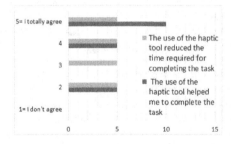

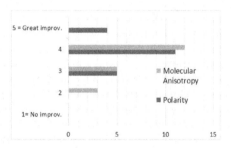

Fig. 9. Evaluation of the role of the haptic tool during the accomplishment of the task

Fig. 10. Evaluation of improvements in the comprehension of molecular phenomena due to the haptic tool

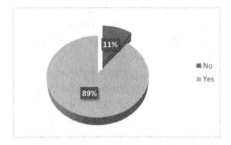

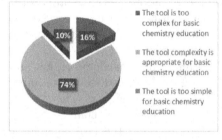

Fig. 11. Can the haptic-based tool generate improvements in chemistry education?

Fig. 12. Student evaluation of the tool complexity

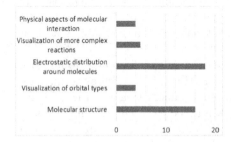

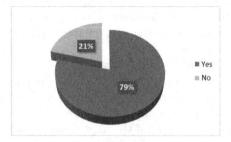

Fig. 13. Specific improvements indicated by the student

Fig. 14. Has the tool improved the student perceived knowledge on molecular phenomena?

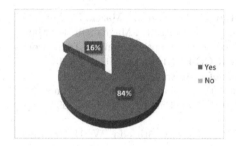

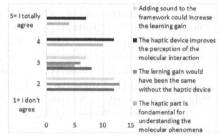

Fig. 15. Has the haptic-based tool improved your spatial abilities?

Fig. 16. Overall evaluation of the haptic-based tool

6 Conclusions

The present analysis helps in understanding how the application can be developed and improved for an educational purpose; the direct interaction with the users of the tool has proven to be fundamental to correctly develop the device features, especially in overcoming the difficulties that students met during the experience. In the present case, even though results are limited to a small number of participants to the test, it is generally demonstrated that the use of the haptic device as a tool for learning chemistry can help the process of understanding molecular properties and features. It is also found that there are significant improvements in the learning time. It should also be noticed that the use of a such innovative instrument enables to highly rise the interest of students in the learning process: indeed, one of the benefits is the strong increase of motivation due to the use of the haptic device. Moreover, students appear to assimilate the concepts presented through the haptic experience in an easier way. It is also noticed that, moving in a tridimentional space, student can understand the different proportions of the involved objects and how the nature and intensities of interactions can be related to spatial properties (e.g., distances from molecule).

Further works will consider the implementation of other kinds of interactions, such as covalent, ionic, and Van der Waals interactions, in order to investigate their differences and impact on the user's learning process.

References

1. Bivall Persson, P., Tibell, L.A.E.: Evaluating the Effectiveness of Haptic Visualization in Biomolecular Education: Feeling Molecular Specificity in a Docking Task. In: Proceedings of 12th IOSTE Symposium, pp. 745–752 (2006)
2. Schönborn, K.J., Bivall, P., Tibell, L.A.E.: Exploring Relationships between Students' Interaction and Learning with a Haptic Virtual Biomolecular Model. Computers and Education 57(3), 2095–2105 (2011)
3. Sourina, O., Torres, J., Wang, J.: Visual Haptic-based Biomolecular Docking. In: Proceedings of International Conference on Cyberworlds, pp. 240–247 (2008)
4. Sauer, C.M., Hastings, W.A., Okamura, A.M.: Virtual Environment for Exploring Atomic Bonding. Eurohaptics (2004)

5. Bergamini, E., Comai, S., Corno, F., Cristini, G., Lanzani, G., Mazza, D., Metrangolo, P., Resnati, G., Terraneo, G., Brero, G., Espinoza, R., Magnanelli, E., Mahmood, K., Mazzoletti, G., Pascali, S., Rizzi, A.: A Haptic-Enhanced Framework for Chemistry Education. In: Proceedings ICCE-ECRICE, pp. 102–106 (2012)
6. Comai, S., Mazza, D.: Usability Assessment of a Multimodal Visual-Haptic Framework for Chemistry Education. In: Campos, P., Graham, N., Jorge, J., Nunes, N., Palanque, P., Winckler, M. (eds.) INTERACT 2011, Part IV. LNCS, vol. 6949, pp. 648–651. Springer, Heidelberg (2011)
7. Berg, J.M., Tymoczko, J.L., Stryer, L.: Biochemistry, 5th edn. W. H. Freeman (2002)
8. Sensable PHANTOM Omni, http://www.sensable.com/haptic-phantom-omni.htm
9. Comai, S., Mazza, D.: Haptic and Visual Rendering for Multi-Modal Exploration of Molecular Information. In: BCS HCI, pp. 221–229 (2010)
10. Berman, H., Nakamura, H., Henrick, K.: The Protein Data Bank (PDB) and the Worldwide PDB. In: Encyclopedia of Genetics, Genomics, Proteomics and Bioinformatics, ch. 4(6) (2005)
11. Dupuis, M., Watts, J.D., Villar, H.O., Hurst, G.J.B.: The General Atomic and Molecular Electronic Structure System Hondo: Version 7.0. Computer Physics Communications 52(3), 415–425 (1989)
12. Leache, A.L.: Molecular Modeling: Principles and Applications, 2nd edn. Pearson (2001)
13. Stone, A.J.: Distributed Multipole Analysis, or How to Describe a Molecular Charge Distribution. Chemical Physics Letters 83(2), 233–239 (1981)
14. Kojić-Prodić, B., Molčanov, K.: The Nature of Hydrogen Bond: New Insights Into Old Theories. Acta Chim. Slov. 55, 692–708 (2008)
15. Politzer, P., Lane, P., Concha, M.C., Ma, Y., Murray, J.S.: An Overview of Halogen Bonding. Journal of Molecular Modeling 13(12), 305–311 (2007)
16. Metrangolo, P., Resnati, G.: Halogen Versus Hydrogen. Science 321(5891), 918–919 (2008)

Augmented Reality Applications in the Engineering Environment

Karle Olalde Azkorreta[1] and Héctor Olmedo Rodríguez[2]

[1] University of Basque Country, UPV/EHU; C/Nieves Cano 12. 01006 Vitoria-Gasteiz, Spain
karle.olalde@ehu.es
[2] Universidad de Valladolid; Campus Miguel Delives s/n. 47014 Valladolid, Spain
holmedor@gmail.com

Abstract. In the area of engineering, we can move much in the way clients generally can interact with models or designs for new products, so we are developing various alternatives for visualization, such as Virtual and Augmented realities based on accurate models with no need of using specific software. In order to have a better and global knowledge of the possibilities we show in this paper the situation and capabilities of these technologies. From models developed with commercial programs and tools for industrial design, we propose a workflow to give everybody a chance to interact with these models. The sectors where these technologies are applied and the services offered are grouped in Industrial production systems and Learning of related disciplines. At the end conclusions will be given with every reference used. With everything, ideas for improving these technologies and the correspondent applications could be suggested to the reader.

Keywords: Collaboration technology and informal learning, Augmented and virtual Reality, engineering, models.

1 Introduction

In this paper we try to analyze the different options we have to represent an object in augmented reality, from 3D design programs and engineering, such as Catia, Solid Edge, Solid Works, Autocad, etc., with the objective of product design or do it more accessible to all potential customers.

Augmented Reality (AR) [1, 2] is a technology in which the vision for the user in the real world is enhanced or augmented with additional information generated from a computer model. The improvement may consist of virtual devices placed in a real environment, or the display of "non-geometric" information about real objects.

The AR allows the user to work with and examine real 3D objects, while receiving additional information about these objects. The AR adds information to the real world of the user. Allows the user to stay in touch with the real environment. This is a clear difference from the Virtual Reality (VR), in which the user is completely immersed in an artificial world, completely separated from the real world. In VR [3, 4] systems there is no possibility for the user to interact with objects in the real world, the AR,

P. Zaphiris and A. Ioannou (Eds.): LCT 2014, Part II, LNCS 8524, pp. 83–90, 2014.

however, does allow users to interact naturally with a world that is a mixture of virtual and real. The AR systems carry the computer to the real world of the user, while the VR systems have the real to the computer world.

However, such applications impose demanding requirements. To combine models actually states that these models are very accurate. This realistic mix requires objects that are introduced in the real scene behave in a very realistic way. To achieve this reality the AR requires a very detailed description of the physical setting.

2   Software CAD

The Computer Aided Design (CAD) software, which we will discuss in this article, refers to the most widely used in the field of both mechanical as aerospace, automotive engineering and many other fields of engineering mainly manufacturing.

What we intend to show in this article, first, is the use which has been given so far to the designs in CAD [5], and different outlets that we provide such software to work at a later stage display through AR.

This kind of software is always expensive and there are students, customers and partners that can't afford to buy licenses. Sharing 3D contents using websites and AR/VR apps based on open standards offers a great chance to make public know our products with no specific investment. There are open technologies to diffuse 3D contents but there are not widely used nowadays because producers of plugins to visualize 3D contents on the web are in advanced. But most used web browsers include native possibilities to visualize 3D contents, it is only a question of developing special websites or adding the needed modifications to the actual websites. There is where the aim of our project lies in.

Basically we will focus on CAD programs [6], we have at our disposal and that has allowed us to see all the possibilities for the AR environment.

In **Table 1** shown below can be seen, the software used and the different extensions that we provide for further treatment in AR.

Table 1. Software CAD and extensions

Software CAD	Main extension	Other extensions
CATIA v5	*.part; *.product	*.stp;*.vrml;*.3dmap;*.3dxml;*.cgr;*.iges;*.model;*.Navrep;*. stl;*.x3d;*.wrl;*.hcg;*.icem
NX 9	*.prt	*.iges:*.stp:*step:*dxf:*dwg:*.model(catia):*.catpart(catia)
Autocad 2014	*.dwg;	*.dgn;*.dxf;*.dws;*.dxx;*.bmp;*iges:*.igs;*.dwf;*.3ddwf;*.pdf ;*.fbx;*.wmf;*.sat;*.stl;*eps
Solid Edge ST5	*.par;*.asm	*.model;*.plmxml;*.prt:*.dwg:*.dxf; *.x_t;*.xgl;*.sat;*.jt:*.part;*.igs;*.step;*.stl;*.3dpdf;*.u3d
Solid Works	*.sldprt;*.sldas m	*.stl;*.iges;*.stp;*.proe;3D XML; *.dxf;*.dwg
Skectup 2013	*.skp	*.mtl;*.obj;*.wrl;*.xsi:*.fbx;*.dwg;*.3ds;*.txt

From the different extensions that provide us with CAD programs, we try to transfer to AR software, making the appropriate changes, and rendered application layers, lighting and even movement, to try to get the effect of visualization features is as real as possible and the user can manipulate as if it were in your hand. Such supplements are obtained from other specific porgrams [7] for it such as the Autodesk 3DStudio, Maya or Blender, the latter of Open Source, and they are specialized in toods rendering, animation or ilumninacion scenes.

3   Web3D

Even more and more websites are tridimensional. This will be generalized when our smart phones and tablets will be able to visualize these characteristics. Having specific hardware to do this is the intention of project AREngine [8]. Several standards like VRML and X3D have been designed by Web3D Consortium [9] but there are also works in progress for AR. For example, ARML [10] is a proposal. Also standardization of a 3D compression format is a must. The big challenge is to compress and stream 3D assets using an effective and widely adopted coder – decoder (codec), in the same way as MP3 is the standard for audio, H.264 for video and PNG/JPEG for images. Then we will see a popular application for 3D transmission on the way as there are popular applications for audio, video and images (see Table 2).

Table 2. A Standard 3D Compression Format?

Audio	Video	Images	3D
MP3	H.264	PNG/JPEG	X3D, MPEG4, COLLADA
Napster	YouTube	Facebook	?

Uses of Web3D could be those proposed by John Vince in Table 3 but related to engineering environment we can consider:

(1) Visualization of product and data, reducing cost of sending samples to the customers, etc.

(2) E-commerce and B2B applications, improving detailed information about products offered.

(3) Learning and training, giving a better approach to the tridimensional appearance to the learners without using authoring tools.

(4) Web improvement, giving 3D to the web.

(5) News and Ad improvement, giving 3D to advertising and commercial web-based reports.

Table 3. AR/MR/VR applications (Vince, 2004)

GROUPS	AR/MR/VR applications
Industrial	Visualizing engineering concepts, Training personnel, Evaluating ergonomic issues, Visualizing virtual prototypes, Visualizing virtual weapons, Exploring servicing strategies, Simulating the interaction of assemblies, Simulating the dynamics of articulated structures, Stress analysis, Distributed product development management, Simulating manufacturing processes, Collaborative engineering on large AEC projects, Machining and pressing simulation, Concurrent engineering, Ergonomics, Virtual prototypes, Visual engineering, Spatial visualization.
Training Simulators	Medicine (Soft body modeling, Minimally invasive surgery, Virtual therapy), Civilian flight simulators, Teaching, Learning, Military simulators (Flight, etc.), Strategic simulators, Train driving simulators, Vehicle simulators, Emergency services
Entertainment and Cultural Heritage	Computer and Video Games, Recreational games, Experiences at Thematic parks and Museums, Tourism and Advertisement
VR Centres	Architecture, Indoor Design, Urban Development, Airport Design, Bridge Design, Human Movement Analysis

Several options have been used to develop Web3D, the most popular are:

(1) Commercial Plugins: Adobe Director [11], Adobe Flash [12], Microsoft Silverlight [13], Cortona [14] and others.

(2) Java Plugins, applet based solutions developed with Java or Java based APIs like Java3D [15].

(3) Ajax3D [16]: X3D based and plugin needed with JavaScript.

(4) WebGL [17]: several JavaScript libraries for HTML5,

(5) X3DOM [18]: that is our choice because of the great community supporting this JavaScript and CSS library with no need of plugin and widely implemented natively on most popular web browsers.

4   X3DOM

While X3DOM community is still working hard to make it a reference for Web3D [19], we have tested several desktop and mobile devices to know the possibilities to access 3D contents using desktop/laptop based systems and mobile based systems.

4.1   Desktop / Laptop Support

The current implementation of the X3DOM fallback model needs an InstantReality plugin, a Flash11 plugin or a WebGL-enabled browser. WebGL-enabled web browsers are available for most platforms. We tested the most usual web browsers on a Microsoft Windows 8.1 Enterprise 64 bits machine and an Apple Mac OS X 10.9.1 (Table 4).

- Internet Explorer: Latest version needed and installing of the Instant Reality plugin, Flash 11, or Chrome Frame.
- Google Chrome [20]: Starting with version 9.x of Google Chrome, WebGL is natively supported.
- Mozilla Firefox [21]: Supports WebGL natively, latest version recommended.
- Safari [22]: Mac only, version 5.1 and newer on OS X (10.6 and above) include support for WebGL but manual enabling is needed.
- Opera [23]: Despite of having no information about support for X3DOM, we tested that it works on Mac OS but it doesn't work on Windows.

Table 4. Desktop/laptop browser support for X3DOM

Web browser	Windows	Mac OS	Linux
Internet Explorer	NO	N/A	N/A
Google Chrome	OK	OK	N/A
Mozilla Firefox	OK	OK	N/A
Safari	NO	NO	N/A
Opera	NO	OK	N/A

4.2 Mobile support

We tested the most usual web browsers on an iOS based device and an Android based device (Table 5):

- iOS: The standard Safari browser does not yet support WebGL. However, there are various ways to enable WebGL via 3rd party solutions, there is no way to visualize 3D content on any web browser without special configuration.
- Android: Sony Ericsson delivered there 2011 Xperia Phones with WebGL support. By doing so, Sony Ericsson is the second mobile phone manufacturer to support WebGL for the default (Android) web browser and standard HTML content. Firefox mobile for Android supports WebGL natively. We improved it works on our Android device and also Google Chrome does.
- Windows Phone: No tests done yet.

Table 5. Mobile browser support for X3DOM

Web browser	iOS	Android	Windows Phone
Internet Explorer	N/A	N/A	N/A
Google Chrome	NO	OK	N/A
Mozilla Firefox	N/A	OK	N/A
Safari	NO	N/A	N/A
Opera	NO	NO	N/A

5   From CAD to AR

As mentioned above, the information transfer from CAD [24, 25] models to the AR is done sometimes in a direct way, through specific software of AR or through intermediaries such as could see Sketchup, Maya or 3DS that allow models to be interpreted by the AR software.

Our proposal allows 3D designers to export their contents developed with usual author tools like Catia, Autocad, etc. to be shown on the Internet inside websites with no need of downloading plugins or any special configuration for the users. On Figure 1 where this process is shown.

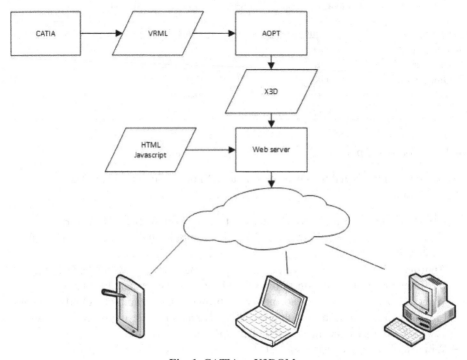

Fig. 1. CATIA to X3DOM

Once the 3D content is exported to standard Web3D format (VRML, X3D, etc.) a customized HTML and JavaScript code is created to display the 3D content in usual Web browsers on PCs, laptops, tablets or mobile phones where users can interact with this 3D content resizing it, changing perspectives, etc. 3D content can be shown as VR or AR. For visualizing as AR more development is needed depending on being location based, marker based or even Oculus Rift [26] based but always using JavaScript and HTML with no commercial plugins.

Once we are able to show our 3D models through the Web3D, 3D printing could be the next step and this could be done with a similar process where instead of producing web pages file formatted for 3D printing are put to be downloaded (STL, stereotype layered, etc.)

6   Conclusions

With the above, we show that the world of AR is very powerful and can have many applications [27] in engineering and that this junction can be very beneficial for all parties involved, both the designer and the potential customer, which the information will reach a more realistic and intuitive way, as it can interact with the model in some cases. At other times we may be of assistance to the formation or maintenance [28] of equipment, both aeronautical and automobile field.

In the area of education, we can see that the interactive with the design can be more realistic, although still alignment errors or loss of information are in place, the AR [29, 30] can provide us a breakthrough in spatial ability student, unimaginable recently time.

In the field of aeronautics and automobile production, major companies like Boeing and Airbus are already making significant evidence for the use of AR in the training of their workers, as well as field maintenance.

There is a promising future for Web3D technologies. Despite of the investment on training for developing this kind of applications, the solutions that can be reached are less expensive than others, not only relating to money, also talking about sustainability. As an illustrative example, augmented books are cheaper to develop than paper books and there is no need of deforestation, virtual furniture for TV programs is cheaper and more sustainable and including 3D objects in a website could be a perfect way to let our customers interact with our products with no need of sending samples.

References

1. González Carretero, E.D., Sánchez Trujillo, S., Escuela Técnica Superior de Ingeniería Civil e Industrial. Sección: Mecánica, Aplicación de la realidad aumentada en la Ingeniería (2010)
2. Ciollaro Rodrigo-Magro, G.A., Juan Nadal, C.: Escola Universitària Politècnica de Mataró. Aplicaciones de la Realidad Aumentada (2011)
3. McDowall, I., Dolinsky, M.: IS & T–the Society for Imaging Science and Technology and Spie. In: The Engineering Reality of Virtual Reality, vol. 8289 (2012)
4. Dangelmaier, W., Fischer, M., Gausemeier, J., Grafe, M., Matysczok, C., Mueck, B.: Virtual and augmented reality support for discrete manufacturing system simulation. Comput. Ind. 56(4), 371–383
5. Summers, J.D.: Comparative study of CAD interrogation capabilities commercial CAD vs. design exemplar (2005)
6. Park, J., Kim, B., Kim, C., Kim, H.: 3D/4D CAD Applicability for Life-Cycle Facility Management. J. Comput. Civ. Eng. 25(2), 129–138 (March-April)
7. Kosmadoudi, Z., Lim, T., Ritchie, J., Louchart, S., Liu, Y., Sung, R.: Engineering design using game-enhanced CAD: The potential to augment the user experience with game elements. Comput. Aided Des. 45(3), 777–795 (March)
8. Anonymous, ARengine (2013), http://www.metaio.com/products/arengine/
9. Anonymous, Web3D Consortium (2013), http://www.web3d.org

10. Anonymous, Tripp, M. L. (n.d.). ARML - An Augmented Reality Standard, `http://www.perey.com/MobileARSummit/Mobilizy-ARML.pdf` (retrieved from ARML - An Augmented Reality Standard)
11. Anonymous, Adobe Director (2013), `http://www.adobe.com/es/products/director.html`
12. Anonymous, Adobe Flash (2013), `http://www.adobe.com/es/products/flash.html`
13. Anonymous, Microsoft Silverlight (2013), `http://www.microsoft.com/silverlight/`
14. Anonymous, Cortona 3D (2014), `http://www.cortona3d.com/`
15. Anonymous, Java3D (2013), `http://www.java3d.org/`
16. Anonymous, Ajax3D (2013), `http://www.ajax3d.org`
17. Anonymous, WebGL (2014), `http://www.khronos.org/webgl/`
18. Anonymous, X3DOM (2013), `http://www.x3dom.org/`
19. Olmedo, H.: Virtuality Continuum's State of the Art. Procedia Computer Science 25, 261–270
20. Anonymous, Google Chrome (2014), `http://www.google.com/chrome`
21. Anonymous. Mozilla Firefox (2014), `http://www.mozilla.com/firefox/`
22. Anonymous, Safari (2014), `https://www.apple.com/es/safari/`
23. Anonymous, Opera (2014), `http://www.opera.com`
24. Altidor, J., Wileden, J., McPherson, J., Grosse, I., Krishnamurty, S., Cordeiro, F., Lee-St John, A.: A Programming Language Approach to Parametric Cad Data Exchange (2012)
25. Chang, H., Kim, K., Kim, Y.: The research of security system for sharing engineering drawings (2007)
26. Anonymous, Oculus Rift (2014), `http://www.oculusvr.com/`
27. Anonymous "Special issue on the applications of augmented reality in architecture, engineering, and construction". Autom. Constr. 33(8), 1–2
28. Anastassova, M., Burkhardt, J.: Automotive technicians' training as a community-of-practice: Implications for the design of an augmented reality teaching aid. Appl. Ergon. 40(4-7), 713–721
29. Olalde, K., García, B., Seco, A.: The Importance of Geometry Combined with New Techniques for Augmented Reality. Procedia Computer Science 25, 136–143
30. Olalde, K., Guesalaga, I.: The New Dimension in a Calendar: The Use of Different Senses and Augmented Reality Apps. Procedia Computer Science 25, 322–329

User Experience Observations on Factors That Affect Performance in a Road-Crossing Training Application for Children Using the CAVE

Aimilia Tzanavari[1,2], Skevi Matsentidou[2], Chris G. Christou[1,2], and Charalambos Poullis[2]

[1] University of Nicosia, Nicosia, CYPRUS
{tzanavari.a,christou.ch}@unic.ac.cy
[2] Immersive and Creative Technologies Lab, Cyprus University of Technology, Limassol, CYPRUS
skevi.matsentidou@gmail.com, charalambos@poullis.org

Abstract. Each year thousands of pedestrian get killed in road accidents and millions are non-fatally injured. Many of these involve children and occur when crossing at or between intersections. It is more difficult for children to understand, assess and predict risky situations, especially in settings that they don't have that much experience in, such as in a city. Virtual Reality has been used to simulate situations that are too dangerous to practice in real life and has proven to be advantageous when used in training, aiming at improving skills. This paper presents a road-crossing application that simulates a pedestrian crossing found in a city setting. Children have to evaluate all given pieces of information (traffic lights, cars crossing, etc.) and then try to safely cross the road in a virtual environment. A VR CAVE is used to immerse children in the city scene. User experience observations were made so as to identify the factors that seem to affect children's performance. Results indicate that the application was well received as a learning tool and that gender; immersion and traffic noise seem to affect children's performance.

Keywords: CAVE, User Experience, Road Crossing, Children, and Training.

1 Introduction

Each year thousands of pedestrians lose their lives in road accidents and millions are non-fatally injured. Many of these are children and occur in accidents when crossing at or between intersections, primarily when children are going to and from school. It is more difficult for young children to understand, assess and predict risky situations, because of poorly developed perceptual and attention abilities especially in settings where they don't have that much experience, such as in a busy city.

Many governments have realized the great importance of road safety education and have developed well-organized initiatives towards increasing awareness and training, especially among young children. Early practical experience is acknowledged by all as the most important factor to improve road safety skills among children. Studies have shown [1] that increasing knowledge does not necessarily improve behavior. Investing on getting practical experience seems to be the key to alleviate this problem.

P. Zaphiris and A. Ioannou (Eds.): LCT 2014, Part II, LNCS 8524, pp. 91–101, 2014.
© Springer International Publishing Switzerland 2014

Current strategies used to train children in safe pedestrian behavior include group education, individualized roadside behavioral training; computer based training and virtual reality training. Virtual reality represents the newest approach and has several advantages: children can engage in potentially risky situations, such as road-crossing, without facing any risk, they can practice without time restrictions, the settings can be adapted according to the child's individual needs (which might include disabilities) and last but not least VR applications are highly engaging.

In the study presented in this paper, we try to study the effectiveness of a specialized VR CAVE application as a learning tool to improve 9-year old children's road-crossing skills. Furthermore, by observing and monitoring children's experience/ behavior we try to identify factors that seem to contribute to successful road-crossing performance in the VR CAVE.   The results of this study are discussed, as well as the next steps towards this research direction.

2   Background

Children's road crossing skills and their behaviour in traffic may be influenced by a variety of factors including demographics and individual differences, cognitive ability, as well as visual, attention and perceptual skills. Much of the literature suggests that young children are less competent in traffic than older children and adults because of poorly developed perceptual and attention abilities, which consequently increases their risk as pedestrians [2], [3], [4]. A more recent study [5] that involved children aged 6 to 11, concluded that younger children took longer to make correct decisions with respect to road crossing and also seemed to be affected negatively by auditory and visual distractions. Keeping the above in mind, it is recommended that children be supervised when crossing roads until they reach the age of nine.

Virtual Reality allows one to do more than just imitate reality. If that was the only goal, then it may be simpler to manufacture physical props with which a participant could practice some procedure. What virtual reality adds is the ability to practice uncommon, expensive and dangerous tasks. Additionally, the operator has more control over what scenarios can be presented to the participant, and can change the scenario in response to performance. The other significant benefit is that performance can be recorded and analyzed.

The effectiveness of virtual reality has been tested in a pedestrian-safety training situations for children since 2002 [6]. Thomson et al. [7] conducted a study with 7, 9 and 11-year old children, looking at their road-crossing judgments before and after training with a computer-simulated traffic environment. Trained children performed better, crossing more quickly, missing fewer opportunities to cross safely and generally demonstrating a better understanding of the factors considered when making crossing decisions. Schwebel et al [8] conducted an important study confirming the validity of human behavior in the virtual world matching the same person's behavior in the real world using an immersive, interactive virtual pedestrian environment.

3 VR CAVE Application for Road-Crossing

3.1 Software and Equipment Used

For the design and development of the immersive application in the VR CAVE environment we used the EON Studio Professional for the implementation, Autodesk Maya and 3ds Max for the 3D modeling and animation production. A road-crossing learning environment was developed. In this environment, there is a crossing, with the crossing button, lights and cars that commute in a street of a city. The child has the opportunity to navigate and interact with the virtual world. The child can press the button at the crossing, wait until cars stop and lights change from red to green and then cross the street.

Fig. 1. VR CAVE, glasses, Xbox controller

The EON REALITY iCube VR CAVE was used to display the 3D virtual environment which was viewed using a pair of active stereo shutter glasses. Interaction and navigation were performed using an Xbox game controller. Both the stereo glasses and the Xbox controller were tracked using a non-invasive infrared position tracker. The former allowed the view of the environment to be updated according to user head movements.

The VR Cave consists of four screens (to the front, left and right of the viewer and one on the floor). Each screen is displayed by one of four HD projectors. The participant stands between the screens and with the help of the active stereo glasses is immersed in the 3D world being displayed (see Figure 2).

Fig. 2. Screenshots from VR CAVE application for road crossing

3.2   The Study

The goal of this research was to design and develop an immersive application in a VR CAVE environment for improving children's road-crossing skills, as well as to study the factors that influence performance.

A city is an environment that it is realistically dangerous for young children especially because of cars, but indirectly because of heavy noise levels and continuous distractions which can disturb concentration. They have to learn how to cross the road safely, identify and avoid cars, recognize and press the crossing button and recognize and interpret traffic signs and lights. Specifically, in the scenario used for this study, the following learning processes are involved:

- The child recognizes, tracks and avoids moving cars within the virtual street scene
- The child recognizes and finds the crossing button, walks to it, stops, and presses it
- The child recognizes the traffic lights and how to interpret them (red light means stop and green means walk)
- The child recognizes the crossing and walks over it, if it is safe to – based on the lights and cars

In this study the main objective was to investigate which factors seem to affect children in their behavior in road-crossing using the VR CAVE environment. Traffic noise was added to study its influence on road-crossing behaviour. It is commonly believed that background noise can affect concentration and can increase stress levels

[9]. Additionally, questions involved finding out whether the children felt immersed, whether the application can be used for educating children to learn how to cross a road safely, the devices were easily used by children and also if it offered an enjoyable experience.

Eleven children (9-10 years old) participated in the study. The evaluation was empirical and was assessed by a pre-test questionnaire, by making observations during the session, and by a post-test questionnaire. Four girls and seven boys between 9 and 10 years old were selected randomly among sixty children of a primary school that had come to the research lab for a visit, as part of an educational excursion. Consent forms were signed by parents/guardians, informing them about the particular study and giving details about their children's participation.

The procedure for each session was as follows. First of all, the child was asked to wear shoes and glasses, which are necessary in order to enter the VR CAVE environment. After that, it was explained to the child how to use the Xbox controller in order to interact and navigate within the environment. For 5-10 minutes, we gave the opportunity to the children to play with the Xbox controller in order to familiarize themselves with it and learn how to handle it and interact with the environment.

The session for each child consisted of four trials: two with traffic noise and two without (with no specific order). The steps that each child was expected to execute during each trial in order to complete the session successfully, were the following:

- Press the button at the crossing box (the child did this by pressing a button on the Xbox controller)
- Look right and left in order to check if cars are coming
- Wait until cars stop
- If the cars stop and the pedestrian lights are green, then cross the road
- Cross the road and get to the other side safely

Participants filled a pre-test questionnaire and a post-test questionnaire. Also, during the session the observers kept a form for each child to record observations. The pre-test questionnaire contained questions related to the child's skills with technology, and electronic gaming habits (e.g. hours per week). It also included questions relating to their subjective level of knowledge of road-crossing, as well as some questions concerning attention and how easily they get distracted. The observation form and the post-test questionnaire focused on specific proposed judgment categories, such as mistakes made, difficult points in interaction, etc.

3.3   Data Analysis

Most children reported in the pre-test questionnaire that they already knew how to cross the street; one child stated that they knew a little, and another one that they knew but never before had the chance to cross a road alone. All children owned one or more electronic devices: PC, tablet and smartphone. They reported using their electronic device for browsing the Web (91%), for playing games (91%), for doing homework (45%), for Social Networking (45%). Most children (64%) reported playing electronic games for less than 5 hours per week, while the rest (36%) said they played for 5-20 hours per week. There were three attention related questions in which children were asked (a) whether their attention gets distracted (e.g. from noise, conversations, etc.), (b) how difficult do they find it to concentrate on a telephone conversation when their favourite TV program starts and (c) how often do they find themselves repeating pieces of text when they are reading. Answers were distributed somewhat evenly when seen for all participants, but a tendency was observed in boys being more easily distracted when reading text, whereas girls had more difficulty concentrating in a telephone conversation (**Error! Reference source not found.**).

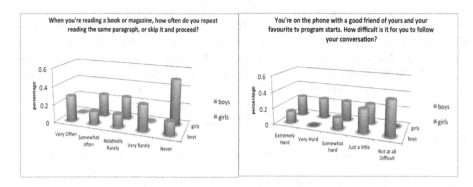

Fig. 3. Boys and Girls responses to attention-related questions

Almost all children verbally mentioned and demonstrated through gestures and facial expressions that they greatly enjoyed the virtual street-crossing experience. The post-test questionnaire results indicated exactly the same. Additionally, only 27.27% of children mentioned that they felt dizziness during their experience, while 64% of the children answered that they got immersed. 91% answered that they felt the whole experience and interaction was compatible with the real world and all of them agreed that the application would be an excellent learning tool. Regarding the adequacy of the application we measured if children found the use of the equipment (hand controller/ glasses/ shoes) restrictive. 55% of children reported founding it restrictive, referring primarily to the glasses being uncomfortable due to them being relatively large and perhaps too heavy for children of their age.

After careful analysis of the data, we observed that boys outperformed girls in all aspects in the four trials. Figure 4 summarizes these findings. Boys did significantly better when it came to waiting for the green light before crossing, look left and right and generally in successfully crossing the road.

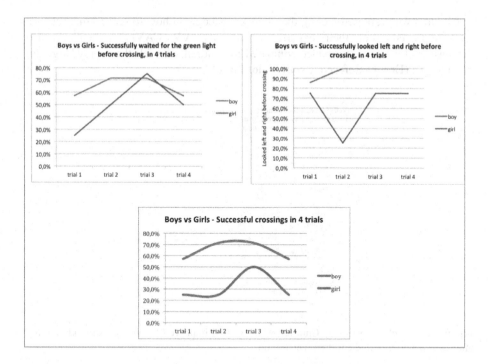

Fig. 4. How Gender Seems to Affect Performance

Another factor that seemed to affect children's performance was their sense of immersion. Children who reported that they felt immersed when interacting with the application did significantly better than those who said they did not (**Error! Reference source not found.**).

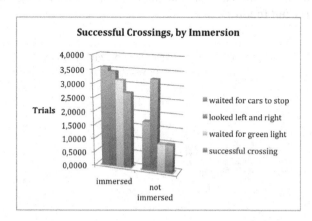

Fig. 5. Successful Crossings by Children who reported being immersed and not

Children who reported feeling that their knowledge on how to successfully cross a road improved after their experience with the VR CAVE application, also demonstrated better performance compared to children who felt their knowledge did not improve (**Error! Reference source not found.**).

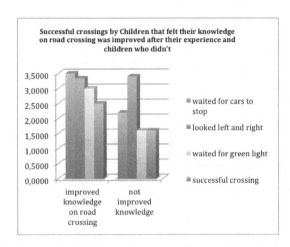

Fig. 6. Successful Crossings by Children who reported improved knowledge on road crossing after their experience and children who did not

Finally, the influence of bakcground noise was studied, offering each subject two trials with traffic noise and two trials without. The starting state was alternated for each subject: so some experienced with-noise in the first trial and others without-noise. Across subjects, noise did not seem to affect performance as such. However, it was observed that subjects who started with a "without noise" trial performed better in all trials compared with subjects who started with a "with noise" trial (**Error! Reference source not found.**).

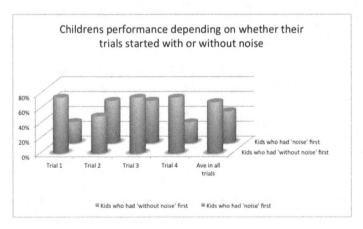

Fig. 7. Children's Performance depending on whether their trials started with or without noise

No particular relation was found between children's responses to attention-related questions and their performance. In Table 1, we report on children's responses to question "Your attention is easily distracted (by e.g. noise, people talking around you, etc.) with possible responses "Yes", "Sometimes" or "Never" and their performance in the four (4) trials, based on successful crossings.

Table 1. Performance observations, by subjective attention level

Question: You are easily distracted (e.g. by noise, by others' conversations, etc.)		To_wait	lookleftright	waitgreen light	Cross_ok
yes	Mean	3.0000	3.2000	2.2000	1.6000
	Std. Deviation	.70711	1.30384	1.64317	1.81659
someti mes	Mean	3.5000	4.0000	3.0000	3.0000
	Std. Deviation	.70711	0.00000	1.41421	1.41421
never	Mean	2.5000	3.2500	2.2500	2.2500
	Std. Deviation	1.91485	.95743	1.70783	1.70783

4   Conclusion

The results indicate first of all that the VR CAVE application for road-crossing training of children can be beneficial as a learning tool. The children who participated in the study (9 year olds) all interacted with the virtual environment smoothly and had no difficulties handling any of the devices. All of them reported to have had a pleasurable experience and most of them felt that they improved their knowledge on safe road crossing. However, a more accurate tool for assessing learning effectiveness would be needed in future studies.

Questionnaire results in combination with user performance observations (waiting for cars to stop, looking left-right, waiting for the green light and successfully crossing) revealed that boys out performed girls in all aspects and that children who reported feeling immersed in the VR CAVE application did much better as well. Indeed gender, as a factor influencing the sense of presence and realness, has been investigated in recent studies [10] reaching similar conclusions: male subjects feel more present than female subjects in virtual environments.

In addition it was noticed that children who felt their knowledge improved after interacting with the application, also did better. Attention-related questions were included in the pre-test questionnaire, but data was not sufficient to draw conclusions that can relate attention levels with performance. In addition, children's responses about their own attention abilities might be seen as not objective enough to draw firm conclusions relating attention to road-crossing ability. A more specialized attention related test would need to be administered to get more conclusive results.

Finally, we were not in a position to draw important conclusions concerning traffic noise, which was added as a distractor in two out of four of the trials, however it was noticed that children who got "no traffic noise" trials first performed better than those who got the opposite. This possibly indicates that traffic noise distracted children at the beginning of their session and affected their overall performance.

Despite the fact that this initial study's population was not very significant so as to safely generalize the results, they are nevertheless promising results and a follow-up, larger scale study is therefore justified.

5   Future Work

A larger scale study is in the immediate future plans. More children have to experience the CAVE application to extract results that can be generalizable. It is believed that factors such as traffic noise (or other distractors) and attention levels might appear to actually have an important influence on successful crossing. Investigating the impact, differences and corresponding factors that influence performance when children have a disability, such as autism, is also being planned.

We have concluded that the VR CAVE environment can be used as an educational tool in road safety with promising results. The application appeared to have contributed to the improvement of children's knowledge about safe road crossing, but a more accurate assessment tool will need to be devised. One of the factors affecting performance, such as immersion, indicates that we need to invest resources on improving the users sense of immersion.

Next steps also involve broadening the collection of scenes of the application, including more road-safety situations one can encounter in a city, such as cyclists, traffic lights that are not working, basic road signs, etc.

Acknowledgement. The research presented in this paper was made possible with the use of the VR CAVE equipment, at the Immersive and Creative Technologies Lab (http://www.theictlab.org) of the Cyprus University of Technology. The acquisition and establishment of the equipment was part of the IPE/NEKYP/0311/02 "VR CAVE" project (http://www.vrcave.com.cy) and is financially supported by the Cyprus Research Promotion Foundation and the European Structural Funds. The authors of this paper would also like to thank the students and parents who agreed to take part in this study.

References

1. Zeedyk, M.S., Wallace, L., Carcary, B., Jones, K., Larter, K.: Children and road safety: Increasing knowledge does not improve behaviour. British Journal of Educational Psychology 71, 573–594 (2001)
2. Connelly, M., Conaglen, H., Parsonson, B., Isler, R.: Child pedestrian's crossing gap thresholds. Accident Analysis and Prevention 30(4), 443–453 (1998)
3. Dunbar, G., Hill, R., Lewis, V.: Children's attentional skills and road behaviour. Journal of Experimental Psychology: Applied 7(3), 227–234 (2001)

4. Whitebread, D., Neilson, K.: The contribution of visual search strategies to the development of pedestrian skills by 4-11 year-old children. British Journal of Educational Psychology 70, 539–557 (2000)

5. Tabibi, Z., Pfeffer, K.: Finding a safe place to cross the road: the effect of distractors and the role of attention in children's identification of safe and dangerous road-crossing sites. Inf. Child Develop. 16, 193–206 (2007)

6. McComas, J., MacKay, M., Picik, J.: Effectiveness of virtual reality for teaching pedestrian safety. Cyber Psychology & Behavior 5(3), 185–190 (2002)

7. Thomson, J.A., Tolmie, A.K., Foot, H.C., Whelan, K.M., Sarvary, P., Morrison, S.: Influence of Virtual Reality Training on the Roadside Crossing Judgments of Child Pedestrians. Journal of Experimental Psychology: Applied 11(3), 175–186 (2005)

8. Schwebel, D.C., Gaines, J., Severson, J.: Validation of virtual reality as a tool to understand and prevent child pedestrian injury. Accident Analysis and Prevention 40, 1394–1400 (2008)

9. Andrews, M.A.W.: How does background noise affect our concentration? Scientific American (January/ February 2010), http://www.scientificamerican.com/article.cfm?id=ask-the-brains-background-noise

10. Felnhofer, A., Kothgassner, O.D., Beutl, L., Hlavacs, H., Kryspin-Exner, I.: Is virtual reality made for men only? Exploring gender differences in the sense of presence. In: Proceedings of the International Society on Presence Research, pp. 103–112 (2012)

Mobile and Ubiquitous Learning

Context Dependent Preference Acquisition with Personality-Based Active Learning in Mobile Recommender Systems

Matthias Braunhofer, Mehdi Elahi, Mouzhi Ge, and Francesco Ricci

Free University of Bozen-Bolzano, Bozen-Bolzano, Italy
{mbraunhofer,mehdi.elahi,mouzhi.ge,fricci}@unibz.it
http://www.unibz.it

Abstract. Nowadays, Recommender Systems (RSs) play a key role in many businesses. They provide consumers with relevant recommendations, e.g., Places of Interest (POIs) to a tourist, based on user preference data, mainly in the form of ratings for items. The accuracy of recommendations largely depends on the quality and quantity of the ratings (preferences) provided by the users. However, users often tend to rate no or only few items, causing low accuracy of the recommendation. Active Learning (AL) addresses this problem by actively selecting items to be presented to the user in order to acquire a larger number of high-quality ratings (preferences), and hence, improve the recommendation accuracy. In this paper, we propose a personalized active learning approach that leverages user's personality data to get more and better in-context ratings. We have designed a novel human computer interaction and assessed our proposed approach in a live user study - which is not common in active learning research. The main result is that the system is able to collect better ratings and provide more relevant recommendations compared to a variant that is using a state of the art approach to preference acquisition.

Keywords: Recommender Systems, Collaborative Filtering, Personalized Active Learning, Cold start, Mobile.

1 Introduction

In the more recent years there has been an explosive growth of the sheer volume of information available through the World Wide Web. For instance, in tourism websites, the amount of travel offers is continuously increasing, making it extremely difficult to select a good hotel or a place to stay, due to the overwhelming number of offers provided and the lack of effective system support. RSs address this "information overload" problem by providing to users recommendations for items that are likely to be appealing to them [1].

Collaborative filtering (CF) is a state-of-the-art technique that generates recommendations by exploiting ratings for items provided by a network of users. A challenging problem of CF is the cold-start problem, i.e., its poor performance

P. Zaphiris and A. Ioannou (Eds.): LCT 2014, Part II, LNCS 8524, pp. 105–116, 2014.

on new items and on new users. In fact, CF requires that an adequate number of ratings is provided by the target user (who is requesting a recommendation), which makes the system knowledgeable about the user's preferences, before relevant suggestions can be generated.

The cold-start problem becomes even more severe for Context-Aware Recommender Systems (CARS), i.e., systems that recommend items by exploiting not only the traditional user and item dimensions but also contextual information [2]. In these systems, it doesn't suffice anymore to have enough ratings of several users for many items; the system must have collected a sufficient number of ratings in the various contextual situations as well. For instance, imagine that a CARS for places of interest (POIs) collected from the users many low ratings for a mountain hiking route, and the users tagged these ratings with "rainy weather", to indicate that the item was always experienced under that contextual situation (which influenced the rating). Moreover, assume that no rating for the same route was tagged with "sunny day", which is a contextual condition expected to make that route much more attractive. In this case, that route would not be recommended to any user during a sunny day since the system could not learn yet that in a sunny day the ratings for this item tend to be higher than on a rainy day.

In order to tackle this problem in a CF system (irrespectively whether is context-aware or not), the user-system interaction typically begins with a rating elicitation process (preference elicitation). When a new user registers, the system proposes a set of selected items for her to rate. If the system is context-aware the user must specify not only her ratings but has to tag each rating with the contextual conditions under which the item was experienced (e.g., a rainy or sunny day). In fact, the ratings that a user provides are not all equally informative of her preferences and equally useful for the RS to generate accurate recommendations (for her and also for other users). For this reason, in the most advanced CF systems, the items selected by the system for the user to rate are computed by an Active Learning (AL) strategy aiming at acquiring a better user profile and ultimately generating more accurate recommendations [3–6].

In this paper we illustrate the application of a novel AL strategy for context-aware rating elicitation that uses the personality of the user within a mobile recommender system for places of interest, which is called STS (South Tyrol Suggests). First, the user personality is acquired with a simple questionnaire. Then, using a customised matrix factorisation model, the system predicts the items that the user is familiar with, i.e., items that the user has experienced in the past, and asks the user to rate them. This prediction is crucial because in our application domain, which is tourism, users cannot experience or try an item during the rating elicitation process, as for instance in the music domain, in which users can listen to a music track on the spot and rate it. Moreover, in the selected domain, user needs are dependent on the context of the travel and are not simply based on the long term preference model. Therefore, any user rating should explicitly indicate the contextual situation of the user while she was experiencing the rated item, i.e., must be tagged with as many as possible contextual conditions which correctly describe the experience of the user.

The proposed AL strategy, by exploiting the knowledge of the user personality, aims at maximizing the utility of the recommendations, which is measured by the appropriateness of the suggestions to the user preference and their relevance to the current contextual situation of the user (requesting recommendations). In order to measure the above mentioned properties we have designed a novel evaluation methodology and conducted a user study [7]. We hypothesised that if the recommendation model is trained with the ratings elicited by the proposed AL strategy then it will recommend items that not only "fit the preferences" of the user (ultimate goal of classical RSs), but also are "well-chosen for the situation" of the user (her contextual situation). In fact, our results show that the proposed AL strategy, compared to a state-of-the-art strategy, elicits ratings that make the recommendations more "context-aware", i.e., better suited for the current situation of the user. Moreover, it acquires more and better ratings, i.e., the acquired ratings are tagged by the raters with more contextual conditions.

In conclusion, the main contributions of the paper are the following:

1. Based on the acquired user personality, we have designed a new algorithmic AL strategy that can be used for preference elicitation in CARS.
2. We have designed an easy-to-use HCI that supports user personality acquisition, context-aware rating elicitation and recommendation in a mobile scenario.
3. We have designed a novel online user study to evaluate our proposed AL strategy with respect to the quality of the generated recommendations.
4. We have shown that the proposed AL strategy outperforms a state-of-the-art one in terms of how well-chosen are the recommendations for the current user situation, which indicates that it is more effective in context-aware recommendation scenarios.

The rest of this paper is structured as follow: Section 2 presents the HCI that we have developed for preference elicitation. Section 3 describes the structure of the user study and the obtained results. Section 4 discusses the related works and positions this work with respect to the state-of-the-art in active learning for collaborative filtering. Finally, section 5 summarizes contributions and outlines the directions for future work.

2 Human Computer Interaction for Active Learning Preference Elicitation

This section describes the experimental design of the user study and the human-computer interaction with STS (South Tyrol Suggests): our Android-based recommender system that provides users with context-aware recommendations for attractions, events, public services, restaurants, and accommodations (for South Tyrol region in Italy).

2.1 Personality Questionnaire

After the user has registered to the system by specifying her username, password, birthdate and gender, she is asked to fill out the Ten-Item Personality Inventory (TIPI) questionnaire [8], so that the system can assess her Big Five personality traits (openness, conscientiousness, extroversion, agreeableness, neuroticism). Figure 1 (left) shows a screenshot of our application where one of the questionnaire statements is illustrated. The full questionnaire includes the following ten statements, answered on a 7-point Likert scale (from "strongly disagree" to "strongly agree"): I see myself as extraverted, enthusiastic; I see myself as critical, quarrelsome; I see myself as dependable, self-disciplined; I see myself as anxious, easily upset; I see myself as open to new experiences, complex; I see myself as reserved, quiet; I see myself as sympathetic, warm; I see myself as disorganized, careless; I see myself as calm, emotionally stable; I see myself as conventional, uncreative.

2.2 Active Learning Strategies

Using the assessed personality (as illustrated in Figure 1, middle), along with the retrieved age and gender as input to one of the two implemented AL strategies (i.e., either the state-of-the-art log(popularity) * entropy [9] or our proposed personality-based binary prediction [7], depending on the experimental group the user belongs to), the system identifies and prompts the user to rate eight POIs, whose ratings are aimed at best improving the quality of subsequent recommendations. The *log(popularity) * entropy* strategy is considered as a baseline in our evaluation (see section 3). We have used it since previous works have compared it with other approaches and reported its excellent performance [4, 6, 9, 10]. In fact, it has been shown that this strategy (or its variation) is one of the bests [4, 6, 9].

Log(Popularity) * Entropy scores each item i by multiplying the logarithm of the *popularity* of i (i.e., the number of ratings for i in the training set) by the entropy of the ratings for i. Then, the top scored items are proposed to be rated by the user (4 in our experiments). This strategy is a *Balanced* strategy [9] in the sense that it tries to collect many ratings, by highly scoring items that are popular (hence can be rated), but also taking into account their relative informativeness (measured by the ratings' entropy), hence finding a balance between the quantity and quality of the acquired ratings.

Personality-Based Binary Prediction first transforms the rating matrix in a matrix with the same number of rows and columns, by mapping null entries to 0, and not null entries to 1. Hence, this new matrix models only whether a user rated an item or not, regardless of its value. Then, this Boolean matrix is used to train an extended version of the popular matrix factorization algorithm. Our model, which is fully described in [7], is similar to that proposed in [11], and enhances the user representation with additional factor vectors that correspond to each attribute in the set of user-associated attributes, in our case, gender, age group and the discretized scores for the Big Five personality traits.

2.3   Contextual Information Acquisition

The acquisition of rating-in-context is a new feature of the rating elicitation HCI that we have designed. During the rating elicitation process, for each of the POIs selected by the AL strategies, the user can specify her rating as well as the value of up to three randomly selected contextual factors (from a set of 14 context factors [12]) in which the POI was visited. From the GUI design view, three contextual factors can better fit into the mobile device and the random selection allows to sample uniformly the impact of every factor on the ratings. Figure 1 (right) shows the snapshot of the system where the user is presented a POI and is asked to rate it, if she has experienced it, and specify the contextual situation, if she remembers it and is eager to give. For instance, here, the user is asked to specify the travel budget, the crowdedness as well as the duration of the stay. We note that such contextual information could help the system to better figure out the contextual situation when the user experienced a POI, and hence help the system to make better predictions and better recommendations.

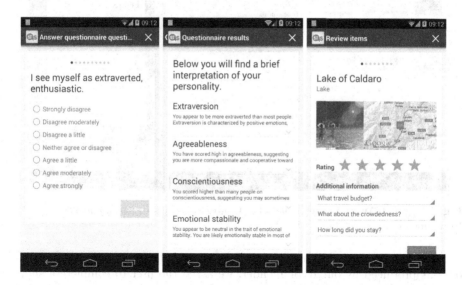

Fig. 1. Personality Questionnaire (left), Big 5 Personality Trait Assessment (centre), and Active Learning (right)

2.4   Recommendation Presentation

After the user has completed this registration procedure (i.e., by filling out the personality questionnaire as well as by rating known POIs), she is finally presented with the suggestions (recommendations) screen, as illustrated in Figure 2 (left). This window provides the user with a list of four POIs that are considered highly relevant taking into account the previously acquired user's ratings as well as the current contextual conditions around the user and the POIs. In order to take into account the current contextual conditions when generating POI recommendations, we use an extended version of Context-Aware Matrix Factorization (CAMF) [13], which, besides the standard parameters (i.e., global average, item bias, user bias and user-item interaction), incorporates baseline parameters for each contextual condition and item pair. This extended version, analogously to our implemented AL strategy, exploits known user attributes to provide accurate recommendations also for users with no or few ratings (more details can be found in [12]). We note that some of the contextual conditions are automatically acquired (e.g., weather conditions, temperature, season and location), whereas others can be specified by the user using a system screen (e.g., mood, budget, means of transport) (Figure 2, middle).

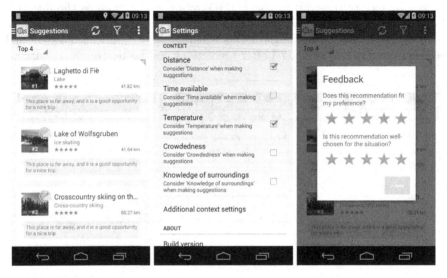

Fig. 2. Context-Aware Suggestions (left), Context Settings (centre), and Feedback on Recommendations (right)

Since we were interested in evaluating the quality of the individual recommendations produced by our recommender, we asked the user to complete a short mobile-based questionnaire (see Figure 2, right) for each of the recommended POIs that popped up after doing a long press on them. The questionnaire contains the following two specific statements to be answered on a five-star rating scale (1 star being the lowest score and 5 stars being the highest score):

- Q1: Does this recommendation fit my preference?
- Q2: Is this recommendation well-chosen for the situation?

These statements are obtained from [14], which provides a standard questionnaire for perceived recommendation quality and choice satisfaction. We chose these statements since they address two important goals of recommender systems, i.e., fitting the preference of the user (general preference) and being well-chosen and relevant (specific preference related to the context).

3   Evaluation Results

The online evaluation methodology presented in the previous section was designed to understand whether the incorporation of human personality into AL can result in eliciting more informative ratings or not. We have formulated the following hypotheses: the proposed personality-based AL strategy (in comparison to the chosen baseline) elicits ratings which result in recommendations that: a) better fit the preference of the user (preference fitting), and, b) are well-chosen for the current situation of the user (context-awareness).

To evaluate these hypotheses we conducted a live user study involving 51 participants who were randomly assigned either to the log(popularity) * entropy strategy group (n = 19) or the personality-based binary prediction item selection strategy group (n = 27). Some users from log(popularity) * entropy strategy group have been excluded because they did not complete the evaluation. Given a particular AL strategy, the (training) rating matrix evolves by including all the ratings entered by users on the training items elicited so far. Using these ratings the RS model is computed and recommendations are generated.

Table 1 summarises the results of the evaluation. It shows the average replies of the users to the two statements mentioned above. Those of the users assigned to personality-based binary prediction Active Learning is 3.56 for Q1 (preference fitting) and 3.31 for Q2 (context awareness). For the log(popularity)* entropy strategy, these numbers are 3.58 (for Q1) and 2.95 (for Q2), respectively. Comparing the results, we observe that both strategies got almost the same average reply to Q1 (no significant difference, $p = 0.43$ for a t-test), while personality-based strategy got a significantly higher average for Q2 ($p = 0.049$). Hence, while both strategies acquired ratings that resulted in recommendations that "fits the preferences" of the users, the proposed personality-based binary prediction strategy outperforms log(popularity) * entropy, by acquiring ratings that result in recommendations that are evaluated to be more "well-chosen".

Table 1. Average users reply to recommendations evaluation questions (numbers in bold indicate significant improvement of one strategy vs. the other). "# of contexts" refers to the average number of contextual conditions entered by a user while rating an item.

	AL Strategies	
	log (popularity) * entropy	personality-based binary pred.
Q1	3.58	3.56
Q2	2.95	**3.31**
# of contexts	1.01	**1.52**

In [7] we have shown that the proposed active learning strategy acquires significantly more ratings than *log (popularity) * entropy*. Here we want to also compare these strategies in term of how many contextual conditions are entered by the users, in order to describe their POI experience, during the rating elicitation process. The users assigned to the variant using the personality-based active learning strategy, by average, have entered 1.52 contextual conditions (out of 3) vs. 1.01 entered by the users assigned to log(popularity) * entropy strategy variant ($p = 0.001$). This result indicates that the proposed strategy acquires significantly more contextual conditions. We believe that this effect is due to the fact that the personality-based strategy selects POIs that are more familiar to the users and hence users may better remember the experience of their visit (and the contextual conditions).

Furthermore, we note that STS was deployed on Google Play on Sep 18, 2013, and until Jan 14, 2014, 465 users have used the system (346 users downloaded it from Google Play). Overall, the system has collected 2,415 ratings and many of the ratings were entered together with a description of the context of the experience. Among the full set of users, 380 (81.72%) have completed the personality questionnaire and 326 (70.1%) went through the active learning phase. This shows that users largely accept to follow the proposed active learning phase to obtain recommendations.

4   Related Works

Most of RSs interactions begin with a sign-up process that includes a preference elicitation phase. In this phase the users are required to enter their preferences, for instance, in the form of ratings to items. After that, the recommender system is able to generate and display a set of personalized recommendations for the user to review or critique. The more informative about the user preferences the available ratings are the higher the recommendation quality is. This is because the ratings given by the users are not all equally useful for the system and informative of the users' preferences and tastes. Indeed, the need to implement more effective sign up processes is one of the main motivations of the research on Active Learning (AL) for recommender systems.

Several AL strategies have been proposed and evaluated [3, 4, 9, 10, 15, 16]. Two methodologies have been used for evaluating AL strategies: either based on conducting *online* or *offline* studies. In the first case, the active learning system interacts with real users and acquires their preferences (ratings) by means of a customary designed user interface. This requires to access an up-and-running recommender system, preferably with a large network of active users. Conversely, in offline evaluations, a pre-collected rating dataset is used to simulate the behaviour of users interacting with the system. However, since the online evaluation is expensive and time consuming, the majority of previous works have focused on offline evaluations [3, 15, 16], while only a few of them have tackled online evaluations [4, 9, 10].

One of these few works which conducted an online evaluation, as a follow up to a preliminary offline study, is [9]. The authors considered six AL strategies: *entropy*, where items with the largest rating entropy are preferred; *random* request; *popularity*, which is measured by the number of ratings for an item, and hence the most frequently rated items are selected; *log(popularity)* ∗ *entropy* where items that are both popular and have diverse ratings are selected; and finally *item-item personalized*, where random items are proposed until the user rates one. Then, a recommender is used to predict what items the user is likely to have seen based on the ratings already provided by the user. These predicted items are requested to the user to rate. In online evaluation, every new user who registers to the system (MovieLens), was presented with a number of movies (10 movies per webpage) selected by one of the active learning strategies described before. This process continued until the user rated 10 or more movies. Then the strategies were compared in terms of the number of pages the users had seen. The authors considered this measure as an indication of "the effectiveness of the signup process". In their results, they have shown that overall the $log(popularity) * entropy$ strategy got the best prediction accuracy while popularity and item-item were the best in terms of the effectiveness of the signup process. It is important to note that there are several differences between their work and ours. First of all, they have not compared the strategies with respect to the recommendation quality (fitting to the user preference, and context-awareness) or the number of acquired contextual conditions. Instead, they focused on the number of pages the users see during the rating elicitation process. Moreover, their RS uses only the ratings while our system uses the users' personality together with their ratings, and hence, can generate personalized recommendations even if the user has not provided any rating. Finally, their system recommends movies through a web interface, while, our system recommends POIs through a mobile interface, which is totally different (due to the limited interaction capabilities in the mobile devices). For instance, the mobile screen size is small and this makes it infeasible to present properly 10 items in a page (as they have done in their work).

In [4] the authors followed up their early work [9] by proposing an AL strategy, called $IGCN$, which is based on decision trees. According to the user rating entered for the asked item a different branch is followed, and a new node, which is labelled with another item to rate, is determined. They also considered two alternative strategies. The first one is *entropy0* that differs from the classical entropy strategy, which we mentioned above, because the missing value is considered as a possible rating (category 0). The second one is called $HELF$, where items with the largest harmonic mean of entropy and popularity are selected. They have evaluated their strategies in an online study after a preliminary offline analysis: for every new user who registered to the RS (MovieLens), a number of movies selected by one of the AL strategies, was shown. After the user had rated 20 movies she took a brief optional survey that collects the users' opinions about the signup process. Then the RS was trained on the ratings entered by the user during the signup process (train set) and generated a set of recommendations to the user. After that, the user could provide any rating whenever she wanted, either by searching movies or using the "rate more movies" feature that presents random movies. Finally, the ratings entered by the user, after the signup process, were used as test set to evaluate the accuracy of the RS. The authors have concluded that, overall, Entropy0 and IGCN performed the best among the considered strategies. It is worth noting that this work has also several differences compared to ours. First of all, they have not asked the users whether the recommendations are well-chosen for the user's contextual situation or not. Moreover, they have asked the users to rate any movie any time they want. In this way, the users were more likely to rate the movies that they like, while we asked the users to evaluate only the recommended items even if they don't like them, hence we better measured the true performance of the RS. Another difference is that, in this work, the users completed a survey in order to globally evaluate the AL items and the sign-up process. We instead asked the users to evaluate, one by one, the recommended items.

We must note that the AL approach illustrated in this paper was originally proposed in [7]. It exploits user's personality information - using the Five Factor Model (FFM) - in order to identify a list of items that are not only useful to rate but also expected to be experienced by the user. Personality is a predictable and stable factor that forms human behaviours. It has been shown that there are direct relations between personality and tastes / interests [17]: people with similar personality factor usually share similar interests and tastes. Earlier studies conducted on the user personality characteristics support the possibility of using this information in collaborative filtering based recommender systems [18]. However, to the best of our knowledge, no previous research work has incorporated the personality of the user in AL for RS. In [7] we showed that the proposed personality-based AL technique increases the number of ratings elicited from the users as well as the recommendation accuracy, measured in terms of Mean Absolute Error (MAE), i.e., the average absolute deviation of the predicted ratings from the true ratings in a randomly selected test set. In this paper, instead, we evaluate the quality of the recommendation list rather than the system accuracy on a random list of items, and we show that there is a positive effect on the "context awareness" dimension of the recommendations.

5   Discussion and Future Work

In this paper, we have proposed a novel AL strategy based on collecting the user personality. We have applied this strategy in the mobile recommender system to elicit context-aware ratings. Also, an easy-to-use HCI has been designed for our application. Using this application, we have conducted an online user study to evaluate our proposed AL strategy with respect to the quality of recommendations. Our results have shown that our proposed AL strategy outperforms a state-of-the-art strategy and it is more effective in context-aware RSs.

We want to finally discuss a number of issues and implications of our research. Most of the current active learning approaches for collaborative filtering implement the *Standard Interaction Model* [3], i.e., the system selects and proposes a set of items to the user to rate only in the sign up process, until she rates a sufficient number of items. An alternative interaction model is the *Conversational and Collaborative Model* [3], which, in addition to allow the user to rate items in the sign-up process, it proposes to rate some additional items whenever the user is motivated to provide more ratings. For instance, in a tourism scenario the system may ask the user to rate a POI when she is visiting it. We call this feature *Proactivity*, and a proactive system asks the user to rate an item when the user is in a better position to provide a reliable rating. For instance, our mobile platforms can help users to rate their experienced items in a ubiquitous manner. In a future work we want to extend the current active learning strategy to become even more proactive, i.e., the system should evaluate the items and select the most useful and appropriate for rating elicitation, not only in the sign-up process, but also in the full operational usage of the system.

Moreover, while there are several types of contextual data that can be automatically obtained from sensors (e.g., weather, temperature, location, daytime, season, and weekday) there are contextual information that can only be provided by the user (e.g., budget, companion, mood, and transport mean). However, not all the contextual factors are equally useful for the system to improve the accuracy. For instance, may not be useful to know the transportation mean of the travel when the user is rating a visit to a museum. In other words, the transportation mean may not have any impact on the experience of the museum and hence should not be used in the predictive model that evaluates if a museum is worth recommending to a user. Moreover, actively selecting the contextual factors that are more informative and relevant to the item is an feature that can also ease the user-system interaction (more meaningful requests are made to the user).

Another issue in active learning for recommender systems concerns the sequential nature of preference elicitation. Although we have shown that identifying a list of well selected items for the user to rate can increase the system performance (number of ratings elicited and recommendation accuracy), this approach may fail to correctly react to the first users entered ratings and may not immediately adapt the remaining rating requests to the user. Hence, sequential AL algorithm in which the items to be rated are selected incrementally by choosing each successive item to be rated based on the users ratings provided to the previously requested items is an interesting area of future research.

References

1. Ricci, F., Rokach, L., Shapira, B., Kantor, P.B.: Recommender Systems Handbook. Springer (2011)
2. Adomavicius, G., Mobasher, B., Ricci, F., Tuzhilin, A.: Context-aware recommender systems. AI Magazine 32(3), 67–80 (2011)
3. Carenini, G., Smith, J., Poole, D.: Towards more conversational and collaborative recommender systems. In: Proceedings of the 2003 International Conference on Intelligent User Interfaces, Miami, FL, USA, January 12-15, pp. 12–18 (2003)
4. Rashid, A.M., Karypis, G., Riedl, J.: Learning preferences of new users in recommender systems: an information theoretic approach. SIGKDD Explorations 10(2), 90–100 (2008)
5. Rubens, N., Kaplan, D., Sugiyama, M.: Active learning in recommender systems. In: Ricci, F., Rokach, L., Shapira, B., Kantor, P. (eds.) Recommender Systems Handbook, pp. 735–767. Springer (2011)

6. Elahi, M., Ricci, F., Rubens, N.: Active learning strategies for rating elicitation in collaborative filtering: A system-wide perspective. ACM Trans. Intell. Syst. Technol. 5(1), 13:1–13:33 (2014)
7. Elahi, M., Braunhofer, M., Ricci, F., Tkalcic, M.: Personality-based active learning for collaborative filtering recommender systems. In: Baldoni, M., Baroglio, C., Boella, G., Micalizio, R. (eds.) AI*IA 2013. LNCS, vol. 8249, pp. 360–371. Springer, Heidelberg (2013)
8. Gosling, S.D., Rentfrow, P.J., Swann Jr., W.B.: A very brief measure of the big-five personality domains. Journal of Research in Personality 37(6), 504–528 (2003)
9. Rashid, A.M., Albert, I., Cosley, D., Lam, S.K., Mcnee, S.M., Konstan, J.A., Riedl, J.: Getting to know you: Learning new user preferences in recommender systems. In: Proceedings of the 2002 International Conference on Intelligent User Interfaces, IUI 2002, pp. 127–134. ACM Press (2002)
10. McNee, S.M., Lam, S.K., Konstan, J.A., Riedl, J.: Interfaces for eliciting new user preferences in recommender systems. In: Brusilovsky, P., Corbett, A.T., de Rosis, F. (eds.) UM 2003. LNCS, vol. 2702, pp. 178–187. Springer, Heidelberg (2003)
11. Koren, Y., Bell, R., Volinsky, C.: Matrix factorization techniques for recommender systems. Computer 42(8), 30–37 (2009)
12. Braunhofer, M., Elahi, M., Ricci, F., Schievenin, T.: Context-aware points of interest suggestion with dynamic weather data management. In: 21st Conference on Information and Communication Technologies in Tourism (ENTER). Springer (2014)
13. Baltrunas, L., Ludwig, B., Peer, S., Ricci, F.: Context relevance assessment and exploitation in mobile recommender systems. Personal and Ubiquitous Computing 16(5), 507–526 (2012)
14. Knijnenburg, B.P., Willemsen, M.C., Gantner, Z., Soncu, H., Newell, C.: Explaining the user experience of recommender systems. User Modeling and User-Adapted Interaction 22(4-5), 441–504 (2012)
15. Harpale, A.S., Yang, Y.: Personalized active learning for collaborative filtering. In: SIGIR 2008: Proceedings of the 31st Annual International ACM SIGIR Conference on Research and Development in Information Retrieval, pp. 91–98. ACM, New York (2008)
16. Golbandi, N., Koren, Y., Lempel, R.: Adaptive bootstrapping of recommender systems using decision trees. In: Proceedings of the Fourth ACM International Conference on Web Search and Data Mining, WSDM 2011, pp. 595–604. ACM, New York (2011)
17. Rentfrow, P.J., Gosling, S.D., et al.: The do re mi's of everyday life: The structure and personality correlates of music preferences. Journal of Personality and Social Psychology 84(6), 1236–1256 (2003)
18. Hu, R., Pu, P.: A study on user perception of personality-based recommender systems. In: De Bra, P., Kobsa, A., Chin, D. (eds.) UMAP 2010. LNCS, vol. 6075, pp. 291–302. Springer, Heidelberg (2010)

Mobile Apps for Older Users – The Development of a Mobile Apps Repository for Older People

Francisco J. García-Peñalvo[1], Miguel Ángel Conde[2], and Vicente Matellán-Olivera[2]

[1] Computer Science Department, Research Institute for Educational Sciences (IUCE)
GRIAL Research Group
University of Salamanca, Salamanca, Spain
fgarcia@usal.es
[2] Department of Mechanical, Computer Science and Aerospace Engineering,
Robotics Research Group, University of León, León, Spain
{miguel.conde,vicente.matellan}@unileon.es

Abstract. The emergence and application of the information and communication technologies have changed the tools that people use in their daily life. However not all the collectives use the technology in the same way. One case to take especially into account is older people. For them technology should be an inclusive factor but it can be also exclusive. The use of mobile devices and mobile apps by older people is an example of this. The devices and the apps are not always adapted for the special abilities or features of older people; moreover they do not always meet their needs. In order to facilitate older people access to mobile apps the present work reviews the usability issues to take into account and poses a repository of apps adapted and classified taking into account usability issues related to older people.

Keywords: Older people, ICT, mobile apps, usability, needs.

1 Introduction

Since the late 1990s access to information and communication technologies (ICTs) has seen tremendous growth —driven primarily by the wireless technologies and liberalization of telecommunications markets. The impacts of ICTs cross all sectors. Research has shown that investment in information and communication technologies is associated with such economic benefits as higher productivity, lower costs, new economic opportunities, job creation, innovation, and increased trade. ICT application also helps to provide better services in health and education, and strengthen social cohesion [1]. ICT has become something natural in people daily life. However all persons do not use it in the same way.

An example of this is older people. Older people are also known as elderly people or senior citizens, however during this work the expression used to name them is "older people" as several experts recommend [2]. What is understood as older people? It depends on the context, in Europe an older person is not the same as in Africa, most developed countries set the age of 65 years to define when a person is older. At the

P. Zaphiris and A. Ioannou (Eds.): LCT 2014, Part II, LNCS 8524, pp. 117–126, 2014.

moment, there is no United Nations (UN) standard numerical criterion, but the UN agreed cut-off is 60+ years to refer to the older population [3]. In this paper this last age is used to consider who is an older person.

These older people have special features and use ICT in a different way from the people that have grown surrounded by ICT. This fact implies a digital gap between the former group, named digital immigrants, and the latter, known as digital natives [4, 5].

Moreover, ICT has high potentiality for inclusion and exclusion for older people. It can help to include older people because ICT and specially, older-adapted ICT, can reduce de digital gap [6], increase social interaction and improve older people quality of life. ICT helps them to access to learning activities, gives them health information, provides a new way to interact with family and friends, etc. [7, 8]. However the use of these technologies is not easy for older people, the devices and technologies are not always adapted to their real needs and they find such technologies and tools expensive [9-11]. Surveys such as "ICT and Older people. Connected to the future" from Vodafone Spain Foundation, show that people between 56 and 70 years are in favour to use new technologies, which implies that exclusion is being reduced. [12].

Mobile technology can be seen as an example. Mobiles are one of the technologies with a greater penetration and acceptation in our society. In 2013 there are more than 6800 millions of subscriptions in the world and more than a mobile device per person in the developed countries [13]. These devices provide access to a complete set of services that can be employed with different purposes. A high percentage of older people in developed countries owned one of these devices, however they use only mobile phones for very limited purposes, such as for calling or texting in emergencies. This is mainly caused because the devices are not adapted to their needs, because they need to learn to use the device and they have been not thought thinking in their special features [12, 14]. Adaption of mobile services and apps is not new [15-17], however in this case a very specific collective is considered.

Given this context, there is a need to facilitate older people mobile apps adapted to them and that facilitate their access to other of the services provided by such kind of devices. To deal with these problems several issues should be taken into account:

- It is necessary to study the usability in this kind of devices and specifically if the devices and apps are adapted older people.
- It is necessary to study what are the apps and tools that this collective want and needs. That is, take into account older people real necessities and not only what the apps developers think they have.
- It is necessary to explore existing repositories of mobile apps for older people.

In order to order to do this the present work studies: the different existing studies about usability in mobile devices for older people, those that consider how the mobile apps included in the devices are adapted for them and which of those apps they are really using. With this information an application for classification, storage and recommendation of mobile apps is defined. It acts as a repository for mobile apps and it is tested with a set of mobile apps and enriched with older people feedback about them.

The paper is structured as follows: the following section (Section 2) presents the related works, including usability studies, necessity surveys and other repositories of tools for older people; after it the approach to carry out the repository is presented and also the evaluation methodology (Section 3); finally (Section 4) some conclusions are posed.

2   Related Works

The idea of the definition of repository of apps is not new, but in this case the apps stored into it are oriented to a stakeholder with very specific abilities and necessities, the older people.

These people use the mobile phones and apps in a different way from other collectives, they interact with mobiles in other ways, they have other worries, need other functionalities, etc. [18]. As the ongoing work consists of the definition of a repository of apps for older people it is necessary to explore the usability of this devices and apps for them and also what they need from this technology.

2.1   Mobile Phones Usability for Older People

The usability measurement of any kind of device or application is not an easy task. It implies to consider several dimensions that can be different depending on the authors, some of most common are the execution time, performance, final user satisfaction and ease to learn [19]. In addition, this dimensions cannot always been applied in the context of mobile technologies given the special features of this devices and that they are continuously evolving [20]. In this sense there are several studies that consider mobile usability such as [20-25]. However they are very focused in the device and no so much in a different final user of the device as a senior citizen is.

Regarding the works that study the usability for older people, Villaseca [26] made a review of different studies in this sense. This study shows that older people require more time to complete tasks on mobile devices [27] and it describes problems such as: the size of the screen to read information, the size of menus and interfaces to enter data such as keyboards (virtual and physical), functionalities such as de drag and drop, the size of the target (the older tend to make errors when tapping a small target), the gap between intended and actual touch locations (the older tend to miss their intended targets due to parallax and the large contact area of each finger) [28-32]. In addition Villaseca [26] also carry out an experience from which they extract that for older people there are also other issues very important related to mobile devices such as: characters in the screen easy to read, buttons easy to use, that the device was easy to learn and operate, keep in contact, good sound quality, etc.

If these and other factors were taken into account to define more usable interfaces it would be possible to compensate performance decrements as present in older adults [18].

These studies present two problems: 1) mobile technologies and mobile interfaces are evolving very quickly, this means that the usability issues considered by them can be old-fashioned in a short period of time; 2) the existing studies are specially focused usability issues of the devices but also apps and mobile operating systems should be taken into account.

2.2 Mobile Phones Usability for Older People

The study of usability in mobile devices apps is not something new; there are several works that explore this issue [33-35]. However in this case the important issue is how to define usable apps for older people.

Usability in apps for older people used to be linked to the requirements they have from this devices [36] (that is discussed in next subsection). For instance some of the features to include in mobile apps and in mobile devices designed for older people are [14]: Memory aids (e.g.: appointments, reminders, address book with photos, personal Information, standardised menus, personalized menus), Visual aids (e.g.: backlight, large text, bold colour, colour scheme and big buttons, etc.), Haptic aids (e.g.: a rubber grip and easy-to hold phones), Features to minimise user error (e.g.: keypad autolock, extra confirmation dialog and noticeable reminders); And safety features (e.g.: panic button and speed-dial).

Authors such as Lorenz and Oppermann [37] describe some requirements for mobile applications: The font size should be between 36pt and 48pt; one-level navigation instead of using menu structures; Arrange the buttons at the bottom of the interface so the input-hand will not hide the screen; Colour-neutral displays for visual impaired users; Redundant user guidance by colour-coding and blinking boxes; and Slow animation speed.

Authors such as Holzinger et al [38] define metrics for the design of applications for the older (not only mobile applications), to do so they establish relationship among some criteria understandable and easy to identify for the older people (Likeability, Controllability, Simplicity, Privacy, Security Familiarity, etc.) with the traditional usability factors (Efficacy, Effectiveness, Satisfaction, Productivity, etc.).

Other authors carried out experiences with tablets that are successfully completed by older people [39]. From this experiences some issues related to the usability of the apps can be highlighted: The representation of web links can vary largely between different websites therefore they are not always perceived and recognized correctly; Simpler applications and features such as gesture control were quickly learnable and useable by the target group; Anglicizes are present when using the World Wide Web and not all the possible older people know them; And the way input fields work is not easy to understand for novice users (the necessity to tap in the input fields to show the virtual keyboard).

From these studies it is possible to see that different criteria is used to define the usability of a mobile app for an older person. Several of them can be grouped to define a classification of factors to take into account. However, in order to deliver a popular application, the mobile application itself must be able to meet the specific needs of senior citizens in their daily life, so these needs should be also considered.

2.3   Older People Specific Needs from Mobile Devices

As the present project aims to define a repository of tools specifically designed for older people, the tools to include in the repository should be usable by older people but also should satisfy their needs. This means that older people needs should be explored. In this sense there are several studies.

VDI/VDE-IT, together with the AAL Association developed a model that classifies the needs of older people for their well being. They considered the following factors [40]: Health and Wellness, Home Care, Chores and Supply with Goods, Safety, Security and Privacy, Mobility, Information, Learning and Education, Social Interaction, Hobbies and Working life.

Other authors such as Plaza et al review this classification [41]. They distinguish between: Health, wellness and home care; Safety, security and privacy; Mobility, Information, learning and education; Chores and supply with goods; Religion/spirituality; Social Interaction; Hobbies and Working Life.

Abascal and Civit defined 6 requirements that mobile communication systems should provide older people: Personal Communication, Security, Social Integration, Access to Education and Labour Market and Autonomy. The apps should satisfy these requirements.

Finally, Gao and Koronios [36] explore different studies about the older people needs related to mobile devices and they needed: Health Monitoring tools, Personal Information tools, Social tools, Leisure and Sales tools, Safety and Privacy services.

It is possible see that most of these classifications take into account more or less the same areas and a combination of the is used as will be described in the Repository Approach section.

2.4   Repositories of Apps for Older People

Regarding with mobile apps repositories, there are not markets of apps specifically designed for older people. However it is possible find communities such as: AppsForOldPeople in Facebook [42], that recommend apps; other recommendation of apps by user communities [43-47]; and sections in the main mobile app repositories that can be related with some of older people needs (e.g.: Google Play and Apps Store have categories for health monitoring apps, home care; chores and supply with goods, etc.).

These initiatives are not defined thinking in older people and do not classify the tools for them. Given this contexts there is a necessity of the definition a repository of mobile apps, that satisfies older people needs, presents tools usable for them and gathers their feedback to classify the applications efficiently for the people of this collective.

3   Repository Approach of Mobile Apps for Old People

In the previous section was described that although there is lot of work about usability in mobile apps for older people, there are not specific repositories for them. The repository should consider the final end-user, the older persons. They have special requirements and characteristics that should be taken into account while designing the repository.

Taking this into account the present work poses a repository with functionalities to satisfy older people needs. These functionalities are:

- Apps Classification. The mobile apps should be classified attending to different criteria:

  o Operative System. The repository should consider Android and iOS apps because they are the most common operative systems for mobile devices nowadays. However it should be flexible enough to add other operative systems (Windows Mobile, FirefoxOS, etc).

  o Attending to older persons needs. In order to do so Plaza et al classification [41] is used because it takes into account a wider range of apps. In this classification will be added the adaptations of mobile phone operative systems for older persons (e.g.: VoiceOver, Talk-Back, Big Launcher, Phonotto) [48].

  o Usability features. The apps will be evaluated taken into account if they include some of the usability features desirable for these collectives (described in section 2.2.). A scale will be defined depending on the number of usability issues considered; the definition of such scale will depend on the evaluation of at least 30 tools for each operative system.

  o Evaluation by older people. The final users of the repository will have the possibility to vote for their favorite tools and report feedback about them. This evaluation can be used to establish the top rated tools in the repository or in an existing category.

  These criteria can be combined to show a specific showcase of the stored apps. For instance a user could be interested on a list of apps filtered by needs and evaluation.

- Apps Evaluation. The user of the repository can evaluate and provide feedback to an application. The evaluation will consist of a score between 0 and 10. The feedback will be free text that later can be evaluated by using qualitative techniques in order to elaborate reports that facilitate recommendations and new classifications.
- Visualization and navigation for older people. All the content shown in the repository should take into account the special characteristics of the final users. Navigation should be simple and contents should provide different aids that for older to decide the tools to use.
- Web and Mobile adapted navigation. The repository should facilitate the navigation both through web browsers and through mobile browsers, so it is possible that some content should be adapted in this last case.
- Advanced search and recommender. The repository should provide a functionality to search for tools based on the name of the tool or the possible classifications. It should recommend the apps for the final user can solve their specific needs. If the

user is registered and have added which are his/her preferences and characteristics the recommender will use this information to suggest tools depending on the old person necessities.

- User and contents management. Functionalities to manage the users, the categories of apps, the recommendations, etc.;
- Download manager. Functionalities to facilitate apps downloading.

In order to carry out this development Drupal Content Management Platform [49] is chosen because its use can reduce the development time and facilitates the definition of a repository with the above described functionalities. Once it has been developed at least 100 apps will be included in the repository and pilots will be carried out with older people. Fig. 1. shows the proposed structured for the app repository.

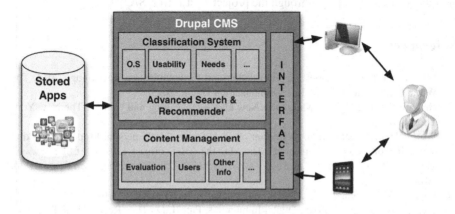

Fig. 1. App Repository description. It includes the store of apps and the Drupal implementation of the repository that can be accessed through a computer and a tablet.

4   Conclusions

The application of ICT to different contexts has associated an impact in the people involved on them. This specially evident in older people, ICT can be for them an inclusive or an exclusive factor. These people have special characteristics and not always the technology is adapted to them. However when it is ICT can open new possibilities for older people to socialize, learn, keep contact with family and friends, etc.

This paper is focused in mobile phones and how they are adapted to older people. It has carried out a review of different aspects related with the usability of the mobile, and the mobile apps for older people, which tools satisfy their needs and if it is possible to find repositories specially designed for them. From this study it was possible to see that there exist different factors to take into account when talking about mobile usability for older people, but not all authors agreed on them nor considered, in addition such factors should be solved by the devices developers that do not always want to do changes in the devices for an specific collective. In addition apps usability features should be taken into account, in this case the different authors present also different conclusions about app usability but in this case is easier to address them when developing tools. However this do not guarantee that an app can be used by older persons, it is important to take into account also if the apps are solving the needs and interests of old people. In this sense several authors present more or less the same areas of interest of older people about mobile applications.

Taking this into account a repository of apps for older people is going to be developed with special attention to usability features and with the idea to satisfy their special requirements.

Acknowledgements. This work is partially supported by the Cátedra Telefónica of the University of León (CTULE13-3) and by the Regional Council of Education of the Junta de Castilla y León through the project MPLE (ref. SA294A12-2).

References

1. ITU: The Little Data Book on Information and Communication Technology 2013. The World Bank - International Telecommunication Union (2013)
2. Graham, J.: 'Elderly' No More. The New Old Age - Caring and Coping. The New York Times (2012)
3. World-Health-Organization, Definition of an older or elderly person. Proposed Working Definition of an Older Person in Africa for the MDS Project (2014), http://www.who.int/healthinfo/survey/ageingdefnolder/en/ (accessed February 20, 2014)
4. Prensky, M.: Digital natives, digital immigrants. On the Horizon 9 (2001)
5. Prensky, M.: Digital Natives, Digital Immigrants, Part II: Do They Really Think Differently? On the Horizon 9 (2001)
6. Burdick, D.: Digital divide or tool for understanding and collaboration: computers and intergenerational relationships. In: 54th Anual Scientific Meeting of the Gerontological Society of Americas, Chicago, USA (2001)
7. White, H., McConnell, E., Clipp, E., Bynum, L., Teague, C., Navas, L., Craven, S., Halbrecht, H.: Surfing the net in later life: A review of the literature and pilot study of computer use and quality of life. Journal of Applied Gerontology 18, 358–378 (1999)
8. Weatherall, J.W.A.: A grounded theory analysis of older adults and information technology. Educational Gerontology 26, 371–386 (2000)
9. Madden, G., Savage, S.: Some economic and social aspects of residential Internet use in Australia. Journal of Media Economics 13, 171–185 (2000)
10. Hernández-Encuentra, E., Pousada, M., Gómez-Zúñiga, B.: ICT and Older People: Beyond Usability. Educational Gerontology 35, 226–245 (2009)
11. Teo, T.: Demographic and motivation variables associated with Internet usage activities. Internet Research-Electronic Networking Applications and Policy 11, 125–137 (2001)
12. Fundación-Vodafone-España: TIC y Mayores (2012)
13. ITU: Mesuring the Information Society. International Telecommunication Union (2012)
14. Kurniawan, S.: Older people and mobile phones: A multi-method investigation. International Journal of Human-Computer Studies 66, 889–901 (2008)

15. García-Peñalvo, F.J., Conde, M.Á., Del Pozo, A.: A Mobile Personal Learning Environment Approach. In: Shumaker, R. (ed.) VAMR 2013, Part II. LNCS, vol. 8022, pp. 132–141. Springer, Heidelberg (2013)
16. García-Peñalvo, F.J., Conde, M.Á.: The impact of a mobile Personal Learning Environment in different edu-cational contexts. Universal Access in the Information Society (in press)
17. Casany, M.J., Alier, M., Mayol, E., Piguillem, J., Galanis, N., García-Peñalvo, F.J., Conde, M.A.: Moodbile: A framework to integrate m-learning applications with the LMS. Journal of Research and Practice in Information Technology 44, 41–61 (2012)
18. Ziefle, M., Bay, S.: How older adults meet complexity: Aging effects on the usability of different mobile phones. Behaviour & Information Technology 24, 375–389 (2005)
19. Abran, A., Khelifi, A., Suryn, W., Seffah, A.: Usability Meanings and Interpretations in ISO Standards. Software Quality Journal, 325–338 (2003)
20. Chamorro-Valor, S.J.: Análisis de usabilidad de dispositivos móviles con diferentes interfaces de usuario. Ingeniería de la Organización, Administración de Empresas y Estadística, vol. Ingeniería en Telecomunicaciones. Universidad Politécnica de Madrid, Madrid (2011)
21. Kjeldskov, J., Stage, J.: New techniques for usability evaluation of mobile systems. International Journal of Human-Computer Studies 60, 599–620 (2003)
22. Coursaris, K., Kim, D.: A Qualitative Review of Empirical Mobile Usability Studies. In: Proceedings of the Twelfth Americas Conference on Information Systems, Acapulco, Mexico (2006)
23. Hussain, A., Ferneley, E.: Usability metric for mobile application: a goal question metric (GQM) approach. In: 10th International Conference on Information Integration and Web-based Applications & Services, pp. 567–570 (2008)
24. Nielsen, J., Budiu, R.: Mobile Usability. Pearson Education (2012)
25. Oehl, M., Sutter, C., Ziefle, M.: Considerations on Efficient Touch Interfaces – How Display Size Influences the Performance in an Applied Pointing Task. In: Smith, M.J., Salvendy, G. (eds.) HCII 2007. LNCS, vol. 4557, pp. 136–143. Springer, Heidelberg (2007)
26. Urdaibay-Villaseca, P.T.: Usability of Mobile Devices for Elderly People. Department of Information Technology, Master of Science in Software and Inforamtion Systems. National University of Ireland, Galway, Ireland (2010)
27. Lin, C.J., Hsieh, T.-L., Shiang, W.-J.: Exploring the Interface Design of Mobile Phone for the Elderly. In: Kurosu, M. (ed.) HCD 2009. LNCS, vol. 5619, pp. 476–481. Springer, Heidelberg (2009)
28. Arning, K., Ziefle, M.: Barriers of Information Access in Small Screen Device Applications: The Relevance of User Characteristics for a Transgenerational Design. In: Stephanidis, C., Pieper, M. (eds.) ERCIM Ws UI4ALL 2006. LNCS, vol. 4397, pp. 117–136. Springer, Heidelberg (2007)
29. Fujioka, R., Akiba, T., Okada, H.: Evaluation of Pointing Efficiency on Small Screen Touch User Interfaces. In: Salvendy, G., Smith, M.J. (eds.) HCI International 2009, Part II. LNCS, vol. 5618, pp. 375–384. Springer, Heidelberg (2009)
30. Jin, Z.X., Plocher, T., Kiff, L.: Touch Screen User Interfaces for Older Adults: Button Size and Spacing. In: Stephanidis, C. (ed.) HCI 2007. LNCS, vol. 4554, pp. 933–941. Springer, Heidelberg (2007)
31. Lee, C.-F., Kuo, C.-C.: Difficulties on Small-Touch-Screens for Various Ages. In: Stephanidis, C. (ed.) HCI 2007. LNCS, vol. 4554, pp. 968–974. Springer, Heidelberg (2007)
32. Kobayashi, M., Hiyama, A., Miura, T., Asakawa, C., Hirose, M., Ifukube, T.: Elderly User Evaluation of Mobile Touchscreen Interactions. In: Campos, P., Graham, N., Jorge, J., Nunes, N., Palanque, P., Winckler, M. (eds.) INTERACT 2011, Part I. LNCS, vol. 6946, pp. 83–99. Springer, Heidelberg (2011)

33. HIMSS: Selecting a Mobile App: Evaluating the Usability of Medical Applications. Healthcare Information and Management Systems Society (2012)
34. Ryan, C., Gonsalves, A.: The effect of context and application type on mobile usability: an empirical study. In: 28th Australasian conference on Computer Science, vol. 38, pp. 115–124 (2005)
35. Zhang, D., Adipat, B.: Challenges, Methodologies, and issues in the Usability Testing of Mobile Applications. International Journal of Human-Computer Interaction 18, 293–308 (2005)
36. Gao, J., Koronios, A.: Mobile application development for senior citizens. In: 14th Pacific Asia Conference on Information Systems, July 9-12, pp. 214–223. National Taiwan University, Taipei (2010)
37. Lorenz, A., Oppermann, R.: Mobile health monitoring for the elderly: Designing for diversity. Pervasive and Mobile Computing 5, 478–495 (2009)
38. Holzinger, A., Searle, G., Kleinberger, T., Seffah, A., Javahery, H.: Investigating Usability Metrics for the Design and Development of Applications for the Elderly. In: Miesenberger, K., Klaus, J., Zagler, W.L., Karshmer, A.I. (eds.) ICCHP 2008. LNCS, vol. 5105, pp. 98–105. Springer, Heidelberg (2008)
39. Werner, F., Werner, K., Oberzaucher, J.: Tablets for Seniors – An Evaluation of a Current Model (iPad). In: Wichert, R., Eberhardt, B. (eds.) Ambient Assisted Living, pp. 177–184. Springer, Heidelberg (2012)
40. Gaßner, K., Conrad, M.: ICT enabled independent living for elderly. A status-quo analysis on products and the research landscape in the field of Ambient Assisted Living (AAL) in EU-27, Berlin, Germany ((2010)
41. Plaza, I., Martín, L., Martin, S., Medrano, C.: Mobile applications in an aging society: Status and trends. Journal of Systems and Software 84, 1977–1988 (2011)
42. AppsForOldPeople, Apps For Old People (2014), http://www.facebook.com/AppsForOldPeople/info (accessed February 20, 2014)
43. PandaApp, Top 10 Best Apps for Older People, Panda App iPhone Channel, http://iphone.pandaapp.com/news/05082013/024405898.shtml (accessed February 2014)
44. Anderson, J.: Best iPad Apps for Senior Citizens, AssitedLiving.com (2014), http://www.assistedliving.com/best-ipad-apps-for-seniors/ (accessed February 20, 2014)
45. Myageingparent, Top iPad apps for the elderly, http://www.myageingparent.com/top-ipad-apps-for-the-elderly/ (accessed February 20, 2014)
46. Myageingparent, More top apps for older people, http://www.myageingparent.com/top-ipad-apps-for-the-elderly/ (accessed February 20, 2014)
47. Actitud50, Aplicaciones móviles para mayores de 50 años, http://www.actitud50.com/es/tecnologia/descargar-aplicaciones-en-moviles-y-tabletas-para-mayores-de-50-anos-20122603.html (accessed February 20, 2014)
48. Pastor, J.: Móvil y tercera edad (II): terminales y apps para el público senior, http://mobileworldcapital.com/es/articulo/137 (accessed February 20, 2014)
49. Drupal, Drupal, https://drupal.org/ (accessed February 20, 2014)

Development of the Learning System
for Outdoor Study Using Zeigarnik Effect

Yuko Hiramatsu[1,*], Atsushi Ito[2], Masahiro Fujii[2], and Fumihiro Sato[1]

[1] Chuo University,742-1 Higashinakano, Hachioji, Tokyo 192-0393
{susana_y,fsato}@tamacc.chuo-u.ac.jp
[2] Utsunomiya University, 7-1-2 Yoto, Utsunomiya-shi, Tochigi, 321-8505
{at.ito,fujii}@is.utsunomiya-u.ac.jp

Abstract. What is the best way to feel the spirit of the location? In Japan, the students of the elementary school and the secondary school have the school trips for several days with classmates. The purpose of those trips is to visit historical areas in Japan or foreign countries to encourage the students to learn about history, culture and nature in a proactive way. However, it is not easy for them to recognize and understand valuable points such as the artistic points and historical points even if they look at the objects or scenery. To solve this problem, we have developed a new learning model for outdoor studies using mobile phone applying Zeigarnik effect that explains human beings takes much interest in uncompleted or interrupted tasks. In this paper, we explain our study model for outdoor study and evaluate the usefulness of our tool though trials.

Keywords: E-learning, Zeigarnik effect, Outdoor study, Mobile Phone, Secondary Education.

1 Introduction

Mobile communication gives us access to others whenever and wherever we want, however it is still important to go to the field in order to know the place or the thing thoroughly. In Japan, students go on several day school trips to encourage students to learn history and nature in more positive way. For that purpose, 87.3 % of junior high schools allow students to walk around the area by themselves in small groups [1]. Such outdoor studies are very precious in the view point of history, architecture and some site-specific art [2], however, they cannot recognize artistic or traditional points and understand the meaning and the value just by look at the objects or scenery. To solve this problem, we have developed a new learning model for outdoor studies using Zeigarnik effects [3]; human beings take an interest in uncompleted or interrupted tasks. This paper examines our learning model for outdoor study, our original application and the results of 2 trials.

---

* Corresponding author.

P. Zaphiris and A. Ioannou (Eds.): LCT 2014, Part II, LNCS 8524, pp. 127–137, 2014.

2   Background

2.1   Children's Mobile Phone Usage in Japan

Increasing the crimes using mobile phones, the Ministry of National Education informed Education Committees of Japan announced that children should not take mobile phones to their schools in 2009. Exceptionally, however, students sometimes use mobile phones while outdoor studying in order to get contact with teachers. In addition after the big earthquake in Fukushima, many parents hope their children to bring mobile phones with GPS. Telephone, e-mail and location technology of mobile phones are regarded as a useful instruments for disaster. However, such special use means just bringing something like a safety box for students.

2.2   Learning for the Several Day School Trips

Before visiting the area, the students learn about history, art, architecture and some special points of place to visit for several hours in the classroom. They can use the Internet by PC to search information where to visit and write down the important points on their notebooks. They sometimes make a leaflet for the school trip, however, they seldom have chances to check with the document when they visit the area.

3   Our Methods for Students to Take an Interest in the Objects

3.1   Characteristic Points of Human Beings from the Viewpoint of Cognitive Science

It is said that "seeing is believing", however, we, human beings do not recognize what we are looking at. For example some like a game named photo hunt. If we can recognize all the things our eyes catch, photo hunt would not be a game. We sometimes don't see the differences between two resembling photos. However, once we have caught the object, we cannot help looking at that particular point. If students walk around the area without any marks, their memory would become ambiguous. We utilize this special quality of human beings and use the quiz as a trigger to focus on the object from the whole scenery in front of them. Then the special point of the object would make a marked impression on their minds.

In addition, we treat the class in which students prepare for their outdoor studies as an incomplete experience. Before the trip students learn the history and specific arts in the area and make some quizzes for the other classmates by making use of the preparation. They do not know what kinds of quizzes are being prepared for each other. Such an incomplete experience rouses human interest in the object. This is on the basis of a version of the Zeigarnik, that tasks that have been completed are recalled less well than uncompleted tasks. Nowadays some engineers have created detailed navigation systems for trips, however, we deliberately create such incomplete experiences for students by a design based on the Zeigarnik effects.

3.2   Related Works

For the Zeigarnik effects, a study made by Greist-Bousquet and Schiffman 1992[4] provided evidence. There are several related works about Environmental psychology and tourism. Pearce & Stringer 1991[5] studied from the view point of physiology, cognition and individual variation etc. Fridgen 1984[6], van Raaij 1996[7], Toshiji Sasaki also studied about this field. T.Sasaki told that we can part a trip into 3 scenes: before the trip, during the trip, and after the trip [8]. We focus to connect before the trip and during the trip using our new application.

4   Quizzes for Site-Specific Learning

4.1   Preparing for the Trip － Using Zeigarnik Effects

On our methods students learn about the area: famous persons, arts, architecture etc. (knowledge input). Then they make quizzes in preparation for the trip (Learning outcomes). They make quizzes about the objects they are interested using our authoring tool, and then they study about the area more. For, if they want to win the game, they should remember many kinds of things. They do not know which quizzes they will be answering and they do not know which course they will be taking until the trip. Teachers make the courses and choose quizzes. In such an incomplete situation, students go to the destination and will complete their study on the trip.

4.2   For Outdoor Learning

Using the quizzes, we make some special points to keep students' eyes on. (Refer to Figure 1) This is an example.

> **Do all dragons have wings on their back?**
>
> 1.Yes. All dragons have wings.
> 2. No. Dragons don't have wings.
> 3. Though Eastern Dragons have wings, Japanese
> Dragons don't have wings.
> 4. There are several kinds of Dragons in Japan.
> Some have wings and some don't have wings.

> Correct answer : 4
>
> There are several kinds of dragons in Japanese legend. Some belong in water and some belong in the sky. The Dragon of the sky, TENRYU has wings. Let's go to the temple and look at the sculpture of a flying dragon.

Fig. 1. An example of the quizzes

After answering this quiz, students will look at the sculpture of the dragon with beautiful wings (Fig.2) at the temple with more interest. The quizzes are triggers to accept objects positively.

Fig. 2. The sculpture of the dragon

4.3   About Our System

Figure 3 shows an outline of our learning model and the behavior of this system. Students use mobile phones to access this system. We named this system as "Stasta eye". "Stasta" is our project name. That is an abbreviation of "Study Studio" and "eye" means to see the visiting location deepler.

- Scene 1: Preparation in the classroom by PCs

Students make quizzes before going to outdoor studying. Teachers input the walking routes, information of emergency call and select quizzes in the classroom. ((1) and (2) in Figure 2).

- Scene 2: Our door studying by mobile phones

When a group of students visit a place, they answer a quiz and find the next place to visit, as in an orienteering game. They compete on points and can also check the status, such as points and location of other groups. Teachers can also access the same information. At the same time, they can upload photos and comments. ((3)(4)(5) in Figure 3)

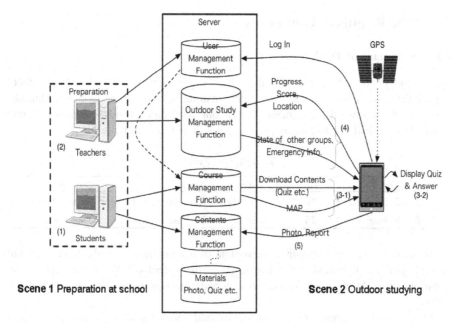

Fig. 3. Outline of our learning model

4.4   As the Safety System for Emergency

In addition to the learning effects, parents and teachers concerned about safety of their children on the school trip.   When we had a big earthquake on 11 September in 2011, many groups on outdoor studying were isolated for several hours.   That became a big problem. Using our application on the trip, teachers can check students' positional information on time and contact with them by several methods: telephone by one push, short mail, SNS. In addition students can know publish shelters around them by the mobile map in which they usually look for next quiz point. See Figure 4. This is the image of pages of our application. Under the icon of the camera, several functions are displayed. One of them denotes emergency call to teacher and one lead to map with shelters.   Students can find these icons in every page if they need.

Fig. 4. Screens of our application, "Stasta Eye"

5   The Results of Our Trials

5.1   Summary of Trials

We should prove safety and efficiency before practical use in junior high school. Especially for outdoor study we had to demonstrate not only in the laboratory but also our door. After several experiments [9] in our workshop "Study Group on School Trips"[10], we had two trials using our orienteering system as table 1.

Table 1. Our 2 trials

	Date	Number	Age	Area	Device
I	15, Sep, 2012	30	16-60	Sumida-city, Tokyo	Smart Phone
II	15, Aug, 2013	35	9-22	3 cities, Tokyo	Tablet PC

At the first trial we ascertained movement of our application at the large area with several groups. We have also investigated the effectiveness of the system by questionnaires. At this time we only researched a part of using application. (Refer to Figure 2)

After having ascertained our system, we had second trial with younger subjects enclosing junior high school students by the cooperation of Academy Camp [11]. Students had a lecture in the room to know about the areas and history to answer the quizzes at the outdoor study. They should keep new knowledge till answering the quizzes. This situation would cause Zeigarnik effects. In order to prove the effect, we performed questionnaires at the next day of the trial. At first trial we performed them when subjects arrived at the goal. If the second subjects remembered the points of quizzes, Zeigarnik effects will be proved.

5.2   The First Trial

Summary. 30 persons (students and adults) formed 8 groups (3 or 4 persons per group) with smart phones and 1 teacher managed them by PC. They walked around the Tokyo sky Tree, where there are many old historical Japanese temples, gardens and architecture. After they answered one quiz, the next point was shown by our application, "Stasta eye". They could also see the point on the map with their smart phones. 10 quizzes were prepared for each group. The teacher could have the information through the PC, such as the telephone number which students use, their location and the score of the quizzes.

Results: Our system worked normally. All groups reached the goal using "Stasta eye" within 2 hours. Teacher got 3 calls from 2 groups using emergency button as a part of testing. The results of questionnaires show us that people were interested in the objects and scenes they saw by answering the quizzes. (Refer to Figure 5 and Figure 6.)

Fig. 5. Impression of using "Stasta Eye"

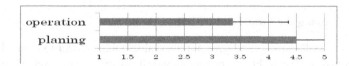

Fig. 6. Evaluation about the planning and the operation（Likert scale）

The evaluation of planning was 4.5/5(Average). It is very high and seems to affect other elements; Planning and operation R=0.312 / Planning and "interesting" R=0.452 (Both results means moderate positive correlation) The evaluation of the operation was 3.36/5(Average). The standard deviation was 1.08. We had high evaluation about the planning and our methods of learning.

5.3   The Second Trial

Summary. 35 persons (pupils and students) formed 7 groups (5 persons per group) with tablets and 1 manager used PC. Before the orienteering with quizzes, they had a lecture about 3 traditional areas, where they would walk around, in the room for 1 hour. After the lecture 2 or 3 groups walked with our application each area. Only the start point and the goal point are same. Answering a quiz, they took pictures or compared their records with other groups.

Results: The results of questionnaires are following.

- The evaluation of our application (Likert scale)

The evaluations were very high level. Though the quizzes are little difficult for younger students, they enjoy the outdoor studying and gave "Quiz" a high evaluation as Figure 7. In addition many students used several functions. 94% of the subjects took photo. 80% of the subjects answer the quizzes (Some elder students didn't answer and encouraged children to answer quizzes). 83% of the subjects input something at tablet.

Comparing with the results of the first trial (Figure 6), evaluation of operation is higher (+1.0 point). At the first trial we used smart phone and second one we use Tablet. The result reflected the differences of interface. The evaluation of quiz was excellent at the second one.

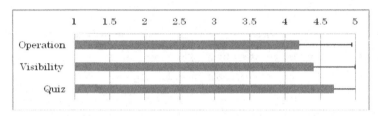

Fig. 7. Results of the application evaluation（Likert scale）

5.4　Comparing the First Trial with the Second One

Comparing 2 trials, we can find several remarkable points. (Refer to Figure8)

The second trial gave higher results about all positive evaluations. Exceptionally the negative item, "difficult" was indicated 17% of the second trial. None said "difficult" at the first trial.

The ages of the first trial were 16-60 years old.　The ages of the second trial were 9-22 years old (Refer to Table 1). Young subjects felt something "difficult", however they also said "interesting".

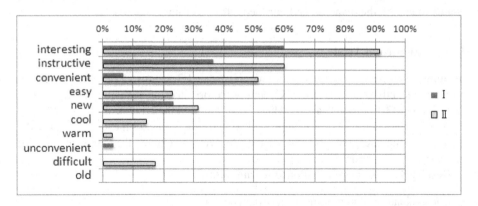

Fig. 8. Impression of 2 trials(1)

This tendency became clearer in the Figure 10 in which we assorted 2 layers about ages in the second trial. (Refer to Figure 9.)　Ages of the second trial are from 9-22 (Average 13.34 years old). Main students are Junior high school students and pupils at elementary school.

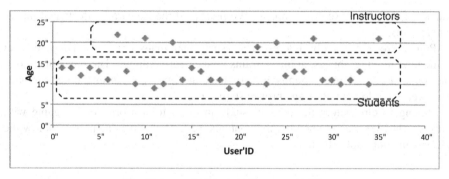

Fig. 9. Ages of subjects at the second trial

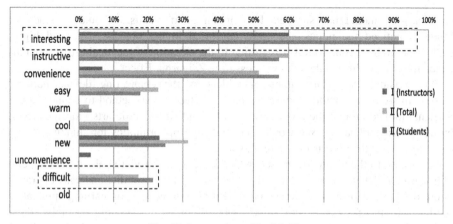

Fig. 10. Impression of 2 trials(2)

II (students) in the Figure 10 means Junior high school students and pupils and they are 28 persons. Comparing "Interesting" with "Difficult", we find younger students interested in our application and felt interesting and convenience, though they felt the quizzes were difficult. In the scene of outdoor studying difficulty isn't necessarily a bad meaning for those students. To learn something is to solve some difficulties. This can gain the feeling of satisfaction from younger students.

- The most impressive place

The students of the second trial answered the questionnaires at the next day of the outdoor study, however, 18 persons (51.42%) answered the points of quizzes concretely. For example 10 years old pupil answered that the bronze statue of Takamori Saigo, who was a famous person on Meiji Restoration, was the most impressively. 13 years old students answered that The Stone Hut at Edo Castle was the best. Those objects were explained in the lecture before outdoor studying and also they answered quizzes at the points. At the first trial in which we didn't have a preparing lecture, only 2 persons (6.67%) answered the points of quizzes and the names of the places were incomplete. We presumed the Zeigarnik effects can makes such results.

Pupils are not usually interested in such inanimate objects.   They look at something moving objects; animals, trains or such active things. There is a big zoo at the same area and many pupils like to look at lions, pandas and other animals, however, they do not notice any bronze statues near the zoo.

Having lecture before the outdoor study in order to win orienteering game with quizzes, they keep and remember the contents well. They have one point to know the place using our application.

6   Conclusion

Our learning model has succeeded to obtain good results for outdoor studying. Students noticed the points and were interested in the objects.   We had higher evaluation in the second trial that is similar to the situation of practical use at secondly education and confirmed the effectiveness of   Zeigarnik Effect.

We consider the smart phone or tablets as the connecting device between classroom study and outdoor study. Zeigarnik Effect is the method to connect them. Students looked around the area, architectures, and site-specific arts more positively by using our application. We would like to design opportunities for students to feel and know about the objects of where they are.

According to the results of the second trial, we also considered about the elements of e-learning. When it comes to use the ICT, we need the usability and easy operation in our daily life. However,   we need different idea in the field of learning application so that the students could find some problems or hard tasks and the solve those matters.Then they get some knowledge and the sense of accomplishment.   Much automatic information is never always necessary for their learning. It is important for students to make chance to think about something positively.

At the next stage we will have chances to use our system at junior high schools, where the whole process inclosing scene 1(Refer toFigure2) perfectly.

Nowadays mobile internet users are increasing year by year throughout the world and some other countries in Asia become to have such several days school trip.   We will use this system to introduce Japanese culture for them.

References

1. The Travel News (July 30, 2010), http://www.travelnews.co.jp/news/kankou/1007301042.html
2. Hatta, N.: The Commitment of 'Place' to the Birth and the Appreciation of Art Works" Shimane. Journal of Policy Studies 8 (December 2004)
3. Zeigarnik, B.V.: On finished and unfinished tasks. In: Ellis, W.D. (ed.) A Sourcebook of Gestalt Psychology. Humanities Press, New York (1967)
4. Schiffman, N., Greist-Bousquet, S.: The effect of task interruption and closure on perceived duration. Bulletin of the Psychonomic Society 30(1), 9–11 (1992)

5. Pearce, P.L., Stringer, P.F.: Psychology and toursim. Annals of Tourism Research 18, 136–154 (1991)
6. Fridgen, J.D.: Environmental psychology and tourism. Annals of Tourism Research 11(1), 19–39 (1984)
7. Van Raaij, W.E.: Consumer Research on tourism:Mental and behavioral consructs. Annals of Tourism Research 13, 1–9 (1986)
8. Sasaki, T.: Kankoo-Ryoko no Sinrigaku, p. 38. Kitaoji Shobo (2007)
9. Hiramatsu, Y., Sato, F., Suzuki, A., Ito, A.: Outdoor Study System for Mobile Literacy. In: PC Conference, Ehime Japan, pp. 463–466 (2009)
10. Study Group on School Trips, http://joyful-shu-gaku.com/
11. Academy Camp, http://academy-camp.org/

Dream Drill: A Bedtime Learning Application

Aya Ikeda[1] and Itiro Siio[2]

[1] DeNA Co., Ltd.
2-21-1 Shibuya, Shibuya-ku, Tokyo, Japan
ikeda.aya@is.ocha.ac.jp
[2] Ochanomizu University
2-1-1 Otsuka, Bunkyo-ku, Tokyo 112-8610, Japan
siio@acm.org

Abstract. There is considerable evidence that sleep supports memory consolidation. Items studied before going to sleep are memorized more efficiently than on other occasions. Consequently, we propose a learning application based on these findings. The system includes an alarm clock, which alarm is set only if a user answers a few questions. We implement a prototype and conduct a field test to evaluate the effectiveness of the system.

Keywords: Memory consolidation, CAI, sleep, learning application, smartphone application.

1 Introduction

Since David Hartley proposed in 1971 that memory consolidation is enhanced by dreaming [1], many studies have been conducted on the relationship between sleep and memory. In recent years, the importance of sleep in memory reactivation has been borne out by neuro-scientific and cognitive-scientific research [2].

Memory is generally classified into sensory memory, short-term memory, and long-term memory [3]. Sensory memory stores sound and image information. The duration of short-term memory is in the order of seconds. In contrast, information can retain in long-term memory until one's death, barring impairment of the brain's function. Long-term memory is classified into declarative and non-declarative memory. The former contains facts and knowledge that we can consciously recall, and the latter contains unconscious skills, procedures, and techniques that we have learned. It is well-known that both declarative and non-declarative memories are consolidated by sleep [2].

Research shows that sleep consolidates declarative memory, but no systems have yet utilized this finding to help with everyday life. Setting an alarm before going to sleep is one of the routines of our daily lives. To utilize this for effective learning, we make a ubiquitous learning system, Dream Drill. The alarm clock application designed for Dream Drill provides a learning opportunity when a user sets the alarm at night and turns it off in the morning. To test the effectiveness of our application, we have conducted preliminary English-language word

P. Zaphiris and A. Ioannou (Eds.): LCT 2014, Part II, LNCS 8524, pp. 138–145, 2014.

Fig. 1. Dream Drill usage scenario

memorization experiments on several Japanese participants [4]. In this paper, we carry out more precise experiment with larger number of subjects in longer period of days. We also present results of learning effect data from a wide variety of users, gathered by making our learning application public through Google Play[1]. These results indicate that learning before bedtime is more effective than at any other time of the day, and also show that our learning system successfully encourages the consolidation of memory.

2   Related Work

Some alarm clocks are employed not only to wake the user up but also to help him/her learn. The TWIST Desktop Digital Alarm Clock [5] displays a formula on the LCD when its alarm sounds. To stop the alarm, the user has to complete the formula by twisting the wheel on the clock. This technique is based on the idea that forcing a user to use his/her brain and body will help him/her wake up easily. However, this technique does not employ sleep effects to promote memory consolidation. This device does not provide any systematic way to make users practice memory enhancement before sleeping.

Various devices and applications have been developed for learning support. For example, MicroMandarin [6] is a location-based application program for language learners whose first language is not Chinese. It provides Chinese word quizzes that correspond to the location of users. However, such devices and applications do not provide any systematic way of making users exercise their memory before sleeping. In this paper, in order to effectively promote memory consolidation by sleep, we propose Dream Drill, a ubiquitous learning system that uses the time before sleep for this purpose.

3   Design of Dream Drill

Dream Drill is a system that supports daily learning before sleep for people whose first language is not English. We used smart-phones as mobile terminals

---

[1] A smart-phone (Android) applications and contents distribution service by Google.

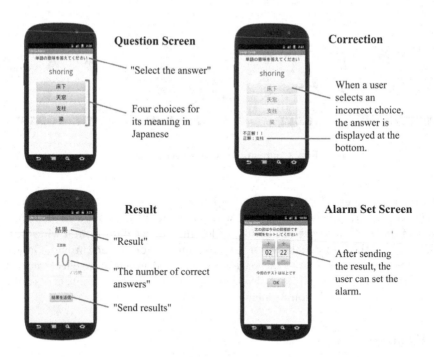

Fig. 2. Question, correction, result and alarm set screens

and built the server using the Google App Engine. The system includes an alarm clock function and the opportunity to perform language exercises before and after sleep. Figure 1 shows the typical scenario for the use of the system. It offers English language word quizzes to users before they set alarms and after they turn them off. We chose an English word quiz, because a lot people want to learn English and memorize English words. The screenshots of the quiz on a smart-phone are shown in Figure 2. The system displays one English word and four options for its meaning in Japanese. Users select one of these words as answer. The system displays "correct" in response to a correct answer and "incorrect" in response to an incorrect one, along with the correct answer to the question. At the end of a turn, the system shows the number of correct answers. Users are able to set the alarm after the completion of the quiz.

On the server side, the database of the system stores information for each user, such as his or her name, a list of question words, correct response rate, the choices, the time taken to answer, and the date and time of each turn (Figure 3). At the beginning of each turn, mobile terminals fetch the words from the server. At the conclusion of each turn, the mobile terminals send data to the server. The server selects words at random for each user in the first version. In the later version, word-sets are selected according to the user's language skill as selected in the setup menu.

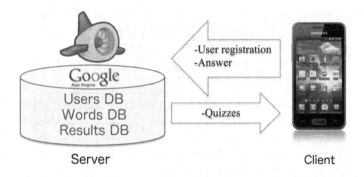

Fig. 3. Server and client configuration

4   Experimentation

Using the system described above, we performed a weeklong experiment with 10 participants to explore an effective way to learn before sleep. We selected difficult English words that were new to all participants. The participants learned the words simply by answering the questions asked by the system. We asked the participants to take these tests three times a day – upon waking up, in the daytime, and before bedtime – and compared the results. We know that a few trials in the experimental log can be noise, such as taking the quiz before a short nap instead of prior to going to sleep for the night, or waking up and taking the quiz only to fall back to sleep, or taking the quiz at an unscheduled time. We consider such data to be noise and remove it manually by referring to our survey questionnaire, which was filled out by each participant.

Table 1 is the trial schedule of the experiment and shows when a subject challenges each word group. The first column represents the name of the word group, the first row represents the days of the experiment while the second row records the time of the experiment (morning, afternoon, and evening). Each word group contains five words and is posed to the users at the scheduled time marked by a capital letter, as shown in Table 1. The letter 'O' (for once) shows a learning trial that poses a questions only once, while 'R' (for repeat) shows a learning trial that will be repeated until the user correctly answers each question two times. 'T' (for test) indicates the final test to measure the effectiveness in each word group. At the beginning of each trial, a questionnaire screen is shown to survey the condition of sleep, such as time elapsed between learning and bedtime, whether the user takes a nap after the last trial, etc. Although not shown in Table 1, this experiment also has dummy word groups to adjust the amount of learning.

Table 2 shows the results of measurement effectiveness. The numbers show normalized scores of the final tests (out of 100). EMD (Evening Morning Double), AED (Afternoon MD), and MAD are the word groups with four trials. EMS

Table 1. Trial schedule for the word groups

	Day1 M	Day1 A	Day1 E	Day2 M	Day2 A	Day2 E	Day3 M	Day3 A	Day3 E	Day4 M	Day4 A	Day4 E	Day5 M	Day5 A	Day5 E	Day6 M	Day6 A	Day6 E	Day7 M	Day7 A	Day7 E
EMD							O	O		O	O					T					
AED										O	O		O	O					T		
MAD				O	O		O	O					T								
EMS													O	O							T
AES													O	O					T		
MAS													O	O		T					
EMR					R	R			T												
AER						R	R		T												
MAR	R	R					T														

Table 2. Average score of effect measurements (out of 100)

EMD	AED	MAD	EMS	AES	MAS	EMR	AER	MAR
89	73	80	73	65	70	87	78	85

(EM Single), AES, and MAS are groups with two trials. EMR (EM Repeat), AER, and MAR are word groups that are repeated until the user successfully answers correctly. In all categories, evening-morning pairs (EMD, EMS, and EMR) recorded the highest scores. Therefore, we concluded that learning before going to bed and upon waking up leads to higher learning effects than at any other time.

5   Field Test

5.1   Method

We released our learning application on Google Play and gathered learning effect data from a wide variety of users. We also offered three courses with different levels of difficulty so that users with varying English language skills could be involved. Users in each skill level can learn 100 English words using our application. During the two-month field test period, 45 Android users downloaded our program, and attempted our 10-word-quiz 170 times.

The program advises users to answer the quiz regularly in the morning, during the day and in the evening. We recommended that learning activities be evenly spread out during the day, i.e., a quiz be taken every eight hours. We also recommended that users take the evening quiz just before bedtime.

In the release version of our application, the quiz schedule has been designed to be much simpler than in the experimental version in order to obtain more useful data. The simplification is also intended to make our application more user-friendly, since we realize that the average Internet user is likely to be less

Table 3. Scheduling word groups (A, B, C,...)

Time	Day1/A	Day1/E	Day2/M	Day2/A	Day2/E	Day3/M	...
Word groups	A & B	B & C	C & D	D & E	E & F	F & G	...

patient than our volunteer subjects. While we tried to evaluate effects in multiple learning trials in the previous experiment, we designed the quiz schedule in the release version to evaluate effects using a single session. Each English word is sequentially presented twice. That is, if a user takes the test regularly, each word is posed in evening-and-morning, morning-and-afternoon, or afternoon-and-evening sessions. The regular quiz schedule is shown in Table 3. Each word group – A, B, C, D, E, F and G – consists of five words, and users try two word groups (10 words) in each quiz. There are 20 word groups for each of the three skill levels, so that each skill level contains 100 words. As shown in Table 3, 10 English words are presented to the user, half of which are new and the other half are words from previous quizzes. The word group A is a dummy group and not used in later analyses. In case a user has missed a quiz, the relevant score is excluded from the analysis.

5.2 Analysis

The words presented to each user can be categorized into the following two groups:

- words of which the user remembers the meaning even before starting the first quiz, and always answers 100% correctly
- words of which the user does not remember the meaning perfectly, and answers with an accuracy of less than 100%

Let X be the number of words in the second group – the words that the user needs to learn and does not answer perfectly in the quiz. Note that even if the user does not know these words, he/she can select the correct answer in 25% of all cases. This is because each question on the quiz offers four options to choose from, and thus, the probability that the user gets the correct answer is 0.25, even when he/she is completely ignorant of the meaning of the word at hand. Given that the total number of the words is N, the number of words that the user remembers 100% correctly even before starting the first quiz is $(N-X)$. We claim that the learning effect of a quiz trial can be measured by the improvement of the rate at which words belonging to the second group above are answered correctly. In the following analysis, we try to calculate the improvement of the rate using the number of correctly and incorrectly answered words.

Firstly, we calculate the number of correctly and incorrectly answered words in the first quiz as shown, respectively, in Formulas 1 and 2 below. Here, we assume that perfectly memorized $(N-X)$ words can be answered correctly, and that inaccurately memorized X words are answered correctly with percentage of α. Formulas 1 and 2 describe the user's initial knowledge of the words in the quiz.

$$C = (N - X) + \alpha X \tag{1}$$

$$I = (1 - \alpha)X \tag{2}$$

Secondly, we calculate the number of correctly and incorrectly answered words in the second quiz. We also assume that inaccurately memorized words, from the second group above, are answered correctly with percentage of β in the second trial. We categorized the words used in the quiz as follows:

- CC words that are correctly and correctly answered
- CI words that are correctly and incorrectly answered
- IC words that are incorrectly and correctly answered
- II words that are incorrectly and incorrectly answered

The two letters in each category refer to the user's performance, respectively, in the first and second quiz. The respective numbers of words in each category is represented by formulas 3, 4, 5 and 6.

$$CC = (N - X) + \alpha\beta X \tag{3}$$

$$CI = \alpha(1 - \beta)X \tag{4}$$

$$IC = (1 - \alpha)\beta X \tag{5}$$

$$II = (1 - \alpha)(1 - \beta)X \tag{6}$$

Using Formulas 4 and 6, the rate α of correct answers in the first quiz trial is calculated as shown in Formula 7:

$$\alpha = \frac{CI}{CI + II} \tag{7}$$

Similarly, using Formulas 5 and 6, the rate β of correct answers in the second quiz trial is calculated as shown in Formula 8:

$$\beta = \frac{IC}{IC + II} \tag{8}$$

Additionally, using α, β, and Formula 3, X is calculated as follows.

$$X = \frac{N - CC}{1 - \alpha\beta} \tag{9}$$

Table 4 shows the results of the field test. The rows labeled by "Evening-Morning", "Morning-Afternoon" and "Afternoon-Evening" represent,

Table 4. Word-learning effect. α and β denote rates (%) of correct answer for uncertain words in the first and second trials. The learning effect is calculated by $\beta - \alpha$.

Timing	CC	CI	IC	II	N(words)	X(words)	α(%)	β(%)	Effect(%)
Evening-Morning	58	11	38	23	130	90.2	32	62	**30**
Morning-Afternoon	43	13	25	24	105	75.5	35	51	**16**
Afternoon-Evening	55	20	33	17	125	109	54	66	**12**

respectively, records in the quiz trials of the times before going to bed and after-waking-up, after waking up and daytime, and daytime and before bedtime. The columns labeled CC, CI, IC and II represent the total number of words answered correctly and incorrectly in the first and second quiz trial, as explained above. The column labeled N represents the total number of words use in the trial. The columns labeled X, α, and β represent, respectively, the number of uncertainly remembered words and the rate (%) of correct answers, calculated formulas 9, 7, and 8. The last column shows the learning effect of the first quiz trial: that is, the improvement in the percentage for answering uncertainly memorized words. These are calculated by $(\beta - \alpha)$. By calculating the difference of the percentages, we can accurately evaluate the learning effect by canceling factors arising out of the difficulty of the quiz and questions correctly answered by chance. The results in Table 4 show that using our application before bedtime is two times more effective for learning than using it in the morning or during the day.

6   Conclusion

We proposed a smart-phone application based on findings that sleep supports memory consolidation. From the results of the experiment and the field test, we found that learning before bedtime is the most effective in memory consolidation. This result indicates the usefulness of our alarm clock design, which provides an opportunity to learn while setting the alarm just before going to sleep. We will continue to improve the functionality and user-interface design of our application to innovate more practical computing devices that support everyday learning activities.

References

1. Hartley, D.: Observations on Man, His Frame, His Duty and His Expectations. Johnson, London (1791)
2. Maquet, P.: The role of sleep in learning and memory. Science 294, 1048–1052 (2001)
3. Squire, L.R.: Memory and Brain. Oxford University Press, Oxford (1987)
4. Ikeda, A., Drill, D.: Learning Application. In: CHI 2012, pp. 1853–1858 (2012)
5. Good friend Workshop TWIST Desktop Digital Alarm Clock, http://1030gfw.com/
6. Edge, D., Searle, E., Chiu, K., Zhao, J., Landay, J.A.: MicroMandarin: Mobile Language Learning in Context. In: Proc. CHI 2011, pp. 3169–3178 (2011)

Sustaining Outside-of-Class CALL Activities by Means of a Student Self-Evaluation System in a University Blended Learning EFL Course

Yasushige Ishikawa[1], Reiko Akahane-Yamada[2], Misato Kitamura[2], Craig Smith[1], Yasushi Tsubota[3], and Masatake Dantsuji[3]

[1] Kyoto University of Foreign Studies, Japan
{yasuishikawa,craigkufs}@hotmail.com
[2] ATR Intelligent Robotics and Communication Laboratories, Japan
{yamada,kitamura}@atr-lt.jp
[3] Academic Center for Computing and Media Studies, Kyoto University, Japan
{tsubota,www-call}@media.kyoto-u.ac.jp

Abstract. This paper is a report on a research project which was conducted on blended learning (BL) in an English as a foreign language (EFL) course at a Japanese university. In this study the BL approach to EFL teaching was defined as a combination of in-class and outside-of-class learning tasks and materials integrated in a single learning environment by a www-based courseware, ATR CALL BRIX (http://www.atr-lt.jp/products/brix/index.html). The use of the courseware outside of class was intended not only to help improve students' TOEIC scores, but also to nurture self-regulated learning (SRL). A student self-evaluation system was implemented in this project. On the basis of the findings of pre- and post-learning questionnaires and interviews with students, it was concluded that the self-evaluation system encouraged students to engage in SRL. Furthermore, pre- and post-TOEIC testing revealed that the students in the project improved their TOEIC scores ($p < .01$; $r = .49$).

Keywords: Self-evaluation system, Blended learning, Self-regulated learning, E-mentoring, English as a foreign language (EFL).

1 Introduction

1.1 Blended Learning: A Definition

Blended learning has been defined as a combination of face-to-face delivery with online delivery [1]. However, there is a lack of satisfaction with the definition that is apparent in the literature. As with other innovations in educational technology, there have been problematic issues with the definition of blended learning as the related technologies have developed [2].

In this study, the BL approach to EFL teaching was specified as a combination of in-class and outside-of-class learning tasks and materials integrated in a single

P. Zaphiris and A. Ioannou (Eds.): LCT 2014, Part II, LNCS 8524, pp. 146–154, 2014.

learning environment by a www-based courseware, ATR CALL BRIX (http://www.atr-lt.jp/products/brix/index.html) which included a learning management system (LMS). The LMS provided a variety of learning materials designed to prepare students for the TOEIC Listening and Reading Test.

1.2   Blended Learning as a Facilitator of Self-Regulated Learning

Self-regulated learning (SRL) is defined as a set of proactive study processes that students use to manage their own learning by making decisions about their own learning goals, by selecting and deploying learning strategies and by self-monitoring their own effectiveness as learners [3].

Nicol & MacFarlane-Dick [4] found that feedback is a key element in the development of SRL as it informs students of the parameters of good learning behavior through self/peer learning performance comparisons enhanced by analytical interaction with instructors and peers. This process facilitates self-assessment and the development of self-esteem, key processes within SRL. Butler & Winne [5] also found that the richer the feedback a learner received, the higher the level of self-regulation. A study by Sadler [6] suggests that when constructive feedback empowers students self-regulatory skills improve. Interaction and feedback facilitates analytical thinking, as learners interpret what they have done or intend to do next, compare their own performance with that of their peers, and with the target performance level that their teacher guides them towards.

The abilities to recognize what good performance is and to gauge one's own performance against performance standards are key factors in the development of reflective learning. Interaction and feedback are important for self-assessment, as self-reflection alone can be a limited and difficult process [7]. Effective self-assessment is based on the critical evaluation of actual personal experiences, in particular the impact on current performance of past success and failure; the analytical observation of peer performance; and the constructive reception of feedback from peers and teachers. A study by Miltiadou & Savenye [8] highlighted the importance of feedback for improving self-assessment in ways that will foster study persistence by allowing learners to accept signs of incremental steps towards target-level success. Thus, the variety of interaction and feedback opportunities BL offers facilitates the growth of SRL through self-assessment skill-building.

Using several case studies from Japanese universities, Goda [9] examined e-learning environments and their capacity to encourage SRL. Goda [9] created a self-regulated learning scale for e-learning based on a study by Wolters, Pintrich, & Karabenic [10] which has 4 categories of SRL strategies; affective, cognitive, help-seeking, and independence-generating. The scale was designed for the purpose of investigating the link between learner types and learner behavior to ascertain what kind of support students require. It was hypothesized that different learner types when engaged in e-learning require different approaches to the provision of appropriate types and amount of support.

At Yamagata University, Japan, the scale was used to determine the influence of e-mentoring in a blended learning course. It was found that e-mentoring had an affect on help-seeking. In a further study, time management was focused on as a SRL target behavior that the use of a LMS could improve, particularly with regards to having too much freedom in terms of the use of time which can lead to postponement of tasks and failure to complete assignments [9].

Kumamoto University in Japan has used a CALL English program to improve students' autonomy and SRL skills. The system allows students to check their own learning progress and amount of time spent on the LMS and compare their learning performance with that of their classmates. The findings of this study suggest that an e-mentor and other forms of support are important in order to increase time spent on SRL activities [9].

Ng, Seeshing Yeung, & Yuk Hung Hon's study with EFL students in Hong Kong [11] shows a correlation between levels of learner satisfaction and two factors: learner self-management of the amount of time and effort invested in learning and the amount of time spent on self-assessment of their learning performance. The study claims that learners who are active in self-assessment have more effective learning outcomes than learners who attend class and engage in few self-assessment processes. Thus, it can be expected that BL practices that involve peer and teacher interaction and a deep engagement with materials will encourage the active learning behavior common in self-regulated learners.

Sagarra & Zapata's [12] study of Spanish L2 learners in the United States claims that how learners acquire information is related to the depth of engagement with the materials and the learning process. For example, resubmitting work in the online phase multiple times and then being encouraged to self-assess each time in the face-to-face phase, prompts critical thinking, and the creation of more opportunities for self-assessment, reflection and satisfaction due to a growing sense of achievement as progress is made toward learning goals. Learners who were active in self-assessment increased their self-awareness of SRL strategies.

Qu [13] found that high levels of engagement in interaction and feedback enhances self-efficacy levels in EFL learners in China. Conventional courses with limited resources, usually the teacher and the students, have low levels of input from peers compared to BL courses. It was found that encouragement and inspiration from teacher and peer feedback that acted as scaffolding built learners' self-confidence. Through engagement with other people, cognitive processes were activated, and as students became increasingly aware of their own weak and strong points, their problem solving strategies improved.

Sanprasert [14] investigated a BL delivery system for Thai EFL students that was designed as scaffolding to create a flexible learning environment based on autonomous learning. Thai students are generally described as being obedient to the point of being over dependent on their teachers. Thus, classroom time assigned to face-to-face interaction may mainly be spent in students listening to the teacher talk. The study acknowledged that it is not easy to radically alter ingrained learner and institutional characteristics; however, if teaching and learning methods shift the classroom power structure, individual capacity may be liberated. Sanprasert [14] found that students who had been described as having low SRL levels became more aware of the importance of their own roles, they gained in confidence at setting goals, and did not just rely on receiving them from the teacher. The students reported that feedback which allowed them to compare their performance with that of their peers was a good source of motivation. While many students still preferred to have face-to-face time with a teacher, blended learning had altered their beliefs and behavior in ways that resulted in more active SRL activities.

A study by Jochum [15] examined the use of blended learning by learners of Spanish and the impact of self-reflection and assessment. The study identified how a BL multiple delivery system prompted SRL. Although the online activities were student-centered and thus, facilitated independent learning and consequently improvements in learner self-esteem, it was concluded that online materials alone do not provide students sufficient output opportunities and feedback. It was found that if online tools are used to provide data on learner progress to teachers and students, teacher and peer feedback can become a rich source for self-reflection which may prompt learners to adapt their learning strategies in the SRL practice phase.

The studies reported above offer encouragement that systematic procedures for student self-evaluations in the BL approach to foreign language teaching may promote SRL. Positive findings are reported on efforts to constructively apply the on-going developments in ICT to create effective combinations of on-line and in-class mentoring in programmed generic e-mentoring and face-to-face in-class teacher and peer mentoring. The studies rest on an assumption that students will use on-line self-evaluation materials and add to it in their own independent and individual ways in class.

In the classroom students must be willing to interact with each other and their teacher as learning colleagues, and not as isolated individuals or in groups that are primarily friendship-based. Based on such constructive attitudes, classroom time can be devoted to interaction between students and their teacher that will support outside-of-class study through problem-solving tasks which depend for success on self- and other-analytical reflection of learning task performances.

The aim of the study reported in this paper was to learn how to recreate the self-reflective independent learning environment that some high-performing students employ to continuously and gradually improve their skills. Professional mentoring for top performers typically relies on self-reflection by students that allows timely critical interventions by the mentor. The aim of our study is to apply this combination of teacher/peer-mentoring and self-mentoring to enhance students SRL effectiveness at the same time teachers become more insightful mentors to the full range of students they teach from the highest to the lowest proficiency levels.

The study reported in this paper explores a way of creating and sustaining student motivation at levels high enough to ensure that a virtuous cycle of reflection, mentoring intervention and performance is created.

2   ATR CALL BRIX

ATR CALL BRIX is a www-based courseware with a LMS, which contains seven different functions: 1) study logs, 2) feedback on the achievement rates of student-set goals, 3) records of the frequency of the use of the materials, 4) a record of time spent on learning, 5) a continuous update of the average score on the TOEIC learning tasks, 6) an evaluation of students' weak points and advice for further learning, and 7) students' rankings in comparison with other students in the course [16].

The courseware was used in conjunction with weekly messages of advice and encouragement from an e-mentor team, student in-class completion of a self-evaluation form in which students reflected on their progress and set personal learning goals, and in-class teacher-student communication in learning tasks.

3   Research Question

The project sought to answer the following research question: Would this project's student self-evaluation system lead to an observable development in student attitudes, knowledge, and skills which characterize successful SRL practices?

4   Student Self-Evaluation System

A student self-evaluation system was implemented in this project which combined e-mentoring outside of class and weekly in-class self-evaluations as part of the course routine.

E-mentoring can be defined as similar to traditional mentoring but accomplished through ICT communication. It is also known as online mentoring, virtual mentoring, telementoring or cybermentoring, utilizing computer-mediated communication tools such as e-mail, listservs, chat groups, and computer conferencing [17], [18], [19]. E-mentoring has been adopted by companies, educational institutions and community programs where face-to-face or synchronous mentoring is not readily accessible, for example where there is a substantial distance between mentor and learner [18]. Compared to e-coaching where the focus is on a single goal or area of performance, e-mentoring involves a more ongoing period of advice to support an individual's development in a more general sense, for example, in achieving their career goals [18]. Within an educational setting, e-mentoring can be said to cover the academic or non-academic needs of the learner such as providing advice regarding the retention of knowledge and enhanced academic performance, or giving encouragement when human relationship problems interfere with study. The term online-tutoring, in contrast, is used when the focus of support is limited to academic areas [20].

For outside-of-class e-mentoring, students were placed in four groups according to their TOEIC scores at the beginning of the semester. An e-mentor team of one teacher and a graduate school student teaching assistant sent different need-based messages of advice and encouragement weekly to the mobile phones of the students in each of the four groups according to how often the students used the LMS learning materials. In addition, a self-evaluation process was a feature of the weekly class. The students reflected on their previous goals and set new goals for the following week in consultation with their peers and the classroom teacher. Fig. 1 shows a flow of the tasks of participants and the e-mentor team in the student self-evaluation system.

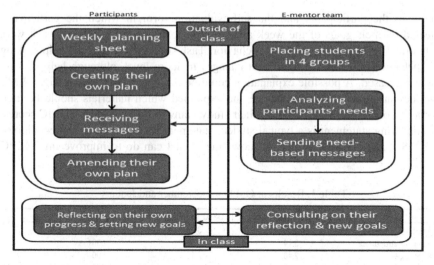

Fig. 1. Flow of tasks of participants and e-mentor team in the system

5   Validation of the Study

5.1   Participants

Twenty nine students at a university in Japan participated in this study. The participants' scores on the TOEIC Listening and Reading Test in September ranged from 295 to 650 (average = 482.59).

5.2   Method

The participants were provided, as out-of-class activities, with the courseware materials for improving their TOEIC scores between September, 2012 and January, 2013. The materials were designed to be completed in eight weeks, and each week the records of the seven LMS materials were compiled. A pre- and post-course, the Online Self-Regulated Learning Questionnaire (OSLQ), was administered in September and in January. It included 24 items which used a 5-point Likert scale for ranking student responses from strongly agree (5) to strongly disagree (1). The OSLQ covered six SRL constructs [21]: setting goals, structuring the learning environment, creating learning strategies, managing time, seeking help, and conducting self-evaluations. The student self-evaluation system was implemented in this project which combined e-mentoring outside of class and weekly self-evaluations as part of the class routine between September, 2012 and January, 2013.

5.3   Results and Discussion

Scores of four out of the six SRL constructs significantly increased as described in Table 1, below. The results indicate that the messages that the e-mentor team sent weekly to the participants and the self-evaluation form in which the participants reflected on their goals of the week and set new goals for the following week were likely effective in encouraging SRL behavior. Task strategy creation and help seeking SRL behaviors showed no significant changes in score level, although help seeking scores decreased. A possible explanation could be that the ATR CALL BRIX's LMS gave the participants adequate advice and explained which materials should be used in order to overcome weaknesses in their study plans to improve their TOEIC scores. The following statement is a typical student statement regarding their appreciation of the LMS: "The LMS is so nice. It shows me what I can do to improve my TOEIC score."

Table 1. Results of OSLQ in September and January

	OSLQ (September)	OSLQ (January)	p	r
Goal setting	2.86	3.26	.002**	.57
Environment structuring	3.14	3.55	.030*	.56
Task strategies	2.40	2.45	1.00	.00
Time management	2.68	3.20	.000**	.66
Help seeking	2.13	2.05	.523	.12
Self-evaluation	2.53	2.83	.043*	.38

$*p < .05; **p < .01$

Furthermore, pre- and post-TOEIC testing was conducted in September, 2012, at the beginning of the semester and in January, 2013, at the end of the semester. The result as is shown in Table 2 revealed that the students in the project significantly improved their TOEIC scores ($p < .01; r = .49$).

Table 2. Results of pre- and post-TOEIC testing

TOEIC score (SD)		Gain	p	r
Pre-TOEIC	Post-TOEIC			
482.59 (91.01)	520 (116.02)	37.41	.009**	.49

$**p < .01$

6   Conclusion

The following research question was the focus of the project described in this paper: Would this project's student self-evaluation system lead to an observable development in the student attitudes, knowledge, and skills which characterize successful SRL practices? The results of the study reveal the student self-evaluation system, an important component of our BL project, encouraged SRL development.

Further research should be conducted to identify which particular types of e-mentoring may be most effective in encouraging SRL.

Acknowledgement. This study was supported by a Grant-in-Aid for Scientific Research (#23242032) from the Japan Society for the Promotion of Science. The data presented, the statements made, and the views expressed are solely the responsibility of the authors.

References

1. Osguthorpe, R.T., Graham, C.R.: Blended Learning Environments: Definitions and Directions. The Quarterly Review of Distance Education 4(3), 227–233 (2003)
2. Motteram, G., Sharma, P.: Blending Learning in a Web 2.0 World. International Journal of Emerging Technologies & Society 7(2), 83–96 (2009)
3. Zimmerman, B.J.: Investigating Self-Regulation and Motivation: Historical Background, Methodological Developments, and Future Prospects. American Educational Research Journal 45, 166–183 (2008)
4. Nicol, D.J., Macfarlane-Dick, D.: Formative Assessment and Self-Regulated Learning: A Model and Seven Principles of Good Feedback Practice. Studies in Higher Education 31(2), 199–218 (2006)
5. Butler, D.L., Winne, P.H.: Feedback and Self-Regulated Learning: A Theoretical Synthesis. Review of Educational Research 65(3), 245–281 (1995)
6. Sadler, D.R.: Formative Assessment and the Design of Instructional Systems. Instructional Science 18, 119–144 (1989)
7. Andrade, M.S., Bunker, E.L.: A Model for Self-Regulated Distance Language Learning. Distance Education 30(1), 47–61 (2009)
8. Miltiadou, M., Savenye, W.C.: Applying Social Cognitive Constructs of Motivation to Enhance Student Success in Online Distance Education. Educational Technology Review 11(1), 1–28 (2003)
9. Goda, Y.: Formative Assessment and Support for Students' Self-Regulated Learning in E-learning. Symposium Summary 7, 85–92 (2012)
10. Wolters, C.A., Pintrich, P.R., Karabenic, S.A.: Assessing Academic Self-Regulated Learning. the Conference on Indicators of Positive Development: Definitions, Measures, and Prospective Validity (2003)
11. Ng, C., Seeshing Yeung, A., Yuk Hung Hon, R.: Does Online Language Learning Diminish Interaction between Student and Teacher? Educational Media International 43(3), 219–232 (2006)
12. Sagarra, N., Zapata, G.C.: Blending Classroom Instruction with Online Homework: A Study of Student Perceptions of Computer-Assisted L2 Learning. ReCALL 20(2), 208–224 (2008)
13. Qu, W.: Stimulating Foreign Language Learning Motivation: From the Perspective of Cognition and Metacognition. US-China Foreign Language 7(10), 34 (2009)
14. Sanprasert, N.: The Application of A Course Management System to Enhance Autonomy in Learning English as A Foreign Language. Science Direct, System 38, 109–123 (2010)
15. Jochum, C.J.: Blended Spanish Instruction: Perceptions and Design Case Study. Journal of Instructional Psychology 38(1), 40–47 (2011)
16. Ishikawa, Y., Akahane-Yamada, R., Kondo, M., Smith, C., Tsubota, Y., Dantsuji, M.: An Interoperable ICT Educational Application for TOEIC Preparatory Study. In: Khosrow-Pour, M. (ed.) Encyclopedia of Information Science and Technology, 3rd edn. Information Science Reference, Hershey (2014)
17. Bierema, L.L., Merriam, S.B.: E-mentoring: Using Computer Mediated Communication to Enhance the Mentoring Process. Innovative Higher Education 26(3), 211–227 (2002)
18. Harrington, A.: E-mentoring: The Advantages and Disadvantages of Using Email to Support Distant Mentoring. Hertfordshire TEC (1999)

19. http://www.coachingnetwork.org.uk/resourcecentre/articles/ViewArticle.asp?artId=63

20. Switzer, J., Stanley, L., Switzer, R.: Student Attitudes and Preferences Toward An E-Mentoring Program. In: Amiel, T., Wilson, B. (eds.) Proceedings of World Conference on Educational Multimedia, Hypermedia and Telecommunications 2012, pp. 2073–2081. The Association for the Advancement of Computing in Education, Chesapeake (2012)

21. Matsuda, T.: Organizing E-Mentors: Development and Management. In: Luca, J., Weippl, E.R. (eds.) Proceedings of World Conference on Educational Multimedia, Hypermedia and Telecommunications 2008, pp. 5308–5313. The Association for the Advancement of Computing in Education, Chesapeake (2008)

22. Barnard-Brak, L., Lan, W.Y., Paton, V.O.: Profiles in Self-Regulated Learning in the Online Learning Environment. International Review of Research in Open and Distance Learning 11(1) (2010)

23. http://www.irrodl.org/index.php/irrodl/article/viewArticle/769/1480

Society@school: Towards an e-Inclusion App for Social Reading

Longo Lucia[1], Guercio Elena[2], Tedde Alessandra[3],
Belluati Maurizio[2], and Actis-Grosso Rossana[3]

[1] Politecnico di Torino
lucia.longo@polito.it
[2] Telecom Italia S.p.A. Torino, Italy
{elena.guercio,maurizio.belluati}@telecomitalia.it
[3]Università degli Studi di Milano-Bicocca
aletedde@live.it, rossana.actis@unimib.it

Abstract. Society@school, a Telecom-Italia Social Reading application designed as a tool for education (presented in its first version at HCI International 2013) turned out to be a useful tool for students with Specific Learning Disabilities (SLD). Social reading could be a way to compensate some SLD, such as dyslexia, allowing a real inclusion of these students in the school system. The design process, aimed at including specific design requirements for SLD students with a user-centered design approach, is presented.

Keywords: Social reading, User Experience, School, User Interface, Social, Inclusion, SLD, Constructivism.

1 Introduction

Society@school is an application for social reading running on IOS, Android and PC Systems. With social reading we refer to the possibility of sharing opinions and annotations inside a community-based group with similar reading interests (such as high-school students of the same course and readers of the same book or reading genre). By using society@school, students and teachers can also find and produce new multimedia contents. In this way, students can be active actors of the educational process, by constructing their studying materials and, in the end, building new knowledge. This process makes reading a social and shared experience.

The theory underlying our app is Constructivism (Vygotsky, 1978), according to which the goal of education should be to become creative through conceptualizations and synthesis of prior experience to create (or construct) new knowledge. According to Vigotsky (1978) every student has a "zone of proximal development" which is the distance between the actual development level, as determined by independent problem solving, and the level of potential development as determined through problem solving under adult guidance (i.e. a teacher) or in collaboration with more capable peers. Therefore interaction and active collaboration between peers is an essential part of the learning process.

P. Zaphiris and A. Ioannou (Eds.): LCT 2014, Part II, LNCS 8524, pp. 155–164, 2014.
© Springer International Publishing Switzerland 2014

In a first trial we asked one secondary school (2 classrooms: 42 students, 3 teachers) to test Society@school in their daily educational activities for 6 months (Guercio et al. 2013). On the base of the feedbacks collected during this trial, we inserted some specific extra tools, such as vocal recording and reading, cognitive maps and text customized format. Furthermore, by testing society@school in the context of use, we realized that our app could be very useful also for students with specific learning disabilities (SLD), an emergent problem in the Italian education system, due to the increasing number of SLD students. Epidemiological data report that 10-20% of school-age population has learning difficulties. In particular, children with Specific Learning disabilities (SLD) are about 5% of the school population (Stella et al., 2009).

Therefore, the goal of the present study is two-folded, being focused on both customizing society@school by defining the appropriate user requirements for SLD stu-dents, and improving the social reading experience for the class group as a whole (i.e. students and teachers). By adopting a user-centered design approach, we consider the designing process as an iterative process, in which users' involvement is requested in every step of the designing process.

We started to define user requirements with both an analysis of scientific literature and a review (and consequent analysis) of the existing tools designed to support SLD in the education system. The second step consisted of a heuristic evaluation of society@school carried out by our UX team, integrating Nielsen's (1993) heuristics with WCGA guidelines for accessible web interfaces. Then we run a participative heuristic evaluation by asking 15 users (i.e. teachers, psychologists, students with developmental dyslexia and their parents) to test the application and to refer their User Experience. Users were let free to use the application with the help of an expert, who was also collecting and stimulating their comments and suggestions, referring each com-ment to the correspondent heuristic (such as navigation, familiarity and so on).

The comparison between expert and participative heuristic evaluations brought to define the designing requirements. Through a quick Balsamiq prototyping, society@school became a cloud-based solution, including not only annotations and notes, comments and links to multimedia extra-contents, highlights and sharing options, but also new functions, which are intended to be useful for both SLD and typically developed students.

2   State of Art

2.1   Dyslexia and Specific Learning Disabilities

Developmental Dyslexia is usually defined as a neurodevelopmental disorder characterized by slow and inaccurate word recognition (e.g. Lyon & Shaywitz, 2003). Although usually considered of constitutional origin, its actual mechanisms remain the subject of intense research endeavor in various neuroscientific areas and along several theoretical frameworks. Developmental Dyslexia causes small but significant anomalies in brain sites involved in the organization of linguistic and cognitive functions of reading (Consensus Conference, 2007) and present a high rate of comorbidity with other SLD (such as dysgraphia, i.e. difficulty in writing, and dyscalculia, i.e. difficulty in calculating) as well as attention deficit hyperactivity disorder (Stella, 2004).

To date it is possible to identify at least four major theories, identifying different causes for developmental dyslexia:

1. Phonological deficit theory - the basis of reading disorder is a persistent impairment of the module for phonology, which pervasively affects various aspects of phonological processing (Catts, 1989);
2. Theory of automation deficit (cerebellar) – the lack of automation would be determined by a cerebellar dysfunction which compromise a more general automation of skills, not only for reading, but also for other motor sequences and, in general, for implicit learning. In addition, this hypothesis seeks to explain the general difficulty shown by dyslexics in performing two tasks at the same time;
3. Theory of visual/auditory impairment (magnocellular) – an impairment in the coordination of visual and auditory stimuli causes a difficulty to respect the correct sequence of letters in a word (as is the case of "cursor", which becomes "rucsor");
4. Theory of attention deficit – The automatic orienting of spatial attention, and in particular a deficit in selective spatial attention, may distort the development of phonological and orthographic representations that is essential for learning to read. In a recent study, Franceschini and colleagues (2012) demonstrated that pre-school children with visual-spatial attention problems are the same who later develop dyslexia. A relevant paper for our goal (Zorzi et al., 2012) shows that in-creasing the space between the letters of a word (and between words in a sentence), improves the speed and accuracy in the reading of dyslexic children. This study confirms the importance of using a specific font for dyslexics and the possibility to customize the page layout of an eBook.

2.2   Compensatory Softwares for SLD

The difficulties arising from dyslexia can be compensated with the help of specific tools. In last decades, a plenty of such tools have been developed for the educational system.

Compensatory software allow people with SLD to achieve a good degree of autonomy, and overall they guarantee to SLD students the opportunity to learn and communicate without depending on a mediator (Peroni et al., 2010).

Below the most common compensatory tools for the Italian education system are reported.

- the "*Talking Calculator*", a calculator with a speech synthesizer that reads numbers and operation signs as you type;
- specific software for writing and reading with lexical prediction and spelling corrections. Most of the existing text editors (such as Office *Word,* OpenOffice *Writer*, or *Writer* Libreoffice) have these functionalities too;

- Digital Voices (synthetic voice like *Loquendo-Nuances*) designed to "read with ears", help dyslexic children by decreasing the cognitive load they usually have when reading;
- Audacity is the best solution to record lectures. It has a free portable version and allows users to record, edit the audio file and save it as MP3;
- *Aplusix* is a French commercial software for arithmetic assistance, available in Italian as well. It helps students in solving calculations by guide them step by step, indicating whether the each single step is carried out correctly;
- *Berlitz* is a useful plug&play program for translations from foreign languages: it instantly translates each single word in 5 different languages (including English, French and Spanish) and is also equipped with speech synthesis;
- the visual organizers to create maps, charts and diagrams (for the study and the summary of written texts) are considered very useful: *SuperMappe Anastasis* with all its useful features is the most used instrument for dyslexics in Italy;
- the "easy to read" books are becoming increasingly popular: those books have typographical choices that make them much more readable, such as big characters, special fonts, increased spacing, not justified alignment, no hyphenation and all key elements for the easy reading;
- *Anastasis* and *Erickson, two of the most influential educational publishers in Italy*, makes available for schools audio books and spoken books read by a human voice and distributed on CD, tapes or MP3.

3   The Design Process to Integrate SLD Requirements in Society@school

After testing society@school in a trial in the city of Trento (Guercio et al. 2013) and according both to the benchmark on the available software and the analysis of literature about dyslexia and SLD, we realized how important it would be to develop society@school towards a real inclusion of all the students in the learning process.

For this reason we focused our analysis on the development of design requirements for SLD students, using the User Centered Design approach, i.e. an iterative process that puts the user in the center in every step of the designing process, from the collection of user requirements to the final evaluation

In particular, we started from a heuristic evaluation of society@school to evaluate if our app, thought for general consumers of the educational world, would be usable also for people with especial needs. After the expert evaluation we interviewed 15 individuals involved at different levels with developmental dyslexia, to find out specific requirements for that type of users. Users' requirements were transformed in designing requirements and inserted in a new low fidelity prototype of society@school. This new version was tested with SLD users before the final implementations.

3.1   Heuristic Evaluation Results

In the heuristic evaluation, we analyzed the application according to the guidelines of both heuristic analysis (Nielsen, 1993) and accessibility. Main results were related to:

- Visibility and feedback: there are no violations of the heuristic of visibility. Moreover, the application is easy to interpret, with good feedback for each user interaction. However, text formatting is not usable for SLD students and a violation of the WCGA principle of visual presentation has been identified: there is no left alignment of the text and there is no division into paragraphs;
- Consistency and standards: the application is consistent and icons are overall intuitive. However, for students with SLD the Text To Speech functionality is too mechanical and without intonation;
- Familiarity and Control: the "back" function is always available and respect "standard de facto" for tablet applications; all the icons are well positioned;
- Navigation: In two cases some weakness were highlighted. In the first case, when the touch screen is tapped to select the text there is no feedback, which left the user with the idea of not having performed the action correctly (a serious break of the principle of visibility and feedback). In the second case, after selecting the text, the context menu could appear at the top or at the bottom of the screen in a random way;
- Flexibility, style and friendliness: in general, standards of flexibility and efficiency for a good usability are respected. Features are simple and designed to avoid technological breakdown. The user interface makes the interaction easy, reducing user's cognitive load by the use of very intuitive icons.

3.2   User Interviews and Test of Application Prototype

To collect specific user's need of SLD needs, we interviewed 15 individuals: four students (three attending high school and one college), three educators, three teachers (one teaching at high school and two at "middle-school", i.e. a school for children aged from 10 to 13 years old), three parents and two psychologists. The interviews were face to face and were different according to the interviewed individual; each interview lasted on average 55 minutes.

Each interview was structured in five different steps. The first step was dedicated to collect information about the role each individual have in the "SLD world". In the second part the questions focused on the most frequent needs of SLD students, on their difficulties and on their learning requirements. The third phase was aimed at collecting information about the most used tools for compensating SLD weaknesses. In the fourth phase each interviewed was given a tablet with society@school, asking them to use it and to refer comments and criticalities to the interviewer. Then the interview was concluded by the last phase, consisting in 15 questions regarding the collaborative learning, aimed at having information about the core of society@school and its possible improvements.

3.3   Main Results and User Requirements for SLD Students

The main needs emerging from interviews involve support in reading, writing, calculation and recovery of grammar and arithmetic rules. In particular, it was highlighted that SLD student should be supported during both homework and exercises at school, with the help of grids for reading, forms, summary tables and mind maps.

It emerged the need for a single solution, which can simultaneously compensate the SLD students' difficulties and integrate the learning process for the whole class-room.

The features requested by the majority of respondents are:

- The app should be ease to use and designed to avoid cognitive overload;
- The app should be synchronized in all devices so that one can write down on his tablet, view and make quick additions on his smartphone, and then double check all on his personal computer at home;
- Readability is a crucial requirement: a specific font should be available; a change in text format (overall enlargement) is requested; justified alignment has to be avoided. Dyslexics prefer to read with left alignment of the text and spacing should be at least 1.5. It should be possible also to change the color of both text and background, as well as screen luminosity, which base-level should be low, to avoid eyes tiring during the reading;
- Collaborative learning and the presence of a social network are two important requirements: all participants think that it could be useful to integrate in society@school some specific features of the most popular social networks (i.e. Face-book) like groups, private conversations, group working, and so on. However, ac-cording to teachers, these functions should be used under their supervision given that, as a teacher said during his interview, "too much freedom could destabilize students". On the contrary, students prefer autonomy and self-organized study;
- Encyclopedia (like Wikipedia) is requested: the whole sample agrees that a vocabulary can greatly help individuals with SLD;
- All the interviewed claimed that personalized study path is necessary and that users should have the possibility to activate or de-activate each different tool, because things change during the year, and some deficits may be compensated;
- Mind and conceptual maps are fundamental functionalities to be introduced;
- Speech synthesis is a significant enrichment: once again, all the 15 participants agree that the use of speech synthesizers can be a valuable aid. It would be optimal to use the synthesizer while surfing the web, taking notes or translating to different languages (without having to change application or system settings). Such a software could be useful for everyone, not only for SLD students. A requested requirement of speech synthesis is "a human voice": robotic voices are disliked by students, who do not use tools with such voices;
- Finally, last requirement was the possibility to record lessons and to translate them in written text.

3.4   From User Requirements Towards a Low Fidelity Prototype

Every collected user requirement was "transformed" in graphical element or navigation option of the App prototype.

- Accessibility for all (Fig. 1): a simple mode to access the App by a friendly GUI has been crested. In particular, we have added an icon button to change the default text format (spacing, alignment left, pronounced edge, special fonts, etc) into a simplified format. By pressing this button the whole preferred options set is available with one click. In this way SLD students could save their set without feeling "different" from the rest of the classroom;

Fig. 1. Activation of simple reading mode

- Multiple devices: Society@school will have a total synchronization between tablet and PC. In fact, all the work done on the tablet, will be visible on the PC and vice-versa. This also allows users not to choose a specific platform (iOS vs Android);
- Modularity: default settings are provided, but they can be modified by the user;
- Readability (Fig.2): text is not justified, line spacing is set a 1.5 at the minimum, the possibility is given to change the space between words and letters, and fonts are sans serif or special (preferably EasyReading, certified by AID - Italian Association of Dyslexia). Background and text colours are set black for text on a parchment-colored background, which makes reading more relaxing;

Fig. 2. Text before and after the activation of simple reading mode

- Interactivity: Interactivity has been already present in the first version, to give the possibility to upload and share both text notes and media files (video youtube, image / photo, audio). In the new version users can also create mind maps and sum-maries as well as underlining, create notes and new text about the reading experience. We have added a translator and a fast link to Wikipedia;
- Speech synthesis: Users could convert text to speech voices. The functionality of audio book has also been included.
- Access Privileges and different interaction for students and teachers: the validation of both textual and multimedia materials is necessary. Teacher, or more in general the administrator, has the role to guarantee safe contents, by deleting notes if they're considered not relevant or dangerous.

3.5   The High Fidelity Prototype

After the design of a low fidelity prototype with Balsamiq (a tool for rapid proto-typing) and a short user test with DSL students, we designed the final functionalities and code for a new version of society@school. Below some screenshot of our application, which maintains all the features of the low fidelity prototype.

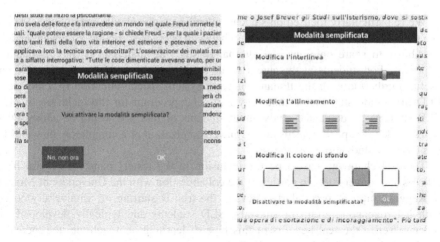

Fig. 3. Activation of simple reading mode and text customization

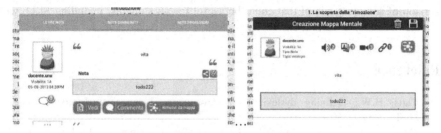

Fig. 4. Creation of a mind map

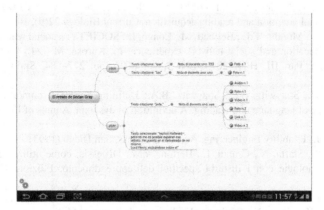

Fig. 5. Mind map visualization

4   Conclusion and Next Steps

The user centered design process seems to fit nicely with the developing process of Society@school for both SLD and typically developed students.

We're particularly focused on students attending high-schools and colleges. At this age (i.e 14-25 years old) the relationship between peers is particularly relevant and the possibility to share opinions and alternative studying materials is thus particularly important. For students at this age a social-reading tool could be very effective and useful. Furthermore, in the Italian education system special attention is dedicated to SLD first-grade students, without any particular program for the inclusion of older SLD students. A dedicated study about students of this age would be addressed in order to identify specific needs and define customization or a completely new tool for this target of students.

The real challenge would be the inclusion in the testers panel of several high-schools and universities. In particular the collaboration with the University of Modena & Reggio-Emilia is particularly relevant: the trial is starting on a university course with heterogeneous group of students (SLD students and typically developed), in order to verify the real benefits of this type of learning approach and the increased level of inclusion of students with SLD.

Our aim is to validate all the choices made in the design process and to develop a version of society@school that could be useful for all students, including SLD, without the necessity to label them as "dyslexic".

References

1. Catts, H.W.: Defining dyslexia as a developmental language disorder. Annals of Dyslexia 39(1), 50–64 (1989)
2. Concensus Conference, Disturbi evolutivi specifici di apprendimento: Raccomandazioni per la pratica clinica definite con il metodo della Consensus Conference (2007)
3. Franceschini, S., Gori, S., Ruffino, M., Pedrolli, K., Facoetti, A.: A casual link between visual spatial attention and reading acquisition. Current Biology 22(9), 1–6 (2012)
4. Guercio, E., Mondin, F.L., Belluati, M., Longo, L.: SOCIETY: a social reading application to join education and social network experience. In: Kurosu, M. (ed.) Human-Computer Interaction, Part III, HCII 2013. LNCS, vol. 8006, pp. 277–284. Springer, Heidelberg (2013)
5. Lyon, G.R., Shaywitz, S.E., Shaywitz, B.A.: Defining Dyslexia, comorbidity, teachers' knowledge of language and reading: A definition of dyslexia. Annals of Dyslexia 53, 1–14 (2003)
6. Nielsen, J.: Usability Engineering. Accademic Press, San Diego (1993)
7. Peroni, M., Staffa, N., Grandi, L., Berton, A.M.: Dislessia: come utilizzare al meglio le nuove tecnologie con i disturbi specifici dell'apprendimento. Edizioni CRA, Bologna (2010)
8. Phipps, L., Sutherland, A., Seale, J.: Access All Areas: Disability, Technology and Learning. JISC TechDis. Stella, G., La dislessia, Bologna, Il Mulino Editore, 2004 (2002)
9. Stella, G., Franceschi, S., Savelli, F.: Disturbi associati nella dislessia evolutiva: uno studio preliminare. Dislessia 6(1), 31–48 (2009)
10. Vygotsky, L.S.: Mind in society. Harvard University Press, Cambridge (1978)
11. Zorzi, M., Barbiero, C., Facoetti, A., Lonciari, I., Carrozzi, M., Montico, M., Bravar, L., George, F., Pech-Georgel, C., Ziegler, J.: Extra large letter spacing improves reading in dyslexia. PNAS 109(28), 11455–11459 (2012)

Sensor Based Interaction Mechanisms
in Mobile Learning

Kai-Uwe Martin[1], Madlen Wuttke[2], and Wolfram Hardt[1]

[1] Computer Engineering, Chemnitz University of Technology, Chemnitz, Germany
{kai-uwe.martin,wolfram.hardt}@informatik.tu-chemnitz.de
[2] Institute for Media Research, Chemnitz University of Technology, Chemnitz, Germany
madlen.wuttke@phil.tu-chemnitz.de

Abstract. This contribution discusses the possibilities for mobile interaction and learning, facilitated by the increasing use of sensors in mobile devices. Each sensor provides information which is useful in certain learning contexts and allows for distinct interaction mechanisms. However a model is required how to collect the sensor data and connect it to the learning environment and content. A suitable architecture is described and the steps of the information flow are explained. Future prospects to enhance mobile interaction with more natural ways of communication supported by sensors are given.

Keywords: Collaboration technology and informal learning, Mobile and/or ubiquitous learning, Personalization, user modeling and adaptation in learning technologies, Technology enhanced learning, sensors, context information, architecture, m-learning.

1 Introduction

Over the last years smart mobile devices reached a significant market share [1]. They are characterized by having advanced calculating powers, high resolution displays, permanent internet access, an app store and social network integration as well as a full scale operating system like Android or iOS. They have essentially reached the technical level of former desktop environments while usability characteristics like display size, resolution and operating systems were standardized and gained a broad acceptance [15].

These devices use special interaction mechanisms like touchscreens and accelerometers which offer a broader and more natural human to computer interaction than previous desktop computers [2]. With increasing success they are used as e-learning devices, which is the focus of the research field mobile learning that can be defined as a special area of technology enhanced learning, where either a mobile device is used or the user himself is mobile and communicates with devices in his environment [3].

However almost all e-learning contents and interaction mechanisms are aimed at desktop devices. For this reason an adaptation to the special characteristics of mobile devices is required to better support mobile learning processes and to fully use their potential [4]. Especially for interaction purposes mobile devices offer more

P. Zaphiris and A. Ioannou (Eds.): LCT 2014, Part II, LNCS 8524, pp. 165–172, 2014.

possibilities and channels than most desktop e-learning environments. Several sensors, primarily used in the mobile interaction and communication processes, have a high potential for mobile learning. In addition, the interaction with the environment, personalization and continuous reachability in social networks can be used to promote learning purposes.

2   Sensors in Mobile Devices

Sensors are converters that measure physical quantities and convert them to signals or data which can be interpreted by users, electronic instruments or applications [16]. Most sensors need to be calibrated which in the case of mobile devices is usually part of the manufacturing process.

Examples for sensors used in current devices are the camera, microphone, accelerometer, gyroscope, GPS, temperature, light, humidity and pressure sensors, orientation sensor, magnetic sensor and the clock as a time measuring instrument. Related are scanners for mobile networks or Bluetooth devices.

2.1   Typical Sensors and Interaction Mechanisms for m-Learning

One important sensor of mobile devices which is usually not present in desktop environments is the accelerometer. It is used to calculate the orientation of the device in space and to measure any motion of the device. Furthermore, it's movement can serve as an indicator of the distraction level the user is experiencing during the mobile learning process. Shaking the device can trigger actions like activating learning content or switching to the next chapter while acceleration can be used to showcase physical processes within learning content.

Most devices, except special ones used for secure business areas, include cameras. With this sensor, it is possible to determine whether the learner is facing the device, if he is focused on the content or elsewhere and to provide augmented reality support [5]. A small variety of facial expressions is also detectable by several phones. A camera can be used to recognize an individual learner, which is useful to offer content according to one's personal learning history and offer other personalization and context features [6]. The camera is also useful to attach pictures or videos of real life situations to learning content and to or to collect further data by scanning codes like QR tags, which provide additional information.

With the microphone it is possible to record annotations of the learner to the learning content, to give commands to the application and to communicate with other learners [7]. The microphone can be used to collect all environmental audio data and connect it to the current learning process, e.g. the audio is repeated when the user repeats the learning process which supports a better knowledge representation. The audio information can also be used to change device parameters like the volume or to request a repetition of the learning content due to a sensed disturbance. In connection with the internet cloud based speech recognition programs can be used to search for answers to questions.

The light sensor measures the ambient light level or illumination in lux. It can give information whether the mobile device is covered or worn in a pocket and when used outdoors of sun position and day or night time. The light sensor is able to adapt the mobile device parameters to the learning environment as it provides the ability to adjust the brightness of the mobile display to the environmental factors. A valuable information for learning is whether the device is covered which means a learning process should be put on hold if it does not solely rely on audio content.

The GPS sensor determines the current location of the mobile device with the help of satellite position information and is able to provide hints about the movement speed of the user and the altitude. Especially the location is an important context information which is especially true for learning purposes as it is one main factor that determines whether the environment is suitable for learning. The location is essential for learning recommendations based on objects or people nearby and a lot of additional information is attainable by combining the location information with content from the internet [12]. It shows whether the user is learning at home, in the library or at the university, where he has learned before. Another example would be whether or not he is moving in a car or public transport, where learning might be possible but only with specific content which has been adapted to a short travel time. With the positional information, situation based mobile learning approaches become feasible.

A clock is able to measure the learning time and to keep track of the learning history. The local time, especially in combination with a calendar, schedule or reminder is able to trigger learning events, request users to learn after intervals and arrange meetings with other learners. In assessments the time is usually a measurement for success. Sessions for learning and other activities can be defined and frequent situations of mobile spare time e. g. while travelling can be identified.

The temperature sensor measures the temperature of the device or the ambient environment. It indicates weather conditions and detects temperature changes, which are further indicators about indoor or outdoor learning situations. Moreover it is more difficult to learn in an unusually hot or cold environment which might be an indicator for adjustment of the learning content.

A proximity sensor measures the position of an object relative to the surface of a device. Usually the sensor is typically used to determine whether a handset is being held up to a person's ear [18] or, within a learning context, it can be used for gesture based control of the content or for an intuitive interaction with a virtual teacher.

2.2 Other Sensors

Other available sensors include the barometer which supports the GPS location service in cloudy weather conditions, the compass or magnetic field sensor, which is also mainly useful for navigation purposes, and the humidity sensor.

In addition to these commonly built in sensors additional wearable sensor systems are available which typically connect to the mobile device via Bluetooth. Especially the biophysiological values of a human body can be measured in this way, often a special watch or wristband is used to collect pulse data, body temperature and motion.

These can also be an indicator for the stress level or exhaustion which is useful in a learning context.

With Bluetooth it is possible to scan for other users in the area using a learning tool or to exchange data between users. Data sent from local objects can be received and some objects can be manipulated and controlled, which offers a wide variety of real world interaction suitable for learning.

Another channel, which has not been previously mentioned in detail is the multitouch screen, which allows for several ways of interaction usable for mobile learning, but is mainly seen as an input device and not as a mobile specific sensor.

Most of these sensors can also be plugged into a desktop computer, but when designing an e-learning environment these cannot be assumed in the same way it is possible for an average mobile device, which is a special characteristic and advantage of a mobile learning environment.

3   Combining Sensor Data to Identify Learning Situations

A combination of collected sensor data can be seen as typical for a special situation the user is experiencing [17]. By defining a range of conditions to match certain situations it is possible to categorize, save and later to recognize them. Some of these situations are more suitable for mobile learning purposes and some need an adaption of the content or the device parameters to maximize the learning support.

Examples are quiet and noisy surroundings, spaces where there is typically less time for learning than elsewhere and times and dates when a learning routine took place in the past and is likely to be repeated in the future. This information could be obtained by recording sensor parameters of such a situation [14]. The captured dimensions of the sensors need to be in a certain range to be classified as a known learning situation.

Based on a recognized learning situation a content proposal mechanism [13], interaction mechanisms or device parameter adjustments to support the learning process can be activated. Examples would be complex content in quiet situations without much distraction, like being in the library or at home, and short learning nuggets in busy situations, like travelling in a public transport.

4   A sensor Based Interaction Architecture

4.1   Technical Collection of Sensor Data

To make the sensor data usable for learning purposes, a service has to collect the data and provide ways for an e-learning application or learning management system to obtain this data. The service collects the data of the selected sensors continuously and, after a filtering process to reduce the complexity, streams it to the applications. A suitable transfer format for the multi-dimensional information is necessary to extract the relevant data and to convey it to the learning application.

4.2   Interaction Architecture

A suggested architecture to work with sensor data to support the interactions in mobile learning is described in the following paragraph. Using a client-server architecture multiple mobile devices can be supported by a server, which hosts the learning content, and a certain mapping logic for sensor data. This data is collected through a context service [8] which aggregates the raw data of all hardware sensors and then filters it to reduce the amount of data to relevant parts needed in the current context.

This data is sent to a server, where a decision making engine maps it to different categories and determines the degree of fulfillment of a certain action or decision. Based on this, a learning situation may be recognized and suitable learning objects can be chosen and sent back to the mobile device [comp. 9].

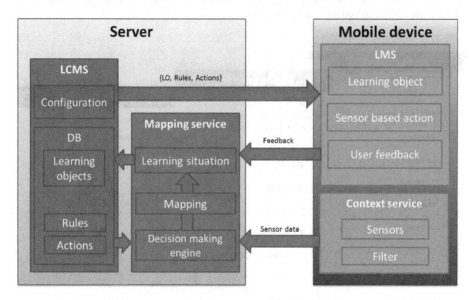

Fig. 1. Sensor based interaction architecture

The learning management system on the client's mobile device delivers the learning object sent by the server to the user. The learner benefits from learning content that is appropriate to the actual context he is currently in. In addition, an assisting mechanism to better support the mobile learning in the recognized situation can be started. An example would be the rise of the volume level or the adjustment of the device's brightness level.

To adjust the decision making process on the server, user feedback data is collected about whether the learning object and assisting mechanisms were appropriate for the learner.

5   Connecting Sensors and Learning Content

To connect the sensors with the learning environment a model which supports sensor data acquisition and the inclusion of the sensor data within the learning content is necessary. Furthermore, if the sensor information is supposed to trigger actions to support the mobile learning process, an event based interaction model specified for the learning content is required.

A set of rules determine the way the sensor is used and how it affects each learning content.

The following figure [Fig. 2] shows mobile learning content which is connected with sensor data. The sensors can be clipped to the learning objects and are indicated by icons. During the learning process the sensors are used to display information in the content or to change device parameters.

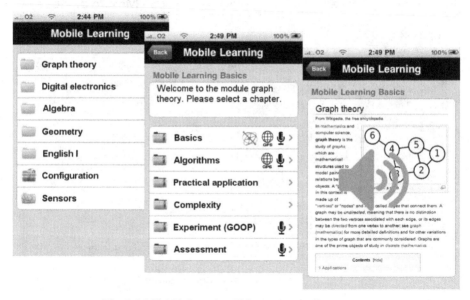

Fig. 2. LMS with Learning Objects connected to sensors

6   Towards a Mobile Pedagogical Agent

A natural form of tutoring and interaction in e-learning is the communication with or through a virtual pedagogical agent. In this context the collected sensor data can serve as a basis for a mobile pedagogical agent to allow a human-like form of interaction with the mobile device. The advantage of such a system would be to have a mobile learning system which is visualized by a face, following the theoretical implications of the persona effect [10]. The sensors would serve as senses and interaction channels for an agent. Furthermore, the sensory equipment could not only be used as a passive source of surrounding environmental information, but result in a pro-actively assessing agent-infrastructure [11]. By implementing aforementioned senses to the pedagogical agent, the transfer of knowledge would be greatly enhanced, since learning software usually does not observe the user's visual attention to the learning material nor does it check for disturbing noises in the learning environment. By opening up these additional channels of non-verbal communication, any e-learning software would be able to adjust its material presentation and enables it to react pro- and retroactively to disruptive occurences.

7   Conclusion

This paper discussed the different sensors available in mobile devices with the focus on enhancing the mobile learning experience. Several techniques to use sensory information for mobile learning purposes were presented and scenarios for practical application, methods for implementation and evaluation are suggested. Using a sensor based interaction architecture, matching rules and the concept of defining specific learning situations from data aquired by sensors is a feasible way to utilize this context information in learning content.

Following this evolution an efficient use of sensor data leads to more natural ways of human computer interaction and thus can be used to further enrich e-learning scenarios and support mobile aspects of learning.

References

1. Franklin, T.: Mobile Learning: At The Tipping Point. The Turkish Online Journal of Educational Technology 10(4) (2011)
2. Roschelle, J.: Keynote paper: Unlocking the learning value of wireless mobile devices. Journal of Computer Assisted Learning 19(3), 260–272 (2003)
3. Rensing, C.: Szenarien und Erfahrungen mobilen situierten Lernens an Hochschulen. DeLFI (2012)
4. Sharples, M., Taylor, J., Vavoula, G.: Towards a theory of mobile learning. In: Proceedings of mLearn 2005, vol. 1(1), pp. 1–9 (2005)
5. Gellersen, H.W., Schmidt, A., Beigl, M.: Multi-sensor context-awareness in mobile devices and smart artifacts. Mobile Networks and Applications 7(5), 341–351 (2002)
6. Taylor, J.: A theory of learning for the mobile age. In: Medienbildung in Neuen Kulturräumen, pp. 87–99. VS Verlag für Sozialwissenschaften (2010)
7. Sarker, S., Wells, J.D.: Understanding mobile handheld device use and adoption. Communications of the ACM 46(12), 35–40 (2003)
8. Chia, Y., et al.: Context-aware mobile learning with a semantic service-oriented infrastructure. In: 2011 IEEE Workshops of International Conference on Advanced Information Networking and Applications (WAINA), pp. S.896–S.901. IEEE (2011)
9. da Silva, L.C.N., Neto, F.M.M., Júnior, L.J., de Carvalho Muniz, R.: Recommendation of Learning Objects in an Ubiquitous Learning Environment through an Agent-Based Approach. In: Putnik, G.D., Cruz-Cunha, M.M. (eds.) ViNOrg 2011. CCIS, vol. 248, pp. 101–110. Springer, Heidelberg (2012)

10. Lester, J.C., Converse, S.A., Kahler, S.E., Barlow, S.T., Stone, B.A., Bhogal, R.S.: The persona effect: affective impact of animated pedagogical agents. In: Pemberton, S. (ed.) Human Factors in Computing Systems: CHI 1997 Conference Proceedings, pp. 359–366. ACM Press, New York (1997)
11. Wuttke, M.: Pro-Active Pedagogical Agents. In: Fakultät für Informatik (ed.) Proceedings of International Summer Workshop Computer Science, pp. 59–62 (July 2013)
12. Wang, S.-L., Wu, C.-Y.: Application of context-aware and personalized recommendation to implement an adaptive ubiquitous learning system. Expert Systems with Applications 38(9), S.10831–S.10838 (2011)
13. Hong, J., et al.: Context-aware system for proactive personalized service based on context history. Expert Systems with Applications 36(4), S.7448–S.7457 (2009)
14. Martin, K.-U.: Delivering complex learning content on mobile devices. In: World Conference on E-Learning in Corporate, Government, Healthcare, and Higher Education, pp. S.161–S.166 (2013)
15. Ally, M. (Hg.): Mobile learning: Transforming the delivery of education and training. Athabasca University Press (2009)
16. Eckardt, D., Hettich, G., Schmid, H.-D.: Sensor for measuring physical dimensions and process for balancing the sensor. U.S. Patent Nr. 4,845,649 (1989)
17. Martin, K.-U., Hardt, W.: Adaptive agent supported mobile learning. In: International Summer Workshop Computer Science 2013, vol. 17, p. S.28 (2013)
18. Hinckley, K., et al.: Sensing techniques for mobile interaction. In: Proceedings of the 13th Annual ACM Symposium on User Interface Software and Technology, pp. S.91–S.100. ACM (2000)

Visual and Spatial Data Integration
in Mobile Application Design

Patricia Morreale, Allan Goncalves, Daniel Church, Steve Holtz,
Joshua Lisojo, Nathaly Lozano, Carlos Silva, and Jason Bonafide

Department of Computer Science, Kean University
1000 Morris Avenue, Union, NJ 07083
{pmorreal,goncalal,churchda,holtzs,jlisojo,
lozanon,salvadca,bonafija}@kean.edu

Abstract. Mobile application design is a strong motivator for student-centered
computing. By including visual and spatial data in a mobile application, students can develop a 3-D implementation which can provide the mobile app users with a virtual experience. The development of a mobile app for a historical
burial ground provides an example of how to integrate database information
with visual and spatial data to achieve s virtual experience. The case study
presented here, using both Android and iOS devices, includes three parts. Initially, an existing database was converted for mobile application access. This
was followed by design integration in support of the desired mobile app features. Finally, the inclusion of an image gallery, with visual and spatial elements, integrated with the mobile application, resulted in a compelling mobile
application, providing a virtual replica of an actual visit to the historical site.

Keywords: Mobile application development, Android, iOS, visual data, spatial
data.

1   Introduction

As part of a student-centered design project, a mobile application ('app') for a historical burial ground was developed by a team of undergraduate computer science students. The mobile app includes a database of deceased people interred in the burial
ground of the First Presbyterian Church (FPC) of Elizabeth, New Jersey, which is
integrated with visual and spatial data to create a virtual experience emulating a physical visit to this historical burial ground.

The idea for the mobile application was initially motivated by the Reverend Higgs,
the religious leader in charge of the FPC. The church is home to a historical cemetery
that contains many local people as well as several well-known individuals who were
important in the history of New Jersey, one of fifty states in the United States. The
cemetery at the church is very old and includes gravestones dating back to the 1700s.
The land itself was used to establish The College of New Jersey, which later became
Princeton University [1]. Buried in this land are important characters from American
history such as James Caldwell and several hundred members who served in the

P. Zaphiris and A. Ioannou (Eds.): LCT 2014, Part II, LNCS 8524, pp. 173–181, 2014.

American Revolution, as well as slaves and commoners. The church and graveyard receive many visitors every year who are interested in the history of the church and the lives of those whom are buried there.

Reverend Higgs, an enthusiastic advocate of technology, requested a mobile application that would begin by introducing the church with a small description. The primary reason for the app comes from the cemetery itself. The mobile application was envisioned as having a search function that would allow anyone with the app to be able to search the cemetery using any search criteria they desired, for example: name, age, or date of birth. The application would provide information on all the deceased in the cemetery who matched the search criteria. Anyone using the app could then select a person and the app provides all the information on that person's gravestone including where in the cemetery the burial plot and headstone can be found. The gravestone information within the application is useful because of the physical age of many of the gravestones has results in some headstone inscriptions no longer being legible.

In addition to the search function, the app provides a map of the graveyard which can be zoomed in and out using pinch gestures, as well as a section with more information about the cemetery, including contact information and a photo gallery. This paper describes the steps to organize, design and develop this app.

2   Organizing Development Groups

The development project was managed and executed by students. The team encompassed a range of programmer expertise. A common method for developing applications is to break up the work that is required among the team of developers, with a team leader [2]. The first task of the team leader was to bring all the developers up to the same level. While all members of the team had prior Java programming experience, there wasn't anyone experienced with the Google Android or Apple iOS APIs.

Fig. 1. Platforms Selected for Development

The Android development environment was provided by the Eclipse Integrated Development Environment (IDE), which was then linked to the Android Software Development Kit (SDK) with an Eclipse plug-in. The Apple iOS development was carried out in the Xcode 4 IDE environment using the Objective-C programming language. In both development environments, the work was divided evenly based on the skills and personal preferences of each team member.

The iOS team had to learn Objective-C and the Xcode IDE, which they did by watching the Stanford iOS video lectures on iTunesU [3] and reading books on iOS development [4]. The team leader created a schedule for watching the video lectures so that everyone in the group would be on the same level. The video lectures also included challenges that the viewer should try to solve with hands-on coding. After a few video lectures, the students were familiarized with the IDE and ready to start the development of the app.

The Android team used a similar approach by reading a book on Android development [5]. The team leader created a schedule for reading the book chapters in order to keep everyone at the same level. The book provided practice applications to provide a hands-on learning experience. After reading the first eight chapters, the team was ready to begin the implementation of the app.

Learning new libraries and a new programming language takes time. For that reason, the project would take more than one semester to be completed, so the milestones were set within a two semester time frame. Each member of the group would be responsible for keeping a blog with progress information. This helped the students maintain focus. Also, it was useful for documenting the project.

Additionally, milestones were used to make sure everyone worked towards the same goal. The initial goal was to have a "skeleton" of the application - the base layout with all of the functionality required to navigate the app, but without content - running on the iOS simulator within a month. For the second milestone, the skeleton would be filled with content and include a functioning map that scrolls and zooms in and out. The third milestone was to implement the search functionality retrieving data from the database. Finally, the fourth milestone was to submit the application to the Apple store, a goal which was expected by the end of the first semester.

3   Designing the App

With a student-centered approach, the team began with a site visit. By physically visiting the site, the students learned the actual physical layout of the burial ground as it existed in the community, and began thinking about how they could replicate this experience for users of the mobile app. During the site visit, photographs were taken, and notes were made regarding engravings on the tombstones.

After brainstorming ideas and sketching the app, the application design that emerged included four primary functions: a home screen, a search page, a map of the cemetery and more information page. To access each of these activities a tab bar was required at the bottom of the application. An initial splash screen was also implemented to provide a perceived short loading time for the app as well a small amount of information about the church while the database is loaded in the background. The home page design selected was a simple image slide show of the cemetery accompanied by a quote from one of epitaphs in the tombstones. The slideshow provided the first visual image of the graveyard and served to familiarize the user with the environment in the cemetery.

Applications can be categorized in two groups: web-based and native client [6]. Initially, the team considered developing a web-based app using HTML5. Facebook and Verizon are examples of apps that chose to use HTML5. In this case, it is easier to update the content server-side and all users will see the changes instantly. However, these apps perform poorly compared to native apps. Users also tend to respond negatively to this format [7]. Generally, native code will run better and the perceived value of the product will be higher, which is why the team chose to develop native iOS and Android apps. If they were to create an HTML5 portal, it would not packaged as an app; instead it would be using a universal URL [8].

4   Development Phases

The mobile application development identified included three parts. First, an existing database had to be converted and organized to support the mobile application access. This was required to pull the database information into the phone effectively and give the user access to it.

Fig. 2. iOS and Android home screen with tab bar navigation

Secondly, the iOS team had to start development ahead of the Android team because the client requested priority for the iOS app. A tab-bar application was developed with four main tabs (Fig. 2). These included the "home", "search", "map" and "more" tabs. The home tab is the entrance to the app and the search tab is what connects the user to those interred in the burial ground. The next tab was "map" (Fig. 3), which displays a map of the entire burial ground in which the user can use pinch gestures to zoom in and out of areas.

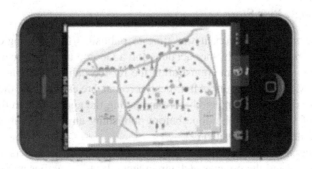

Fig. 3. The map

The "more" tab is a sub-menu that links to three different options: the first option is "plan your visit". The second option is an image gallery (Fig. 4), and the third is "contact", which provides the user with contact information. The inclusion of an image gallery, with actual photos from the historical burial ground, adds visual data [9, 10]. The spatial data is provided by the map of the entire area. The inclusion of visual and spatial design elements with database integration make a compelling mobile application, providing a close replica of the experience one would get by actually visiting the historical site.

Fig. 4. The image gallery

Third, the Android team had to use the iOS app design as a reference to make the app work the same way in both iOS and Android devices (Fig. 2). This presented a set of difficulties because of the differences in developing for the two platforms. It was useful to read other developers perspective on developing for both platforms [11].

5   Mobile Application Deployment

5.1   The Google Play Store

After developing an application, it was time to publish it to the Google Play store. Before that can be done, a publisher account and a Google merchant account must be created. There is a $25 one-time registration fee for the publisher account and no fee for the Google Merchant account. After these accounts are established, there were still a few important details to complete before uploading the application to the market. A full checklist of what should be done before publishing an application can be found on the Android developer website [12].

The first several points on the checklist are there to ensure an understanding of the publishing process and the policies and agreements. It also specifies an understanding of the billing process and pricing of the application. The next section of the checklist involves checking the application itself for certain criteria. At the time, the Google Play store did not allow applications bigger than 50MB.

Another important quality of an app for Android devices is that the application itself must be ready for the various devices and screen sizes. An app could look quite different on a larger screen than on a smaller one. This was an error that the Android team encountered during this mobile application development; images being displayed were not filling the screen on larger phones as they were on smaller phones.

Before an app can be published, it must be signed and given its own private key to use for future updates. Eclipse makes the signing process of an 'apk' simple. Private keys must be valid until the date specified by the Android market. Properly signing and compiling the 'apk' can be done by using the Export action in Eclipse. Export gives the option to create a new key for new applications or using an existing one for updating older applications. Once exported, signed, and compiled, the app is ready for the app store. After the app is sent to the store, the final item on the checklist is to support users after launch.

5.2   The Apple App Store

Publishing an app on Apple's app store requires an Apple developer account, which one can register for free at the Apple Dev Center website. However, Apple also requires developers to join the iOS Developer Program, which costs $99.00 per year for individual accounts. There is a good tutorial on how to create the developer account [13].

Apple requires every app run by iOS to have a signed Apple Certificate, which is done by creating a profile in the iOS Provisioning Portal and using Xcode to sign the app. There are two types of profiles: the *developer profile* allows the developer to test the app on his own device, but the app cannot be distributed, while the *distribution profile* is used to sign the app before publishing it to the app store.

The app must then be submitted to the iTunes Connect portal, where all of the app store configurations should be filled in. This includes the app name, description, icon, price and screen shots. After submission, a few weeks may be needed for Apple to review the app for approval.

6   User Experience

The "FPC Cemetery" app intends to create a near 3-D virtual experience of physically visiting the historical burial grounds. It does so by providing visual and spatial data in the form of a map of the graveyard, as well as images of the individual tombstones and an image gallery of the cemetery. However, the app actually offers more than the experience of a typical visit to the burial grounds. It offers the ability to search (Fig. 5) the database by name or using other queries, such as age at death and whether or not the interred was a veteran.

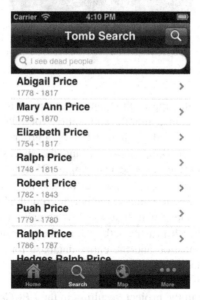

Fig. 5. The search tab

Furthermore, the search feature is integrated with the map, so each record in the search has a detailed section (Fig. 6) including personal information of the deceased, an image of the tombstone, the epitaph—which is no longer legible in some of the tombs, cause of death, and location of the tombstone in the map. The app is capable of creating a memorable user experience for the curious person who does not plan to physically visit the site. The mobile app is also a great tool to guide those who decide to visit the cemetery in person, as detailed information and the complete cemetery map (Fig. 3) are available as the actual physical environment is navigated.

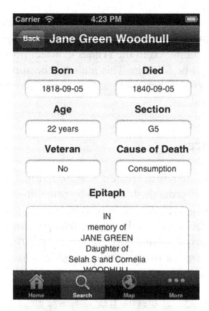

Fig. 6. Tombstone details

7   Conclusion

This paper has described the approach taken by a team of undergraduate students to organize, design and develop a mobile application for iOS and Android handheld devices. It has explained in detail the steps taken by a group with no prior knowledge for the development of a working prototype and the successful deployment of the FPCCemetery app in both the Andriod and Apple iOS marketplaces. The design of the mobile app interface was a collaborative effort and the resulting product provides a user experience comparable to being in the burial ground. However, the information available from the app is superior to that which is actually available during a visit to the First Presbyterian Church in Elizabeth, NJ, as the tombstone data is clearly presented in the mobile application and the entire database for the site is searchable by query. Clear, detailed information provided by the app is superior to information available to visitors to the physical FPC site.

The students involved in the project, resulting in the *FPCCemetery* app available in both the Apple and Android stores, are proud of their accomplishment. Starting very little knowledge of mobile application design, by consensus the team developed an outstanding mobile application, operable on two platforms, which provides a virtual 3-D rendering of a visit to a historical burial ground. This experience is now available to visitors who live far from the area, who are interested in seeing where their ancestors or predecessors are interred, as well as historians who want to investigate death patterns related to age at death and year of death.

References

1. Scharff, C., Verma, R.: Scrum to Support Mobile Application Development Projects in a Just-in-time Learning Context. In: Proceedings of the 2010 ACM ICSE Workshop on Cooperative and Human Aspects of Software Engineering (CHASE 2010), pp. 25–31 (2010)
2. The First Presbyterian Church of Elizabeth, NJ (2012), http://fpcenj.org/FPCENJ/History.html (accessed: September 14, 2012)
3. Stanford iOS Development Video Lectures (2012), https://itunes.apple.com/us/itunes-u/developing-apps-for-ios-sd/id395631522&sa=D&sntz=1&usg=AFrqEze3iy_maj-hijdGbv9MaBjUttYdhg (accessed: September 12, 2012)
4. Neuburg, M.: Programming iOS 5, 2nd edn. O'Reilly (2012)
5. Darcey, L., Conder, S.: Sams Teach Yourself Android Application Development in 24 Hours, Sams (2010)
6. Mobile Application Development Best Practices. AT&T (2012), https://developer.att.com/home/develop/referencesandtutorials/whitepapers/Best_Practices_Mobile_Application_Development.pdf (accessed: November 26, 2012)
7. Constine, J.: Facebook Speeds Up Android App By Ditching HTML5 and Rebuilding It Natively Just Like the IOS Version. TechCrunch (2012), http://techcrunch.com/2012/12/13/facebook-android-faster/ (accessed: September 17, 2012)
8. Packaged HTML5 Apps: Are We Emulating Failure? Groovecoder (2013), http://groovecoder.com/2013/01/07/packaged-html5-apps-are-we-emulating-failure/ (accessed: February 20, 2013)
9. Shirazi, A., Bahzadan, A.: Technology-Enhanced Learning in Construction Education Using Mobile Context-Aware Augmented Reality Visual Simulation. In: Proceedings of the IEEE 2013 Winter Simulation Conference (WSC), pp. 3074–3085 (2013)
10. Medicherla, P., Chang, G., Morreale, P.: Visualization for Increased Understanding and Learning using Augmented Reality. In: Proceedings of the 11th ACM SIGMM International Conference on Multimedia Information Retrieval (MIR 2010), pp. 441–444 (2010)
11. Coover, B.: Building the same app for iOS and Android. Coovtech (2012), http://coovtech.com/posts/nearby-now-for-ios-android/ (accessed: April 12, 2013)
12. Publishing Checklist for Google Play (2012), http://developer.android.com/distribute/googleplay/publish/preparing.html (accessed: March 11, 2013)
13. Ambrozio, G.: How to Submit Your App to Apple: From No Account to App Store, Part 1. Raywenderlich (2012), http://www.raywenderlich.com/8003/how-to-submit-your-app-to-apple-from-noaccount-to-app-store-part-1 (accessed: February 20, 2013)

Exploring Simulated Provocations

Supporting Pre-Service Teachers' Reflection on Classroom Management

Mathias Nordvall[1], Mattias Arvola[1], and Marcus Samuelsson[2]

[1] Linköping University, Department of Computer and Information Science, Linköping, Sweden
{mathias.nordvall,mattias.arvola}@liu.se
[2] Linköping University, Department of Behavioural Sciences and Learning, Linköping, Sweden
marcus.samuelsson@liu.se

Abstract. The purpose of our research project is to explore the design of game-like simulations that allow pre-service teachers to explore and experiment with problematic classroom situations to develop proficiency in classroom management. The research problem for this paper is how to design a plausible, valuable to learn, and interesting game-like simulation that also is usable and opens up for reflection on and understanding of the scenarios in the simulation. We used 'research through design' and combined interaction design and game design to develop the SimProv simulation. 21 pre-service teachers were invited to evaluate it in a play session with constructive interaction and questionnaires. Sim-Prov consists of text-based scenarios where pre-service teachers can take actions corresponding to classic leadership styles. The results show that it provides a plausible, valuable, exploratory, playful, but not always interesting experience for pre-service teachers. The participants did engage in reflective discussions about the choices they made.

Keywords: Serious Games and 3D virtual worlds for learning, Technology enhanced learning, Design, Simulation, Classroom management.

1 Introduction

There is a lack of authentic learning opportunities for pre-service teachers where they can experience the provocations and conflicts that will be a part of their future professional life. Provoking such situations for practice purposes with actual students would be ethically problematic, and not allow for adequate reflection during the situation.

Lectures, seminars and books do not prepare pre-service teachers enough for the reality they are about to face when they start working. The forthcoming reality-chock, that as many as one out of five realize, gives them no other choice then leaving the profession within then first three years of service. One major reason is a lack of tools for managing students troublesome behavior and managing critical situations that may occur in the classroom. Their response to classroom conflicts might therefore be punishment even though it is not effective, which they actually have learned in their teacher education [1-3].

P. Zaphiris and A. Ioannou (Eds.): LCT 2014, Part II, LNCS 8524, pp. 182–193, 2014.
© Springer International Publishing Switzerland 2014

The purpose of our research project is to complement existing approaches to learning classroom management. We aim to explore the design of game-like simulations that allow pre-service teachers to explore and experiment with problematic classroom situations to develop a self-reflective understanding of such situations. An understanding like that is critical for developing proficiency in classroom management.

2   Theory

A benefit of computer-based simulations is the possibility to support learning by creating variation in situations that would otherwise be difficult to vary in a natural context [4]. A premise of our simulation is to allow pre-service teachers to experiment with different actions in order to explore the variation and learn to discern the aspects of the classroom situation that are critical to manage it. What we will vary are the events in the classrooms and the feedback that pre-service teachers get on their choice of strategy.

Edman Stålbrandt [5] has conducted a significant study of simulations for learning classroom management and supporting reflection on such issues. Her simulations were linear animations with sound, text and images. After engaging with the simulation her participants took part of a seminar, scaffolded by questions for discussion and reflection. Her results indicate that the sound in the simulation carries emotional content while the text carries the facts. The role of the graphics was less obvious in her results. She also observes that a scenario has to have enough complexity, and be a genuine dilemma in order to work. She furthermore concluded that theoretical reflection was difficult, even though she provided questions for discussion as scaffolding to support reflection. This points toward a need for a mentor or a teacher that can facilitate the theoretical reflection. Edman Stålbrandt also notes that a simulation needs to be embedded in a didactic structure with clear connections to relevant learning objectives. We follow Edman Stålbrandt's results, by situating our simulation in a course structure, and paying attention to what happens before the play session and afterwards. We also expand on her work by developing an interactive game-like simulation where users can make choices and observe outcomes of them.

3   Research Problem

The research problem focused on in this paper is how to design a plausible, valuable to learn and interesting game-like simulation that also is usable and opens up for reflection on and understanding of the scenarios in the simulation.

4   Method

The project spans two parts: the design work and the evaluation of the resulting proposal. Methods for these both parts are covered below.

4.1   Design Method

The classroom simulation was developed in a process that combined interaction and game design practice in a 'research through design' process [6]. Theories, methods as well as empirical evidence from research on education have informed the interaction design and game design through a co-design approach. Fundamental design issues have been explored in a series of workshops with five participants with knowledge in teachers' education, classroom management, interactive learning environments, cognitive science, interaction design and game design. The scenarios that form the basis for the design have been developed in tight cooperation between a game design researcher, and a classroom researcher (also is a teacher and teacher educator) whom has conducted extensive field studies in Swedish classrooms. The field studies form the foundation for the scenarios in the simulation. Design artifacts produced during the process have included written scenarios, sketches, and examples of similar systems, as well as demos of possible future directions (e.g. head mounted virtual reality).

4.2   Evaluation Method

21 pre-service teachers participated in the evaluation of the simulation. 15 of them were studying to get the license as vocational teachers, and 6 of them studied to become special educational needs teachers. The vocational teachers already had experience from serving as teachers, and took part of a study program that would complement their earlier education and earn them a teacher's license. The participants collaborated in pairs or triads during the play session, which took between 1 and 2 hours depending on the discussions. Videos were recorded of the pre-service vocational teachers play sessions if they agreed to that. In-game actions and conversation in five pairs and one triad were recorded. The pre-service teachers were also invited to watch a replay of the session.

The study was conducted in collaboration with a course on social relations, leadership, conflict management and professional ethics. The play session itself was a mandatory exercise in the course, but participation in the study was voluntary.

The participants were welcomed and informed about the structure and goal of the exercise before sitting down in pairs or triads to play the game-like simulation. They played in front of a computer and explored the story together. It was necessary for them to discuss the events in the simulation and decide mutually which actions they wanted to take. This set up facilitated a constructive interaction where they shared ideas and experiences about appropriate leadership in the classroom. Between each scenario event, the participants were asked to answer three questions concerning the authenticity of the events: do you believe the event can happen in school (is plausable); do you believe the event would be valuable to be able to handle; and do you believe the event is described in an interesting manner?

After they had played through the entire scenario they were asked to individually fill out a Post-Study System Usability Questionnaire (PSSUQ, version 3) [7-8]. The three questions for each event provide an assessment of the content, while the PSSUQ is concerned with the overall usability of the simulation. Questions 7, 8, and 9 in the Information Quality category of PSSUQ were in the end excluded because 16, 5, and 9 users respectively thought the questions were not applicable to the current system. It is in PSSUQ not uncommon that the Information Quality questions are judged more harshly than the other questions and items can to a limited extent be removed if they are not applicable to the system [8].

In-game actions and conversation in five pairs and one triad of pre-service vocational teachers were video recorded. The transcribed recordings made it possible to study their constructive interaction (CI) and how they understood and reflected around the scenarios in our simulation. This is a method that Miyake [9] describes as useful to understand iterative processes of understanding.

5   Results

There are two kinds of results from our study: the resulting proposal from the design process, and the results of the evaluation of our proposed design.

5.1   Design Results

The aim of the game-like simulation, SimProv, is for pre-service teachers to learn classroom management through play and reflective discussions of experiences with their peers. The simulation consists of text-based scenarios made up of a series of events were the pre-service teachers can take actions corresponding to classic leadership styles. The scenarios depict variations of problematic situations that occur in classrooms. It is possible to redo previously made choices in order to encourage exploration of alternative approaches.

Using text as a medium for communication has a long tradition in computer game development and the first truly social Internet games where people could meet in groups and talk to each other were entirely text-based. This tradition stretches back to the 70's when the first Multi-User Dungeon (MUD) was made [10-11].

Pre-service teachers in Sweden are according to [12] less knowledgeable and have a less positive to technology than the general population in their own age range. Text was therefore seen as a suitable medium to use as it can be easily displayed in a web browser. This is beneficial from a social accessibility perspective, since most people in Sweden today use the web on a daily basis, even if they do not necessarily play computer games. Using text allows the SimProv simulation to be distributed easily to people that wants to use it without requiring large downloads or installations. From a development perspective it requires less time commitment to write text scenarios than developing full-scale 3D computer game scenarios. This allows scenarios to be built and tested without requiring a large time investments by the development team.

Text scenarios do, however, come with drawbacks. Text does not necessarily capture the constant changes that happen dynamically in a classroom as a result of the interaction between students and teachers. The text is also unable to provide visual cues that more closely correspond to the behavior that can be observed directly in the classroom. The reader is instead both invited, and required, to imagine how the textual descriptions would play out in reality.

The multi-modal communicative aspects of student behavior are currently not known, so building computer-based animated avatars could lead multi-modal cues in the scenarios that are not naturally present in a physical classroom. Identifying such multi-modal cues in classrooms is a current on-going work. It is therefor, for the time being, more appropriate to invite players to instead imagine those aspects based on their experiences from the classroom.

Fig. 1. Screenshot from the first hypertext version of SimProv

The current version of SimProv is accordingly a hypertext scenario and event-focused text-based simulation of conflict and disturbances that occur in classroom environments. Figure 1 is a screenshot from the first hypertext version of SimProv.

It currently contains two scenarios; the first scenario consists of six interlinked events that take place in the morning at the start of a class, and the second scenario consists of seven events that take place during a lesson when the class is just about to change from one task to another. Each event is presented with an introduction text that describes what is currently happening in the classroom together with four different choices that the pre-service teachers can choose between. These four choices correspond to the classical manager styles authoritative, authoritarian, democratic, and laissez-faire styles [13]. When one of these are selected the pre-service teachers are taken to a new screen that shows the progression of the event together with 1-4 new choices that are variations of the previously selected teaching style. After a choice is selected the pre-service teachers playing the simulation are taken to the resolution of that particular event, and they can continue in the scenario with the event that follows.

The idea behind the simulation is that it is explored rather than played and it is therefore possible to not only move forward through the events, but also step back and redo earlier choices to explore alternative ways of resolving the events.

The scenarios are not intended to be normative, so there are no scores for the different choices. The classroom is seen an environment that is complex and dynamic. It has a unique context depending on the participants and their histories, and situations can unfold and change rapidly. It was therefore more natural to make descriptive scenarios as authentic as possible so pre-service teachers can make choices that feels suitable for them, reflect on those choices, and use them as discussion points when talking about leadership with other pre-service teachers.

5.2   Evaluation Results

The evaluation of our proposed design has two quantitative parts with questionnaires, and one qualitative component where we have analyzed the constructive interaction in play sessions with the pairs and triads of pre-service teachers. The three parts are described below.

Is the Event Authentic? Figure 2, shows the results of the three questions asked after each event regarding its authenticity: Do you believe the event can happen in school (Exists); do you believe the event would be valuable to be able to handle (Valuable); and do you believe the event is described in an interesting manner (Interesting)? .

The participants rated that they believed that the described events could happen in school, with the exception of event 5, and to a lesser extent event 4. Event 5 unfortunately contained a bug that linked about half of the participants directly to event 6, which caused a lot of participants to give blank answers. Most participants believed it would be valuable to be able to handle the situations described in the events well. Participants that did not agree had different and varied reasons for objecting. For example that they believed they could handle it already, or that there were worse situations to worry about. The last question asked was whether they thought that the events were written in an interesting way, and the responses here were more critical with at least 20 percent of the participants answering no to this question for every event. The overall impression is that the participants see the scenario events as authentic, but that the storytelling needs improvements to make the events more interesting.

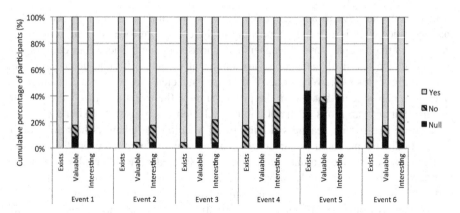

Fig. 2. All participants' self-reported perception of the authenticity of the events

Is it Usable? The PSSUQ results on the dimensions of System Quality, Information Quality, Interface Quality, and Overall Quality are presented in Figure 3. Mean values from Lewis' database [7] of other systems evaluated with the PSSUQ are included for the readers' benefit as a general indication of the level of usability of the current design.

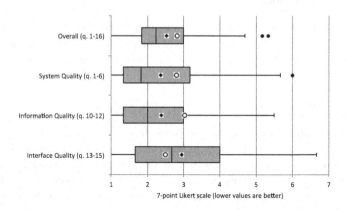

Fig. 3. All participant's responses to the Post-Study Usability Questionnaire

The median line in the box plots separate the 2nd and 3rd quartiles while the black diamonds show the mean values. The mean values from Lewis' database are shown with the white circles. Each of the 16 items on the questionnaire is answered on a 7 point Likert-scale. A value of 1 means that the participant agrees strongly with the statement, and a value of 7 means that he or she strongly disagrees. Lower values are better than higher values. The particular questions that make up a category are given in the parenthesis.

The Overall Quality median for all items was 2.23. The System Quality median was 1.83. The Information Quality median value was 2.00. The Interface Quality category median value was 2.67. The mean values from Lewis' database was for the Overall Quality 2.82 compared to our system's 2.53, System Quality was 2.80 compared to our system's 2.37, Information Quality was 3.02 compared to our system's 2.38, Interface Quality was 2.49 compared to our system's 2.95. SimProv scores accordingly as good or better than the average system on all dimensions with the exception of Interface Quality.

Does it Open Up for Reflection and Understanding? The Constructive Interaction of the pre-service vocational teachers showed that the simulation worked well in stimulating reflective discussions on how to understand the classroom situations, on options, and on reactions from the pre-service teachers. The example below shows a couple of pre-service vocational teachers discussing how to start a lesson, where two students, Philip and Oliver, is missing:

Excerpt 1.

712	1: I don't know what do you think?
742	2: I don't know anyone?
746	1: which one suite the best, no
753	2: Hmm
808	2: Could be
823	2: Perhaps this is the best one (points at option number 3)
824	1: Yes, I think so to, because one those after all reflect about, I am pretty sure, or
832	2: But, the fact is that it is Tuesday morning, where they out of school during the Monday and no on Tuesday?
837	1: Hmm
838	2: Or is it every Tuesday?
840	1: Hmm
844	2: It, but eh, but I do not know, I perhaps mostly get stuck on the fact that
858	1: It depends on how one interprets it
901	2: Yes, but eh, but even so probably would, I think I would choose that one (points at the screen)
918	2: Because just being silent, accordingly
920	2: I never ever just sit and wait

The excerpt above, two minutes out of a session that lasted 53.16 minutes, shows how two vocational teachers move between understanding and non-understanding. The excerpt starts with an interaction where they try to find out how the other one understands the scenario. In this part both of them express their non-understanding. That shifts in line 823 where one of them expresses how he thinks, based on his reflection on the scenario. In the following lines the pair of them jointly articulate their shared understanding. This can be described as *identification*. This goes on to line 844 where one of them raises a question, based on his non-understanding. The other one states then that it depends on how one interprets it. This can be described as *objection*.

Then in line 901 there is a new shift, towards understanding, where one of them express how he would choose. The other one follows up the argument by saying that sitting quiet is not an option. This could be described as a *suggestion*.

During the sessions some of the participants discussed the choices and what they actually would do in a situation as the one described. The following excerpt shows such a discussion with a pair of vocational teachers. They are discussing a situation where a student during the teacher's instructions for lesson raises his hand and asks if they cannot do something fun during the lesson.

Excerpt 2.

1145	2: What shall, I just point at an option that I think we could do and then we can have a discussion (points at an option on the screen)
1212	1: Yes
1215	1: Yes, it depends, sure I can change my behavior depending on the students way to behave, depending on the students situation, but if I mean that it is important to clear this thing out, then it would be, then this would be the right thing to do (point as one option)
1225	2: I would be irritated at the him; asking what we should do even before I had had a chance to explain that
1230	1: Hmm
1231	2: Yeah, then I should be irritated on him
1235	1: Yes... hell, the you must be irritated every day
1238	2: Yes I am (laughs)
1239	1: Because I get such a, every day I actually get such, if I have 20 student then 19 of them would as such a thing
1247	2: Okay, yes, no, but, hey, one can be irritate in different ways
1252	1: Yes
1253	2: One can be irritated without being aggressive so to say
1255	1: Yes of course, eh, ok (points at the first opinion on the screen)
1303	2: Or that one (points at the second option) when get astonished about such as question (laughs)
1310	1: Yes, yes, one can actually chose that option, but if one has written, in this situation we actually had written the content and mode on the white board, then why should they ask
1322	2: Hmm
1325	1: Then one becomes a little bit like that (points once again at the second option on the screen) I would have done hat, I think
1330	2: Hmm
1332	1: To react
1334	2: You don't react, you just continue
1337	1: Yes, eh
1338	2: Okay, yeah that's right
1340	1: Eh, I would stand beside my list, and if they, if they have such a question I would point at the list, in principle
1346	2: Me to, but I would be irritated when I stand by that point (laughs)

1351	1: Okay, (laughs), yeah but, yes but we perhaps can add that (points at option two)
1404	1: Let me know if you disagree, no, no (points at option three)
1411	3: It's okay
1424	1: If I didn't react then I wouldn't loose my track
1425	2: No
1433	2: I like that idea about a stop sign
1434	1: Yes
1441	1: Yes, but I won't choose anyone of these options
1442	2: No
1446	1: But eh, it of course depends on the situation and in what way the students ask their question
1452	2: Hmm
1457	1: Shall we move backwards and try another one.

This excerpt with three pre-service vocational teachers shows three aspects (a) how pre-service teachers moved back and forward between options in the scenario, (b) how they actually would do in such a situation, and (c) a degree of playfulness. The excerpt describes parts of a discussion about different ways to handle the first 5-7 minutes of a lesson. The excerpt also shows different strategies for the pre-service teachers. In this excerpt two of the participants shared and argued about ideas while the third one mostly listens.

This excerpt shows how some of the pre-service teachers experimented, moving back and forward between the options in the scenario events. The three pre-service teachers tried all four options, before choosing which one they actual would pick. While figuring that out, they read and discussed the consequences that followed on each of the four options. These, more or less, authentic reactions forced them to describe, argue and put forward their thoughts on the scenario and on proper ways to act as manager of the classroom.

The excerpt also contains information about how pre-service teachers choose between options in the scenario and what they think they actually would do in such a situation in real life. The discussion in the excerpt shows different standpoints about provocations and what a provocative behavior could be. In line 1235 where one of the vocational teachers questions the others' idea about being irritated and the consequences that would follow of being an irritated teacher. With questions like that this triad also discussed ways of conduct as a manager of a classroom.

Finally, the excerpt also contains a degree of playfulness. In line 1346 one of the pre-service teachers argues for a way of managing the situation. The other pre-service teachers find that argument reasonable in one way, but they would like to add the right to be irritated. This argument, or way to behave, was actually presented by that pre-service teacher. This represents another level of social playfulness, where participants challenged each other's approaches to managing the classroom situation.

6   Discussion

The purpose of our research project is to explore the design of game-like simulations that allow pre-service teachers to explore and experiment with problematic classroom situations to develop proficiency in classroom management. The research problem focused on in this paper is how to design a plausible, valuable to learn, and interesting game-like simulation that also is usable and opens up for reflection on and understanding of the scenarios in the simulation.

We designed SimProv with the aim of supporting pre-service teachers' learning of classroom management through play and through reflective discussions of experiences with their peers. The simulation consists of hypertext scenarios made up of a series of events where the pre-service teachers can take actions corresponding to classic leadership styles. The scenarios depict variations of problematic situations that occur in classrooms. It is possible to redo previously made choices in order to encourage exploration of alternative approaches.

In the evaluation, the majority of the participants thought that the scenario events could happen, and that they were valuable to learn to manage. The majority found the descriptions interesting, but improvements can be made to the event descriptions. The simulation was also on the whole considered usable. In the constructive interaction, the participants moved between articulating understanding and non-understanding. They also experimented by testing different choices in the scenario events. The interaction indicated a degree of playfulness in discussion around choices made in the simulation and the possible choices that could be made in an actual classroom and their consequences.

Our approach follows Edman Stålbrandt's results [5], by situating our simulation in a course structure, and paying attention to what happens before the play session and afterwards. In contrast to the work by Edman Stålbrandt, SimProv offers the pre-service teachers choices with observable outcomes and opportunities for play. The constructive interaction between the peers also shows a level of reflection on their choices. These results are indeed promising, but further thought needs to go into if and how more scaffolding for reflection is needed after the play session, and how that relates to concepts introduced before the session. Scaffolding for reflection could include questions for discussion or support by a mentor.

Future work in the project will focus on improving the scenarios, making sure they are experiences as existing events that are interesting and valuable to learn to manage. It would do well to focus time in future iterations on improving the quality of the writing of the events. As noted by Edman Stålbrandt it is also important to make sure that the simulation has sufficient complexity and true dilemmas to be interesting [5]. Issues left to investigate include the relative merits of adding graphics, sound and dynamic behavior to the currently hypertext simulation. It would be interesting to see if that would lead to improvements in Interface Quality.

To conclude, the SimProv game-like simulation for classroom management provides an exploratory experience. It is a viable candidate for complementing more traditional education in classroom management, since the pre-service teachers engaged each other in reflective discussions about the choices they made and consequences. Reflection is necessary for successful experiential learning, which SimProv successfully helps to facilitate.

Acknowledgements. Thanks to Eva Ragnemalm and Gunnel Colnerud for joint work on SimProv. Supported by The Swedish Research Council, ref 2011-4741.

References

1. Lewis, R.: Classroom Discipline and Students' Responsibility: The Students' View. Teaching and Teacher Education 31, 173–186 (2001)
2. Woolfolk Hoy, A., Weinstein, C.S.: Student and Teachers Perspectives on Classroom Management. In: Evertson, C.M., Weinstein, C.S. (eds.) Handbook of Classroom Management: Research, Practice and Contemporary Issues. Lawrence Erlbaum Associates, Mahwah (2006)
3. Lewis, R., Romi, S., Katz, Y.J., Xing, Q.: Students' Reactions to Classroom Discipline in Australia, Israel and China. Teaching and Teacher Education 24, 715–724 (2008)
4. Bowden, J., Marton, F.: The University of Learning. Routledge, London (2004)
5. Edman Stålbrandt, E.: Simulerade Skoldilemman: Redskap för Utveckling av Reflektionsförmågan? Åbo Akademi, Åbo (2013)
6. Zimmerman, J., Forlizzi, J., Evenson, S.: Research Through Design as a Method for Interaction Design Research in HCI. In: Proceedings of the SIGCHI Conference on Human Factors in Computing Systems, pp. 493–502. ACM, New York (2007)
7. Lewis, J.R.: Psychometric Evaluation of the PSSUQ Using Data from Five Years of Usability Studies. Int. J. Hum. Comput. Interact. 14, 463–488 (2002)
8. Sauro, J., Lewis, J.R.: Quantifying the User Experience: Practical Statistics for User Research. Morgan Kaufmann, San Francisco (2012)
9. Miyake, N.: Constructive Interaction and the Iterative Process of Understanding. Cognitive Science 10, 151–177 (1986)
10. Bartle, R.: Hearts, Clubs, Diamonds, Spades: Players who Suit Muds. J. Mud Research 1(1) (1996), http://www.mud.co.uk/richard/hcds.htm
11. Bartle, R.: Designing Virtual Worlds. New Riders, Indianapolis (2004)
12. Svingby, G.: Simulerad Lärarpraktik. Slutrapportering för Projekt 2010/2005 "Spel och Simuleringar: Ett Utvecklingsprojekt inom Ramen för KK-stiftelsens Satsningar på IT i Lärarutbildningen. Malmö Högskola, Malmö (2011)
13. Lewin, K., Lippitt, R., White, R.: Patterns of Aggressive Behavior in Experimentally Created "Social Climates". The Journal of Social Psychology 10, 271–299 (1939)

Rapid Prototyping for Mobile Serious Games

José Rouillard[1], Audrey Serna[2], Bertrand David[3], and René Chalon[3]

[1] LIFL Laboratory, University of Lille 1,
F-59655 Villeneuve d'Ascq Cedex, France
jose.rouillard@univ-lille1.fr
[2] Université de Lyon, CNRS
INSA-Lyon, LIRIS, UMR5205,
19 avenue Jean Capelle, F-69621 Villeurbanne Cedex, France
audrey.serna@insa-lyon.fr
[3] Université de Lyon, CNRS
Ecole Centrale de Lyon, LIRIS, UMR5205,
36 av. Guy de Collongue, F-69134 Ecully Cedex, France
{bertrand.david,rene.chalon}@ec-lyon.fr

Abstract. Mobile Serious Games are new kind of Serious Games which are running on mobile devices, mainly on Smartphones. With continuously increased power and User Interface facilities, they constitute an alternative to the usual entertainment applications proposed on Smartphones. To design and implement such applications, a methodological assistance and development support are required. In this paper, we present our contribution to rapid prototyping for Mobile Serious Games in which we propose to augment *App Inventor for Android* framework with a methodological assistance. This proposition is based on a study in which we asked to 116 students to use this framework for the development of mobile applications. The results are presented (thematic domain, targeted users, components used...) and we discuss the relevance of using such a tool to achieve rapid prototyping for mobile Serious Game.

Keywords: Human-computer interaction, Serious Games, Mobile learning, Prototyping, App Inventor.

1 Introduction

To use mobile devices, as smartphones, for other purpose than entertainment seems an interesting orientation in order to exploit the small size of these devices and their contextualization facilities, and user's availability anywhere (in transportation, in waiting moments, ..) to devote this time to a more helpful activity, as learning. Mobile Learning or M-Learning refer to this kind of learning, which can be either context independent, using user's availability to learn in any location or context dependent, taking into account user's location (geographical, logical, ...).

Serious Games (SG) are pedagogical games that educate, train and inform ([2], [3], [6], [7], [9]). SG were initially introduced to support sophisticated learning in

P. Zaphiris and A. Ioannou (Eds.): LCT 2014, Part II, LNCS 8524, pp. 194–205, 2014.
© Springer International Publishing Switzerland 2014

contextual situations in which learners play their roles in an authentic scenario (or working situation) expressed by a simulator. Company management investments or gaining new market places are archetype scenarios used for SG. For this kind of SG a well-organized design process allowing team working is needed [4], as well as a development infrastructure, an IDE, allowing developing a simulator and user interfaces for all users [1]. These heavy applications require usually several years of developments [8].

In the following section, we present related work and state of the art around the notion of SG. We present next how to expand an existing framework, App Inventor for Android, for rapid prototyping for mobile SG.

2   Previous Work on Designing Serious Games

2.1   Situated and Mobile Serious Games

Previous works conducted at LIRIS laboratory are aimed to design learning environments, in particular SG, which are supported by the use of technologies and that relied on situated learning theories.

From a general point of view, some guidelines are aimed to design situated learning environments [10], such as providing authentic context and activities and supporting learners' collaboration, reflection and articulation for the construction of knowledge and abstractions. In addition, the learning environment should allow learners to observe different aspects of a situation by adopting different roles or perspectives.

SGs meet intrinsically a part of situated learning environments requirements since they usually integrate role-playing aspects and provide coaching and feedback elements embedded into the activities. In addition, the advances of technologies in the field of HCI can foster the authenticity of activities and offer tools to help learners in reflecting on their actions, reasoning and building their knowledge together. Mobile technologies offer interesting perspectives thanks to their characteristics such as connectivity, mobility and context sensitivity. Mobile SG (M-SG) can be able to extract, interpret and use contextual information in order to adapt its content to the authentic context. Other features, such as augmented reality, can be easily deployed on recent mobile devices, and can be used to favor learning professional gestures in a real-life situation (learning by doing paradigm).

In previous work [1], we argued that these technologies, in particular mobile devices, should be integrated into more global learning systems forming a set of heterogeneous platforms. This point of view addresses several issues at different granularity levels. For example, at the highest abstraction level, the learning game should be able to adapt its content to each learner experiences. At a lower level, the combination of platforms should be managed dynamically: the system should be able to distribute the users interfaces (redistribution mechanisms [11]) in order to increase collaborative and authentic aspects.

To explore these concepts, we proposed different scenarios integrating mobile or collaborative aspects in global learning environments (SEGAREM project described in next section). We also explored lighter applications using scenarios [1] and paper-based prototypes at the earlier stages of a user-centered design approach [12] to measure the collaborative potential of a learning scenario using tangible interactions on multitouch tabletops. This evaluation gave us some hints on the design quality but to go further in the evaluation, we need to implement the game and test some synchronization aspects.

2.2   SEGAREM Project and the Le(a)rnIT Prototype

The implementations of SGs are highly cost and time consuming, and rapid prototyping tools are necessary to develop and test different solutions to foster collaborative and contextualized activities. In SEGAREM project (which lasted 3 years – 2010-2012) we developed a SG prototype called Lear(n)IT aimed at teaching the Lean Manufacturing methodologies [13]. Players' goal is to manufacture as many products as possible in a limited production time. Each learner plays an operator role in the industrial production line to understand the complexity of its dynamicity and how to improve it. Raw materials and processed materials are moved between the player's tables by a warehouseman handling a cart. After each simulated working sequence, the teacher and learners debrief their working experience in order to find improvements to apply to the production line (as presented in the lectures).

From the hardware perspective (see Figure 1), three tangible interface-supported tabletops (MT1 to MT3), a Samsung Surface 2 tabletop, an Android Tablet (Ta), an Android smartphone, and classical personal computers compose the learning environment. The Tablet and Smartphone are used as mobile interfaces to convey raw materials and processed products, while tabletops (workstations) have a specific position defined by game rules and in-game debriefings. The spatial configuration between tabletops is very important in defining object flows and is crucial to the optimization process.

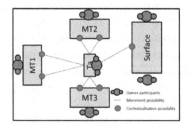

Fig. 1. Physical arrangement of participants and devices in Lear(n)IT

From an interaction perspective, the production line is supported by 4 augmented tabletops and a tablet. Each workstation waits for material to enter its input area in order to transform it. These materials are moved between tables using the tablet carried by the learner playing the warehouseman role. Material processing tools are represented by tangible interfaces directly on each table, where materials are also digitally represented.

In SEGAREM we designed several toolkits to develop the prototype, which can be reused for helping in developing further projects. Despite these toolkits, developing such a complex serious game which involves several users and devices is a very time consuming task and required high programming skills. Rapid prototyping tools are necessary to develop and test different solutions to foster collaborative and contextualized activities.

3   Mobile Serious Game Design and Implementation Support

The SGs for mobile devices are a transposition of initial SG orientation taking into account new characteristics related to mobility. If SGs and M-SGs are known to help learners develop specific skills, they are not so widespread mainly because of implementation cost. "Their use has proven to be promising in many domains, but is at present restricted by the time consuming and costly nature of the developing process." [8].

Basically, we can consider two classes of SGs: complex SGs and simpler Mobile SGs. Complex SGs require a development by teamwork with specialized actors, complex simulator and have a significant cost. Aldrich considers the estimated cost of this kind of SGs between 10 and 300 thousand dollars [15].

M-SG must be light, at first individual with short sessions, but progressively also multiplayers. In this way, the design and development of M-SG is different from conventional SG design and implementation. Individual design and implementation are prevailing, in order to privilege innovation and creativity. Designers, who are neither design specialists nor experienced implementers, should be assisted in these activities (designing and programming) by providing methodological and implementation supports. Thus, this research focuses on:

- Concerning programming issue, visual programming by assembly various components is an interesting and proven approach: it can be seen as an end-user programming method.
- Concerning methodological issue, the architectural approach allows us to propose a model of thinking based first on an interactive application structure (architecture) organized in 5 categories of components: HCI, contextualization, data management, treatment and communication, then its increasing by introduction of two SG oriented components: SG springs and SG engines.

We are going to present in the following section how App inventor can be used in such context and what are the strengths and weaknesses of this tool for developing SGs.

3.1   Developing Serious Games with App Inventor

From a development point of view, rapid prototyping and end-user programming are interesting approaches to speed up and increase the quality of produced applications.

App Inventor for Android framework is a tool for rapid prototyping based on visual programming. It is aimed to facilitate the design and deployment of Android applications. The main advantage to use App Inventor for Android is that actors are not necessarily supposed to be computer scientists or programming developers. By manipulating (drag and drop on visual blocks) components from palettes and snapping them together, this Google and MIT tool allows to generate usable and powerful applications, that can be used, for instance, in the SG's world.

The App Inventor design editor is composed of 9 palettes of components that are the following (in version 2): User interface, Layout, Media, Drawing and Animation, Sensor, Social, Storage, Connectivity, Lego® Mindstorms®. It allows developers not to spend too much time learning programming skills (Java), but instead, to explore technologies actually related to the mobility of users and ergonomic matters.

We tested this framework with a consequent group of students, who programmed in a short period devoted to class works a lot of interactive applications, games and serious games.

3.2   Experimentation

We have conducted a study involving 79 projects, developed by 116 students from 5 different classes. Students were asked to use App Inventor to develop mobile applications, games and serious games on Android smartphones and tablets.

Among those 116 students, 60 (51.72 %) had a personal Android smartphone, and 8 (6.90 %) had already developed a mobile application. The students worked at least during 10 hours (5*2 hours) at university, to produce the final version of their mobile application, with the advices of a teacher. They used ACER Stream, Liquid MT and Z2 Duo Android smartphones to test and package their applications.

The topics of the mobile applications developed by the students were mainly oriented towards tools & utilities, games & entertainment, social, sport, and travel aspects. The categories of targeted users chosen by the students are the following: All public (46.84 %), Adult (44.30 %), Other (24.05 %), Adolescence (15.19%), Childhood and pre-adolescence (1.27%). The category "Other" was used to specify particular users such as disabled people, professionals, etc.

Figure 2 presents the palettes of component used by the students, in order to develop their mobile applications. For each palette, the first column indicates the number of projects (among 79) that used this component, and the second column is the percentage associated. For example, as we can see, 79 Android applications (100% of the projects) used the Button component

The great majority of the developed mobile applications are non-collaborative (single user mode). Only one project used a Bluetooth communication in order to play a collaborative pong game, and 12 projects used a TinyWeb component, allowing data exchanges on the Internet network.

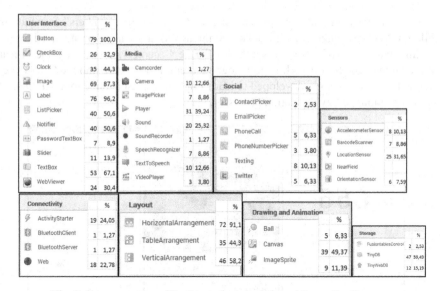

Fig. 2. Components used by the students in their mobile applications

It's interesting to notice that various sensors were employed by student developers: 25 projects among 79 (31.65 %) used a "LocationSensor" component (GPS), 8 (10.13 %) used an "AccelerometerSensor", and 6 (7.59 %) used an "OrientationSensor" (compass). Figure 3 shows the blocks needed to detect automatically the location of the user, and the resulting interface of this implementation on a real Android device.

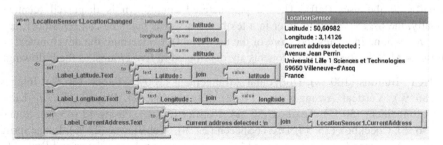

Fig. 3. Detecting latitude, longitude and current address, with the location sensor component of App Inventor

Among the 79 projects, we consider that 14 applications can be seen as prototypes of interesting M-SG, and we are focusing on those projects in the following section.

3.3   Focus on 14 M-SG prototypes

Those M-SG prototypes are applications that are really connected to the user environment and that used various components, such as barcode scanner, accelerometers, compass, shake detection, etc. In such applications, users can play and learn, by interacting with the (serious) games.

Figure 4 (left) presents an application called "I learn the numbers" in which the children have to enter (touch canvas components) a number pronounced by the machine with a Text-To-Speech synthesis. Figure 4 (center) presents a game to learn various things about horses (how to recognize them, how to care and feed them, etc.). Figure 4 (right) is a game developed to learn English: the users have to touch the right number pronounced by the digital professor, etc.

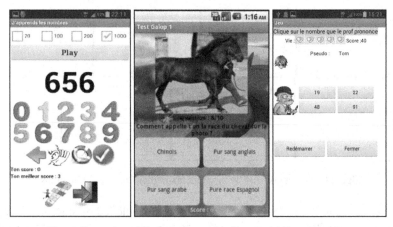

Fig. 4. Examples of Serious Game developed with App Inventor

Figure 5 is an example of application developed by students with App Inventor, for fighting against Alzheimer's disease. Some words are presented, textually and vocally, to the user (left). Then a parametered countdown is displayed (center). Finally, the user is asked to enter in a textbox the words that s/he can remember, and the smartphone indicates the score of the user (right). Concerning the development of those 14 M-SGs, the used components are distributed in five groups, as the following:

- HCI : Buttons (100 %), Horizontal Arrangement (100%), Labels (86 %), Images (86 %), Vertical Arrangement (71 %), Canvas (64 %), Player (57 %), Table Arrangement (50 %), Textbox (50 %), Notifier (50 %), Password (43 %), Sound (36 %), Checkbox (35 %), TextToSpeech (29 %), WebViewer (29 %), ImageSprite (29 %), Slider (27 %), ListPicker (14 %), Image Picker, VideoPlayer and Ball (7 % each);
- Contextualization: Location (29 %), Accelerometer (21 %), BarcodeScanner (7 %) and Orientation (7 %);
- Treatment: Clock (43 %);
- Data management: TinyDB (50 %), TinyWebDB (14 %) and FusionTableControl (7 %);
- Communication: Web (14 %) and PhoneCall, (7 %).

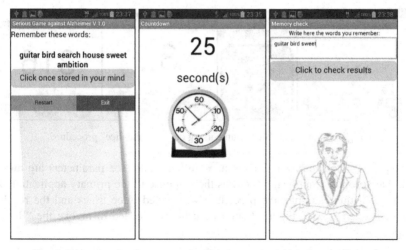

Fig. 5. Example of serious game for fighting against Alzheimer's disease

4   Facilitating the Implementation of Mobile Serious Games

From a methodological point of view, it seems important to indicate that an analysis of the target interactive application can be driven by its architectural structure, which is mainly based on five aspects: HCI, Sensors, Data management, Communication and Treatments (computational behavior of the application). These five architectural aspects are not too far from components categories of App Inventor framework. In this way the mapping between these two views is relatively easy.

In order to increase applicability of App. Inventor framework, three directions can be explored:

- Elaboration of new components, which increase the scope of application behaviors. Main orientation seems be "Treatment components", i.e. reusable computational behaviors to be used in future applications;
- Creation of composite components obtained by interconnection of existing components, and use of them as basic components;
- Merge of existing applications and manipulation of their components in order to create new applications.

4.1   Facilitating the Implementation of Mobile Serious Games with App Inventor

Figure 6 presents the "421 game", developed with App Inventor. Each time the user touches a dice, a random number procedure is invoked and the result is displayed in the calling application.

Fig. 6. Example of "421" game using our "roll the dice" procedure

When the random number is chosen, x milliseconds (see parameter) are awaited before that secondary application returns the response to the primary application, and kills itself. In this example, the procedure was called three times and the resulting number obtained is 316. Figure 7 shows the blocks needed to invoke the "Roll the dice" procedure.

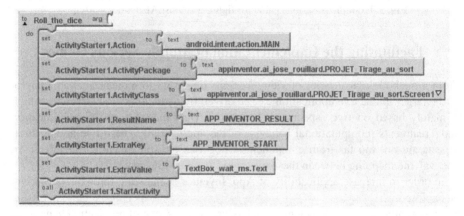

Fig. 7. The "Roll the dice" procedure is calling another activity with parameters, to get a result

With this kind of patterns and pre-programmed procedures, we believe that developers of M-SG would be more efficient with App Inventor. It would reduce their development time and would help to generate some safe and robust M-SG.

4.2   Going Further Towards Mobile Serious Games

App Inventor provides a range of interesting components in these 5 categories: HCI (Input, Output, Layout, animation), contextualization (sensors), data management (local or web DB), communication and collaboration (social aspects), but it offers relatively limited components for treatments and meta-treatments. To go further towards M-SG development, it is interesting to take into account the following three additional aspects: game principles, game engine and more complex treatments.

Regarding game principles, Mariais and al. [14] propose some motivating factors and important characteristics to take into account in SG:

- Being in competition (form of competition: independent actions, sequential, data, time or position actions, calculation type of victory)
- Playing a role (special abilities associated with a role)
- Being subject to chance (the impact of involving an element of chance)
- Managing a high-risk situation (qualification of the crisis situation)
- Acting collectively (choice of cooperation / collaboration methods)
- Receiving recognition (type of information sharing, personalization, feedback/notifications)

Regarding the collaborative aspects of M-SG, it could be interesting to model game playing behaviors in order to provide a game playing management engine. We identified at least 6 game playing behaviors, which can be expressed by corresponding engines:

1. No constrained individual actions: the users (players) are able to work separately without coordination and data evolution: exploration of a compartmented universe;
2. Sequential game between players: each player can action only one in a predefined order;
3. Time organized players' participation (playing schedule);
4. Data constrained players' participation managed by data accessibility and update;
5. Real time synchronization, update of data and players locations;
6. Management of team of players' game participation with cooperation.

These engine behaviors can either be proposed as new components, in relation with previous extension suggestions, or as component patterns, which can be recomposed during the game development.

Finally, for complex treatments, a set of new "Treatment components" can be added to App. Inventor in order to facilitate their integration by composition. We are proposing an open-ended list of fairly generic treatments:

- Score, ranking and awards calculation;
- Interval related random calculation;
- Timer, scheduler and overall time management;
- Choosing characters and avatar routines;
- General and particular calibrations (user profile, sensors' accuracy, etc.).

5   Conclusion

In this paper we have shown the relevance of using App Inventor to achieve rapid prototyping for M-SGs. We have observed that, without coding in Java, 116 students succeeded in developing 79 real prototypes (APK easily generated for Android smartphones and tablets) in a short time (around 10 hours). We focused our study on 14 mobile applications that can be considered as interesting M-SG. Indeed, the user can really learn relevant information by playing and interacting with those prototypes.

In the design and development of M-SGs it is very important to detect the user's context and to offer information and data related to this context (location, orientation, time, device's features...). With such kind of tools, it becomes relatively easy for designers to integrate mobile applications features and sensors, such as GPS, barcode scanner, accelerometer, orientation sensors, video/camera recorders, etc., that certainly improve the usability of the developed M-SGs. The weaknesses of using App Inventor for M-SGs are related to the poor possibilities to reuse existing blocks and/or patterns already developed in other projects.

Our main contribution was to propose a methodological helping for the design and implementation of M-SGs designed with App Inventor. We illustrated this possible reuse of patterns with an example (Roll the Dice) invoking a StartActivity component with parameters.

In the close future, we will provide more M-SGs patterns and/or super-components, in order to facilitate the implementation of applications related to pedagogical and learning concerns. We will also work around the notion of context awareness and pedagogical learning style available within tools like App Inventor, in order to improve the tutoring activity and the collaboration in M-SGs. Our next job will be to measure and evaluate the usability of M-SGs developed with App Inventor enhanced with the propositions made in this work.

References

1. George, S., Serna, A.: Introducing Mobility in Serious Games: Enhancing Situated and Collaborative Learning. In: Jacko, J.A. (ed.) Human-Computer Interaction, Part IV, HCII 2011. LNCS, vol. 6764, pp. 12–20. Springer, Heidelberg (2011)
2. Rouillard, J.: Developing a multimodal application for a scientific experiment on smartphone: case study, tools and results. In: Tools for Mobile Multimedia Programming and Development. Part of the Advances in Wireless Technologies and Telecommunication Book Series, pp. 68–80. IGI Global (2013)
3. Wakefield, J., Smith, D.: From Socrates to Satellites: iPad Learning in an Undergraduate Course. Creative Education 3, 643–648 (2012)
4. Parsons, D., Petrova, K., Ryu, H.: Mobile Gaming - A Serious Business! In: Proceedings of the IEEE Seventh International Conference on Wireless, Mobile and Ubiquitous Technology in Education, WMUTE 2012, pp. 17–24. IEEE Computer Society, Washington, DC (2012)
5. Cortez, C., Nussbaum, M., Santelices, R., Rodriguez, P., Zurita, G., Correa, M., Cautivo, R.: Teaching science with mobile computer supported collaborative learning (MCSCL). In: Proceedings of the 2nd IEEE International Workshop on Wireless and Mobile Technologies in Education, pp. 67–74 (2004)
6. Susi, T., Johannesson, M., Backlund, P.: Serious games – An overview. School of Humanities and Informatics. University of Skövde, Sweden (2007)
7. Riedel, J.C.K.H., Hauge, J.B.: State of the art of serious games for business and industry. In: Proceedings of the 17th International Conference on Concurrent Enterprising, ICE 2011, pp. 1–8, 20–22 (2011)
8. Marfisi-Schottman, I., George, S., Tarpin-Bernard, F.: Tools and Methods for Efficiently Designing Serious Games. In: Proceedings of the 4th Europeen Conference on Games Based Learning, ECGBL, Copenhagen, Denmark, pp. 226–234 (2010)
9. Michael, D., Chen, S.: Serious games: games that educate train and inform. Thomson Course Technology, Boston (2006)

10. Herrington, J., Ron, O.: Critical characteristics of situated learning: Implications for the instructional design of multimedia, pp. 253–262 (1995)
11. Balme, L., Demeure, A., Barralon, N., Coutaz, J., Calvary, G.: CAMELEON-RT: A Software Architecture Reference Model for Distributed, Migratable, and Plastic User Interfaces. In: Markopoulos, P., Eggen, B., Aarts, E., Crowley, J.L. (eds.) EUSAI 2004. LNCS, vol. 3295, pp. 291–302. Springer, Heidelberg (2004)
12. Vahdat, M., George, S., Serna, A.: Wizard of Oz in Designing a Collaborative Learning Serious Game on Tabletops. International Journal of Information and Education Technology 3(3), 325–329 (2013) ISSN 2010-3689
13. Delomier, F., David, B., Benazeth, C., Chalon, R.: Situated and colocated Learning Games. In: 6th European Conference on Games Based Learning (ECGBL), pp. 139–151. Academic Conferences and Publishing International Limited, Cork (2012) ISBN 978-1-62748-068-0, ISSN 2049-0992
14. Mariais, C., Michau, F., Pernin, J.-P.: The Use of Game Principles in the Design of Learning Role-Playing Game Scenarios. In: ECGBL 2010 Proceedings, Copenhague (2010)
15. Aldrich, C.: The Complete Guide to Simulations and Serious Games. Pfeiffer, USA (2009)

Creating Universal Designed and Trustworthy Objects for the Internet of Things

Trenton Schulz

Norsk Regnesentral – Norwegian Computing Center,
Gaustadalléen 23a, Kristen Nygaards hus, NO-0373 Oslo, Norway
Trenton.Schulz@nr.no
http://www.nr.no

Abstract. The Internet of Things promises to connect different kinds of devices, allow for new ways of interaction, and make our lives easier. But, we need to be able to trust that the Internet of Things will protect our security and privacy. It should also be universally designed so that anyone can use it regardless of ability. We applied a user-centered approach to looking at user-centered trust in the Internet of Things, including universal design issues. We conducted an evaluation with 85 participants of a security assistant that can present security and privacy information to users. The evaluation included participants who were either elderly, had vision impairment, or had dsylexia. Participants found the information useful, but there was confusion about how the UI worked. We present an updated security assistant and future areas for research in trust and the Internet of Things.

Keywords: Internet of Things, trust, universal design, usability, accessibility, security, privacy.

1 A Promising Future

As more devices gain the ability to communicate with each other, we are presented with a new idea, the Internet of Things (IoT), where objects will automatically exchange information and help make it possible to live more efficiently, collaborate more easily, and live independently for longer. The IoT gives us an opportunity for ensuring these new interaction methods and services are universally designed so the greatest amount of people benefits. Yet, these objects will be entrusted to gather data about their users and their users' habits. The IoT can also make it much easier for anyone to find out more about where we go, what we do, and who we do it with. To realize the benefit of the IoT, users need to trust that their data will be treated safely and that the objects will function correctly.

How do we create this trust? What sort of guidelines can one follow to present this information in an accessible and usable way that can be understood by as many people as possible? We have examined trust issues in the IoT with a user-centered approach, particularly in the area of smart homes, smart offices, and e-voting.

First, we examine the IoT and the definition of trust that we used during our investigation. Next, we look at a *security assistant* that can help users in presenting security and privacy information. We will also document how this information was made accessible to people with different disabilities like dyslexia and vision impairment and how

P. Zaphiris and A. Ioannou (Eds.): LCT 2014, Part II, LNCS 8524, pp. 206–214, 2014.

we evaluated the security assistant. Then, we look at the results from a user evaluation in a smart home apartment. Finally, we conclude with an updated security assistand and possible areas for future research in trust and collaboration systems.

2 The Internet of Things, User-centered Trust, and Universal Design

The *Internet of Things* (IoT) was first used by Ashton [1] in 1999 to refer to the idea of uniquely identifiable objects (things) and their virtual representations in an Internet-like structure. The idea of how the IoT will be implemented depends on the technology. For example Bassi and Horn [2] describe how RFID technology can be used to create an IoT for tracking objects, and Vermesan, Harrison, Vogt, Kalaboukas, Wouters, Gusmeroli, and Haller [3] presents the argument of the IoT being an integral part of the future Internet, with things being involved in everything from the power grid to your clothing. We went with the latter definition as it gave us a broader base for potential users to understand the implications of the IoT.

Trust is another term that has different meanings in different disciplines. In our investigations, the two disciplines where we had the most conflict, was between computer science and social sciences. In information security, Quirin, Fritsch, Husseiki, and Samson [4] point out that the ITU-T X.509 standard defines trust as an entity functioning the way it is expected to. Further, Quirin et al. state trust in information security is always, "...the correct function of a technical component that is important for the system security." From a user's perspective, this manifests itself in the authenticity of hardware or a service and usually involves some sort of certification or public key infrastructure. This means looking at the areas of online transactions and banking [5, 6]. In other areas of computer science, Yan, Kantola, and Zhang [7] try to lay out a theoretical approach for describing trust in human-computer interaction.

In social sciences, a focus area is interpersonal trust, which is not only about the expectation that things will do what they claim, but also the risk involved for the person required to trust (*trustor*). Mooradian, Renzl, and Matzler [8] examine how personality can affect the willingness to trust someone and share knowledge. Bansal, Zahedi, and Gefen [9] discuss how an individual's perception of risk in providing health information online can affect the success of a healthcare websites.

Since we were working in a cross-discplinary investigation, we struggled to find a definition of trust that could be accepted by the different disciplines. After much discussion, we settled on the definition presented by Döbelt, Busch, and Hochleitner [10, p. 23], "A user's confidence in an entity's reliability, including user's acceptance of vulnerability in a potentially risky situation." The focus on the user being willing to take the risk and use an object emphasized our focus on user-centered trust, but we still highlighted the technical component from computer science that the other entity should function as advertised. Döbelt et al. try to make a distinction between trust and *trustworthiness*. A user trusts something, but an object does not trust; it is instead trustworthy if it is trusted by the user.

The concept of *universal design* was introduced in the mid-1980s by the architect Ronald Mace, and has since then been adopted in many fields, including the design of

ICT [11]. Many think of universal design as design for people with disabilities. Yet, the general intention of universal design in ICT is to design an object so that it can be used by as many people as possible, i.e., mainstream technology for everyone, including the elderly and people with disabilities. The emphasis is on avoiding unnecessary special solutions and to provide equality and equal opportunities to participate in the society [12]. For ICT, this normally means adding bits of semantic information so it is *accessible* via assistive technology (AT) without extra set up.

Finally, the concept of universal design has two aspects: a process and a result. That is, universal design denotes (*a*) a design process or an approach and (*b*) a design that can be used by as many people as possible.

3   User Evaluations

In the past, we have examined how users perceive trust in the IoT by designing a model [13] and in virtual reality environments [14, 15]. This work was combined with a study on presenting trust information and resulted in a set of guidelines [16] for an interface for presenting trust information (Fig. 1) called the *security assistant*. The security assistant is divided into multiple layers. Layer 1 is a high-level assessment of the situation coded into four different levels: 1 (lowest) to 4 (highest). The security level is also conveyed by using colors. Layer 2 provides a simplified explanation of the levels along with a recommendation if the user should proceed or not. Layer 3 is targeted at users desiring more information about what factors and state have determined the security level. Layer 4 is for users that are curious about different terms in information security and want to find out their meaning. The idea is to provide users with the security level at a glance, but allow users to check the resulting layers to find out why this security level was chosen to build their trust in the security assistant.

After the general layout of the security assistant had been decided, we began looking at ways to make it more accessible, especially to AT. We made sure that no essential information was conveyed by one only modality. For example, the colors are used as an aid to display the security level, but this information is also presented as numbers that can be read and interpreted by AT. However, the security level number needs to be presented to the AT in a usable way. While a sighted user has the position and highlighting to see the indicated security level, this context is not sent to AT by default. Instead, an AT like a screen reader only says "1. 2. 3. 4." We added context so that the security level instead read, "Security Level 4 of 4, Excellent Security." This matches the intent of what the graphics are showing.

Normally, people in the IoT are interested in accomplishing some task and security and privacy are only a secondary goal. We wanted to make sure that the security assistant's information was understandable to as many people as possible. Graf et al. [16] found that the term "security" was most understandable term when discussing privacy, security, and trust issues with the potential users. In addition, we went through the text presented in the Layer 2 recommendation so that it was easy to understand for the majority of users, and we worked to reduce the amount the text so that people with dyslexia could easily read it.

We wanted to test the security assistant in a variety of environments and decided to perform the evaluations in a smart home, smart office, and e-voting environment.

Fig. 1. The security assistant showing the first two layers of security information (*left*) and the detailed information (*right*)

So, we needed to make these environments and prototypes accessible for people with disabilities. We went through the different mobile applications and devices that were under development and made adjustments as was done with the security assistant itself. To help ensure that things worked with accessible technology, an accessibility expert worked with the developers at a two-day workshop where everyone worked with the prototypes and AT to find deficiencies.

We performed a user evaluation of the security assistant with 85 participants in Germany, Austria, and Norway. The tests in Germany used a virtual reality setting where users navigated the environment using a Kinect. The tests in Austria used a laboratory environment, and the tests in Norway were conducted in a smart home apartment.

Before beginning the evaluation, participants were surveyed about their general feelings about technology, trust, and privacy. Then, participants performed nine different tasks in the smart home and smart office environments using a phone or tablet and other objects in the environment depending on the task. Half of the participants received a low security environment and half received the high security environment. As they performed each task, participants were asked to evaluate their opinion of trust, both in the environment and in what was presented by the security assistant. Participants were then asked to provide their overall opinion of the security assistant. Finally, in Austria and Norway, participants finished the evaluation by participating in an e-voting scenario for a housing cooperative.

We evaluated 23 participants in Norway (Fig. 2). The participants consisted of five visually impaired using TalkBack (Android's screen reader application), seven visually impaired depending on text enlargement (either via software or a magnifying class) and good contrast, five with reading and writing difficulties, and six elderly.

Fig. 2. A participant testing out the medicine cabinet in the bedroom of the smart home apartment in Norway; *photo source: Aftenposten/Robert McPherson* [17]

After the evaluations were completed, the answers to the surveys were compiled to understand participants' opinions on trust in the different situations and their opinions on the security assistant. For looking at accessibility, we entered the notes from each user session into a digital system. These notes included observed behavior and comments from the participants. We used an open-code process, often used during the first steps of a qualitative analysis as described by Crang and Cook [18, p. 137] to group these observation and comments into different themes. These themes were then used as the basis for determining the accessibility of the security assistant.

4   Participants' Feelings on Trust and Accessibility

This is a summary of the participants opinions on using the security assistant and their experiences with the accessibility features. Detailed findings information for trust and universal design is provided in a separate report report [19].

Participants generally accepted the advice that they were given during the tasks, regardless of whether or not they are in a high security or low security environment. Most of the participants only looked at the first two layers of the security assistant (the security level and recommendation); few bothered to look at the details in Layer 3. One of the reasons for this could be that participants had to swipe the screen to the left to get access to the third and fourth layers. The hint that more information was available via this gesture was not obvious and few users recognized this.

Trusting the security assistant was an issue for some participants. They would ask, "where does the security assistant get this information?" and "how does the security assistant know this?" This indicates that even if the information provided by the security assistant is accurate, a user needs to trust the source of the information and its messenger.

Some participants misunderstood how the security assistant worked. The security assistant reports on security, but some participants would tap on the security level to change it. Changing the security level was *not* intended (and didn't work), but it could be that the user interface for showing the security level (Fig. 1) may have been mistaken for buttons. None of the participants that used TalkBack to access the security assistant had this problem. This indicates TalkBack gave enough contextual information.

After it was understood that they could not change the security level from the security assistant, they were able to complete tasks. Most participants understood the concept of the security assistant, but felt they needed help to learn how it worked. The assistant helped some to realize the flow of information and how much implicit trust they were giving the objects around them. Others complained about being interrupted by the security assistant during the different tasks. Since we were evaluating the security assistant, it was necessary to be interrupted, though some participants tapped through for the final tasks.

Almost all participants with disabilities were able to complete the tasks in the evaluations and were able to get the information from the security assistant. Testing in the real world environment revealed issues with contrast and text size that we didn't not discover during development. Even though we attempted to use good color contrast and a large text size, the resolution of a screen, its color gamut, and glare due to its position in the environment resulted in less contrast and smaller text than we expected. Part of this could have been prevented by getting a higher quality display and making sure that text is a minimum physical size (i.e., measuring the size in millimeters not points or pixels), but sometimes the screen needs to be tested in the environment it's intended for to see how well it works.

Participants using TalkBack had problems using was the medicine cabinet. The medicine cabinet had a built-in screen that used its own version of TalkBack. However, this version of TalkBack was different than the one on the phones and tablets. It couldn't be upgraded and used a much different metaphor for interaction that made it difficult to use; participants using TalkBack had to give up and move on.

There were also some differences in using TalkBack between the phone and tablet that were used during the evaluation, but this did not stop the participants from completing the tasks. However, we found that the order of the information could have been presented in a more optimal way. First, TalkBack reads the security level (Layer 1). Then, TalkBack would read information about the security level and the recommendation (Layer 2) before going to the buttons to continue or cancel the action. This matches the visual layout of the security assistant (Fig. 1), but it did not match how many non-TalkBack participants used the security assistant; most looked at the security level and then pushed one of the buttons at the bottom of the screen. It probably would have been better for TalkBack to read buttons after the security level, curious users could then be informed that additional information was available.

5 Summary and Future Work

Overall, there are some issues with the security assistant, but the evaluation shows that the security assistant is a tool that can present privacy, security, and trust information in different situations to a varied group of users. In addition, the focus on universal design made it possible to uncover deeper accessibility issues due to placement or set up of information and highlights the value of real world testing by people with disabilities.

We used the information from the evaluation to improve the design of the security assistant (Fig. 3). For example, we changed the design of the security level indicator to make it more obvious that it is presenting information and not a control for changing the security level. Besides the swipe gesture, we have also added a button to make it more obvious that information in Layers 3 and 4 can be accessed. This will help determine if users need the progressive disclosure of information or are satisfied with only the first two layers. We also made the *Cancel* and *Accept* buttons change size depending on what the assistant recommended. For example, the *Cancel* button would take more space if the assistant felt one should not continue.

Fig. 3. The updated security assistant

For future research, work needs to be done to indicate that people can trust the security assistant. Our evaluation showed that sometimes the security assistant got in the way. How and when should the security assistant show its info? Also, the IoT has the potential to be ubiquitous, and we may not always have a device like a smartphone with us; what other methods and objects might be effective for conveying the security and trust information?

We created a set of guidelines [20] for creating new interfaces in the IoT. The guidelines provide principles based on usability heuristics and experience from past usability projects, and they detail how we created the final version of the security assistant. There is also information about designing accessible applications for Android mobile devices and how to include universal design throughout a project. The document is written to be applicable in areas outside the IoT.

User-centered trust and universal design can be applicable in other areas. For example, collaborative and learning environments need users to exchanging information and determine what they should do with it. Yet, the environment still needs to respect users' security and privacy, and it should be possible to use it regardless of ability. Everyone can benefit from having a safe environment for exchanging ideas and working together.

Acknowledgments. This research was funded as part of the uTRUSTit project. The uTRUSTit project is funded by the EU FP7 program (Grant agreement no: 258360). Thanks to Mark Summerfield and Wolfgang Leister for proofreading the article.

References

1. Ashton, K.: That 'Internet of Things' Thing. RFID Journal (2009),
   http://www.rfidjournal.com/article/view/4986
2. Bassi, A., Horn, G.: Internet of Things in 2020: A Roadmap for the Future (2008)
3. Vermesan, O., Harrison, M., Vogt, H., Kalaboukas, K., Wouters, K., Gusmeroli, S., Haller, S.: Internet of Things Strategic Research Agenda. In: Sundmaeker, H., Guillemin, P., Friess, P., Woelfflé, S. (eds.) Vision and Challenges for Realising the Internet of Things, ch. 3, pp. 39–82. Publications Office of the European Union, Luxembourg (2010)
4. Quirin, T., Fritsch, L., Husseiki, R., Samson, F.: Ergänzende und alternative Techniken zu Trusted Computing. Tech. rep., Sirrix AG security technologies, Bochum (2010)
5. Wang, H.: Review of studies on online consumer trust. In: Second International Conference on Computational Intelligence and Natural Computing, pp. 97–100. IEEE (September 2010)
6. Law, K.: Impact of Perceived Security on Consumer Trust in Online Banking. Master, AUT University, Auckland, New Zealand (2007)
7. Yan, Z., Kantola, R., Zhang, P.: Theoretical Issues in the Study of Trust in Human-Computer Interaction. In: IEEE 10th International Conference on Trust, Security and Privacy in Computing and Communications, pp. 853–856. IEEE (November 2011)
8. Mooradian, T., Renzl, B., Matzler, K.: Who Trusts? Personality, Trust and Knowledge Sharing. Management Learning 37(4), 523–540 (2006)
9. Bansal, G., Zahedi, F., Gefen, D.: The impact of personal dispositions on information sensitivity, privacy concern and trust in disclosing health information online. Decision Support Systems 49(2), 138–150 (2010)
10. Döbelt, S., Busch, M., Hochleitner, C.: Defining, Understanding, Explaining TRUST within the uTRUSTit Project. Tech. rep., CURE, Vienna, Austria (2012)
11. The Center for Universal Design: About UD (2008),
    http://www.ncsu.edu/ncsu/design/cud/about_ud/about_ud.htm
12. Aslaksen, F., Bergh, S., Bringa, O.R., Heggem, E.K.: Universal Design: Planning and Design for All (1997), http://home.online.no/~bringa/universal.htm
13. Leister, W., Schulz, T.: Ideas for a Trust Indicator in the Internet of Things. In: Leister, W., Dini, P. (eds.) SMART 2012—The First International Conference on Smart Systems, Devices and Technologies, No. c, pp. 31–34. IARIA, Stuttgart (2012)
14. Schulz, T., Tjøstheim, I.: Increasing Trust Perceptions in the Internet of Things. In: Marinos, L., Askoxylakis, I. (eds.) HAS/HCII 2013. LNCS, vol. 8030, pp. 167–175. Springer, Heidelberg (2013)
15. Busch, M., Hochleitner, C., Lorenz, M., Schulz, T., Tscheligi, M., Wittstock, E.: All In: Targeting Trustworthiness for Special Needs User Groups in the Internet of Things. In: Huth, M., Asokan, N., Čapkun, S., Flechais, I., Coles-Kemp, L. (eds.) TRUST 2013. LNCS, vol. 7904, pp. 223–231. Springer, Heidelberg (2013)

16. Graf, C., Busch, M., Schulz, T., Hochleitner, C., Fuglerud, K.S.: D.2.7 Updated Design Guidelines on the Security Feedback Provided by the "Things". Tech. rep., CURE, Vienna, Austria (2012)
17. Hexeberg, A., McPherson, R., Færaas, A.: Ville du bodd i et hus hvor alt er koblet til Internett? (May 2013), http://www.aftenposten.no/nyheter/iriks/Ville-du-bodd-i-et-hus-hvor-alt-er-koblet-til-Internett-7192204.html
18. Crang, M., Cook, I.: Doing Ethnographies. Sage Publications Ltd., Los Angeles (2007)
19. Busch, M., Wolkerstorfer, P., Hochleitner, C., Schulz, T., Fuglerud, K.S., Tjøstheim, I., Leister, W., Solheim, I., Lorenz, M., Wittstock, E., Dumortier, J., Vandezande, N., Petro, D.: D6.3 Design Iteration II – Evaluation Report. Tech. rep., CURE, Vienna, Austria (2013)
20. Klein, M., Wolkerstorfer, P., Hochleitner, C., Fuglerud, K.S., Schulz, T.: D2.8 Final UI-Guidelines for the Trust Feedback Provided by the IoT. Tech. rep., CURE, Vienna, Austria (2013)

Prototyping M-Learning Course
on the Basis of Puzzle Learning Methodology

Krzysztof Szklanny and Marcin Wichrowski

Polish-Japanese Institute of Information Technology Warsaw, Poland
{kszklanny,mati}@pjwstk.edu.pl

Abstract. The aim of the "Puzzles for Nomad" project is to improve the system of education by filling gaps in job seekers' competencies in an informal way (incidental learning). That would enable graduates, especially of humanities, to adjust their skills to the needs of the modern workplace using an innovation teaching method based on puzzles (puzzle learning). The first stage of the project was to create and test a mobile prototype.

The distinctive, innovative features of our system are:

- puzzle learning – course contents follow the chosen methodology by integrating problem-based learning with the presentation (Presentation Practice Performance) methods, ensuring high levels of interaction with the user. The didactic process is carried in pre-planned stages or according to scenarios;
- learning outcomes ascribed to each stage, content is broken into stages of the learning process in accordance with the methodological approach;
- monitoring, testing, methodology and course organization are relevant to the pre-defined learning outcomes – we developed a procedure and a special qualifying questionnaire to check whether the expected learning objectives can be achieved and verified using our system of incidental learning;
- verification of the final product – a course developed by an expert is subject to review with respect to the criteria outlined in the correctness questionnaire at the methodological and technical levels;

All the elements described above form an adaptive system for incidental learning, which is innovative not only with regard to the problem it tackles (mechanisms for the adaptation of informal education to the current job market) but also forms of learner support (distance learning with the use of mobile devices adjusted to the needs and skills of learners), and target groups (learners and content providers, corporate users).

The system was based on the pilot course, a series of studies into the needs and opinions of users, and usability studies. These actions ensured high quality of user interface ergonomics in line with the rules of Human-Computer Interaction. Both the process of entering courses into the system and its use by students have been subject to in-depth usability tests.

The proposed system functionalities and the results of research, as well as the developed methodology, can be used to create similar m-learning systems.

Keywords: Methodologies for the study of computer supported collaborative learning and / or technology-enhanced learning, Mobile and/or ubiquitous learning, Open educational resources, Puzzle Learning, Nomad Education.

P. Zaphiris and A. Ioannou (Eds.): LCT 2014, Part II, LNCS 8524, pp. 215–226, 2014.
© Springer International Publishing Switzerland 2014

1   Introduction

According to [2] m-learning (mobile learning) is a kind of e-learning which is based on the use of mobile devices (PDAs, mobile phones, notebooks or tablets) anywhere at any time. The progress made in these technologies in recent years has influenced everyday life [1,12] and the quality of distance learning [7]. These rapid changes inspired the authors to conduct research concerning the potential of m-learning in Poland. In the first part of this work we analysed whether Polish students were ready for joining m-learning courses. In the second part we investigated tuition-free online courses run in Polish as the language of instruction from the point of view of their relevance for the graduates of humanities. It turned out that all free m-learning courses [9] do not meet the requirements of either the methodology or multimedia quality of the courses. Following this observation a new methodology was proposed basing on [3,9] research. Next, we prepared a pilot course testing the proposed methodology. The obtained results showed that the proposed model meets the expectations of project beneficiaries, both from the point of view of methodology and organisation and presentation of materials.

2   Motivation and Background

According to the data published by the Ministry of Labour and Social Policy, job centres in Poland have observed an increase in the number of the unemployed with higher education diplomas – from nearly 4% in 2002 to 11.7% in 2012 (ca. 250 000 people). A quarter of the total number of unemployed persons are graduates of economy and administration, 15% of pedagogy and related fields, 14% of social sciences and 8% of humanities. In comparison – graduates of technical and engineering faculties account for only 8% of all university graduates. Another worrying phenomenon is the fact that many graduates accept job offers which are below their qualifications or in another field [13]

Young graduates exhibit high flexibility in terms of job seeking and the need to develop new skills. Focus group research involving 30 persons proved that the main motivator behind job change (taking a job other than the learned one) is the lack of opportunities to fulfill one's ambitions and no perspectives of further growth. Those data are consistent with the research done by the Public Opinion Research Centre in January 2013 (Occupational Mobility and Elasticity)

72 % of survey participants said they were ready to spend their free time improving their qualifications. A survey conducted as part of our project confirmed those findings. Our respondents admitted that they could devote 6.5 hours per week to learn new things (however there was a large standard deviation of 3.4). As far as preferred methods and organizational forms were concerned, most respondents pointed to individual learning (40%) conducted online (23%). In a study of older learners the percentages of participants of online courses was even higher (58%) with 78% assessing the content of e-learning courses well [8].

3   Analysis of the Popularity and Usage of Mobile Devices in Poland

Prior to launching the pilot course, a survey was conducted regarding the use of mobile devices among the user group. The results previously reported in [11] were compared with the data for the most popular mobile devices in Poland. A comparison was made in order to find out if similar devices are used by the selected target user group i.e. graduates of humanities.

In [11] it was reported on the use of mobile technologies in Poland and the Western World. The report also contained information regarding ways of creating multimedia elements for mobile devices, and ways in which users interact with them with a special emphasis on practices of User-Centered Design. A key difference between the project's target group and mobile users in Poland and the world in general is a smaller popularity of tablets. A total of 23 % respondents from the target group admitted to having owned a mobile phone for less than 6 months. Only 17% were planning to buy a new one in the near future. In the target group of 80 learners:

- 98% of respondents own a mobile phone
- 88% own a portable computer
- 10% own a tablet
- 58% had participated in e-learning courses before, and 78% of these described their attitude towards e-learning as positive
- 13% had participated in distance courses using mobile devices, and 55% of these described their attitude towards this type of content presentation as positive
- 70% watch films on their mobile phones
- 49% use their phone to acquire knowledge
- 24% are planning to buy a phone with the Android OS in the near future, and 7% with iOS
- 5% would not find time for mobile learning, 30% would spend about 30 minutes a day, 53% no more than 30-60 minutes, 10% 2-3 hours.

4   The Analysis of Resources of Online Courses Available in Polish

In order to assess the resource quality of free-of-charge distance learning courses, the resources were analysed and the following hypotheses verified: [9]

- There is a lack of clear and well-defined goals, following the recommendations of National Qualifications Framework;
- The content rage of offered courses is not large (a handful of subjects dominate);
- The presentation method is the most popular, interaction with a user is limited to summative assessment;
- Summative assessment does not allow for the reliable monitoring of the attainment of learning outcomes by a learner;

- Content featuring elements of mathematics and logic are not adjusted to meet the needs of our project's beneficiaries;
- Technical aspects of courses, including the multimedia, navigation and graphics of the user interface are often poor quality.

Resources which were analysed had to meet several criteria:

- They are public and easily accessible;
- They are free and require the maximum of free-of-charge user registration; free content is not limited to a demonstration (e.g. first lesson);
- They refer to the knowledge and skills relevant to the beneficiaries of the project as jobseekers [9]
- They are not limited to an e-book.

103 courses were examined, most of them available at http://kursolandia.pl, of which 61 were initially selected for further analysis. In the end the selection process identified 50 courses to be subject to further scrutiny.

Our research proved that currently available online courses are limited in scope, with many lacking any clearly defined learning objectives, which makes proper analysis impossible. Only a handful of courses have learning goals, but even then the type of final assessment used is inadequate. Courses often lack the definition of target audience, in which case it is difficult to say whether the methodology, forms and didactic means are relevant to the abilities and needs of our project beneficiaries. In all analysed courses the presentation mode dominated, and interactivity was limited to simple tasks done as part of ongoing assessment and closed questions which constituted final assessment. Some courses had nice-looking graphics but in most cases multimedia elements were irrelevant and served aesthetic rather than didactic purposes.

Furthermore, some materials were published in the e-book format and presented as online courses, which might be misleading for a user and lead to negative opinions about e-learning. On the other hand, solutions which seem fine from the methodological point of view, such as PARP Academy, are not aimed at the beneficiaries of our project.

To sum up, the analysis showed that the current offer of free-of-charge distance (online) courses does not provide our project beneficiaries with opportunities to adjust their competencies to the needs with the Polish job market [9].

Our analyses led to conclusions that the most important features of a system meant for incidental learning of our target group, i.e. the graduates of humanities, should be the following:

- Conformance to the fundamental rules of education, including the need for acquired knowledge to be operative and practical, the need for high interactivity (learner activity), appeal to many senses, individualisation, differentiation of methods and assessment forms;

- relevance of content in relations to the needs of the job market and integration of final (summative) assessment with a system for the management of competencies;
- agreement of course objectives with the National Qualifications Framework;
- use of methods, forms and means appropriate to the needs, abilities and preferences of learners (e.g. it is advisable to incorporate elements of learner participation and cooperation).

5   Methodology Based on Elements of Puzzle-Learning

Puzzle Learning is a new teaching and learning methodology focused on solving different kinds of problems using puzzles [3,4]. It is possible to increase the student's mathematical awareness and problem solving skills by discussing a variety of puzzles. Such a methodological approach relies on standards requiring from a teacher to define a problem, present a puzzle to illustrate it, in order for the learner to see the complexity of the problem in question. Then the teacher lets the learners deal with the puzzle, providing feedback whenever necessary. At the next stage, the teacher explains the theoretical background related to the problem and checks the skills mastered by the students. The initial program is followed by subsequent presentation of the wider context of the problem and, finally, final assessment of the predefined learning outcomes [6]. This methodology allows students to take an active part in solving tasks and thus promotes better understanding of the presented issues. Students can use these methods for solving problems in different fields. It is the opposite of passive approach to studying, like reading without understanding and rote learning of ready-made solutions.[5]

The three basic rules of Puzzle-Learning are:

- Rule 1. Make sure you understand the problem and all key terms used to define it.
- Rule 2. Do not trust intuition; calculations are more reliable.
- Rule 3. Calculations and reasoning will be more constructive if you create a model for the given problem, defining its variables, limitations and objectives. [3]

Below we present an example of a puzzle used in the course.

General teaching aim of the puzzle:

- To develop problem-solving skills.

Learning outcomes:

- Knowledge: the user defines the sense (rationale) of defining assessment criteria in situations where problems are not adequately defined.

Puzzle 1 (Fig.1.):

- You have two sand timers – a 2-minute and a 5-minute one. You want to have soft-boiled eggs and you prefer eggs boiled for 3 minutes. How can you do this using the two devices described above?

Ongoing monitoring:

- A user should have the opportunity of using the sand timers, one at a time and simultaneously. When a sand timer's top bulb is empty, the user should have the opportunity of throwing an egg into the water.

Correct answer:

- The best way is to use both sand timers simultaneously. When the 2-minute one is empty, there will be enough sand for the next 3 minutes in the other one; therefore it is the right time to throw in the eggs.

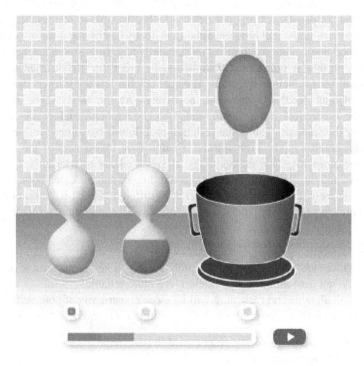

Fig. 1. The graphic presentation of the described puzzle

Basing on the above methodology used in the pilot course, we broke the teaching/learning process into stages presented in the table.

Table 1. Stages of the didactic process of the pilot course

Stage	Actions	
Introduction	Stage 1	• Choosing learning outcomes • Explaining the subject of the lesson (unit) • Shaping a learner's motivation
Problem/puzzle	Stage 2	• presentation of the problem or puzzle illustrating the given problem
	Stage 3	• providing the learner with an opportunity of solving the problem/puzzle (providing tips)
	Stage 4	• providing the learner with feedback
	Stage 5	• presenting lesson goals (the problem illustrated by the puzzle)
Knowledge	Stage 6	• presentation of the knowledge related to the chosen subject
Skills	Stage 7	• testing of acquired knowledge and the ability to apply it in practice (ongoing assessment) • tips for further learning
Consolidation	Stage 8	• presenting a broader perspective • generalisation of the learnt material more examples
Summary	Stage 9	• presenting the importance of the gained knowledge and skills
Final verification (testing)	Stage 10	• verification if the goals of the lesson have been attained.

In order to prepare a course using the puzzle-learning method, it is necessary to use the course template. That forces a user to follow a set sequence of course design and development stages:

- Formulate the expected outcomes
- Find out who the learners are, what are their cognitive skills and personality traits
- Define what knowledge, skills and social competencies are necessary to reach the learning goals
- Set detailed, measurable, realistic and observable learning outcomes
- Develop monitoring tools, such as tests checking whether concrete outcomes have been reached
- Pick teaching/learning strategy, decide whether to use presentation mode or searching mode with the elements of puzzle learning
- Fill-in a qualifying questionnaire and a questionnaire which will be the basis for course approval at the concept stage. Both questionnaires are verified by a methodology specialist.
- Prepare a scenario and multimedia. Fig. 2 presents a template of a scenario divided into screens, with learning outcomes, core and optional multimedia and navigation.

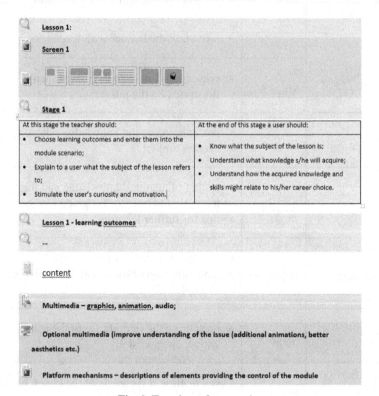

Fig. 2. Template of a scenario

When filled-in this template allows for a course to be entered into its mobile version.

6   Construction of the First Mobile Version of the Pilot Course

It was decided that the course should run on mobile devices because that was consistent with the character of the project, i.e. Nomadic Learning. Research was carried into the preferred resolutions of audio, video, static graphics and animations. Then decisions regarding the technology utilised in the pilot study were based on the devices and multimedia formats favored by the target group. Currently one of the most frequently used solutions for developing content for multiple mobile platforms is HTML5 combined with CSS3 and JavaScript, whose operation is actively supported by the latest mobile web browsers. That ensures similar display of content and consistent interaction on many platforms without additional effort. jQuery Mobile is a very popular free-of-charge solution offering predefined graphic and interaction components (widgets). The pilot course was developed using this particular technology.

The course uses a minimalist user interface which allows for simple transitions between screens with the help of large, easily visible buttons. Interactivity is provided by means of timed quizzes, illustrations appearing upon clicking and audio/video players. Course scenario depends on previous answers, which are remembered by the application.

The course uses the Responsive Web Design technology, which helps adjust the content to mobile device screens of different sizes. Below we present screenshots from the mobile version of the course on the examples of a smartphone (Fig.3.) and a tablet (Fig.4.).

Fig. 3. Mobile version of the course on smartphone

Fig. 4. Mobile version of the course on tablet

7   Evaluation of the Pilot Course

In the last stage of our research we set out to verify our hypotheses. The results confirm that the incidental-learning model allows to attain educational goals, however the effectiveness of the learning process depends on many factors – didactic, technical and pertaining to the attitudes of learners, as well as their self-study competencies. Our results suggest that it is easier to reach an objective related to the area of 'application' rather than 'knowledge', the most difficult being 'comprehension'. To confirm the observations more extensive research needs to be conducted.

In some cases negative effectiveness of learning was observed, which, together with data on self-regulation of the learning and assessment processes (e.g. the time between starting a course and attempting a final test), casts doubt on whether the failing participants took their learning seriously. Disregarding those data, however, could adversely affect the reliability of results because with the single-choice questions, from the point of view of statistics, the number of chance incorrect hits should equal the number of correct answers [10].

Despite the above-mentioned limitations, the results allow us to conclude that the proposed model meets the needs of the students from both perspectives - methodology and structure. Research results serve as guidelines to be used in the further stages of the project, i.e. work on a number of new courses.

On the basis of obtained results, the following recommendations have been formulated for the authors of methodology books, courses, and for the teachers:

- content should be broken into small 15-45-minute thematic blocks (lessons) which would focus on a very limited (one to three) detailed operating objectives;
- a screen should not contain too much text;
- problems discussed should be illustrated with examples and multimedia elements, especially if they refer to abstract-symbolic explanations;
- the didactic process should combine the stages of problem-solving with presentation, in order to balance theory with its practical applications;
- the didactic process should incorporate interactivity and tests verifying content comprehension and skills acquisition (ongoing assessment);
- testing questions should contain clear explanation of assessment criteria, especially in the case of open questions (final assessment).

8   Future Work

Currently we are working on the development and implementation of a full e-learning platform and an m-learning platform which will base on previous assumptions and the results of the pilot test. The e-learning platform will feature an extended module for lecturers/editors allowing for the easy publication of courses and accompanying materials on the platform. We envisage the option of creating moderated courses (i.e. with a lecturer) in a distance and blended models, as well as non-moderated ones (without a lecturer/moderator). The platform will enable the creation of a course structure with the use of ready-made templates and designing a unique structure with the help of a drag&drop menu. We plan to give course authors access to a puzzle editor so that they could add more advanced logical tasks. Below we present first models of the platform showing selected functionalities.

Both the e-learning and the m-learning platforms will be subject to detailed evaluation whose aim is the analysis of the usability of applied user-interface solutions. That will help identify main problems which users might encounter while working with the platform and propose solutions which should enhance the ergonomic quality of the analysed interfaces.

Usability testing will be carried in controlled conditions at PJIIT, where individual users will be observed by a moderator/researcher while doing pre-defined tasks. User interactions and actions will be registered by a program recording screen content in a video form. Those recordings will be subject to further analysis. Users will also be encouraged to share their remarks regarding the tested platform ("Thinking Aloud Protocol"), which will also be recorded. After the usability test, the user will complete a satisfaction questionnaire to express his/her opinions on working with the platform. The research will be followed by a final report describing the usability tests with the lists of the problems that emerged, organised according to predefined priorities and illustrated with relevant screenshots, user comments, questionnaire results as well as their interpretation.

Regular usability tests will enable platform modification, which should help maintain its high reliability and ease-of-use both for students and teachers.

Acknowledgements. The authors would like to thank the whole team of Nomad i.e Ania Muniak, Maciek Słomczyński, and Dorota Sidor. The Project is an innovative testing project developed as part of Action 4.1.1 Enhancing didactic potential of school, Human Capital Operational Programme 2007-2013.

References

1. Allan, J.: Nomadic Learning to Teach: Recognition, Rupture and Repair. In: Rethinking Inclusive Education: The Philosophers of Difference in Practice. Inclusive Education: Cross Cultural Perspectives, vol. 5, Book Section, pp. 117–130. Springer, Netherlands (2008), http://dx.doi.org/10.1007/978-1-4020-6093-9_8, doi:10.1007/978-1-4020-6093-9_8
2. Tsvetozar, G., Evgenia, G., Angel, S.: m-learning: a new stage of e-learning. In: Proceedings of the 5th International Conference on Computer Systems and Technologies (CompSysTech 2004), pp. 1–5. ACM, New York (2004), http://doi.acm.org/10.1145/1050330.1050437, doi:10.1145/1050330.1050437
3. Zbigniew, M., Matthew, M.: Puzzle Based Learning. In: Proceedings of the 2007 18th Conference of the Australasian Association for Engineering Education, AAEE 2007, School of Computer Science, Melbourne, Australia, pp. 1–8 (2007), http://hdl.handle.net/2440/44940, 9780975717219, 0020076199, en, AAEE in association with the University of Melbourne, http://www.cs.mu.oz.au/aaee2007/papers/paper_25.pdf, Puzzle-based learning, Conference paper
4. Michalewicz, Z., Michalewicz, M.: Puzzle-based learning: Introduction to critical thinking, mathematics, and problem solving. Hybrid Publishers, Melbourne (2008) ISBN 9781876462635
5. Raja, S., Nickolas, F., Zbigniew, M.: Puzzle-based learning. J. Comput. Sci. Coll. 25(3), 7 (2010)
6. Fezile, O., Nadire, C.: Basic elements and characteristics of mobile learning. Procedia - Social and Behavioral Sciences 28, 937–942 (2011) ISSN 1877-0428, http://dx.doi.org/10.1016/j.sbspro.2011.11.173
7. Pérez-Sanagustín, M., Ramirez-Gonzalez, G., Hernández-Leo, D., Muñoz-Organero, M., Santos, P., Blat, J., Kloos, C.D.: Discovering the campus together: A mobile and computer-based learning experience. Journal of Network and Computer Applications 35, 176–188 (2012), doi:10.1016/j.jnca.2011.02.011
8. Dorota, S.: The report on methods, forms of education in distance education (2013)
9. Maciej, S.: The Report onExamination of the quality of free tuition courses (2013)
10. Maciej, S.: The Report on evaluation ofpilot course (2013)
11. Krzysztof, S.: The Report on the mobile technology used in the learning (2013)
12. Ravi, T., Kumar, S.: Usefulness of M-Devices in Education: A Survey. Procedia - Social and Behavioral Sciences 67, 538–544 (2012) ISSN 1877-0428, http://dx.doi.org/10.1016/j.sbspro.2012.11.358; http://www.sciencedirect.com/science/article/pii/S1877042812 05344X, Keywords: m-learning; education; information
13. Mc Kinsey Report – Education to Employment, designing a system that works

Posture and Face Detection with Dynamic Thumbnail Views for Collaborative Distance Learning

Takumi Yamaguchi[1], Haruya Shiba[1], Masanobu Yoshida[1], Yusuke Nishiuchi[1],
Hironobu Satoh[1], and Takahiko Mendori[2]

[1] Kochi National College of Technology, 200-1 Monobe, Nankoku, Kochi 783-8508, Japan
[2] Kochi University of Technology, 185 Miyanokuchi, Tosayamada, Kami-city,
Kochi 782-8502, Japan
{yama,shiba,myoshida,nishiuchi}@ee.kochi-ct.ac.jp,
{satoh.hironobu,mendori.takahiko}@kochi-tech.ac.jp

Abstract. In this paper, we describe the use of a collaborative TERAKOYA learning system developed to help students actively study anywhere on a local area network (LAN) linked to multipoint remote users. In this environment, if many students send questions to a teacher, it is difficult for the teacher to provide answers quickly; furthermore, the teacher is largely unable to determine the degree to which each student has understood the course materials, because he or she cannot observe the students and their reactions in person. In this paper, we discuss a graphical user interface (GUI) system that prioritizes student screens by changing the GUI on the teacher's computer; more specifically, thumbnails of student screens zoom dynamically in proportion to each student's understanding level. By sorting these priorities on his or her screen, the teacher can observe each student's work and support their thinking process at each student's individual pace.

Keywords: Advanced Educational Environment, Ubiquitous Learning, Distance Education.

1 Introduction

In today's environment of ubiquitous computers, promoting the use of computers in school is very important. E-learning and learning through web content, however, are passive methods, and it is difficult to cultivate comprehensive active learning, which has recently gained prominence. Because active learning requires learner participation, computers are expected to complement classroom lectures. Systems for computer-based active learning enable in-class participation by transparently manipulating the input instruments of the students and the teacher. Several researchers have suggested that the challenge in our information-rich world is not only to make information available to people at any time, at any place, and in any form but also to specifically say the right thing at the right time in the right way [1]. In particular, the fundamental pedagogical concern is to provide learners with the right information at the right time and place in the right way instead of enabling them

P. Zaphiris and A. Ioannou (Eds.): LCT 2014, Part II, LNCS 8524, pp. 227–236, 2014.

to learn at any time and at any place [2]. Moreover, as Jones and Jo [3] point out, educators should aspire to combine the right time and place learning with a transparent method that allows students to access lessons flexibly and seamlessly. Such an approach is a calming technology for ubiquitous computing environments and adapts itself to student needs by supporting specific practices.

In our present study, we have developed a new collaborative learning system called TERAKOYA [7] for remedial education, which helps students actively study anywhere on a LAN linked to multipoint remote users, as shown in Fig. 1. The TERAKOYA learning system provides both interactive lessons and a small private school environment similar to basic 18th-century Japanese schools called terakoya. In particular, the system provides an interactive evening lesson that uses tablets on a wireless LAN (WLAN) and custom-built applications that link students in the dormitory and at home with a teacher in the school or at home. In this new system, students and the teacher cooperate and interact in real time by using a personal digital assistant (PDA) [4]. This system can be used to submit and store lecture notes or coursework using a tablet.

We define TERAKOYA as a new evolving virtual private school realized on a network, which certainly distinguishes it from the 18th-century terakoya. TERAKOYA is a system for simultaneously achieving the following:

(1) Small group lessons for students, like those at a private school in which the teacher serves as the leader.

(2) Interactive lessons that provide dialogue with the teacher and allow students' work to be checked and thinking processes to be supported by online collaboration.

(3) Lessons enhanced by mutual assistance that can clarify any misperceptions in a student's thinking processes and provide appropriate support for each student via the opinions and answers of other students.

In short, TERAKOYA is an educational support system that can flexibly adapt to the learning demands of many students by applying a private school model for small group lessons. Therefore, as noted above, the TERAKOYA system realizes personal learning support for students in a dormitory or at home from a teacher in the school or at home.

In the original terakoya environment, it was not easy to keep students focused on learning, except for students with a high willingness to learn. Conversely, our TERAKOYA system is a more flexible learning environment that allows teachers to switch freely between the conventional terakoya environment and the mutually supportive environment using teacher-centered learning or self-paced learning, as needed. Because of this flexibility, we view our system as able to reach a wide range of vulnerable students and accommodate contemporary student attitudes toward learning. In addition, our system is expected to allow teachers to provide additional learning assistance to students with less additional work for the teacher than supplementary lessons conducted in the classroom or dormitory.

In this paper, we consider a realistic scenario of dynamically providing an interactive lesson for students in an active learning environment in their own living space. A serious problem occurs when many students send questions to the teacher; it is very difficult for the teacher to quickly answer all such questions. In addition, the teacher is largely unable to determine the degree to which each student understood the course content, because the teacher cannot observe individual student reactions. Accordingly, the GUI of our system prioritizes student screens through changing GUI interfaces on the teacher's computer. More specifically, these windows are shown as thumbnails that zoom dynamically based on student understanding levels. The teacher can then sort these as per priority. Using this approach, the teacher can observe student work and support their thinking process much more effectively. The teacher can also clarify any misperceptions in their thinking processes, providing appropriate support for each student.

In this paper, we present the basic configuration of a system that provides the dynamic delivery of full-motion video while following target users in a ubiquitous learning environment. The delivery of full-motion video uses adaptive broadcasting; the system can continuously deliver streaming data, including full-motion video, to the teacher's display as thumbnails of student screens. Because it maintains information about each user's attitude in real time, the system supports the user wherever he or she is without requiring a conscious request to obtain their information. Below, we describe a prototype implementation of this framework and a practical application.

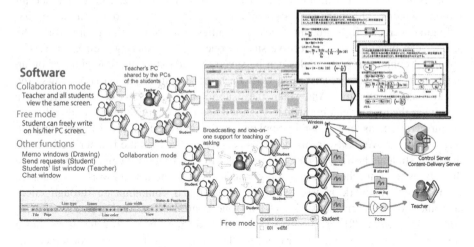

Fig. 1. Framework of TERAKOYA learning system

2 Basic Configuration

Our configuration consists of tablets, a server machine, and software to enable collaboration among the tablets over a WLAN, which covers the campus, the dormitory, and student and teacher homes. The interactive system software consists of server software, authoring software for the teacher, and client software for students. The authoring software synchronizes with clients via server software, and the system operates in either collaboration mode or free mode. The authoring software is launched on a teacher's computer with a 12-inch XGA display; its main functions are to distribute teaching materials, select collaboration mode or free mode, give a specific student's computer permission to write, view a student's screen, share files between a specific student's computer and another computer using the client software, and submit coursework using remote control from the teacher's computer. The main functions of the client software are browsing lecture notes, storing learning materials, and submitting coursework. Using the authoring software, teachers can view student screens as thumbnails; overall, the thumbnail view can display 50 client computers. When students submit coursework from their computers, the filenames are displayed in the order of submission on the teacher's computer. Thus, a teacher can immediately confirm the submission status of student coursework.

In collaboration mode, the display on the teacher's computer is shared and displayed on computer screens of up to 50 students. Each student computer serves as an electronic board on which they can write. All students in the class can view the activity of a selected student on their own screens when that student is completing his or her coursework. Furthermore, students with write access can post messages regarding their coursework; the teacher can control the write access rights of the students' screens. All students can browse through or view these group discussions.

In free mode, a student can freely write on the teaching material and coursework made available by the teacher on his or her screen. The teacher can then watch all student screens, although each student's writing is displayed only on his or her individual screen. If a student faces difficulties completing the coursework, the teacher can provide hints or receive student questions by sharing their screens. The displayed content in both modes can be saved on each student's computer or on an external memory device, such as a USB flash drive. Students can freely browse the saved data at any time. And when they submit their coursework to the teacher's computer, the teacher can immediately mark it and then later evaluate it in detail.

Furthermore, as one possible implementation, the system can support multiple servers, with server software used for data exchange between the teacher's client and that of a student; however, student computers in the dormitory cannot communicate directly with a teacher's computer connected with another network on campus, because each network is isolated by a firewall. To communicate through client computers on different networks, at least one control server and a steady network connection via TCP/IP are necessary for data exchange between a teacher's and a student's client. By using a server that runs the server software as a control server, our system can provide multipoint remote lessons via connections anywhere on the campus and in the dormitory. In addition, it can even be accessed from student homes.

Because interactive lessons are provided, each client is required to continuously maintain its connection to other computers. Thus, the traffic load between the server and clients grows when the number of connected users increases. Consequently, network hardware must provide adequate system performance for real-time information sharing. The system is optimized to work smoothly with one server machine and 50 client computers, each with a 12-inch XGA display, for one lesson; the network speed is maintained at 500 kbps or less for each connection. To limit the amount of data exchange between the client machines, all teaching materials and coursework are sent to the screens of all students when each interactive lesson begins.

After the lesson begins, the system sends only their own written data and the data controlled by the teacher to student screens.

If many students send frequent questions to the teacher, it is very difficult for the teacher to quickly provide answers. In addition, the teacher largely has no means to determine the degree to which each student understood the course materials, because the teacher cannot directly observe students and their reactions. By conducting a pre-survey requesting freeform advice in the subjective evaluation, we received useful comments, such as "It may take some time before a student's question gets a response from the teacher."

Accordingly, our advanced GUI is configured to prioritize student screens by changing the GUI interfaces on the teacher's computer. Thumbnails are blinked, sorted, and scaled on the basis of student viewing and other parameters. In particular, the thumbnails of each student's computer is zoomed dynamically based on their understanding level, as shown in Fig. 2. If the student screens can be sorted on the basis of their priorities on the teacher's screen, the teacher can observe student work and support their thinking process as an effective teaching aid. The teacher can also clarify any misperceptions in student thinking processes, providing appropriate and individualized support for each student

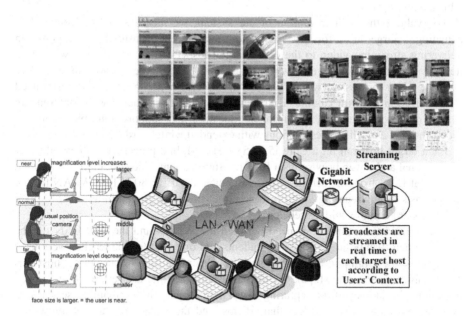

Fig. 2. Overview of GUIs for viewing student screens as thumbnails on the teacher's computer; student screens are zoomed dynamically based on their attitude

3   Practice and Evaluation

As a prototype for applying this system to a real lesson for students in campus, we assembled 20 computers. The proposed learning system was implemented in a pilot evening class. After conducting this class, the feasibility and practicality of the system in helping the students study actively and willingly was verified by observation and questionnaires. Using this system, a teacher in his/her office on the campus sent instructions or learning materials to all student PCs via the network. On receiving this material, the students could note their views and answer the questions in the learning material on their PC screens using the stylus pen attached to their tablet PCs. They could also submit their answers as an image to the teacher.

Because the students' PC screens were visible on the teacher's PC screen, the teacher could check the students' work and support their thought processes by online collaboration. The teacher could also identify any misinterpretations in their thought processes and provide appropriate clarification to each student by combining the images drawn on their PC screens and by verbal communication through the headset, respectively. In an investigation of the system, it was observed that students who were uninterested in a normal class exhibited a different attitude in the pilot evening lesson: they concentrated more, studied the coursework, and frequently sent their questions to the teacher. Consequently, it became easier for the students to ask questions to the teacher in a face-to-face interaction. In addition, it was very satisfying for students when their queries were answered immediately and therefore, their work could be adjusted appropriately.

To evaluate the implementation of our system, we measured its performance in actuating a target host for broadcast and subsequently measured the response in delivering streaming video to the entire target host. For this experiment, we used a delivery server and from five to twenty target hosts. The delivery server ran on a Core i7 (3.4 GHz) processor with Windows 7 Professional and the self-customized BigBlueButton [8] with Ubuntu; BigBlueButton is an open source web conferencing system developed primarily for distance education that supports multiple audio and video sharing, as well as presentations with extended whiteboard capabilities.

Each target host ran on a Core i5 (2.53 GHz) Mobile processor with Windows 7 Professional and a web browser as a BigBlueButton client. The system interconnected via a Gbit LAN from the server on our campus to an IEEE 802.11g/n WLAN for the target hosts. The streaming video for one target host was played in a 320×240-pixel (QVGA size) window with a webcam.

We verified the connection speed between the WLAN and the Gbit LAN for the server. When twenty target hosts for students and one host for the teacher were used on campus, the minimum throughput speed between the server and a target host was 12 megabits per second (Mbps). We also measured the time lag before a target host's actuation; the latency from capturing a webcam to passing a streaming server's IP address to a target host was less than 10 ms, and the latency of the web browser's connection between a streaming server and a target host over a TCP connection was set to minimum.

We also implemented a questionnaire survey to investigate the subjective impression of our prototype system. The test subjects were ten students in the department of electrical engineering, all in their twenties. We assumed that subjects in their twenties were well-versed with the use of computers in their daily life. We explained and demonstrated to the subjects how to use our prototype system before they filled out the questionnaire, which included the several questions. Next, questionnaires on the subjective impression were evaluated using the following five-point rating scale: Better (5), Slightly better (4), Fair (3), Slightly worse (2), and Worse (1).

Subjects evaluated our system favorably, focusing on the system's operability. The subjects' rating of the ease of use of the system increased to more than 4 points after conducting the supplementary lesson, whereas the comparison with using a notebook was low and decreased to less than 3 points. The reason for this result was that the response of the stylus pen was slightly slow, as reported in student comments. The ratings regarding the ability to concentrate during the supplementary lesson showed that, because it was possible to concentrate on the teacher's explanations without taking notes and to concentrate on hearing the teacher's voice using the headphones without other noises, this system helped students concentrate better. Furthermore, other evaluations of our system by these users indicated greater effectiveness. In particular, the subjects' rating of their wish to continue the supplementary lessons using this system increased to 5 points.

Regarding the educational impact, the subjects felt that the supplementary lessons using our system had the same effect as a face-to-face class. Further, their desire to attend supplementary lessons in the future increased. Overall, the subjects' rating regarding the benefits of studying was also high (more than 4 points), because all students answered that the supplementary lessons taken using our system were more useful for forming the habit of studying, whereas study time outside of the supplementary lessons was slightly low (less than 4 points). Regarding study time, two students answered "slightly yes," whereas one student answered "slightly no." Thus, one student had more incentive to study for the course because of the supplementary lessons, whereas the other students felt that the lessons were sufficient.

These ratings of the supplementary lessons provided by our system suggest that our system can achieve the same outcome as a face-to-face class if the supplementary lessons are provided as multipoint remote interactive lessons. Further, the evaluated value of our prototype system for these users might prove greater with more familiarity and experience using our system. As freely provided advice in the subjective evaluation, we received useful comments such as "It is inconvenient that the voice is interrupted sometimes," "It may take some time before a student's question gets a response from the teacher," and "We want more time to do a lot of exercises."

Because we need to analyze the evaluations of teacher performance, we will conduct this analysis and discussion as a future work.

4   Related Work

Studies of interactive support systems used in class with a pen-based interface focus on the way in which the system helps students answer questions and use the teaching materials with an electronic board, a PDA, or information and communication technology (ICT) equipment. To compare our TERAKOYA system to such related work, we weighed two technical areas: interactive systems [5] and active learning environments [6]. Both incorporate pen-based computers [6,13].

AirTransNote [5] is an interactive system that provides a mechanism for improving the interactive feature by using a PDA via WLAN in a normal class. The system is highly compatible with legacy interfaces using pencil and paper because it involves manipulating a stylus pen.

Livenotes [9] allows listeners to share slides on their tablet PCs and discuss issues with other listeners by collaborative note-taking in a shared space. The concept of the system, a new cooperative learning practice, fosters goals similar to those of our system. We particularly focused on a small private school environment on a LAN linked to multipoint remote users rather than collaborative learning among peers connected in small groups, as in Livenotes.

Classroom Presenter [10] is an alternative tablet PC note-taking system based on a broadcast model. The instructor can add annotations to his/her own slides, which are broadcast to all students. Students can also annotate their slides and provide aggregated feedback on the instructor's slides. However, there is no support for small-group student interaction.

Tablet PCs with a stylus pen are becoming increasingly common in engineering classrooms, as they provide the instructor with an extended set of educational tools. Even as a direct replacement for the traditional blackboard, they have many advantages [6,13]. One of the most important advantages is that the tablet PC enables the instructor to seamlessly switch between a standard blackboard-type interface to one of the many multimedia programs or materials to enhance the presentation of difficult subjects. The tablet PC clearly offers many advantages over the traditional blackboard approach for improving the overall learning experience of the students [11]. Ubiquitous Presenter [12] is a web-based extension to Classroom Presenter and facilitates distance learning.

Although each of these related systems is interesting, our system has numerous distinguishing features. First, our system makes it easier for students to ask the teacher questions just as they could in face-to-face interactions. Second, it is very satisfying for students to have their queries answered immediately, which is achieved by directly connecting the teacher and the students. Third, students may feel a sense of security and of being looked after, because the psychological distance between the teacher and each student is less. As a result, students can maintain their study concentration longer than in a normal remedial education class. Thus, the TERAKOYA system not only expands the accessibility of popular tablet support methods, but also accommodates a wide variety of learning styles by leveraging a transparent and calm learning environment.

5   Conclusions

In this paper, we detailed how our system helped students study actively anywhere on a LAN linking multipoint remote users; our system provides an interactive evening lesson using tablets and custom-built applications both in the dormitory and at home such that students and teachers can remain in their own living spaces. As a prototype, our proposed learning system was implemented in a classroom with a teacher in the teacher's on-campus office. Our implementation employed a handwritten electronic whiteboard with verbal and non-verbal information. By conducting the test, the effectiveness of our system in helping students study actively and willingly as an example of "right time, right place learning" was verified.

In addition, our system was configured to help the teacher quickly answer student questions. Thus, the teacher can better observe the degree to which each student understood the course materials by observing students and their reactions in real time. Our GUI implementation prioritizes student screens by changing the thumbnails on the teacher's computer; the thumbnails zoom dynamically based on each student's level of understanding. By sorting out these priorities via the GUI, the teacher can observe student work in real time and support each student's individual thinking process.

Using our system, the teacher distributed instructions or learning materials on all student screens via the network. On receiving these materials, students could note their views and answer questions in the learning material on their computers using pens attached to their tablets. They could also submit their answers as an image to the teacher. Because student screens were visible on the teacher's computer, the teacher could check student work and support their thinking processes via direct online collaboration. The teacher could also clarify any misperceptions by providing appropriate support for each student.

In conclusion, we feel that more specific and effective education programs are required. We would like to further evaluate the impact this system can have on the understanding and motivation of students. We would also like to study various configurations of our new interactive system under active learning conditions, including the development of a new interaction system realized by adding entities. Our system is an ambient human interface system, which materializes as a friendly advisor that gives users natural awareness through making real images via a network to follow users. We would like to work toward realizing such an ambient human interface system of user-oriented ubiquitous computing through implementing this system.

Acknowledgments. This study was partially supported by a Grant-in-Aid for Scientific Research (C, Area #1602, Project No. 24501236).

References

1. Fischer, G.: User Modeling in Human-Computer Interaction. Journal of User Modeling and User-Adapted Interaction (UMUAI) 11(1-2), 65–86 (2001)
2. Ogata, H., El-Bishouty, M.M., Yano, Y.: Knowledge Awareness Map in Mobile Language-Learning. In: Proceedings of the Sixth IEEE International Conference on Advanced Learning Technologies (ICALT), pp. 1180–1181 (2006)

3. Jones, V., Jo, J.H.: Ubiquitous learning environment: An adaptive teaching system using ubiquitous technology. In: Proceedings of the 21st ASCILITE Conference, pp. 468–474 (2004)
4. Roschelle, J.: Unlocking the learning value of wireless mobile devices. Journal of Computer Assisted Learning 19(3), 260–272 (2003)
5. Miura, M., Kunifuji, S., Sakamoto, Y.: Practical Environment for Realizing Augmented Classroom with Wireless Digital Pens. In: Apolloni, B., Howlett, R.J., Jain, L. (eds.) KES 2007, Part III. LNCS (LNAI), vol. 4694, pp. 777–785. Springer, Heidelberg (2007)
6. Hurford, A., Hamilton, E.: Effects of tablet computers and collaborative classroom software on student engagement and learning. In: Proceedings of Frontiers in Education Conference, FIE 2008, pp. S3J-15–S3J-20 (2008)
7. Nishiuchi, Y., Matsuuchi, N., Shiba, H., Fujiwara, K., Yamaguchi, T., Mendori, T.: Evaluation of TERAKOYA Learning System Linking Multi-point Remote Users as Supplementary Lessons. In: Proceedings of the 18th International Conference on Computers in Education (ICCE 2010), pp. 486–488 (2010)
8. BigBlueButton: http://www.bigbluebutton.org/
9. Kam, M., Wang, J., Iles, A., Tse, E., Chiu, J., Glaser, D., Tarshish, O., Canny, J.: Livenotes: a system for cooperative and augmented note-taking in lectures. In: Proceedings of the SIGCHI Conference on Human Factors in Computing Systems (CHI 2005), pp. 531–540 (2005)
10. Anderson, R., Davis, P., Linnell, N., Prince, C., Razmov, V., Videon, F.: Classroom Presenter: Enhancing Interactive Education with Digital Ink. IEEE Computer 40(9), 56–61 (2007)
11. Stickel, M.: Impact of lecturing with the tablet PC on students of different learning styles. In: Proceedings of Frontiers in Education Conference (FIE 2009), pp. M2G-1–M2G-6 (2009)
12. Wilkerson, M., Griswold, W.G., Simon, B.: Ubiquitous presenter: increasing student access and control in a digital lecturing environment. In: Proceedings of the 36th SIGCSE Technical Symposium on Computer Science Education (SIGCSE 2005), pp. 116–120 (2005)
13. Ando, M., Ueno, M.: Analysis of the Advantages of Using Tablet PC in e-Learning. In: Proceedings of the 2010 10th IEEE International Conference on Advanced Learning Technologies (ICALT), pp. 122–124 (2010)

Technology@school

Collaborative Tools in the Primary Classroom: Teachers' Thoughts on Wikis

Andria Agesilaou, Christiana Vassiliou, Sotiroula Irakleous, and Maria Zenios

Cyprus University of Technology, Limassol, Cyprus
{agesilaou.andria,christivass,irakleoussotiroula,
mkzenios}@gmail.com

Abstract. The purpose of this work-in-progress study is to examine the attitudes of primary school teachers in Cyprus on the use of wikis as a mean to promote collaborative learning in the classroom. A survey investigation was undertaken using 20 questionnaires and 3 semi-structured interviews. The survey results indicate a positive attitude of teachers in Cyprus to integrate wikis in primary education for the promotion of cooperation. As such collaborative learning activities among pupils are being encouraged.

Keywords: wikis, primary education, collaboration, collaborative learning, educators.

1 Introduction

By upgrading the Web from Web 1.0 to Web 2.0, various and different tools appeared in the online space. One of the most popular technological tools is the wiki [10]. Wikis are a popular tool with many possibilities, which we see embodied in many areas of human life. Education is one of the places where wikis find perfect fit, according to experimental studies have been done [4].

Higher education primarily led the way for inclusion of this multimedia tool in the learning process, as a means of promoting the co-construction of knowledge among students. Although its use is spreading widely in schools, however, elementary education is presently out of this application. Moreover, there are few studies done to study this aspect [10]. Based on the assumption that wikis are used for implementation of educational objectives it is expected that sooner or later they will become integrated into primary education.

The purpose of this research, therefore, is to contribute to the literature on the use of wikis in primary education and to form a complete picture of the attitudes of Cypriot primary school teachers for: (a) the wikis as a tool for collaborative learning and (b) as a tool that they intend to use in the future in their teaching work.

Among the concepts of solidarity, mutual respect and mutual help, educationalists wish to instill in children the concept of cooperation. In order to cultivate a spirit of cooperation among students, an approach that starts from the early learning years is needed. For this reason, the primary school teachers have a very important role in achieving this goal. It is vital to promote cooperation rather than competition among

P. Zaphiris and A. Ioannou (Eds.): LCT 2014, Part II, LNCS 8524, pp. 239–247, 2014.
© Springer International Publishing Switzerland 2014

students. The wikis can offer collaborative environments capable, through their structure and features, to support the co-construction of knowledge by students and contribute to the completion of cooperative activities [4-10].

2   Research Questions

1. What are the attitudes of primary school teachers for promoting collaborative learning in the context of formal education through the use of wikis?
2. Are primary school teachers willing to use the wiki in their classroom for activities promoting cooperation and targeted learning?
3. In what way, according to the views of teachers, the use of wikis within primary education can help students to processing collaborative projects?
4. What should be the role of the teacher during the use of a wiki for collaborative processing projects for students, according to the views of primary school teachers?

3   Methods

3.1   Research Procedure

The study is based on a mixed approach for the data collection. Specifically, quantitative and qualitative methodology is used in order to crosscheck the data and achieve valid and reliable results. The data collection tools were a questionnaire consisting of 29 questions and a semi structured interview. The questionnaire consists of four parts, and includes closed questions and open-ended. The first two parts, include the closed questions, the third part includes open-ended questions and finally the fourth part refers to demographic questions, to examine whether the factor of sex or experience in primary education, influence the opinions of teachers. Firstly, we gave the questionnaire to the participants and when the procedure was completed, we started the interviews. The analysis of the questionnaires was made through Microsoft Office Excel using tables and charts and the analysis of the interviews followed the qualitative content analysis.

3.2   Research Participants

Participants of the study were working teachers in public sector education, and specifically in public primary schools. Twenty teachers (7 men and 13 women) aged 26 and above took part in the study. The average of the years participants had been working in schools is 11,6 years. An important element of the sample selection was the experience of teachers, so we avoided reaching out to primary teachers who did not practice the profession. The sample of this study is characterized as a convenience sample and we ought to make clear that it was not in our first criteria not to include participants from the private education sector, but it was something that came up after. From the sample of 20 participants, we selected three of them for the procedure of the interview.

4   Literature Review

Cooperation is an essential skill that should characterize both adults and kids. The last years, great efforts are made to integrate cooperation activities into the educational system, since cooperation is considered a necessary skill for the integral development of the person (Partnership for 21st century skills, 2009; Kay, 2011). The advantage of this cooperation implies the integration of cooperative learning in an education system, which should base its operation on a model that meets the 21st century [5].

As al result, learners initially are characterized by a host of skills of the time and point of readiness, since they can cope with the demands of society [10].

Dillenbourg defines collaborative learning as "a situation in which two or more people learn or are in the process of learning something together." [3] [page. 1]. One definition [1] states that "cooperative learning is a system of learning methods, in which students work with interaction and interdependence in small heterogeneous groups to achieve common goals" [page 61]. The existence of a group of people is necessary, in order to achieve learning through communication between them, either in person-contact, whether in an asynchronous or synchronous discussion via a mobile device [3].

The concept of cooperation ensures central role in Web 2.0 technologies, since these technologies are characterized by various factors such as interaction, active user participation and communication between them at any time and any place [10]. As a Web 2.0 technology, wikis are characterized as collaborative learning tools that promote cooperation [10]. It is worth mentioning that the word wiki comes from the Hawaiian "wiki wiki", which means that something is done quickly [13].

4.1   Features of Wikis

There are certain unique characteristics that can be used to describe this technology. Through the wiki the user can create content and then edit it in a collaborative way. Users may add, delete and change the content of the wiki in which they are members. Additionally, wiki gives them the potential of asynchronous discussion, which gives them the opportunity of reflection and critical thinking on the content, by any user separately in its own time and space [10].

4.2   Teacher Role

The characteristics of wikis although differ depending on usage, the owners and the architecture of the page, are believed to have the potential as a technology to enhance collaborative activities and be a source of knowledge and learning space [11]. Prerequisite for the proper and complete use of wikis is the knowledge around this technological tool on the part of teachers [4]. Teachers should help in their own way, so that each child feels comfortable to the idea of use of a wiki in the learning process [8]. In education, however, should be emphasized and the role of the teacher to use technology, to apply it correctly and produce the desired results. The role of the teacher is to guide the collaborative knowledge building [10].

The wiki, being a tool for carrying out cooperative activities, allows the teacher to observe how students organize and coordinate their cooperation to solve a problem, and thus achieve a project [7]. It is important that the teacher will seek to carry out a collaborative activity through the use of the wiki, be well aware of the capabilities and features of this technology in order to prepare and train their students properly. This process takes time and students should practise not abruptly, but gradually and methodically. Research states that the educational use of wikis is based on the preferred learning model of education [2].

4.3   Learner Role

Through wikis, students assume new roles, which in traditional teaching could not be possible to have. In roles like the one of the producer, content is created by the student. They can also act as commentator enabled by the functionality of the wiki to comment and reflect on data posted from others in a wiki. Finally there is the role of the classifier, since each member of a wiki has to classify the activity. These roles characterize the users of a wiki [13]. As a result of these different roles, users are given the opportunity for the organization and construction of knowledge. Corollary of this is the association of wikis with the theory of social constructivism of Vygotsky [13].

An additional requirement for the use of wikis, relates to the fact that the users need to participate actively in collaborative writing, therefore they must have developed the ability of expressing themselves very well. This will eventually enable the active involvement of learners in the process of problem solving and constructive cooperation between them [10]. Research emphasizes that through a tool such as a wiki, one can form groups of students, which will be invited to create content through cooperation with each other, exchanging ideas and opinions on the subject they are studying and developing skills of autonomy and responsibility for their own personal learning [4].

4.4   Social Constructivism

Social constructivism, according to Vygotsky, emphasizes on student interaction for building and creating their own learning and knowledge [12]. Two models of learning that meet the characteristics and capabilities of a wiki, is constructivism and collaborative learning [2]. Both of these models do not follow traditional methods of teaching where the teacher is an authority and the student passive receiver of information and knowledge.

According to the principles of social constructivism, opportunities exist for students to develop concepts based on their prior knowledge and understanding. It is necessary, therefore, to have appropriate tools that will allow students to discover new knowledge and support them in their efforts in a creative way [2].

4.5   Wikis and Learning Communities

Research indicates that successful use of a technological tool such as the wiki needs to develop a framework of intersubjectivity [10]. Within a collaborative wiki one may create teach communities, which can be compared to learning experiences that are gained as part of participation and negotiation" [4]. An indispensable factor for the successful creation of learning communities is intersubjectivity when creating content that will be hosted by the wiki. There must be an exchange of views and ideas, interaction and negotiation between participants that identify the elements considered under all members group, and thus will be incorporated in their field [10].

It is worth noting that according to earlier research wikis create communities of practice that are identified as particularly important to the educational process [13]. Theory reinforces the importance of communities of practice, indicating that interaction between individual experience and social cognitive structures may result in knowledge creation [13]. This collaborative process of building knowledge in a wiki, leads to the creation of so-called "architecture of participation", after users - students, collaborate and interact to produce and compose the subject of their study. In line with the views of teachers who studied the capabilities of a wiki, this can facilitate learning by creating a learner-centered educational process [13].

4.6   Challenges

Like any technological tool, and so wikis, have to face various challenges in the effort to integrate them into the educational process. When handling a collaborative activity in a wiki, the risk that users-learners focus more on the technological tool, rather than to the study topic-problem which is called upon to resolve, exists. Meanwhile, a wiki hardly presents the individual's work, which can create confusion for the distinct roles that every member of a team has to carry. It should also be noted that the production of content by any user is not considered guaranteed within a wiki, since there can be no absolute accuracy of the content generated by each separately. These challenges, however, can be overcome by promoting the idea that the contribution of each team member is considered equally important in the process of studying a subject through a wiki [8].

The various challenges of wikis were considered in a survey conducted in higher education [11]. The latter aimed to determine whether the use of wikis in collaborative learning environments, as part of learning the Japanese language at an early stage was helpful and contributed in blended learning scenarios where face-to-face contact and interaction through technology were combined. Research indicated emerging challenges such as the difficulty in creating and modifying the content of a page wiki, the uncertainty about the nature of activities undertaken, difficulties on deciding the structure that should be followed, and the need for more direct interaction within groups and issues about leadership among team members [11].

Cooperation may be both a catalytic and a limiting factor in achieving a common goal, as on the one hand, students can recognize the positive results from the use of technology in learning and on the other, the difficulties on the process followed at several points, depending on the weaknesses that characterize each part of the wiki. This may be due to lack of adequate training in techniques involving the wiki and student information from the teacher to the stage and type of activities that should be carried out [11]. Some of these challenges stem from the lack of effective coordination for the work done and the different time and space cooperation takes place in an environment wiki [7].

Research on the integration of wikis as a collaborative learning tool in primary education, revealed that the characteristics of the particular technological tool fosters cooperation between learners, even young school children [13]. Users of wikis characterized by anxiety about the criticism they would receive from the rest of what had been written. Teachers are the ones who have to reduce the stress levels of the students and to emphasize that the main objective of processing an activity in a wiki, is a form of collaboration between users, which requires honesty and sharing thoughts and ideas [13].

The wikis seems to offer opportunities for developing the important skills of cooperation and integration of knowledge, which are required by learners of all ages.

5   Discussion

The analysis of the data showed some really important findings. To begin with the first research question that is related to the attitudes of primary school teachers about wikis and the collaboration learning, positive attitude is identified. Most of the teachers who participated in the research and specifically 14 out of the 20 participants agreed with the statement that the use of wiki leads to collaboration when it is used in the classroom. The same positive attitude is noted from the participants about the use of wiki and collaboration outside of the classroom door (13 out of 20 were positive). Only one participant disagreed with the statement that wikis results to collaboration when they are used outside the classroom. A positive attitude is observed in total due to the educators who believe that the use of wikis leads in the achievement of collaborative learning.

Furthermore, the second research question which refers to the degree of availability of teachers to use the wiki in the classroom mainly for the implementation of group assignments, a positive attitude is identified as well. We found that 15 out of the 20 participants showed positive attitudes about the use of wiki in their own classroom and about the attainment of group work. Only one participant showed negative attitude with the use of wiki in his own classroom for team work.

Continuing with the third research question relating with primary school student's willingness to implement team work using wikis based to the technological features of them, results indicate that teachers are willing to try them in their classrooms. More specifically primary school educators have noted the characteristics of the wikis which make group work flexible and feasible. Features as the asynchronous discussion, the content editing, the post of multimedia content from the students, characteristics noted by earlier research [4 -10] make the use of wiki really important for the achievement of collaborative learning. In summary, educators believe that wikis facilitate team work and the "entrance" of them in the classroom will be good for the children, due to the fact that collaboration skills will be approved and the group work will be based on interaction between students.

The last research question refers to the role of the educator in the classroom when wikis are the means to achieve group assignments. Our 20 informants agree on their views on the role of the teacher. They believe that teachers must have the leading role when wiki is used, indicating that educators have to participate with their students during the process of collaborative learning through wikis. They also suggest that they have to give feedback to the students at regular time intervals. Specifically six out of the 20 participants completely agreed with the statement that the teacher has to have the leading role. Moreover, 12 of the 20 teachers also agreed with the specific statement. Also, 15 teachers agreed with the statement that during the process of the use of wiki and the implementation of assignments, educators have to give general and specific feedback to the students. These characteristics of the teacher role are also mentioned in the literature [8].

These results that derived from the analysis of the questionnaire data were compared with the data collected from the semi-structured interviews. In total three interviews were taken. Through the qualitative analysis of the interviews, the same positive attitude is shown from the teachers. It is worth noting, however, that through the interviews some problems were referred from the participants about the use of wiki in Cyprus classrooms. First of all, the one interviewee noted the lack of computers and in general the lack of technological equipment in Cyprus schools, that makes the use of wiki difficult. Further, another problem expressed by the second interviewee refers to the lack of time in the classroom. The uses of wikis were considered to be too time consuming for an overloaded curriculum. The third interviewee said that despite the fact that wiki technology is very important and the use of it will result in collaborative learning, one needs to specify the characteristics that students must have to achieve this. Appreciation to the work of others, discussion with the group you work with about the content of the assignment, respect to all the members of the team and communication between the students were among the qualities required from the students.

In summary, the analysis of the semi-structure interviews emphasized the positive attitude of educators about wikis. Interviews also pointed the vital role the teachers must have during the implement of assignments using wiki technology. They further highlighted the main problems that are likely occurring from the use of wiki in a typical Cyprus classroom. These mainly relate to the lack of infrastructure in schools, the time pressures and overloaded curriculum which specifies the material educators have to cover in a specific time schedule as indicated by the Ministry of Education and Culture of Cyprus.

6   Conclusion

The ultimate purpose of conducting the current research was to examine the views of primary school teachers in Cyprus about wikis as a tool that can be integrated into education and promote collaborative learning. The importance of this work-in-progress study lies in its attempt to illuminate the field of wiki use in Cyprus primary schools and teachers' views in particular.

Results indicate that the teachers have a quite positive attitude towards the use of wikis in primary education, since according to their views they promote collaboration among students and learning outcomes based on the implementation of the learning objectives set on each lesson. Also in accordance with their views, wikis and the ways in which they work lead to the development of collaborative skills to students.

Further, teachers appear to be willing to incorporate wikis into the learning process, for achieving objectives in different subject domains of the curriculum. Teachers note, however, difficulties exist in the introduction of wikis in Cypriot primary education, the main reasons being logistical and related to infrastructure in schools and lack of time on the part of teachers to cover the teaching material.

Finally, despite their positive attitudes, teachers stress the importance of equity in the integration of wikis in education. They believe that their role in processes of collaborative learning enabled through the use of wikis should be prescriptive, with continued participation and feedback to learners to maximize learning.

Implications of the study point to the need to consider the use of wikis in the primary classroom as part of collaborative learning activities. Further study needs to explore further questions on teacher attitudes and existing uses of wikis in larger populations in Cyprus schools.

References

1. Charalampous, N.: Collaborative Learning: from theory to practice. Pedagogical Institute of Cyprus (2000), http://users.sch.gr/kliapis/NeofytF.pdf (retrieved); (Χαραλάμπους, Ν.: Συνεργατική Μάθηση: από τη θεωρία στην πράξη. Παιδαγωγικό Ινστιτούτο Κύπρου (2000))
2. Cole, M.: Using Wiki technology to support student engagement: Lessons from the trenches. Computers & Education 52(1), 141–146 (2009)
3. Dillenbourg, P.: Introduction: What do you mean by 'collaborative learning'? In: Dillenbourg, P. (ed.) Collaborative learning: Cognitive and computational approaches. Pergamon/Elsevier Science Ltd., Oxford (1999)
4. Grant, L.: Using Wikis in Schools: a Case Study, Futurelab, 1-10 (2006)
5. Kay, K.: 21st century skills: why they matter, what they are, and how we get there. In: Bellanca, J., Brandt, R. (eds.) 21st Century Skills. Rethinking How Students Learn, pp. xiii–xxxi. Solution Tree Press, Bloomington (2011)
6. Korompili, S. (n.d.): The need for guiding strategy in libraries of educational institutions, pp. 109–116, http://eprints.rclis.org/10707/1/14psab018.pdf (retrieved) (Κορομπίλη, Σ. (n.d.).: Η αναγκαιότητα της καθοδηγητικής στρατηγικής στις βιβλιοθήκες εκπαιδευτικών ιδρυμάτων, pp. 109–116)
7. Larusson, J.A., Alterman, R.: Wikis to support the "collaborative" part of collaborative learning. International Journal of Computer-Supported Collaborative Learning 4, 371–402 (2009)

8. O'Bannon, B.W., Lubke, J.K., Britt, V.G.: You still need that face-to-face communication.: drawing implications from preservice teachers' perceptions of wikis as a collaborative tool. Technology, Pedagogy and Education, 1–18 (2013)
9. Partnership for 21st Century skills Framework definitions (2009), http://p21.org/storage/documents/P21_Framework_Definitions.pdf (retrieved)
10. Pifarré, M., Staarman, J.: Wiki-supported collaborative learning in primary education: How a dialogic space is created for thinking together. International Journal of Computer-Supported Collaborative Learning 6(2), 187–205 (2011)
11. Ramanau, R., Geng, F.: Researching the use of Wiki's to facilitate group work. Procedia - Social and Behavioral Sciences 1(1), 2620–2626 (2009)
12. Schunk, D. Learning Theories: An Educational Approach. Athens: Metaixmio. (2010) (Schunk, D.: Θεωρίες Μάθησης: Μια εκπαιδευτική προσέγγιση. Αθήνα: Μεταίχμιο (2010))
13. Wheeler, S., Yeomans, P., Wheeler, D.: The good, the bad and the wiki: Evaluating student-generated content for collaborative learning. British Journal of Educational Technology 39(6), 987–995 (2008)

Computer Assisted Individual Approach
to Acquiring Foreign Vocabulary of Students Major

Nadezhda Almazova and Marina Kogan

Dep. of Linguistics and Cross-Cultural Communication,
St. Petersburg State Polytechnical University, St. Petersburg, Russia
almazovanadia1@ya.ru, m_kogan@inbox.ru

Abstract. Multiple challenges for organizing an effective ESP language course for non-linguistics post-graduate students at St. Petersburg State Polytechnical University (SPbSPU) are inherently rooted in the broad spectrum of students' majors in ESP classes. Diversity of students' academic interests calls for new approaches and for tailoring the course in accordance with the students' needs. Our study represents an approach to individualizing the course by introducing data-driven learning (DDL) elements into the syllabus. More specifically, our approach is aimed at having post-graduate students getting concordances of their readings corpora for identifying unfamiliar vocabulary. The paper describes the recommended software for concordance building, concordance-based activities with unfamiliar vocabulary and the way of controlling the vocabulary acquisition. Test results show steady progress in independent vocabulary acquisition among the experiment participants. Questionnaires show they see the usefulness and efficiency of DDL approach to identifying and learning unfamiliar vocabulary.

Keywords: data-driven learning (DDL) approach, teaching methodology, ESP course for post-graduates, concordance building software, knowledge rating, unfamiliar vocabulary.

1   Introduction

The problem of acquiring new lexis in specific purpose language (SPL) courses is traditionally in the focus of attention of both practical teachers, and methodology researchers [5, 17, 19, 24]. They argue the importance of forming teaching/learning strategies aimed at developing the students' ability to read words correctly, to know the meaning of a word within several different contexts, to use words both in reading and writing, as well as to use word-learning strategies.

Before answering all these questions a teacher, as well as students, should see quite distinctly what certain tasks they can fulfill without assistance but only mastering vocabulary. Basing on the research of Carver [3], Hu and Nation [15], and Chung and Nation [4] have come to the conclusion that at least 98 % coverage of the running words is needed for unassisted reading. Should it be acquired from extensive reading advocated by Cobb et al. [6], Day and Bamford [9], Hornst [11], and Pigada and

P. Zaphiris and A. Ioannou (Eds.): LCT 2014, Part II, LNCS 8524, pp. 248–257, 2014.

Schmitt [22], or is there any measurable learning from hands on concordancing [7] or an interactive on- line database, the idea supported by Horst et al. [12]?

The problem seems to be rather acute for Russian postgraduate students of Polytechnic University whose major covers different fields of sciences and humanities. Their study course comprises, as an obligatory part, taking an exam in the English language. The exam is mainly based on reading and comprehending special literature (scientific articles, monographs, etc.) which is demonstrated in adequate translation or interpreting. Adequacy implies the necessity of students' mastering their major vocabulary substantially in a pre-exam period at English classes. Translation is a common activity for many of them. A wide range of professionally -oriented lexis encourages intelligent uses of appropriate translation strategies as well as appropriate reading and test doing strategies. In this particular case a teacher must be very strategic about what vocabulary should be learned first, how a learning process should be organized, what word-learning strategies are preferable.

In spite of the fact that there have been several textbooks produced to teach academic vocabulary, examples are [16, 25] and papers devoted to technical vocabulary identifying and acquisition [4, 5], a teaching methodology here is of vital importance, because the problems a teacher faces are numerous. The situation turns out to be rather unpredictable when students with various major have English classes together. Not only their major is different, the level of English can be incomparable (from pre-intermediate to upper-intermediate). It is quite obvious that the learner-centered individual approach to learners in order to promote their interest to and the efficiency of learning their major vocabulary seems next to impossible to be implemented in a group of 20-30 students having classes once a week within a period of 90 minutes as it is often the case for ESP classes in post-graduate groups in Russian Universities [1]. All these factors predetermine some practical limitations to the current teaching context, and a vocabulary component of an ESP course seems to be quite challenging for a teacher, as far as all these issues must be taken into consideration.

One of possible ways of making the process of mastering major vocabulary more efficient is a tandem-learning described in one of our articles [23]. Another one is described here and is based on integrating computer in teaching context with the aim of eliminating those "postgraduate numerous class" minuses. It is based on DDL (data-driven learning) approach adapted to our circumstances. The main difference of our approach from what is described in the majority of publications on applying DDL in language teaching and learning is that we develop activities for concordances built by post-graduate students from their major reading corpora in English. We were inspired by T. Cobb and his colleagues' idea of intensifying work with unfamiliar vocabulary through different activities with the concordance of the text which students have to read [6, 7, 13].

The activities depend on the features of the concordancer program available. For example, karTatekA allows analysis of a different lists (frequency list, inverted list, wordlengths list), lemmatization of words which provides an opportunity to unite all word family members in a single card and then to gain access to all contexts from the card, creating lexical and grammatical homonyms, word segmentation, and word element and morpheme search etc. [1]. The serious obstacle towards its wide implementation is that it requires a very time-consuming procedure of preparing text in an original pdf format for building concordance with a sentence-length minimal context.

Being convinced that the idea of using concordances of reading corpora for intensifying vocabulary work is very promising and fruitful we decided to develop activities with different tools freely available on T. Cobb's *Compleat Lexical Tutor* website (http://www.lextutor.ca/) for consequent post graduate students' independent work.

Against this background the main research questions are thus:

1. Is the usage of this DDL adapted method efficient?
2. Does it reflect research interest or has it large uptake in practical teaching?
3. What is the learners' reaction to it?
4. Are the students largely successful in their outcomes?

2   Method

2.1   Features of Software Used

The concordance building software chosen was Text-based concordance tool from Comleat Lexical Tutor website developed and supported by Tomas Cobb at Université du Québec à Montréal (http://www.lextutor.ca/ http://www.lextutor.ca/concordancers/text_concord/). It is a free-available on-line resource with a number of unique features considered by Diniz [10] and described in a series of T. Cobb and his colleagues' publications [e.g., 6, 12, 13]. Among the features not mentioned in the above papers but highlighted by Boulton [2], who found them typical of the most reputable websites, are its availability from any computer around the world via stable Internet –connection, its extremely low possibility of crashing, changing interface, moving site or being removed from the web. Even though Compleat Lexical Tutor does not offer the same conventional types of text searches as many other concordancer type programs do, and does not allow saving output concordance automatically on a hard disk, we decided to use this resource in our research because of

- simplicity of the original text (usually available in pdf format) preparation for getting its concordance;
- the maximum size of the text affordable for uploading to build concordance (up to 50 000 words) meets the needs of our post graduate students whose compulsory reading corpus of specialized papers consists of 47 000 words on average;
- unique features of the resource such as the *Text-based Range*, allowing users to upload up to 25 of their own texts and see how many of them each word appears in, and in which texts each word appears, and the *Vocabulary Profile* feature which analyses users' uploaded texts and compares their texts to the most-frequent-words-in-English word list and/or to the Academic Word List composed by Coxhead [8].

2.2   Analysis of Questionnaire Data

The data were collected from two achievement tests (Test 1 and Test 2) and the questionnaires completed by the experiment participants, post graduate students, totaled 6. The experiment participants were to build a concordance of their reading corpora using corresponding tools from *Compleat Lexical Tutor* website, to make up a list of 100 unknown words using a wordlist of the concordance, and to send it to the instructor. Basing on T. Cobb's and other researchers' works we could expect that the majority of unknown words will be of infrequent occurrence in the selected texts. To our surprise students reported from 30 to 50% words as unknown which are rather frequent in their corpora (with frequency more than 10). The recommended algorithm of studying the unknown lexis depended on the unknown word frequency in the student's corpus. For high-frequency words they were asked to read concordance lines and extended contexts from their papers to understand the meaning of the unknown word, and then to verify their guessing using a dictionary. For low frequency words they had to start with the same step, but taking into account a low probability of correct guessing based on one or two examples of the word usage, they were recommended to search for the word or word combinations using Multi-concordance tool on T.Cobb's website and in case of failure to find more examples there (which can be the case if the unknown item belongs to the specialist vocabulary) to use the *Google>books* query search before looking it up in a dictionary. As we showed [1] this is a very effective search tool for finding plentiful examples of usage of specialist lexis in domain-specific sources of usage in specialized and specialist contexts which are underrepresented in general on-line corpora such as BNC and COCA.

The questionnaires were completed after Test 2 because some questions implied the reflection on the Tests results. The respondents were from different departments, majoring in nanotechnology, physical electronics, physics of semiconductors, electric devices, economics, and finances; all but one of the respondents were male; the average age is 22. They all have been studying English for years, but have had different breaks in formal training. To decide if the usage of DDL adapted method was efficient we asked the students about their favourite strategies of memorizing new vocabulary. According to their answers, using an electronic bilingual dictionary and making up vocabulary lists were the most widespread strategies of dealing with unfamiliar vocabulary, "making no special efforts in hope that they will become familiar in a "natural" way (through reading, watching films, speaking to native speakers, etc.) sooner or later" was a second frequent choice; one third of respondents prefer using synonyms and guessing meaning from the context. The students use the same strategies reading different types of texts including specialized texts of their major. Usually most of them read specialized texts carefully just once, with only one student reporting that he does this twice. Nobody of the experiment participants has heard about DDL approach in language learning before the course.

The questionnaire asked students to rate strategies they used to clarify the meaning of the unknown words in their corpus according to the following five-point scale:

1 = never
2 = once or twice
3 = fairly often
4 = very often
5 = almost always

The results are presented in Fig. 1. The mean ratings on the ordinate axis show that for both high frequency words and low frequency words the students very often tried to guess their meaning from the nearest context (which means the concordance lines of their texts) or extended contexts. For low frequency words they also often used electronic mono- and bilingual dictionaries and *Google>books* query search, a new resource for them. Nobody used online corpora on a regular basis dealing with the unknown words from their texts. But many of them gave a try to this resource, new and unusual for them.

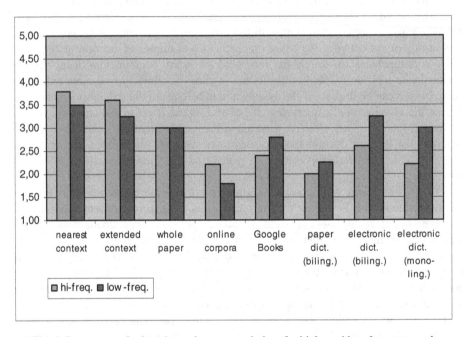

Fig. 1. Strategy use for learning unknown vocabulary for high- and low frequent words

They did pay attention to collocations of the unknown words with other words but often failed to notice grammar peculiarities (e.g., co-occurrence of articles, prepositions, commas, the place of words in the sentence, etc.). They reported that they did not encounter unknown words among off-list words produced by VocProfile tool. This means that the examples of the usage of single unknown words can be found in the BNC and COCA on-line corpora, and that the students know the specialist vocabulary well enough. However, the latter might be an illusive impression because the automotive word frequency range analysis deals with single words, not with word collocations. As a result, two- and multiword terms remain undetected.

Despite the multitude of examples of single frequent words usage (e.g., the number of tokens in COCA is 2048 for *turbine* and 175604 for *head*) there are no examples of the two-word terms from the specialist field (e.g. *turbine head* which is the difference between the static head and the losses through the installation) [1].

Some of other questions were in the form of statements on a 5-point Likert scale, from 1= strongly disagree to 5=strongly agree. They all found the concordance of their corpora which provides the wordlist helpful (M=4) in identifying unfamiliar vocabulary, the way of controlling and assessing the progress in mastering unknown vocabulary stimulating (3.6) and all but one would like to have similar tests during the whole course. They think that the activities with their texts based on using different tools from T. Cobb website are effective and useful for studying unknown vocabulary (4). There is only one "refuser" who did not like the method at all and is not likely to use it in future. Other participants are planning to continue to use this resource in their language studies after the end of the course. Taking into account the fact that this resource was absolutely new for them and training in the computer lab was very limited (actually only one academic session was allocated for the purpose) we feared that the students would find the resource difficult to use. To our surprise all participants except "the refuser" reported that it was not difficult to use the resource, with only one student pointing out that, overall, it is time-consuming. As for tools=activities most useful for learning unknown vocabulary their opinions divided. Text-based concordance and multi-concordance tools were the most frequent choice, with Text-based range, List_Learn and VocabProfile also mentioned. Two students are so enthusiastic about the DDL approach in language learning that they are ready to go further and master concordancer-type programs which can be installed on their PCs.

2.3   Testing Unfamiliar Vocabulary

Each of two tests contained 20 words selected randomly from 100 unknown word lists provided by the students. During the test they were to estimate a knowledge rating of the words according to the following scheme developed by Horst and Meara [14] and later used by Cobb and his colleagues [6].

    0 = I don't know what this word means
    1 = I am not sure what this word means
    2 = I think I know what this word means
    3 = I definitely know what this word means

and then provide translation equivalents for items they had given 3 and 2 points. Test 1 was conducted 2 weeks after they had identified 100 unknown words from their reading corpora. After another 3 weeks Test 2 was conducted. It contained items from Test1 which were given 0 or 1 points and those which were translated incorrectly. The rest words were selected randomly from the original 100 wordlist except for the words which had been included into Test 1. The students did not know the results of Test 1, and did not know which words we were planning to include into Test 2. So, they are supposed to have worked with all the words from their lists using different strategies until Test 2. After completing Test 2 the students were asked to correct their translations from Test1 using the concordance or the context for the cases when they gave the correct translation of lemma but ignored a word morphology, e.g. *corrode –* *korrozia, which is a noun in Russian. By the next class they all submitted correct translations for these words. The results of the tests are presented in Tables 1 and 2.

Table 1. Word knowledge rating at Test 1 and Test 2

	Average number of words for each category from 6 lists of 20 words	
	Test 1	Test 2
0 (not known)	2.5	2.0
1 (rather unsure)	4.5	4.0
2 (less unsure)	4.5	2.6
3 (known)	8.1	11.4

Table 2. Translation results

	Average number of words translated correctly	Percentage of words with correct translation	Average number of words marked as "known"	Average number of "known" words translated correctly	Ratio of "known words" to words translated correctly from this category
Test 1	10.5	53	8.1	7.6	0.93
Test 2	14.4	72	11.4	10.2	0.90

The results show that the average number of words in the first three categories decreased while the number of words marked as "known" increased according to the students' self- evaluation. The test results prove that their self-evaluation is correct: they translated correctly 91.5% words marked as "known".   Back to the questionnaires, they think the results of the tests are valid (3.8) for making conclusions about the degree of learning the rest of the words from the given group (of 100 words). They estimate that they do not know about 0.5-2% words in their reading corpus, which is within 230 – 950 words for their corpora of an average size of around 47 000 words.

We did not take into account the results of the "refuser" who did not use DDL approaches while working with the unknown vocabulary. We have good reasons to suspect that he did not use his favourite strategy (bilingual dictionary) either, because none of the words from Test 2 was marked as "known" by him, and only 3 words were translated correctly. On the other hand, he marked as "not known" only 3 words. This can be regarded as an illustration of the conclusion – very encouraging, in our opinion – made by some researchers that there is the learning impact of even one or two encounters with a new word (though to capture it, very sensitive measures are required) [13]. We used so called "active recall" [18], the most difficult for learners way of testing and, probably, the only possible for us having to deal with lists of 100 words each. Our "refuser" definitely encountered unfamiliar words at least a couple of times, selecting them from the wordlist and then copying them into a special file.

2.4   The Analysis of Unknown Vocabulary

We have conducted the analysis of the vocabulary that our students are unfamiliar with using the software from VocabProfile section of *Compleat Lexical Tutor* website. The results are presented in Fig. 2. Curve 1 shows the distribution of all words from the students' 100 word lists of unknown words, a total of 611 tokens. Curve 2 shows the distribution of words found in more than one of 100 word lists. The total number of such words is 70, including 9 words unfamiliar to the half of the students.

According to the plot most of the first hundred unknown words from the students' reading corpora belong to the first – fifth thousand frequency bands of the *most-frequent-words-in-English* BNC-COCA word list. The majority – 185 tokens or 153 words excluding re-occurrences for curve 1, and 32 tokens for curve 2 – belong to the third band. The possible recommendations could be as follows.

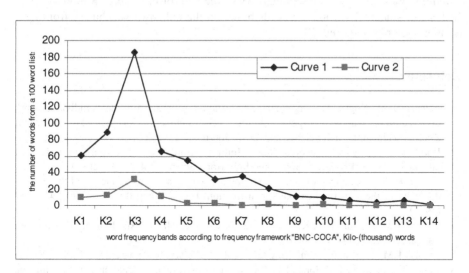

Fig. 2. The distribution of the experiment participants' unknown words according to the frequency framework «BNC-COCA»

The students could be recommended to revise the first – forth thousand frequency band word lists from List_Learn section of the T. Cobb's website. It allows users to detect unknown words looking sequentially through the word list of a given frequency band. Then the meaning of an unknown word could be understood from a number of BNC examples, with the most telling of them being stored on the user's PC. Hopefully by the end of the course post-graduate students will be able to expand their vocabulary till 5 000 General English words and collocations in accordance with the Russian National Standards requirements, following this algorithm independently. The words unknown to different students are to be accumulated in a special bank so that foreign language teachers could develop vocabulary training exercises and use them in the ESP post-graduate classroom.

3   Conclusions

The small sample in the present study needs extending though the results so far have been promising in terms of what learners do with their reading corpora to identify the unknown vocabulary and learn new words using DDL approach which is new for them. They are largely successful in their outcomes and the progress in acquiring new vocabulary proven by tests. It is important to notice that they achieved these results focusing on the unknown words, not re-reading carefully their texts several times as participants of a similar experiment described in [6] did.

The described algorithm could be recommended for introducing this DDL adapted method into the ESP post-graduates course for organizing their individual work in the course taking into account generally positive feedback, small amount of special training required, and a relative simplicity of the control procedure. A more detailed analysis of students' vocabulary needs based on the unknown vocabulary from their reading corpora is required.

References

1. Almazova, N., Kogan, M.: Organizing polytechnic post-graduate students individual work on required reading corpora (wihtin ESP course). Universitetskii Nauchnyi Zhurnal=Humanities and Science University Journal 6, 13–25 (2013)
2. Boulton, A.: Beyond concordancing: Multiple affordances of corpora in university language degrees. Procedia – Social and Behavioral Sciences 34, 33–38 (2012)
3. Carver, R.P.: Percentage of unknown vocabulary words in text as a function of the relative difficulty of the text: Implications for instruction. J. of Reading Behavior 26(4), 413–437 (1994)
4. Chung, T.M., Nation, P.: Technical vocabulary in specialized texts. Reading in a Foreign Language 15(2), 103–116 (2003)
5. Chung, T.M., Nation, P.: Identifying technical vocabulary. System 32(2), 251–263 (2004)
6. Cobb, T., Greaves, C., Horst, M.: Can the rate of lexical acquisition from reading be increased? An experiment in reading French with a suite of on-line resources. In: Raymond, P., Cornaire, C. (eds.) Regards sur la didactique des langues secondes, Éditions logique, Montréal, pp. 133–153 (2001)
7. Cobb, T.: Is there any measurable learning from hands-on concordancing. System 25(3), 301–315 (1997)
8. Coxhead, A.: A new academic word list. TESOL Quarterly 34(2), 213–238 (2000)
9. Day, R.R., Bamford, J.: Extensive Reading in the Second Language Classroom. Cambridge University Press, Cambridge (1998)

10. Diniz, L.: Comparative review: Textstat 2.5, AntConc 3.0, and Compleat Lexical Tutor 4.0 Language Learning & Technology 9(3), 22–27 (2005)
11. Horst, M.: Learning L2 vocabulary through extensive reading: A measurement study. Canadian Modern Language Review 61(3), 355–382 (2005)
12. Horst, M., Cobb, T., Nicolae, I.: Expanding academic vocabulary with an interactive on-line database. Language Learning & Technology 9(2), 90–110 (2005)
13. Horst, M., Cobb, T.: Growing academic vocabulary with a collaborative online database. In: IT-MELT 2001: Information Technology & Multimedia in English Language Teaching, Kowloon, Hong Kong (2001)
14. Horst, M., Meara, P.: Test of a model for predicting second language lexical growth through reading. Canadian Modern Language Review 56(2), 308–328 (1999)
15. Hu, M., Nation, I.S.P.: Vocabulary density and reading comprehension. Reading in a Foreign Language 13(1), 404–430 (2000)
16. Huntley, H.: Essential Academic Vocabulary. Houghton Mifflin, Boston (2006)
17. Joe, A., Nation, P., Newton, J.: Vocabulary learning and speaking activities. English Teaching Forum 43(1), 2–7 (1996)
18. Laufer, B., Goldstein, Z.: Testing vocabulary knowledge: Size, strength, and computer adaptiveness. Language Learning 54(3), 399–436 (2004)
19. Nation, I.S.P.: Learning Vocabulary in Another Language. Cambridge University Press, Cambridge (2001)
20. Nation, I.S.P.: Teaching Vocabulary: Strategies and Techniques. Thompson Heinle, N.-Y. (2008)
21. Nation, P., Chung, T.: Teaching and testing vocabulary. In: Long, M.H., Doughty, C.J. (eds.) The Handbook of Language Teaching, pp. 543–559. Blackwell Publishing Ltd., Hong Kong (2009)
22. Pigada, M., Schmitt, N.: Vocabulary acquisition from extensive reading: a case study. Reading in a Foreign Language 18(1), 1–28 (2006)
23. Popova, N., Kogan, M.: Didactic Links as means of Profiling Technology Realization for Masters of Linguistics. In: Proceedings in the 1st Global Virtual Conference workshop, pp. 185–189. Publishing Institution of University of Zilina, Zilina (2013)
24. Read, J.: Assessing Vocabulary. Cambridge University Press, Cambridge (2000)
25. Schmitt, D., Schmitt, N.: Focus on Vocabulary. Longman Pearson Education, White Plains, NY (2005)

Immersive Creative Classrooms within the Zones of Educational Priorities in Greek Primary Schools

Antonios Besios[1], and Niki Lambropoulos[2]

[1] 152nd Primary School of Athens, Miliaraki 57-59, Athens, 11145, Greece
[2] Wire Communications Laboratory, Dept. of Electrical and Computer Engineering,
University of Patras, Greece
26504, Rion-Patras
adonisbessios@gmail.com, nlampropoulou@wcl.ee.upatras.gr

Abstract. Nowadays, ICT and Social Media utilization in primary schools becoming more challenging provided that the educators aiming at not only transferring knowledge but also at developing shared meaning and common skills within creative classrooms (CCR). In this way both the teachers and the students can work on and share experiences to support co-creativity and idea generation also having wide presence in related educational communities. CCR refer to innovative learning environments that fully embed the potential of ICT to innovate learning and teaching practices. Such environments are proposed to bring forward 'online presence' on an interface for shared knowledge to occur by enhancing trust and reliability. The teachers of Art and Theatre subjects at the 152 Primary School in Athens, Greece supported the Zones of Educational Priorities the school was chosen for. In the case study presented, presence and co-creativity are developed under CCR umbrella with the use of social media and Web 2.0 tools as well as best practices are shared within the wider Greek teachers' community network.

Keywords: Online Presence, Creative Classrooms, Immersive Experience, Zones of Educational Priorities, Social Media, Web 2.0 Tools.

1   Introduction

Greece is in the middle of a severe economic crisis, which is also related to an educational crisis. Education is generally acknowledged as one of the crucial components of personal and professional development. The integration of Information and Communication Technology (ICT) in education as well as the social and collaborative nature of the Internet provided another medium for communication and training; however, despite the advantages, the crisis exists. In his foreword for the United Nations Educational, Scientific and Cultural Organization [1], Daniels said that within a short time ICT has become one of the basic building blocks of the modern society. Furthermore, the current shift occurring in the Web from a static content environment where end users are the recipients of information—defined as Web 1.0—to one where they are active content creators—defined as Web 2.0—can be

P. Zaphiris and A. Ioannou (Eds.): LCT 2014, Part II, LNCS 8524, pp. 258–268, 2014.
© Springer International Publishing Switzerland 2014

described as a transition to a more distributed, participatory, and collaborative environment [2]. Web 2.0 is a platform where "knowledge-working is no longer thought of as the gathering and accumulation of facts, but rather, the riding of waves in a dynamic environment" [3]. To Berners-Lee [4], the Web is not only a technological tool but also a social phenomenon that enables collaboration and creativity.

ICT is the backbone of the knowledge economy and has been recognised as an effective tool for promoting economic growth and development [5]. Organisations, educational institutions and business have been investing in the use of ICT in Education, or in what ESRC now calls Technology Enhanced Learning (TEL). Nevertheless, teachers' education has been severely criticized on the grounds of both quantity and quality [6]. Economic advantage will accrue to a population that acquires competencies in processing information into knowledge and applying it in work and everyday life. These competencies are not only related to using the devices but also working on procedures that give access to information and skilfully transforming information into knowledge. As this is the task of the educator, educational systems will become a national resource as important as the traditional factors of production-land, labour, and capital. This in turn would cause educators to become more important, their productivity and their wages should increase, but they can also expect the nature of their jobs to change with a great deal of specialization.

In Greece, teachers' training is mainly conducted within the universities pedagogical departments; also the Greek National reform Programme suggested the introduction of Pedagogical and Teaching Certificate for future teachers, following the PGCE (Postgraduate Certificate in Education) British example. Implementation of the integrated in-service training programme was suggested for the "New School". It is estimated that the number of those who are to be trained, until December 2013, will rise to approximately 150,000. Greek in-service teachers' training at the moment is limited to level B offered to the ones who have attended courses outside the school (KEK). Further training has stopped from any other organisation and only the school advisors support the active teachers in their work. This gap was filled within the ZEP by constant internal training focused on teachers' problems and actual needs.

In regard to the educational staff working at the 44th and 152nd Primary Schools of Athens, and the 110th Nursery School of Athens, there are 43 teachers, 7 nursery school teachers, 2 educational psychologists, 1 social worker and scientific staff occasionally visiting the schools; these are, one individual responsible for ZEP, one researcher on learning difficulties, a schools management consultant, the school advisor of the area and the ZEP project manager.

1.1   Online Social Awareness and Presence

Web 2.0 tools and social media offered the glue to stick together the CCR characteristics into place. The authors created a unique for a Greek school multiple uses of the social media and tools available to create presence in the Greek educational world and communities. The web 2.0 platforms WordPress, Slideshare, Facebook and YouTube, the Greek educators' platform and ZEP Community of

Practice within the Greek School Network were utilized so to connect, exchange and synthesize knowledge and experiences as well as present the project in the outer world. A new webpage was developed with Joomla (http://152dim-athin.att.sch.gr) used as an official and more 'permanent' way to link all other tools and communities together. Social media tools keep people constantly informed and connected whereas the project outcomes and best practices are presented interactively with diverse audiences, sharing our views, news and opinions. The blog http://blogs.sch.gr/152dimat/ was used as an online diary facilitating users to interact; it is directly connected to the Community of Practice developed on the Greek School Network platform (http://blogs.sch.gr/groups/zep-patisiwn-152odim-athinwn/). Social media tools provide a great, and necessary, way to increase communication and engagement with the Greek educational audiences. Such communication and engagement facilitate school's presence by making efforts and project outcomes known to students, parents and other stakeholders. Such strategy includes the right messages with little perseverance towards targets also merging formal with informal learning and exchange of best practices. School self-organisation and self-connected was possible as the needed educational staff was doubled due to the participation to the specific ZEP also offering flexibility in the timetable and decision making. According to [7], what a learner has learned is displayed when they talk to other learners. Therefore, the importance of social awareness is evident is learning theories related to social interaction and social organization. We now consider not only information and knowledge transmission but also social and dialogical interactions; social learning theories revolve around such meaning and thus understanding created through discussions. Learning derives from social interactions; an individual's cognitive structures and processes can be made apparent by their interaction with others [8].

According to [9] social presence is the degree of salience of the other person in a mediated communication and the consequent salience of their interpersonal interactions. Other studies referred to the concepts of immediacy as psychological distance [10]) and intimacy as the interpretation of the degree of interpersonal interactions [11]. In online conversations social presence awareness has been defined as the degree by which a person was perceived as 'real' [12]. Presence is concerned with self-representation, self-locality, self-organisation and self-assessment. Co-presence is concerned with group-representation, group-locality, group-organisation and group-assessment. If both can be facilitated via Web 2.0 tools and the use of Social Media the learners have the opportunity to observe themselves and to learn and reflect on their behaviour with other group members.

2   CCR within ZEP at the 152nd Athens Primary School

Creative Classrooms (CCR) refer to innovative learning environments that fully embed the potential of ICT to innovate learning and teaching practices [13]. The policy of Zones of Educational Priorities (ZEP) constitutes a strategic choice of certain European states in order to fight functional illiteracy and school failure. The importance and the contribution of this policy in the reduction of school failure are underlined in reports of experts of the Organization for Economic Co-operation and Development (OECD), European Union.

As the 152nd Primary School of Athens was chosen for ZEP, the Headmaster of the School also considered implementing CCR within ZEP. The IT teacher collaborated with the Fine Arts and Theatre teachers so facilitate the project implementation by utilizing ICT as the collaboration medium as well as bringing the teachers' together as the information and collaboration human hub. The teachers worked in all kinds of couples or in triads, however, the ICT teachers was the catalyst for each one of them. According to [13], innovating in Education and Training (E&T) is a key priority in several flagships of the Europe 2020 Strategy: for example the Agenda for New Skills and Jobs, Youth on the Move, the Digital Agenda and the Innovation Agenda. CCR require innovative pedagogical practices in detail at organizational, curricular, and assessment levels, but also the systemic capability (at micro, meso and macro level) which involves the whole schools community practices on a larger scale. Such implementation is directly associated to content and curricula, assessment, learning practices, teaching practices, organization, leadership and values, connectedness, and infrastructure.

Zones of Educational Priorities (ZEP) were initially implemented in the UK, and elsewhere in the English-speaking world such as New Zealand, South Africa, Australia and particularly successfully in France. ZEP are targeted plans per geographical region for students living in deprived areas. ZEP deal with school failure and consequently early school leaving and promote social inclusion. Zones of Educational Priorities are set up by Ministerial Decisions. School units of primary and secondary education, operating in regions with a low total educational indicator, with a high rate in early school leaving, with a low rate in tertiary education, as well as with low social/economic indicators, namely a low synthetic indicator of prosperity and growth and an indicator of high poverty risk, are becoming ZEP parts.

The objective of ZEP is the equal integration of all pupils into the school system through the operation of support actions about the strengthening of educational outcomes, such as mainly the operation of reception classes, classes of remedial teaching, summer school classes and classes where pupils' mother tongue is taught. The project was implemented in the school year 2010-2011 in its pilot phase through three ZEP in the region of Attica where Athens is, including approximately 20 schools of all levels (ISCED 0, ISCED 1, ISCED 2) and with a follow-up and assessment plan of the action. The scope of the action is that the services offered by the ZEP meet the special educational demands of the local student population.

ZEP purpose is to provide assistance to students who need help within the educational process for equal opportunities for all. The special educational needs of some students are the result of either learning difficulties or social inequalities. Special educational activities for students with learning difficulties have been designed and implemented in many educational systems with the help of psychology and special education. The rapid rise of capitalism in some cases caused the emergence of a new economic and social class; besides the common features of poverty, unemployment, low living standards for many families, small houses, etc there is also another common element: the families are concentrated in areas where they can survive financially. The houses in such areas are small and old, near industrial areas or ports with underdeveloped infrastructure, minimum open spaces, sometimes dodgy and deprived areas.

As such, this creates a new reality for educational policy designers since they have to deal with an educational need regarding individual students, usually a few in each school, but within entire districts. These students' characteristics from deprived areas are: low self-esteem, tendency towards crime, low academic performance particularly in language and mathematics, frequent absence from the school, lack of robust parental responsibility, inability to support learning difficulties at home, also considering the weak financial situation, poor personal health care, poor nutrition, etc. It is therefore clear that such problems are highly social and have a direct impact on the students' school life. Without a radical intervention from outside, these characteristics create a self-sustaining vicious circle regenerated in these deprived areas, supported by them and simultaneously contribute to their perpetuation.

Zones of Educational Priority are an initiative in which the education system is trying to eliminate educational inequalities resulting from social inequalities via specific educational activities. As such, one target is to provide all students of the region equal opportunities in higher education and the labour market.

All citizens that belong to ZEP areas constantly receive social and educational interventions and welfare benefits; however, such discrimination only enhances it and prevents their active participation in the Greek society. Their basic individual human rights are already compromised. As such, an expensive educational intervention is f no meaning to the student coming from a family with unemployed parents; s/he will return into a packed family room with no power and no heating, quietness to read, food to eat or clothes to change, and even a vision for hope. Such intervention should take the form of thunderstorms and has to be multipurpose, discreet and sudden.

3   Social Media and Web 2.0 Tools Utilisation within CCR

The Headmaster of the 152nd Primary School of Athens together with the school teachers decided to adopt the CCR characteristics within ZEP. The teachers of Art and Theatre subjects at the 152nd Primary School in Athens, Greece supported ZEP is implementing based on the British examples. These teachers along with the classroom teacher work together in the same classroom environment using ICT to merge and converge the educational activities from different subjects. In this way not only the students do benefit from the technology enhanced learning activities but also the teachers themselves participate in an in-service training on the knowledge, skills and competencies required to work in such creative class-room activities. In the case study presented, virtual museums visits and videoconferences along with associated experiences were mapped in Inspiration to support students' collaborative writing for an eTwinning program.

The main CCR characteristics and reference parameters (building blocks) were incorporated as interface and tools characteristics and uses as follows:

Content and Curricula - Innovating timetables. Innovative, flexible and tailor-made timetable was used within the official curriculum borders as well as the books adjusted to the curriculum. However, the ICT use offered the new tools especially for external collaboration with other students and teachers via the eTwinning program for sharing timetables and facilitate time management. It offered a boost to teachers' confidence as well despite the economic, professional and social teachers' devaluation with a direct impact on their teaching performance with absence of vision. This project supported 90-100-150 paid teachers' working hours; this is unlikely to continue, and almost impossible to sustain good practice and extend costs.

Assessment. Innovative ICT-enabled assessment approaches can better capture 21st century skills implemented in the use of social media and Web 2.0 tools. However, sustainable and innovative formative assessment in the school everyday life is most of the times without particular practical use due to the absence of initial coherency.

Learning practices across disciplines / subjects. In social media and Web 2.0 tools implemented within CCR, a variety of learning materials were organized thematically to foster "horizontal connectedness" and enable learners to analyze and understand things by multiple perspectives. These tools offered innovative ways to retrieve information from different domains and to create rich multimodal content. Also, everyone was free to try and fail, encouraged and experiment; such philosophy has radically changed the cross-curriculum approaches as until the project implementation, these approaches were difficult to be realized.

As the ICT, Arts and Theatre Education teachers were co-teaching together with the normal classes teachers, some interesting insights were revealed: a) teachers are disassociated to other teachers' subjects due to deeply rooted attitudes and lack of solid and substantial in-service training b) teachers for specialized subjects do not come from pedagogical departments, and thus, pedagogical training is absent; also, there are not familiar with the reality of primary school everyday life. Furthermore, some teachers come from secondary education carrying also false concepts about primary education. As a result, they do not realize, and as such, inspire the students that are in an important subject as they view it as 'playtime'. This is in contradiction to their CCR related teaching practice.

Teaching practices. CCR require that teachers effectively play new roles as mentors, orchestrators, and facilitators of learning and act as role models of creativity and innovation. Therefore, the skill sets of professional teachers should shift from subject knowledge towards expertise in pedagogy and orchestration of CCR management strategies towards creative learning. Innovative teaching practices should be supported by updated, targeted, and inspiring initial education and in-service training (Kampylis et al., 2013). As such, the teachers for special subjects such as ICT, Arts and Theatre education acquire the missing pedagogical experience, learn new strategies, and overall, reconsider the classroom management strategies. Unfortunately, the teachers who gained these experiences do not stay in the school for another year; this is due to different work arrangements, teachers hired by the hour, seconded teachers etc. Consequently, there is knowledge, skills, competence and experience diffused in other schools; however, because of lack of sustainability, everything has to start from scratch again every year in the 152nd Primary School.

Learning-by-creating. CCR actively engage the students as content creators in order to nurture creative imagination, innovation attitude and authentic learning in real contexts. ICT offered the means for working together in teams, co-designing, co-creating, and communicating the actual learner-generated content via Web 2.0 tools and media. Such great and added value offered by new technologies and art classes as well as the important contribution to increase the cultural and therefore human capital via students' participation in culture products. which can these courses serve in school there are groups of teachers, students, there are communities that are involved in a project and act drafted by design, common goals and collaborative practices.

Facilitating peer-to-peer collaboration: Social media and Web 2.0 tools in CCR constantly encourage peer collaboration so students learn to think both independently and with others, enabling them to consider a plurality of perspectives working on synchronous and asynchronous online collaboration to enhance co-creative learning in teams.

Organization. This dimension captures the organisational practices in CCR, and refers to the macro, meso and micro levels, implying a progressive breadth and depth of action to meet local circumstances and needs. This requires a broader involvement with the local communities and authorities; however, the communication is always one way, from the school towards them making great efforts to disseminate the extracted best practices on a local, regional, national and European level.

Leadership and values. CCR currently operate within the ZEP and by definition the work in located in situ within a context of educational structures and values that strongly influence learning objectives and pedagogies, promote equity and guarantee access to quality education for all supporting and facilitating all teachers' initiatives. Social media and Web 2.0 tools are used in a peripheral way extract information and opinions about decision made about school activities.

Connectedness. The pervasive and participatory cultures in anchored in the social and emotional factors that profoundly affect the relationships among school members have a significant impact on their level of engagement and motivation especially within a ZEP. Social media and Web 2.0 tools in CCR offered new possibilities for students to connect with multiple other actors, teachers to interrelate their subjects and exchange experiences and best practices. This is feasible by everyone's conscious and continuous involvement creating and maintaining bonds between teachers and students engaging them in current and future projects.

Infrastructure: For the Social media and Web 2.0 tools in CCR implementation within the ZEP, a dynamic ICT infrastructure is there to support the needed information and experience exchange as well as providing the creative activities medium and platform to improve and accelerate innovative teaching and creative learning as well as disseminate best practices and projects outcomes and results.

As a result, such multi-faceted collaboration promoted the use of computers in ICT-enabled innovation for learning for the teachers' in-service training developing Social media, Web 2.0 and CCR associated knowledge skills and competencies as well as pedagogical approaches and evaluation techniques related to, to name a few: opening up to ICT-enabled innovation and co-creation with the use of Social media and Web 2.0 tools in art and theatre along with the everyday educational school subjects; utilizing available technologies on idea generation and sharing on collaborative writing; working on communication using diverse media to exchange ideas, experiences and best practices; enhancing extreme collaboration between supposedly irrelevant subjects in cross-curriculum approaches; and supporting mutual respect, control as well as taking responsibility in identifying and supporting each other's gaps within the implementation process for collaborative writing.

4   Immersive Factors and Design Attributes into CCR

Immersive eXperience (iX) [14], as with User Experience (UX), is the creation of immediate, deeply immersive, meaningful and memorable learning experience within the previously suggested CCRs. There are specific immersive factors, conditions and associated iX Design attributes that enable and enhance the user's engagement and activity on platforms that require such actions.

Immersive Factors

1. Clear goals as challenge level and skill high level
2. Concentration and focused attention
3. Loss of feeling
4. Distorted sense of time
5. Direct and immediate feedback
6. Balance between ability level and challenge
7. Sense of personal control over the situation or activity
8. The activity is intrinsically rewarding, so there is an effortlessness of action
9. Lack of awareness of bodily needs
10. Absorption into the activity.

iX 10 Design Attributes

1. Common purpose
2. Powerful Online Presence   and Co-Presence
3. Engagement
4. Virtual Collaboration

5. Zone of Proximal Flow (ZPF)
6. Connectedness and Inter-Connectedness
7. Engagement in Compelling & Memorable Activities
8. Sense of Belonging

5   Discussion, Conclusion and Future Work

In-service training within schools can be individualised and self-paced; there are more opportunities to access diverse learning resources; learning is based on activities and experience (active and experiential learning) within groups (collaborative learning); time and cost are less because of the in-service manner and the use of the electronic form of resources; and communication is nonlinear. Nevertheless, there are several obstacles: institutional, instructional, technical, and personal. Consequently, ICT utilization in primary schools depends, among other reasons, upon the levels of teachers' expertise in the ICT use with the aim of Immersive Experience engaging Web tools and Social Media for educational purposes. Facing the 2020 challenge for the whole of Europe, educators are aiming at not only transferring knowledge but also at developing creative classrooms (CCR) so for the students to work on and share immersive experiences towards co-creativity and idea generation.

The results were impressive as with the theater education (dramatizations in dialogues, role plays, recitations and vocal exercises, emotional control - control behaviour) and with visual artists and musicians (construction artworks, maquettes, posters, collective works, familiarization with new materials, tools and thus, possibilities, new techniques, sand art, graffiti, exhibitions, choirs, concerts, attend concerts, acquaintance with musical instruments and types of music); all facilitated by ICT infrastructure.

Other CCR case studies [15] report results reports that the use of ICT empowered the development of learner's soft skills, such as problem solving and communication with real-world context and actors, and the fostering of multiple modes of thinking through a variety of learning materials. Such innovative approaches impact not only on learning practices, but also on content and curricula, connectedness, leadership and values, teaching practices, and infrastructure.

The use of Web 2.0 tools and Social Media within the ICT infrastructure presupposes that the learning practices need to widen up across disciplines / subjects and thus, the teaching approaches were adjusted to such customization. Innovative learning environments enable learning by creating and facilitate peer-to-peer collaboration in multiple and diverse ways as with the ICT and Arts teachers in our school. The organization was also supported, including the flexible timetable compared to the other Greek schools, indicating a distributed leadership approach rather than a top down decision making. Such approaches enabled inter-connectedness and a sense of belonging to the school community of practice, working towards specific targets and goals. The project funding also supported the school to acquire a solid and functional ICT infrastructure that all of the above could not be realized without it. Web 2.0 tools and Social Media supported collaboration, connectedness and internal school innovation so to modernize learning and teaching practices. Lastly, such unique implementation helped in the extraction of best practices and shedding light to innovative and key elements that are widely implemented in the ZEP Greek schools. The results from the project now used as best practice within all schools in the Greek Educational Action Zone. Implications revolve around the extraction of best practices while using the discussions to explain, evaluate and further discover new uses and re-uses of existing material and approaches.

Our proposition to integrate the Immersive factors and design attributes within the learning platforms, social media and Web 2.0 tools can offer memorable experiences for both the teachers and the students, building sustainable learning communities towards lifelong learning sustainability. Our next research work will be focused on the design, implementation and evaluation of such implementation within Immersive environments such as the use of Serious Games and augmented reality and in-depth analysis so to provide a more coherent study, more accurate and evidence-based.

Acknowledgement. This project was co-funded by the European Union and the Greek government under ESPA.

References

1. UNESCO (2002), Information and Communication Technology in Education – A Curriculum for Schools and Programme for Teacher Development. Paris: UNESCO, http://unesdoc.unesco.org/images/0012/001295/129538e.pdf (retrieved October 22, 2007)
2. Delich, P.: Pedagogical and interface modifications: What instructors change after teaching online. Published doctoral dissertation, Pepperdine University, Malibu, CA (2006), http://proquest.umi.com/pqdlink?Ver=1&Exp=09-09-2012&FMT=7&DID=1144195631&RQT=309&attempt=1
3. Downes, S.: E-learning 2.0. eLearn Magazine. Association for Computing Machinery, Inc. (2005), http://elearnmag.org/subpage.cfm?section=articles&article=29-1 (retrieved April 12, 2006)
4. Berners-Lee, T.: Berners-Lee warns of changes ahead. Computing Magazine (2007), http://www.computing.co.uk/computing/analysis/2186086/berners-lee-warnschanges-ahead (retrieved June 17, 2007)
5. Chen, D.H.C., Kee, H.L.: A Model on Knowledge and Endogenous Growth. World Bank Policy Research Working Paper 3539 (2005), http://info.worldbank.org/etools/library/latestversion.asp?135703 (retrieved October 22, 2006)
6. Thompson, A., Schmidt, D.A.: Winter 2006-2007. Journal of Computing in Teacher Education (JCTE) 23(2) (2007)
7. Lambropoulos, N., Faulkner, X., Culwin, F.: Supporting Social Awareness in Collaborative E-learning. The British Journal of Educational Technologies (BJET) 43(2), 295–306 (2012)
8. Palinscar, A.S.: Social constructivist perspectives on teaching and learning. Annual Review of Psychology 49, 345–375 (1998)
9. Short, J., Williams, E., Christies, B.: The Social Psychology of Telecommunications. John Wiley & Sons, London (1976)

10. Wiener, M., Mehrabian, A.: Language within language: Immediacy, A channel in verbal communication. Appleton-Century-Crofts, New York (1968)
11. Argyle, M., Dean, J.: Eye contact, distance and affiliation. Sociometry 28, 289–304 (1965)
12. Meyer, K.A.: Quality in distance education: Focus on on-line learning. Jossey-Bass, San Francisco (2002)
13. Bocconi, S., Kampylis, P., Punie, Y.J.: Scientific and Policy Reports.Innovating Learning: Key Elements for Developing Creative Classrooms in Europe. eLearning Papers n. 30 (September 2012), http://www.elearningpapers.eu, ISSN: 1887-1542
14. Lambropoulos, N., Tsotra, P., Kotinas, I., Mporas, I.: Composites Ideas in COMPOOL Immersion: A Semantics Engineering Innovation Network Community Platform. In: Ozok, A.A., Zaphiris, P. (eds.) OCSC/HCII 2013. LNCS, vol. 8029, pp. 385–394. Springer, Heidelberg (2013)
15. Kampylis, P., Law, N., Punie, Y., Bocconi, S., Brečko, B., Han, S., Looi, S.-K., Miyake, N.: ICT-enabled innovation for learning in Europe and Asia - Exploring conditions for sustainability, scalability and impact at system level. JRC Scientific and Policy Reports (2013)

Enhancing Online Learning Activities
for Groups in Flipped Classrooms

Reecha Bharali

School of Informatics and Computing, Indiana University, IUPUI
535 W. Michigan Street
Indianapolis, IN 46202
rbharali@iupui.edu

Abstract. Flipped classrooms have been the latest trend in online learning. They have been accepted as a novel model because of an application based environment with the students. In this paper, the flipped classroom model has been studied in the context of online classrooms. The author vents in the context of groups in online classrooms and tries to understand the match within the flipped classroom scenario. This study is conducted with instructors and students to understand this attitude towards online classrooms and to integrate them with the flipped structure. Key requirements are identified from the study; which are proposed to influence the design of such a platform. Finally from the study the gaps are recognized, and the author proposes a novel platform for online group activities with a focus on flipped classroom scenario.

Keywords: flipped classroom, online learning, groups.

1 Introduction

Flipping the classroom, has become a buzzword in the last several years. Flip teaching is a form of blended learning technique in which students engage in learning new content online by watching video lectures. The homework is done in the class with the instructor offering more personalized guidance and interaction to the students; instead of lecturing. The students do lower levels of cognitive work outside of class. They are engaged in reviewing the lectures, viewing the support materials. The students focus on application, analysis, synthesis of content in class, where they have the support of their peers and instructor. The Wikipedia mentions flipping changes the role of teachers from "sage on the stage" to "guide on the side". This allows them to work with individuals or groups of students throughout the session. The instructor acts a facilitator of the student's activities and discusses with them their misconceptions [5]. A Flipped Classroom would look very different from the setting of a traditional classroom. There would no necessity of students sitting in individual desks facing the instructor while, they lecture, because of the high interactive nature of the classroom students, instead might sit at tables or desks pushed together. Students are off by themselves working on problems and the concepts that they have learnt in the

P. Zaphiris and A. Ioannou (Eds.): LCT 2014, Part II, LNCS 8524, pp. 269–276, 2014.

lectures, which they reviewed before coming to the class. [12] It may appear that flipped classroom are chaotic, loud, or even messy, but the action and collaboration taking place in the flipped classroom will help in student learning. Students are motivated to try out the problems for they are free to commit mistakes as they aware instructors regard that as a part of the learning process. Flipped Classroom stress on the students working interactively with each other. Students learn by doing and by asking questions to both the peers and the instructors. Though the classroom design in such a scenario may highly depend on the instructor, course and institution. Thus, the interaction within the classroom increases. There is a dynamic of increasing the student interactivity among students.

2   Problem Space

In flipped classrooms, there arises a scenario of working together in groups. Students need to interact more with each other because of the dynamics of the classroom. It can be both for helping or seeking help. Thus, a variable of class interactivity added with instant communication among the peers. In such a classroom students often form their own collaborative groups, which may be to the geography of the class or due to student preferences. Students help each other and learn from each other, instead of relying on the teacher. The teacher might not be regarded as the sole disseminator of knowledge.[13] Flipped classrooms let students carry out meaningful activities instead; that helps them do get engaged and learn. With the advent of such a scenario, in modern day classrooms, leads to the demand and need of course content beyond pdf's and power point, audio and video lectures. For there must be more supplementary materials that can help in in-class activities, in flipped classrooms. Materials that are more organized and that can help enhance students to learn. Working in groups, as well as peer learning, are keys to this set of a classroom environment. As flipped classrooms, support group collaboration in learning by doing. As the flipped classroom setting remains no longer isolated to one individual rather the platforms on which the students work should be group centered instead of being self-centered. A novel platform in such a scenario is where activities can be carried out for collaborative and co-operative learning activities. In such an environment, the students may not require reviews from the instructor but can take benefit from the peers through such platforms. Peer inter-action, review, recommendation can be integrated into platforms to enhance learning activities.

Flipped Learning Classrooms can be supported by active learning strategies for better experiences with peer learning. There is a demand for higher enriched material that can support students while the class is in progress. The flipped class-room matches with the traditional classroom scenario, but the need of a flipped classroom are very different in an online classroom. However, flipped classroom can inculcate the scenario from its traditional classroom into an online platform. There needs to be a novel scenario where even the students of the online courses can maintain the asynchronous nature of the online classrooms. At the same time be a part of interactive learning activity in the online environments.

As students working in the flipped classrooms are definitely not working in isolation. [8]There can be possibilities where students can be connected through the online classrooms.

2.1 Learning Models

Flipped classrooms provide free class time for hands-on work. Flipped Class-room stress on the students working interactively with each other. Students learn by doing and asking questions. Thus, the interaction within the classroom in-creases. There is a dynamic of increasing the student interactivity among students. Students tend to help each other, a process that benefits both the average, advanced and poor learners in the classroom. It justifies the main objective of the flipped class-room. Active Learning; which is to activate the higher order thinking and maximize the class learning time.[8] Active learning forms as the base of such higher order learning that acts on learning by doing.

Adaptive learning strategy is also being supported in many platforms currently. Brusilovsky in his paper proposes an architecture based on adaptive learning that integrates the benefits of the modern Learning Management Systems and educational material repositories. [4] Atkinson et al.'s GOALS tried to develop active learning strategies in an online environment for graduate students. They designed a course that incorporated knowledge from different forms of technology. Learners received voicemails that explained their assignments. It is a learner centered environment; injecting the responsibility of learning on learners. [1,11]

2.2 Understanding the Domain

Based on the reviews from literatures and linking the dots. The prospect of online flipped classroom was sought for as a challenge. It was believed that flipped classroom in an online settings need to be enhanced. For, group activity in online settings is sought for as challenging. The study tries to investigate how can group interaction in a peer learning environment be increased in an online flipped classroom scenario? What enhancements/ features are required for peer to peer interaction in such a case? If there is a novel product that can fulfill these needs of the stakeholders?

3   The Design Study

The study was designed to understand the general attitude of students towards working in groups in online environments. The study tried to understand what challenges were faced and what challenges were expected in online environments while working in groups. The three questions that seemed as a gap that were asked with its break up into minor questions that directed the answers of the interviewed user group. The study was designed to generate data to understand if there exists a gap to work in groups in online environments. The general perception was to understand, from the users, if there can be a novel hypothetical product that can satisfy the gap that is being found in the study conducted.

3.1   Demographics

A set of 10 students and 10 instructors are interviewed across different disciplines to understand the attitudes towards group learning activities. The instructors and students belonged to Informatics, Visual Arts, Business, Engineering, Liberal Arts and Medicine. The diversity in the user set was supposed to give a varied set of results but as the study followed a qualitative approach such diversity was supposed to understand if there are differences in different fields of study or if the pattern found was same. However difference in areas of study has not been taken into consideration in the study.

3.2   Design Study Process

Semi Structured Interviews. The questions that were asked were designed to answer the questions that raised from the existing literature. The questions were targeted to get valuable data for better insights into design synthesis. The interviews were conducted in the natural environment of the user. The interviewer asked the questions over a period of an hour. The interview took notes in paper sheet with the key points of the questions were written. Over the interview, sticky notes that were attached below the key points whenever the interviewer felt something was important, however to comfort the user some of the important points were not noted. However to not miss the interview the entire interview was audio recorded. The putting up of a sheet was an important way to keep up with the interview time without the interviewer being distracted.

The questions that were asked to the students were

- Do you think online learning classes like blogs and forums help you in any form?
- What is your opinion in group learning in online classes?
- Are you comfortable in working on a project in a group or learning a new concept in a classroom?
- Do you know your peers in the online learning classroom?
- Would you like feedback from them? If yes, can you tell why?
- Do you think group work helps you learn technical skills?
- Do you have an opinion on the time management issue in an online group work?

The questions that were asked to the students were modified to suit the perspective of the instructor.

The Survey. A paper survey was conducted. A set of ten questions. They were respectively being modulated to understand the differences in student and the instructor attitude. The survey was responded after an in-person interview. The survey was generally responded in a time of 2 minutes to 5minutes.

3.3 Analysis of Results

The analysis of the results led the author to come across various concerns. The method of affinity diagram was used to analyze the qualitative data collected. All the quotes that had been received from the interviews were put up in small notes which were then tried to be grouped. Once the data was grouped the respective categories were named. After the categories had been named the relations between each element was looked forth and extrapolated.

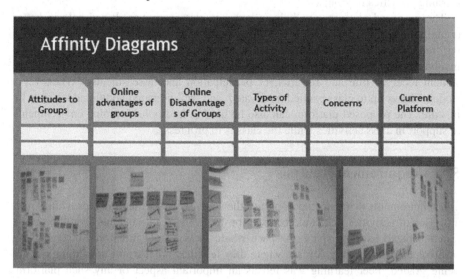

3.4 Synthesis of Results/ Requirements

The results were varying. With respect to a negative when it comes to volunteer in taking part in activities online, and, however, the theme of a hypothetical novel product was very positive. The interviewees were adding features and functionalities to the product. Some of the common issues that were observed from the instructors was the need of interactive content that don't need management. Some of the dissatisfaction using major LMS in such a scenario were mentioned with the naming of a few. The need of participation of each member of the team, the need of each student been evaluated without being veiled by the performance of other. There was a major concern about individual performance and evaluation across all the instructors.

Students complained that group activities break the self-paced nature of online learning environments. There is no noise in the online classrooms when they participate in groups. They don't feel connected and don't feel the need to connect with other users in an online environment. There was a high support for a face to face meeting in an online environment if there is a group activity. The said that they would try to have a hangout with the person they have been engaged in a group activity.

4   Design Synthesis

The study highly supported the hypothetical idea of a novel platform which supports the scenario of working together in groups, in flipped classrooms. Based on the study, a conceptual design defining the features of the platform where group activity can be enhanced is provided. The proposed platform is a new interactive communication platform that provides richer contextual environment to enhance the feature of online learning activities in groups.

The proposed platform can help in better in-class activities. It can help in better organized and motivated activities in a peer learning environment. The platform looks into the kind of enhancements that are required for peer to peer interaction and the involvement of interactive media. The students are offered an environment where student receives title and rewards for participation and, assessments. Whenever a student shows up to class excited, motivated, and well prepared additional rewards lie in store. The proposed platform can also be used in traditional learning environments to support in class activities while the class is in progress.

5   Requirement Analysis

The requirements that came up as part of the study were peer learning, providing with a playlist of activities that could be used for the learners, the students should be given a personalized learning space. A space where they are not monitored but receive a positive aura of learning. A place where they feel they are learning something but not being graded. Peer learning was felt as an important aspect of any such platform. These would be the key rules while interacting with any person. The students also would like to interact within a small group where they have the capacity to remember each other's name and skill. As a general feedback, the interviews stressed on Audio and video feedback from the studies. However from a design perspective this might not be an apt thing to do. The student also expressed interest where they are being evaluated by their peers. But it does not make the student feel discouraged. Instead of being evaluated they wanted frequent feedbacks from the environment. There is a need of interactive content. A content that expresses its form in a more expressive manner so that they can visualize their concepts. Though interactivity is not much stressed. Students said that they would want interactive tools to play with which are not very distracting due to their fancy features. The concepts of blogs and forums are criticized. However, they were found important features of the submission as well as evaluation. There should be a lot of peer learning going on. Gamification was something all the interviews carried with theme though the word was not explicitly used in the interviews.

The extrapolation of requirements was from the raw interview data that was received while interviewing. Various design methods were used like the 5why method; the author also used brainstorming methods to analyze the data from the interviews.

6   Design Ideas

A set of design ideas was put up with the features and functionalities of such a platform. A range of such twelve items was listed. They being gamification, socialization, interaction, rewards, noise, learning, activity, fun, peer learning, peer challenge, content aggregation and feedback. They were then arranged with a hierarchy to decide the core of the platform. Features and functionalities for the design ideas were decided on this.

7   V-Learn, a Concept

V-Learn is a platform that suits an environment where students can participate in group activities online. It's a platform that is self-paced. The students need not be synchronously present in the platform. A group is formed based on common interests by the platform. The students can be a part of activities that are based on the lessons that are being released for a particular week. Each student participates in the platform and completes a set of activities that are based on the lessons for the week. But the students' progress is based on the group's progress. They would receive instant notifications from the platform for advancing in the week's task. The students can challenge different groups together. In many cases, there are chances of discrepancies where the group activity in such a platform becomes peer led.

V-Learn is a conceptual model which can be a fit for students looking into the platform for enhanced learning activities and to feel the noise within the classes. Adding socializing features add to the demands of the platform being demanding.

8   Limitations of the Study

The study was conducted with a set of 20 users to understand the attitude of the users towards the attitude towards the online learning environment. The knowledge from this was used to understand the attitude towards these studies. The users were not directly part of the flipped classroom arena but were active participants of online classrooms. The users belonged to different majors that might have led to multiple features being included in the interface.

9   Future Work

The proposed platform has not been developed and tested with the users. The platform would look for testing its hypothesized design with prototypes. The demographics of the user also may be a concern with respect to the discipline.

Acknowledgements. The author would like to thank Indiana University-Purdue University, Indianapolis for letting use the facilities and resources. The author would also like to thank the participants in the study for the valuable opinions which helped in the design of the study.

References

1. Atkinson, T., Atkinson, R.H., Smith, D.: GOALS (graduate online active learning strategies). Journal of Computing Sciences in College 17(3), 251–264 (2002)
2. Bade, D., Nüssel, G., Wilts, G.: Online feedback by tests and reporting for elearning and certification programs. In: Proceedings of the 13th International World Wide Web Conference on Alternate Track Papers & Posters. ACM (2004)
3. Bower, M.: Groupwork activities in synchronous online classroom spaces. ACM SIGCSE Bulletin 39(1) (2007)
4. Brusilovsky, P.: KnowledgeTree: A distributed architecture for adaptive e-learning. In: Proceedings of the 13th International World Wide Web Conference on Alternate Track Papers & Posters. ACM (2004)
5. Cold, S.J.: Partially flipped: experiences using POGIL. In: Proceedings of the 13th Annual ACM SIGITE Conference on Information Technology Education. ACM (2013)
6. Courte, J.E.: Comparing student acceptance and performance of online activities to classroom activities. In: Proceedings of the 8th ACM SIGITE Conference on Information Technology Education. ACM (2007)
7. Dillenbourg, P.: Over-scripting CSCL: The risks of blending collaborative learning with instructional design.Three worlds of CSCL. Can we support CSCL? 61–91 (2002)
8. Kachka, P.: Understanding the flipped classroom: Part 2. Faculty Focus (2012)
9. Mejias, L.: Effects of introducing an interactive teaching and learning activity (TLA) in the engineering classroom. In: 2012 7th International Conference on Computer Science & Education (ICCSE). IEEE (2012)
10. Moreno-Ger, P., et al.: TrivialCV: Competitive activities for the classroom integrated in a Moodle Virtual Campus (2013)
11. Rutherfoord, R.H., Rutherfoord, J.K.: Flipping the classroom: is it for you? In: Proceedings of the 13th Annual ACM SIGITE Conference on Information Technology Education. ACM (2013)
12. eLearning Industry, Concepts, http://elearningindustry.com/the-flipped-classroom-guide-for-teachers (accessed on February 21, 2014)
13. Take Part, I learned it on YouTube, http://www.takepart.com/article/2011/11/11/how-youtube-changing-education-embracing-flipped-classroom (accessed on February 21, 2014)

Does CMC Reduce Foreign Language Classroom Anxiety?

Adel Jebali

Concordia University, Montreal, Canada
adel.jebali@concordia.ca

Abstract. Many researchers have proposed that anxiety related to second language learning, especially in the classroom, has a negative impact on the performance of learners. To reduce this anxiety, some authors propose to use computer-mediated communication (CMC) to realize oral tasks while others believe that the effects of this mode of communication is comparable to the effects of the face-to-face (FTF) communication. In order to provide an answer to this question, a systematic measurement of the performance of learners during oral interactions conducted through these two modalities must be obtained as the comparison cannot be made without this measurement. This paper is a preliminary study with 20 learners of L2 French in which the degree of anxiety beforehand was measured with [1] Foreign Language Classroom Anxiety Scale (FLCAS). These learners completed a communication task through Skype and also responded to a post-task questionnaire on their perceptions of anxiety, FTF and CMC. Performance during the CMC was measured in order to verify the effects of anxiety on their performance. The comparison was made with their performance in another FTF communication task. The results show that all the students performed better in FTF than in CMC and that even the most anxious learners obtained better results in the former.

Keywords: FLCAS, CMC, FTF, anxiety, French L2.

1   Introduction

Anxiety about second language learning (henceforth L2), especially in the context of the classroom, is the most studied individual difference that distinguishes L2 learners. Although the concept is psychological, the linguistic and educational implications are an object of study in their own right for both education and language teaching specialists. It is for this reason that the effects of this anxiety on L2 learning as well as the best ways to overcome these effects are part of the most discussed research topics in this area.

In this context, one of the most prevalent ideas among researchers in CALL is to associate computer-mediated communication (CMC) with a significant reduction of learners' anxiety and thus with a better performance in oral exchanges, either on an online platform or via a tool of synchronous communication [2-4]. This assumption is

P. Zaphiris and A. Ioannou (Eds.): LCT 2014, Part II, LNCS 8524, pp. 277–287, 2014.
© Springer International Publishing Switzerland 2014

however not unanimous and some studies tend to show that this mode of communication does not allow learners to perform better than within face-to-face (FTF) communication [5, 6].

I believe that one cannot opt for either of these hypotheses without measuring learner performance in these two types of communication, and especially learners who are subject to this particular type of anxiety. The means used to achieve this comparison is to conduct an empirical study with learners of different levels of competence by exposing them to the two communication modalities and thereby measuring their performance. A measure of the degree of anxiety of these learners is also required to focus on those learners who tend to be anxious in the specific context of L2 learning regardless of the type of communication.

The goal of this study is to measure the impact of foreign language anxiety on the quality of exchanges and to further probe the perception of learners about the potential role of computer-mediated communication in reducing this anxiety. To achieve this goal, I conducted an empirical study with a small group of 20 French L2 learners whose level is intermediate – to – advanced (B2[1]). These learners were exposed to both modalities of communication and their performance was measured in these two contexts. The study is preliminary, but the results are generalizable to other learners.

In the second section of this paper, I will present the concept of foreign language anxiety. In the third section, I present the methodology for the data collection. The results are presented in the fourth section followed by the discussion in section five.

2   L2 Anxiety

In this section, the concept of foreign language anxiety, as defined in L2 acquisition studies, will be presented. The negative effects it can have on learning will be presented.

2.1   The Concept

Foreign language anxiety is not a psychological trait that can manifest itself in any learning process. It is only related to the specific process of L2 learning. Many experiences have shown that learners who do not experience anxiety in other types of learning become anxious while learning an L2 [7-9], which is explained by the fact that L2 learners feel helpless when deprived of the comfort given by their first language (L1) to express themselves or to undertake communication tasks.

According to [1], this is a specific anxiety reaction: "We conceive foreign language anxiety as a distinct complex of self-perceptions, beliefs, feelings, and behaviors related to classroom language learning arising from the uniqueness of the language learning process." (p. 128) The authors further explain this phenomenon by "the importance of the disparity between the 'true' self as known to the language learner

---

[1] According to the Common European Framework of Reference for Languages.

and the more limited self as can be presented at any given moment in the foreign language" (p. 128).

2.2   Effects of Anxiety on Language Learning

The importance of this psycho-educational phenomenon is explained by the negative effects of this particular anxiety on the performance of learners [1, 10-12]. In fact, many researchers have noted a significantly worse performance in anxious subjects when it comes to performing cognitive tasks, such as making a judgment, analyzing situations, making decisions, etc. [13]. Language learners' performance, for example, is affected, and we note the presence of more errors, the non-use of certain forms which are well assimilated, lack of cohesion and some deviation from the norm already learned (grammatical, sociolinguistic, pragmatic). These effects are also found among learners of all proficiency levels according to [13] : beginners, intermediate and advanced. However, it seems that beginners tend to be more affected by anxiety than the others according to [14].

2.3   CMC and Anxiety

To mitigate the negative effects of this anxiety, some researchers have proposed that teachers work their personal attitudes and their teaching [15]. Others have proposed instead to work on another part of the learning environment: educational technologies. [2-4, 16-19] believe that CMC can help decrease of the apprehension to communicate (one facet of L2 learning anxiety), since according to them, the physical distance between the interlocutors and the use of a tool that prevents learners from feeling intimidated due to FTF meaning negotiation significantly reduces the anxiety of these learners. This point of view, however, is not shared by all. Indeed, [5, 6] have achieved results which tend to show the contrary; that this mode of communication does not reduce the anxiety of learners and thus, it is not different from FTF communication.

Researchers do not agree on the effect of CMC, whether synchronous or asynchronous, on the language anxiety of L2 learners. If the widespread idea was a correlation between the use of these technologies and the improvement of the performance of learners, especially in synchronous communication, the latest research seems to cast doubt on these claims. However, what is lacking is an empirical study of the performance of learners, measured in both FTF and CMC contexts, regardless of the degree of anxiety of these learners. The purpose of this study is to fill this gap.

3   Methodology

3.1   Participants

Participants in this study are French L2 learners enrolled in an oral communication course (B2 level) at Concordia University (Montreal, Canada) during the 2013 Fall semester.

Twenty ($n= 20$) students participated in this study, 16 of which were women and 4 of which were male. The age of participants ranged from 19 to 40 years old. The students had various first languages, such as English, Romanian, Russian, Spanish, Mandarin, Arabic and Urdu.

3.2   Data Collection

To perform this study, I used three main sources to gather data: the FLCAS, a questionnaire and two tasks (one computer-mediated and one FTF).

FLCAS. [1] proposed the FLCAS (Foreign Language Classroom Anxiety Scale)[2] to measure the anxiety of learners related to foreign language classes and to the Support Group for Foreign Language Learning at Texas University back in 1983. This test is composed of 33 items which are evaluated on a Likert-like scale which allows respondents to indicate for each item whether they strongly agree, agree, are neutral, disagree or strongly disagree with the statement in the item in question.

CMC Task. This task was performed via Skype. To do this, I split the participants into pairs (10 in all). Both participants of each pair were shown   two nearly identical images, on which there were 10 differences (a task adapted from [20]). The transmitted image was only visible to its receiver. The following instructions were given: "Each of you has received an almost identical image to the image received by the other participant. There are 10 differences between these two images. You have about 15 minutes to find the 10 differences. Ask questions to your partner to discover them. You may ask a lot of questions. For example: I see X on my image; do you see the same thing? Where is it exactly? What color is it? , Etc." I also specified to the participants that the purpose was to describe the images as precisely as possible to find as many differences as possible. The score shown in the results is related to the number of differences found by each participant.

Questionnaire[3]. The questionnaire was administered after the CMC task was performed and before the FTF task. The aim of this questionnaire is twofold: to determine respondents' perceptions about the task itself and to determine their digital profile. I asked them questions like "Are you at ease when you use the computer to communicate?" accompanied with a Likert-like scale and some open-ended questions about their daily use of ICT.

FTF Task. This task was designed to test the performance of the participants FTF to compare it to their performance in a mediated context. The task was to discuss a topical subject in Montreal, Quebec and Canadian news and it was the "Charte de la laïcité" (Charter of secularism) at that time. To start this discussion, I posted a short video found on YouTube (a debate between Minister Bernard Drainville and

---

[2] See Appendix 1.
[3] See Appendix 2.

sociologist Gérard Bouchard in the Radio-Canada show "Tout le monde en parle"). The debate was taped to verify the performance of each participant afterwards. The score shown in the results is related to the language performance of each participant during this debate.

4   Results

Data from all these measurement instruments were encoded in Excel then in SPSS (version 21, for Windows).

4.1   Participants' Profile

The goal of the questionnaire was to define the "digital profile" of the participants through their use of computers in everyday life (video games, chat, email, work, or school, social networks). 17 of them (85%) said they are comfortable or very comfortable when using the computer to communicate. One respondent expressed being uncomfortable in this context, two said they were neither comfortable nor uncomfortable. With respect to other activities through computer or other media, very few respondents spend time on video games (0 hours / week for 90%). On the other hand, work related to studies monopolizes 20 or more hours per week for 40% of them. Emails occupy, meanwhile, between 1 hour and 10 hours per week for the vast majority of learners. Finally, social networks monopolize between 1 and 20 hours weekly and one respondent indicated "a lot" as an answer. In all, the use of computers to communicate (on social networks, through the tools of synchronous communication or by email) monopolizes at least 10 hours per week, for the vast majority of respondents (95%). One respondent seemed to have a different profile: less than one hour for email, one hour for CMC, 0 for social networking, 0 for video games and 3 hours only for work related to studies. This person is also one of the respondents who indicated that they are neither comfortable nor uncomfortable performing communication tasks by computer. The respondent who expressed being uncomfortable in this context spent 10 hours for email, 0 for synchronous communication, 10 for social networks, 0 for video games and 10-15 hours on computer tasks related to studies.

Therefore, the vast majority of the participants in this study use communication technologies (computers, tablets, cellular phones) to perform various communication tasks on a daily basis. This finding is of great importance for this type of research, since it proves that subjects have a great ease in the use of communication technologies and also perceive their utility.

4.2   Language Anxiety

The results from the FLCAS (see table 1) show that language anxiety is not widespread in the group. Items indicating a moderate or high degree of anxiety received a high percentage of responses "Disagree" and "Strongly disagree". This is the case, for example, of item 17 (*I often feel like not going to my language class*) with 75% of respondents who did not agree with its content compared to only 15% who did agree. This is the case of item 19 also (*I am afraid that my language teacher is ready to correct every mistake I make*) with 75% of respondents who disagree and only 10% agree.

On the other hand, item 5 (*It wouldn't bother me at all to take more foreign language classes*) received more favorable responses from 90% of participants while only 5% disagreed. This clearly shows that respondents were comfortable or very comfortable with French as a second language and feel very little anxiety in the classroom or even when communicating with native speakers.

Table 1. FLCAS, Results of selected items

Item	Strongly agree	Agree	Neither agree nor disagree	Disagree	Strongly disagree
2	25%	20%	0%	35%	20%
5	15%	75%	5%	5%	0%
10	5%	50%	20%	20%	5%
13	0%	20%	30%	35%	15%
17	0%	15%	10%	45%	30%
18	5%	50%	20%	25%	0%
19	0%	10%	15%	65%	10%
21	10%	5%	15%	50%	20%
25	5%	10%	15%	55%	15%
26	5%	25%	20%	30%	20%
27	0%	15%	30%	45%	10%
29	5%	10%	20%	55%	10%
31	5%	5%	25%	50%	15%

A one-way ANOVA shows that in the group in general, anxiety score has no effect on the CMC performance: $F (15, 4) = 3.093$ p = *ns*. This is also the case for the performance of learners in FTF context: $F (15, 4) = 1.261$ p = *ns*. It is for this reason that we need to verify the performance of the most and the least anxious learners in these two contexts.

The most anxious learners in my corpus are identified as subjects 12, 15, 18 and 20. The anxiety score is measured by the responses to the FLCAS items. The maximum score is 66 (always strongly agree or strongly disagree); a score of 33 still means a high degree of anxiety (always agree or disagree). The most anxious subjects obtained a score ranging from 25 to 35. The least anxious had scores of 0 (not anxious at all) in some cases, and 16 in the worst case.

Concerning the four most anxious learners, I found that their performance in FTF communication task is better than their performance on Skype.

Table 2. Overall performance of the most anxious learners

Subject	Anxiety score	Skype	FTF
12	25	60%	90%
15	29	40%	85%
18	33	30%	85%
20	35	0%	80%

The least anxious learners show comparable results. However, surprisingly enough, subject 6, whose anxiety score is 0, obtained 0% on Skype and 85% in FTF.

Table 3. Overall performance for the least anxious learners

Subject	Anxiety score	Skype	FTF
6	0	0%	85%
2	2	50%	90%
10	2	50%	90%
19	2	30%	80%
4	3	40%	70%
7	4	50%	85%
3	5	30%	95%
9	5	30%	85%
17	5	50%	95%
13	8	50%	85%
14	9	60%	90%
5	10	40%	100%
11	11	70%	90%
8	14	50%	85%
16	15	40%	85%
1	16	70%	85%

Therefore, it seems that the communication modality has an effect on the performance of learners, but not the effect expected by many CALL studies. In fact, the performance of the participants was better in FTF than on Skype. This is the case for both the more anxious and the least anxious subjects.

5   Discussion

Learners in this group are intermediate-to-advanced (B2 level). My experiment seems to show that learners who have reached this level of proficiency in the target language (French) have little anxiety even if some of them had high scores. They generally performed well in tasks, which seems to demonstrate that they have learned to manage anxiety and its effects are well controlled at this stage of L2 acquisition. This confirms the assumptions made by [14], according to whom "a clear relationship exists between foreign-language anxiety and foreign-language proficiency." (p. 272-273): beginners tend to be more anxious and their performance is more severely affected by foreign language anxiety.

If learners of French L2 in this study perform better in FTF than on Skype, this demonstrates that the hypothesis of [5, 6] is verifiable. However, two variables should be considered and taken into account: the type of tasks assigned to learners and the number of participants.

With respect to the type of tasks, it would be more appropriate if the assigned FTF and CMC tasks had similar degrees of difficulty, even though these tasks should be different. With respect to the number of participants, more participants from the same level (B2), but also participants from the lower levels (A1, A2 and B1) should be recruited.

6   Conclusion

The results of this study seem to indicate that language anxiety does not affect the performance of intermediate - advanced learners, as no significant relationship was found between the levels of anxiety and the performance of learners in FTF and CMC contexts. In addition, it seems that learners, whether the most or the least anxious, performed better in face-to-face communication than in computer-mediated communication using Skype.

It should be noted that this study is preliminary and exploratory in nature. To settle the question of whether computer-mediated communication improves the performance of learners, by reducing their language anxiety, a larger scale study needs to be conducted, including participants with varying levels of proficiency in the L2.

Acknowledgment. I would like to thank Leslie Redmond for her invaluable help.

References

1. Horwitz, E.K., Horwitz, M.B., Cope, J.: Foreign-Language Classroom Anxiety. Modern Language Journal 70(2), 125–132 (1986)
2. Abrams, Z.I.: The effect of synchronous and asynchronous CMC on oral performance in German. The Modern Language Journal 87(2), 157–167 (2003)
3. Kern, R.G.: Restructuring classroom interaction with networked computers: Effects on quantity and characteristics of language production. The Modern Language Journal 79(4), 457–476 (1995)
4. Warschauer, M.: Comparing face-to-face and electronic discussion in the second language classroom. CALICO Journal 13(2 & 3), 7–26 (1995)
5. Arnold, N.: Reducing foreign language communication apprehension with computer-mediated communication: A preliminary study. System 35(4), 469–486 (2007)
6. Baralt, M., Gurzynski-Weiss, L.: Comparing learners' state anxiety during task-based interaction in computer-mediated and face-to-face communication. Language Teaching Research 15(2), 201–229 (2011)

7. Macintyre, P.D., Gardner, R.C.: Anxiety and 2nd-Language Learning - toward a Theoretical Clarification. Language Learning 39(2), 251–275 (1989)
8. Macintyre, P.D., Gardner, R.C.: Language Anxiety - Its Relationship to Other Anxieties and to Processing in Native and 2nd Languages. Language Learning 41(4), 513–534 (1991)
9. Macintyre, P.D., Gardner, R.C.: The Subtle Effects of Language Anxiety on Cognitive Processing in the 2nd-Language. Language Learning 44(2), 283–305 (1994)
10. Ganschow, L., Sparks, R.L., Javorsky, J.: Foreign language learning difficulties: An historical perspective. Journal of Learning Disabilities 31(3), 248–258 (1998)
11. Horwitz, E.K.: Foreign and second language anxiety. Language Teaching 43, 154–167 (2010)
12. Sheen, Y.: Recasts, Language Anxiety, Modified Output, and L2 Learning. Language Learning 58(4), 835–874 (2008)
13. Tóth, Z.: Foreign Language Anxiety and the Advanced Language Learner: A Study of Hungarian Students of English as a Foreign Language. Cambridge Scholars Publishing, Newcastle (2010)
14. MacIntyre, P.D., Gardner, R.C.: Anxiety and Second-Language Learning: Toward a Theoretical Clarification*. Language Learning 39(2), 251–275 (1989)
15. Young, D.J.: Language anxiety in second-language acquisition: Using a wider angle of focus. In: Georgetown University Round Table on Languages and Linguistics 1995, pp. 398–411 (1995)
16. Bump, J.: Radical changes in class discussion using networked computers. Computers and the Humanities 24(1-2), 49–65 (1990)
17. Lee, L.: Online interaction: negotiation of meaning and strategies used among learners of Spanish. RECALL-HULL- 13(2), 232–244 (2001)
18. Perez, L.C.: Foreign language productivity in synchronous versus asynchronous computer-mediated communication. Calico Journal 21(1), 89–104 (2003)
19. Roed, J.: Language learner behaviour in a virtual environment. Computer Assisted Language Learning 16(2-3), 155–172 (2003)
20. Silver, R.: Input, output, and negotiation: Conditions for second language development. In: Social and Cognitive Factors in Second Language Acquisition: Selected Proceedings of the 1999 Second Language Research Forum (2000)

Appendix 1: Foreign Language Classroom Anxiety Scale (FLCAS)

1. I never feel quite sure of myself when I am speaking in my foreign language class.
2. I don't worry about making mistakes in language class.
3. I tremble when I know that I'm going to be called on in language class.
4. It frightens me when I don't understand what the teacher is saying in the foreign language.
5. It wouldn't bother me at all to take more foreign language classes.
6. During language class, I find myself thinking about things that have nothing to do with the course.
7. I keep thinking that the other students are better at languages than I am.
8. I am usually at ease during tests in my language class.
9. I start to panic when I have to speak without preparation in language class.

10. I worry about the consequences of failing my foreign language class.
11. I don't understand why some people get so upset over foreign language classes.
12. In language class, I can get so nervous I forget things I know.
13. It embarrasses me to volunteer answers in my language class.
14. I would not be nervous speaking the foreign language with native speakers.
15. I get upset when I don't understand what the teacher is correcting.
16. Even If I am well prepared for language class, I feel anxious about it.
17. I often feel like not going to my language class.
18. I feel confident when I speak in foreign language class.
19. I am afraid that my language teacher is ready to correct every mistake I make.
20. I can feel my heart pounding when I'm going to be called on in language class.
21. The more I study for a language test, the more confused I get.
22. I don't feel pressure to prepare very well for language class.
23. I always feel that the other students speak the foreign language better than I do.
24. I feel very self-conscious about speaking the foreign language in front of other students.
25. Language class moves so quickly I worry about getting left behind.
26. I feel more tense and nervous in my language class than in my other classes.
27. I get nervous and confused when I am speaking in my language class.
28. When I'm on my way to language class, I feel very sure and relaxed.
29. I get nervous when I don't understand every word the language teacher says.
30. I feel overwhelmed by the number of rules you have to learn to speak a foreign language.
31. I am afraid that the other students will laugh at me when I speak the foreign language.
32. I would probably feel comfortable around native speakers of the foreign language.
33. I get nervous when the language teacher asks questions which I haven't prepared in advance.

Appendix 2: Questionnaire (in French)

1) L'ordinateur

- Êtes-vous à l'aise lorsque vous utilisez l'ordinateur pour communiquer?
Très à l'aise   À l'aise   Neutre   Mal à l'aise   Très mal à l'aise

- Dans le cadre de ce cours, est-ce que la communication par Skype était plaisante?
Beaucoup aimé Aimé   Neutre   Pas aimé   Pas du tout aimé

- Prière d'indiquer le nombre d'heures que vous passez en utilisant un ordinateur/une tablette/un téléphone intelligent

a) Pour les courriels : environ ___ heures par semaine

b) Messagerie instantanée (Skype, Messenger, etc.) : environ ___ heures par semaine

c) Réseaux sociaux (Facebook, Twitter, Tumblr, etc.) : environ ___ heures par semaine

d) Travaux pour vos cours : environ ___ heures par semaine

e) Pour jouer : environ ___ heures par semaine

2) L'expérience de communiquer via Skype en français

- Cette expérience était stressante.

Tout à fait d'accord   D'accord   Neutre   En désaccord   Tout à fait en désaccord

- Cette conversation a fait baisser mes sentiments de nervosité quand je parle français.

Tout à fait d'accord   D'accord   Neutre   En désaccord   Tout à fait en désaccord

- Je pense que j'aurais mieux parlé si cette conversation était face à face.

Tout à fait d'accord   D'accord   Neutre   En désaccord   Tout à fait en désaccord

- Utiliser Skype m'a permis de bien comprendre ce que disait mon partenaire de conversation.

Tout à fait d'accord   D'accord   Neutre   En désaccord   Tout à fait en désaccord

- Cette activité ajoute quelque chose de positif à ce cours.

Tout à fait d'accord   D'accord   Neutre   En désaccord   Tout à fait en désaccord

The Role of Educational Technologist in Implementing New Technologies at School

Birgy Lorenz, Kaido Kikkas, and Mart Laanpere

[1] Institute of Informatics, Tallinn University, Narva Road 25, 10120 Tallinn, Estonia
[2] Estonian Information Technology College, Raja St 4C, 12616 Tallinn, Estonia
{Birgy.Lorenz,Kaido.Kikkas,Mart.Laanpere}@tlu.ee

Abstract. In 2005, a new profession called "educational technologist" was introduced in Estonian schools. At first, the idea was confusing for many school principals, because of the seeming overlap with the job descriptions of existing ICT support specialists or ICT managers. Other principals interpreted the role of the educational technologist as a technology-savvy teacher who could take responsibility for teaching with technology in some subject domains so that the rest of teachers would not have to bother them with constantly changing landscape of technology. According to the data from the Tiger Leap Foundation (2012), almost 7% of Estonian schools had hired an educational technologist by 2012 – in most of the cases by re-allocating the salary fund of IT support specialists. The position is usually funded by local municipalities, not from the state budget. This paper is reflecting upon the case study data collected from 13 Estonian schools where educational technologists had been employed, the focus group interviews were conducted with 29 persons working in the field of educational technology. The study gives an overview of the current situation by defining the emerging profession of educational technologist on the level of professional practice. We also describe the arguments for establishing such a new position in school and the main challenges of a new specialist starting his/her career in this dynamic field.

Keywords: educational technologist roles, implementing new technologies, learning environments, assessing teachers, training methods and principles, mixed expectations.

1 Background

The latest report from the European Commission reveals that some EU countries do better than others with integrating new technologies in teaching and learning. For example, in Ireland, Finland, Norway, Estonia, Czech Republic, Denmark, Malta, teachers and students seem to apply technology more often [23]. The change has been fast, as only 10 years ago Estonian teachers were struggling to have even minimal access to computers and internet [17]. The aforementioned EC report gives good input to change the Tiger Leap[1] programs and rewriting the Estonian Information Society

---

[1] The Tiger Leap Foundation is an Estonian government initiative to distribute resources and knowledge about how to use technology at schools.

P. Zaphiris and A. Ioannou (Eds.): LCT 2014, Part II, LNCS 8524, pp. 288–296, 2014.
© Springer International Publishing Switzerland 2014

Strategy 2006 that focused in the near future [6]. To share best practices is also important as teachers can learn from each other [21] and also see the change not only to support education change in order to use technology, but see it as a countrywide innovation effort to reach information society [7].

The value and role of the educational technologist has usually been discussed in the context of school reforms [2]. The problems with technology are not for those who have not grown up with it [12]. At the same time there is a bigger need than ever to teach more people at the same time (distance learning, e-learning etc.). Educational technologists are needed to push teachers to find ways to reach the pupils and students in a meaningful way using technology. Attempts to change learning have given mixed results, some might even say that nothing has really changed in higher education, except the amount of technology being used [18]. However, technology-enhanced learning is still powerful driving force in education to raise interest and find patterns of learning and try to automate processes where teacher is not needed to help the student [10].

When we looked at the technology-related roles at school we saw a lot of positions that had overlapping job descriptions: ICT manager [3], administrator, ICT support, computer teacher, educational technologist and sometimes others too. Some companies training ICT personnel and principals have tried to propose solutions by dividing the process tasks between them, e.g. the principal deals with strategy, core teachers with education leadership, ICT managers with technology and educational technologists with e-learning [19]. Investigating different educational technologist job instructions developed in Estonia we also saw common lines about supporting e-learning [15] and skills that overlap also with common teachers' knowledge [24]. Teachers' professional development should also include mastering technology used in their field, this should not be left to someone else [11]. Teachers should differentiate learning process [25], use inquiry-based teaching [4], flipped classroom [20] and mobile learning [22] as well as other opportunities that arise. However, help is needed as most of the teachers are not still ready to face that challenge by themselves [9].

The Estonian national curriculum is in an implementing phase – the old one is gone, the new one is still taking off. A group of educational technologists led by Ingrid Maadvere (a leading educational technologist in Estonia) has analyzed the information from the curricula that involves use of ICT. Various ICT skills and knowledge of new methodology are needed by teachers on all levels [16].

Some people have started to talk about a new age of learning (learning 3.0 or social learning) that increases student participation, blurs the teacher-student relationship, changes the environment and time [13]. This brings along a lot of new issues as teachers abandon teacher-centered learning styles and focus on pushing students to learn actively [1]. A good example of this is Kathy Schrock (a popular American educational technologist) who has published a lot of information on her website "Kathy Schrock's Guide to Everything"[2].

---

[2] Kathy Schrock's Guide to Everything
http://www.schrockguide.net/index.html

2   Methods

The methods used to investigate the role and challenges of the educational technologist are data analysis, focus group interview and survey among experts. We used grounded theory [5]:

- stage 1: analysis of the job description (ET). Different job descriptions are used at different schools; they are also different in secondary and higher education. As these have been discussed at some courses training ETs at Tallinn University, we used the course transcript as well as web search (as some descriptions are put up to school websites). . We coded the main ideas and used them in stages 3 and 4 to analyze priorities;
- stage 2: analysis of blog posts about school environment and challenges of 13 working and studying ETs that have participated in 2011-2012 at the Infrastructure course at Tallinn University (http://taristuseminar.blogspot.com/). We collected tips, tricks and challenges that we used also in stage 3 and 4 to conduct the survey and interview;
- stage 3: focus group interview and discussion – "what is the most important and why in the tasks of educational technologists?" (18 ICT specialists, educational technologists or computer teachers from different Tallinn schools participated);
- stage 4: a survey among the experts (11) was carried out and the results discussed with ETs trainers (3). The questionnaire consisted of background information; job description, everyday tasks and priorities; how to motivate colleagues, management of ICT; and exemplary cases (e.g. about choosing a cloud system for the school and implementing it).

These four stages gave us information about the tasks that should be solved in a school environment by ETs as well as best practices how to implement new things and some tricks that are used to motivate others to use technology.

3   Results and Discussion

3.1   Overall Ideas of the Position

The technology-driven changes in Estonian society have produced good results, bringing the country to the top ten in overall freedom [14] and according to Freedom House[3] Estonia ranks among the most wired and technologically-advanced countries in the world [8]. Schools have also taken part in that innovation and have implemented a lot of changes over the last 10 years. At the same time, the occupation of educational technologist is not very old and only 7% of Estonians schools have got the position. Schools that have special support to teachers have shown more interest towards using technology and sharing best practices.

---

[3] Freedom House is an independent watchdog organization dedicated to the expansion of freedom around the world.

Looking at the big picture, it seems that educational technologist is still a "side" job with its description being different in every school. On the one hand, it is useful for the schools as they have someone providing help where it is needed. On the other hand, for the others it is often unclear who "the educational technologists" are and what should they do? The most popular task seems to be to participate everywhere to pick up knowledge (e.g. to be aware of the current trends); support teachers through training activities and participate in extracurricular projects with students. At the same time, according to their official job descriptions their main goal is to emphasize e-learning practices, consult not only teachers but also board, as well as analyze the results of local studies and find out the school's standing in them. For now, these seem to be not so important in the minds of the focus group. Addressing the challenge, we found out that the main problem is in the mixed signals and needs of the school board and teachers as well as the sheer extent of the problems that should be dealt with at the same time.

Competency-related problems can be solved with additional training, but also clarifying the job descriptions (ICT manager, environments administrator, website manager, ICT help, educational technologist, computer teacher). Training for educational technologists is provided by Tallinn University (a separate master's program), BSC Koolitus (a short program of 80 hours), Estonian e-Learning Development Centre (supporting seminars and training activities) as well as other web-based e-learning courses from abroad. New people usually come from the fields of pedagogy, andragogy, informatics or other similar backgrounds featuring customer support in some form.

Other challenges faced by schools include overworked teachers, not enough resources in any level and no clear vision for the future as there are also some educational reforms going on – e.g. to separate primary and secondary schools from gymnasiums. There are also issues with employing extra help (psychologists, special needs teachers, social pedagogues) that is regulated by the law. So school leaders have to make decisions whether to repair the roof, get more qualified help or purchase equipment. All are needed, but which one is the most important?

3.2 Educational Technologist Tasks and Power

The focus group interviews about the tasks of educational technologists revealed the top priorities that schools are struggling with right now - they strive to employ an ET that a) has all the necessary skills and knowledge; b) is able to train less knowledgeable teachers in the ICT area; c) can participate in international projects and d) support students. And even if all this is achieved, the ET does not have resources left to investigate the school to find actual problems and difficulties, or to advise the school board at important decisions (see Table 1).

Table 1. Priorities of the tasks of ETs

nr	Opportunity, Task	Impor- tance	Remarks
1	**Participate in different courses (online, real life, seminars) to be aware of the current trends**	**highest**	More skilled ET-s can share knowledge
2	Write projects for the school to get more funding for new technologies	low	Even if the school needs more resources and the ET has the skills to get them, usually it is not their task
3	**Participate as a supporting person in various projects with students (eTwinning, Comenius)**	**high**	An ET task is to train teachers. Sometimes they end up as project managers
4	**Train teachers inside your schools (in groups to individual)**	**high**	Skilled colleagues mean better results in using ICT
5	Advise the school board in technology-related decisions	low	Skilled management means better leadership
6	Perform research at schools (teachers-students skill level, feedback to services, innovation)	lowest	To make informed decision one needs data to support it
7	Train community: students, parents, teachers from other schools, partners	low	This promotes the school. Better reputation means better students and teachers will apply to study or work
8	Help teachers when they use technology in their classrooms (co-teaching)	average	A typical ET task. The only threat seen is to 'hijack' the lesson from the actual teacher
9	Create learning materials for others	average	Create materials for other teachers to learn, not for students. Still an unclear area.
10	Manage different e-learning sites/environments or networks for the school	low	Some schools also employ an ICT-administrator. Mixed results here, depending on personal interests and skills of people
11	Update a personal blog and link repository for others to use	average	One of the ET tools for sharing knowledge. To promote e-learning there must be a personal example

The experts (actual education technologists working at schools) stated that their job is to influence people to use technology, but without any power given to them. Their job is like that of a servant - to provide information, tools and have a lot of patience and good mood. Only 2 of 11 experts interviewed were members of school board. Also, only 42% of them work full time. This means that they have second job somewhere else or have extra tasks to do. At least all of them had official instructions and goals from the management about what they were expected to achieve and do.

A typical ET is thus expected to develop and support e-learning (share knowledge, train people); help others to develop their skills on ICT and support them, they must keep up with the new trends and environments; maintain and administer online learning environments; and also create new media learning materials. As if the ET is supposed to attend all kinds on seminars to learn the trade of all other teachers and then do their work as well (by creating their study materials and even giving their lessons) - it is a little similar to the 'teacher-oriented' learning style with students supposed to use technology but in reality, the teacher is doing the entire task with students being a passive audience. Thus, the ET's should be careful not to cultivate learned helplessness (especially among older teachers who would passively use the technology but refuse to learn from it) - to make things worse, many ET's are evaluated by the count of learning objects and courses they create, tempting them to 'score all the goals' by themselves.

3.3   Suggestions How to Grasp the Nettle

When starting to work as educational technologist, the first goal was suggested to be to get an idea what is going on at the school. Suggestions to get the basic knowledge of other teachers ICT skills were usually a) make a survey or interview, b) let them write a self-evaluation essay, c) observation, d) communicating and asking for evidence of ICT usage, e) doing something together. At the same time the subject (specialty) skill is not measured and it is a problem. While the teacher can master the content of her/his topic, they probably do not know the newest teaching methods. When ICT methods are presented the technologist relies on teachers' skills to recognize valuable tools for the content. As ICT seems difficult for teachers, it is really hard to determine how it would help the lesson when the teacher sees only the trouble with using technology. The solution is to push ordinary teachers to get involved in teacher support communities and also in some extent receive training in the national curricula goals for different subjects.

The second step would be to get people motivated. One way for an ET is to know the subject of the teacher and then smuggle in ICT skills (usually by personal example of either by the ET him/herself or some 'success stories' of others). Efforts by teachers should be noted and complimented. For some people, the whole process must be divided into small steps, doing them first together and then letting them try on their own. On the contrary, some others would like to study on their own - they only need the starting impulse (starting a blog would be a good example of a possible way) and perhaps some support (sending interesting web links etc). Some advanced ones can be asked to join the educational technologist training or made to present something to the colleagues. Some people worry constantly about their workload - they must be convinced that the new technology will decrease it (it is a slippery road to go, as this cannot always be guaranteed). Some kind of point system (to measure progress) can also help, as can direct benefits (added salary, free time etc) - but the latter are very difficult to do at schools due to a serious financial plight.

The management must be informed as well, usually by monthly to yearly meetings where goals and results are reported. Some ET's use private blogs to record their progress, others use mailing lists.

At the same time the support of management was the biggest issue reported from the ETs. Some leaders are not open to hear suggestions or even don't like technology (an example: a school leader states that "our school has no e-learning option", at the same time the ET reports that there are over 100 e-learning courses at that school"), the management is often not participating in training events, reports are asked, but nobody discusses them or even share them with others ("ET: I don't know why I even report, when nothing changes").

Measures to increase ICT usage includes:

- mandatory courses;
- optional courses with strong suggestion from the management;
- continuity ("repeat until they get it");
- dividing tasks/learning skills into smaller units ("I train only 15 minutes and teach 1-3 new tricks during that time");
- arguments of "old" and "new" ("Times has changed, we will never get the old times back");
- compliments;
- reliance on personal example until others start to follow;
- teaching only those that are interested ("I can't reach everybody");;
- sharing the resources only when the teacher writes a motivational letter and agrees to do more than just to use the device on her/his classes ("I ask them to train others, share materials etc);
- including questions about using ICT and innovative teaching to the work evaluation interview; when they want to get the "points" they must use technology and change;
- bottom up pressure (teach students to help teachers or ask them to complain about lack of interest when teachers use traditional methods);
- threatening teachers and management that other schools are already using all this technology and the school will lose good teachers, students and reputation.

So there are different approaches to achieve the goal – from the balanced and supporting approaches to the aggressive fear tactics. Different schools are used to different management styles to get the results. When calm and positive ET is recruited to a somewhat edgy environment then in the starting years the goal should only be to make oneself visible using the same means. Likewise, it is not advisable to make rapid or eclectic changes in a peaceful, slow-moving environment. The first year tasks should be also to build relations and work with those who are open to it. From the second year on when people already know the ET it is advised to push people to achieve more and widen the circle involved. The most important advice was never to try to reach more than 3 big goals in one year as that would be the optimum.

4   Conclusion

The most important step to start with is to clarify different positions and job descriptions. When school leaders expect to employ "whatever" to solve all the ICT challenges nothing will change. Different jobs need different people and personalities. Facilities that involve ET's (the Educational Technologist Society, universities, companies and other trainer/employers of ET's) should strive to promote the exact nature of the profession - most of all among school management but also future ET's.

Educational technologists are a key factor in how the technology is implemented at a school. When she/he has the support and power from management then the work succeeds, otherwise it is almost impossible. The ET tasks are to know what is going on (at school but also in the area of using ICT in an educational setting), find the ways to motivate people to use ICT and inform the management about the results. To do that, he/she must be as important as management themselves or have the unlimited support. Tools to achieve that vary from praise to scare. For a starting ET the most important goal is to make one visible, the second is to gather people that are interested at using ICT in classes. To change the school culture the ET must be patient - to change old habits and spread new values is a marathon rather than a sprint.

In the longer run, the other supporting systems also must change rapidly. Use of technology in the classes is written to the national curriculum, but there are no sanctions when it is not used at the learning environment. The Ministry of Education should raise the level of expectations to use ICT and present evidence of that during the teacher training process at universities as well as professional development, but also when teachers apply to raise their qualification to senior or mentor teacher.

Acknowledgements. This research was supported by the Tiger University Program of the Information Technology Foundation for Education.

References

1. Bean, J.C.: Engaging ideas: The professor's guide to integrating writing, critical thinking, and active learning in the classroom. Jossey-Bass (2011)
2. Davidson, J.: A new role in facilitating school reform: The case of the educational technologist. The Teachers College Record 105(5), 729–752 (2003)
3. Doucek, P., Maryska, M., Novotny, O.: Requirements on the competence of ICT managers and their coverage by the educational system–experience in the Czech Republic. Journal of Business Economics and Management (ahead-of-print), 1–24 (2012)
4. Duffy, T.M., Raymer, P.L.: A Practical Guide and a Constructivist Rationale for Inquiry Based Learning. Educational Technology 50(4), 3–15 (2010)
5. Glaser, B.G., Strauss, A.L.: The discovery of grounded theory: Strategies for qualitative research. Aldine de Gruyter (1967)
6. Eesti infoühiskonna arengukava 2013, Majandus- ja kommunikastiooniministeerium, eelnõu (2006), http://www.mkm.ee/failid/AK21nov.rtf (retrieved)
7. Eesti infoühiskonna arengukava 2020 koostamise ettepanek, Infoühiskonna arendamisest Eestis (2012), http://infoyhiskond.eesti.ee/files/Infoyhiskonna%20arengukava%20koostamise%20ettepanek_10-09-2012.pdf (retrieved)

8. Freedom in the net: Estonia, Freedomhouse (2012), http://www.freedomhouse.org/report/freedom-net/2012/estonia (retrieved)
9. Fullan, M.: The new meaning of educational change. Routledge (2013)
10. Goodyear, P., Retalis, S.: Technology-enhanced learning. Sense Publishers (2010)
11. Hughes, J.: The role of teacher knowledge and learning experiences in forming technology-integrated pedagogy. Journal of Technology and Teacher Education, 277–302 (2012)
12. Lawless, C., Kirkwood, A.: Training the educational technologist. British Journal of Educational Technology 7(1), 54–60 (1976)
13. Levy, S., Yupangco, J.: Overcoming the Challenges of Social Learning in the Workplace, LEarning Solutions Magazine (2008), http://www.learningsolutionsmag.com/articles/85/overcoming-the-challenges-of-social-learning-in-the-workplace (retrieved)
14. McMahon, F., et al.: Towards a Worldwide Index of Human Freedom, Fraser Institute (2013), http://www.fraserinstitute.org/research-news/display.aspx?id=19170 (retrieved)
15. Maadvere, I.: Üldhariduskooli haridustehnoloogi ametijuhend (2010), http://www.scribd.com/doc/25866605/Uldhariduskooli-haridustehnoloogi-ametijuhend (retrieved)
16. Maadvere, I. IKT uues riiklikus õppekavas, Tallinna Haridusamet (2010), http://www.tallinn.ee/est/haridusasutused/g7677s51441
17. Marandi, T., et al.: IKT ja Eesti koolikultuur, Tiigrihüppe SA) (2003), http://www.tiigrihype.ee/sites/default/files/tekstifailid/IKT_ja_Eesti%20koolikultuur_2003.pdf (retrieved)
18. McNutt, L.: Tension, Frustration and Compromise in the Field, An Exploratory Study of the Habitus of Educational Technologists (Doctoral dissertation, National University of Ireland Maynooth) (2010)
19. Mets, U.: IT tervikpilt, IT arendusprojektid, haridustehnoloogia juhtimine materjalid. BCS Koolitus (2011)
20. Miller, A.: Five best practices for the flipped classroom (2012), http://appliedlinguisticsclass.eportalnow.net/uploads/1/0/4/5/10458746/culturally_responsive_differentiated_instruction_narrowing_gaps_between_best_pedagogical_practices_benefiting_all_learners.pdf (retrieved April 16, 2012)
21. Niemi, H., Kynäslahti, H., Vahtivuori-Hänninen, S.: Towards ICT in everyday life in Finnish schools: seeking conditions for good practices. Learning, Media and Technology 38(1), 57–71 (2013)
22. Peters, K.: M-Learning: Positioning educators for a mobile, connected future. Mobile Learning 113 (2009)
23. Survey of Schools: ICT in Education: ICT in Education. Benchmarking Access, Use and Attitudes to Technology in Europe's Schools, European Commission DG Communications Networks, Content & Technology, SMART-Nr 2010/0039 (2013), http://ec.europa.eu/information_society/newsroom/cf/dae/itemdetail.cfm?item_id=9920 (retrieved)
24. Tipp, V.: Kes on haridustehnoloog (2010), http://www.scribd.com/doc/31144190/Kes-on-haridustehnoloog (retrieved)
25. Vaughn, S., Bos, C.S., Schumm, J.S.: Teaching students who are exceptional, diverse, and at risk in the general education classroom. Pearson (2011)

Facilitating Student Reflection through Digital Technologies in the iTEC Project: Pedagogically-Led Change in the Classroom

Sarah McNicol[1], Cathy Lewin[1], Anna Keune[2], and Tarmo Toikkanen[2]

[1]Education and Social Research Institute, Manchester Metropolitan University,
799 Wilmslow Road, Didsbury, Manchester M20 2RR, UK
[2]Learning Environments Research Group, Aalto University, PL 11000, 00076 Aalto, Finland
S.McNicol@mmu.ac.uk

Abstract. During the Europe-wide iTEC project, student reflection has been supported through the development of two dedicated digital tools: TeamUp and ReFlex. Using these tools, students are able to monitor their progress, thus gaining a greater awareness of their learning achievements and an appreciation of the new skills they have developed. Although TeamUp and ReFlex have been well-received by teachers and students, the use of audio-visual tools to support reflection was novel for most and the project evaluation highlighted the need for detailed guidance if these technologies are to be exploited to their full advantage.

Keywords: Reflection, audio-visual tools, scaffolding, digital tools.

1   Introduction

iTEC1 is a four year European Commission-funded project which aims to transform the way that existing and emerging technologies are used in teaching and learning throughout European schools. Within iTEC, teachers are encouraged to adopt reflection as a key learning activity, to support independent learning and critical thinking and increase students' confidence, self-awareness and motivation. Although a wide variety of methods and tools can be used to support reflection, from diaries and logbooks to wikis, blogs, and video diaries, in iTEC, the emphasis has been on using audio-visual tools. In particular, student reflection has been supported through the development of two dedicated digital tools: TeamUp and ReFlex, as well as the use of existing audio-visual reflection tools such as VoiceThread2, a cloud application which allows the upload and sharing of over fifty types of media and commentary using microphone, webcam, text, phone or audio-file upload.

---

[1] http://itec.eun.org
[2] http://voicethread.com/

P. Zaphiris and A. Ioannou (Eds.): LCT 2014, Part II, LNCS 8524, pp. 297–308, 2014.

2   Supporting Reflection

Reflection can be defined as a process that allows the learner to "integrate the understanding gained into one's experience in order to enable better choices or actions in the future as well as enhance one's overall effectiveness" [1]. The benefits of reflection as a vital component of the learning process are well rehearsed; as Hinett comments, "The benefits of reflection and associated techniques such as self- and peer-assessment speak for themselves. Students develop interpersonal skills, improve confidence and sustain motivation for their studies by monitoring and taking responsibility for their own development" [2]. Fuher argues that students are often better able to recognise their thoughts simply by documenting them [3], while more challenging forms of reflection push students to think in new ways and develop alternative explanations for experiences and observations, as demonstrated by Eyler and Giles [4]. The act of reflection therefore promotes independent learning and critical thinking as we "make sense of what we've learned, why we learned it, and how that particular increment of learning took place" [5]. Through reflection, students also learn to organise and express their thoughts, increasing confidence and self-awareness. As they become more aware of their progress, motivation can increase.

As Rogers points out, however, reflection remains a challenging concept for educators to apply in practice in spite of the potential for positive outcomes [1]. For example, research involving higher and continuing education students found that many do not initially understand how reflection may help them and feel that reflection is over-emphasised, failing to see its relevance to their learning [6, 7]. Moreover, there is limited evidence of adoption of reflection in primary and secondary school contexts [8]. This is particularly true in relation to 'live reflection' [9], or as Schön termed it, 'reflection-in-action' [10], that is, reflection conducted during the learning processes rather than after the events. Yet evidence suggests that supporting student metacognition and self-regulated learning can lead to 7-9 months additional progress [11]. Therefore, there is a need to identify how to support teachers engaging with student reflection as part of their pedagogical repertoire.

From Dewey [12] onwards, various models have been developed to describe and support, or scaffold, the reflection process and many follow a similar format, with an initial descriptive stage, followed by a more critical evaluation, which is then used as the basis for determining future actions. For example, the Driscoll Cycle (or 'What? So What? Now What?' framework), which can be mapped onto Kolb's Experiential Learning Cycle, starts with a description of the event, followed by an analysis of the event, which is then used to determine future actions [13]. Prompt questions are a common means of helping students to reflect and to make sense of their learning. An example is articulated learning (AL), as described by Ash and Clayton, which is structured in accordance with four guiding questions:

1. What did I learn?
2. How, specifically, did I learn it?
3. Why does this learning matter, or why is it significant?
4. In what ways will I use this learning?

They found, however, that students need more than just the four questions structuring the AL to achieve deep, critical learning [14]. Alongside these process frameworks, models have also been developed to classify students' reflective activities. For instance, Kember et al devised a series of coding categories for reflective thinking, which range from 'habitual action' to 'premise reflection', the latter suggesting a, "significant change of perspective" [15].

2.1   Reflection and Technology

Lin et al identify four ways in which theoretical frameworks suggest that technology can provide powerful scaffolding for reflection, namely, process displays (displaying problem-solving and thinking processes); process prompts (prompting students' attention to specific aspects of processes while learning is in action); process models (modelling of experts' thinking processes so that students can compare and contrast with their own process in action); and forums for reflective social discourse (creating community-based discourse to provide multiple perspectives and feedback that can be used for reflection). They argue that technology can often ensure that scaffolds to enhance reflection to occur in ways that are difficult to achieve in more traditional learning environments, for example, through guided prompts at critical points. They also describe the "leverage provided by technology to display learning processes in multiple formats, such as graphics, text, animation or audio" [16].

In a practical context, it has been demonstrated that technology can be used effectively to support reflection [17]. Audio-visual formats (eg video, multimedia web applications) are increasingly being used as an effective medium for reflection, particularly for pre-service and practicing teachers [18, 19, 20]. More recently, Voicethread has been used to student reflection in a higher education context [21, 22]. However, the use of audio-visual formats to support reflection is not always effective [17]. For instance, in a case study comparing written and multimedia reflection methods, Holland and Purnell found no evidence that using technology enhanced students' level of reflection and it may actually have hindered the reflective process as narratives were read from a prepared script. Furthermore, staff judged that all the multimedia reflections contained less reflection than written work [23]. In school contexts in particular, whilst potential for the use of blogs and e-portfolios to support reflection in school contexts has been noted [9, 24], there is little evidence of innovative uses of technology to support formative assessment and reflection in primary and secondary schools [25].

3   iTEC: Innovative Technologies for Engaging Classrooms

The iTEC school pilots are being delivered over four years (2010-14) in five overlapping 18-month cycles involving both primary and secondary schools. The number of European countries involved varies between cycles, as does the number of teachers (each of whom runs pilots with 1 to 3 cohorts, or classes, of learners). During the four cycles which have been completed to date, 278 cohorts from 17 countries participated in Cycle 1; 421 cohorts from 15 countries in Cycle 2; 407 cohorts from 18 countries in Cycle 3 and 874 cohorts from 19 countries in Cycle 4. A team from the Education and Social Research Institute (ESRI) at Manchester Metropolitan University (MMU) in the UK is responsible for the evaluation of iTEC. Each country has a national co-ordinator who oversees the project and supports teachers. At the end of each cycle, teachers who have participated complete an online questionnaire about their experiences, focusing on their use of the iTEC technologies, including reflective tools, as well as more general benefits, enabling factors, challenges encountered and potential for innovation. National co-ordinators conduct one or more case studies in their country each cycle, involving lesson observation and interviews with teachers, headteachers, ICT co-ordinators and students. These are returned to the evaluation team as case study reports (cycles 1-3 only, two per cycle) or transcripts (all cycles, one per cycle). In cycle 4, national co-ordinators also conducted a focus group with a sample of teachers from their country. In addition, members of the evaluation team have gathered data through the observation of project activities such as training sessions and webinars. The focus of the evaluation has altered slightly during each cycle to adapt to the needs of the project, so the precise questions asked within the survey and interviews have changed, meaning direct comparison between cycles is not possible for all measures.

Qualitative data are analysed using Nvivo. Transcriptions and notes are initially coded thematically using a conceptual framework from the SITES2 study [26], but an iterative approach is adopted with the initial framework being modified to incorporate new codes to reflect emerging themes. The survey comprises both open-ended and closed questions; the open-ended questions are translated into English using Google Translate and then analysed using Excel, while the closed questions are analysed using SPSS.

3.1   Audio-visual Reflection Tools in iTEC

The two prototype audio-visual reflection tools created as part of iTEC, TeamUp[3] and ReFlex[4], are open source tools, which will continue to be available beyond the project and are free to use and adapt. TeamUp (Fig. 1) has been used throughout the project[5]. This prototype tool allows teachers to create teams of students based on shared interests and/or other criteria such as gender. It also offers the facility for groups of students to record 60-second audio 'newsflashes' in the style of news bulletins which are stored with an image of themselves or work they are engaged in at the time of recording. When recording the 'newsflash' students are prompted on screen to respond to three points (highlighted at 20 second intervals): what they have done, what they will do next, and any problems encountered. This enables the group to reflect on their progress in group projects or learning activities, as well as achievements and future needs of work in progress. The audio-visual reflection recordings of a group are available to other students and their teacher. Anyone with

---

[3] https://sites.google.com/site/itectectester/
services/teamup

[4] https://sites.google.com/site/itectectester/services/
reflex

[5] Although in Cycle 1 data was not collected on the use of TeamUp as a reflection tools specifically.

access to the classroom space may listen to the recording of any group and create recordings for any group. For example, the teacher can use the reflections to monitor progress and inform assessment. Although focus lies on creating reflections of work in progress throughout project, teachers are advised to ask students to record a final reflection at the end of the project summarising activities, explaining how problems were overcome, and outlining next steps. ReFlex (Fig 2) is a more recently developed prototype; it enables students to build up a series of 60-second audio-clip reflections about their learning which are subsequently displayed on a timeline. Students can use ReFlex as a learning diary which also helps the teacher to monitor students' activities; it is intended to be used to facilitate one-to-one guidance sessions between the teacher and the student. A student's recordings are only available to themselves and their teacher. ReFlex also has a 'time capsule' feature, where the student can record a 'note' and send it to the future as a milestone or learning goal.

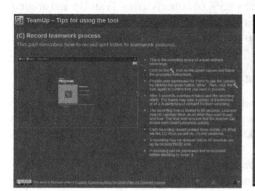

Fig. 1. Extract from TeamUp manual

Fig. 2. Screenshot of ReFlex 'reflection space'

The reflection tools used within the iTEC project can therefore be said to focus on the 'process display' [16] feature of scaffolding as students used the tools to make their problem-solving and thinking processes more visible and later review these as a means of reflecting on progress. In addition, it could be argued that TeamUp includes a simple implementation of 'process prompts' [16].

Teachers participating in the project have been implementing packages of learning activities[6] in their classrooms, in many cases within a 'learning story', or narrative exemplifying how a package of learning activities may support learning and teaching in the classroom. This has usually been in the form of a 'project' taking place over several lessons. In each cycle to date, teachers have been presented with the packages of learning activities and two to three learning stories, all designed to inspire teachers to do things differently and make more use of technology in their pedagogical practices. For example, during the last project cycle the learning activities have suggested a design-based learning process, in which students are asked to develop ideas and to question a design-brief, explore the context of their ideas through methods, such as mapping and stakeholder interviews, and to iteratively develop an

---

[6] http://itec.aalto.fi/learning-stories-and-activities/

artefact. These resources are not intended to be prescriptive and as a result each individual implementation can be unique as teachers adapt them to meet their needs and to fit with the technology infrastructures in their schools. Each package of learning activities has included one dedicated to reflection, focussing on project progress, perceived challenges and future plans. Teachers were asked to decide how many times their students would record reflections, with a recommendation that it should take place at the end of each day of project activity.

To date, Reflex has only been used by a small number of teachers (27 of those participating in Cycle 4). TeamUp has been more widely trialled however. During the second cycle of the project, TeamUp was used to record reflections with 30% of cohorts whilst an alternative tool was used in 33% of cohorts (n=262). The corresponding figures for Cycle 3 were 28% and 21% (n=334). In C4, 30% of cohorts[7] used TeamUp to record student reflections (n=424). During Cycles 2 and 3, teachers listened to the recordings made by 85% of cohorts using TeamUp and around three-quarters (74% and 77%) asked their students to listen to the recordings. In Cycle 2[8], the majority of students were asked to record reflections 1-5 times.

3.2   The Benefits of Reflection Using Audio-Visual Tools

The evaluation has found that reflection using iTEC digital tools has enabled both students and teachers to monitor the progress of their work by giving them a greater awareness of the progress they were making:

> *Students and the teacher reviewed their recordings next time. It was easy to follow projects' progression. (Finland, teacher, C3)*

Students in a class in Israel discussed how, initially, they viewed the time they spent reflecting as time wasted; some felt frustrated because they felt this meant less time for what they considered to be learning. However, after using TeamUp for several weeks, their opinions changed and they began to see its value as a project management tool. They came to realise TeamUp was, "not only as a technical tool but also as a way of learning" (Israel, student, C4) as it enabled them to appreciate the learning process and to consider each stage, rather than only focusing on the final outputs:

> *TeamUp really helped us in planning - think about what we did and what they are going to do at the next meeting. It made me think about the process and not just on the object [learning output]." (Israel, student, C4).*

Using the iTEC tools, students were also able to reflect more generally on their learning development and to identify new skills they had acquired. Teachers

---

[7] Data on number of cohorts was not provided in all cases in Cycle 4; this figure is calculated on the assumption that those teachers for whom no data is available ran the activities with one cohort.

[8] This question was not asked in other cycles.

commented that recording reflections helped to develop students' skills in self-evaluation; as they became "more aware of the learning process" (Spain, teacher, C4) and they were able to see how they were developing as individuals:

It forces students to think about their work, become aware of the work we have been able to do, and skills they have developed. (Spain, teacher, C3)

This realisation could be motivational for students as it made them aware of the progress they had made and encouraged them to undertake further work:

It also stimulates you to work, because you know that if you do so you will have a lot to record and you can listen to the progress you have made. (Israel, student, C4)

As well as reflecting on their progress and development as individuals, students engaged in peer-to-peer learning as they shared their individual reflections with each other. Students believed that the iTEC tools supported them in reflecting on their work as a group, not just as individuals and also helped them to "connect to the group" (Israel, student, C4). Students felt that documenting their reflection in some way was crucial and using technology to support reflection had notable advantages over traditional methods such as written journals. Although students commented that the process was more important than the tool itself, they believed that the act of recording (and listening back to) their reflection made them think more critically about their comments and encouraged them to construct their statements more clearly than they might do in a written document :

If you write it on a page, maybe you invest less time on the phrasing. But if you must also speak and hear yourself talk, then you must express it correctly.[...]You hear just what you say, and what intonation, so it requires you to speak more to the point, concisely and clearly. (Israel, students, C4)

Using digital tools to support reflection also had benefits for teachers. It enabled them to monitor individual and group progress more effectively and learn from students' reflections, using these to better appreciate where students were struggling and to identify where they needed to make changes to their pedagogical approach or provide additional support.

What I really liked was the various types of feedback. What we did today, and what the kids summarized, namely what they liked and what they disliked, why it was different [...] I learnt things about the kids that I would not have known otherwise (Hungary, teacher, C4).

3.3   Challenges of Using Audio-Visual Tools for Reflection

There were a number of challenges experienced in using audio-visual tools for reflection however. This was not unexpected as the use of digital tools to support reflection was clearly new for both students and teachers:

Some tasks, such as reflection or showing the work produced by students, were carried out using ICT. Normally I do not use ICT for the accomplishment of these tasks. (Portugal, teacher, C4)

As TeamUp and Reflex were new tools which neither teachers nor students had used before, it took some time for both groups to become familiar with them. To help students learn how to use the tools, a teacher in Israel tutored one student from each group, who was then responsible for supporting the other group members in their use of TeamUp.

Both tools were being refined and developed over the course of the project, so using prototype technologies meant that technical problems, such as a lack of infrastructure, equipment or support, could be a challenge:

...there were some connection problems and some problems with the use of Flash for video recording on some computers (Spain, teacher, C3).

Furthermore, although using digital tools to support reflection was appealing to some students, others were less comfortable being asked to record their reflections:

Recording was just embarrassing, some couldn't even record their voice (Portugal, teacher, C4)

Other challenges identified did not merely relate to audio-visual methods of reflection, but to the activity of reflection more generally. Time was a common barrier to reflection. As well as the problems of technical bugs and unfamiliarity, as described above, this was partly due to the fact that reflection was often seen a supplementary activity, rather than an integral part of the learning process.

Another frequently mentioned problem was students' lack of evaluation skills; case study teachers often felt that students tended to simply describe the process they had undertaken rather than reflecting on the successes and challenges experienced and the significance for their learning development. As reflection was something students were not used to doing many, and especially younger students, found it difficult to express their thoughts. As teachers explained:

It is not always easy to look at our own work from 'outside', the children often find it difficult to formulate their ideas (Hungary, teacher, C4)
...they [students] hardly made reflections, they simply told [the story of] what they made. Reflection as a method is very popular, but it is not easy for primary students to evaluate their own work. (Lithuania, teacher, C4)

Student attitudes could also present a challenge. Some students did not understand the value of reflection, regardless of the method used, and were therefore reluctant to take part in this learning activity. For example, a teacher referred to the problem of, "convincing students of the usefulness of this type of work" (Portugal, teacher, C4).

4   Discussion

As evidence from the evaluation of iTEC demonstrates, audio-visual tools can be used to support student reflection and offer a number of potential benefits, including being motivational for students; supporting project planning; and facilitating peer-to-peer learning and group work in general. While the technical challenges of using audio-visual reflection tools are not too challenging to overcome with adequate support, and are likely to diminish over time, pedagogical and organisational issues are likely to present more persistent barriers. Perhaps the greatest challenge is that reflection, in any format, is not yet considered an integral aspect of the learning and teaching process in many European schools, hence the perceived lack of time for reflection; poor understanding of its relevance; and paucity of student skills reported in the iTEC evaluation.   As Stephens and Winterbottom suggest, routine, structured reflection methods are less commonly used in schools compared to higher education [8].

Critically, as Boud and Walker point out, "reflection is not solely a cognitive process: emotions are central to all learning" [27]. The iTEC evaluation found student attitudes to be critical; if students did not appreciate the value of reflection, or were uncomfortable using audio-visual approaches, this proved to be a significant barrier. Teacher attitudes are equally important. Lin et al describe how, regardless of the medium used for reflection, the role of the teacher is crucial: "Providing students with tools for reflection does not guarantee that they will use them appropriately, if at all. Teachers are crucial in creating classroom norms and structures that increase the value that students place on reflection" [16].

Even if both teachers and students appreciate the value of reflection however, as Welch points out, it is not enough to tell students to "go and reflect"; rather, some form of scaffolding is necessary to help students to structure the way in which they reflect on their learning and to make sense of their experiences [28]. The guidance provided to support the use of TeamUp initially focused on three questions: 'What we did?' 'What we're going to do?' and 'Any problems?', echoing the tripartite reflection structure of the Driscoll Cycle [13] and similar models. From Cycle 3 onwards, this guidance was expanded to include two additional prompt questions: 'Did you overcome the challenges? (How?)'; and 'What challenges can you foresee?'[9]. However, the evaluation findings suggest that students, and their teachers, required still more detailed guidance and support to make effective use of the TeamUp tool. This need for a more detailed structure is unsurprising given similar findings reported elsewhere [14]. Although iTEC students were generally able to master the first component of reflection: describing an experience, they found analysing this and reflecting on it to determine future actions to be more challenging. Students clearly needed more support in these specific aspects of reflection.

As Holland and Purnell reported, although digital tools may have potential to enhance reflection activities, there is a danger that, in practice, they may in fact detract from critical reflection, especially if audio-visual tools are seen merely as an extension of written formats whereby students prepare and record a script [23]. Analysis of the

---

[9] http://itec.eun.org/c/document_library/get_file?uuid=665ee1c5-aae2-475b-a94c-724cb44931e7&groupId=10136

evaluation data from iTEC offers a number of suggestions as to the ways in which teachers and students may make more effective use of digital tools to support reflection, capitalising on the inherent strengths of this format, rather than simply regarding it as a direct replacement for a written reflective journal. Some possible methods of enhancing the use of audio-visual reflection tools are described below. These are organised according to the four ways in which technology can provide powerful scaffolding for reflection identified by Lin et al [16]. Although it has not been possible to explore all of these within the timeframe of the project, they suggest ways in which iTEC resources, and similar audio-visual tools, could be further exploited in the future.

4.1   Process Display

Developing 'Newsflashes'. One of the potential strengths of the TeamUp tool is the use of the idea of a 'newsflash' which will be familiar to students from television news bulletins. This concept might be further developed, for example, by students devising a headline which sums up their experiences in a few words, along with the use of images illustrating their 'reflection story'.

4.2   Process Prompts

Interview Structure. Lin et al discuss the use of process prompts embedded in digital tools to scaffold reflection [16], but another approach may simply be for one student to interview another, thereby providing the prompts for their reflection, and then reversing roles. Students can be assisted in devising their own prompts, or these can be provided by the teacher. The interview can be recorded and revisited by the student.

Thinking Hats. A widget based on de Bono's Thinking Hats[10] has been used to support reflection by a number of iTEC teachers. Feedback indicates that students found this approach helpful as a means of looking at their project from different perspectives in order to analyse their learning experiences. This suggests that integrating this widget with the audio-visual reflection tools used may help in scaffolding.

4.3   Process Models

Peer Tutors. Peer tutors can help to overcome basic technical challenges and a lack of relevant ICT skills. These students can be trained by the teacher in the use of the digital reflection tools and then recognised as 'experts' who are able to support other members of their group in using the technologies.

---

[10] http://exchange.smarttech.com/
details.html?id=c22fce6f-b61f-4bf2-a3ad-cd714228ee82

4.4   Reflective Social Discourse

Paired Reflection: Paired reflection may help to reduce the embarrassment students may experience when recording themselves and making reflections orally. Two students discussing their progress and reflecting in this way can be a more natural, and less pressured, setting than a single student speaking aloud to a camera.

Imaginative and Creative Approaches. Audio-visual tools might also be used to support more creative and imaginative approaches to reflection, such as the use of metaphors, poems or sketches to both describe and analyse learning.

5   Conclusion

The use of digital tools to support reflection was novel for most iTEC teachers and students and, although such tools were well-received, the evaluation highlighted the fact that detailed guidance needs to be provided if these technologies are to be exploited to their full advantage.

Acknowledgements. TeamUp, ReFlex and the iTEC Learning Activities were developed by the Learning Environments Research Group at Aalto University, Finland (http://legroup.aalto.fi). Thanks to all the teachers and students involved in the iTEC evaluation and to the national co-ordinators and their colleagues involved in data collection. Thanks also to Maureen Haldane, iTEC work package 5 co-lead investigator during Cycles 1-3. iTEC is coordinated by European Schoolnet (EUN) and co-funded by the European Commission's 7th Framework Programme.

References

1. Rogers, R.: Reflection in Higher Education: A concept analysis. Innovative Higher Education 26, 37–57 (2001)
2. Hinnet, K.: Improving Learning Through Reflection – Part One (2002),
   http://www.heacademy.ac.uk/assets/documents/resources/
   database/id485_improving_learning_part_one.pdf
3. Fuher, C.: Response Journals: just one more time with feeling. Journal of Reading 37(5), 400–405 (1994)
4. Eyler, J., Giles, D.E.: Where's the Learning in Service-learning? Jossey-Bass. Jossey-Bass, San Francisco (1999)
5. Race, P.: Evidencing Reflection: Putting the 'w' into reflection (ESCALATE Learning Exchange) (2002), http://www.escalate.ac.uk/exchange/Reflection
6. Francis, D.: Reflective Journal: A window to preservice teachers' practical knowledge. Teaching and Teacher Education 11(3), 229–241 (1995)
7. Langer, A.M.: Reflecting on Practice: Using learning journals in higher and continuing education. Teaching in Higher Education 7(3), 337–351 (2002)
8. Stephens, K., Winterbottom, M.: Using a Learning Log to Support Students' Learning in Biology Lessons. Journal of Biological Education 44(2), 72–80 (2010)

9. Crook, C., Fisher, T., Harrop, H., Stokes, E.: New Modes of Technology-enhanced Learning: Developing successful practice. Becta, Coventry (2010), http://dera.ioe.ac.uk/1535/

10. Schön, D.A.: Teaching Artistry through Reflection-in-action. In: Educating the Reflective Practitioner, pp. 22–40. Jossey-Bass Publishers, San Francisco (1987)

11. Higgins, S., Katsipataki, M., Kokotsaki, D., Coleman, R., Major, L.E., Coe, R.: The Sutton Trust-Education Endowment Foundation Teaching and Learning Toolkit. Education Endowment Foundation, London (2013)

12. Dewey, J.: How We Think. D. C. Heath, New York (1933)

13. Driscoll, J.: Practising Clinical Supervision: A Reflective Approach for Healthcare Professionals, 2nd edn. Bailliere Tindall Elsevier, Edinburgh (2007)

14. Ash, S.L., Clayton, P.H.: The Articulated Learning: An Approach to Guided Reflection and Assessment. Innovative Higher Education 29(2), 137–154 (2004)

15. Kember, D.: Determining the Level of Reflective Thinking from Students' Written Journals Using a Coding Scheme Based on the Work of Mezirow. International Journal of Lifelong Education 18(1), 18–30 (1999)

16. Lin, X., Hmelo, C., Kinzer, C.K., Secules, T.J.: Designing Technology to Support Reflection. Educational Technology Research and Development 47(3), 43–62 (1999)

17. Kori, K., Pedaste, M., Leijen, Ä., Mäeots, M.: Supporting reflection in technology-enhanced learning. Educational Research Review 11, 45–55 (2014)

18. Maclean, R., White, S.: Video Reflection and the Formation of Teacher Identity in a Team of Pre-service and Experienced Teachers. Reflective Practice 8(1), 47–60 (2007)

19. Rich, P.J., Hannafin, M.: Video Annotation Tools Technologies to Scaffold, Structure, and Transform Teacher Reflection. Journal of Teacher Education 60(1), 52–67 (2009)

20. Leijen, A., Lam, I., Wildschut, L., Simons, P.R.-J., Admiraal, W.: Streaming Video to Enhance Students' Reflection in Dance Education. Computers & Education 52, 169–176 (2009)

21. Augustsson, G.: Web 2.0, Pedagogical Support for Reflexive and Emotional Social Interaction Among Swedish Students. Internet and Higher Education 13, 197–205 (2010)

22. Olofsson, A.D., Lindberg, J.O., Stödberg, U.: Shared Video Media and Blogging Online: Educational technologies for enhancing formative e-assessment? Campus-Wide Information Systems 28(1), 41–55 (2010)

23. Holland, L., Purnell, E.: Does the Use of Multimedia Technology Change or Improve First Year Information System Students' Level of Reflection? Reflective Practice 13(2), 281–294 (2012)

24. Hartnell-Young, E., Harrison, C., Crook, C., Pemberton, R., Joyes, G., Fisher, T., Davies, L.: Impact Study of e-portfolios on Learning. Becta, Coventry, UK (2007), http://dera.ioe.ac.uk/1469/1/becta_2007_eportfolios_report.pdf

25. Luckin, R., Blight, B., Manches, A., Ainsworth, S., Crook, C., Noss, R.: Decoding Learning: The proof, promise and potential of digital learning. Nesta, London (2011)

26. Kozma, R.B. (ed.): Technology, Innovation and Educational Change: A global perspective. International Society for Technology in Education, Eugene (2003)

27. Boud, D., Walker, D.: Promoting Reflection in Professionals Courses: The challenge of context. Studies in Higher Education 23(2), 191–206 (1998)

28. Welch, M.: The ABCs of Reflection: A template for students and instructors to implement written reflection in service-learning. NSEE Quarterly 25, 22–25 (1999)

Which Is More Effective for Learning German and Japanese Language, Paper or Digital?

Reina Shimizu and Katsuhiko Ogawa

Faculty of Environment and Information Studies
Keio University, Kanagawa, Japan
{t10438rs,ogw}@sfc.keio.ac.jp

Abstract. Recently, many people often say how practical is the digital media. Moreover, there are many researches on this topic that compare the use of paper and the digital media, but unfortunately, only the moment in which the user is actually using one of these two media is taken into account. We researched a group of Japanese and German subjects about their ability to remember some words on the next day, three days later and a week after they first tried to memorize them. The results demonstrated that users who want to learn in a short term should use digital media, only if they have a lot of experience using digital media in general. But if the user wants to learn something in a long term, might prefer to use Paper.

Keywords: paper digital learning memorizing language.

1   Paper vs. Digital

Digital media, especially electronic books, has been brought to public attention recently. This is not only in Japan but also in the world. The electronic media has more to offer other than photo and music. People are now considering to study using tablet-type devices. We have known paper for a long time, but many people are not thinking about the importance of paper. The learning curve of paper and digital needs to be examined in detail era. The hidden charm of paper can cause favorable effects for learning, so the reason why this is so effective deserves careful attention.

We based our research on testing with the method of flash cards for learning and memorizing. Many Japanese and German students use paper for learning, but digital flash cards Applications are also rising as well as the use of the Smartphone is spreading. Several comparative studies have been made on learning curve of paper and digital media, but apparently there has been no study that tried to see the results in the long run. In this article, we would like to see comparatively the learning curve after one day, three days and one week that can be offered with paper or with digital media.

Many people feel that they can memorize better using paper than using digital media. The learning curve with paper seems to be better than with digital in the long run and there are not only differences from paper and digital media but also among languages. The factor can be their mother tongue (naturally learned) and a foreign language (knowledge acquired through taking lessons).

P. Zaphiris and A. Ioannou (Eds.): LCT 2014, Part II, LNCS 8524, pp. 309–318, 2014.
© Springer International Publishing Switzerland 2014

2   Experimental Methods

Japanese subjects have been tested from 15th July 2011 to 29th July 2011. German subjects have been tested from 5th July 2013 to 26th July 2013. The term for testing each subject was eight days.

2.1   Japanese Subjects

20 students were tested. They all belonged to Keio University in Japan. The number of women and men were equal. The average age of subjects were 20.1 years old. The youngest person was 18 years old and the oldest person was 24 years old. None of the subject had eyesight problems. The average length of experience time using Smartphone was 22.8 months. Three people had never used Smartphone. The largest experience time using Smartphone was 84 months. The average experience using PC was 8.22 years. The shortest was 3 years and the largest was 15 years. In Japan, the English study program begins generally over the age of 12. The average time for learning English was 7.1 years. Two people of the tested users studied English abroad.

2.2   German Subjects

The number of students was the same as in the test in Japan, but they belonged to Martin-Luther University Halle-Wittenberg in Germany. The number of women and men was equal too. A range of age was 19 to 31 years old. The average of age was 22.25 years old. As the Japanese users, the German users did not have eyesight problems either. The average time of experience using Smartphone was 11.95 months. Seven people had never used Smartphone. The largest experience was 48 months. The average experience time using PC was 8.992 years. The shortest was 8 months and the largest was 15 years. In Germany, the English study program begins generally over the age of 10. The average time for learning English is 13.25 years.

2.3   Methodology for Testing

It was investigated the influence of digital as well as paper media by testing how the students remembered the words on the following day, three days later and a week later. This means that the test was conducted several times, in order to verify how well the knowledge was learned after having used the paper or the digital media.

One part of the experiment was made on paper, and the other was made in an Apple iPod touch, but the designs had the same character size. Subjects who took the experiment used both media.

Fig. 1. Vocabulary flash cards ground by a ring (Paper), iPod (Digital)

2.4   Contents of Flash Cards

Each flash card set (in paper and digital media) had 10 words in English and 10 words in their mother tongue (Japanese words for Japanese subjects and German words for German subjects).

In the case of Japanese subjects, difficult ideograms were chosen for the test. In Japan, the Japan Aptitude Kanji Test is an examination in which is questioned how many and how complete is one's knowledge of Japanese Characters. For our test, we used ideograms that had the same level of difficulty as in that examination.

In the case of German subjects, the selected words were technical vocabulary from various fields. This was made to preserve the same level of difficulty as in the case of Japanese words for Japanese people.

2.5   Process

Subjects were given 2 minutes to learn 20 words in each media; 10 subjects started to learn with digital media, and the other 10 subjects started to learn with Paper. There were a set of rules: first, "The user has to see all of the words at least once in 2 minutes" following this rule, there is no difference between the amount of time dedicated to each word. Second, "The user can not take off the ring of paper flash cards". When the users do not use a ring to ground the cards, they can use the flash cards with too many directions. Third, "The user must use the iPod touch only in horizontal position", because when the user uses iPod touch vertical direction, the letter size gets smaller to fit the screen size.

There were some subjects who have never used digital media, so before beginning the experiments, they trained in how to use the digital flash cards. In case of the German subjects, they had to practice also how to use the paper flash cards. In figure 2, it is shown how normal flash cards are in Germany. They use paper flash cards without a ring.

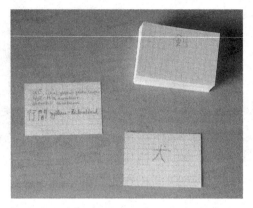

Fig. 2. Paper flash cards in Germany

On the next day, three days later and a week after memorizing words, subjects received a mail with the test. This test consisted in 20 words: 2 that belonged to the group of the 10 already learned in paper and 2 to the group of words learned in the digital media. Those 4 words among the group of 20 were known for them. The rest 16 words were new vocabulary.

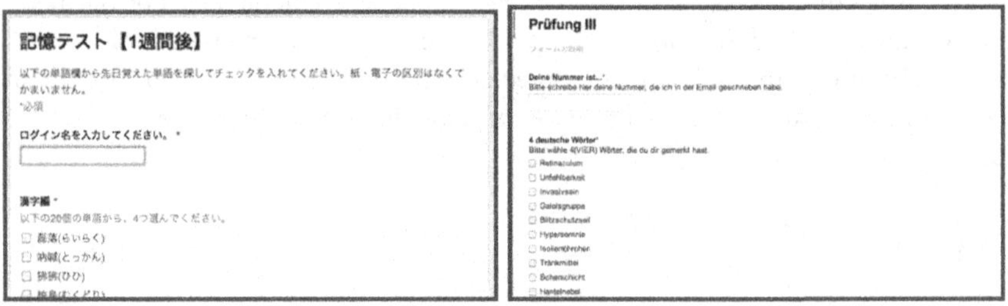

(a) In Japanese	(b) In German

Fig. 3. Test

3   Results

Each word was given a score of 1 point. The number of subjects is 20 and each subject can have maximal 2 points. In brief, the maximal scores are 40 points. The graphs below show the results with average scores.

3.1   Results of Japanese Subjects

The results show that subjects could memorize more words in Japanese or English when using paper flash cards than when using digital media as a learning tool.

Only comparing the results of English vocabulary after one day, points scored for digital media were higher. But this is believed that happened if the users had many years of experience using digital media. During the next tests, having more experience or not having experience at all, did not make any difference: the results showed that paper flash cards resulted more effective.

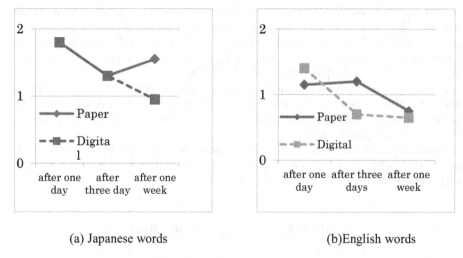

(a) Japanese words   (b)English words

Fig. 4. Results with Japanese subjects

3.2   Results of German Subjects

The results of German words with German subjects are similar to the results of Japanese words with Japanese subjects. But the results of English words with German subjects are somehow different from the same test but with Japanese subjects.

Graph 3: Results of German word (left) / Graph 4: Results of English word (right)

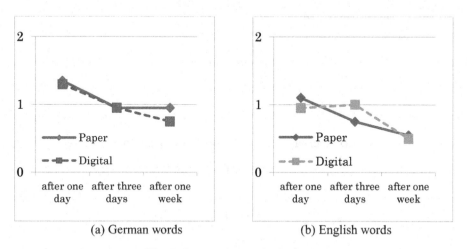

(a) German words   (b) English words

Fig. 5. Results with German subjects

3.3   Individual Results

Patterns for individual results. We made five patterns for analyzing individual results.

First type is "Keep". Subjects in this pattern collected always same point on the following day, three days later and a week later. Ex) (1 point, 1 point, 1 point) or (2 points, 2 points, 2 points). Usually, memory decrease gradually, that is why this pattern is called positive pattern. When subjects couldn't any points, it showed a negative pattern, so we separated this from "Keep" type.

Second type is "Reborn". Subjects in this pattern collected once bad results on three days after memorizing the words, but results on a week later is the same as in the first test. Ex) (2 points, 1 point, 2 points), (1 point, 0 point, 1 point). This pattern is also considered a positive pattern.

Third type is "Little Increase". Result is rising on three days later or on a week later. Ex) (1 point, 1 point, 2 points), (1 point, 2 points, 2 points). Those three patterns are positive pattern.

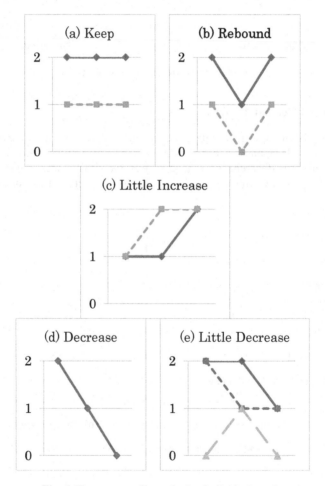

Fig. 6. Five patterns for analyzing individual results

Forth type is "Decrease". This pattern occurs when the result fall rapidly. Subject that follow this pattern collected 2 points on the following day, but 1 point on three days later and no point on a week later. It's a negative pattern.

Fifth type is "Little Decrease". Result shows a decrease three days later or on a week later. Ex) (2 point, 1 point, 1 points), (1 point, 2 points, 1 points). Those two patterns are negative patterns.

Individual results of Japanese subjects. We used patterns that are written in section "Patterns for individual results".

In the case of Japanese words with Japanese subject, type "Little Decrease" is majority by both media. But in the case of paper, many subjects were included in positive patterns. 13 of 20 subjects were in the "Keep", "Reborn" or "Little Increase" group. In the case of digital, only 4 subjects followed a positive pattern. No one is "Decrease" by using paper, but there were 4 subjects in "Decrease" by using digital.

In the case of English words with Japanese subject, "Little Decrease" were majority. This graph shows that there is not a large difference between paper and digital. 2 subjects couldn't any points by using digital media. This shows us that the use of digital could be poorer than paper.

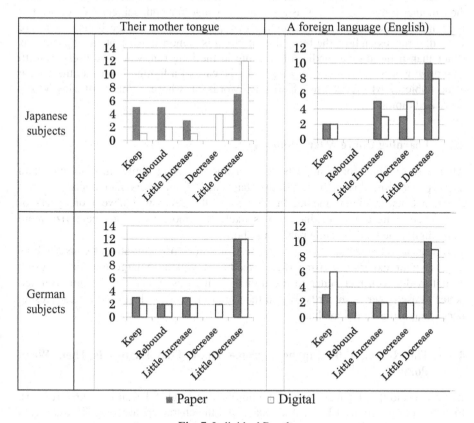

Fig. 7. Individual Results

In the case of German words with German subjects, taking into account positive patterns, paper and digital seem to be similar. But only in digital, subjects were included "Decrease" pattern. Same numbers of subjects were included in "Keep", "Reborn", "Little Increase" and "Decrease" by digital.

The results of English words seem not to be a lot of changes from the results of German words. But by using paper, the number subjects who were included in the pattern "Decrease" raised, and by digital, the users who follow the pattern "Keep" increased.

4   Discussion

4.1   Learning Curve in the Long Run

In the case of Japanese words with Japanese subjects and German words with German subjects, results on a week later by paper were better than by digital. (Paper: Digital) = (32, 18), (19, 15). In the case of English words with Japanese subjects or German subjects, results on a week later were same. (Paper: Digital) = (13, 13), (11, 10).

Japanese words for Japanese subjects and German words for German subjects were their mother tongue. English was a foreign language for both subjects. When we use foreign language, this is translated into our mother tongue by the brain. There are some differences on how the brain does it. So, it is demonstrated that using paper was better than using digital media for learning in the long run, when the users want to memorize words in their mother tongue. In the case of a foreign language, there were some subjects who could not learn any words or whose memory of new words decreased rapidly.

4.2   Learning Curve After a Short Time

After a short time, some subjects could memorize using digital media better than using paper. But this is believed that happened if the users had many years of experience using digital media. In the future, the users will have more years of experience using digital media, so it is likely that more users can memorize more using digital media than using paper in a short time.

If you have to memorize words for test on tomorrow, you should consider how large is your experience using digital media. If you have large experience using digital media, you had better to use digital flash cards. When you do not, you had better to use paper flash cards. But in the long run, you can learn more steady using paper than using digital media.

4.3   The Reason Why Japanese People Think That English Is Their Weak Point

It is often said that Japanese people are not good at English because of three reasons. First, the construction of English language and the characters are very different from Japanese. On the other hand, is also said that the English education in Japan is not good because they only teach grammar.

It is quite likely to believe that is not good for learning that people is under the impression "I am not good at English".

The results of Japanese words with Japanese subjects were better than the results of English words test. The reason why this happens is because not only Japanese is their mother tongue, but also because Japanese words are ideograms. Japanese ideograms have many meaning. For example, the ideogram 清 (sei) is constructed by two parts: left part is "water" and right part is "blue". The meaning of the ideogram is "clean" or "pure". People can grasp the meaning just by seeing the parts of the ideogram. But English for Japanese people is a foreign language and the letters itself do not have a meaning. Those aspects make the difference.

In the case of German subjects, the results of English words were similar to the results of English words in the case of Japanese subjects. But the results of German words are not as well as the results of Japanese words, this is believed to happen because German letters itself do not contain a meaning.

It has been recognized that when a person has negative awareness, the learning curve can be lower than with a positive awareness.

5   Conclusion

We conducted research with Japanese and German subjects. They memorized 10 words in their mother tongue and 10 words in English. On the next day, three days later and a week after memorizing words, the subjects took a test. It was demonstrated that users who want to learn in a short term should use digital media, but only if they have a lot of experience using digital media in general. In the case that the user wants to learn something in a long term, might prefer to use Paper. That was a common point between Japanese subjects and German subjects, not only the average results but also the individual results show that evidence. Positive patterns became visible when the participants used paper flash cards, and negative patterns often appeared when using the digital media, especially when subjects wanted to learn more vocabulary their mother tongue.

There are differences not only on the selected medium, but also in the language. The results of Japanese words with Japanese subjects were better than the results of German words with German subjects. Japanese words and German words were in their own mother tongue, however we could observe why the results of Japanese vocabulary have so many points compared to the German results: first, Japanese is the mother tongue for Japanese people. Second, in English as in German, each letter itself has no meaning; but in Japanese (in the case of this experiments) each letter itself has a certain meaning.

In the future, we want to make new set of flash cards so that people can memorize more words and enjoy studying. For the new set of flash cards and enhancing the accuracy of the experiments, we had better to make more iterations and test in various situations.

References

1. Keio-University; Human Performance Laboratory (HPL), 人間工学ガイド: 感性を化学する方法 (Ningen Kogaku Gaido: Kansei wo Kagaku suru Houhou). Scientist-Press, Tokyo (2009)
2. 酒井邦嘉(Sakai, Kuniyoshi), 脳を創る読書 (Noh wo Tsukuru Dokusho)". Tokyo: Jitsugyo no Nihon Sha (2011).
3. 高野健太郎(Takano, K.), 大村賢悟(Omura, K.) and 柴田博仁(Shibata, H.). Comparison between paper books and electronic books in reading short stories. 2011-HCI-141(4), 1–8 (2011)
4. 柴田博仁(Shibata, H.) and 大村賢悟(Omura, K.). Comparison between paper books and electronic books in reading to answer questions. 2011-HCI-141(5), 1–8 (2011)
5. 山内悠輝(Yamauchi, Yuki) and 永岡 慶三(Nagaoka, K.). Comparison on Reading Behaviors between Digital Book and Printed Book for Satisfaction and Speed, 453-110 27–32 (2011).
6. 清水玲那(Shimizu, R.), 橋口恭子(Hashiguchi, K.) and 小川克彦(Ogawa, Katsuhiko). Which is More Effective for Learning German and Japanese Language, Paper or Digital? (2012)
7. 赤堀侃司(Akahori, K.). Learning Effectiveness Using Non-verbal Information with a Mobile Terminal Camera Function, 7-1 29-37 (2013).
8. Morris, M.R., Brush, A.J.B., Meyers, B.: Reading Revisited: Evaluating the Usability of Digital Display Surfaces for Active Reading Tasks. InL Tabletop, 79–86 (2007)

Monitoring Teachers' Complex Thinking while Engaging in Philosophical Inquiry with Web 2.0

Agni Stylianou-Georgiou[1], Alexios Petrou[1], and Andri Ioannou[2]

[1] University of Nicosia, Department of Education,
Nicosia, Cyprus
[2] Cyprus University of Technology, Limassol, Cyprus
{stylianou.a@unic.ac.cy,petrou.a}@unic.ac.cy,
andri.i.ioannou@cut.ac.cy

Abstract. The purpose of this study was to examine how we can exploit new technologies to scaffold and monitor the development of teachers' complex thinking while engaging in philosophical inquiry. We set up an online learning environment using wiki and forum technologies and we organized the activity in four major steps to scaffold complex thinking for the teacher participants. In this article, we present the evolution of complex thinking of one group of teachers by studying their interactions in depth.

Keywords: complex thinking, critical thinking, creative thinking, caring thinking, philosophy for children, philosophical inquiry, technology integration, wiki, forum, WikiSplit.

1 Introduction

This study is an attempt to advance the current instructional design approaches in online and blended learning settings. Our approach was inspired by the principles of the "Philosophy for Children" (P4C) program [10] and exploited web 2.0 technologies to scaffold and monitor the development of teachers' complex thinking while engaging in philosophical inquiry.

Briefly, P4C aims to allow children to acquire complex thinking skills through play and the development of a community. Since its development [10], this program has been used successfully in many schools worldwide and a few scholars have discussed its success in promoting students' complex thinking [11]. To date, P4C has not been used with adult learners, such as pre-service or in-service teachers. Moreover, the role of technology in P4C has not been explored.

In this study we aimed to help in-service teachers develop complex thinking while they engage in philosophical inquiry using web 2.0 technologies. We first sought to understand how collaboration and critical thinking unfolds within a small group of teachers in our technologically mediated environment. We then examined their interactions, in more depth, in order to understand how their arguments evolved as they discussed a philosophical dilemma and wrote a, so called, thinking-story (e.g., an

P. Zaphiris and A. Ioannou (Eds.): LCT 2014, Part II, LNCS 8524, pp. 319–327, 2014.

essay) to be used as a springboard for debate in a classroom environment. Finally, we discuss how WikiSplit [7] – a combined wiki-forum tool -- assisted the development of complex thinking.

2   Theoretical Framework

The main purpose of the P4C program is to promote complex thinking by developing critical thinking, creative thinking and caring thinking. The philosophical dialogue helps children improve reasoning ability and acquire metacognitive skills, as is the awareness of how they think [8]. According to Lipman [1], critical thinking in the context of this program, is promoted by and as a result of interactions that occur in a community of inquiry. He argues that critical thinking is a complex process involving the development of personal and social experience [9]. During the development of this kind of thinking, an emphasis is put on the process (in contrast to the product) of philosophical debate in a community of inquiry. As Haynes points out, philosophical inquiry is not a 'tool-kit' approach to promoting independent thinking [5]. The process is dependent on the quality of interaction and dialogue engendered, rather than rigidly following a step-by-step procedure. The dialogue in its strict meaning as dia-logos is an active and critical method of communication [1]. Fisher [3] supports that dialogue leads to the development of thinking. Creating meanings is a dialogical process. Meaning does not have static identity. It is a result of different voices. It is important for children to be exposed and actively engage in inquiry where different voices, ideas and perspectives are present.

Children in the program have the opportunity to monitor the way their peers think and critically evaluate the various arguments. Therefore, they become more sensitive to the opinions of others and they engage in dialogue, rather than parallel monologue. Lipman defines this type of thinking as caring thinking [1]. As Haynes [5] points out "caring thinking involves caring enough to make the effort to hear what others are saying and developing the capacity to see the merits of each point of view[…] caring for self and others through learning detachment from the need to be right or certain about everything" (p. 46). Creative thinking is also encouraged in the p4C program. Philosophical - logical thinking is encouraged through creative activities and creativity is cultivated through reasoning ability.

Fostering the above types of thinking in the P4C program occurs by means of praxis [1]. To enable this praxis, Lipman developed seven novels with accompanying manuals. The novels serve as springboards for debate [9]. Their central characters learn to resolve their problems through their powers of reasoning. The story is presented and the children take time to think of their own questions. Then, these questions are discussed briefly before one is selected for more extensive discussion. The presentation of different positions gives the opportunity for all participants to share their thoughts and collectively judge which of these sites are dominant and which are not, by developing arguments. The argumentation ability is an important objective of the P4C program. Children are encouraged to support their positions reasonably and recognize whether their opinions are valid and reliable. Also they are asked to correct possible flaws, seeking more evidence to substantiate their opinions, especially when they contradict. Alternative stimulus materials have evolved since Lipman's original materials. In the UK, Fisher [2] has produced a series of books. In general, P4C involves students and their teacher sharing a short story that stimulates thinking. In our study we use the term thinking-story to refer to this type of story. To date, P4C has not been used with adult learners, such as pre-service or in-service teachers, even though there is a great need for teachers to understand the importance of complex thinking and how it can evolve through collaboration within a community of inquiry. In this study, we examine the discourse of a group of teachers in order to understand how arguments evolve while engaging in a debate and collaborative writing of a thinking-story.

3   Method

Participants. The community of inquiry under investigation was composed of seven students (mean age 25 years old) attending a graduate course on Learning Theory at a private university in Southeastern Europe.   In addition to the domain-expert instructor, the course was tutored by an instructor of philosophy and a learning technologist. Students within the community of inquiry were randomly separated in two smaller groups (3 vs. 4 students) to engage in an online debate on a philosophical dilemma. Each group was randomly assigned to support one of the two aspects presented in the dilemma: "The phenomenon of euthanasia to people in cases of severe illness is completely unacceptable" vs. "The phenomenon of euthanasia is acceptable to the people in case of severe illness" [12]. The goal of each group was to produce a thinking-story, which could be used as a springboard for a debate on the topic of euthanasia in the K-12 classroom.

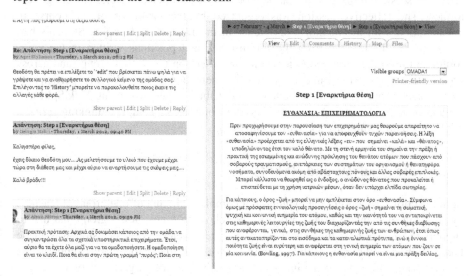

Fig. 1. WikiSplit (forum on the left, wiki on the right)

Research Context. The online debate was supported by WikiSplit [7] – a combined wiki-forum tool which aimed to facilitate students' discussion during the debate as well as their collaborative writing of the thinking-story. In forum-mode group members discussed the dilemma. In wiki-mode the position of the group was recorded as a result of their negotiation in forum-mode.

In WikiSplit, the activity was organized in four major steps to scaffold students' complex thinking. Three steps involved the argumentation process and one step involved the collaborative writing of the thinking-story.

In step 1, each group was asked to discuss initial arguments and list initial ideas for the support of their assigned aspect of the dilemma.

In step 2, the position of the group was reconstructed based on arguments offered by the other group.

In step 3, both groups attended a lecture on critical thinking and were asked to improve their arguments and synthesize their final position as a group.

In step 4, participants were asked to collaborate in writing a thinking-story using the key arguments of their group.

Each of the argumentation steps lasted a week whereas the final step (step 4) of collaborative writing of the thinking-story lasted two weeks. The discussion that occurred during each step within each group in forum-mode (within-group interaction) and the position of each group in wiki-mode was not visible to the opponent group until the end of each step. At the end of each step, the positions of the two groups were revealed in order to allow for across group interactions.

Data sources. Data sources included the group's discourse from the forum mode and the group texts from the wiki-mode during the four steps (3 steps of argumentation and 1 step of collaborative writing of the thinking-story). We also videotaped a 2-hour reflection session of the argumentation process that took place in a class meeting face-to-face. The reflective session was organized by the instructor of the course in collaboration with the mentor / researcher in the field of philosophy. Students had access to the discussions from the forum-mode and positions written in the wiki-forum and used the think-aloud technique to reflect on the within group (and across group interactions) while engaging in the argumentation process. Finally, participants were asked to provide written feedback about their experience using WikiSplit and explain how the technology assisted the development of complex thinking (critical thinking, creative thinking and caring thinking).

4   Data Analysis and Results

In this section, we present the evolution of complex thinking of one group of teachers by studying their interactions, in depth. We chose to focus on the group that had to support the position against the euthanasia phenomenon. This decision was made based on the fact that most of the literature that was available to students supports this position. Therefore, we were interested to study how the arguments of the group would evolve throughout the three steps of the argumentation process.

Coding the discourse. The analysis focused on coding occurrences of the evolution of the quality of arguments within the group's discourse. Table 1 presents the first coding scheme that was used in the study. While studying group's discourse, the arguments used were assigned a code based on their nature. Ethical arguments that are used to support why the phenomenon of euthanasia is unacceptable were coded as arguments "1, 1.0.1, 1.0.1.1 and 1.1". Arguments that relate with medical science ethics and the legal and political aspects of the euthanasia phenomenon were coded as "2, 2.0.1, 2.1, 2.1.1, 2.2". Finally, the theological argument supporting the value of life as a gift provided by God was coded as argument "3". As we observe from the numbers in Table 1, group members focused on the main categories of each type of argument (1, 2, 3) during the argumentation process (step 1-3). We also observe that in step 2 there was a lot of discussion regarding the theological argument. This was the main argument that was used by the group. Another interesting observation is that during the collaborative writing of the thinking-story (step 4), the group focused on fewer arguments: the ethical and the theological argument supporting the value of life even at the presence of pain. A reason to explain this finding is that the participants, being in-service teachers, chose to focus on arguments that would be easier to discuss with children when addressing the euthanasia phenomenon.

Table 1. Number of Messages for Each Type of Argument During the Steps of Philosophical Inquiry

Argument Code	Type of Argument	Debate: Step1 (forum-mode)	Debate: Step2 (forum-mode)	Debate: Step3 (forum-mode)	Thinking-Story Step 4 (forum-mode)
1	Ethical argument: the value of life	1	8	17	3
1.0.1	Ethics of pain		2	2	4
1.0.1.1	Ethics of pain using examples			1	
1.1	Human weakness- disability of arguing for the value of life due to illness	4	13	5	5
2	Selfishness vs ethics of medical science vs science ethics	2	11	14	
2.0.1	Patient's life beyond medicine: possibility of improving patience's health			2	1
2.1	Law prohibiting euthanasia to doctors	2	5	8	
2.1.1	Selfish financial incentives of doctors			5	
2.2	Legal and political dimension of euthanasia			3	
3	Theological argument: the value of life	5	15	7	3

Analysis of chronological visuals. To understand more about the process of collaboration we examined visual representations of the group's coded discourse in chronological order by generating an Excel scatter-plot– see Figure 2. The time of the contribution runs at the top of the diagram for the duration of the activity (5 weeks) and each time-point on the visual represents a collaborator and his/her contribution in the thinking process. The visual presents the four steps of the activity (Step1-3 of the argumentation process and the step of collaborative writing of the thinking-story), as well as the concurrent use of the wiki and forum modes of WikiSplit. These visuals were inspired by the CORDTRA visualization technique [6]. The visual of Figure 2 was first inspected for general patterns of arguments of philosophical inquiry, across steps 1-3 and the groups' thinking-story. Then, the collaboration process was examined in more depth by going back and forth between each visual and the group's discourse. That is, we needed to zoom into the group's discourse and wiki activity, while using the CORDTRA as a pointer to interesting patterns. This in depth analysis revealed that the design and scaffolding of the activity (in four steps), as well as the affordances of WikiSplit for collaboration (i.e. hiding the within-group interactions at each step), facilitated the discussion during the debate and the process of the collaborative writing of the thinking-story. In particular, the discussed arguments around the philosophical dilemma (forum-mode) were summarized in wiki-mode and were then well integrated into the thinking-story 'resulting in a creative product that was a group effort and outcome of all participants' input and negotiation. This provides evidence that creative thinking was cultivated through reasoning ability.

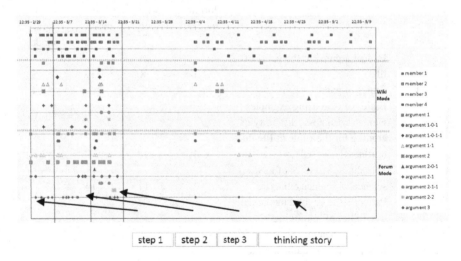

Fig. 2. Chronological Visual of Discourse Activity- Arguments

Critical thinking in collaborative argumentation. After identifying the nature of the arguments used during the collaborative interaction of the group members, we aimed to understand the development of critical thinking during collaborative argumentation. As shown in Table 2, we focused on studying six critical thinking skills: interpretation, analysis, evaluation, inference, explanation and self-regulation.

Table 2. Critical Thinking Skills Coding Scheme [5]

Critical Thinking Skill	Description
Interpretation • categorization • decoding significance • clarifying meaning	To comprehend and express the meaning or significance of a wide variety of experiences, situations, data, events, judgments, conventions, beliefs, rules procedures, or criteria. The three sub-skills of interpretation are categorization, decoding significance, and clarifying meaning.
Analysis • examining ideas • detecting arguments • analysing arguments	To identify the intended and actual inferential relationships among statements, questions, concepts, descriptions, or other forms of representation intended to express belief, judgment, experiences, reasons, information, or opinions. The three sub-skills of analysis are examining ideas, detecting arguments, and analyzing arguments.
Evaluation	To assess the credibility of statements or other representations which are accounts or descriptions of a persons, perception, experience, situation, judgment, belief, or opinion; and to assess the logical strength of the actual or intended inferential relationships among statements, descriptions, questions or other forms of representation.
Inference • querying evidence • conjecturing alternatives • drawing conclusions	To identify and secure elements needed to draw reasonable conclusions; to form conjectures and hypotheses; to consider relevant information and to deduce the consequences flowing from data, statements, principles, evidence, judgments, beliefs, opinions, concepts, descriptions, questions, or other forms of representation. The three sub-skills of inference are querying evidence, conjecturing alternatives, and drawing conclusions.
Explanation • stating results • justifying procedures • presenting arguments	To state the results of one's reasoning; to justify that reasoning in terms of the evidential, conceptual, methodological, criteriological, and contextual considerations upon which one's results were based; and to present one's reasoning in the form of cogent arguments. The sub-skills under explanation are stating results, justifying procedures, and presenting arguments.
Self-Regulation • self-examination • self-correction	To self-consciously monitor one's cognitive activities, the elements used in those activities, and the results deduced, particularly by applying skills in analysis and evaluation to one's own inferential judgments with a view toward questioning, confirming, validating, or correcting either one's reasoning or one's results. The two sub-skills of self-regulations are self-examination and self-correction.

Table 3 addresses the occurrences of critical thinking skills during the three steps of argumentation. Overall, Interpretation and Analysis are the most dominant skills applied during the discourse while Explanation and Self-Regulation are the less frequent skills. Therefore, there was not a progressive development of more sophisticated levels of critical thinking throughout the three steps of argumentation. However, the fact that "Interpretation" and "Analysis" are more frequent in step 2 compared to step 1, implies the development of caring thinking due to across group-interactions. Group members tried to comprehend, decode the significance, clarify the meaning and analyze the arguments of the opponent group. Within the framework of P4C, we can assume that the group members cared enough to make the effort to interpret and analyze what the opponent group was saying (arguments presented in the text appearing in wiki mode). Therefore, caring enough to develop the opponent group's thinking resulted in development of their own critical thinking.

Table 3. Critical thinking skills in group's discourse during debate

Critical Thinking Skill	Debate: Step1 (forum-mode)	Debate: Step2 (forum-mode)	Debate: Step3 (forum-mode)	Total
Interpretation	2	18	13	33
Analysis	6	21	21	48
Evaluation	3	6	7	10
Inference	2	3	5	16
Explanation	0	1	5	6
Self-Regulation	1	2	3	6

The role of the technology was important during the development of caring and critical thinking, since hiding the discourse of the opponent group during each step and revealing their position at the end of the step forced the group members to identify more arguments, and evolve their thinking regarding the phenomenon of euthanasia.

5   Discussion and Conclusions

A community of philosophical inquiry evolves as it matures. In our study, we noticed that through praxis, in-service teachers were empowered to engage in reasoning, demonstrating a better understanding not only of their thoughts regarding the phenomenon of euthanasia but the thoughts of the other members in their group as well as the broader community of inquiry that was created within WikiSplit. Reasoning is hardly touched upon in school education. Therefore, most teachers are not trained to be aware of patterns of reasoning, and often have difficulty in determining whose patterns are valid or fallacious. We suggest that if teachers learn how to reason and monitor how their own thinking evolves within a community of inquiry, they will be able to guide their students to develop complex thinking when P4C is applied in a school setting. We also provided teachers the opportunity to engage in the process of writing a thinking-story instead of applying a ready-made story or manual.

Our research used a variety of methods to explore the development of complex thinking (consideration of participation, interaction visualization). The results of the data analysis show that there are interesting observations pertaining to the collaborative processes that occur and technology can be used to monitor the evolution of the thinking process. Web 2.0 technologies can mediate the development of complex thinking as defined in the P4C program. We are aware that our results are tentative and require replication. Although firm conclusions cannot be drawn solely based on a case study, the currently presented work can indicate future research paths in terms of how to best integrate tools and structure to promote the development of complex thinking within a community of inquiry framework.

References

1. Daniel, M.F., Auriac, E.: Philosophy, Critical Thinking and Philosophy for Children. Educational Philosophy and Theory 43(5), 415–435 (2011)
2. Fisher: Stories for thinking. Nash Pollock, Oxford (1996)
3. Fisher: Dialogic teaching: developing thinking and metacognition through philosophical discussion. Early Child Development and Care 177(6&7), 615–631 (2007)
4. Hawkins, J., Pea, R.D.: Tools for bridging the cultures of everyday and scientific thinking. Journal for Research in Science Teaching 24, 291–307 (1987)
5. Facione, P.A.: Critical Thinking: What it Is and Why it Counts, pp. 1–22. California Academic Press, Millbrae (2006)
6. Haynes, J.: Children as Philosophers: Learning through Enquiry and dialogue in the primary classroom. Routledge (2008)
7. Hmelo-Silver, C.E., Liu, L., Jordan, R.: Visual representation of a multidimensional coding scheme for understanding technology-mediated learning about complex natural systems. Research and Practice in Technology-Enhanced Learning Environments 4, 253–280 (2009)
8. Ioannou, A., Stylianou-Georgiou, A.: Mashing-up wikis and forums: A case study of collaborative problem-based activity. Educational Media International 49(4), 303–316 (2012)
9. Lipman, M.: Philosophy goes to school. Temple University Press, Philadelphia (1988)
10. Lipman, M.: Thinking in Education. University Press, Cambridge (2003)
11. Lipman, M., Sharp, A.M., Oscanyan, F.S.: Philosophy in the classroom. Temple University Press, Philadelphia (1980)
12. Trickey, S., Topping, K.J.: 'Philosophy for children': a systematic review. Research papers in Education 19(3), 365–380 (2004)
13. Tzavaras, J.: A Manual of Philosophy: Teaching philosophy using the dialogical method and the searching inquiry. Dardanos Press, Athens (2006) (in Greek)

Developing an Effective ESP Curriculum Integrating CALL

Rumi Tobita

Ashikaga Institute of Technology, Life Systemics, Tochigi, Japan
rtobita@ashitech.ac.jp

Abstract. This study introduces a compilation of the eight-year trial at a Japanese technical college involving an effective CALL training program for EFL learners to meet ESP curriculum goals: to develop global engineers who can work in the real-world environment and exchange ideas globally. According to the survey based on needs research, e-Learning software such as voice recognition software had been introduced and its effective usage discussed. As e-Learning materials were deemed a passive learning method, a Text to Speech (TTS) system was introduced to resolve this issue. Training using TTS systems was conducted in various settings, including metacognitive strategies and autonomous learning, such that students could more actively engage in the training. As one element of the subsequent development of an effective ESP curriculum, an original overseas training program and near-infrared spectroscopy (NIRS) were also introduced and applied to evaluate the effectiveness of e-Learning systems.

Keywords: CALL, curriculum development, e-Learning system, voice recognition, TTS, overseas training program, NIRS.

1 Introduction

Concerning the globalization and internationalization of our society, development of English communication skills was crucial for EFL teaching in Japan. However, Japanese engineering students' English skills were declining and far from achieving English debating or presentation levels. Therefore, designing and developing effective courses and curricula to meet ELF goals for acquiring communication skill has been a critical need.

In the field of educational technology, Attitude-Treatment Interaction (ATI) is an important element in planning to develop an effective curriculum. [1] As ATI's concept and theoretical framework suggest that instructional strategies' effectiveness for individuals depends upon their specific abilities and optimal learning is achieved when the curriculum matches the learner's aptitude, the most suitable training had to be applied to the less motivated EFL learners. [2-3]

In addition, English for Specific Purposes (ESP), which is designed to meet specific learner needs, is another essential element of an effective curriculum. [4-5] According to ATI and ESP development methods, the present study conducted needs

P. Zaphiris and A. Ioannou (Eds.): LCT 2014, Part II, LNCS 8524, pp. 328–338, 2014.

analysis-based research to identify the area of training upon which the curriculum concentrated. The survey revealed that in a situation where one observed declining English skills and lack of student motivation, the integration of CALL training in EFL programs had gained much attention. [6-7] Moreover, the importance of interactivity within an e-Learning community of instructors and learners had been emphasized to increase learners' motivation. To follow this trend, e-Learning software such as voice recognition has been integrated into EFL classes since 2006.

2   Comprehensive Overview of Integrating CALL

Concerning integration of CALL into ESP curriculum performed in the past years, the process could be summarized into several stages based on the TTS systems and methods applied toward different categories of EFL learners. Below Table 1 describes the comprehensive overview of each CALL training program integrated into the curriculum based on each phase of study which details are explained later.

Table 1. Transition of curriculums during each phase of application of CALL

(a) Curriculum during Phase 1

	Required Course	Class Division	Content	CALL
Freshman	English 1	Based on the degree of academic achievement	Composition	Communication 911* Database 3000*
Sophomore	English 2	Mixed level	Reading	SpeaK!* & metacognitive strategies (* = trial program)

(b) Curriculum during Phase 2 & 3

	Required Course	Class Division	Content	CALL
Freshman	Freshman English	Based on the degree of academic achievement	Reading & e-Learning	Speak! & autonomous learning approach & original oversea training program** (** = elective program)
Sophomore	Sophomore English	Based on the degree of academic achievement	Reading & e-Learning	

(c) Curriculum during Phase 4 & 5 (Note: Phase 5 was applied to selective classes only)

	Required Course	Class Division	Content	CALL
Freshman	English 1 & 2	Based on the degree of academic achievement	Reading & e-Learning	Speak! & autonomous learning approach & original oversea training program** & online lesson** (** = elective program)
Sophomore	English 3 & 4	Based on the degree of academic achievement	Reading & e-Learning	
Junior	Comprehensive English 1 & 2	Mixed level	Technical English	
Senior	Comprehensive English 3 & 4	Mixed level	TOIEC	

3   Phase 1: Pilot Study of Integrating CALL

Before CALL could be officially integrated into the curriculum, the e-Learning material and its effectiveness had to be evaluated to determine whether it would be useful for both EFL learners and teachers. Further, as the effectiveness of the curriculum using e-Learning materials should be consistent with ATI and ESP, three types of e-Learning software were used in the trial for observing and evaluating the effects of the software.

The initial software, "English Communication 911[Obunsha (2004)]," was introduced in 2004 and was used in a pilot program intended to improve students' communication skills through digital methods. The computer gave students several phrases to practice, and by evaluating students' pronunciations and providing feedback, it enabled students to develop listening and speaking skills. [8]

The second trial software, "Database 3000 [Kiriharashoten (2004)]," was installed in 2005 and allowed more upper level students to access the software simultaneously. It also provided an environment wherein students could learn English at their own preferred time and location in the school. [9-10]

The third trial software, "SpeaK! [Lighthouse (2005)]," was the initial voice recognition software using a Text to Speech (TTS) system. EFL learners read the text aloud, listened to their pronunciation, and responded to the TTS system's individualized feedback immediately, and the system enabled them to monitor their training progress [Fig. 1 & 2].

Fig. 1. Sample of SpeaK! - Text insertion

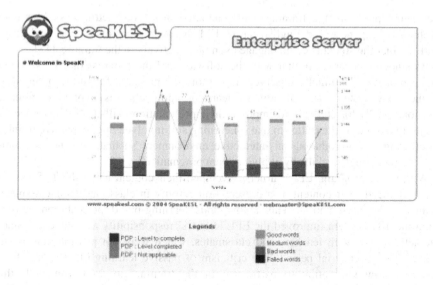

Fig. 2. Sample of SpeaK! - Progress monitoring

During this trial, to solve the concern that e-Learning systems make EFL learners passive, metacognitive strategies such as self-monitoring were applied. By this method, students observed themselves objectively and recognized their weaknesses so that they could concentrate on areas that needed improvement. Further, as students' learning was video recorded and fed back as part of their evaluation, they could visually understand the areas that need to be concentrated to improve their skills. [11]

Although each trial software produced certain benefits and progress in English skill development, the TTS system using "SpeaK!" produced better learning outcomes; therefore, it was selected for integration into the CALL training program in future ESP curricula.

4   Phase 2: Developing a CALL-Based Curriculum

Although it could be observed that increasing of skills from the tests of the three e-Learning software programs during the two year trail period, such as progress in EFL learners' skills and improvement in the EFL curriculum along with the effect of metacognitive strategies, criticism remained that training using e-Learning materials provided a very passive type of learning. Therefore, to overcome this issue, enhance the curriculum's effectiveness, and achieve higher goals by using the TTS system, "SpeaK!" was fully integrated into the curriculum with additional improvements. [12]

Because the TTS system enabled EFL learners to create their own content and simply insert any text of their choice and the students could self-select their English lesson contents and modify them to meet their interests, they exhibited active participation and involvement in the training. Further, to gain greater effects from the e-Learning program, the training was conducted in various settings, such as team teaching by Japanese and English native EFL teachers, peer evaluation, and group work, so that the students could engage even more actively in the training. [13]

As students became familiar with the software and the progress of TTS system's application was continually observed, to explore the potential for further integration of the TTS system, an autonomous learning approach was applied combining additional tasks for students to improve their presentation skills.[14] This objective sought to overcome the criticism that e-Learning still involved largely passive training by creating and introducing an interactive environment so that the students could improve their English skills by applying them pragmatically.

Within this program, EFL learners developed their content using the TTS system and introduced their content as a presentation activity in class, and their classmates evaluated the presentation. This autonomous learning-based presentation activity using the TTS system improved the EFL learners' responsibility and students gained interactive skills with teachers and classmates, which were not possible during the initial TTS system trial period. The criticism of passive learning often results from observing low motivation to participate in the training program. But with this presentation method, students could interact with the audience in their own field of interest and maintain a higher level of motivation throughout the curriculum. [15][Fig. 3 & 4]

Fig. 3. Curriculum scene using SpeaK! training

Fig. 4. Integrating SpeaK! along with presentation scene

5   Phase 3: Subsequent Development

In 2008, as a part of the subsequent development of an effective ESP curriculum, an original overseas training program was developed and adopted to train engineering students to improve specific English skills in their fields of interest, giving them the opportunity to think about their future work options in the global market and become global engineers.[16] Though many colleges had their own overseas program, most of which were limited to language training and even outsourced to third party training companies, the focus was on not only improving students' language skills but also engineering students to create their individual vision and direction, which will motivate them to realize the need to study English and understand the international environment.

The program was conducted five times. It included training sessions on topics such as visiting overseas companies related to the students' engineering fields, discussion with Japanese engineers working in the global market, and participating in lectures given onsite. Through personal conversations with workers in the companies, the students could not only gain international knowledge but also realize the importance of learning English and developing English communication skills. As this overseas training program provided a real-world environment where students could practice their knowledge and skills, students could exercise their skills learned through the TTS system training and evaluate their achievement. Moreover, as motivation was, as always, an important element in students' persistence in the English training program, interaction with people abroad and developing familiarity with the real-world environment significantly affected their attitude toward involvement in the training.[Fig.5]

Fig. 5. Lecture by the engineer of Microsoft at Redmond Campus

6   Phase 4: Pilot Study of Integrating HCI-Based CALL

Although the overseas training program was developed for EFL learners to practice their English skills in the real world, it also served as a means to evaluate the results of the e-Learning program. As the students had to interact with people other than teachers and colleagues for the first time, it was also important to evaluate the program's effectiveness to identify areas for future development of the curriculum and usage of a TTS system and e-Learning materials.

The development of ESP curricula using a TTS system had been recognized in previous training programs, but the overseas training program provided a certain impact and reflection point regarding the integration of CALL. Moreover, to increase the students' English skills, additional training for use in the real world, Human–Computer Interaction (HCI) became an important element for focus and analysis; therefore, we added improvement of communication skills in a live environment as an objective in developing a curriculum using a TTS system for training. [17]

To address the HCI concerns and improve EFL learners' communication skills, a special trial course was designed by combining the TTS system with an online English lessons called "ONE'S WORD ONLINE" [ONE'S WORD, INC. (2010)] which was a training system having a live oversea instructor over Skype. The instructors were chosen in the Philippines to minimize the impact of the time lag between the instructors and learners in Japan. Using this system, students could communicate with instructors and improve their interaction and correspondence skills. In addition, TTS systems involving movies were introduced to facilitate students' development of an active learning attitude in the overseas training program.

This combination using the TTS system, online English lessons and movies enabled students planning to participate in study abroad programs to create their own digital content to improve their knowledge in their field while becoming more actively involved in the training and discussing it with overseas instructors. Often, movies depict the natural circumstances of everyday life; therefore, students developed the TTS content by using their favorite movie scripts to build their communication skills.[18][Fig. 6]

Fig. 6. Training scene using online English lesson "ONE'S WORD ONLINE"

From this training, it could be said that, HCI is a key factor in developing and integrating CALL into an e-Learning curriculum. With this analysis and subsequent improvement of the curriculum, students could actively participate in gaining knowledge in their field of interest while improving their communication skills with a live instructor, thus effectively preparing to use their skills in the real-world environment when visiting overseas. The improved curriculum increased student motivation and attention in the e-Learning program; as a result, students who participated in the overseas training program scored significantly higher scores on their TOEIC Test. [Table 2]

Table 2. Result of t-test

	N : Participants of overseas training program	Mean	SD	t-test (two-tailed)
Pre Test	10	67.8	17.55	
Post Test	10	77.4	12.87	4.995**

**(p = 0.001)

7 Phase 5: Applying NIRS to Course Design

Although the effectiveness of various teaching methods and materials has improved, an assessment based on traditional paper and pencil tests has revealed its limitations. Recently brain activity has become subject to monitoring by technologically innovative instruments. These technologies provide data that reveals the results of teaching and learning; therefore, a few researchers have noted that these data can be utilized to assess the effectiveness of EFL teaching in Japan. With this newly developed technology, the present study examined the effectiveness of analysis using Near-Infrared Spectroscopy (NIRS) for EFL listening training from the perspective of brain science to propose a well-matched combination of listening materials and training methods for EFL learners. [19]

The present study used NIRS to analyze the amount of blood flow in the brain while learners were learning English. It then examined the relationship between brain activities and learning outcomes to identify the most effective combinations of learners' characteristics and English conversational skills teaching materials.

NIRS is widely recognized as a practical non-invasive optical technique to detect the hemoglobin density dynamics response during functional activation of the cerebral cortex. The primary application of NIRS to the human body uses the fact that the transmission and absorption of NIR light in human body tissues contains information about changes in hemoglobin concentration. When a specific area of the brain is activated, the localized blood volume in that area quickly changes.

The greater the amount of blood flow, the hemoglobin oxygenation increases; measuring the amount of blood can thus indicate the state of brain activation caused by differences among teaching materials. This experimental technique indicated the well-matched combination of listening materials and training for EFL learners. As these new technologies could improve the accuracy of the evaluation of CALL integration effectiveness, such technologies have further potential for improving e-Learning methods and curriculum development. [Fig. 7 & 8]

Fig. 7. Experimental using NIRS

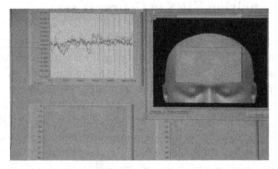

Fig. 8. Data of experimental evaluation

8   Conclusion

Through this study, various curricula integrating CALL have been developed and evaluated during the past eight years. Each curriculum achieved certain goals for EFL learners to gain knowledge and develop English communication skills to support their future in becoming global engineers who could actively participate in the real-world environment. However, though CALL is not criticized to the extent that it was in the past as a passive type of learning, recent developments in evaluation methods, such as NIRS, have revealed areas for improvement remain in achieving higher goals and better results for the students.

Concerning TTS systems for CALL, technology has improved, and many new functions have been added to make learning easier. Further, the digital environment has become much more accessible than before; EFL learners can communicate with people around the world using free software and many more e-Learning materials for English study are now available.

However, the availability of more options does not mean that CALL integration alone can achieve optimal effectiveness. From an educational technology standpoint, as consideration of ATI and ESP is critical in developing an effective curriculum, teachers' involvement cannot be overlooked.

Previous studies [12-15] have made it increasingly obvious that even though EFL learners could achieve certain goals from the TTS system itself, the results are insufficiently effective to gain practical English skills for application in a real-life environment. Therefore, it is suggested that teachers should test and evaluate the effectiveness of e-Learning material, add an interactive approach and methods, and provide a live environment with HCI elements so that the EFL learners gain not only knowledge but also practical experience in using English skills in a real-world environment. In addition, with recent scientific and technological evaluation approaches such as NIRS and digital evaluation provided in addition to traditional test results, these outputs could be used to develop even more effective curricula.

Even after combining these elements, areas of improvement in content and methods remain for achieving higher goals through active involvement with teachers. Such involvement is not an easy task for teachers as they will have to keep up with constantly evolving e-Learning technology and evaluation methods, and challenges always arise when developing new curricula. However, as past studies have revealed HCI to be an important element when integrating CALL, teachers should always consider the effectiveness of the interaction between students and e-Learning materials as well as the application of new technologies in order to organize and utilize the available resources to develop the most effective curricula for EFL learners.

References

1. Cronbach, L.J., Snow, R.E.: Aptitudes and Instructional Methods: A Handbook for Research in Interactions. John Wiley & Sons Inc., New Jersey (1977)
2. Tobita, R., Fukuda, Y.: An Experimental Study on the Combination of Treatments and Tasks in Listening Practice. Language Laboratory 36, 117–127 (1999)
3. Tobita, R.: An Experimental Study on the Use of Metacognitive Learning Strategies of Reading Comprehension in English Learning. Bulletin of Saitama Women's Junior College 13, 207–234 (2002)
4. Dudley-Evans, T., John St., M.: Developments in ESP: A multi-disciplinary approach. Cambridge University Press, Cambridge (1998)
5. Douglas, D.: Assessing languages for specific purposes. Cambridge University Press, Cambridge (2000)
6. Tobita, R., Kuniyoshi, H.: The Needs Analysis of English Learners in a Technological College. Ashikaga Institute of Technology Collaborative Research Center Annual Review 7, 160–174 (2006)
7. Tobita, R., Miyazaki, M., Ochiai, M.: Curriculum Development based on Needs Analysis of English Education–Comparison between Technical and Co-medical Universities-. Ashikaga Institute of Technology Collaborative Research Center Annual Review 8, 161–178 (2007)
8. Tobita, R., Miyazaki, M.: Oral Practices Using Voice-Recognition Software and Video. Paper Presented at TESOL (Teachers of English to Speakers of Other Languages) 38th Annual Convention and Exhibit, Long Beach, California, U.S.A (2004)
9. Tobita, R.: Effective Course Design When Applying New Technology. Paper Presented at TESOL (Teachers of English to Speakers of Other Languages) 39th Annual Convention and Exhibit, San Antonio, Texas, U.S.A. (2005)

10. Tobita, R., Sato, T., Kuniyoshi, H.: Utterance improvement among communication skills with voice-recognition program. Paper Presented at FLEAT 5 (Foreign Language and Technology) 5th Convention, Provo, Utah, U.S.A. (2005)
11. Tobita, R., Miyazaki, M., Kuniyoshi, H.: Utterance improvement communication skills using voice-recognition software. Paper Presented at the 3rd International Conference of Multimedia Language Education of APAMALL, Asia-Pacific Association of Multimedia-Assisted Language Learning, Tainan, Taiwan (2005)
12. Tobita, R., Nakayama, A.: Utterance improvement using voice-recognition software. Paper Presented at 18th International Symposium on Theoretical and Applied Linguistics in Thessaloniki, Greece (2007)
13. Tobita, R., Nakayama, A.: Effective way of using voice-recognition software to improve communication skills. Paper Presented at AILA 2008 (15th World Congress of Applied Linguistics) in University of Duisburg, Essen, Germany (2008)
14. Tobita, R., Matsuoka, Y.: A Study Regarding the Effective Use of E-Learning System in Technical College. Ashikaga Institute of Technology Collaborative Research Center Annual Review 9, 177–187 (2008)
15. Tobita, R., Matsuoka, Y.: Study of Developing E-Learning Materials for Engineering Students. Ashikaga Institute of Technology Collaborative Research Center Annual Review 10, 129–135 (2009)
16. Tobita, R.: Development of Overseas Training Program for Global Engineers. Bulletin of Ashikaga Institute of Technology 44, 97–111 (2010)
17. Tobita, R.: Effective Course Design Using e-Learning System and Online English Lessons. Paper Presented at CALICO (The Computer Assisted Language Instruction Consortium) 2011, University of Victoria, B.C., Canada (2011)
18. Tobita, R.: Development of effective course design using voice recognition and online lessons. Paper Presented at World CALL 2013, Glasgow, Scotland (2013)
19. Perani, D., Abutalebi, J.: The neural basis of first and second language processing. Current Opinion in Neurobiology 15(2), 202–206 (2005)

HCI Requirements for Young Primary School CALL Learners

Monica Ward

School of Computing, Dublin City University, Ireland
Monica.Ward@computing.dcu.ie

Abstract. This paper looks at the HCI requirements of young learners in the context of Computer Assisted Language Learning (CALL) resources. It explains the motivation behind the project and the specific deployment context. It outlines some key components that must be taken into account when developing materials for this learner group. For example, the learners cannot read, so no text can be used on the screen. Colors and images are very important to make the material attractive and intuitive for the users. It shows that using HCI observations from other researchers, along with a structured approach, combined with an agile paradigm can produce useful, usable CALL resources in a limited resource context.

Keywords: young learners, HCI, CALL, primary school, agile paradigm.

1 Introduction

This paper looks at the Computer Assisted Language Learning (CALL) HCI requirements for young primary school learners. It outlines the deployment context of the CALL resources and the particular HCI considerations that have to be taken into account when developing resources for young learners. Young learners differ from adult learners in several respects and psychology, art, design, physiology and ergonomics must be taken into account when considering their HCI requirements.

From a psychological point of view it is important to understand the learners and their requirements, in order to design suitable CALL resources for them. Designing and developing CALL resources for any user group must include analysis, design, development, testing, and implementation stages [1]. The analysis phase for this project was carried out in conjunction by the class teacher and it was determined that there was a learner need and that it was feasible to build CALL resources for the learners. In this scenario, the pedagogical design was driven by the teacher, who wanted CALL resources that were aligned with her classroom teaching. The lack of integration of CALL resources with classroom activities is one of the reasons why CALL resources are not as successful as they should be in the primary school context [2].

Obviously, the User Interface (UI) has to take into account the preferred aesthetics of the target users (which may differ from adult learners). For example, colors, font size, buttons, text (or no text) are some areas of difference with adult learners. An

P. Zaphiris and A. Ioannou (Eds.): LCT 2014, Part II, LNCS 8524, pp. 339–348, 2014.

agile software development paradigm was used in the development of the CALL resources for a number of reasons. An agile paradigm is useful when dealing with an unfamiliar context, so it was useful in this project. Young learners have a different physiology than adult learners and this too must be taken into consideration when design CALL resources for them. Also, ergonomics are just as important for young learners as they are for adult learners, although sometimes there is limited scope to change the ergonomics of the deployment context. Testing is a key part of any software development and it was important to carry out both formative and summative testing as part of the project. The implementation phase of the project involved first training the learners with the resources and then letting them use them at their own pace.

This paper provides an overview of the project from a HCI perspective, and outlines what worked in this context and provides some suggestions for future projects in this domain.

2   Background

2.1   Motivation and Deployment Context

In Ireland, most children start primary school at 4 or 5 years of age. The first year of primary school is called Junior Infants. Children study a range of subjects, including English, which is one of the national languages, along with Irish. In Junior Infants the children learn the alphabet in synthetic phonetic form. The aim of this project was to develop English spelling resources that would allow the students to practise what they learnt in class, at their own pace and to repeat exercises as often as they wanted. The CALL resources would also enable the teacher to monitor the progress of each student. Currently, it is difficult for the teacher to monitor each student individually in real-time. Sometimes it can be difficult for her to see how quickly and effectively each individual student is mastering the material. One of the aims of the CALL resources was to provide a tool for the teacher to see what each student was able to do and what presented difficulties. The teacher would be able to see at a glance, in real-time, what each student was doing, as well as the class overall.

In 2010, the government introduced a free pre-school year for children. This means that most children have attended an authorised pre-school before starting primary school and they can recognise letters and sounds to some extent on entry into primary school. This aims to ease the transition from pre-school to primary school for the children. In Ireland, schools in or close to cities, the schools may be single sex schools, but outside of these areas, the schools are mixed. The school in this study is a boys' school and there were 24 boys in the class. In order to comply with Ethics guidelines, the boys' parents were asked to sign a consent form. Not all parents signed the form, perhaps due to loosing it rather than any objections so data usage statistics were recorded for 17 boys. However, all boys got a chance to use the system.

The school has a computer room with 19 PCs, of which only 16 worked. The PCs were rather old, and had older monitors that took up a lot of space. The keyboard just about managed to fit on the table and space was very limited. The students had one 30 minute session in the computer lab per week. The students were reasonably competent computer users (e.g. they were familiar with the keyboard and mouse, and know how to click on icons). Young primary school CALL learners are only beginning to learn to read and write in their first language (L1). Therefore, when developing CALL resources for this target learner group, there can be no written instructions and this presents special. Furthermore, the look and feel of the CALL resources has to be clear and appealing to the students, as well as being pedagogically appropriate.

This paper looks at the HCI requirements of Junior Infant students (i.e. 4-5 year old pupils at the Preoperational stage of development [3] in a primary school in Ireland. Often the students had to share a PC with another student, and while this has HCI implications also, the focus of this paper in on the design of the CALL resources in particular (see [4] for HCI with children). This school would be fairly typical in Ireland in terms of computing resources, teacher computer literacy, class size and student ability.

2.2   CALL Resource Overview

The teacher wanted CALL resources that would enable the students to reinforce their prior learning and allow them to test themselves with regards to spelling words. There were four exercise types developed for this purpose. The easiest exercise for the students was the matching exercise, in which the student was shown three different images and had to match the correct word with the correct image. The next easiest exercise was the mixed-up word exercise, in which the students where shown the letters of the word jumbled up and had to spell the word correctly. The final two exercises were cloze exercises, in which the students had to spell the word. In the first of the cloze exercises (single cloze), the students just had to spell one word, while in the other cloze exercise (the multi-cloze exercise) they had to spell three words. Students worked on a different set of words each week, and this set was closely aligned with what they had studied the previous week in class. For example, "pin, sit, pat, tap" was one group of words that was used at the start of the project.

Students could check their progress through the exercises by clicking on a progress button and it would show them how many gold star they had and how many more they needed to get to complete all the exercises. There were several analysis features available to the teacher. The most important one was the real-time student progress monitor. This showed who was logged in, what exercises they had attempted and how successful they were at those exercises. This enabled the teacher to check that the lesson was proceeding more or less as planned.

3   Planning, Analysis and Design

Planning and design are key phases in the genesis of any software project [5], including CALL resources. Planning determines if the project will go ahead, if the project is feasible and defines the scope of the project. Analysis works out what the project requirements are and what the will be the scope of the project. [1] has designed a very use grid (Global-Local-Differential-Targeted) that takes into account the main 'players' in the learning process (learners, teachers, pedagogy, technology, content and other actors (e.g. society)).

HCI design must take into account including what the users want and expect and what users find enjoyable and attractive [2]. A user-centred approach [7] was adopted in which the teacher was consulted regularly during the planning, design and development stages of the project – this is especially important when the CALL developer may be unfamiliar with the needs and abilities of the target learner group. The key is to keep it simple and avoid functionality creep [8]. Learners had mainly a user role in the design process [9], but as an agile software development paradigm [10] was used throughout the project they also had a testing role.

4   HCI Design

The young learners in this project were only starting to learn the letters of the alphabet and could not yet read (apart from a few very simple words). The need to avoid written instructions of any kind, including names on buttons, might seem trivial, but it is quite challenging. It means that images, colors and UI design must be intuitive and clear. The learners have to be able to navigate their way through the resources, with minimal teacher interaction. The images used in the resources need to be clear and non-confusing. Sometimes, it can be difficult to find suitable images, especially ones that work with older monitors and are age-appropriate. This section provides an overview of the considerations given to colors, images and other HCI features in the project.

4.1   Colors

Colors and coloring are very important when designing computer resources for children, especially when no written instructions are used. Children have positive reactions to bright colors [11]. For this reason bright colors were used for each different exercise type. Light purple was used for the mixed-up word exercise, yellow was used for the matching exercise, light green was used for the single word cloze exercise and cyan was used for the 3-word cloze exercise. It was important that the colors were bright, attractive and sufficiently different in order for the children to be able to distinguish between them. The school involved in this project is an all-boys school and this had to be taken into account when considering suitable colours for the different components of the CALL resources. For example, the boys associate pink with being a girls' color and would not be favourably disposed to seeing it on any of the exercises.

4.2   Images

Images were central for the CALL resources. One of the most important concepts of the CALL resources was that the children could use the resources on their own, without the teacher working with them. This would allow them to work through the exercises at their own pace. This is very important in the Junior Infant class, as indeed other primary school classes, as there will be quite a range of abilities within the student group, and it can be difficult for the teacher to make sure that all students are working to their ability. As no written words could be used, in order to be able to spell a word, the students needed to see an image of the word. This meant that only words that could have an easily identifiable image were chosen for the exercises (generally nouns, but sometimes verbs and adjectives). The images had to be child-appropriate. For this reason, cartoon images were generally used, as not only did they appeal to the students, but they tended to have brighter colors and appeared clearer on the screen.

Not only were images needed to depict the exercise words, images were also required for the buttons of the application. Images were needed for standard button types such as 'home', 'go back', 'next' and 'correct'. Furthermore, images were also needed to indicate 'correct' or 'incorrect' to the students, and colourful cartoon faces were used for this purpose (yellow, smiling face for correct, blue, unhappy face for incorrect).

4.3   Other HCI Issues

Design consistency is very important ([6], [12], [13]). In this scenario, it was especially important as there were no written instructions and it would not be possible for the teacher to spend time with each student individually in the lab to explain how each exercise worked. Each different exercise had to have the same look and feel as the others. The same buttons had to be in the same place and have the same functionality. This contributes to easy of learning, remembering and use.

Other design issues included avoid drag-and-drop interaction, as this can often be problematic for young children [14]. In the mixed-up exercise, there were two possible options for allowing the students to rearrange the jumbled up letters. One was to allow them to select a letter and drag it to the spelling line. The other option was to allow them to click on the letter and the system would automatically place it in the spelling line for them. Both options were testing with young learners and the drag and drop option proved problematic (as more manual/mouse dexterity is required for this movement). The learners can check if their answer is correct by clicking on the check button and they see a happy face if the answer is correct and an unhappy face if it is incorrect. However, sometimes the students would forget what they had done or would want to see how they were progressing and allowing learners to view their progress [15]. Fig. 1 shows an example of a cloze exercise (for the word pin).

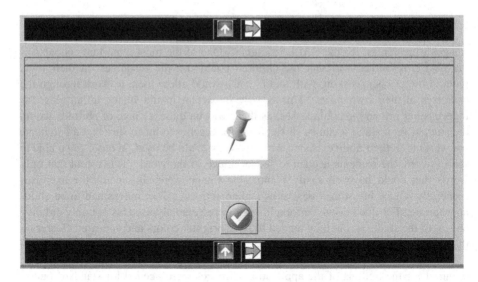

Fig. 1. Example of mixed up exercise (pin)

5   Development and Testing

5.1   Development

One important consideration in this project was the desire to have a relatively short turn-around time for the actual development of the CALL resources. There had been some discussion with the class teacher for several years about the possibility of developing suitable resources, but for a variety of reasons there was no progress beyond the discussion stage. From the start of this project, there was a determination that working CALL resources would be developed and deployed during the primary school year. This meant that existing resources would be reused to speed up the actual development process. In this regard, Hot Potatoes CALL authoring software was reversed engineered to provide a template for the generation of English spelling exercises. This facilitated the speedy and flexible generation of language exercises on a week-by-week basis. Also, in order to make sure that the students were able to use working parts of the software, even if the full suite of resources was not complete, an agile software development paradigm was adopted. The agile software development paradigm focuses on iterative and incremental development. In the case of this project, it meant that the students could use the basic version of the software and avail of new features as they became available (typically on a weekly basis). The CALL developer, the teacher and the students were learning throughout the project and modifications could be made very quickly if an error was detected or a potential enhancement identified.

For example, it became apparent that some of the images were not as clear as they should have been. Some mechanism was required to make it obvious to the learner what the word was. It was decided to add an audio component to the system, so that the students could hear the word being spoken, as well seeing a suitable image. Due to the agile approach, it was not that difficult to add this feature and have it ready for the following week.

5.2   Testing

While testing with the target learner group is important in the design and development of any CALL resource [11], it is particularly important when working with a learner group that is very distinct from a more familiar learner group [4]. Testing can reveal that the 'obvious' may not be that obvious to the target learners. Also, target learners can point out things that may be missed by the designer. It is really important to check out the suitability and feasibility of CALL resources with someone from the target learner group before real-world deployment, especially when a non-successful initial encounter with the CALL resources may inhibit future use of the resources. [16] and [17] provide guidelines and insights for testing with young learners which were useful during this phase.

As part of the testing process of this project, several young learners took part in the testing of the CALL resources. They were given minimal guidance in how to use the materials and were asked to use the system. Their interaction with the system was observed and important points were noted. They tried both the drag-and-drop and click versions in the mixed-up exercises, and, as expected (see [14], there were some difficulties with the drag-and-drop interaction. Therefore, as mentioned previously, the click option was adopted in the final version of the system. The young learners also helped out in choosing the images for some words. Several different images were shown to the learners and they picked the 'best' or their favourite one. The learners tested all parts of the system to make sure it was usable and worked as expected.

The other target user, i.e. the teacher, also had a chance to test the system. She tested the learners' part of the system as well as the teacher component. The teacher testing component was less extensive, due to the limited functionality of that part of the system, and the fact hat the teacher was a competent adult that could test the system fairly quickly.

6   Training and Implementation

6.1   Training

Providing training to the learners is a key component of successful CALL deployment [18]. If suitable training is not provided, the learners may not know how to use the system or may not be able to exploit it to it is full potential. Training is often overlooked, but it is important. It does not have to be long or overly complicated, especially if the system is well-designed, but it is important to give it sufficient consideration when rolling-out a system. One extra consideration in this particular scenario is that there could be no written instructions or help information for the learners as they could not read. Normally, a user guide or help facility would be provided with CALL resources. This guide would give an overview of the material and instructions on how to use the system. However, as a written guide was not an option, it was really important that the learners were trained on the system. In fact, the importance of making the user interface intuitive for the learners was a key consideration at the design stage of the product.

Therefore, the CALL resources had to be easy to use, easy to learn and easy to remember. The learners were shown how to use the CALL resources and were able to use them without too many problems – colour coding the components helped greatly in this regard. During the training process, an Interactive White Board (IWB) was used to show the learners how to use the system. They were shown step-by-step each different exercise and then given a chance to try it out for themselves. The learners had no particular difficulties in using the CALL materials.

6.2   Implementation

The students had access to the computer lab once a week for 30 minutes. Sometimes the teacher used this lab session to work on maths resources or other educational games with the students. For the duration of the project, the students worked on the CALL resources during their allocated computer time. This meant that there was an onus on the CALL developer to produce useful and educationally valuable software for the students if they were going to use their scare computer time on the CALL resources. Due to the fact that there were 24 children in the class and only 16 working computers, the children often had to share a PC. This meant that one boy logged in and his partner worked with him on the exercises. This impacted negatively the monitoring feature of the CALL software as the scores and usage of the system may not have reflected the ability of the logged in user (as he may have been assisted by his partner).

7   Discussion

There were several lessons learnt from this real-world deployment of CALL resources for young primary school learners. It is possible to design and develop clear, colourful, easy to use CALL resources using a modified authoring tool for this target learning group. It is important to use a user-centred design approach that includes input from the teacher and someone from the target learner group itself. It can be difficult to find suitable, unambiguous, age-appropriate images and persistence may be required when seeking out images. One helpful addition is the use of sound, which can help disambiguate images and make it clear to the learner what the image contains. While learners in the target group may have similar characteristics, there should be room for variation and customisation, and this would be one recommendation for future CALL projects in this area. For example, one of the students did not like the image shown for an incorrect answer (sad, blue face) and would cover his eyes if it showed up. In fact, this was a good student and generally the sad face only appeared when his partner was doing the exercises. In this situation, it would be good if the images could be customised for each student. It would add to the complexity, but could be feasible.

The CALL resources would also benefit from additional audio features. Initially, there were no audio features as it felt that it would not be feasible in the lab where one student would be able to hear the word being spoken, while his partner could not. However, in practice, this was not an issue as the boys were used to sharing headphones and would let their partner hear the word as well. In the light of this fact, it would be nice to add an audio feature to the progress monitoring screen that would play different music based on the learner's progress to date.

While this project was a success in terms of providing the teacher and students with curriculum aligned CALL software that they could actually used, there are still areas for improvement. Some of them are pedagogical related. For example, students learn 'sh' as a single sound e.g. 'shell'. In the mixed up exercise, the 'sh' can be shown as one unit, and the students are fine with that. When they have to actually spell the word, they have to type the letter 's' and then the letter 'h' and this can cause confusion. There are other issues related to the lack of computers available in the lab and one possible workaround for this is for some students to work on the same exercises printed on paper, while they wait their turn for a computer.

The issue of evaluation is a difficult one in the CALL context. There was no attempt in this project to compare this group of students with a peer (control) class, as there are so many reasons why this would not be feasible. The determination of success of the project was determined by the teacher and the students. Their qualitative feedback showed that they liked the system, that they found it easy to use and had not major suggestions for improvements. This feedback has to be tempered with the knowledge that children in this age group tend to want to please adults and that they may find it difficult to express their feelings [16]. However, informal interaction with the boys revealed that they did actually enjoy using the resources and kept asking me for more the next year. The teacher was happy with the CALL resources and felt that it did what she wanted it to do and that it was of value to her students.

8   Conclusion

In summary, this paper discusses how a CALL authoring tool was adapted and customised to the needs of this learner group. Some specific HCI considerations for the target group include using bright colors and 'obvious' images for buttons as no text could be used. The manual/mouse dexterity of the learners must be taken into account, so that their effort is focused on answer the exercises and not the actual process of system input. This paper reports on the deployment of these young learner oriented HCI CALL resources and the lessons learnt in the process. It shows that it is possible to produce and deploy useful materials in a relatively short space of time and with very limited resources. Some suggestions for future research in this area include the enhanced customisation and audio features, which could make the materials more attractive and assessable to the learners. The UI in this project looks very simple, because it is very simple. However, simple is not a bad thing and in this case it was exactly what was required and it as what worked.

References

1. Colpaert, J.: Design of online interactive language courseware: conceptualization, specification and prototyping: research into the impact of linguistic-didactic functionality on software architecture. PhD diss., Universiteit Antwerpen (2004)
2. Ward, M.: The Integration of CL Resources in CALL for Irish in the Primary School Context. PhD diss., Dublin City University, School of Computing (2007)
3. Piaget, J.: Science of Education and the Psychology of the Child. Orion Press, New York (1970)
4. Bruckman, A., Bandlow, A., Forte, A.: HCI for kids. The human-computer interaction handbook: Fundamentals, evolving Technologies, and emerging applications, 428–440 (2002)
5. Sommerville, I.: Software Engineering, 9th edn. International computer science series. Addison-Wesley, Harlow (2010)
6. Galitz, W.O.: The essential guide to user interface design: an introduction to GUI design principles and techniques. Wiley.com (2007)
7. Abras, C., Maloney-Krichmar, D., Preece, J.: User-centered design. In: Bainbridge, W. (ed.) Encyclopedia of Human-Computer Interaction, vol. 37(4), pp. 445–456. Sage Publications, Thousand Oaks (2004)
8. Resnick, M., Silverman, B.: Some reflections on designing construction kits for kids. In: Proceedings of the Conference on Interaction Design and Children. Boulder, CO, pp. 117–122 (2005)
9. Druin, A.: The role of children in the design of new technology. Behaviour & Information Technology 21(1), 1–25 (2002)
10. Martin, R.C.: Agile software development: principles, patterns, and practices. Prentice Hall PTR (2003)
11. Boyatzis, C.J., Reenu Varghese, R.: Children's emotional associations with colors. The Journal of Genetic Psycholog 155(1), 77–85 (1994)
12. Ozok, A., Salvendy, G.: Twenty guidelines for the design of Web-based interfaces with consistent language. Computers in Human Behavior 20(2), 149–161 (2004)
13. Koyani, S.J., Bailey, R.W., Nall, J.R.: Research-Based Web Design & Usability Guidelines. National Institutes of Health (2003)
14. Inkpen, K.M.: Drag-and-drop versus point-and-click mouse interaction styles for children. ACM Transactions on Computer-Human Interaction (TOCHI) 8(1), 1–33 (2001)
15. Butler, Y.G., Lee, J.: The effects of self-assessment among young learners of English. Language Testing 27(1), 5–31 (2010)
16. Hanna, L., Risden, K., Alexander, K.: Guidelines for usability testing with children. Interactions 4(5), 9–14 (1997)
17. Donker, A., Reitsma, P.: Usability testing with young children. In: Proceedings of the Conference on Interaction Design and Children, College Park, MD, pp. 43–48 (2004)
18. Hubbard, P.: Learner training for effective use of CALL. In: New Perspectives on CALL for Second Language Classrooms, pp. 45–68 (2004)

Collaboration, Learning and Training

E-Portfolios – Fostering Systematic Reflection in Social Work Education

Patricia Arnold[1] and Swapna Kumar[2]

[1] Faculty of Applied Social Sciences, Munich University of Applied Sciences, Germany
[2] School of Teaching and Learning, University of Florida
patricia.arnold@hm.edu, swapnak@ufl.edu

Abstract. Learning technologies in higher education open up new possibilities for academic professional development due to the flexibility in time and place they offer. For professional students it is important to develop a critical distance to their daily practice and a capacity for reflection. E-portfolio technology is considered to be suitable to help to develop such a reflective critical stance. In this paper we argue that in order for e-portfolios to foster reflection, a robust educational design with careful "scaffolding" is needed. We present a design in social work education that was meant to gradually develop students' ability to reflect, while using a mixture of technologies. With three exemplary e-portfolios, we re-construct how students reflected on their professional trajectories, how they used the technology and how this was fostered by the educational design. A critical discussion leads to recommendations for using e-portfolio technology for fostering reflection in other settings.

Keywords: e-portfolios, learning technologies, professional students, social work education.

1 Introduction - The Challenge of 'scaffolding' e-portfolios

The integration of learning and collaboration technologies in higher education opens up new possibilities for lifelong learning and provides non-traditional populations with access to universities. Generally, such technologies increase flexibility for students as regards time patterns for studying, choice of location, possible mobile device usage, etc. Study programs that are aimed at practitioners offer them academic professional development while meeting the demands of family commitments and continuing to work in their field. Although using learning and collaboration technologies in such programs for flexibility and virtual collaboration is valuable, a robust educational design is needed to provide a meaningful professional trajectory for students and to help them embrace a critical approach to their field. Learning and collaboration technologies have to be purposefully chosen and thoughtfully implemented so that students acquire a critical distance to their daily practice, a willingness to incorporate new perspectives and the ability to systematically reflect (cf. the notion of "digital habitat" by Wenger, White & Smith 2009). Without a capacity for reflection, students will not be able to become "reflective practitioners" (Schön, 1983), a goal of many academic programs for professional students.

P. Zaphiris and A. Ioannou (Eds.): LCT 2014, Part II, LNCS 8524, pp. 351–362, 2014.
© Springer International Publishing Switzerland 2014

In this paper we present the use of e-portfolio technology to foster reflection in students who are working professionals and study alongside their jobs. E-portfolios have been termed both an innovative method and a technology for learning, teaching and assessment. E-portfolios are digital documentations of students' work within a study program, where students use specialized e-portfolio software or a combination of other learning technologies to build the portfolio and its contents. E-portfolios include students' reflections on learning processes and products as well as instructor or peer feedback, all collected in a variety of multimedia formats and arranged in an individual fashion to suit the individual learner's situation. The process of digital documentation of growth, articulation of reflection, and exposure to peer reflections can develop students' ability to take a critical stance towards their daily practice and entrenched work routines. E-portfolios are therefore generally regarded as a valuable tool for fostering students' reflective capacities (cf. e.g. Barrett 2003, Bäcker, Cendon & Mörth 2011, Bauer & Baumgartner 2012).

On the other hand e-portfolios within educational designs are by no means a straightforward and simple issue, they are accompanied by limitations, possible risks and pitfalls (cf. Meyer et al. 2011): E-portfolios do not comprise or represent software that students or teachers use in their daily lives, therefore some introduction to the concept and the technology is needed. As with any new technology, students run a risk of "over-acting," e.g. including too many items and applying insufficient selection criteria (Reinmann & Sippel 2011). Likewise, students might "over-reflect". They might reflect only because it is required of them, resulting in only personal remarks (ibid.) or "defensive-reflect" to avoid bad grades (Häcker 2005). The assessment of e-portfolios is problematic and no processes have been documented about students' participation in the development of assessment criteria.

In this paper we argue that it is not the e-portfolio technology as such that helps students develop their capacity for professional reflection but the use of e-portfolios in a carefully constructed educational design that provides "scaffolding" for students in building up their reflective capabilities. We use the term "scaffolding" according to Brown, Collins & Duguid's (1989) cognitive apprenticeship model where it refers to a learning environment that provides carefully thought-out support for acquiring certain skills. We present an educational design in social work education in an online degree program that combines a mixture of carefully selected learning technologies (including "mahara" as specialized e-portfolio software) with explicit scaffolding within the educational design to foster reflection.

2   Theoretical Framework – Schön's "Reflective Practitioner"

According to Schön (1983, 1987), a "reflective practitioner" is a professional expert who deals competently with challenging real-world situations through different forms of reflection. Schön contended that problems that are clearly defined can be resolved with technical expertise, but problems in practice are usually fuzzy, involving unstable and complex situations and conflicts of interest. He perceived a gap between "professional knowledge" and actual practice, concluding that two types of reflection could be of great significance in such situations.

Schön asserted that the "reflective practitioner" masters both "reflection-in-action" and "reflection-on-action." "Reflection-in-action" occurs during the action itself when the expert draws on a blend of prior experiences, expert knowledge, his/her feelings and intuition to deal with a challenging new professional situation. "Reflection-on-action" refers to the practitioner's analysis of his actions after they take place. The expert reflects on his/her approach to the situation, reactions and actions, and resolution of the problem with the aim of understanding his/her behavior but also possibly improving it in a similar future situation. "Reflection-on-action" often includes the documentation of actions in a given situation. Reflective practice that includes the two types of reflections helps to bridge the gap between academic knowledge and actual practice. According to Schön, reflective practice is an integral component of any study program for educating expert practitioners who aim to continuously improve their practice through reflection.

Schön's framework is particularly valuable in social work education because social workers and social educators are confronted with many ill-defined situations and problems in their practice, where a combination of academic knowledge and prior experiences could be greatly valuable to resolve difficult situations. The program that provides a context for this study therefore aims for students, who are practicing professionals, to "recapture their experience, think about it, mull it over and evaluate it. It is this working with experience that is important in learning" (Boud, Keogh & Walker 1985, 18). The educational design of the program, which is offered partially online, thus deliberately includes activities that facilitate reflection in action and reflection on action, thus providing students with opportunities for enacting a reflective practice.

The use of e-portfolios within this educational design seems particularly appropriate as e-portfolios enable a) reflection by the individual and b) reflection with the community when the individual shares with peers and reflects on issues common to all. In addition, e-portfolios are a suitable means to document one's own professional learning trajectory and the process of creating a meaningful documentation in itself "nudges" students to reflect on their learning, their actions taken, etc., thus fostering especially "reflection-on-action". E-learning technologies allow for organizing the individual documentation, individual and collective reflections as well as a general exchange of ideas and feedback concerning the professional learning trajectory, in many media formats.

3   Context – Reflection within the Online Degree Program

3.1   Online Degree Program BASA-online

The program "BASA-online" that serves as a case study in this paper enables students with professional experience in the social field to obtain a bachelor's degree in social work. As students work in the social field alongside their studies, the degree program combines online modules (75% of the study time) and face-to-face tuition (25% of the study time). Online modules are based on the communication and collaboration affordances of the learning management system OLAT, which contains learning resources presented in a variety of multimedia formats (text, audio, video, etc.), forums for discussion as well as live classroom features to facilitate synchronous collaboration and discussion, mainly in small working groups. In all modules, students' professional experience is used as a point of departure for the inquiry into a certain topic, and for connecting theoretical concepts directly with social work practice. Interweaving academic knowledge and student's work experience is an overall design feature of the program.

3.2   Module "Scientific Theory-Practice Transfer"

The online module "Scientific Theory-Practice Transfer" (STPT) runs over four semesters and was especially designed to accompany students' personal learning trajectory, during which they integrate academic knowledge into their professional practice and, in turn, their academic research endeavors are inspired by their daily work challenges. In addition, this module provides multiple opportunities for a "reflective practice", i.e. opportunities for reflection–in-action as well as reflection-on-action. As a key part of the reflective practice students build a personal-e-portfolio to document and reflect on their personal learning trajectory and their individual "scientific theory-practice-transfer". To support students' learning processes and facilitate the attainment of these goals, a careful selection of additional learning technologies is used: the software mahara for creating the e-portfolios as well as a specialized peer-counseling platform (http://www.kokom.net) that is also used by professionals in social work organizations (for details of this platform cf. Arnold 2011). Working on the assumption that neither of these technologies fosters reflective capacities per se, an educational design was crafted that provided "scaffolding" for reflective processes as well as for building a meaningful e-portfolio by means of these different technologies.

In detail, the scaffolding consists of four tasks that require different forms of reflection and the usage of specialized technologies. The complexity of the tasks gradually increases, and at the same time the scaffolding by design and/or technologies "fades out". The four tasks correspond to the four semesters and are described here according to the (1) task, (2) technology, and (3) scaffolding elements. The module STPT starts with a face-to-face seminar that gives students an overview of the module's aims, general structure, activities and technologies used. The rest of the module is delivered entirely online.

First Semester: (1) Students go through a "peer counseling" process. A student who is confronted with a challenge in his or her working context presents the "case" to a small group of fellow students. The group then discusses the case online, following the 10-step model of peer counselling according to the Heilsbronn model (Spangler 2012), an established model for peer-counselling in the social realm. (2) In terms of technology the specialized platform kokom.net is used where the 10-step-Heilsbronn model is mapped within the software and the software therefore "scripts" the peer-counselling process of the small working groups. (3) Scaffolding of reflective practice as well as adequate appropriation of the technology is high within this task: The choice of a challenging problem at work is a clearly defined starting point, the counselling process follows the 10 steps and reflection-in-action and reflection–on-action are clearly supported by these concisely defined steps. In addition, students' reflection on practice is also guided by an evaluative discussion at the end of the first semester, which uses a structured feedback form, and focuses on the personal gain, the assessment of the method and the technology, as well as the potential for further usage after completion of the study program. The platform has a very intuitive "look & feel" and includes ample material on how to use it, including a video tutorial.

Second Semester: (1) Students have to choose a key theoretical concept in social work, such as "inclusion" or "empowerment", and create instructional material on the topic, aimed at practitioners in the social field, e.g. guidelines, an introductory reader, or a resource website, etc. The focus within this task is on the usefulness of the "product" for practitioners. All "products" are showcased at the end of the semester, to be peer-reviewed by the other students as regards their practical usefulness. Finally, instructors also provide feedback to the working groups. (2) Collaboration and showcasing takes place on OLAT, using synchronous and asynchronous collaboration features of the learning management system. (3) Scaffolding for reflection is less in that students have more room to make their own decisions compared to semester one where the software walks them through the 10-step process. Students find the process of choosing a topic and creating a "useful product' challenging but the task structure and examples from previous student cohorts provide support. Usage of OLAT does not need any scaffolding as it is students' "digital habitat" in the degree program.

Third Semester: The task focuses on issues of professional identity. Students first discuss articles describing professional identities and roles in social work. Then, students select a "case" from their practice, this time identifying a conflict in their own professional behavior or role that might have arisen due to their learning trajectory within the study program and discuss the "case" again using the peer counseling method from the first semester. At the end, they share a personal statement on their own concept of professional identity within their working area. (2) Again kokom.net is used as technology. (3) Students' reflection during this semester is more challenging because they have to distance themselves from their daily work practice in order to reflect on professional identity and possibly recognize role conflicts triggered by their academic studies. The three elements of the task gradually increase in difficulty. The "scripting" for the counselling process, also supported by the technology and the familiarity with the kokom.net as technology due to previous usage provides some support.

Fourth Semester: Designed as "reflection-on-action", students are asked to document and evaluate their own theory-practice-transfer process during the module (or within the overall program) in an e-portfolio. Students need to present three "learning products", giving reasons for their selection, commenting on the products in hindsight, and integrating any feedback from peers, instructors or retrospective self-evaluation. In addition, students should comment on their overall learning trajectory, condense it with an overarching motto or narrative. (2) The e-portfolio is built with mahara, integrating texts or other material created within the module on OLAT or kokom.net. (3) The only scaffolding provided here as regards reflection is the suggestion of two sets of guiding questions for creating the e-portfolio and some examples of previous student cohorts. For mahara, standard how-to manuals are provided.

Table 1. Overview Module "Scientific -Theory-Practice-Transfer"

#	Task	Technology	Scaffolding
1	Peer-counselling on workbench case	OLAT & kokom.net	• Individual reflection on practice • Collective reflection on practice • Sharing reflection with learning community • Video tutorials and personal support
2	Creating guidelines on key theoretical concepts	OLAT	• Individual reflection on theory • Collective reflection on theory • Giving and receiving feedback
3	Peer-counselling on professional identity	OLAT & kokom.net	• Social worker statements on professional identity • Individual reflection on professionalization • Collective reflection on professionalization
4	Creating e-portfolio on learning trajectory	OLAT, kokom.net & Mahara	• Providing guiding questions and e-portfolio examples • How-to manuals for mahara

4   E-Portfolios – Re-Constructing Reflection

In this section we present three e-portfolios as products of the final task in semester four of our educational design. The three e-portfolios vary greatly in the approach adopted by the student for reflecting on the learning trajectory and compiling this reflection as a visible and sharable product on mahara. In the following section we proceed to discuss how they used the technologies in their portfolios, and how their final product might have been influenced by the scaffolding in our design as well as by the different technologies used.

4.1   E-Portfolio A – "All in Flux"

Student A titles her e-portfolio "all in flux" and presents herself as a student with three adult children for whom obtaining an academic degree is an import part of her aspirations in life. Her portfolio starts with a longer personal intro containing her motivation for study, her general experience and philosophy in life. As her first product she presents her BA thesis and reflects on the study program. Using strong visual clues she argues that studying does not mean creating "heaps" of knowledge but rather building a growing network of knowledge. She highlights the most valuable insight gained from her studies for her professional future by using a strong visual of a train buffer. This visual is accompanied by a statement that she refuses to "act as a buffer zone" as a social worker in the future. In her second product, she presents and reflects on the group work from the second semester where her group created a product for institutions in early childhood education. Her part in the project was to find an appropriate language for communicating research results that would strike a balance between insider scientific language and daily life imprecision. Thirdly, she presents notes taken during the peer-to-peer counselling process and reflects on her initial assessment of the usefulness of the tool and method based on her current perspective. The closing remark summarizes how her overall behavior has changed due to her academic studies: she now adopts a critical stance everywhere and e.g. requests sources for information, even in small talk conversations.

4.2 E-Portfolio B – Scientific Theory-Practice-Transfer

Student B is a comparatively young student, working as a nurse in early childhood education. For the title of her e-portfolio she adopts the module name: "STPT by B". For documentation and reflection she selects the key study products within the module, albeit in a different order: (1) Her understanding of her professional identity as a future social worker, (2) the peer counselling process she was involved in and (3) the group work on a theoretical concept in social work, presented to practitioners. She produced a video as supporting documentation in which she explains her changing views on professional identity, indicating that her statement on professional identity was the most important part of her module. However, she does not explicitly explain her chosen order of products. Overall, her e-portfolio is structured by three elements: (1) a personal intro und a future perspective, (2) the description of the three study products and a commentary on each from her current perspective and (3) supplemental resources to support her documentation and reflection (the study products as such, descriptions of the peer counselling method or other relevant texts as well as the video).The common thread that runs through the different parts of the e-portfolio is the theme of how important it is to intertwine theory and practice: For example, in her personal closing remarks she emphasizes how much she appreciated being able to study alongside her job as she could repeatedly apply newly acquired academic knowledge into her practice.

4.3 E-Portfolio C – Autoethnographic Reflection

Student C has adult children and works in a Montessori school. Her e-portfolio contains a variety of elements: (1) a summary of her personal history, (2) a variety of quotes that guide her through life, (3) a vivid image that supports colorfully her praise of "the great diversity of opportunities in life" as well as (4) a playful section with the text capture "Space" and an empty space created in the portfolio by spreading the single letters out over many lines. In addition, she (5) declares her passion for writing. As *study products* she creates two separate mahara *views*[1], one titled "My encounter

---

[1] Technical term in mahara denoting a subset of the e-portolio, in which certain artifacts are arranged with comments in a particular layout. Access rights can be granted particularly for each view in mahara.

with autoethnography", referring to a qualitative research method she used for her BA thesis and a second *view*, titled " Task: creating an e-portfolio" where she documents and reflects on the process of working on this task of creating an e-portfolio itself[2]. In the first *view* she comments on the method of autoethnography from her current standpoint and weaves in a diary entry from when she was actually working with the method and deeply enjoying it. Supporting documentation includes her thesis, her favorite text on the method and scans of handwritten notes taken while reading through the literature to understand this special method. The second view takes the form of a small autoethnographic study of the task at hand, creating the e-portfolio. It comprises an introspection of her first initial resistance to yet another task and tool, a scan of handwritten notes taken when the task was introduced, quotes by instructors explaining the task which resonated immediately with her ("to look back on traces of a study program"), a text and a self-created image of how she gradually understood what a portfolio means as well as an excerpt of a documentation where she and a fellow student "played" with mahara to come to terms with this new tool. At the end she reports how she inwardly smiled when she suddenly realized how her own conclusion statement in her BA thesis "reflection and introspection are important for any educational process" matched the task of the portfolio creation.

5   Discussion – Scaffolding for Reflection

The three e-portfolios selected for this paper represent the diversity of the e-portfolios in the cohort and the different elements and levels of reflection present in all the e-portfolios. Based on the three sample e-portfolios presented above, this discussion focuses on the ways in which the educational design and scaffolding provided within it influenced the final products, students' e-portfolios and students' demonstrated reflection in those portfolios. The actual processes of reflection and technology appropriation that led to the final product were not part of a formal investigation as this educational design was not developed for research purposes but to facilitate reflection within a study program for professionals in social work education. We also discuss students' usage of the different technologies OLAT, kokom.net and mahara in the module as well as any supplemental technology they might have used to reflect and to present their reflections.

5.1   Students' Reflection and E-portfolios

Reflecting the diversity of adult professional students in BASA-online and corresponding to prior research on the capabilities of e-portfolios for students to customize and individualize their learning (e.g. Bauer & Baumgartner 2012), the e-portfolios that resulted from the educational design of the STPT module varied. Nevertheless, all the students achieved some level of reflection as demonstrated in their e-portfolios (for more details cf. Arnold & Kumar in press) - these ranged from those that closely followed the scaffolding guidelines and structure provided to those

---

[2] In her cohort the number of study products to be contained in the portfolio was not specified.

who absorbed those guidelines, making them their own and rising to reflect on their actions and their growth during the study program. The three e-portfolios presented in this paper mirror this spectrum of student reflection in the e-portfolio products at the end of the STPT module.

Student B responded to the guiding questions ("which are the study products and what do I think of them now") for constructing an e-portfolio in a very literal way, while using all the reflective elements from the first three parts of the STPT module. The scaffolding clearly helped her reach a basic level of reflection and build the e-portfolio. However, with the exception of her video on her professional identity development, she did not add any retrospective reflection or commentaries to her portfolio in addition to the elements previously produced in the educational design. It is possible that she chose to adhere to the structure provided, and that the scaffolding prevented her from exploring new dimensions, or, that she lacked the time to do so as a busy working professional. In contrast, Student A loosely used the set of guiding questions provided for structuring the e-portfolio, and included reflective statements written during the different parts of the STPT module, but incorporated them into a bigger narrative, with a focus on the perceived impact of the study program on her personal and professional development. Further, she went beyond just including elements from the other parts of the module (Student B) by reflecting back on her earlier work from her current perspective. She appears to have benefited from the scaffolding in this respect because she integrates earlier individual reflections into her personal narrative "all in flux" that, according to her, is her main takeaway from the study program in a nutshell.

Student C's e-portfolio reflects the other end of the spectrum, in that she did not explicitly follow the guidelines or structure provided, but used the many degrees of freedom inherent in the previous tasks in the module and had the confidence to take the task to another level. The structure of her portfolio is only vaguely guided by the questions provided. She adopted an autoethnographic approach to the task at hand, demonstrating her learning from the study program, and expanding the required reflection-on-action on her learning trajectory by documenting her reflection-in-action to create the e-portfolio. In her case, the scaffolding appears to have provided her with structures that resulted in reflection and to have also instilled in her the confidence that any creative solution of the assignment would be appraised if it was well argued and convincingly presented. This student interwove the collective dimension with her individual reflection, presenting notes from the shared playful "sandbox" session that she and a fellow student used for coming to terms with mahara.

5.2   Students' Use of Technology for Reflection

The educational design of the program scaffolded not just reflection, but also the integration of specific technologies for specific activities to help students become comfortable with those technologies while becoming reflective practitioners. Although student A successfully reflected on her learning trajectory in the study program, she used the basic features of mahara, writing linear text, using text sections with headlines, incorporating documents for download as documentation and inserting images for illustration of her statements. Her strongest design elements were "snappy" photos that provided strong visual clues for her statements as well as different text colors to differentiate statements from different points in time. The educational design appears to have succeeded in that she used mahara to convey her reflective statements and to emphasize them with visual clues. Going beyond how Student A used mahara, Student C adopted basic features of mahara in an authentic personal fashion, by using basic features of text sections, images and files for download but additionally adding a layer of creativity. She represented "space for introspection" in her e-portfolio by emphasizing space and using single letters in paragraphs, or inserting special characters in the headlines like symbols for musical notes. The educational design appears to have influenced her learning trajectory in a similar way to the reflective stance she adopted: it helped her to gain confidence, adopt a playful attitude, and to allow herself creativity in her solutions.

Although Student B's e-portfolio was found to most closely following the scaffolds or structures provided in the module, and did not transcend to reflection on the learning trajectory in the study program, she demonstrated the maximum reflection on her technology usage and advanced usage of mahara. Although the other parts of her e-portfolio lacked an explicit explanation of why she did what she did, she eloquently explained why she "dared" to produce a video herself, that after having dealt with many different technologies in the course of her study program, this seemed a doable task. She reported initial difficulties handling both OLAT and kokom.net but attributed her increased media competency, i.e. venturing into the new territory of producing a video on her own, to the study program. Her growing confidence in dealing with technology was a subject in her reflections on her learning trajectory. Additionally, she situated her thoughts within a definition of media design, thus connecting her video well with her e-portfolio theme of combination of theory and practice. In general, student B used more advanced features of mahara for her e-portfolio, mapping her internal structure of (1) personal information, (2) study products, (3) supporting documentation into a three-row-layout. In addition, with her homemade video on her professional identity development, she made use of mahara's multimedia features, and thereby adds a lot of authenticity to her documentation and reflection.

6   Conclusions

In this paper we investigated how e-portfolio technology can help students to develop reflective capacities. We argued that in order for the technology to support students' reflection, an educational design that scaffolds individual and collective reflection as well as technology use is needed. We presented such a design in social work education, using mahara as e-portfolio software, kokom.net for peer-counselling processes and OLAT as a standard learning management system. We then used three resulting e-portfolios to re-construct how students reflected on their professional trajectories and how the e-portfolio task, the software used as well as the scaffolding in the design interacted to support students' reflection.

Generally, the educational design with its in-built scaffolding seemed to have worked in this setting. The portfolios clearly showed reflection-on-action with respect to students' learning trajectory to become qualified social workers, albeit in different forms, on different levels and with different interaction as regards the technologies. The diversity does not come as a surprise as all students in BASA-online were adult learners and working professionals in the social field who bring a wide range of experiences to the program. Based on their individual learning and personalities, students adopted the processes of reflection scaffolded in the educational design and made them their own. Furthermore, the educational use of e-portfolios is regarded as a means for personalization of educational processes. This personalization was apparent because students interacted with the technologies provided in different ways and chose to present their reflections using supplemental technologies, or not, based on their acquired comfort level with technology in the study program. Likewise, students' responses to the scaffolding varied: whereas some "clung" to the structure provided and do not go much beyond it, while others used it as a "trampoline" to reach a completely different level of reflection. Some students demonstrated basic use of technology but were very creative in the way they represented their reflection, while others' intensive use of technology provided them with new ways of expressing themselves and spurred them on to reflect in ways that they would not have done so otherwise. Although the use of technology played a role in the level of reflection reached, the scaffolding in the educational design appears to have been more important for the reflective processes that folded into the e-portfolios.

Despite the success of the current educational design for e-portfolio production, we would like to provide additional scaffolding in the future for the production of multimedia elements, thereby enabling a more intensive use of the multimedia features the e-portfolio software affords. It would also be interesting to explore whether increasing students' ability to use multimedia would deepen their reflection. In terms of research design, in this study we focused on the educational design to facilitate reflection-on-action and the creation of e-portfolio products, analyzing the e-portfolios at hindsight. If expanding our research to multimedia effects, we would use a different research design, additionally studying the reflection processes, capturing some reflection-in-action elements, and considering factors such as students' inclination to write, gender issues, etc.

Acknowledgements. This work was supported by the Federal Ministry of Education and Research in Germany (BMBF) within the framework of the "Quality Initiative for German Higher Education" and the university's development project "Well Equipped for the Future" (duration 2011-2016) within this initiative.

References

1. Arnold, P.: Online peer-to-peer counseling as a new collaborative format in studying social work. In: Proceedings of 7th International Conference on Technology Supported Learning & Training, Berlin (November 30-december 2, 2011)
2. Arnold, P., Kumar, S.: Crossing Professional Thresholds with Networked Learning? An Analysis of Student E-Portfolios Using the Threshold Concept Perspective. In: Bayne, S., Jones, C., de Laat, M., Ryberg, T., Sinclair, C. (eds.) Proceedings of the 9th International Conference on Networked Learning (in press, 2004)

3. Bäcker, E.-M., Cendon, E., Mörth, A.: Das E-Portfolio für Professionals. Zwischen Lerntagebuch und Kompetenzfeststellung. In: Zeitschrift für E-Learning, vol. 3, pp. 37–50. Studienverlag, Innsbruck-Wien-Bozen (2011)
4. Barrett, H.C.: Electronic portfolios. In: Kovalchick, A., Dawson, K. (eds.) Educational Technology: an Encyclopedia, ABC-CLIO, Santa Barbara (2003)
5. Bauer, R., Baumgartner, P.: Schaufenster des Lernens. In: Eine Sammlung von Mustern zur Arbeit mit E-Portfolio. Waxmann, Münster (2012)
6. Boud, D.J., Keogh, R., Walker, D. (eds.): Reflection: turning experience into learning. Kogan Page, London (1985)
7. Brown, J.S., Collins, A.: Situated Cognition and the Culture of Learning. Educational Researcher 18, 32–42 (1989)
8. Häcker, T.: Das Portfolio als Instrument der Kompetenzdarstellung und reflexiven Lernprozesssteuerung. In: Tramm, T., Brand, W., (eds.), bwp@ Berufs- und Wirtschaftspädagogik – online, No. 8 (2005), http://www.bwpat.de/ausgabe8/txt/haecker_bwpat8-txt.htm (February 06, 2014)
9. Meyer, T., Mayrberger, K., Münte-Goussar, S., Schwalbe, C. (eds.): Kontrolle und Selbstkontrolle. VS Verlag für Sozialwissenschaften, Wiesbaden (2011)
10. Reinmann, G., Sippel, S.: Königsweg oder Sackgasse? E-Portfolios für das forschende Lernen. In: Meyer, T., Mayrberger, K., Münte-Goussar, S., Schwalbe, C. (eds.) Kontrolle und Selbstkontrolle, pp. 185–202. VS Verlag für Sozialwissenschaften Wiesbaden (2011)
11. Schön, D.: The reflective practitioner. How professionals think in action. Basic Books, New York (1983)
12. Schön, D.: Educating the Reflective Practitioner. Jossey-Bass, San Francisco (1987)
13. Spangler: Gerhard Kollegiale Beratung, 2nd expanded edn. Mabase, Nürnberg (2012)
14. Wenger, E., White, N., Smith, J.D.: Digital habitats: stewarding technology for communities. CPsquare, Portland (2009)

European Citizens and Their Trust in Social Networks

Gianmarco Baldini[1], Ioannis Kounelis[1,2], Jan Löschner[1], and Mariachiara Tallacchini[1]

[1] Institute for the Protection and Security of the Citizen
Joint Research Centre (JRC), European Commission, Ispra (VA), Italy
[2] Royal Institute of Technology (KTH), Stockholm, Sweden
{gianmarco.baldini,ioannis.kounelis,jan.loeschner,
mariachiara.tallacchini}@jrc.ec.europa.eu

Abstract. In information and communication technology (ICT) trust has been considered as a crucial component of digital interactions. Trust has been dissected in a variety of potential meanings and dimensions and through the merging of trust in humans and trust in machines. In this paper, we investigate the role and the aggregation of trust in social networks and blogs and how it relates to knowledge production, and its connections to concepts such as reputation and sustainability in the European context. Moreover, we discuss knowledge production in information and communication technology and its relationship to user trust. We develop a view on the co-production of knowledge and trust and propose a policy management framework to support the users in their trusted use of social networks and blogs. This is presented based on an e-health use case analysis considering web based reputation and developing a new reputation scheme.

Keywords: trust, social networks, European citizens, collaboration, reputation, e-health.

1 Introduction

The relations between trust and modes of knowledge production have been widely explored by scholarly work in sociology of science, where they have been shown as an essential part of the renewal of the social contract between science and society [1, 2]. On the one hand, the involvement of lay citizens in the making of science and the concept of peer-production of knowledge between experts and non-experts are envisaged today as strategic ingredients to improve scientific and technological learning processes and make them more robust and trusted. On the other hand, trust is increasingly needed in all relationships –be they related to knowledge, personal, professional, and social life.

In information and communication technology (ICT) trust has been considered as a crucial component of digital interactions, and has been dissected in a variety of potential meanings and dimensions –and through the merging of trust in humans and trust in machines. Trust and confidence have different shades of meanings. However, here we propose to define trust as the level of confidence, which an entity can ensure

P. Zaphiris and A. Ioannou (Eds.): LCT 2014, Part II, LNCS 8524, pp. 363–374, 2014.

to another entity or entities for specific services and in given context [3]. Even if trust has been often used with reference to human beings, trust can also be associated to a machine or digital system (e.g., web site), which points out the importance of analysing and measuring the level of trust in a digital society.

In ICT knowledge production has entered the debate as a possible path to trust as it represents a vehicle for valued and respected relationships. Collaboration in knowledge processes has been at the core of the most traditional scientific community ethics –namely the so-called "ethos" of science. Today, knowledge co-production can contribute to trusted ICT digital interactions [4, 5]. European citizens' values and fundamental rights provide a specific framework that needs to be explored, together with its opportunities and challenges.

In this paper, we investigate the role of trust in social networking services and how it relates to knowledge production, and its connections to concepts such as reputation and sustainability in the European context. In comparison to conventional social networks, there are important differences to be considered:

1. The persistence of information about individuals, which impacts the personal sphere in particular its privacy or security,
2. The possibility to provide real-time updates on the life of the individuals thanks to the pervasiveness of the internet and wireless communication,
3. The possibility of masquerading behind a web page, which can become both a protection of the individual and a liability if used by malicious entities.

We expand in this paper the concept of social networking services to include other forms of citizens' interactions through digital technologies (e.g., blogs). In continuously changing digital ecosystems, where new technologies appear in the wider context of the internet and have an impact on the ethical sphere of the citizen (e.g., wearable sensors, e-health), it is very important to define a model for trust providing a measurable level of confidence and trust to the citizen as user. This trust model must be technology agnostic to address the future evolution and it must be flexible enough to support different contexts or different regulations/policies defined at national or European level. In particular, we will investigate potential future extensions of social network services regarding mobility, wearable sensors (e.g., including medical devices) and the increasing role of eGovernment services. This paper also reviews the existing models of trust in literature (e.g. reputation or credential based, institutional) and their applicability to social network services.

On the basis of the previous considerations a new model of trust based on a policy management approaches is proposed and described. This model is applied qualitatively to the scenario of social networking services and blogs related to the domain of e-health, where entities (e.g., research centres, e-commerce sites) from different domains with different levels of reputation can provide information and services. On the one hand, this is an area where citizens are increasingly looking for information and knowledge to improve awareness and make informed decisions regarding their personal health. On the other hand, considering the wide range of offers (both in terms of information and products) available on the web, there is an increased risk that the provided information could be dangerous or incorrect. The potential consequence of an absence of trust indicators in these sites is that the citizen can be exposed to considerable risks both for personal information (i.e., privacy), and for his/her health and safety, as incorrect or inappropriate information and products can be harmful rather than beneficial. Finally, the paper also links the provision of trust in this domain to supporting more sustainable and safe ecosystems as indicated in [6].

This contribution is structured as follows. The next section introduces knowledge production in information and communication technology and its relationship to user trust. In section 3 we introduce a policy management framework. In section 4 we discuss mechanisms to support reputation in the Web, and in section 5 we illustrate the discussion with some online examples. In section 6 we present an e-health use case and the analysis of a new reputation scheme. Finally, we provide some conclusions and an outline of our future work.

2   Co-production of Knowledge and Trust

The relations between modes of knowledge production and ethical behaviour have been at the core of the intertwined foundations of the validity and ethical soundness of science as well as of the trustworthiness of the scientific community. Indeed, the most traditional framing of the so-called 'ethos' of science — as portrayed, for instance, by Robert Merton [17]—interprets scientific practices as simultaneously generating and replicating sound knowledge and moral conducts, in a co-production of epistemic and normative dimensions [16]. As known, four main characters compose the 'ethos' of scientific knowledge as a certified stock of knowledge and a set of cultural values: universalism, communism, disinterestedness, organized scepticism. Universalism refers both to the universal character of scientific knowledge and to its not being bound nationalities or cultures; communalism entails that scientific results are the common property of the entire scientific community; disinterestedness assumes that common good and not personal gain is the purpose of the scientific endeavour; organized scepticism means that scientific claims must be exposed to the peers' critical scrutiny before being accepted.

Altogether, these elements were deemed reliable in constituting and legitimizing the scientific community as a polity composed by 'peers.' In fact, at the same time these criteria refer to the knowledge practices embodied in scientific work and to the values that, while informing and guiding scientists' conducts, consolidate and reproduce science as a cognitively and morally trusted social system.

After the neo-positivist vision of science as neutrally objective has been mostly abandoned, reference to scientists' trustworthiness, namely their moral credibility, has become an integral part of the validity of science, both internally (within the community of experts) and externally (in the relations with society). In the redefinition of the relations amongst scientists, institutions, and the public, the rebuilding of trust has turned out as critical to the renewal of the social contract between science and society, in the face of scientific failures in preventing unforeseen consequences of new technologies —e.g. in the health and food sectors in the EU. A lack of trust was at the base of what EU institutions have called citizens' 'unease' with science, namely their hesitant and unconfident behaviour towards technological innovation. Moreover, due to both the widespread dissemination of knowledge and the availability of technologies, scientific knowledge started happening in diverse social environments other than universities, academies, research centres [1, 2].

In the last two decades, ICT have increasingly and capillary encouraged a different mode of knowledge, relying on the spontaneous and collaborative creation and sharing of knowledge by scientists and lay people, experts and non-experts, meeting through the web in virtual communities and social networks. This co-produced, or crowd sourced, knowledge reveals a special value when it is shaped as 'commons-based peer production' of knowledge, namely when all parties involved are recognized as peers within the community [4, 5]. From this perspective, it is important to specify that, while 'crowd sourced' knowledge merely refers to a project soliciting participants' contributions, 'peer production' implies the genuine and as freely as possible sharing of those contributions amongst all participants [15].

This extended community of peers shows relevant similarities with the traditional scientific community in the mutual interconnectedness of its epistemic and moral foundations. As Benkler and Nissembaum have pointed out [4], *"socio-technical systems of commons-based peer production offer not only a remarkable medium of production for various kinds of information goods but serve as a context for positive character formation."* In fact, *"the emergence of peer production offers an opportunity for more people to engage in practices that permit them to exhibit and experience virtuous behavior"*.

As known, the traditional ethos of science has revealed its limitations and rhetoric when, from ideal set of relevant epistemic and ethical criteria, it has become a self-referential and black-boxed way to establish validity and legitimacy —e.g. in science-based policy models, where political decisions claim to be neutrally based in scientific facts [18, 19]. In a similar way, peer production of knowledge needs to adopt deeper justifications towards the dynamically quest for trustworthiness.

In fact, if, on the one hand, the equal involvement of experts and lay people in knowledge-making as peers has become an essential ingredient in improving the scientific and technological learning processes and in making them more robust, transparent, and trusted; on the other hand, these overall processes have to constantly sharpening and deepening their search for trust through both technical and non-technical, human-based, criteria.

This unending search towards trust, namely trust as a process rather than a product, has a special meaning within the EU and for its citizens. Not only trust has been a critical element in the relations between the EU institutions and European citizens, but it is also an essential part of the European vision of rights and science policy [24].

3   Trust and Reputation in Regulatory Frameworks

In the European Commission, the concept of Trust belongs to one of the pillars of the Digital Agenda: the Third Pillar of Trust and Security [7], which is the basis for various actions of the Digital Agenda, including Action 28: Reinforced Network and Information Security Policy, Action 35: Guidance on implementation of Telecoms rules on privacy and Action 37: Foster self-regulation in the use of online services. This pillar is related to Data Protection Directive (namely Directive 95/46/EC) [8], which regulates the processing of personal data within the European Union. This directive is currently ongoing a review and a new regulation will supersede the existing provisions. Beyond the specific concept of privacy and data protection, trust services have been proposed as part of the recent regulation on electronic identification and trust services for electronic transactions in the internal market [10]. In the wider context described in this paper, there is a clear need to establish new guidelines or a regulatory framework to evaluate the level of trust in web services. A step in this direction is the definition of Privacy Seals [11], namely the development of *"an EU website labelling system, modelled on the European Privacy Seal, certifying a site's compliance with data protection laws (…) that (…) should include a thorough impact assessment and must avoid duplication of existing labelling systems"*. Public and private seals have been already developed in some European countries such as Germany, where the e-Ten project developed EuroPriSe4. In a similar way, the French Data Protection Authority is developing privacy seals for trainings and audits. In the USA, privacy seals are provided by private companies like TRUSTe [12]. However, despite these efforts, privacy seals may not be enough to guarantee that a user can fully trust a web service and its contents.

In the USA, the National Strategy for Trusted Identities in Cyberspace [9] highlighted the need to increase the level of trust of internet services towards the user. The main proposed approach, called Identity Ecosystem, is based on identification of the individuals and entities operating in the cyberspace in a way that can protect their privacy. Some of the main elements of the Identity Ecosystem described in [9] are:

- The subject of a transaction: a generic citizen or an application
- An identity provider, which is for establishing, maintaining, and securing the digital identity within the Identity Ecosystem.
- An attribute provider is responsible for the processes associated with establishing and maintaining identity attributes. Note that a subset of the real identity can be used or a new identity can be created for a specific context.
- An accreditation authority assesses and validates identity providers, attribute providers, relying parties, and identity media, ensuring that they all adhere to an agreed-upon trust framework.

Note that the Identity Ecosystem foresees the application of policies and standards even if a clear description of the related technical solutions is not included [9]. The Identity Ecosystem does also support change of the context or different roles, with different levels of access, so that specific roles (e.g., a doctor) can have access to personal data when there is a crisis or similar change of context from a "normal" situation. These features are also present in the framework we describe in this paper.

Communication with peers in the light of a cross border situation with different legal frameworks and possibly natural language barriers challenge even more the reputation mechanisms.

4   Mechanisms to Support Reputation in the Web

In [13], the authors describe various signal processing techniques, which can be used to support the security of reputation systems on the web: bayesian reputation systems where the reputation scores of a web entity can be updated on the basis of observations; belief theory based on probability; fuzzy logic and others. In [13] the most probable attacks to reputation mechanisms and related countermeasures are also identified.

One of the main drivers for attacks to reputation is the economic gain. For example, e-commerce web sites are increasingly based on reputation mechanisms to give an estimate of the reputation of a seller or a buyer. The feedback mechanism in eBay is well known, but also other web sites use a review-based approach where customers of an online or physical (e.g., restaurant) merchant can provide a review on the received service. On the basis of the positive or negative reviews, a host application or web service can create a sorted reputation list of the merchants. This review mechanism does not exist at the moment for all the online services. The healthcare information sites described in the introduction may also benefit from a simple feed-back/review mechanism but, as described in [14], there are various techniques to at-tack such a simple mechanism and undermine the overall reputation framework. For example, malicious users can generate fake feedbacks by creating a large number of pseudonyms in reputation frameworks where the feedback is linked to an identity. Instead, in reputation frameworks based on reviews where the identity is not strongly enforced, professional paid writers can generate any type of positive or negative review. The overall impact of these coordinated and even profit-driven manipulations can be a significant distortion of the reputation scores and a degradation of the overall reputation framework, which eventually undermine the level of confidence of the users.

Other popular reputation frameworks, which have been proposed for the online world, are based on the evolution of old-fashion approaches. One approach could be based on the collection of evidence from organizations, which have the objective or the professional capacity to provide impartial (or at least non intentional partial) feedbacks, which can be used to build trust. One example is a consumer organization. Another approach could be based on the opinion of experts, which are also supposed to be impartial. The model of the movie or restaurant critics can be reapplied to the online world. Both approaches have some strong disadvantages. In fact, their provided evidence is costly to collect and can become outdated very quickly with the evolution of web services; moreover, the large number of online web services requires, in order to be validated, a large number of experts in different fields. Under such circumstances it is difficult to build a proper business case and to support the reputation framework in a consistent way.

There is the need to define new models of reputation, involving both technical and non-technical criteria, which can overcome the limitations described before.

5   Online Examples

In our days a continuous growing number of often concurrent online services are dealing to gain clients. The business case is based on increasing membership numbers assuring a profitable service. An example already mentioned in this paper is eBay. The use case is becoming more sensitive in respect to security and data protection when the trust level concerns the user directly, for example in respect to his personal health. The historical "reputation framework" is the relationship between the medical doctor and his patients. Already in 2000 the EU founded in the framework of its Action Plan for Internet User Security the certification and rating of Trustworthy and Assessed Health Information on the Net. A digital trust mark for health information was proposed to assist users in assessing the trustworthiness of medical offerings on the Internet and to make the glut of information on the World Wide Web more transparent. Currently, the patients once getting sick stress social networks and seek for peers to get advice, decide treatments and self-medicate. An example is [22], which focuses its efforts: "*on offering readers and visitors to our site objective, trustworthy, and accurate health information, guided by the principles of responsible journalism and publishing. Our editorial philosophy is to use relevant and accurate content to promote a healthy lifestyle and facilitate disease prevention, as well as to offer clinically significant, medically reviewed information for those who are seeking answers to their health questions.*"

Web services such as online pharmacies use labels such as the "Trusted Shop Guarantee" [20] to proof the quality of service in respect to the security of transactions. The label itself uses trust marks and customer reviews as ranking criteria. The pharmacy actively encourages its clients to recommend the service in social networks such as Facebook [21]. In a number of cases the rankings published by the service providers only refer to the part of the service such as the timeliness of the delivery, but not to the level of knowledge in respect to the health problem.

6   Proposed Reputation Model

The reputation model proposed in this paper is based on the following elements:

- An authentication and authorization mechanism to ensure that only authenticated and authorized entities can contribute to the content of a social networks site.
- A policy management framework, where policies are defined to mitigate some of the limitations of reputation schemes that are described in section 3.

6.1   The Generic Policy Management Framework

The main objective of a policy management framework is to support the definition and application of policies in an ICT system. A policy defines the type of actions which can be executed in a specific context, what should be executed, who is allowed to execute these actions and under which condition. Policy management frameworks are usually based on an Event-Condition-Action (ECA) enforcement rule. In other words, an ICT system or a component of an ICT system receives an *event*, which requests a specific *action*. This *action* can be executed only if a *condition* (or more than one condition) applies. Usually the policy management framework provides two distinct functions: a) the policy reasoning which implements the logic to decide if an action should be performed and b) the policy enforcement, which actually enforces the rule. The policy reasoning process can be implemented through an extraction of a possible solution by composition or decomposition of pre-defined policies. This can be defined as the policy database. These two functions are usually implemented in two elements of the policy management framework: the Policy Decision Point (PDP) also called the Policy Engine because it implements the reasoning function and the Policy Enforcement Point (PEP).

The ECA rule is activated when an element of the ICT system (for example a node in a social networking site) receives an event, which triggers a chain of operations. The event includes information related to the original requester of the event, the type of service requested, the assets and resources on which the service must operate and so on. For example, an event can simply be the request of read access to a record. The event is processed by the PEP component in the node. This processing may include the extraction of the relevant information (type of service, source of the requester, as on which service must operate). Once processed, the PEP executes a policy query to the PDP, which can be hosted by another ICT system in the social networking sites. It is important that the communication between the PEP and the PDP is secure against eavesdropping, and that it ensures the integrity of the exchanged messages. The PDP examines the request and identifies the correct policy to adopt on the basis of the requested service and the *context*. With the word *context,* we mean the existing boundary conditions at the time the request has been received. These boundary conditions could be the number of other users already authenticated in the system, the specific condition of the social networking site (under maintenance), which may prevent the execution of the service request and so on.

On the basis of the content of the service request and the context, the Policy Reasoner in the PDP chooses the specific policy in the space of the policy database. The PDP then replies to the PEP with the policy itself. The PEP enforces the policy in the node. The PDP and PEP relationship is described in Figure 1.

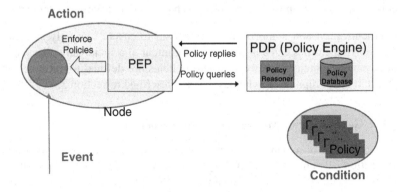

Fig. 1. Policy Management Framework

6.2   The Use of the Policy Management Framework in Social Networks

As we described before, the policy management framework must be combined with an authentication and authorization mechanism to ensure that only authenticated entities can insert content in the social network site. Any authentication technology can be used (e.g., sign-on, credentials). In the authorization phase, the authentication entity is associated to a specific role and type entity. In the example of the social networking site for medical equipment and medicines, the authenticated entity can be a doctor, a researcher, the representative of a consumer association or the representative of a product manufacturer or just a generic citizen. In all these cases, it is important to embed in the system the role of the authenticating entity. While some roles can provide information, which is supposed to be impartial (e.g., a doctor or researcher), in some other cases the provided information can be quite detailed but not impartial, due to a business interest (e.g., the representative of the product manufacturer).

The role of the entity is used in the PDP to understand the particular policy to be applied. For example, a social networking site can have a feedback/comments section, which provides reviews of a specific product. If a potentially partial entity (e.g., the representative of the product manufacturer) would like to provide a comment to the reviews section, the PDP can intercept this request and deny the provision of the content. This approach can be applied to any section of the social network site, so that only appropriate comments are posted in specific areas. In another example, the PDP can check the number of entities, which provided past reviews, and deny a new contribution if an entity has already provided too many reviews to increase the positive or negative feedback on a product.

The policy framework can also be used to implement intelligence in the social networking site to improve the overall robustness of the web site against security/privacy attacks. For example, they can intercept a security or privacy attack by denying a service request, which tries to have access to many instances of personal records of the social networking site. In this context, policies can be used not only to deny or allow data breaches but also to emit notifications to the administrators of the social networking site in case of suspicious behavior of entities during authentication.

New policies can be created at any time in response to a change in the context to address the misbehavior of an entity, which can be a contributor or a product manufacturer. For example, if the administrator of a website receives a notification that there is a suspect medical product in the market, a policy can be immediately implemented to deny procurement of this medical product by users.

The adoption of a policy management approach can be used to mitigate the challenges presented in section 3 in the following ways:

1. *Fake feedbacks in the review mechanism.* In this threat to the reputation mechanism of the social networks, fake feedbacks are generated to alter the review rate of a specific product or evaluation of a cure. This threat can be mitigated through the definition of policies, which can be triggered to analyze patterns or anomalies in the provided feedback. Two examples are identified: in the first example, specific patterns or commonalities can be identified and analyzed like similar feedbacks or feedbacks originating from users with the same IP address or the same location. In the second example, when an entity is applying for a new feedback review, the policy can request a "similarity" check on all the existing feedback/reviews against the opinion of the experts. Note that the policy management approach can also be applied in the authentication/authorization phase to detect the generation of a large number of pseudonyms. While some information can be faked (name, surname), a check can be done against the originating IP address or the provided physical address to detect anomalies. This check can be

implemented in the policy itself. In this way, we can prevent the generation of a large number of pseudonyms.

2. *Reputation frameworks based on reviews where the identity is not strongly enforced.* In this threat, entities can provide contributions but there is no link to the identity of the entity or its role. In the proposed framework, this threat is mitigated by the authentication and authorization mechanism, where the entity's identity and role are recorded and used in the policy management framework. In addition, policies can be used to highlight the content provided by the entities and their level of reputation in the social networks. This will give an immediate indication to the user of the social networks on how much the contribution can be trusted.

3. *Evaluation of the trust of the presented content.* The policy framework can implement additional checks on the validity of the information provided. To achieve a substantial level of trust, the provided content must be supported by scientific studies. The policies can implement a check on the presence of scientific studies on a specific medical cure or the results from scientific trials on a medicine.

4. *Natural language barriers of users.* The policy framework can define a policy agnostic to the natural language to support interoperability within a domain in a cross border environment.

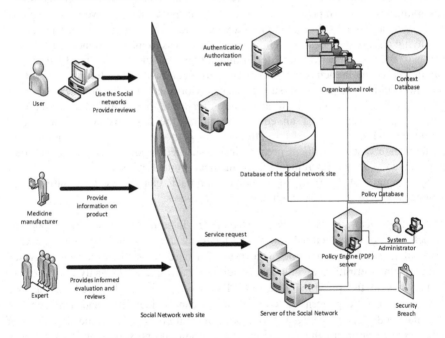

Fig. 2. Policy Framework for a Social networking site

The overall elements of the proposed framework are shown in Figure 2. The PEP components must be implemented and deployed in the main servers of the social networking site, while the policy engine/PDP function can be implemented and hosted in a specific server, which has access to various sources of information in the system, including the database of the social networking site, the policy database and the context database. The Authentication/Authorization server takes care of authenticating the user and matches their identity to a predefined organizational role. As described before, the policies can also be used to mitigate security threats and to notify the system administrators.

7 Conclusions

The evolution of the Web services and applications can support new ways of knowledge production, where both experts and lay people can participate as peers. One example of this evolution is the social network, which can support the collaboration in the knowledge processes, which has been at the core of the most traditional scientific community ethics –namely the so-called "ethos" of science. An essential element for an effective knowledge production is trust among the entities, which collaborate through the social networks.

The idea that valid knowledge and ethical behavior should generate each other in the scientific community, as traditionally portrayed in sociology of science, has re-emerged in relation to the specific features of peer-production of knowledge made possible by the web and ICT. However, here reliability of both knowledge and human behaviour require that trust is constantly renewed through a continuous process involving technical and non-technical criteria. In other terms, the knowledge process should encompass also the knowledge and commitment towards the adoption of shared reliable policy agreements and mechanisms. Support for trusted collaboration can be quite challenging both at an organization and technical level and this paper has highlighted some of the most significant challenges in this area. It remains difficult to build successful business cases and to support in a consistent way the reputation framework.

Future developments will explore more in detail how more advanced forms of the policy management framework, such as presented in [23], can support more effective knowledge production and trusted collaboration in social networks.

References

1. Gibbons, M., et al.: The new production of knowledge: the dynamics of science and research in contemporary societies. Sage, London (1994)
2. Nowotny, H., Scott, P., Gibbons, M.: Rethinking science: knowledge in an age of uncertainty. Polity, Cambridge (2001)
3. Ion, M., Danzi, A., Koshutanski, H., Telesca, L.: A peer-to-peer multidimensional trust model for digital ecosystems. In: 2nd IEEE International Conference on Digital Ecosystems and Technologies, pp. 461–469 (2008)
4. Benkler, Y., Nissenbaum, H.: Commons-based Peer Production and Virtue. The Journal of Political Philosophy 14(4), 394–419 (2006)
5. Benkler, Y.: The Penguin and the Leviathan. Random House, New York (2011)
6. Jin-Hee, C., Chan, K.S.: Building Trust-Based Sustainable Networks. IEEE Technology and Society Magazine 32(2), 32–38 (2013)

7. European Commission: Digital Agenda for Europe. COM, 245 (2010), http://ec.europa.eu/digital-agenda/ (accessed December 17, 2013)
8. European Parliament and Council: Directive 95/46/EC of the European Parliament and of the Council of 24 October 1995 on the protection of individuals with regard to the processing of personal data and on the free movement of such data. Official Journal L 281/31 (1995)
9. The White House: National Strategy for Trusted Identities in Cyberspace (2011), http://www.whitehouse.gov/sites/default/files/rss_viewer/NSTICstrategy_041511.pdf (accessed January 15, 2014)
10. European Parliament and Council: Regulation of The European Parliament and of the Council on electronic identification and trust services for electronic transactions in the internal market. COM/2012/0238 (2012)
11. European Parliament: European Parliament resolution of 15 December 2010 on the impact of advertising on consumer behavior. Official Journal of the European Union, C 169 E/58 (2012)
12. Truste, http://www.truste.com (accessed February 7, 2014)
13. Yan, S.: Security of Online Reputation Systems: The evolution of attacks and defenses. IEEE Signal Processing Magazine (29), 87–97 (2012)
14. Yang, Y., Feng, Q., Sun, Y.: Dai.Y.: Reputation trap: An powerful attack on reputation system of file sharing p2p environment. In: 4th Int. Conf. Security and Privacy in Communication Networks (SecureComm 2008), Istanbul, Turkey (2008)
15. Ball, M.: 23andme's First Patent (2012), http://madprime.org/articles/2012/05/23andmes-first-patent (accessed January 30, 2014)
16. Jasanoff, S.: States of Knowledge: The Co-production of Science and Social Order. Routledge, New York (2004)
17. Merton, R.K.: Science and Democratic Social Structure. In: Social Theory and Social Structure, pp. 604–615. Free Press, New York (1968)
18. Tallacchini, M.: Between uncertainty and responsibility: precaution and the complex journey toward reflexive innovation. In: Vos, E., van Asselt, M., Everson, M. (eds.) Trade, Health and the Environment: The European Union Put to the Test, pp. 74–88. Routledge, London (2014)
19. Wynne, B., et al.: Taking European Knowledge Society Seriously. European Commission, EUR 22700 (2007)
20. Trusted Shops, http://www.trustedshops.eu/ (accessed February 7, 2014)
21. Facebook, VfG Versandapotheke Österreich, https://www.facebook.com/VfG.Apotheke.at (accessed February 5, 2014)
22. Healthline, http://www.healthline.com/health/about-healthline (accessed January 15, 2014)
23. Neisse, R., Doerr, J.: Model-based Specification and Refinement of Usage Control Policies. In: Eleventh International Conference on Privacy, Security and Trust (PST), Tarragona, Spain (2013)
24. Funtowicz, S., Strand, R.: Models of Science and Policy. In: Traavik, T., Lim, L.C. (eds.) Biosafety First: Holistic Approaches to Risk and Uncertainty in Genetic Engineering and Genetically Modified Organisms, pp. 263–278 (2007)

Towards Aggression De-escalation Training with Virtual Agents: A Computational Model

Tibor Bosse and Simon Provoost

VU University Amsterdam, Department of Computer Science, The Netherlands
t.bosse@vu.nl, s.j.provoost@student.vu.nl

Abstract. Serious gaming based on Virtual Reality is a promising means for training of aggression de-escalation skills. By enabling trainees to interact with aggressive virtual characters that respond in a realistic manner to different communicative approaches, they can learn to apply the appropriate approach at the right time. To facilitate the development of such a training system, this paper presents a computational model of interpersonal aggression. The model consists of two sub-models, namely an 'aggressor model' and a 'de-escalator model'. In the long term, the former can be used to generate the behaviour of the virtual characters, whereas the latter can be used to analyse the behaviour of the trainee. The functioning of the model is illustrated by a number of simulation runs for characteristic circumstances.

Keywords: virtual training, aggression de-escalation, cognitive modelling.

1   Introduction

Aggressive behaviour against employees in the public sector, such as police officers, tram conductors, and ambulance personnel, is an ongoing concern worldwide. According to a recent study in the Netherlands, around 60% of the employees in the public sector have been confronted with such behaviour in the last 12 months [1]. Being confronted with (verbal) aggression has been closely associated with psychological distress, which in turn has a negative impact on work performance [12]. Responses to aggression range from emotions like anger and humiliation through intent to leave the profession, and verbal aggression by customers may even impair employees' recognition and working memory [17]. In case of severe incidents, employees may even develop symptoms indicating post-traumatic stress syndrome [5].

To deal with aggression, a variety of techniques are available that may prevent escalation [2, 16]. These include (verbal and non-verbal) communication skills, conflict resolution strategies, and emotion regulation techniques. The current paper is part of a project that aims to develop a serious game [18] for aggression de-escalation training, based on Virtual Reality. VR-based training has proven to be a cost-effective alternative for real world training in a variety of domains, including military missions [11], surgery [8] and negotiation [13].

P. Zaphiris and A. Ioannou (Eds.): LCT 2014, Part II, LNCS 8524, pp. 375–387, 2014.

In the training environment envisioned in the current project, a trainee will be placed in a virtual scenario in which aggression plays a role (e.g., dealing with a domestic violence case), with the goal of handling it as adequately as possible. The emphasis is on dyadic (i.e., one-on-one) interactions. The trainee can observe the events that happen in the scenario (e.g., a virtual character starts offending her), and has to respond to this by selecting the most appropriate action from a multiple choice menu. During the task, she is 'monitored' by a software system that observes her behaviour, analyses this, and provides personalised support [9].

To realise an effective training system, it is crucial to understand the dynamics of the processes related to interpersonal aggression. More specifically, when focussing on dyadic interactions, knowledge is required about how aggression builds up in person A (the aggressor), and what person B (the de-escalator) can do to make it go down again. In the current paper, such knowledge is formalised in terms of a dynamic computational model of interpersonal aggression. Basically, this model consists of two separate sub-models, one for the aggressor and one for the de-escalator.

The remainder of this paper is structured as follows. In Section 2, a brief overview is provided on the literature on aggression and de-escalation of aggression. Based on this literature, the computational model of interpersonal aggression is presented in Section 3. Next, Section 4 describes a number of illustrative simulation runs that were produced on the basis of the model, and Section 5 is a conclusion.

2   Aggression and Aggression De-escalation

In this section, first an overview is presented on the relevant literature on aggression. This is followed by a description of a generic protocol for aggression de-escalation, and a more detailed description of some de-escalation approaches.

2.1   Aggression

According to a report by the Dutch Ministry of the Interior and Kingdom Relations, one of the main aspects to take into account when dealing with aggression is its *nature* (see [16], p.13). The psychological literature distinguishes two important theories regarding the nature of aggression. First, the *frustration-aggression hypothesis* [4] tells us that aggression flows forth from a person's goals being frustrated. Such a person is likely to be angry with respect to whatever stopped him from achieving his goal. By the carry-over effect, the anger can be transferred to new situations as well [3]. The second important theory is the *social learning theory* which states that aggressive behaviour is learned through positive reinforcement. The essence of this theory is that if a person has used aggression to achieve a goal in the past, and if this behaviour was successful, then by operant conditioning (s)he will be likely to follow the same behavioural pattern in the future.

Under the frustration-aggression hypothesis, aggression is of a *reactive* nature, meaning that it is an angry reaction to a negative event that frustrates a person's desires. In the social learning theory, aggression can be considered to be of a *proactive* nature, since the aggression is not a response to a negative event, but is used instrumentally to achieve a goal. One of the primary means of differentiating between reactive and proactive aggression seems to be the respective presence or absence of anger [15]. Based on observations in animals, it has been proposed that reactive aggression is *hot-blooded*, and that proactive aggression is *cold-blooded*. In the former a lot of physiological arousal is visible, whereas this is not the case in the latter [7]. Although this physiological distinction seems strongly rooted in our culture, for example when we talk about a violent act being committed 'in cold blood' versus 'in the heat of passion', direct evidence for it in humans remains relatively sparse. As an example, in an empirical study on children from 6-11 years old, reactive aggression was found to correlate with both skin conductance reactivity and non-verbal signs of anger [10].

Anderson [2] interprets the anger in the frustration-aggression hypothesis as suggested by Lazarus [14], namely as an appraisal of injury to self-esteem that accompanies a loss of control over the situation. Verbal aggression then, is an attempt to regain control over the situation, and restore self-esteem. Aggressive behaviour thus serves the function of relieving the tension caused by the injury to the aggressor's self-esteem. According to this theory, escalation of aggressive behaviour into physical violence is caused by a continuous build-up of tension until a person loses all self-control. This process can be described as a cycle of escalating aggression; see Figure 1, taken from [2]. This paper provides us with a list of behavioural cues and warning signs that can typically be observed during the build-up of aggression, such as 'loud speech', 'tense posture', 'flushed face', and so on. Although these cues and signs will be subject to interpersonal differences, in general we should be able to assume that the more apparent they become in a person, the higher the tension. From here on out, we will also assume that the non-verbal behavioural cues we just mentioned are an expression of physiological arousal caused by anger, which in turn provides us with a way of distinguishing between reactive and proactive aggression.

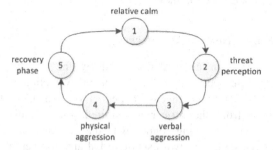

Fig. 1. Five phases in the cycle of aggression (taken and formatted from [2])

2.2   Aggression De-escalation

It is common for employees who are likely to be subjected to aggression to receive some form of training on how to manage these situations. Such training involves the use of protocols that describe the decision making process for de-escalation. One such protocol is the 'exemplar protocol for aggression management' (Figure 2), used for training of people employed in the Dutch public services [16].

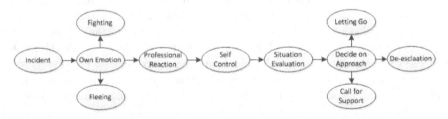

Fig. 2. Exemplar protocol for aggression management (translated and formatted from [16])

The model starts with an incident of aggression occurring. Such an incident invokes a certain amount of stress in an employee, i.e. an *emotional state*, following the naturally occurring fight-or-flight response. This response prepares the person to either flee or fight, both of which can be considered undesirable when dealing with mere aggression. Instead, what is required from employees is a professional reaction; they should recognize their own stress response and regulate it, for example by means of breathing techniques or controlling their thoughts. In the ensuing state of self-control, employees should be able to evaluate the situation on its relevant properties, most importantly on the *nature* of the aggression (reactive or proactive)[1] and the aggressor's level of *tension*. Both have been explained in the previous section.

Having evaluated the situation, there are three principal decisions employees can make. First, when it is not too severe, employees can choose to simply ignore it and let it slide. Second, if de-escalation is considered to be promising, it should be pursued. Third, if de-escalation seems impossible, employees should call for support from colleagues or the police. In case of letting things slide or calling for support, the interaction between employee and aggressor ends. In the next section, this decision making process is elaborated on in more detail.

2.3   Aggression De-escalation Approaches

In a model for aggression de-escalation used by the Dutch police [20], four approaches are distinguished, which depend on an evaluation of the state of the aggressor (see also [16]). First, in case a person is in danger of losing control, *supportive* behaviour from the officer is required, for example by ignoring the conflict-seeking behaviour, making contact with the aggressor and actively listening to what he has to say (see [2] for two lists of verbal and non-verbal *do's and don'ts*). Second, in case the person is actually losing control, a more *directive* approach is called for. In this case employees are to show the aggressor that there is a limit to how far he can pursue his behaviour, and point out its consequences. Third, in case the

---

[1] Discussions with domain experts in public transport confirmed that the ability to distinguish between reactive and proactive aggression is a key element in their training program.

aggressor is actually losing control to the extent that he becomes violent, employees have to *guarantee their own safety*, judging for themselves whether to abandon the conversation, leave, or call for support. And fourth, in case the aggressor starts to *relax*, it becomes possible for employees to do the same thing. They should now attempt to regain contact with the aggressor and re-evaluate the situation. When we relate these four approaches to the cycle of aggression (Figure 1), they seem to match with phase two to five of the cycle. However, it is important to realise that the influence of the de-escalator is not depicted in Figure 1. In other words, the figure shows the 'natural' development of aggression in case no intervention takes place; if instead the de-escalator uses one of the approaches mentioned above, other transitions are possible than the ones shown in Figure 1, (e.g., back from phase three to two). The four approaches mentioned above are of particular interest when dealing with reactive aggression. In [10] it is suggested that interventions aimed at reactive aggression should focus on hostile attribution biases. People with such a bias are more likely to perceive others as threatening. Hence, in such a case the supportive approach, in which the employee makes an attempt to understand the aggressor, may be beneficial. Instead, interventions aimed at proactive aggression should focus on an alteration of the contingencies associated with the aggression (e.g., by making the aggressor aware of what will happen if he continues to behave aggressively). This can be considered as an instance of the directive approach to phase three. Hence, when dealing with proactive aggression, it might be better to skip the supportive approach altogether and directly move to the directive approach. This distinction between the approaches recommended in case of reactive versus proactive aggression is an important feature of the model presented in the next section.

3   Computational Model

This section provides a description of the computational model of interpersonal aggression. First, in Section 3.1, a global overview is presented of the model and the modelling approach that was used. Next, Section 3.2 and 3.3 briefly describe the models of the aggressor and the de-escalator, respectively. Because of space limitations, the main part of this description is given on an abstract level. A complete description of the model is provided in [19].

3.1   Global Overview

The following model is meant to simulate the interaction between an aggressive person (the aggressor) and a person that attempts to calm the aggressive person down by means of de-escalation (the de-escalator). Both are modelled as individual agents that together form a multi-agent system (see Figure 3).

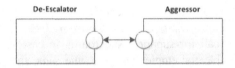

Fig. 3. Global overview of the interaction between de-escalator and aggressor

As for the communication between the two agents, we will distinguish between non-verbal and verbal communication and behaviour, globally corresponding to the verbal and non-verbal cues, and to the various approaches that can be taken towards aggression that we identified in Section 2. This behaviour is performed and observed by both agents. We will consider verbal behaviour to be what a person is saying and how this is being said, and non-verbal behaviour to be all other observable cues, such as pacing around or making erratic gestures.

To formalise the model, the LEADSTO language is used as a basis [6]. This language is based on the assumption that dynamics can be described as an evolution of states over time. The notion of state as used here is characterised on the basis of an ontology defining a set of physical and/or mental *state properties* that do or do not hold at a certain point in time. To formalise state properties, an *ontology* is specified in a (many-sorted) first order logical format as a finite set of sorts, constants within these sorts, and relations and functions over these sorts. State properties are formalised by n-ary predicates over an ontology, such as performs(aggressor, action(physical_violence)) or has_value(emotional_state, 0.8)). Next, dynamic relations can be expressed with the 'leads to' operator $\twoheadrightarrow$. More specifically, the expression A $\twoheadrightarrow$ B indicates that if state property A holds at time point t, then state property B will hold at time point t+Δt.

In the model presented below, most state properties refer to a concept that has a numerical value (e.g., the emotional state mentioned above). In such cases, the respective influence of state property A on state property B is represented as follows:

$B(t+\Delta t) = B(t) + \eta_B(A(t)*\omega_{AB} - B(t))$

Here, ω_{AB} is a connection strength indicating how much the activation of state A influences the activation of state B, and η_B is an update speed parameter used to give the updating of state B a gradual nature.

Similarly, it is also possible to have multiple state properties influence one state property. For example, the influence of states A1 and A2 on state B is denoted by:

$B(t+\Delta t) = B(t) + \eta_B(A1(t)*\omega_{A1B} + A2(t)*\omega_{A2B} - B(t))$

3.2   The Aggressor

A graphical representation of the aggressor model is provided in Figure 4. In this figure, state properties are depicted by circles and dynamic properties by arrows. The circles on the left denote observations of the agent, the circles on the right (communicative) actions, and the remaining circles internal states. Most of these states are formally represented as a real number between 0 and 1.

As can be seen from the figure, a central role in the aggressor's behaviour is played by the two internal states. The *emotional state* is a concept introduced to simulate the level of tension experienced by the reactive aggressor via a real number (where 0 represents no tension and 1 maximal tension). This state is assumed to reflect the phase of the cycle of aggression in which the aggressor resides. In a similar fashion, the *belief about benefit* is a concept introduced to simulate the proactive aggressor's tendency to show aggressive behaviour. However, since proactive aggression is referred to as more 'cold-blooded' (see Section 2.1) than reactive aggression, we here use the more neutral term 'belief'. Basically, this concept can be thought of as the agent's expectation about the benefit of pursuing aggressive behaviour, and its dynamics could be described by a 'cycle of believed benefit'[2]. To highlight the fact that the emotional state mainly plays a role in the reactive aggressor and the belief about benefit in the proactive aggressor, different colours are used in Figure 4: the red arrows are only used for the reactive, and the blue arrows for the proactive aggressor (and the black ones for both).

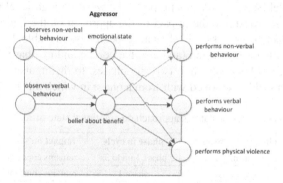

Fig. 4. Overview of the aggressor model

Regarding the dynamics of both internal states, for both of them holds that they are influenced by the observed (verbal and non-verbal) behaviour of the de-escalator. More specifically, the observed non-verbal behaviour (e.g., the extent to which the de-escalator has a flushed face, again represented in the domain [0,1]) has a direct (linear) impact on both states. Instead, the observed verbal behaviour is represented as a qualitative concept that has one of the following values: [letting_go, supportive, directive, call_for_support] (see the approaches discussed in Section 2.3). Depending on whether or not the observed approach matches the phase in which the aggressor resides (in the cycle of aggression or the cycle of believed benefit), the value of the relevant internal state will either increase or decrease.

---

[2] However, this cycle has only three phases, since the phase in which a supportive approach is effective (i.e., phase 2 of the cycle of aggression) does not exist. Hence, this phase is skipped for this cycle.

As an example, assume that a proactive aggressor who resides in phase 2 of the 'cycle of believed benefit' is confronted with a directive approach. Since this is the correct approach for this phase, the value of the believed benefit will decrease. This effect is represented by the following LEADSTO rule (where θ_{2a} and θ_{2b} are thresholds to define the lower and upper bound of phase 2, and η and ω play the role as explained in Section 3.1):

Example 1 - From observed directive approach to a decreased belief about benefit
has_nature(aggressor, proactive) &
observed(aggressor, has_value(verbal_behaviour, directive)) &
observed(aggressor, has_value(non_verbal_behaviour, NVB)) &
belief(aggressor, has_value(benefit, B)) &
B >= θ_{2a} & B < θ_{2b}
$\twoheadrightarrow$ belief(aggressor, has_value(benefit, B + η * (NVB * ω - B)))

Due to space restrictions, we will not provide the complete set of LEADSTO rules used for the model (see [19] for this purpose). However, a high-level overview of the knowledge used to determine the impact of the approach on the internal states of the reactive and proactive aggressor is shown, respectively, in Table 1 and 2. Note that phase 3 of the cycle of aggression (and also the corresponding phase 2 in the cycle of believed benefit) has split into two sub-phases, to distinguish a phase in which the aggressor can still be reasoned with from a phase in which this becomes futile.

Table 1. Impact of de-escalator's approach on emotional state of reactive aggressor

observed approach	phase in cycle	impact on state
letting go	phase 1 up to 3a	remains constant
supportive	phase 1	remains constant
supportive	phase 2	decreases
supportive	phase 3a	increases
directive	phase 1 up to 2	increases
directive	phase 3a	decreases
call for support	phase 1 up to 3a	remains constant
any approach	phase 3b up to 4	increases

Table 2. Impact of de-escalator's approach on believed benefit of proactive aggressor

observed approach	phase in cycle	impact on state
any approach	phase 1	remains constant
letting go	phase 2a	remains constant
call for support	phase 2a	remains constant
supportive	phase 2a	increases
directive	phase 2a	decreases
any approach	phase 2b up to 3	increases

As shown in the right hand side of Figure 4, the intensities of the emotional state and the believed benefit determine on their turn the intensity of the (non-verbal and verbal) behaviour of the aggressor, as well as whether the aggressor erupts into physical violence. The details of these rules are not shown, but are relatively straightforward: the aggressiveness of both the non-verbal and verbal behaviour is represented by a real number in the [0,1] domain, of which the value is determined based on the relevant states (see Figure 4) by using the generic formula shown in Section 3.1. The (binary) decision whether or not to perform physical violence is implemented by checking whether the internal state exceeds a certain threshold.

3.3   The De-escalator

A graphical representation of the de-escalator model is provided in Figure 5. The input and output state of the de-escalator are similar to those of the aggressor, however the internal states are rather different. Roughly, the dynamics of the de-escalator's internal processes can be split into three sub-processes. First, as shown in the lower part of the figure, the emotional state of the de-escalator is updated based on the observed (verbal and non-verbal) behaviour of the aggressor, and has in turn an impact on her own non-verbal behaviour.

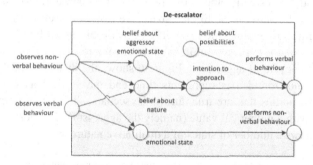

Fig. 5. Overview of the de-escalator model

Table 3. Knowledge used by the de-escalator to evaluate the nature of aggression

observed verbal behaviour	observed non-verbal behaviour	nature of aggression
non-aggressive	any intensity	non-aggressive
aggressive	low intensity	proactive
aggressive	high intensity	reactive

Next, as shown in the upper left part of Figure 5, there is a sub-process related to the evaluation of (both the nature and the intensity of) the aggressor's emotional state. This process corresponds to the 'situation evaluation' task shown in Figure 2. More specifically, evaluating the nature of the aggression boils down to deciding whether we are dealing with reactive or proactive aggression (or no aggression); this is done on the basis of the knowledge shown in Table 3. Evaluating the intensity of the aggression comes down to deciding in which phase of the cycle the aggressor resides.

Finally, as shown in the upper right part of Figure 5, the evaluation of the aggressor's emotional state serves as input for a decision about which approach to select. For this, the knowledge described informally in Section 2.3 is used, of which Table 4 gives a systematic overview. The 'belief about possibilities' serves as an extra condition that needs to be fulfilled before the de-escalator actually executes a selected approach. The possible values of this belief (and of the actual verbal behaviour that is performed) are again the following: [letting_go, supportive, directive, call_for_support].

4   Simulations

To study the behaviour of the model, a number of simulation runs under different parameter settings have been generated using the LEADSTO software [6]. These simulations have been chosen such that they cover the spectrum of possible scenarios that can be encountered. More specifically, they comprise scenarios in which successful de-escalation takes place and scenarios in which the situation escalates, both for reactive and proactive types of aggressors. The latter set of simulations includes cases of escalation that are caused due to different types of mistakes by the de-escalator, such as a failure to remain calm, to judge the nature or intensity of the aggression, and to correctly apply the protocol. The entire set of simulations is included in [19]. Because of the limited space, we restrict ourselves in this section to showing one illustrative simulation run. The scenario discussed here involves a case where the de-escalator is successful in calming down a reactive aggressor that resides in phase 3 of the cycle of aggression. Figure 6 shows the dynamics of the simulation run. Here, the horizontal axis represents time and the vertical axis represents the various state properties that are true during the scenario. The upper graph displays a state property with a numerical value (namely the aggressor's emotional state) and the lower graph shows a number of states of a qualitative nature.

Table 4. Knowledge used by the de-escalator to decide upon which approach to use

aggressor's nature	phase in cycle	selected approach
non-aggressive	any phase	letting go
reactive	phase 1	letting go
proactive	phase 1	letting go
reactive	phase 2	supportive
proactive	phase 2a	directive
reactive	phase 3a	directive
reactive	phase 3b or higher	call for support
proactive	phase 2b or higher	call for support

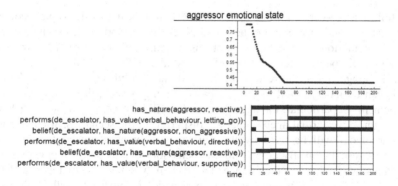

Fig. 6. Example simulation - scenario with successful aggression de-escalation

As shown in the graph, almost immediately the de-escalator (correctly) concludes that she is dealing with a reactive aggressor (time point 10). In addition, she judges the aggressor's level of tension as rather high, and as a result she decides to take a directive approach (time point 12-28). This causes the aggressor to calm down a bit, such that the de-escalator can now switch to a supportive approach (time point 28-60). Since this is again the 'correct' approach, the aggressor calms down even further, and eventually the situation is resolved. Although this is only one example, it clearly illustrates the dynamics of the interaction between the approach taken by the de-escalator and the nature and intensity of the other person's aggression.

5   Conclusion

Aggressive behaviour against public service workers is an ongoing concern worldwide. To improve professionals' de-escalation skills in encounters with aggressive individuals, Virtual Reality-based training is a promising means. By enabling trainees to interact with aggressive virtual characters that respond in a realistic manner to different communicative approaches, they can learn to apply the appropriate approach at the right time. In this paper, a computational model of interpersonal aggression was presented, which will be used as a first step in the development of a VR-based training system.

The model consists of two separate sub-models, namely an 'aggressor model' and a 'de-escalator model'. The aggressor model makes a distinction between reactive aggression (i.e., a response to a negative event that frustrates the person's goals) and proactive aggression (i.e., an instrumental type of aggression used to achieve a certain goal) [7, 15]. In addition, the dynamics of aggression are modelled as a cyclic process that passes through five consecutive phases [2]. The de-escalator model is based on a standard protocol used for training of employees in public services in the Netherlands [16]. This model prescribes appropriate reactions for a variety of circumstances, which can be related to the phases mentioned above. The functioning of the combined model was illustrated by a number of simulation runs for characteristic circumstances.

In follow-up research, a more extensive evaluation of the model is planned. While doing that, we will also explore the possibilities of the model to reproduce different emotion regulation strategies, as well as cognitive biases. Another interesting extension might be to include the role of context and environmental stimuli.

On the longer term, the results of this study are useful because the implemented models can be incorporated in the VR-based training system that is currently under development. In particular, the aggressor model will be used to control the behaviour of the 'aggressive virtual agents' that are displayed in the scenarios, whereas the de-escalator model will be used by the training system as a prescriptive model for adequate de-escalation. By comparing the behaviour of this de-escalator model with the actions performed by the trainee, the system will be able to make a detailed analysis of her performance, allowing it to provide personalised feedback in case of mistakes. Indeed, after further evaluation, both models will be integrated into our system, thus providing a more theoretical foundation to VR-based training of aggression de-escalation.

Acknowledgements. This research was supported by funding from the National Initiative Brain and Cognition, coordinated by the Netherlands Organisation for Scientific Research (NWO), under grant agreement No. 056-25-013.

References

1. Abraham, M., Flight, S., Roorda, W.: Agressie en geweld tegen werknemers met een publieke taak. In: Onderzoek voor Veilige Publieke Taak 2007 - 2009 - 2011. DSP, Amsterdam (2011) (in Dutch)
2. Anderson, L.N., Clarke, J.T.: De-escalating verbal aggression in primary care settings. Nurse Pract. 21(10), 95–98,101–102 (1996)
3. Angie, A.D., Connelly, S., Waples, E.P., Kligyte, V.: The influence of discrete emotions on judgment and decision-making: A meta-analytic review. Cognition & Emotion 25(8), 1393–1422 (2011)
4. Berkowitz, L.: Whatever Happened to the Frustration-Aggression Hypothesis? American Behavioral Scientist 21, 691–708 (1978)
5. Bonner, G., McLaughlin, S.: The psychological impact of aggression on nursing staff. Br. J. Nurs. 16(13), 810–814 (2007)
6. Bosse, T., Jonker, C.M., van der Meij, L., Treur, J.: A Language and Environment for Analysis of Dynamics by Simulation. International Journal of Artificial Intelligence Tools 16(3), 435–464 (2007)
7. Dodge, K.A.: The structure and function of reactive and proactive aggression. In: Pepler, D., Rubin, H. (eds.) The Development and Treatment of Childhood Aggression, pp. 201–218. Erlbaum, Hillsdale (1990)
8. Graafland, M., Schraagen, J.M., Schijven, M.P.: Systematic review of serious games for medical education and surgical skills training. The British Journal of Surgery 99(10), 1322–1330 (2012)
9. Heuvelink, A., Mioch, T.: FeGA: A cognitive Feedback Generating Agent. In: Proceedings of the Seventh IEEE/WIC/ACM International Conference on Intelligent Agent Technology (IAT 2008), pp. 567–572. IEEE Computer Society Press (2008)

10. Hubbard, J.A., Smithmyer, C.M., Ramsden, S.R., Parker, E.H., Flanagan, K.D., Dearing, K.F., Relyea, N., Simons, R.F.: Observational, Physiological, and Self-Report Measures of Children's Anger: Relations to Reactive versus Proactive Aggression. Child Development 73(4), 1101–1118 (2002)

11. Hulst, A., van der Muller, T., Besselink, S., Coetsier, D., Roos, C.: Bloody serious gaming: experiences with job oriented training. In: Proceedings of I/ITSEC 2008, Orlando, Fla, USA, pp. 375–385 (2008)

12. James, A., Madeley, R., Dove, A.: Violence and aggression in the emergency department. Emerg. Med. J. 23(6), 431–434 (2006)

13. Kim, J., Hill, R.W., Durlach, P., Lane, H.C., Forbell, E., Core, C., Marsella, S., Pynadath, D., Hart, J.: BiLAT: A game-based environment for practicing negotiation in a cultural context. International Journal of AI in Education 19(3), 289–308 (2009)

14. Lazarus, R.S.: From Psychological Stress to the Emotions: A History of Changing Outlooks. Annual Review of Psychology 44, 1–21 (1993)

15. Miller, J.D., Lyna, D.R.: Reactive and proactive aggression: Similarities and differences. Personality and Individual Differences 41(8), 1469–1480 (2006)

16. Ministry of the Interior and Kingdom Relations (2008). Handboek agressie en geweld - voorkomen, beperken, afhandelen. Technical Report for the Programme 'Veilige Publieke Taak' (April 2008), http://www.rijksoverheid.nl/documenten-en-publicaties/rapporten/2008/03/12/handboek-agressie-en-geweld.html (in Dutch)

17. Rafaeli, A., Erez, A., Ravid, S., Derfler-Rozin, R., Treister, D.E., Scheyer, R.: When customers exhibit verbal aggression, employees pay cognitive costs. J. Appl. Psychol. 97(5), 931–950 (2012)

18. Ritterfeld, U., Cody, M., Vorderer, P. (eds.): Serious Games: Mechanisms and Effects. Routledge, New York (2009)

19. Provoost, S.: A Computational Model of Aggression De-escalation. M.Sc. Thesis, VU University Amsterdam. (2014), http://hdl.handle.net/1871/50480

20. de Vries, R.: Reader Sociale Vaardigheden. Technical Report, Police Academy of the Netherlands, School voor Politiekunde (2011) (in Dutch)

Mosca

A Case Study on Collaborative Work – Combining Dimensions while Learning

Sílvia Castro

Escola Superior de Educação do Instituto Politécnico de Santarém, Santarém, Portugal
silvia.castro@ese.ipsantarem.pt, silvia.r.c.castro@gmail.com

Abstract. *"Mosca"* was an art project developed by art students, on a context of formal education, the project was designed in a collaborative learning mode. Throughout the presentation of this project one will reflect, on an empirical basis, as an actor and observer, upon the working platforms and the dimensions which were experienced in a very active and intuitive way: the physical and the virtual dimensions, used in order to create a physical event.

Keywords: art education, collaborative learning, virtual dimension, social media, project design.

1 Introduction

"MOSCA", the art project that will be presented in a very brief way was at first developed in a formal education context, with art students.

Together students had to conceive, plan, produce, set and promote their art exhibition, in a physical space, within the local community.

Along the development of the project due to some constrains, such as time, integration and cooperation, virtual platforms and virtual tools came to be suggested and utilized being part and playing an important role in this collaborative learning process.

The use of those platforms was very intuitive by the whole group, one will identify the tools and how the use of these tools contributed to the design of the project and bowed the project into a much more interactive and dynamic learning experience to the group, improving by consequence the outcomes.

As a teacher who adopts collaborative learning as a method, it is a constant to ponder upon practices, learning processes and outcomes. As Walker [1], I can identify the dimension of the teacher within this method as "a facilitator and mentor": (…) A teacher's role... is to respond quickly to questions, to coach individual groups, to identify common difficulties, and to suggest new approaches." Consequently one can draw a line of thought according to Dillenbourg [2] and try "(…) to understand the role which (…) variables play in the mediating interaction". As a teacher, to understand these variables can lead to the improvement of skills in a mediating process, which can reflect on the quality of learning processes.

P. Zaphiris and A. Ioannou (Eds.): LCT 2014, Part II, LNCS 8524, pp. 388–396, 2014.
© Springer International Publishing Switzerland 2014

Now that this project terminated, it seems to be important to reflect on how physical and virtual dimensions intertwine, as variables and can become a plus for art students learning processes in order to integrate these dimensions in a more precise way, concerning collaborative learning future projects in my practice.

As it is a very recent project, one can only bring it in an empirical level, sharing the experience.

In a first moment one will build some considerations on collaborative learning, followed by context, than:

- the group will be characterized
- the project will be presented in a very brief way
- some of the important stages of the project will be mentioned
- there will be the identification of the tools which were used
- how these tools were used by the group
- finally, ponder upon group results and collaborative learning through the use of technology.

2   Some Considerations on Collaborative Learning

Doise [3] states "… it is above all through interacting with others, coordinating his/her approaches to reality with those of others, that the individual masters new approaches".

Through collaborative learning each individual brings his/her own experience and knowledge to a team, meaning, an individual experience turns into a plural experience, transforming the whole team, causing a certain impact, during this process of interaction and in the end, this learning experience which is acquired evolves to another level of knowledge within each involved participant. According to Dillenbourg [2], "individual development allows participation in certain social interactions which produce new individual states which in turn, make possible more sophisticated social interaction (…)", in this line of thought one dares to add that through this level of "social interaction" social engagement comes hand in hand, raising a learning experience inter learners and reinforcing acquired knowledge through experience.

As little as the contribution might be it will enforce any kind of outcome, and the whole sphere of involvement: it will affect the producer, the user, the whole learning experience.

Translated in English language, "MOSCA", the name of the project that was chosen by the students, means, "FLY".

The fly, was taken as the concept of this gather venture as it was taken as a starting point to conceptualize multiple ways and perspectives, just like the insect's vision: multiple.

Around the same theme/concept, which was open enough to bring their personal contributions students produced a body of work, resulting an in an exhibition that mirrored their own multiple perspectives on contemporary world.

3   The Context, the Working Group and the Project

The project was developed in a formal education context, within the duration of a semester.

The learning unit in which the project took place, sets very clear objectives, the student has to:

- Identify different kinds of institutions where artists can operate
- Know the functional structures in the Visual Arts system; acquire a real understanding on how those structures operate in order to be able to relate to them, envisioning an integrated career in arts, along with his/hers inherent creative production.
- To have contact with institutions which can promote a cultural event
- To have an opportunity to experience the real implications of the production of an exhibition
- Experience the impact of his/her art works and experience in a real ground basis the level of involvement with and within a community.

In one's experience, involving students in a collaborative learning platform has its advantages: strengths motivation, promotes autonomy, creates the awareness that working with peers can be an advantage and quite an enriching and creative process. As the level of interaction rises, students also learn about ways to facilitate problem solving individually and collectively.

In former years, in the learning unit's context, students were invited to organize their graduation show and two exhibitions took place, mirroring a collaborative work and reflecting the students academic works on the majors of the degree of Visual Arts and Multimedia, evidencing the academic context of the event.

Both exhibitions were characterized by a wide variety of works, involving different mediums such as painting, sculpture, video animation, digital painting, and other mediums.

This year, as I accompanied the students, in other learning units, on the two previous years, one was familiar with the work of each individual, each student's capability and fragilities, and correspondent level of interaction in the group. Relational proximity with the group allowed to take the chance and confer students with even more autonomy, opting to challenge them to create their own works in an autonomous way, either creating individually or collectively, instead of exhibiting academic exercises which would not reveal so much their own personal approaches on art.

Fig. 1. The group photo, in the opening night of the exhibition

The class was quite large, composed by 34 students.

In a collaborative learning and working method, students were invited to develop their own exhibition project: conceiving, planning, producing (the works and the exhibition), setting and promoting the event – it was a design project which had to be very well planned as it involved so many stages and was not facilitated with such a large group of participants.

The first stages of the project's design happened on a physical dimension, in the classroom, as a whole team.

In the practice of art education, students learn to act as critical individuals and learn how to be active on their own educational process, similarly to the collaborative learning process; with this project students brought that attitude and learnt as a group. As the group started to be active, every week there would be different topics to reflect upon, practical matters to manage and major decisions to the project.

First, we reflected upon the identity of the group, some brainstorming sessions occurred to achieve this goal and after followed the search for the motto of the exhibition: "MOSCA".

The decision where the exhibition would take place, according to the concept, was also taken in the classroom, as a whole group.

After these stages, it was necessary to take in consideration the timings and actions such as the budget and activities to fundraise the project, a plan had to be built constrained by the length of the semester in order to achieve all the learning objectives, according to the formal academic context.

It was decided that for the fundraising two major events would happen:

- An art market in the city centre, by the Christmas time.
- A dinner ceremony, cooked by the group with all the students of the course, including alumni.

4   Combining Dimensions - Combining Communication

To promote both activities as fundraising and others similar that would follow, such as the communication design of the event, the class had to be split in smaller groups.

Randomly, the students were free to choose the preferred activity and the peers to work with. Though there were split groups for specific tasks, collaborative mode was kept and fundamental, all the members worked as a whole.

In order to achieve all the learning objectives and bring the exhibition as an outcome in "useful" time we opted to work with different dimensions of communication.

A parallel path of communication started to be drawn on a virtual dimension, by using some platforms that were used every time we would have to make a decision but would not be able to be physically present. This form of communication was for internal functionality and later was also used for external communication with the community.

Fig. 2. Page of the Art Market, promoted through the *Facebook*

5   Facebook Branching

Given the formal education context, as mentioned above, every week we would meet in the classroom/studio, on a physical dimension and in a virtual dimension, it was proposed the regular use of a social network. We created a working group on Facebook it was our main virtual platform to work, though others have came to be used.

During the project: GoogleDrive and YouTube were used, in the end three virtual platforms contributed for this project.

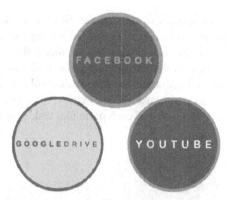

Fig. 3. The three virtual platforms that were used in the project

Fig. 4. Facebook was the main platform used by the group, the other platforms were worked in a integrated mode

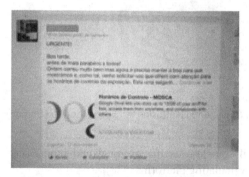

Fig. 5. One of the urgent moments the group had to deal via *Facebook*

Facebook was the main virtual platform in use but along the project the other two: GoogleDrive and Youtube were used in an integrated mode, meaning Facebook came to be the main frame of work on virtual ground though branched and complemented with the other two platforms.

Googledrive was used specifically to create files that would concern careful planning, as the platform allows constant access and editing tools, to all members.

Youtube was used to share videos that would touch the subject matter of the project and would be shared on the Facebook's group and was also used to promote the activities of the group and document the processes involved on the project.

The group made an adequate use of the virtual platforms, we have worked according to the grade of complexity of each particular task or purpose.

Fig. 6. The three platforms were used for different purposes

The use of email was less as the group would report activity on *Googledrive* through *Facebook*, articulating platforms.

One can only think about the advantages on combining a physical and virtual dimension, as they resulted to be quite complementary but also playing different roles.

6   The Results

1. In a physical dimension: the classroom

In the classroom, meetings came to be a place to conceptualize, orientate and manage practical matters but also were managed interpersonal problems that came not to be so evident in the virtual dimension that was in use. Apparently, the group was much more emotive when physically present as critics came to happen much more in this kind of dimension. Critical thought was more marked.

In the classroom, our meetings would also be used to share results and make a brief of the previous week activities and the activities that would have be developed on the week that would come.

2. At distance, on the virtual dimension, groups:

— Have met to organize, produce and promote the event
— Have made contacts concerning the production of the event
— Have reported results and managed production details
— Worked together on the creative process of communication materials
— Interacted in the production of communication materials

It seems that in this dimension there was a higher level of efficiency on problem solving, positive feedback was regular between peers and suggestions were well embraced with active and autonomous response of the group.

Shared information was constant in the working group as several students took the initiative to share the information about the work of other artists.

3. After combined dimensions, some results

In a moment such as a setting of an exhibition, a sense of pressure is quite normal and the need to have the ability to deal with last minute resolutions is necessary. In the case of a collective exhibition interpersonal matters normally add, due to pressure. By the moment of the setting of the exhibition the group revealed a different and better quality level concerning problem solving and it seemed to have acquired better communication skills. One can associate that working in the two different dimensions of communication might have contributed.

The promotion of the event, which was worked on the virtual dimension, produced on Facebook and on Youtube, seems also to have had impact on the local community and in the media.

By means of physical and virtual communication products, the group managed to gather around two hundred people in the gallery, in the opening evening, and frequent visitors during the rest of period.

The local media were also very supportive about the project.

7   To Conclude

Within a complex project, which involved several work fronts, the large number of involved people became an advantage. One's opinion is that the design process and the use of social media played a essential role. Combining dimensions of communication was and can be an advantageous working and learning method, not only to produce but also to develop qualities of interaction.

The "MOSCA" project was possible on a very short term due to high levels of engagement of active individuals but also by means of combining physical and virtual working platforms, the two platforms were a common ground to each individual of the group, this can mean that collaborative work can be quite empowered by the interaction of individuals on a physical dimension but on a virtual dimension as well, depending on the levels of digital literacy of each work group.

Individuals analyze and solve problems in a different way depending on dimensions, physical or virtual.

There are also procedural problems that come from the physical or virtual dimension.

The combination between the two dimensions can allow the reduction of physical and virtual blanks, this might be considered regarding the quality of interaction or concerning problem solving at a more practical level.

8   To Visualize

To watch the video of the set up of the exhibition
The event that was create on Facebook
The page of the project on Facebook
The event that was created on Facebook for the Art Market
To watch how the Art Market happened

References

1. Miller, H.M.: Learning Collaborative: a working paper (1997),
   http://www.math.grin.edu/~walker/coll-learning/index.html
   (February 19, 2014)
2. Dillenbourg, P., Baker, M., Blaye, A., O'Malley, C.: The evolution of research on collaborative learning (1996), http://tecfa.unige.ch/tecfa/publicat/dil-papers-2/Dil.7.1.10.pdf
3. Doise, W.: The development of individual competencies through social interaction. In: Foot, H.C., Morgan, M.J., Shute, R.H. (eds.) Children helping Children, pp. 43–64. J. Wiley & Sons, Chichester (1990)

A New Way to Community Services
Communication with Administration

Habib M. Fardoun[1], Daniyal M. Alghazzawi[1], Antonio Paules Ciprés[2],
and Sebastián Romero López[3]

[1] King Abdulaziz University,
Faculty of Computing and Information Technology,
Information Systems Department,
21589 Jeddah, Saudi Arabia
{hfardoun,dghazzawi}@kau.edu.sa
Information Systems Department,
Albacete, Spain
sebstian.romero@gmail.com
[2] European University of Madrid,
Madrid, Spain
apcipres@gmail.com
[3] University of Castilla-La Mancha
Computer College of Albacete

Abstract. In this paper we are going to describe the architecture of community services by mean mobile devices. We opt for a direct communication between the mobile users and server information and where users interact directly from their mobile devices and the cloud system, by leaving a record of the accused and requested data. As result of this improvement in the process, we have a platform that saves costs and time management to users of these services in the instantiation and regular payments to government claims.

Keywords: Mobile devices, Cloud, Community Services, Administration, Citizens.

1   Introduction

In this article we are going to perform some community services where the architecture is defined by the mobile devices. The increase in both mobile and tablet mobile devices between citizen has been exponential over the past years. The 63.2% of mobile users has one of these types of devices. Despite being the most expensive and the recession experienced by the country, this rate exceeds the rate of the United Kingdom (62.3%), France (51.4%), Italy (51.2%) and Germany (48.4%). [1]

All these mobile devices have 3G, 4G broadband Internet connection or WiFi, where the speed of data transmission is suitable for communication with the offices of the city government. The public administration have public information offices and records for the entry of the official documentation and communication of official bulletins, on the other hand, it has a system for regular payments, in which citizens make their payments by mean of bank transfer, obtaining the subsequent receipt or by mean a payment of the fee bill for that service.

P. Zaphiris and A. Ioannou (Eds.): LCT 2014, Part II, LNCS 8524, pp. 397–407, 2014.
© Springer International Publishing Switzerland 2014

In this case we opt for a direct communication between the mobile users and server information, instead of using a cloud large system, we will try to make a simple system where users interact directly from their mobile devices and the cloud system, by leaving a record of the accused and requested data by checking the activity log or the parameters required. With a system like this, we would have a platform that would save costs and time management to users of these services in the instantiation and regular payments to government claims.

2   State of Art

Currently the communication systems with public administration are provided by the citizen's office, each public administration has a different system, the region's city hall, the county, the central government in its officiate, this is true for both traditional offices and Web sites that offer online services to citizens. [2]

In a system of these characteristics we should find:

- Agility sending and receiving documents.
- Agility in the processing and validation.
- Agility in doubts' resolution.
- Permission to run multiple processes simultaneously.
- Direct and personalized attention with users
- Integration of different services offered by different public entities.
- Authentication and electronic registration of incidents.
- Generating warnings for electronic confirmation of income or output registration.

We have to keep in mind that administrative systems are normal instances and we can find many instances according to each of the different public administrations. The process that we have to undertake is explained below:

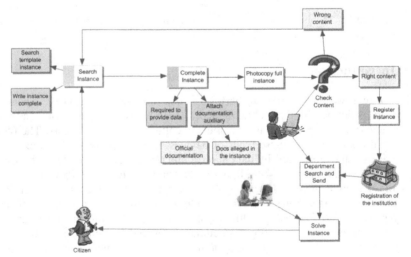

Fig. 1. Current Operation

As we can see, there are different parts in the creation of a request's receipt. First citizens must search the standard instance for creating an ordinary paper or fill out a pdf. For that we need to complete the instance with the required arguments and the necessary documentation. Once the instance is done, the officer proceeds to check in order to perform a verification of the information's correction. After that, they proceed to the instance registration at the registry office and to the request delivery to the officer, who must solve the instance, and send this resolution to the citizen.

There is no direct communication between the instance's solver and citizens so that an error in the documentation not controlled makes the process starts again. Once the instance is opened, this is closed with this resolution and must be restarted again to make every step. Bank transfer or deposit in banks, nowadays makes payments to public administration, fees and administrative penalties.

As we can see now the information system that manages these requests is limited to a web page and an email where the instance is processed. There are no payment gateways or personalized online citizen services. The realizations of these management processes are performed in complex ways and sometimes repeatedly, until citizens receive the reply to their bureaucratic paperwork with the state's administration of the local regions.

We must realize that the administrative process must comply with state law, law of the local region, municipalities and counties. All the regulations depend on each other and regulations and laws complement the higher laws [3]. A system like this would be included in the e-Government for the transparency and the improvement in the communication with the citizens. Thus, we allow them to carry several different operations out, especially those where multiple agencies are involved, without the need for contacting each of them [4]. A single access point reinforces citizen participation in democratic processes because the citizens can easily use administrative procedures and the most convenient way to express their needs to public servers. [5]

3   Objective

Our main goal in this research is approaching a way that enables a system like this to streamline its operations, both for making payments to the administration and for the creation of instances in the process. Since the instance or the administrative process is opened until it ends, considering that the arguments to this fact are included within the process.

Reception and agility of information is done by making the data process be validated by an expert or whoever has to solve the instance and calling for applications in real time or within a short period. It is not the same making a medical demand that making a request for information. This categorization of instances is performed by the administration itself. Therefore officials treat instances and applications in one way or another depending of specific criteria. This fact is well accepted always that it speeds up the process [8][9].

In the previous section we referred the legal rules of public administration and the administrative procedure, as we can see, there are many laws and amendments, which must be followed [5] joined to the law of administrative procedure [6].

4   Definition

Our definition does not controvert the current legislation, we intend to make a system in where different platforms can interact, users can make inquiries and the different administrations can use it in order to streamline their official paper works [10][11].

The cloud system must fulfil the existing law, or in other words, the cloud system as a whole must receive the approval of the official register, as all the regulations would be adjusted to the existing law and also the administrative act would be guaranteed by the different legislations. In the Cloud systems, layers can be added depending on the complexity level of the system itself. We will add to this architecture two very significant layers: the legislative layer, where the instances will be linked to meet the administrative act and the administrative procedure; and the layer monitoring and its resolution, where all the instances and procedures will be accommodated to their completion and archiving.

5   Architecture

In an architecture that solves these needs, we need a big storage for instances and attachments. Therefore we need a cataloguing system for them through the departments that will be associated to the platform and the space for placing on record along the time [12].

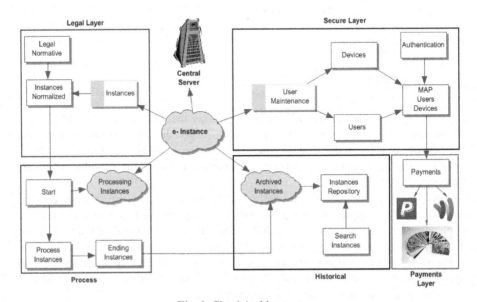

Fig. 2. Cloud Architecture

As we can see above in the diagram, we can also find the layers of an operating system of these features [13]. We can meet below a description of them:

- **Legal Layer:** In this layer, instances are constructed from legal formalities. In the construction of instances by departments we obtain a normalized instance, which is also listed for various agencies. This layer must have a cataloguing system that allows users to find the instance. This layer contains also legal regulations in order to allow the worker to build the instance according to current regulations.
- **Secure Layer:** In this layer the mapping between the user device and the end user is done. In this way we get a safe access, users will only have access from devices discharged by the system, thus we increase the security. There are two ways to do this: the citizen goes to the city centre for the first time and discharge his mobile application or by accessing the electronic ID card and thus authenticate the user on the device.
- **Process:** This layer is where the build process instance and its verification is done, this request is received by the employee of the department, who receives the instance, and once started the process, the communication procedure between the citizen and the worker is established in order to include documentation and data necessary to complete the instance. This is currently done by instances and resolutions. At this point we make the full resolution in an administrative procedure in order to expedite the process and reduce inconveniences to citizens.
- **Historical:** Once the instanced is resolved, this instance is stored in a repository so that the system's stakeholders can have access to it, in this section we have to remember that we must store all the contents and also the different laws which the formation of the instance and its resolution are based, because the legislative layer must remain updated and instances once are completed are not retroactive.
- **Payment Layer:** This layer is where the payment of taxes is made in the administrative procedures. The payment is stored in the historical order to allow the user's processes the request and receipt of payment in the proper department. It is usual that the payment rate be associated to an official document that starts an instance without further complexity.

The figure below shows the system logical structure by using FOBT [7]:

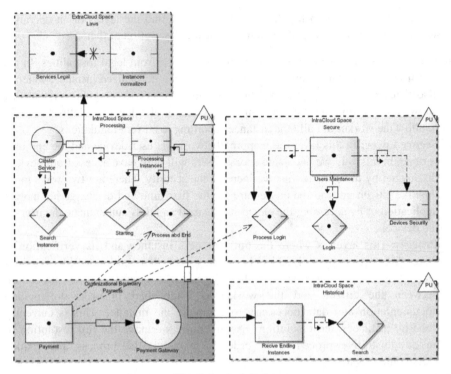

Fig. 3. Logical design

As we can see in this logical design, we establish the different parts of the system in the cloud and the performance. The logical process is developed in the cloud even during the interaction with users; in this way we can increase the safety and speed in the development of the instances.

These objects in the cloud are shared in memory spaces allocated to both users and can perform jumps between processes with no time for the user. We must remember that the transaction time is minimal, but bandwidth is limited to a server of these characteristics due to that the number of users connected simultaneously is elevated. By placing all the business logic in the cloud, the design differs from what we are used to, for example, for each transaction or process's change, the validation is performed by login in order to record all the user steps in the database. Further, we can use external systems to the cloud, where modifications are done by another department and employ a service bus for both to communicate the cloud with outside and to allow receiving data from other applications, through the buses where we control the bandwidth and security.

6   Study Case

This study case reports the receiving instances in the secretary of the education department as we can see at the following screenshot:

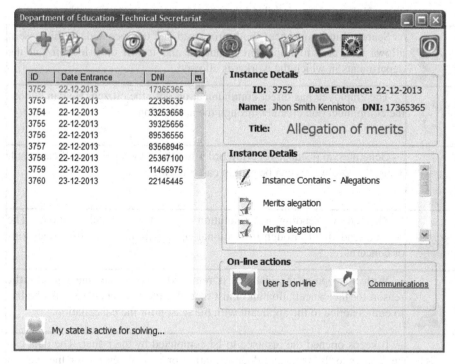

Fig. 4. Screen of Technical Secretariat

The worker has access to all instances assigned by the registry. He proceeds to review the request and processes the resolution. We see that the interface section "Online actions" allows the worker to contact with the active user through the application. From this screen the user can perform the following actions:

Table 1. Icons

	The worker performs an internal instance. Sometimes it is necessary to proceed with interdepartmental requests in order to clarify the legislation which solves citizens' instances.
	The worker performs the selected instance processing, allowing him to make the resolution of this instance.
	This option allows the worker to add the resolution to outstand, in order to see that it is an instance in process and should be handled as soon as possible.

Table 1. (*continued*)

	Search Button instances, both processed and unprocessed. In this case it allows to access to important instances, and it will only look for at the departments in which the worker is allowed.
	The employee has direct communication with the citizen. He can choose the communication channel through the application.
	Generates an instance report in order to send it by regular certificate mail. Thus, the resolutions can be sent in case they are necessary.
	This allows sending the resolution report to an email recipient. The service sends mail through institutional email with the resolution, questions or concerns.
	With this option the instance is removed. The worker must justify the reason for the cancellation and must record it into the database. Also he has to emit a notice to the applicant with the reason for the cancellation.
	It keeps opened the instance to be completed by the issuer. The data can be: complete the instance, documentation or a legal reason for the request can be closed.
	Allows searching the law regulations to perform the resolution of the instance or application.
	Settings panel of the application.
	The application detects the availability of the user through the application in order to the worker can contact to the citizen to inform him about the requested incidents.
	Communications are stored in the system. Citizens can perform queries that will be queued in the system and then the worker will contact him depending on the need.
	With this option, the employee may make a change of state to inform the citizen that he is working on the resolution of his/her instance.

The application is installed into the citizens' terminals to allow them to create instances and to send them directly to the registration [14]. As we see in the following illustration, it is a simple and usable application where the user fills his court and claims the documents necessary for the registration.

Fig. 5. Application into citizen's mobile terminal

Table 2. Mobile icons

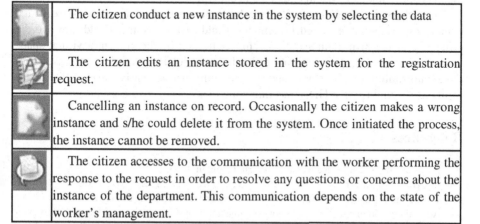

	The citizen conduct a new instance in the system by selecting the data
	The citizen edits an instance stored in the system for the registration request.
	Cancelling an instance on record. Occasionally the citizen makes a wrong instance and s/he could delete it from the system. Once initiated the process, the instance cannot be removed.
	The citizen accesses to the communication with the worker performing the response to the request in order to resolve any questions or concerns about the instance of the department. This communication depends on the state of the worker's management.

The application has not the save option, this is due to optimization of resources in the cloud system [15]. The system itself detects the changes and saves the changes as well as we can also see that do not have the export option. This is because in this way the unique existence of the instance is fully guaranteed for privacy and it won't have problems with the country´s legislation, because the data is stored in a secure system without the possibility of modifying the set of data instances or request sent. We have previously named the PayPal option. In this case we have determined that the worker performs the request for the payment of the application after their revision, thus we reduce the citizen's costs.

7   Conclusions

This is a paper that begins a new research line integrating the e-democracy. We understand that the administration must allow to the citizens the quick send of instances and to reduce the time necessary to their request even when these are wrong and must be solved. A system of these characteristics creates many questions and others that all of you are going to ask during the presentation. Therefore we need a system that answers this question: Is it possible to certify a Cloud system in which the system is included into the administrative procedure?

We have asked to judges and state lawyer and in both cases their answer has been easy, the content can be modified and falsified. Facing this fact we have made this thought: if I were able to treat, inside of the own Cloud system, the instances like non modifiable objects, in other words, to make a copy of them in a system non accessible from outside and that it were possible to make a copy from inside of the Cloud (Everyone knows about RAID systems in the hard disks). This makes us to think about another difficult question to solve, but it is possible that in the future it will be solved from the operating system. The theme is that the operating systems oriented to e-democracy systems give to citizens a safe space for storage with intern copy, allowing the access to one of the system's layers and the realization of a copy of that memory space to other system updated and encrypted with biometrical data.

The technologic evolution will come but before we need to make aware to the administration that an elevated investment would save costs and would improve the efficiency of the own administration. The set formed by the citizen, a virtual space with biometric encryption, a section of hard disk inviolable where the processes with the administration can be stored and sensible information can be saved, all of these form the e-AdministrativeHD, a meeting point to access to citizen's data.

References

1. Eurostat (Statistical Office of the European Communities),
   http://epp.eurostat.ec.europa.eu/statistics_explained/
   index.php/Telecommunication_statistics#Main_tables
2. Administración electrónica y gestión documental. Consideraciones a la luz de la Ley para el Acceso Electrónico de los Ciudadanos a los Servicios Públicos. Carlota Bustelo y Elisa García-Morales. El Profesional de la Informacion 17(1), 106–111 (January-February 2008) ISNN 1386-6710

3. Glassey, O.: Developing a one-stop government data model. en Government Information Quaterly 21(2), 156–169 (2004)
4. Yong, J.S. (ed.): E-Government in Asia, Time Editions, Singapur (2003)
5. Leyes del procedimiento administrativo, http://legislacion.060.es/procedimiento_administrativo_regimen_juridico-ides-idweb.html
6. Ley 11/2007, de 22 de junio, de acceso electrónico de los ciudadanos a los Servicios Públicos. «BOE» núm. 150, de 23 de junio de, páginas 27150 a 27166 (17 págs.) (2007)
7. Service-OrientedModeling Framework, http://www.sparxsystems.com.au/somf
8. Ammons, D.N.: Municipal Benchmarks: Assessing local performance and establishing community standards (2012) ISBN: 978-0-7656-2660-8
9. Lance Bennett, W., Wells, C., Freelon, D.: Communicating Civic Engagement: Contrasting Models of Citizenship in the Youth Web Sphere. Journal of Communication 61(5), 835–856 (2011), doi:10.1111/j.1460-2466.2011.01588.x
10. Nam, T.: Suggesting frameworks of citizen-sourcing via Government 2.0. Government Information Quarterly 29(1), 12–20 (2012)
11. Meijer, A.J.: Networked Coproduction of Public Services in Virtual Communities: From a Government-Centric to a Community Approach to Public Service Support. Public Administration Review 71(4), 598–607 (2011), doi:10.1111/j.1540-6210.2011.02391.x
12. Feller, J., Finnegan, P., Nilsson, O.: Open innovation and public administration: transformational typologies and business model impacts. European Journal of Information Systems 20, 358–374 (2011), doi:10.1057/ejis.2010.65
13. Fardoun, H.M., Ciprés, A.P., Alghazzawi, D.M.: CSchool-DUI for Educational System using Clouds. In: Proceedings of the 2nd Workshop on Distributed User Interfaces: Collaboration and Usability, Conjunction with CHI 2012 Conference Austin, Texas, USA, pp. 84–695 (2012) ISBN-10
14. Fardoun, H.M., Zafar, B., Altalhi, A.H., Paules, A.: Interactive Design System for Schools using Cloud Computing. Journal of Universal Computer Science 19(7), 950–964 (2013)
15. Fardoun, H.M., Cipres, A.P., Alghazzwi, D.M.: Distributed User Interfaces in a Cloud Educational System. In: Distributed User Interfaces: Usability and Collaboration, pp. 151–163. Springer, London (2013)

Online Collaboration: Individual Involvement Used to Predict Team Performance

Walkyria Goode and Guido Caicedo

ESPAE-ESPOL, Guayaquil, Ecuador
{wgoode,caicedo}@espol.edu.ec

Abstract. Social media – with its collaborative and interactive functionalities – is an ideal platform for collaboration. Several teams were asked to create material using a content management system. Log records were analyzed to measure group and individual participation. Direct and indirect measures of involvement are used as predictor variables. A model is proposed that uses system-tracked data to forecast team performance.

Keywords: collaboration, collaborative computing, team performance.

1 Introduction

Educators and researchers have been experimenting with social media technologies (e.g. blogs, wikis) for collaborative learning. Social media stimulates knowledge construction by emphasizing collaboration and interaction. Active learning is accomplished through dialogue and connections within online communities, information is exchanged and content is collaboratively created [3].

An advantage of using social media tools in a team oriented educational environment is that these tools record logs of individual team member involvement. Educators usually rely on peer- or self-reports of team members' participation. The logged data can be used to establish the degree of team participation. This note is a first step into investigating the relationship between team participation and team performance in an online learning setting.

1.1 Collaboration and Teams

A team is a group of people with complementary skills that are committed to a common goal, performance objectives and a process that holds them mutually responsible [6]. Team members need to understand the skills required to create effective and synergistic results. Attributes of successful teams include outcome interdependence and participation [10,6].

Outcome interdependence involves the encouragement of all team members to contribute. Personal benefits depend on successful goal achievement by the rest of the team members. Interdependence leads individuals to share responsibilities and increases collaborative social interaction [12]. A synergistic environment is created

P. Zaphiris and A. Ioannou (Eds.): LCT 2014, Part II, LNCS 8524, pp. 408–416, 2014.
© Springer International Publishing Switzerland 2014

when – through collaboration – individuals achieve goals at a superior level. Research on student groups in an international business degree program found that interdependence predicts team learning behavior [11].

Effective team participation entails equitable sharing of information and workload that promotes the exchange and integration of information. Studies have shown that participation fosters learning by acquiring, sharing and constructing knowledge [4,7]. Teams with unequal participation or teams with instances of social loafing / free riding produce lower quality results and poor satisfaction [8]. Fair workload distribution is positively related with performance and satisfaction [10].

It is hypothesized that effective team participation will contribute to higher team performance. Students will value outcome interdependence.

1.2   Background

The study was performed as part of a graduate business course assignment. Teams of students were assigned to collaboratively author blogs related to class material.

2   Study

2.1   Method

Using regression analysis, the study evaluates the contribution of team participation to the prediction of team performance. Performance is measured by the grade each blog entry received. Team participation is represented by direct and indirect measures. The number of edits made in a blog and participation rates are considered direct measures. A participation rate indicates the proportion of team members that worked on each specific blog. Indirect measures for team participation are the number of views and comments made by team members in their blogs. The model proposed is represented in Table 1.

Table 1. Model for Team Performance

Model	$TP = \alpha + \beta_1 PR_i + \beta_2 E_i + \beta_3 C_i + \beta_4 V_i + \varepsilon_i$	
Dependent Variable	TP: Team Performance	
Independent Variable	Direct Measures	PR: Participation Rate
		E: Number of Edits
	Indirect Measures	C: Number of Comments
		V: Number of Views

2.2   Participants

The sample for this study consisted of 21 students enrolled at the final year of a MBA program. There were 10 females and 11 males. The average age was 31, with a standard deviation of 4.9 years. Sixteen students worked full time and all possess an undergraduate degree. Group size ranged from 3 to 5 students. There were a total of 5 groups. Students stayed in the same group throughout the course.

2.3   Materials

The instructor created team blogs in a content management system using the WordPress platform (http://wordpress.com). This system allows collaborative authoring and recognizes three types of roles: (i) An Editor can publish, edit, and delete any posts, moderate comments, upload files/images and manage categories, tags, and links, (ii) An Author can edit, publish and delete their posts, as well as upload files/images, (iii) A Contributor can edit their posts but cannot publish them. All team members were assigned Author roles and one member in each team was designated Editor.

2.4   Procedure

Teams published a weekly blog during an eight-week period. Entries were concise essays of a topic of interest covered in class. To promote creative and associational thinking, each entry had to include three references to relevant articles or websites. Requirements specified word count, type of reference (one academic and two non-academic) and proper use of APA style [1]. All members were expected to contribute.

Before deadline, the instructor would comment on the blog providing feedback regarding requirements. Each entry was graded. Students were allowed to comment on their own blogs and enter additional references.

Towards the end of the course, students filled out a peer evaluation form as part of their team project and a survey for extra credit. The survey was used to evaluate several social media tools used in the classroom.

3   Results

Teams varied in group size. Participation rate is not affected by group size. However, the total number of edits, comments and views can be influenced by group size. These measures were evaluated as both totals and weights (i.e. total number of edits versus number of edits weighted by group size). Both analyses resulted in similar tendencies. For ease of comprehension, totals will be reported in this note.

All team members were expected to participate in the creation of each blog entry. However, this was not the case, resulting in different participation rates per blog within each team. Figure 1 uses a modified version of a treemap to graphically represent how team members contributed to each of the eight blog entries. Contribution is defined as the number of edits a team member made. A treemap is space-constrained display of data as nested rectangles [9]. Each post is given a rectangle (B1, B2, etc.) and is tiled with smaller rectangles representing the individual contribution of each team member (P1, P2, Q1, Q2, etc.), individual contributions are measured in percentage and add up to 100%. In Teams P, S and T, all team members participated to a certain degree. In Team Q, team member Q2 did not contribute at all. In Team R, team member R3 published almost all posts. These different rates of contribution are expected to affect a team's performance.

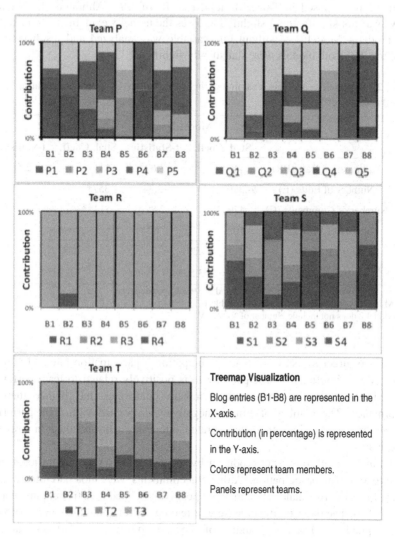

Fig. 1. Team Member Contribution per Blog Entry per Team

A multiple regression analysis was used with blog entries as the units of analysis (i.e. the grade of an entry is the dependent variable). There were five groups and eight entries per group (See Table 2). Two models were compared:

Model 1: $TP = \alpha + \beta_1 PR_i + \beta_2 E_i + \beta_3 C_i + \beta_4 V_i + \varepsilon_i$ (1)

$$\text{Model 2:} \quad TP = \alpha + \beta_1 PR_i + \beta_2 E_i + \beta_3 C_i + \varepsilon_i \tag{2}$$

Model 1 (proposed in Table 1) yielded an R^2 of .291. Although, the Number of Views was not significant, it slightly increases the model's explained variance (R^2). A new model – Model 2 – without this variable was analyzed and resulted in an R^2 equal to .283. Both models were statistically significant.

Table 2. Regression analysis examining the contribution of team participation on team performance (N=40)

	Model 1		Model 2	
	Strd. Coeff.	t-Statistic	Strd. Coeff.	t-Statistic
Participation Rate (PR)	.446*	2.62	.431*	2.58
Number of Edits (E)	-.390*	-2.34	-.357*	-2.27
Number of Comments (C)	.479**	2.89	.514**	3.33
Number of Views (V)	.102	.62	-	-
R^2		.291		.283
F-Statistic		3.59*		4.73**

**, * Statistically significant at the 1% and 5% levels, respectively.
Model 1 is equivalent to the Model in Table 1.
Model 2 does not include Number of Views (V).

The two direct measures of team participation – participation rate and number of edits – were significant. Participation rate is positively related to team performance (See Figure 2(a)). If more team members contribute, the higher their team performance. The number of edits is negatively associated with team performance (See Figure 2(b)). Blogs that incorporated numerous edits resulted in lower team performance.

The number of comments produced by team members was a significant indirect measure of team participation. Although, comments were not part of the grading policy, higher performance appears to be positively related to active commentary (See Figure 2(c)). The other indirect measure of team participation – the number of views – was dropped in Model 2. Number of views is positively – but not statistically significant- related to team performance (See Figure 2(d)).

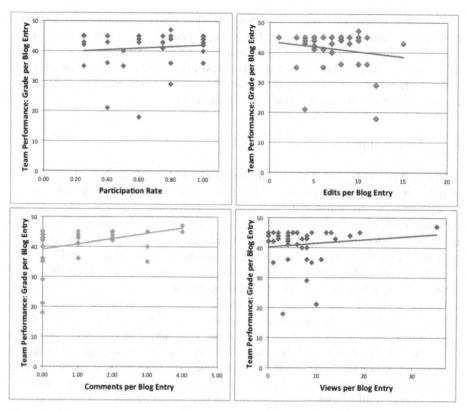

Fig. 2. Team Performance: Grade per Blog Entry (50/50) by (a) Participant Rate, (b) Edits per Blog Entry, (c) Comments per Blog Entry, (d) Views per Blog Entry

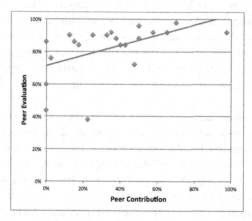

Fig. 3. Outcome interdependence: Peer evaluation by peer contribution

Outcome interdependence is evident in the positive relationship between participation and performance, as shown in Figure 3. The integration of more individual contributions results in blogs with higher grades. Students were intuitively aware of this outcome. Peer evaluation data is positively correlated with contribution, $r(21)= .51$, $p< .05$. Students gave higher ratings to team members with more contributions and punished free-riders with lower ratings.

4   Discussion

Team members were notified that participation was an integral component of the team project and that all individuals were expected to consistently participate. Nevertheless, teams showed different participation rates. Log data illustrate the presence of social loafing and the lone wolf phenomenon. A lone wolf is an individual that has a preference to work alone and dislikes group work. This individual is committed to achieve goals without the contributions of the rest of the team [5].

Although students generally do not endorse social loafing, fear of confrontation permits the existence of free-riders. Students mentioned that doing somebody's workload is easier than having an argument that could negatively affect team dynamics. In addition, the team usually does not trust the quality of work from a free-rider. A lone wolf considers the rest of the team to be subpar and prefers to not share the workload. The erroneous belief that a team product can be of high performance without the contribution of some team members is demonstrated in this study. Participation rate helps to predict team performance. Assignments developed by teams in which all or almost all team members contributed received higher grades than those by teams with poor participation rates.

An interesting finding relates to the negative relationship between the number of edits and team performance. It appears that the more effort teams put into developing their blogs, the lower grades these blogs received. This finding is based on quantitative data. The logs indicate the number of edits to a blog and not what type of edits were involved. A qualitative analysis has not been performed. Edits could have been directed towards the form and not the substance of a blog. It is believed that this is most likely the case. Teams showed concern towards the aesthetics of the blogs and were highly competitive on the type of media (images, slide shares, videos) their blogs contained.

The number of times members commented on their team blogs was considered as an indirect measure of team participation. Commentary is interpreted as an indicator of an individual's interest for the team product. Interest for a team product usually renders into active participation developing that product. The number of comments positively contributes to predict team performance. Blog entries with more comments received higher grades than those with fewer to no comments.

High outcome interdependence involves the encouragement of team members to participate. Teams reap from the benefits of their collective knowledge. Social loafing and the lone wolf phenomenon suggest that students are marginally aware of the benefits of outcome interdependence. However, the relationship between peer evaluation and contribution implies that members internally developed a reward system of sorts. Hard working team members received higher ratings than those who do not contribute.

Teams that actively participated in content creation benefited from a richer collaboration environment. The quality of their blogs was superior and was reflected in their grades. Active participation – in this context – implies greater involvement from all team members. It does not equal more work. Blogs with many edits indicate team members putting considerable effort into their authoring. However, this effort was not focused and resulted in lower quality assignments.

The resulting model serves to forecast performance and collaboration in a social media setting. Team participation rates and interest (as measured by number of comments and possibly number of views) positively predict performance. Effort - as measured by number of edits – is negatively related to performance. Type of effort was not measured.

4.1   Limitations

There are several limitations that need to be acknowledged and addressed regarding the present study. First, the study analyzes a single course. A replication is scheduled to increase the statistical power of these results. Second, the author was the instructor for the course. A social desirability bias could have influenced student survey responses. Social desirability is the tendency of individuals to seek approval [2]. In an attempt to minimize this bias, the survey was part of a set of surveys administered for extra credit towards several courses. Third, the type and quality of effort should be included in the model. This data will be incorporated in subsequent analyses.

References

1. American Psychological Association, Publication Manual of the American Psychological Association. American Psychological Association, Washington, DC (2010)
2. Crowne, D.P., Marlowe, D.: A new scale of social desirability independent of psychopathology. Journal of Consulting Psychology 38, 349–354 (1960)
3. Duffy, T.M., Cunningham, D.J.: Constructivism: Implications for the design and delivery of instruction. In: Jonassen, D. (ed.) Handbook of Research for Educational Communications and Technology, pp. 170–198. Simon & Schuster Macmillan, New York (1996)
4. Edmondson, A.: Psychological safety and learning behavior in work teams. Administrative Science Quarterly 44(2), 350–383 (1999)
5. Feldman Barr, T., Dixon, A.L.: Exploring the "Lone Wolf" phenomenon in student teams. Journal of Marketing Education 27(1), 81–90 (2005)
6. Katzenbach, J.R., Smith, D.K.: The Wisdom of Teams: Creating the High-performance Organization. Harvard Business School Press, Boston (1993)
7. Pfaff, E., Huddleston, P.: Does it matter if I hate teamwork? What impacts student attitudes toward teamwork. Journal of Marketing Education 25(1), 37–45 (2003)
8. Salomon, G., Globerson, T.: When teams do not function the way they ought to. International Journal of Educational Research 13(1), 89–100 (1989)

9. Shneiderman, B.: Tree visualization with tree-maps: 2-d space-filling approach. ACM Transactions on Graphics (TOG) 1, 92–99 (1992)
10. Tarricone, P., Luca, J.: Successful teamwork: A case study. In: HERDSA 2002, pp. 640–646 (2002)
11. Van den Bossche, P., Gijselaers, W.H., Segers, M., Kirschner, P.A.: Social and cognitive factors driving teamwork in collaborative learning environments: Team learning beliefs and behaviors. Small Group Research 37(5), 490–521 (2006)
12. Wageman, R.: Interdependence and group effectiveness. Administrative Science Quarterly 40, 145–180 (1995)

Interface Design for a Real-Time Collaborative Editing Tool

Nurul Naslia Khairuddin

Faculty of Computer Science, University of Malaya, Kuala Lumpur, Malaysia
nurul.naslia@gmail.com

Abstract. The topic Computer Supported Cooperative Work (CSCW) has been introduced since almost three decades now. Many tools have been invented to support different situations in cooperative work. Example of CSCW tools are instant messaging (IM), email, real-time document editor, forum, blog, group decision support system, electronic meeting room, voice chat, video conference and Real-Time Collaborative Editing (RTCE) tools. A study was conducted to investigate the advantages and disadvantages of applying CSCW approach on a class of multicultural undergraduate students as they plan their software project in virtual environment. Analysis of the gathered data was done focusing towards the problems faced during the discussion sessions. Solutions were derived based on the problems identified and an RTCE tool was designed aiming to assist small scale software project planning process in virtual collaborative environment while supporting group awareness for effective teamwork.

Keywords: CSCW, RTCE, Group Awareness.

1 Introduction

In 1984, the term Computer Supported Cooperative Work (CSCW) was first coined by Irene Greif and Paul Cashman [1]. The term came up to describe their research interest in the workshop they organized in Massachusetts, which was focusing on supporting work activities using computer systems.

There are many benefits provided by using the CSCW approach. Teams that are spatially dispersed but working on projects where communication is essential need a medium to connect their group members. With the use of CSCW tools, the team members can attend the discussion sessions at their own space. This reduces or eliminates the commute time and cost, as well as leasing or buying cost for a physical discussion area. Document storage space and maintenance costs and document searching time can also be reduced significantly [2].

Despite the advantages that CSCW can offer, the effectiveness of virtual teamwork highly depends on the CSCW tool used and the team members' individual behaviours that differ mostly affected by their cultures. In a virtual team, it is crucial to have good shared understanding among the team members through language [3]. In addition, "as team members communicate, they tend to filter information through

P. Zaphiris and A. Ioannou (Eds.): LCT 2014, Part II, LNCS 8524, pp. 417–428, 2014.
© Springer International Publishing Switzerland 2014

their cultural 'lenses', thereby giving rise to a potentially broad range of misinterpretations or distortions" [4]. Miscommunications can be reduced with the use of CSCW tools [2, 5].

Real-time collaborative editing (RTCE), also known as real-time distributed collaborative writing systems (RDCWS) or synchronous collaborative authoring (SCA) is an example of a CSCW tool. It is a groupware that allows multiple users to access, view, and edit the same computer file synchronously using globally dispersed computers.

Awareness in the CSCW context is defined as "an understanding of the activities of others which provides a context of your own activity" [6]. Group awareness refers to the knowledge of each other's state and activity in a collaborative work. Mendoza-Chapa et. al [7] defined group awareness as "a mental state of the users generated by their mutual interactions and by their interactions within the workspace".

Group awareness is crucial for effective virtual collaborative work. It has been proven that group awareness helps to simplify communication, improve coordination and assist convention in a shared workspace [6, 8-11]. Group awareness ensures understanding among group members in their discussion when using the tool [7, 11-13]. An extensive review on awareness support in distributed software development research papers was recently done by Steinmacher et. al [14].

2   Research Methodology

A study was carried out to investigate some of the RTCE tools' weaknesses using a chosen RTCE tool. The participants of the study were 25 undergraduate students majoring in Software Engineering. The study was done while they were working on their Project Management course assignment that took 30 percent of their final grade for the course. The students were given a task to plan a software project virtually and submit their project plans as their course assignment. All the study sessions were done during their course's laboratory sessions. The students came from different cultures and there were even minorities of different nationalities. Data were collected during the study using several data collection methods: recording, observation, surveys, document analysis and interviewing.

The 25 students were divided into five teams of five. They were grouped in the best way to achieve equal teams with the highest diversity degree as possible. Each team consisted students of both genders, two or more cultures, and with each team members' CGPA average equals to 2.90 ± 0.02. The list below provides the individual attributes of the students and the values they take:

- **Gender**: female, male
- **Education level**: second year Computer Science undergraduate students
- **Study major**: Software Engineering
- **CGPA**: from 0.00 to 4.00
- **Race**: China Chinese, Malaysian Chinese, Malaysian Indian, Malaysian Malay, Palestinian Arab
- **First language**: Arabic, Cantonese, English, Malay, Mandarin

During the laboratory sessions, the students' seats were pre-arranged. They were instructed to sit far from their own team members to disallow face to face communication among any team members and to set the virtual project team mood. However, there was a high possibility for them to meet face to face at any time other than the discussion sessions. This might have ruined the 'virtual' settings but the best that could be done to control the off-record discussions was by informing them that their marks would depend on their contribution seen in their conversation history.

To obtain enough data for analysis, three laboratory sessions were conducted with two hours allocated for each session. The students were assisted and monitored by a tutor. After each laboratory session, a set of questionnaires was distributed with the requirement that the questionnaires be completed and returned before they leave. The students' conversation history and project planning documents were accessed to understand their work flow and team management. A presentation session was also held after the submission of their completed assignment to clarify certain ambiguities regarding the students' opinions and behaviours during the laboratory sessions and the results seen in their final deliverables.

3   RTCE Tool Selection

There are many RTCE freeware that provide basic features and require payments for pro versions with more added features. However, some of the pro versions are overrated. The features they provide are not much compared to the free versions yet they are costly. Some tools provide many extra features but lack in quality and performance. A virtual team needs to find the most suitable tool that can assist their work best. Different tools are targeted for different types of work and some tools are still new and unstable.

During this research, the most suitable RTCE tool for students' software project planning was searched. All found tools were personally tested to choose the one that is the most suitable for laboratory assignment use. Table 1 shows the summary of RTCE tools that were tested.

During the tool search, there was no existing RTCE tool found that is perfect for undergraduate students project planning. However, a set of Google[1] applications seemed to be the most suitable for the study use. It supports the creation and edit of various file types which are useful for project planning documentations as well as the text chat feature.

The students could use GMail[2] to share files to team members. In this application too, the chat history is retrievable and the links to the teams' shared documents are given in emails. Google Docs[3] was chosen for the students to do their project planning documentation as its interface is simple and the functions are adequate.

There were concerns that led to the choosing of Google applications over the others for the study use. Requirements and constraints include the following:

---

[1] http://www.google.com
[2] http://mail.google.com
[3] http://docs.google.com

Table 1. Summary of existing RTCE tools review

Application name	File type support	Platform	Free version features	Text chat support
Amy Editor	text, source codes	web-based	full	no
Cacoo	diagrams, drawings	web-based	limited or pro for academic plan	yes
CoCKEditor	text	web-based	full	yes
Collabedit	text, source codes	web-based	full	yes
Conceptboard	text, drawings	web-based	limited or pro for 30 days trial	no
Dabbleboard	text, diagrams, drawings	web-based	limited or pro for 30 days trial	yes
FlockDraw	drawings	web-based	full	yes
Gobby	text, source codes	desktop application	full	no
Google Docs	word document, presentation, spreadsheet, form, diagrams	web-based	full	yes
LucidChart	diagrams	web-based	limited or pro for 14 days trial	yes
MeetingWords	text	web-based	full	yes
MoonEdit	text, source codes	desktop application	full	no
PiratePad	text	web-based	full	yes
PrimaryPad	text	web-based	limited or pro for 3 months trial	yes
ShowDocument	text, drawings	web-based	limited or pro for 30 days trial	yes
Squad	text, source codes	web-based	limited or pro for 10 days trial	yes
SubEthaEdit	text, source codes	desktop application	full for 30 days trial	no
Sync.in	text	web-based and desktop application	limited or pro for 30 days trial	yes
TitanPad	text	web-based	full	yes
Twiddla	text, drawings	web-based	limited or pro for 30 days trial	yes
ZohoWriter	text	web-based	limited or pro for 15 days trial	yes

- **Drawing diagrams and tables feature:** A project planning documenting tool requires a simple diagram or table drawing feature. It should be able to at least support the drawing of the simplest diagrams such as the activity chart and also tables to represent project schedule or milestones. Google Docs supports various file types such as the word document, presentation, form and spreadsheet, as well as diagram drawings.

- **Limited learning time:** It was easier to conduct the study using Google applications as most of the students were already familiar with them. Only a few minutes were needed to brief the students on the applications at the beginning of their first laboratory session. The sessions needed to start off immediately as only four weeks were given by the course lecturer to conduct this research with the course's students.

- **Price:** Google applications are free for public usage. Therefore, all the recorded data in Google servers can be accessed at any time after the laboratory session for data collection or revision. Most of the other good applications' pro versions require payment per user per month and the maximum period offered for trial is only 30-days. 30 days is not sufficient to do the study and data collection from all 25 participating students' accounts.

- **Email feature:** Emails enable the students to send offline messages to their team members while allowing them to attach files and links. Team members who were absent during a discussion session would not have the access to the missed session's chat conversation, but would not be missed out if the shared messages are sent via emails to both present and absent members. It would also be more convenient for the students to be able to share ideas, articles or links and have them saved in a separate storage with proper message subjects instead of having to search in the conversation history. GMail can be opened from Google Docs and to use all the Google applications require only one username per person.

It would be best if the RTCE tool supports IM so that the students can discuss and document their work together at the same time in just one page. There were three ways to use IM by Google, one is a chat application and the other two are chat features integrated in other applications. These were Google Docs text chat, Google Talk application and GMail text chat.

The most important feature that was needed in this study is the ability to support group chatting and the ability to save and retrieve chat conversation history. The conversation history was needed to identify the active and passive students, to see the relevance of the students' discussion, and also to check if the flow of the students' planning process was done the correct way.

Table 2. IM mediums by Google

	Google Docs Chat	Google Talk	GMail Chat
Group chat	√		√
Chat history		√	√
Email notification		√	√
No additional setup required	√		√
No need to start any extra application aside from the email and real-time document editing applications	√		√
Provides adequate chatting features to assist the project planning discussion	√	√	√

Table 2 summarizes the three IM mediums. The chat feature integrated in Google Docs might be very convenient for the students to use while they write and edit their documents (as it is located on the right panel of the same page) but it does not support chat conversation history archiving. Using it is still possible, but the users would need to copy and paste their chat conversations onto a document and save them manually. Chat windows other than Google Docs' can also be placed on the right panel of the same page as they can be moved around. Google Talk application does not support group chat. Therefore, GMail chat was the best option and was eventually chosen for the study.

4   Results

The advantages of using RTCE tools identified from the study are listed as below:

- From the compiled completed questionnaires, 92 percent of the students said that they really enjoyed doing their assignment virtually. This result supports other researches stating that students enjoy online chat to face to face chat [15-17]. Some of the students also mentioned that virtual discussions are more exciting than face to face discussions. The minorities who did not enjoy the virtual discussion sessions gave their reason that they do not prefer to stare at the monitor screen for too long.
- None of the students agreed that cultural issues strongly affected their group communication during the assignment discussion sessions. As long as the members are using the same language well and have the right level of knowledge for the project, the project should be able to run smoothly.
- To most of the students, virtual discussions enabled them to complete their project faster. This might be because the students needed to attend and be punctual for the discussion sessions as the laboratory sessions are a part of their Project Management course's requirements, thus require less effort to get the team together. Even for students who had problems to be present at the laboratory, they could still join the discussion sessions if they had internet connection elsewhere.

Complaints from the students and detected problems were also collected and analyzed. Some of the problems reported were:

- Google **account creation errors** and **internet disconnections** during discussion during the first laboratory session. The errors came from Google for some students when they were creating their account probably because there is a limit to a number of accounts that can be created per IP address at one moment.
- They were constantly **editing the same part of the document**.
- **Difficulties to draw diagrams** in Google Docs. Some of the students had to draw the diagrams elsewhere and then paste them onto the document.
- **Deadbeats**. There were some participants who were present during the discussion sessions but did not contribute much due to lack of knowledge, uncomfortable with the written language used, laziness or shyness. Weak language skills could be the cause for students' shyness and anxiety about making errors [18-19].
- A lot of time needed to re-explain and update the team's progress to an **absentee** of the previous laboratory session. Chat conversation history will only be accessible by a user if the user attended the session. Users who were supposed to join the

discussion but were not present at slotted sessions had difficulties catching up with the team's progress.

CSCW tools' users are of different cultures and from different regions with different mind settings. CSCW tools should incorporate awareness mechanisms to improve team communication thus strengthen the team relationship and understanding. During this research, it was found that most CSCW tools do not have good group awareness support. This would cause ineffective teamwork and produce bad quality deliverables. The CSCW tool development team must consider this issue seriously as this globally dispersed and multicultural group of people will be having limited options in developing good team communication in virtual space compared to face to face meetings.

From these findings, possible solutions to the problems were derived, while considering group awareness support. The solutions are expected to reduce the communication problems and improve the teamwork effectiveness, thus produce better quality deliverables. Considering conversational, workspace and contextual awareness, a few RTCE tool features were suggested and an RTCE tool interface was designed. Details are provided in the next section.

5   The RTCE Interface Design

Based on the discussion in the previous section, an RTCE tool for undergraduate students was designed. The tool would consist of three main components:

- **Real time document editor**: Allowing users to create documents (text, drawings and spreadsheets), have them shared with multiple users and edit in real time environment.
- **IM**: Allowing multiple users to chat and discuss via simple text messaging as they are working on the same document.
- **Email or private messaging**: Allowing users to send offline messages and include attachments to the intended users including those who are not able to attend the slotted virtual discussion sessions.

The RTCE tool should also support these added features that are not well supported or have yet to be supported by the RTCE tools that were used in this study:

1. **Telepointers** [20-24]: When a user moves his pointer, the other users should be able to see the movement to know the user's current activity. Each should be assigned with different colour to represent the identity of the pointers' owners. It is suggested that, telepointers that have been idle for at least 15 seconds should disappear from the other users' view to avoid confusion and mess. This feature supports awareness of presence and action in workspace awareness.
2. **Work modification alert** [25-26]: As another user is modifying a part of a document, the original author of the document part should be notified. A simple text notification would do, with a clickable link that would direct the original author straight to the paragraph that is being modified. This feature supports awareness of action in workspace awareness.

3. **Relaxed-WYSIWIS (What You See Is What I See) view sharing** [8, 11, 27-29]: The users will be able to see which part of the document the other users are currently viewing. Being able to view all online users' viewports at a fixed panel might take a lot of space and is not necessary. It is enough for a temporary viewport to only appear as a user mouse over a username. This feature supports awareness of presence in workspace awareness.

4. **User profile info** [30]: The users who are working on the same document should be able to see at least a brief profile of each other by clicking at the user's colour code in the list of users. This would help the team to distribute the work in a more efficient way by maximizing each user's expertise on the relevant sections of the document. This feature supports awareness of identity in workspace awareness.

5. **Paragraph freeze**: This feature is to avoid multiple users editing the same part of the document at the same time. Once a user has started typing in a paragraph, the tool should not allow any second user to disturb the typing process until the first user has finished typing the paragraph. Other users however can still continue editing the other parts of the document. This supports awareness of turn-taking in workspace awareness and might reduce the problem mentioned by some of the students in the compiled questionnaires that they kept modifying each other's work that were still being typed in.

6. **Recorded chat conversation** [31-33]: All chat conversations done in Google Docs are not recorded. Only those conversations that happened in the GMail text chat feature can be retrieved from GMail. It would be useful if all the chat conversations in the RTCE tool will be automatically saved and they are retrievable for later revisions. As we learned from the laboratory session results, it took a lot of time for the other team members to explain everything to the member who has missed the previous session. It would make the work smoother if they could just retrieve their previous session's chat conversation, select relevant conversation using checkboxes and forward them to the absent user in an offline message so the absent user could study and be prepared to join the next session. This feature supports contextual awareness and also awareness of conversational context in conversational awareness.

7. **Wake idle or inactive users**: To solve the problem of deadbeats, the tool might be able to encourage the students to contribute by incorporating a new feature which sends a notification to the idle user via a pop-up with a ping to let the user know that he has been idle for too long and should start taking part in the discussion. In this case, the tool should keep track of each user's idle time and check if it has exceed the maximum idle time limit set by the team leader or the document creator. The team leader or other members should be notified too so that they will try to help bring the passive member into the discussion. This feature supports awareness of presence and conversational context in conversational awareness.

8. **Instant translation** [34-35]: Another known cause for idle users is unfamiliarity with the language used in the discussion. Students who were having problems understanding or typing the language used in the discussion could not really contribute their ideas as they found it difficult to explain their opinions. One of the 25 students was known to be very weak in English by looking at his writing

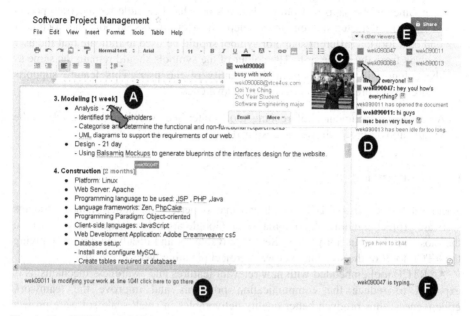

Fig. 1. The RTCE tool design: (A) telepointer; (B) modification alert to original author; (C) user profile info; (D) idle user notification; (E) user availability status; (F) typing cue

skills in the questionnaire answers he submitted and his team's conversation history. It can be seen in the conversation history that he was not actively sharing ideas during the discussion. An extra feature to help this type of users work better is to have an automatic translation feature. The user whom is already aware of his own weakness in the written language used in the discussion could pre-set his preferred language and later during the virtual discussion, he could just mouse over a word to see its meaning in the selected language. This feature supports contextual awareness.

9. **'Who is typing' cue** [11, 36-37]: In most IM tools including Google Talk and GMail chat, users are notified at the chat window if there is another user typing in the group conversation. This notification allows more organized conversation and avoids clash of words at the same time. This feature supports awareness of turn-taking in conversational awareness.

10. **One conversation at a time**: Since the online users are all discussing on the same document, one chat conversation is enough. The chat tool however should allow username tagging as a user types his message in the chat conversation. This feature is yet to be seen on any of the reviewed RTCE tools. This username tagging would allow the users to create attention to specific online member while everyone else could also see the discussion, be aware of any issues arose and join the discussion if needed. This feature supports awareness of multiple concurrent conversations in conversational awareness.

11. **Availability status display** [38-42]: All users who are accessing the document will automatically appear on the chat list and once they go offline, their

usernames will disappear from the list. If a user has been idle for a certain period of time (no detected movement on telepointers or cursors on both the document and chat tool), a different shape or symbol should be used to indicate that the user is away from the discussion. The colour of the symbols should remain the same as the colour will only represent the identity of the user. This feature supports awareness of presence in conversational awareness.

A real time document conferencing tool's interface was designed based on the discussion above. Fig. 1 shows the designed tool's interface.

6   Conclusion

There was no existing RTCE tool found that is perfect for undergraduate students software project planning. A combination of Google applications was identified to be the most suitable, but not perfect. Several advantages and disadvantages of applying the RTCE tool for the students' software project planning were analysed.

An RTCE tool embedded with new relevant features and awareness mechanisms is expected to reduce the communication problems and improve the teamwork effectiveness, thus produce better quality deliverables in small scale software project planning. However, the presented RTCE tool interface design is yet to be tested. Future work includes the development of a working RTCE tool based on the ideas and design presented in this research.

References

1. Grief, I.: Computer Supported Cooperative Work: A Book of Readings. Morgan Kaufmann, San Francisco (1988)
2. Kamel, N., Davison, R.: Applying CSCW Technology to Overcome Traditional Barriers in Group Interactions. Information and Management 34, 209–219 (1998)
3. Powell, A., Picolli, G., Ives, B.: Virtual Teams: A Review of Current Literature and Directions for Future. Data Base for Advances in Information Systems 35(1), 6–36 (2004)
4. Kayworth, T., Leidner, D.: The Global Virtual Manager: A Prescription for Success. European Management Journal 18(2), 183–194 (2000)
5. Shachaf, P.: Cultural Diversity and Information and Communication Technology Impacts on Global Virtual Teams: An Exploratory Study. Information and Management 45(2), 131–142 (2008)
6. Dourish, P., Bellotti, V.: Awareness and Coordination in Shared Workspaces. In: Turner, J., Kraut, R. (eds.) Proceedings of the 1992 ACM Conference on Computer-Supported Cooperative Work, pp. 107–114. ACM Press, New York (1992)
7. Mendoza-Chapa, S., Romero-Salcedo, M., Oktaba, H.: Group Awareness Support in Collaborative Writing Systems. In: Proceedings of 6th International Workshop on Groupware, pp. 112–118. IEEE Press, Washington, DC (2000)
8. Gutwin, C., Greenberg, S.: Support for Group Awareness in Real-Time Desktop Conferences. In: Proceedings of the 2nd New Zealand Computer Science Research Students Conference. University of Waikato, Hamilton (1995)

9. Gutwin, C., Penner, R., Schneider, K.: Group Awareness in Distributed Software Development. In: Proceedings of the 2004 ACM Conference on Computer Supported Cooperative Work, pp. 72–81. ACM Press, New York (2004)
10. Raikundalia, G., Zhang, H.: Novel Group Awareness Mechanisms for Real-time Collaborative Document Authoring. In: Proceedings of the 9th Australasian Document Computing Symposium. The University of Melbourne, pp. 33–40 (2004)
11. Tran, M.H.: Supporting Group Awareness in Synchronous Distributed Groupware: Framework, Tools and Evaluations. PhD Thesis, Faculty of Information and Communication Technologies, Swinburne University of Technology (2006)
12. Tran, M.H., Raikundalia, G., Yang, Y.: Using an Experimental Study to Develop Group Awareness Support for Real-Time Distributed Collaborative Writing. Information and Software Technology 48, 1006–1024 (2006)
13. Lambropoulos, N., Culwin, F.: Group Awareness in Online Work, Learning and Games. In: Proceedings of the 24th Human-Computer Interaction Conference, Dundee (2010)
14. Steinmacher, I., Chaves, A.P., Gerosa, M.A.: Awareness Support in Distributed Software Development: A Systematic Review and Mapping of the Literature. Computer Supported Cooperative Work 22(2-3), 113–158 (2013)
15. Gross, E.: Adolescent Internet Use: What We Expect, What Teens Report. Applied Developmental Psychology 25, 633–649 (2004)
16. Ling, Z.: A Study on the Motivational Power of Internet Chat. Journal of Northern Sichuan Education College 4, 72–74 (2007)
17. Edwards, J., Helvie-Mason, L.: Technology and Instructional Communication: Student Usage and Perceptions of Virtual Office Hours (VOHs). Journal of Online Learning and Teaching 6(1), 174–186 (2010)
18. Cheng, X.: Asian Students' Reticence Revisited. System 28(3), 435–446 (2000)
19. Tong, J.: Some Observations of Students' Reticent and Participatory Behaviour in Hong Kong English Classrooms. Electronic Journal of Foreign Language Teaching 7(2), 239–254 (2010)
20. Greenberg, S., Gutwin, C., Roseman, M.: Semantic Telepointers for Groupware. In: Proceedings of the 6th Australian Conference on Computer–Human Interaction, pp. 54–61. IEEE Press, Washington, DC (1996)
21. Dyck, J., Gutwin, C., Subramanian, S., Fedak, C.: High-Performance Telepointers. In: Proceedings of the 2004 ACM Conference on Computer Supported Cooperative Work, pp. 172–181. ACM Press, New York (2004)
22. Xia, S., Sun, D., Chen, D.: Object-Associated Telepointer for Real-Time Collaborative Document Editing Systems. In: International Conference on Collaborative Computing: Networking, Applications and Worksharing, San Jose (2005)
23. Hu, J.-P., Zeng, G.-Z., Dong, J.: Telepointers and Cooperative Awareness Technology in Collaborative Writing. Computer Engineering and Science 7 (2006)
24. Sánchez, J., Strazzulla, D., Paredes, R.: Enhancing Interaction and Collaboration in Multimedia Rooms with Multilayered Annotations and Telepointers. In: Proceedings of the VIII Brazilian Symposium on Human Factors in Computing Systems (2008)
25. Tran, M.H., Raikundalia, G.K., Yang, Y.: Split Window View and Modification Director: Innovative Awareness Mechanisms in Real-Time Collaborative Writing. In: Proceedings of the Conference on Human Factors. Australian Computer Society, Darlinghurst (2002)
26. Ignat, C.-L., Oster, G., Molli, P., Skaf-Molli, H.: A Collaborative Writing Mode for Avoiding Blind Modifications. In: 9th International Workshop on Collaborative Editing Systems. IEEE Distributed Systems Online (2007)

27. Gutwin, C., Roseman, M., Greenberg, S.: A Usability Study of Awareness Widgets in a Shared Workspace Groupware System. In: Proceedings of the ACM Conference on Computer-Supported Cooperative Work, pp. 258–267. ACM Press, New York (1996)

28. Gutwin, C.: Workspace Awareness in Real-Time Distributed Groupware. PhD Dissertation, University of Calgary (1997)

29. Tran, M.H., Yang, Y., Raikundalia, G.: Supporting Awareness in Instant Messaging: An Empirical Study and Mecahnism Design. In: Proceedings of the 17th Australia Conference on Computer-Human Interaction: Citizens Online: Considerations for Today and the Future, pp. 1–10. CHISIG of Australia, Narrabundah (2005)

30. Moreno, M., Vivacqua, A., de Souza, J.: An Agent Framework to Support Opportunistic Collaboration. In: Favela, J., Decouchant, D. (eds.) CRIWG 2003. LNCS, vol. 2806, pp. 224–231. Springer, Heidelberg (2003)

31. Chen, D., Sun, C.: Real-Time Text Chat via Collaborative Editing Systems. In: Proceedings of the ACM CSCW 2002 Workshop on Collaborative Editing, New Orleans (2002)

32. Pereira Meire, A., Borges, M.R.S., de Araújo, R.M.: Supporting Collaborative Drawing with the Mask Versioning Mechanism. In: Favela, J., Decouchant, D. (eds.) CRIWG 2003. LNCS, vol. 2806, pp. 208–223. Springer, Heidelberg (2003)

33. Adesemowo, A.: Affective Gesture Fast-Track Feedback Instant Messaging (AGFIM). Master Dissertation, University of Western Cape (2005)

34. Rutkas, A.: Language Translation Module for Instant Messaging Systems. In: Proceedings of International Conference on Modern Problems of Radio Engineering, Telecommunications and Computer Science, pp. 630–631 (2008)

35. Yang, C.-Y., Lin, H.-Y.: An Instant Messaging with Automatic Language Translation. In: 3rd IEEE International Conference on Ubi-Media Computing, pp. 312–316 (2010)

36. Erickson, T., Smith, D., Kellog, W., Laff, M., Richards, J., Bradner, E.: Socially Translucent Systems: Social Proxies, Persistent Conversation, and the Design of 'Babble'. In: Proceedings of the SIGCHI Conference on Human Factors in Computing Systems, pp. 72–79. ACM Press, New York (1999)

37. Tran, M.H., Yang, Y., Raikundalia, G.: Conversational Awareness in Text-Based Computer Mediated Communication Awareness Systems. Human-Computer Interaction Series, vol. 3, pp. 313–333 (2009)

38. Viegas, F., Donath, J.: Chat Circles. In: Proceedings of the SIGCHI Conference on Human Factors in Computing Systems, pp. 9–16. ACM Press, New York (1999)

39. Neustaedter, C., Greenberg, S., Carpendale, S.: IMVis: Instant Messenger Visualization. In: Proceedings of the 2002 ACM on Computer Supported Cooperative Work Video Program, p. 6. ACM Press, New York (2002)

40. Avrahami, D., Hudson, S.: Responsiveness in Instant Messaging: Predictive Models Supporting Inter-Personal Communication. In: Proceedings of the SIGCHI Conference on Human Factors in Computing Systems, pp. 731–740. ACM Press, New York (2006)

41. Waite, B.: BuddySpace RFID: An Instant Messaging Application using RFID to Provide Presence Information. Master Dissertation, B. Thomas Golisano College of Computing and Information Sciences (2006)

42. Zhang, X., Law, C.-F., Wang, C.-L., Lau, F.: Towards Pervasive Instant Messaging and Presence Awareness. International Journal of Pervasive Computing and Communications 5(1), 42–60 (2009)

If I Do Not Like Your Online Profile I Will Not Hire You!

Birgy Lorenz and Kaido Kikkas

[1] Institute of Informatics, Tallinn University, Narva Road 25, 10120 Tallinn, Estonia
[2] Estonian Information Technology College, Raja St 4C, 12616 Tallinn, Estonia
{Birgy.Lorenz,Kaido.Kikkas}@tlu.ee

Abstract. Today, both employees and employers are active online. A lot of people live their lives through personal online social networks. Online social networking sites are an easy tool to screen potential employees online profiles and for human resource management to use in recruitment processes. The screening process includes Internet and social networking site search that will provide not only professional but also personal information. Investigating personal information, however, may be considered violation of privacy. Our study goals are to find out how common it is to do background checks on possible future employees in Estonia, how students feel about such a practice and how they maintain their public profiles. Methods used to gather information were a survey among employees (n=34), pupils (n=117) from five high schools, students (n=91) from one university, and a case study that involved pupils (n=54) and students (n=38). Results reported in this paper will give an overview of our understanding of the accuracy of online profiles, common practices, unspoken risks, and maybe even frustration from the side of future employees. The results of this study can be applied to improve youth-related Internet safety training modules and programmes.

Keywords: Internet safety strategies, online profile, privacy management, privacy rights.

1 Background

Rapid spread of the Internet has led to a situation where at least one-third of the North and South American as well as European online population have a profile on a social networking site [6] and a mobile phone [9]. People are using social networking sites and they can update their profiles everywhere. Online profiles are also used to gather information when these people apply for a job.

The aim of this paper is to answer the following questions: does management screen future employees' online profiles and does it have any preconceptions about this; how do students feel about been screened; what are the students' strategies to maintain their public profiles? This study is needed to understand how to train students in Estonia to enhance their Internet safety awareness level in privacy for the Safer Internet Centre in Estonia SIC EE II programme[1].

---

[1] European Schoolnet InSafe Network programme in Estonia years 2012-2014.

P. Zaphiris and A. Ioannou (Eds.): LCT 2014, Part II, LNCS 8524, pp. 429–439, 2014.
© Springer International Publishing Switzerland 2014

To investigate this matter further, we must understand recruitment processes in use nowadays and whether they can violate personal privacy as well as differences between young people's and adults' behaviour on the Net.

1.1   Privacy and Online Profile

Privacy has changed from a purely philosophical and legal matter to a technical [18] and behavioural issue [24]. Nowadays people need protection not only from government and companies, but also from each other [26, 28].

It is easy to make decisions based on preconceptions [14]. For example, it is assumed that people are able to create social networking site profiles that are accurate [2]. From a positive angle, an online profile could extend a person's social capability; from a negative angle, it may result in excessive but undesired attention. Potential employees really don't understand what information about themselves might leak out into a public arena [17] or how ordinary posts or comments might be misunderstood [30]. It has also become ever easier (and especially in small states or small countries) to recognize a person's identity and profile, and understand his or her connections to others [16]. A number of issues also have risen from a weak understanding of policies such as user or privacy agreements [8]. This highlights the question: whether or not to join social networking sites in the first place [27].

Employees point out that using online screening to find workers or make other employment decisions are a) inaccurate, irrelevant or in some other way false, so that this might lead into an unfair decision making b) lack accountability c) lead to violation of employees' legitimate expectation of privacy [5]. Students show an awareness that companies will screen their online profiles, but one-third of the mare against such a practice because their profile is usually not about their professional life [31]. Our interest lies in finding out if this the case also in Estonia.

1.2   Internet Usage by Youth

Young people use more online services (social networking sites, blogging), and have fewer profiles and fragmented interactions between their groups [15]. Personal data can also be uploaded online by others (such as friends, family, or institutions) and this information might be incorrect, not to say damaging to an individual [11]. As young people are more visible online than older people, it makes recruitment processes sometimes seems unfair [13]. To deal with online privacy there is an option to use different strategies like selective information sharing, advanced strategic information sharing, self-censorship of information, multiple identities on multiple platforms and false information, or social strategies like social steganography [19].

1.3   Employers' Practices on Social Media

Earlier, in order to find a worker to employ a company advertised in newspapers or made personal enquiries. To find out more about the potential employee, the employers interviewed potential candidates or spoke to the referee or former employers mentioned in the person's application form or in his or her resumé [10].

Nowadays, because companies hire employees via online services, company websites or even current employers, management also faces ethical dilemmas with regard to whether to do an online background search or not [7, 3, 25]. Screening future workers [23] has given good results in finding highly skilled employees quicker [4]. Still management needs guidance on how to deal with their findings in a socially responsible manner [1, 21, 22]. Using social media in employment is undergoing a transition in terms of behavioural norms, regulations, and law. Dealing with online privacy problems in compliance with corporate social responsibility is still a matter that is under dispute [12, 20].

2   Methods and Data

We focused my study on high school and university students and companies that could employ them in the future. We wanted to find out (a) the situation in Estonian companies – do they screen future employees and do they act on the results they find. About students, I wanted to understand (b) how they feel about being screened, but also (c) how they manage their profiles, and (d) what are the basic challenges and common strategies (if any) used to deal with too much public information.

Firstly, to investigate this matter about three first questions (a-c), we chose to undertake an online survey among students and human resource management staff, using a mixture of open and close-ended questions. We used a Likert scale [29], with both closed and open answers, to assess their decisions (e.g. "feelings about doing screening or being screened"). To analyse open answers we coded them into a group of four, e.g. 1. "value screening as a good tool to know about the person", 2. "don't mind or don't care about screening", 3. "find it offensive" and 4. "it is not a valid method to find workers".

The two surveys – among the students and the human resource management personnel – were structured in different ways and had varying questions:

- The student survey consisted of 19 questions: background information, Internet-using habits and online profile issues, preparation before the job interview and expectations from the employer. To investigate the student's opinions on the topic, we used an online survey method - we wanted to include students from five different high schools all over Estonia, as well as students from one university that are future technical specialists. Our initial assumption was that the university students would be the best of the group (in terms of having information on how to behave online as their future work is related of data protection, programming secure applications or managing company websites, helping users to make better decisions etc.) and students from high schools would be an average knowledge group about Internet safety. I also wanted to get better comparative information about how young people act when they have different backgrounds (age, life experience).
- The human resource management staff survey consisted of 11 questions: background information, how they find new employees, preparation before the job interview, rules and regulations in the company regarding taking photos/videos etc. To investigate a position and perceptions of the people working in management

positions, we also decided to use an online survey - such an approach enabled us to phrase questions that employers might not want to answer in person (because the questions might include things that might be considered unethical or violating privacy). We used my own connections to get interviewees in the companies involved; hence, our sample is a convenience sample.

Secondly, so as to investigate two final research questions (c-d) the strategies used by the students to manage their public profile I used a case study method. To construct the cases we used the help of students (30 groups of three to four students) that assembled the online profile of a volunteering group member via online screening (Google.com, Pipl.com, Webmii.com, Youtube.com) in 15 minutes. The main results give good feedback about the personal data on the Net and about its accuracy. The group discussed what is out there, who had posted the data, and whether they consider the information valid. People who were volunteering to be screened evaluated the overall findings according to accuracy on a scale that ranged from 1-10 (1 - "it is not me" to 10 - "it is completely me"); would they hire themselves; how would they describe their online behaviour; was there something surprising for them; and would they now change something (try to remove something (photos, videos), delete their account, change their behaviour, etc.).

This method gave us information about the possible results that people working in management positions might be getting while doing the screening. We also tried to code the findings into groups, but this was difficult as the outcome is not only dependent on the activity level and knowledge about Internet safety. This exercise was part of an Internet safety training session that was conducted in a lecture about privacy and Internet safety that also changed participants' behaviour toward the problem in a process, so the results gave us a quick snapshot of what did they feel in these circumstances.

The survey of students had 117 high school students (pupils) who participated from five Estonian schools (two from the capital, Tallinn, and three from outside it) and one university that focuses on computer science and technology (91 students). The participants' male/female ratio was almost equal. 13% of pupils worked full time and 15% part time as well 70% of students worked full time and 10% part time. Analysing the data, there were no special differences between non-working and working students and pupils. The main difference related to age and the education that comes with that.

The survey on the management staff had 34 participants. Most of the organizations had the background in education (n=9) or technology (n=11) and were used to employing people over 18 years old (n=30). The companies use job portals (n=19), their own website (n=13), current employers' help (n=20), and social networking sites (n=12; examples included Twitter and Facebook) to find their future employees.

In the case study exercise, I used students from one of the high schools surveyed (54 participants) and one set of education-related university students (38 bachelor students with backgrounds in computer science, education and new media). Thirty participants were screened in that process (18 from high school and 12 from university).

3   Results

This section describes young people's perceptions about pre-employment screening practices, employers' practices with regard to background checks, and strategies to manage personal online profiles.

3.1   Young People's Perceptions about Pre-employment Screening Practices

The results from the survey offer information about the inconsistent behaviour and expectations of the students and pupils. The most important finding is that 86% of the students and 68% of the pupils from the sample believe that they will be scanned before the job interview. 99% of the participants who answered the survey were already screening their own online profile themselves; 85% were happy with the results. 33% of the students and 50% pupils had tried to remove information (pictures, videos, comments) from the Net, and 8% of students and 18% pupils had done so without any visible luck. Both groups state that only 20% of the information has been put online by them, so they can't be responsible for it. 80% of the online data was there because schools, friends and even parents had put the information online.

In the end, only 36% of the pupils and students agree it is useful for a company to "scan" a candidate before the job interview. Against scanning are 18% of students and 22% of pupils – they even thought that it is improper to think about doing that. Some participants see this process as a violation of equality and transparency as some people have more information online than others. They also pointed out that "work is only done for 8 hours a day", and they have the right to meet friends, party and spend their free time as they wish – so that their online profile should not be considered representative of who they are at work. Since they accept a lot of friends' invitations, people whom they don't really know in real life (either because of online gaming or since it is common to accept "friends of the friends even when you don't know them in person"), the younger participants argued that the saying "show me your friends and I will tell you who you are" does not apply as a principle any more in the information age. Some also mentioned that information is usually not updated frequently, and some accounts may be forgotten about or even hacked into. In the end, they stated that in their work life they can be a different person than in the rest of their life; thus, whatever they do in their private life, it is not valid to think that they would be "lazy", "rude" or "unreliable" in a work context.

3.2   Employers' Perceptions about Background Checks

Twenty-five employers in the sample stated that they definitely scan information on potential employees that is easily found using either Google or social networks. Twenty-one employers pointed out that they believe that information that they obtain is accurate (even when it might not be), 11 think it is suspicious when they don't find any information about the candidate, and 28 will stop the selection process with that person if they find a particular example of behaviour that they don't like, such as aggressiveness, racist comments, heavy partying, and loose personal habits.

At the same time, employers stated that it is positive when they do not find a lot about the candidate online; as they interpreted such a finding as meaning that the person is aware of their image and skilful in using it for their own benefit. In the job interview, the management will discuss a) if the interviewee has read anything about the company (n=28), b) does the job candidate know anybody from the company (n=17) and c) only 9 will ask the candidate to comment about any information found online.

3.3   Strategies to Manage One's Online Profile

In terms of online privacy awareness, questions were asked about how easily students give away their right not to have a photograph or video taken of them. The results show that the high-school pupils in the sample were apparently more aware of taking advantage of "party pictures" than students, who were not very concerned about who is taking their photos and where they upload them. They also ask permission from others less often if they are the photographer (see figure 1).

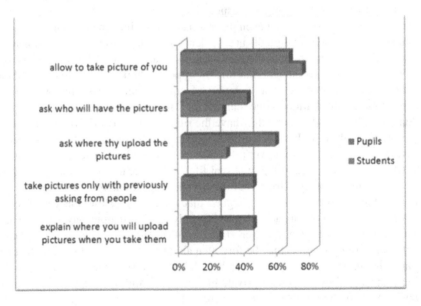

Fig. 1. In the evening, at a party, you…

The results from the case study exercise revealed that there are some differences between pupils' and students' strategies. Among the high-school pupils in the sample, there were mainly three different strategies mentioned so as to deal with privacy and identity management: a) **I don't post information to the Net, others post about me** (meaning: I don't take responsibility for what is on the Internet) b) **I post most of the data about myself and a lot of information** (meaning: I post so much positive information that, if there is something negative about me you will not think it is important) c) **I lie about almost everything that I post online** (meaning: I deliberately post false information as I feel that you should not rely on online information). The main goal for the pupils sharing the latter viewpoint was to teach others a lesson.

The university students also proposed three main ways to manage their online profile: a) **"search and destroy"** (this group consisted of mostly of students who had computer science as their major and hence they were aware of their online behaviour – they had "picture perfect" online profiles that had been tweaked. They had asked everybody they knew to delete everything that they did not like or had made their environments closed to the public or had created fake accounts); b) **I hadn't googled myself before, and now I must change my online habits to be more private** (usually this group consisted of students majoring in education who were a bit more worried about the findings. The justification was that they would not want other students or employers to know about their personal life); c) **I already know something, but not all** (in this group there was a mix of people from different study majors who had already done some online searching about themselves. They were not so worried about their profile. However, since half of the members of this group had found some data about themselves that they hadn't put up (e.g., a lecturer had uploaded homework that should have been private; some people were part of emailing lists that were public; some had had pictures tagged that should not have been online in a first place) they felt a bit betrayed or violated by others.

In the strategy part of the case study we presented three ways that exploit the audience in matters of privacy from pupils and from students. On the one hand, pupils divided their habits regarding the level of activity and the content of information. On the other hand, students divided themselves regarding the level of knowledge. Compared to the study by Oolo and Siibak [19] which grouped Estonian students' online privacy strategies into five main categories, the participants in my sample mainly talked about practices that could be understood as selective information sharing and self-censoring information. Only a few of the participants pointed to having multiple online identities, providing false information, or adapting to various social privacy strategies. Only one student claimed to be practicing strategic information sharing.

In conclusion, the participants in our case study exercise did not find any discriminating facts or pictures about themselves online. At the same time, in more than half of these cases (who were mostly students), participants were able to obtain the person's home address or phone number, different online usernames, and a picture or the location where they grew up or went to school. Friends and circles of acquaintances were visible in both groups. There was lots of information about the pupils that had put online by schools or companies that provide extra curricula activities to young people (such as arts and sports): this also gives away pupils' real location area. Searchers also found out that, when a person has created an example Facebook account using an age that is under 18, then the trace is not as visible as that of people who are over 18 whose accounts were public until the person decided to make it private.

4   Discussion

The main aim of this study was to gain information about the attitudes of future employees and company management towards online screening, and young people's privacy strategies while maintaining a public profile. The clash about online profile management, privacy and being a "nice" employee is basically about a worker's right to have personal and private life or not.

The findings of our online surveys suggest that employees and employers are not on the same page when it comes to their attitudes towards online behaviour. Every company would like to have nice and respectful people working for them, be it in real or online life. Employers also argue that what is online and publicly available is everybody's data, and if the workers did not want these facts to be found, then why did they put them up there in the first place. The other finding is that there is a fine line between spying on people without permission and being aware of the company image. This also emerged from the literature review which shows that, on one hand, online screening is a good tool for the company to find highly qualified workers quickly, but at the same time it probably violates people's rights to do that [1]. At the same time, from the employees' side not everyone was worried about the issue.

Most students and pupils were unconcerned or believed that their online profile showed their real image. But what about those that were not happy? Young people soon to enter (or who have entered) the labour market argue that 80% of the data that is online is not posted by them but by others (such as friends, relatives, partners, and schools). It is one of the basic rights of individuals to ask not to have a picture taken of them or to be presented in a way that they do not like. 50% of the students have successfully removed comments, pictures or other media from the Internet, so at least some of them are aware of the tools available they can help them to manipulate an online profile and present a nice online profile about themselves. 22% of pupils claimed that they have had no success in cleaning up their online profile. Some students also suggested that if you yourself put more information up online, then it might be helpful – as the positive will shine more. In smaller countries there is also an issue about having too many online friends. For example in Estonia, the notion of "six degrees of separation" does not apply, as the country has a "two degree model": for example, if a person has 100 friends then s/he is already visible to too many people [16].

Various online privacy strategies that were proposed by Oolo & Siibak [19] were also found to be dominant among my sample. I found good strategies like "time to time screen your profile yourself" or "be more active than your friends to post information". This means that young people are really trying to take responsibility for what information is on the Net about them. At the same time, maintaining an online profile is hard work – one must be aware of it all the time. We also found examples of rejections of reality whereby some pupils post false information in order to feel safer or to "make others ask the truth from me". As they posted mixed information, such as that "they live under plastic bag" or "eat rubbish" or "have been in prison", they perhaps did not understand the bad side of the fake image. As an example, employers explained that, when they come across this kind of information, they probably might not want to meet or interview this kind of job applicant.

Young people make mistakes on the journey towards adulthood and getting a job. However, there is always a potential problem that someone else can post something about another person which is hard to remove from the Internet (as a result of tagging pictures and videos in a traceable account). The best way is not to get into that position in a first place. The other challenge is that institutions (such as school or work or even family) should also be more considerate with regard to what kind of information they place on websites, for example, personal information, and pictures of children's childhoods. As not everybody asks for permission before putting up information (whether people or companies) the solution is that when one feels violated, others should know about the problem.

5   Conclusion

The rising use of Web 2.0 tools and social networks has raised serious issues about personal privacy and identity management. Companies require that their offices will search out information, ask around for background information, or find other sources if they are not allowed to do that. This at the same time might be violating peoples' rights to privacy. Solutions in this matter are: a) more should be done in high school and university e.g., through careers guidance, to ensure that young people know how recruitment processes work - so it would not come as a surprise to them only at the time they begin to search for jobs; b) to make the recruitment process more visible and transparent. Usually private companies cannot be asked to do that directly (for example, by proposing a law), but it probably can be done effectively in the government sector. Good standards will usually find followers. To discuss these issues more publicly is a must.

Displaying a nice online profile is becoming more important than ever. Some students already have the skills to manipulate their online profile or even destroy information, yet most don't. Personal privacy regulations state that, in their personal life, people don't have to be so nice, they may have their own opinion, friends and may also have problems, for example, with the police. This should not be taken into account when they apply for a job. Still, if there is something wrong, they will not be asked for an interview. Advice for future workers would include: look into your own behaviour, and do not repeat the mistake of letting everybody take pictures or videos about you. Try to "search and destroy" information online when it seems to be damaging your online profile. The best thing is to prevent all of this happening in a first place.

In the end, if the people don't stand up for their rights or are not interested in how companies find their workers, online screening will keep growing. Online screening doesn't always provide accountability and fairness in recruiting processes, as anyone can post whatever they wish to online about anyone. Screening will probably violate a person's equality rights in the process. Most people are happy with their self-online image, but to maintain a perfect online profile is hard work and no one is protected from other people's misuse of information.

Acknowledgements. This research was supported by a Swedbank Estonia scholarship with regard to corporate social responsibility studies through Tartu University Centre of Ethics and by the Tiger University Program of the Information Technology Foundation for Education.

References

1. Clark, L.A., Roberts, S.J.: Employer's use of social networking sites: A socially irresponsible practice. Journal of Business Ethics 95(4), 507–525 (2010)
2. Counts, S., Stecher, K.: Self-presentation of personality during online profile creation. In: Proc. AAAI Conf. on Weblogs and Social Media, ICWSM (2009)
3. Coutu, D.: We googled you. Harvard Business Review 85(6), 37 (2007)
4. Dafoulas, G.A., Pateli, A.G., Turega, M.: Business-to-employee co-operation support through online job interviews. In: Proceedings of the 13th International Workshop on Database and Expert Systems Applications, pp. 286–292. IEEE (2002)
5. Davis, D.: MySpace Isn't Your Space: Expanding the Fair Credit Reporting Act to Ensure Accountability and Fairness in Employer Searches of Online Social Networking Services. Available at SSRN 1601471 (2007)
6. Facebook statistics by Country Socialbakers (2013), http://www.socialbakers.com/facebook-statistics/ (retrieved)
7. Falcone, P.: Ninety-six Great Interview Questions to Ask Before You Hire. Amazon Books (2009)
8. Gindin, S.E.: Nobody Reads Your Privacy Policy or Online Contract: Lessons Learned and Questions Raised by the FTC's Action against Sears. Nw. J. Tech. & Intell. Prop. 8(1) (2009)
9. Global mobile statistics 2013 Part A: Mobile subscribers; handset market share; mobile operators MobiThinking (2013), http://mobithinking.com/mobile-marketing-tools/latest-mobile-stats/a (retrieved)
10. Goffin, R.D., Boyd, A.C.: Faking and personality assessment in personnel selection: Advancing models of faking. Canadian Psychology/Psychologie Canadienne 50(3), 151 (2009)
11. Henson, B., Reyns, B.W., Fisher, B.S.: Security in the 21st Century Examining the Link Between Online Social Network Activity, Privacy, and Interpersonal Victimization. Criminal Justice Review 36(3), 253–268 (2011)
12. Hirsch, D.: The Law and Policy of Online Privacy: Regulation, Self-Regulation or Co-Regulation? ExpressO (2010), http://works.bepress.com/dennis_hirsch/1 (retrieved)
13. Hoofnagle, C., King, J., Li, S., Turow, J.: How different are young adults from older adults when it comes to information privacy attitudes and policies? Available at SSRN 1589864 (2010)
14. Leenes, R.: Context Is Everything Sociality and Privacy in Online Social Network Sites. In: Bezzi, M., Duquenoy, P., Fischer-Hübner, S., Hansen, M., Zhang, G. (eds.) Privacy and Identity. IFIP AICT, vol. 320, pp. 48–65. Springer, Heidelberg (2010)
15. Lenhart, A., Purcell, K., Smith, A., Zickuhr, K.: Social media & mobile internet use among teens and young adults, pp. 155–179. Pew Internet & American Life Project, Washington, DC (2010)

16. Lorenz, B., Kikkas, K.: Socially engineered commoners as cyber warriors-Estonian future or present? In: 2012 4th International Conference on Cyber Conflict (CYCON), pp. 1–12. IEEE (2012)

17. Madejski, M., Johnson, M.L., Bellovin, S.M.: The failure of online social network privacy settings. Department of Computer Science, Columbia University

18. Nissenbaum, H.: Protecting privacy in an information age: The problem of privacy in public. Law and Philosophy 17(5), 559–596 (1998)

19. Oolo, E., Siibak, A.: Performing for one's imagined audience: Social steganography and other privacy strategies of Estonian teens on networked publics. Cyberpsychology: Journal of Psychosocial Research on Cyberspace 7(1), article 7 (2013), doi:10.5817/CP2013-1-7

20. Pollach, I.: Online privacy as a corporate social responsibility: an empirical study. Business Ethics: A European Review 20(1), 88–102 (2011)

21. Sanchez Abril, P., Levin, A., Del Riego, A.: Blurred Boundaries: Social Media Privacy and the Twenty-First Century Employee. American Business Law Journal 49(1), 63–124 (2012)

22. Schoening, K., Kleisinger, K.: Off-Duty Privacy: How Far Can Employers Go. N. Ky. L. Rev. 37, 287 (2010)

23. Slovensky, R., Ross, W.H.: Should human resource managers use social media to screen job applicants? Managerial and legal issues in the USA. Info 14(1), 55–69 (2012)

24. Smith, H.J., Dinev, T., Xu, H.: Information privacy research: An interdisciplinary review. MIS Quarterly 35(4), 989–1016 (2011)

25. Smith-Butler, L.: Workplace Privacy: We'll Be Watching You. Ohio Northern Law Review 35 (2009)

26. Solove, D.: A Taxonomy of privacy. University of Pennsylvania Law Review 154(3), 477–564 (2006)

27. Zheleva, E., Getoor, L.: To join or not to join: the illusion of privacy in social networks with mixed public and private user profiles. In: Proceedings of the 18th International Conference on World Wide Web, pp. 531–540. ACM, New York (2009)

28. Tene, O.: Privacy: The new generations. International Data Privacy Law 1(1), 15–27 (2011)

29. Trochim, W.: Likert scaling, Research Methods Knowledge Base (2006), http://www.socialresearchmethods.net/kb/scallik.php (retrieved)

30. Wang, Y., Norcie, G., Komanduri, S., Acquisti, A., Leon, P.G., Cranor, L.F.: I regretted the minute I pressed share: A qualitative study of regrets on Facebook. In: Proceedings of the Seventh Symposium on Usable Privacy and Security, p. 10. ACM (2011)

31. Vicknair, J., Elkersh, D., Yancey, K., Budden, M.C.: The Use of Social Networking Websites as a Recruiting Tool for Employers. American Journal of Business Education (AJBE) 3(11) (2010)

Collaboration, Knowledge Sharing and Digital Environments: What about Argumentation and Questioning Skills?

Maria José (Zé) Loureiro[1,4], Francislê Neri de Souza[2,4], Anna Bezerra[2,3,4], and Ana Rodrigues[2,4]

[1] ccTICua
[2] DE-Universidade de Aveiro
[3] AES-Garanhuns, Brasil
[4] Didactics and Technology in Education of Trainers of University of Aveiro, Portugal
(CIDTFF - Centro de Investigação Didática e Tecnologia na Formação de Formadores)
{zeloureiro,fns,anna.cecilia,arodrigues}@ua.pt

Abstract. This work aims at explaining one online platform (ArguQuest) whose main objective is to stimulate learning through argumentation and questioning in a collaborative virtual environment. It is expected that students clarify their knowledge by explaining what they know to their peers. They have to make themselves precise and clear so that their peers can understand them and the ideas they want to express.

In this online environment students are invited to discuss topics in dyads, in a certain number of modules where the level of discussion centered on arguments and questions become deeper. In some points they are invited to discuss the contents with other dyads and, to conclude, an argumentative map is presented by the system and changed or not by the participants.

Conclusions of studies developed in Brazil and Portugal reveal that the platform stimulates peer discussion develops questioning and arguing skills.

Keywords: collaboration skills, Argumentation, Questioning, eLearning platform.

1 Introduction

The context of online learning promotes innovative educational environments where collaboration plays an important role due to the characteristics of online communication. Furthermore, these educational contexts encourage discovery, motivation and the diversification of strategies. Assuming that questioning and argumentation skills promote active and reflective learning as well as critical thinking, two very important competences in the promotion of students' awareness about their metacognition. This work aims at explaining the challenges of an online platform (ArguQuest) whose main objective is to offer strategies that stimulate learning through argumentation and questioning in a collaborative virtual environment. Collaboration leads students to clarify their knowledge since they have to explain what they know to

P. Zaphiris and A. Ioannou (Eds.): LCT 2014, Part II, LNCS 8524, pp. 440–449, 2014.
© Springer International Publishing Switzerland 2014

their peers and therefore must be extremely clear so that the others can understand them and the ideas they want to convey. Thus, they structure and consolidate their knowledge. These beliefs have long been discussed and acknowledged by different authors and more recent studies, like the ones developed between 2008 and 2010 in the Netherlands at Utrecht University, in Singapore at Nanyang Technological University, and in England at the school of Education of Kings College, are a few good examples.

As previously mentioned, this paper presents an on-line platform (ArguQuest) where students are invited to discuss topics suggested by the class, by the teacher or by themselves in peers and in successive modules where the level of discussion based on the meaning of arguments or questions gets deeper and deeper. In some points of the discussion they are also invited to debate the contents with the other groups and, to finalize, the system puts forward an argumentative map about the discussion and explanations presented, that students can construct themselves or change according to their discerning. Despite having been detected some technical limitations, as well as a few difficulties due to some students' lack of experience working in on-line environments, the studies reveal that the platform stimulates motivation and peer discussion and at the same time develops questioning and arguing skills.

In addition, taking into account that two studies were made in Higher Education, one in Pernambuco, Brazil and another one in Aveiro, Portugal, in order i) to test the stability and functionality of the platform and ii) to assess the pedagogical issues related to its use, this paper also intends to address their main conclusions.

2   Theoretical Framework

In learning digital environments, different methodologies are used emphasising collaborative work, in both e-learning or b-learning approaches and giving particular importance to knowledge co-construction and sharing. It is a belief that in the interaction and negotiation processes, trying to overcome conflict and reaching consensus with their peers, students build, reflect and strengthen their knowledge, as they have to justify their opinions, counter argument and become more enlightened decision makers about their own learning and the paths they choose in order to learn. Thus, "they develop their ability to coherently express their points of view, enrich their persuasive intelligence and refine their knowledge" [1, 251].

In fact, these work methodologies favor learnings based on socio-constructivism and pro-active learning, allowing students to recreate themselves during the learning processes as they are confronted with new perspectives, with new ways of acquiring concepts, procedures, knowledge and skills, in line with Vygotsky's thinking [2].

Dealing with new perspectives and learning processes is something that comes about as students, in these learning digital environments, tend to establish new relationships with peers. These are learning relationships in the sense that students learn with others, for the others reinforcing their own learning in richer interactions since they are constantly confronted with others and constantly reconstructing their learning strategies, their own thinking and knowledge. At the same time all of these learning paradigms promote autonomy and critical thinking, as they have to make choices and take decisions [3, 4, 5, 6, 7]. It involves high level rational and reflective thinking [8], being focused on decision making processes. As [9] states, it demands detailed analysis and evaluation by exploring ideas and concepts, going through questions and arguments, in construction and deconstruction processes of their content.

Consequently critical thinking requests high skills as interpretation, analysis, deduction and the explanation of all considerations brought to the dialogue as well as the discussion about the evidences or contexts levels in which thoughts and judgments are based.

Another statement and suggestion of literature is that it is not possible to conceive the development of critical thinking without the challenges of questioning and arguments' formulation, which leads to deeper questioning and arguing skills. This is therefore one of the most stimulating strategies in the learning and teaching processes as the voice is given to students so that they actively participate in their knowledge construction.

As a matter of fact, argumentative skills are essential to the appropriation of information and knowledge concepts: when the student selects his reasons, considers and discusses or refutes his or other's topics, he structures and organizes his own thinking in a more adequate way, which means that he learns, by the meaning of the argumentative exercise. Student intensifies and expands the knowledge about the topic.

Student's curiosity is what stimulates best their knowledge acquisition because they learn based on their interest or need and so the contents that promoted his learning need and awareness are better learnt. Obviously the student needs to identify what he knows and doesn't know and it often happens that he has to design critical non structured incidents in a very confident environment so he can express his "non knowledge areas" through questioning [10].

In what the situation of online learning is concerned, students recognize the importance of the social role that it promotes and the importance of the interaction in learning stimulation. Some students in certain online learning situations may eventually consider their posts or contributions as not adequate [3]. But even in those circumstances, in which they dislike their performance or don't see it in as a successful accomplishment, and see themselves or fell like less productive and /or displaced, they identify advantages in online collaborative learning.

In students' statements, it is not only the relation between learners that is mentioned. As a result of interviews and questionnaires performed with undergraduates, [11] and [12] refer that in online situations, the learners, the teacher and the tutor become more present, more visible and more available. In a face-to-face class the teacher has no time to pay attention and to help all the students in their doubts and concerns as it is impossible to attend to all solicitations. On the contrary, online teachers answer to every questions, they are there to help learners solve their problems, they take the time to be with each student and each group in a more rentable and proficuous way.

[11] also concluded that in a normal classroom situation, teachers' questions are poor, of a low cognitive level and without a pedagogical intention. Usually they are

out of context confirmation questions and with only an academic intention. Consequently, students are not stimulated to ask questions but only to give answers, so when they do ask their questions; they belong to a very low reasoning level and are contextless.

Once there are no constrains about the physical presence and others' evaluation, students can establish a more private relationship with their teacher or tutor and with their colleagues within the group or dyad where they feel comfortable to expose their doubts, fears and/or uncertainties, having more time and attention in this process of accompanied and supported learning.

When ArguQuest platform began to be planed, designed and structured there were no online platforms with the purposes this one was aimed at. There were other platforms for argumentation development but no online tools for the improvement of questioning and argumentation in an intended, deliberated, articulated and intersected way [13], [12].

The present study aims to explain the functioning and potentialities of the online interface as well as the steps the students have to perform on this online platform that brings together questioning and argumentation skills so that they both promote and support each other. It also intends to report the conclusions of two case studies developed in 2013.

According to [14] there is a strong connection between these two skills. Through the questioning process, students confront each other about opposing views, generating an episode of questions and answers, in order to refute, concede or justify their ideas and therefore achieving new arguments. Thus, a new and deeper level of reasoning and questioning will be achieved in these continuing and iterative argumentation episodes, which promote reasoning and critical thinking.

An explanation of the platform's organization will now be presented so that the movements and iterative episodes can be better understood.

ArguQuest is organized in four dimensions that correspond to four levels of interactions proposed by [11]: i) brainstorming; ii) collaborative training; iii) collaborative discussion and finally iv) the final product of the reflexive debate and process.

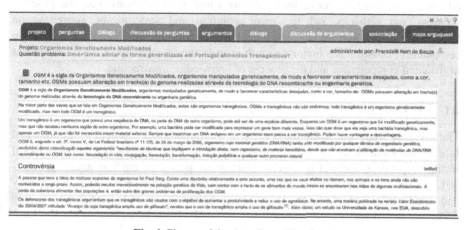

Fig. 1. Phases of the ArguQuest Plataform

The four dimensions of the platform interface are organized in nine steps that the students have to follow so that all the dimensions are considered. Once they move from one step to another, they can always comeback to verify and even correct, or modify some of their contributions to the discussion, in order to make them more profound and critical.

In the platform the steps they have to follow are represented in figure 1: i) project – where they define one topic for discussion or enroll themselves into a topic already defined; ii) questions – they elaborate questions to elucidate concepts and better understand the topic; iii) dialogue – the questions are discussed in dyads and the best ones are reformulated and chosen; iv) questions' discussion – in this step all the group can check, analyze, evaluate and give opinions on others' questions; v) arguments - in this part of the process some arguments are presented; vi) discussed within the dyad - dialogue; vii) and debated in big group - arguments' discussion; viii) after all that pathway it is now the moment to cross questions and arguments – association; ix) creation of a conceptual map in order to visualize doubts, explanations, arguments and reasons given for and against the debated topic – ArguQuest map.

It is important to remark that during all the stages of the questioning and arguing process the platform offers the students prompts or scripts under the form of "sentence openers" for the elaboration of arguments and / or questions. This option is connected with the proposals of authors who considered the inestimable help of such system support: they constitute guidelines that can positively interfere with the interaction, suggesting further formulation, facilitating discussion and achievement. This also leads to a self-regulating learning and to a facilitator of peer feedback [15], [16].

As it was mentioned before, in the dyad online interaction within the platform students are guided to learn by inquiring, searching, proposing, replying, reacting, discussing, supporting, refuting, agreeing, i.e., they refine their questions and arguments and build more sense about concepts or problems, through an active attitude of arguing and questioning.The fact that the platform allows to visit and revisit the scripts of students, with all their forward and backward movement, advances and retreats, corrections, additions and reformulations, i.e., the process, progress and setbacks and the own evolution and structure of awareness on knowledge acquisition by the meanings of a more reflexive and metacognitive competence, constitutes a major research asset in the research about the development of the cited competences and the process of knowledge construction.

2.1   1st Case Study

The first case study was led in the context of a community of practice, with online and face to face methodologies, in a superior institution of the state of Pernambuco, Brasil in the scope of a doctoral research. During the period of the investigation, 2011-2013, 70 university professors formally registered as participants in the community and used different interfaces for their communication and interaction, mainly Facebook and Skype.

In February 2013 the group was invited to participate in 3 training session about "ArguQuest pedagogical applications". 16 professors showed their interest in the participation and made their sign in the platform. However, the time chosen for the training and the conjugation with Portuguese hour for the collaboration of one of the authors of the platform, corresponded to a time of high online traffic in Northeastern Brazil and the poor connections had unexpected consequences and only a few number of registered members attended and participated in the training.

After a content analysis in the 3 sessions with no more than 5 professors each, it was evident that in spite of the difficulties of connecting to the others, the fact that the session was guided in skype and the platform was a novelty motivated the professors who asked several questions concerning the functions of ArguQuest and understood its potential founded on the dynamic of learning centered on students and the possibility of integrate this software in their teaching and learning pratices.

As referred, a lot of constraints occurred during the training and the professors who participated in the sessions had no opportunity to finish an ArguQuest learning episode in the platform. Only the 4 first steps of the platform were worked, until the discussion of the questions made about the topic proposed: "Quotes for the end of discrimination in Brazilian Education".

However, after the training and tanks to the PDF of the interaction's registration, is was possible to verify that the number of questions and their level of refinement was much bigger than in the other platforms. The fact that the sentence openers support the questions elaboration and that the system guides the participants in the formulation, discussion and refinement of questioning, is a valid way to improve the capacity of enrich questioning by filtering and converting it into a more suitable, complete, subtle and complex formulation.

As a matter of fact, these participants were grownups, educated, professors, and the level of questions in ArguQuest could be attributed to these reasons. Nevertheless, being adults, those participants are not informatics natives, so the platform and its interrelated parts could appear to them like complex and make them dismiss. It was exactly the contrary and the prove that, in this context, ArguQuest made them improve the questioning competence, is the comparaison with the written interactions in skype and facebook.

Moreover the interaction between participants became richer, once there was an evolution from categories connected with "declarations of agreement" and "formulation of questions" to "clarify statements" with "proposals and negotiation" for "the knowledge construction".

The software was also evaluated by the participants in the sessions, through a Likert scale questionnaire, and they all agreed that the platform was easy to use and operate with. They also stated that the users' tutorials and the administrator of the projects were very helpful in understanding the functioning. Some of the constraints pointed out by the users, were about the lack of time to work in the platform and to develop the project, as well as the fact that lots of colleagues didn't show up which was not easily understandable for the present little group, because they found the platform very interesting and with plenty of possibilities for the teaching and learning procedures.

2.2   2nd Case Study

The second case study was lead in the context of a graduate students' master in the teaching of 1st and 2nd cycles of basic teaching, which means, 6 to 12 children teaching. The 15 graduate students of the University of Aveiro, were attending the curricular unit "Integrated sciences didactics". Two of authors of this study were the professors of that unit. The discipline occurred during the second semester of 2013 and the data collection happened in March.

On the scope of the curricula contents, a project was beginning in ArguQuest platform under the topic of "Genetically Modified Organisms", "GMO". The problem/question was: Should we adopt in Portugal "GMO"?

The aims of the research study were to identify i) the perception of users about ArguQuest and its impact to promote questioning and arguing skills; ii) the promotion of critical thinking thought the discussion in ArguQuest and iii) the evolution of argumentative and questioning skills.

The methodology used in this bLearning specific case was a qualitative and exploratory one witch data were collected on the basis of a survey group interview and the scripts analyzes registered on the platform background with all movements of the intervenients, teachers, tutors and students.

The data were submitted to a content analysis based in categories of the questions and arguments formulated in both contexts: individual and dyad or group work, as well as the final product, the ArguQuest map which was moreover the target of a face to face debate.

The analyses of critical thinking was based in the several categories and moments [17] and they concluded that the categories the more used were connected to elementary and elaborated clarification, highlighting the capacity of analyses of arguments and the elaboration or answer to questions of clarification or challenging and to define terms or analyze definitions, in a first place.

It is a logical evolution that, while the discussion follows up, the students tend to turn to a more evaluative attitude, estimating the integrity and significance of deductions and making and evaluating value judgments. In the end they mainly took decisions and reformulate principles in an implicit and strategic way to obtain agreement within the dyad and the group and arrive to better results in the discussion and in the conceptual map they aim at developing in a rich schematically metaphorical representation.

In what the questions and arguments are concerned, the analyses of the growth of these competences was based in a SOLO (Structure of Observing Learning Outcome) adapted for this propose [12]. In this case study the first four dimensions of the hierarchy's levels in the capacity of understanding the contents' complexity were showed in different levels according to the development of the work and the progress of the dyads and group discussions.

The lower level, i) the pre-structural, that corresponds to very poor or usual questions; ii) the uni-structural, were questions and arguments establish basic relations with isolated contents; iii) the multi-structural , a more complex one were questions and arguments are connected to more than one content; iv) the relational, were questions and arguments are mainly use to enlarge knowledge and relate the parts with the wholly domain in discussion. The last dimension related to v) abstraction allows to generalize knowledge and moreover to transfer it to new complex situations and problem solving.

In this use of ArguQuest the first four dimensions were verified in students reasoning and, as for the domains about critical thinking, the tendency of argumentation and questioning skills' use, was to deeper and deeper the organization and the complexity of inquiring, suggesting, retorking, reacting, refuting, agreeing augmented and turned into a more complex thinking and cognitive exercise with satisfactory outcomes.

3 Conclusions

The platform ArguQuest, despite the constrains showed in both situations, mainly connected with i) the lack of time to a better dedication to the projects developed which led to a poor use of some of the components and steps of the platform, namely the argumentative part, in the case of the first group, and the argumentative map, in the case of the last one, and ii) the technical problems due to bad internet connections, different time zones in the case of Brazil, and de the bugs still existent in the platform because of the novelty of this work interface in both cases, it has still proven to be a very stimulating interface to promote interaction and deeper skills and the richness of the discussions developed in both cases. Moreover it proves, mainly in the second case, that argumentation and questioning skills have a strong interaction and interdependence that promotes each other's development and refinement.

These studies confirm what recent studies by [14], stand for: argumentation is considered a verbal, social and rational activity, important to convince about the acceptability of ideas and statements, as well as questioning, which is also fundamental for the process of question-generation and for the use of quality questions, having the two competences a very important role in the training and development of critical thinking skills.

Moreover the two studies, developed in completely different contexts, reach conclusions similar to the ones found in literature, as questioning is considered a complementary process that supports argumentation by helping to stimulate cognitive disagreement [14]. When we think about other contexts, in areas where argumentation is highly demanded like philosophy, law, languages, marketing and publicity, we realize that those areas will gain with the use of such tools that help to develop transversal competencies to such different areas of knowledge.

In what further studies are concerned, a group of 25 Brazilian Chemistry teachers and professors are, in this moment, attending an internship in Aveiro's university where they are already using the platform for their course's report. In the first session, there was no technical problems and all the teachers began using ArguQuest easily so, the first conclusion, is that the platform is quite user friendly.

Another project that will take place during the second semester of the present school year consists in doing an experimental use of the platform with young students, whose teachers are the undergraduates that were a part of the second study described in this paper. This experiment will allow to test the platform with the youngest and will also eventually help us to monitor how the first year teachers transfer their behavior, in what the use of the platform is concerned, from the role of students that they had, to the one of teachers, monitors and facilitators that they have this year.

Furthermore, the authors of ArguQuest expect the different testing contexts to foster a better perspective about the platform's strengths and weaknesses in order to improve its development in the future. Summing up, although it will take some time, we shall strive for a high quality product which should safeguard and guarantee excellent level learning processes able to promote argumentation, questioning and critical thinking competences effectively.

Acknowledgements. This work is funded by FEDER funds through the Operational Programme of Competitiveness Factors - COMPETE and by National Funds through FCT - Foundation for Science and Technology under PEst-C/CED/UI0194/2011 project.

References

1. Loureiro, M.J., Pinho, A., Pereira, l., Moreira, A.: Arguing On-line in Order to Learn How to Argue. In: Mendes, J., Pereira, I., Costa, R. (eds.) Computers and Education: Towards Educational Change and Innovation, pp. 251–260. Springer (2008)
2. Vygotsky, L.S.: Thought and Language. The M.l.T. Press, Massachusetts (1986) (Kozulin, A. (ed.), Kozulin, A. (trans.))
3. Curtis, D., Lawson, M.: Exploring Collaborative On-line Learning. Journal of Asynchronous Learning Networks (JALN) 5(1) (2001)
4. Tolmie, A., McAteer, E., Harris, R., Chappel, H., Marsden, S., Lally, V.: Characterising on-line learning environments. In: Banks, D., Goodyear, P., McConne, D. (eds.) Networked Learning 2002: 3rd International Conference Proceedings, Sheffield, UK, pp. 63–69 (2002)
5. Tickner, S.: Charting Change in Networked Learners: What can we learn about what they learn? In: Banks, S., Goodyear, P., Hodgson, V., McConnell, D. (eds.) Proceedings of the Third International Conference on Networked Learning 2002: A Research Based Conference on e-learning in Higher Education and Lifelong Learning. Lancaster University and The University of Sheffield (2002)
6. Cho, K., Schunn, C.D.: Seven Cognitive Factors that Make Learning Successful in Networked Collaboration. Learning Research and Development Center, 246–251 (2003)
7. Loureiro, M.J.: Construção do discurso argumentativo num contexto de eLearning no ensino superior (2007) (U. Aveiro, Ed.)
8. Tenreiro-Vieira, C., Vieira, R.M.: Literacia e pensamento crítico: um referencial para a educação em ciências e em matemática. Revista Brasileira de Educação 18(52) (2013)
9. Facione, N.C.: Critical Thinking:What It Is and Why It Counts. In: Critical Thinking and Clinical Reasoning in the Health Sciences: An International Multidisciplinary Teaching Anthology (2013)
10. Teixeira-Dias, J.J., Pedrosa de Jesus, H., Neri de Souza, F., Watts, D.M.: Teaching for Quality Learning in Chemistry. International Journal of Science Education 27(9), 1123–1137 (2005)

11. Neri de Souza, F., Watts, D.M., Moreira, A.: e-Questioning Tutorial. In: Teaching and Learning 2008: Achieving Excellence and Quality in Education. Aveiro (2008)
12. Loureiro, M.J., Neri de Souza, F.: A Presença de Questões em Mapas Argumentativos: Onde se Cruzam. In: Pereira, L., Cardoso, I. (eds.) Reflexão Sobre a Escrita. O Ensino de Diferentes Géneros de Textos, pp. 269–288. Universidade de Aveiro, Aveiro (2013)
13. Gürkan, A., Iandoli, L., Klein, M., Zollo, G.: Mediating debate through on-line largescale. Information Sciences 180(19), 3686–3702 (2010)
14. Chin, C., Osborne, J.: Maio 04). Supporting Argumentation Through Students' Questions: Case Studies in Science Classrooms. Journal of the Learning Sciences 19(2), 230–284 (2010)
15. Kanselaar, G., Erkens, G., Prangsma, M., Jaspers, J. (n.d.): Using Tools in Computer Supported Collaborative Argumentation (February 12, 2014), http://edu.fss.uu.nl/medewerkers/gk/files/boulder_CSCL2002.pdf (retrieved December 07, 2002)
16. Weinberger, A., Fischer, F., Stegmann, K.: Computer-Supported Collaborative Learning in Higher Education: Scripts for Argumentative Knowledge Construction in Distributed Groups. In: CSCL 2005 Proceedings of th 2005 Conference on Computer Support for Collaborative Learning 2005: The Next 10 Years!, Taipei, Taiwan, pp. 717–726 (2005)
17. Neri de Souza, F., Rodrigues, A.: Questionar e Argumentar Online: Possibilidades de Pensamento Crítico com a Utilização do Arguquest®? In: I Seminário Internacional Pensamento Crítico na Educação. Universidade de Aveiro (2013)

Active Ageing – Enhancing Digital Literacies in Elderly Citizens

Ana Loureiro[*] and Maria Barbas

Instituto Politécnico de Santarém & CIDTFF/Universidade de Aveiro, Portugal
{accloureiro,mariapbarbas}@gmail.com

Abstract. Being digital and information literate is crucial in nowadays society, although not every citizen has the necessary means and resources to achieve these skills, especially the elderly ones. Therefore it is necessary to develop ways to help them to enhance their digital and information competences. In this paper we will present an ongoing project that was designed and implemented with the goal to provide elderly citizens with the necessary skills of a networked society, contributing for an active ageing. The methods used were based on a set of hands on workshops delivered by a team of voluntary students and teacher, with the help of collaborators from a nursing home. The workshops were developed accordingly with the detected needs of a group of elderly citizens, based on the answers of an implemented questionnaire.

Keywords: active ageing, digital literacy, elderly citizens, ICT, inclusion.

1 Introduction

We live in a networked society, in an era of sharing and collaboration, brought by the exponential growth of the Internet - in particular the Web 2.0 and Social Web services – and the faster development of the Information and Communication Technologies (ICT). Citizens all over the world are more dependent of ICT, *"becoming increasingly central to many people's lives, making it possible to be connected in any place at any time"* [1] They are no longer mere passive receivers of information and knowledge, instead they are active and reactive - searching, creating, sharing and commenting on content of multiple contexts, contributing to the collective intelligence. Collective intelligence is seen as *"a form of universally distributed intelligence, constantly enhanced, coordinated in real time, and resulting in the effective mobilization of skills"* [2]. We can only have this diversity if we have the collaboration and cooperation of all citizens of our society. But mastering the technologies doesn't seem to be accessible to everyone. Digital literacy and information literacy are now key concepts of this networked society; therefore, every citizen should hold competences on this matter. Every day new and different gadgets, applications, widgets arise expecting *"us to know or be able to guess, what, where and when to connect, click, double-click, tap, flick, scroll"* [1]. Being able to deal with all those demanding of the networked society is not always easy, especially for those with

---

[*] Corresponding author.

P. Zaphiris and A. Ioannou (Eds.): LCT 2014, Part II, LNCS 8524, pp. 450–459, 2014.

some sort of technological disadvantage – being the elderly one of the most affected groups in society.

The European Union's population structure is changing and becoming progressively older – at the beginning of 2010, there were 87 million people aged 65 and over in the EU, more than 17 % of the total population. In response to demographic challenges being faced within Europe, the European Union designated 2012 as the European Year for Active Ageing and Solidarity between Generations [3]. The general goal was to facilitate the creation of an active ageing culture in Europe based on a society for all ages. As Europeans live longer and healthier lives, governments are looking for ways to involve elderly citizens more in society and to keep them active.

Active ageing means growing old in good health and as a full member of society, feeling more fulfilled in our jobs, more independent in our daily lives and more involved as citizens. No matter how old we are, we can still play our part in society and enjoy a better quality of life. The challenge is to make the most of the enormous potential that we harbor even at a more advanced age [4]. Active ageing can give senior citizens the opportunity to continue to work and share their experiences, to continue to play an active role in society and to live their lives as healthy, independent, and fulfilled as possible. The European Year for Active Ageing and Solidarity between Generations, appealed precisely on taking actions in very different areas: employment, social protection, education and training, health and social services, housing and public infrastructure. Given the fact that we are living in the society of knowledge and information or networked society it is also imperative to provide all citizens with skills in digital and information literacy.

Digital literacy refers *"to the awarenesses, skills, understandings, and reflective approaches necessary for an individual to operate comfortably in information-rich and IT-enabled environments"* [5]. It is thus the ability a person has to perform, effectively, tasks in digital environments - including the ability to read and interpret media to reproduce data and images through digital manipulation, and evaluate and apply new knowledge in digital environments [6]. On the other hand information literacy *"is the adoption of appropriate information behaviour to identify, through whatever channel or medium, information well fitted to information needs, leading to wise and ethical use of information in society"* [7].

Despite the fact that being digital and information literate is crucial in nowadays society, and as already mentioned, not every citizen has the necessary means and resources to achieve these skills, especially the elderly ones. Therefore it is necessary to develop ways to help them to enhance their digital and information competences.

In this paper we will present an ongoing project that was designed and implemented with the goal to provide elderly citizens with the necessary skills of a networked society, contributing for an active ageing. The methods used were based on a set of hands on workshops delivered by a team of voluntary students and teacher, with the help of collaborators from a nursing home. The workshops were developed accordingly with the detected needs of a group of elderly citizens, based on the answers of an implemented questionnaire.

2   Theoretical Framework

On nowadays society, *"jobs and their skills requirements are constantly evolving. Concepts such as critical thinking, multi-tasking, collaboration and team work are increasingly strategically relevant. E-skills can provide the opportunities to meet these fast-changing requirements of the knowledge-based society and achieve a better position to overpass global competitive challenges"* [8]. This calls for citizens with digital and information literacy competences that provide certain digital infrastructures and also citizens with digital skills to use them. Therefore, a digitally literate society is a precursor to a knowledge-based society, requiring specific skills from their citizens, including from elderly citizens to facilitate an active ageing. Those specific skills are characterized by:

- transdisciplinarity;
- social intelligence;
- adaptive and computational thinking;
- literacy in social media;
- virtual collaboration;
- and cross-cultural skills, among others.

Thus, to be digitally literate involves:

- know how to access information and know how to collect it from virtual and digital environments;
- manage and organize information in order to be able to use it in the future;
- evaluate, integrate, interpret and compare information from multiple sources;
- create and generate knowledge by adapting, applying and recreating new information;
- communicate and relay information to different and varied audiences through appropriate means.

Access to information is a way to access knowledge. Parallel to digital literacy it is crucial to develop competences on information literacy. A citizen, to be information literate, *"must be able to recognize when information is needed and have the ability to locate, evaluate and use effectively the needed information"*, available all over the Internet [9].

Despite these facts, in Portugal, accordingly with the latest data from 2013 [10], 64 % of the Portuguese population use the computer and the Internet; those, only 20, 2 % of elderly citizens (between the ages of 65 and 74) use the computer and merely 18, 6% use the Internet. Plus the range of elderly citizens in the Portuguese society is growing, accordingly with the 2011 census [11] 19, 15% of the population is over 65 years old.

The necessary transition to an economy and society based on knowledge leads us to think, work and meet in a network. In this context is required to promote the appropriation of digital literacies throughout the Portuguese society, namely the elderly citizens. To achieve this goal it's necessary to propose and implement innovative initiatives for digital inclusion and increasing digital literacy and skills. The ability to develop those skills is intrinsically related with the concept of lifelong learning, which is the pursuit of knowledge permanent and continuous, performed on a voluntary basis and self-motivated, for reasons both personal and professional, improving social inclusion, active citizenship and personal development as well as the competitiveness and employability [12].

3   Active Citizenship | Grandparents 2.0

As mentioned before, active ageing means taking more and no less out of life as you age, both at work and at home or in the community, affecting each person individually, but also society as a whole. Thus, given this context, we intend to build this project, fostering intergenerational dialogue between students and seniors. Moreover, 2013 was the European Year of Citizens, focusing on the rights that all people automatically enjoy throughout the European Union because they are European citizens. Every day, 500 million Europeans enjoy these rights, which also benefits the European economy. So, if Europeans are better informed and know better utilize their rights as individuals may benefit more, which will also bring benefits for the EU economy and society. Moreover, with the project *Cidadania Activa | Avós 2.0* (Active Citizenship | Grandparents 2.0) is intended to meet the Digital Agenda for Europe 2020 strategies, which reports that over "*50% of Europeans use the internet daily – but 30% have never used it at all! Moreover, disabled persons face particular difficulties in benefiting fully from new electronic content and services. As ever more daily tasks are carried out online, everyone needs enhanced digital skills to participate fully in society. The Digital Agenda tackles the digital divide*" [13]. Therefore, the project aims to contribute to the "*Pillar VI: Enhancing digital literacy, skills and inclusion*" and especially the actions:

- Action 57: Prioritize digital literacy and competences for the European Social Fund
- Action 59: Prioritize digital literacy and skills in the 'New skills for jobs' flagship
- Action 60: Increase participation of women in the ICT workforce
- Action 61: Educate consumers on the new media
- Action 62: EU-wide indicators of digital competences
- Action 64: Ensure the accessibility of public sector websites
- Action 65: Helping disabled people to access content
- Action 126: Grand Coalition for Digital Jobs and Skills

Within the *Agenda Portugal Digital* [14], we hope to contribute to the objective for the promotion and use of online public services, in order to be used by 50% of the population by 2016, in particular the measure aiming to improve literacy, skills and digital inclusion, in particular:

- Develop skills for the Digital Economy;
- Promoting digital inclusion and regular use of the Internet.

One way to promote active ageing and develop their skills in digital literacy, undergoes provide better ways of access to information and other forms of communicating, including Web, allowing to bridge the gap between elderly citizens and the community.

Active Citizenship I Grandparents 2.0 thus intends to provide Portuguese senior citizens with skills in digital literacy, particularly regarding the use of social networking and online communication tools, contributing to the increase of competences in the use of the services available on the Internet.

The project has its roots in a wider national Portuguese programme from *FCT* (Foundation for Science and Technology) which intends to develop the ICT skills in people with disadvantaged backgrounds and to improve their inclusion in society – *Rede TIC & Sociedade* (ICT & Society Network) [15]. To develop this wider project a network of stakeholders was required (cf. Fig. 1.), which aims to mobilize a number of contact points that increase the synergies for the appropriation of digital literacies throughout the elderly citizens, contributing for their active ageing and taking them into the web 2.0 era. The stakeholders involved were working in a voluntary basis. This network will contribute to the:

- reduction in the percentage of non-Internet users among info-excluded citizens;
- mobilization of an operational infrastructure that aims to include: space, equipment and trainers;
- development of training material for digital literacies enhancement;
- improvement of the levels of perceived trust (safety and usefulness).

Fig. 1. Project's Stakeholders

Focused on a strategy for digital inclusion and the development of digital and information literacy, will cover a range of activities, such as:

- Propose and implement innovative initiatives and promoting the inclusion and increasing digital literacy;
- Promote the improvement of ICT skills through the development of digital content available for free;
- Promote guidelines for the effective and efficient use of infrastructure, equipment and resources available to the network;
- Support the sharing among the collaborators of the Network.

With the Active Citizenship I Grandparents 2.0 we will focus on the development of digital literacies among elderly citizens, fostering them into a networked society.

We felt the need to develop such a project because it was detected the feeling of social isolation and loneliness among elderly citizens once that many of them are away from their families and friends.

3.1 Social Isolation and Loneliness in Elderly

The feeling of loneliness appears associated with a small relationship network, being associated with social isolation, which triggers some disturbances in self-esteem and quality of life for the elderly. Social loneliness occurs when a person feels a lack of belonging to the community or in establishing social ties, leaving a mixture of feelings of rejection, anger and non-acceptance. Emotional loneliness happens when one feels the lack of personal and intimate relationships. You cannot mitigate the loneliness replacing it with another form of relationship, being emotional loneliness the most painful form of isolation that a person can suffer [16]. In fact, loneliness is a subjective feeling, associated with the quality of social interaction and not with the quantity of social contact, and may be due to the emotional pain of losing someone very special, a sense of exclusion or marginalization of social ties [17].

Some causes related to the inherent feeling of loneliness are mainly due to population isolation. Elderly living in rural areas are more prone to loneliness than elderly living in urban centers. The weak physical state, widowhood, low yields, diseases and lack of friends are agents that also contribute to the loneliness. On the other hand, contact with other individuals can contribute to the adoption of healthy habits as well as contribute to increased personal control, helping to psychological well-being of the elderly [18]. There are several strategies that help the elderly to combat loneliness: meet new people and mingle with them, participating in voluntary social activities at a local level, integration into acquaintanceship groups, seek to recognize their rights and duties as a citizen, take care of mental and physical health, understand the natural changes associated with ageing, and find or retrieve new channels of communication between individuals from the same generation [19]. Healthy ageing is closely related to the promotion of independence and the prevention of loneliness and social isolation [20]. Sociability in the elderly is crucial for the prevention of several problems, contributing for their health, quality of life and well-being.

3.2   ICT As a Way to Fight Social Isolation and Loneliness

ICT has been an asset to the dissemination of information and knowledge through various digital tools, ensuring forms of socialization that will benefit elderly on the fight of the loneliness and social isolation. On the other hand, virtual tours of museums, libraries and shopping centers are also one of the most sought after activities [21], plus the elderly in addition to sending e-mail, still seek to gather information about hobbies, news, health information and updates on the weather [22].

The access of elderly to the social networks and other ways of online contact, such as email, chat rooms, newsgroups, hangouts and videoconference, will ensure contact with friends and family and can be fostered through training sessions. Digital inclusion is the democratization of access to information technologies, to allow the insertion of every citizen in the information society and also simplify their daily routine, maximize time and its potential. An info-inclusive is not one that simply takes advantage of technology and networks to exchange emails or doing research, but one that boasts of its potential to improve their living conditions. Thus, digital inclusion is not just "literate" citizens regarding the use of technology but improve social frameworks from its use and application .It is intended that the elderly obtain greater autonomy, knowledge, social participation, personal development and skills that will foster relationships with others. The contact with technologies allows the elderly to redefine its insertion in the nuclear family and in society, promoting intergenerational relationships. The use of computers and tablets and the access to the internet allows other ways of communication and interaction, providing also ways to solve a problem situation, such as access to various services of daily-life - home banking, post office, health center, finances, supermarket.

3.3   The Pilot Study

Previously to a wider action a pilot study was implemented in order to understand the viability of the project. In order to understand the needs of the elderly citizens concerning the digital literacies a questionnaire was applied. The target were elderly citizens from a nursing home, in a total of 14 answers – chosen due to their proximity and facility to reach out. The detected needs in terms of ICT skills were varied (cf Fig. 2.) – the need to learn how to use a search engine and how to edit content in a word document are among the most requested ones.

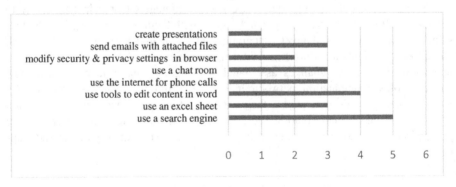

Fig. 2. Detected training needs among elderly citizens

Also the ability to send emails with attached files, use a chat room or make a phone call through the internet were mentioned by the elderly citizens. This necessity arises from the need to have a closer and more often contact with their family and friends, helping to reduce the sense of isolation.

Bearing in mind these needs a set of hand on workshops, covering those topics, were designed to be delivered to the elderly citizens in the selected nursing home.

The nutshell team (cf. Fig. 3.) for this project was constituted by students from a social education course, the ICT teacher, the course coordinator, the nursing home director and their employees and the elderly citizens – all done in a voluntary basis.

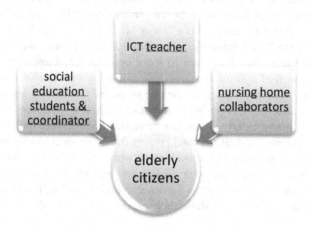

Fig. 3. Nutshell team

The training sessions were provided in the nursing home facilities with the resource of personal computers and tablets.

Although the study is ongoing, the following results are expected:

- Reduce digital exclusion among the elderly citizens;
- Development, dissemination and maintenance of a set of basic, useful and functional digital resources aimed at helping citizens in the development of digital and informational literacies;
- Mobilization of a set of physical, functional and useful features, addressed to the inclusion;
- Promote the importance of improvement of digital and information literacy as an emerging need for elderly citizens;
- Develop a sense of belonging to a community that can stay on time, which can strengthen, allowing further collaboration.

By the end of the project we expect to contribute to a more active, healthier and happier ageing among elderly citizens.

4   Final Considerations

Despite our health declines as we grow old, a lot can be done to cope with this decline. And quite small changes in our environment can make a big difference to people suffering from various health impairments and disabilities. Active ageing also means empowering us as we age so that we can remain in charge of our own lives as long as possible. Provide citizens with competences on digital and information literacy is a way to contribute for an ageing with quality and independence, giving the opportunity to the elderly to feel as part of the modern and networked society. Initiatives like the one we presented here not only contribute for an active ageing but also to the strengthening solidarity between generations and for the lifelong learning. Information and digital literates holds a *"set of skills needed to find, retrieve, analyze, and use information (...) Ultimately, information literate people are those who have learned how to learn. They know how to learn because they know how knowledge is organized, how to find information, and how to use information in such a way that others can learn from them. They are people prepared for lifelong learning, because they can always find the information needed for any task or decision at hand"* [9]. A better informed citizen, elderly or not, is a more successful citizen and will have ways to bridge the gap between their past and present lives – being provided with tools that allow them to fully integrate the nowadays networked society. Plus the *"greater the number of collective intellects with which an individual is involved, the more opportunities he has to diversify his knowledge and desire"* [2], and by giving the possibility of elderly citizens to share their experiences online the better the society will be.

Acknowledgements. The research was co-funded by FEDER (Programa Operacional Fatores de Competitividade – COMPETE) and FCT (Fundação para a Ciência e a Tecnologia – Project PEst-C/CED/UI0194/2011. Research Center "Didática e Tecnologia na Formação de Formadores" – CIDTFF, Departamento de Educação, Universidade de Aveiro, Portugal).

References

1. Mieczakowski, A., Clarkson, J.: Ageing, Adaption and Accessibility: Time for the Inclusive Revolution!, Engineering Design Centre. University of Cambridge (2012)
2. Lévy, P.: Collective intelligence. Mankind's emerging world in cyberspace. Perseus Books, Massachusetts (1997)
3. Eurostat European Commission, Active ageing and solidarity between generations. A statistical portrait of the European Union 2012 (2012), http://epp.eurostat.ec.europa.eu/cache/ITY_OFFPUB/KS-EP-11-001/EN/KS-EP-11-001-EN.PDF (retrieved)
4. European Union, European Year for Active Ageing and Solidarity between Generations (2012), http://europa.eu/ey2012/ey2012main.jsp?catId=971 (retrieved)
5. Martin, A., Ashworth, S.: Welcome to the Journal of eLiteracy! JeLi 1(1) (2004)

6. Jones-Kavalier, B., Flannigan, S.: Connecting the Digital Dots: Literacy of the 21st Century (2006), http://connect.educause.edu/Library/ EDUCAUSE+Quarterly/ConnectingtheDigitalDotsL/39969 (retrieved)
7. Webber, S., Johnston, B.: Information literacy in the United Kingdom: a critical review. In: Basili, C. (ed.) Information Literacy in Europe, pp. 258–283. Italian National Research Council, Rome (2003), http://dis.shef.ac.uk/sheila/webber-johnston-uk.pdf (retrieved)
8. McCormack, A.: The e-Skills Manifesto. European Schoolnet, Belgium (2010) ISBN: 9789490477301
9. International Federation Library Association, About the Information Literacy Section (2012), http://www.ifla.org/en/about-information-literacy (retrieved)
10. Pordata, Indivíduos que utilizam computador e Internet em % do total de indivíduos: por grupo etário – Portugal (2013), http://www.pordata.pt/Portugal/ Individuos+que+utilizam+computador+e+Internet+em+percentagem +do+total+de+individuos+por+grupo+etario-1139 (retrieved)
11. Governo de Portugal, Ano Europeu do Envelhecimento Ativo e da Solidariedade entre Gerações. Programa de Ação (2012), http://www.igfse.pt/upload/docs/ 2012/Programa%20A%C3%A7AoAnoEuropeu2012.pdf (retrieved)
12. Loureiro, A., Bettencourt, T.: The use of virtual environments as an extended classroom – a case study with adult learners in tertiary education. Procedia Technology (2013) (to be published) ISSN: 2212-0173, doi: 10.1016/j.protcy.2014.02.013
13. European Commission, Digital Agenda for Europe, http://ec.europa.eu/ digital-agenda/en/our-goals/pillar-vi-enhancing-digital-literacy-skills-and-inclusion (2012) (retrieved)
14. Governo de Portugal, Agenda Portugal Digital (2012), http://www.portugaldigital.pt/ (retrieved)
15. FCT, Rede TIC& Sociedade. Unpublished document (2014), http://www.ticsociedade.pt/
16. Weiss, R.: Loneliness: The experience of emotional and social isolation. The MIT Press, Cambridge (1973)
17. Freitas, P.: A Solidão nos Idosos. Percepção em Função da Rede Social. Tese de mestrado Inédita em Gerontologia Social Aplicada. Universidade Católica Portuguesa, Centro Regional de Braga, Faculdade de Ciências Sociais (2011), http://repositorio.ucp.pt/ bitstream/10400.14/8364/1/SOLID%C3%83O%20EM%20IDOSOS.pdf (retrieved)
18. Ramos, M.: Apoio Social e Saúde entre idosos. Sociologias 7 (2002)
19. Neril, A., Freire, S.: E por falar em boa velhice. Papirus, Campinas (2000)
20. Chau, F., Soares, C., Fialho, J. & Sacadura, M.: O Envelhecimento da População: Dependência, Ativação e Qualidade. Relatório de projeto financiado inédito, Centro de Estudos dos Povos e Culturas de Expressão Portuguesa, Faculdade de Ciências Humanas, Universidade Católica Portuguesa (2012), http://www.qren.pt/np4/ np4/?newsId=1334&fileName=envelhecimento_populacao.pdf (retrieved)
21. Pasqualotti, A., Barone, D., Doll, J.: As tecnologias de informação e comunicação na vida de idosos com sintomas de depressão: significado, experiências e relacionamentos. Renote 5(2) (2007), http://seer.ufrgs.br/index.php/renote/article/ view/14381/8277 (retrieved), ISSN 1679-1916
22. Jantsch, A., Machado, L., Behar, P., Lima, J.: As Redes Sociais e a Qualidade de Vida: os Idosos na Era Digital. IEEE-RITA 4, 173–179 (2012), http://rita.det.uvigo.es/ 201211/uploads/IEEE-RITA.2012.V7.N4.A2.pdf (retrieved)

Reflective Thinking: Exploring Blog Use by Adult Learners

Maria Mama Timotheou

Faculty of Humanities and Social Sciences
Open University of Cyprus, Cyprus
mamatimo@cantab.net

Abstract. This paper investigates the enhancement of reflective thinking in the context of online and distance adult education, through blogging as part of a course activity. A multi-case was conducted involving content and thematic analyses. The results show that students appreciated the reflection process that blogging engaged them into, while their motivation to further explore and use blogs to improve their learning experiences was increased. Factors affecting blog interaction are also identified, while the findings are associated with the key components of a theoretical framework for reflection in an attempt to link theory and research on reflective thinking.

Keywords: student reflection, critical thinking, blogging, adult education, case study, web-based course, online learning environments, perspective change, model of reflection.

1   Introduction

The popularity of distance and online education has indisputably increased over the last decade; a vastly growing number of higher education institutions worldwide, driven by the 'learning for anyone, anywhere, anytime' imperative, offer blended and/or purely online and distant courses on undergraduate and postgraduate levels [1]. With respect to this new academic paradigm, a great body of research has been devoted on the examination of the effectiveness of web-based programs and the conditions for optimized teaching and learning in online environments [2]. Certainly the field is relatively young and it is not surprising that findings on the quality of the online educational experiences, especially when compared to face-to-face formats, are rather inconclusive [3-5]. In this paper, we attempt to discuss how internet technologies and more specifically blog usage, may impact upon and improve students' online learning experiences by enhancing their reflective thinking and practices.

2   Reflection: A Key Element in the Learning Process

In this attempt, we should first define 'reflection'. John Dewey is considered the first scholar to have introduced the concept of reflective thinking in 1933 and defined it as

P. Zaphiris and A. Ioannou (Eds.): LCT 2014, Part II, LNCS 8524, pp. 460–466, 2014.
© Springer International Publishing Switzerland 2014

«Active, persistent, and careful consideration of any belief or supposed form of knowledge in the light of the grounds that support it, and the further conclusions to which it tends» [6]. Despite the early introduction of the term by Dewey, it was not until the late '80s that researchers and academics started devotedly exploring the importance of reflection for learning. Indeed, over the last decades, reflection has been acknowledged as a crucial cognitive process and a key element in learning [7]. Learner-centred pedagogies identify the value of reflection in being a conscious process, according to which the learner purposefully attempts to make links between existing understandings, thoughts and experiences, with new information. Reflection embraces evaluation and analysis strategies, and is, thus, regarded a form of metacognition, crucial in view of the complicated objectives of today's education and the versatile requirements of our information society and its workplace [8, 9]. Particular emphasis has been placed in the literature on the importance of reflection in the context of adult learning, which is of interest in this review. In fact, critical reflection consists a major principle in Malcolm Knowles's theory of adult learning [10], while studies have proved that reflective strategies, accomplished through experiential practices, have the potential to establish meaningful learning experiences [11] and motivate adult learners [12].

Even though reflection is considered essential to teaching and learning and often set as a major educational goal, scholars have pointed out that its accomplishment can be challenging. This is often attributed to a lack of systematic definition of its elements, which in turn makes it difficult to «be taught, learned, assessed, discussed and researched» [13], and then to the fact that it is socially and culturally sensitive, making it highly context-specific and requiring strict structure in the educational environment [14]. Taking these challenges into account, we reviewed the literature in search of a comprehensive framework to understand reflection [8, 15, 16]. The metacognitive model of reflection proposed by McAlpine et al. [8], focuses on higher education, proved to be a guiding theoretical framework developing our understanding of reflection. In their paper, the authors describe the model and coding scheme resulting from their research study of six university professors who were considered excellent teachers and who provided data on their planning, instructing and evaluating of their students. They claim that their model incorporates the key theoretical concepts of the reflective process but also describes how these concepts are operationalized. According to the model [8], reflection is an ongoing process, composed of six prime components as outlined below and also presented in Figure 1:

- Goals, which translate into decisions
- Knowledge, which represent cognitive structures
- Action, which transforms cognition into behaviours and enacts plans
- Monitoring, which requires feedback during enactment
- Decision making, which reflects the influenced action, and
- Corridor of tolerance, which defines the acceptable limits for change.

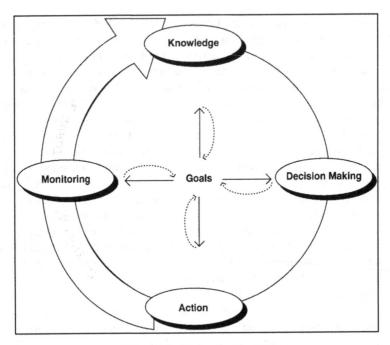

Fig. 1. Model of reflection [8]

Two more aspects are highlighted by the authors; the first is 'time of reflection', according to which reflection may be continuous and synchronous with an action (reflection-in-action) or asynchronous, meaning that it can occur or after an action (reflection-on-action). The second important aspect is 'spheres of reflection'; these are categorized into the practical sphere, which emphasizes improvement of actions in a specific context, the strategic sphere, which aims at generalizing approaches across contexts, and the epistemic sphere which represents knowing on a metacognitive level how reflection works and what it factors may influence it.

3   Reflection in Online Learning Environments

Technology-supported environments have been consistently associated with pedagogically meaningful practices and improved learning experiences, and research devoted to the incorporation of educational technologies, particularly web-based ones, in higher education has been extensive [17, 18]. Synchronous and asynchronous interaction formats, social networking, less-structured environments, multimedia incorporation and representation, unlimited choice over resources and personalization, are just some of the features of information and communication technologies reported to enhance the educational process [19], enabling constructivistic, self-directed and collaborative approaches to learning and knowledge acquisition [20].

With specific respect to the facilitation of reflective thinking, internet technologies have been analogously claimed, in theory and in research, to provide authentic opportunities for learners [21]. Such activities may include creation of multimedia such as podcasts [22], development and maintenance of e-portfolios [23], engagement with distant learning objects [21], creation and contribution to wiki sites [24], online gaming [25] and others. This paper is particularly concerned with blogging, as an activity for enhancing learner reflection.

The literature presents several other studies that have investigated blog use for educational purposes [26-28]. Three main categories of reflection are identified with regards to blogging: Self-directed, peer-inspired and collaborative reflection. We consider self-directed reflection as the process when a learner reflectively contributes to her own blog or shares thoughts and ideas on an educational topic addressed in a third party blog, driven by her individual pursuit of learning and knowledge acquisition. Furthermore, we understand peer-inspired reflection as the process in which a learner reflects on another person's message (whether posted on her own blog or a third party blog), and purposefully comments or discuss further that message. We distinguish peer-inspired reflection from collaborative reflection in that learners engaged in the latter, attempt to create and maintain a blog on a topic towards a collaborative construction of knowledge.

In view of the dramatic change that (formal and informal) education faces with the growth of the web-based tools, it is key to collect additional practices and accumulate evidence on how reflection can be prompted in online and virtual spaces. This paper aims to contribute towards this direction addressing self-directed and peer-inspired reflection during blog-based activities.

4   Methodology

A multi-case study of 6 (out of 19) participants in a course within a graduate program at a US university, was conducted. The study sample was based on volunteer participation. Participants fell within the 35-45 age group, with four of them holding teaching posts and two working at administrative positions. The course was offered exclusively online, and aimed at preparing participants to design and deliver online learning programs in both formal and informal settings. It ran over a 4-month period and was moderated by a single tutor. Instruction and communication occurred asynchronously throughout the course. Participants were expected to contribute to the online discussion and accomplish weekly activities assigned by the tutor. Three data sets were collected; the first set included participant messages on the discussion board. The second set included their responses to a brief questionnaire on online reflection. Great emphasis was particularly placed on the third data set which included the participants' assignments on an individual blog activity. According to the activity, participants were asked to follow and comment on an educational blog of their preference, and then describe and reflect on that experience. As shown in Figure 2, data were analysed qualitatively, using content and thematic analyses.

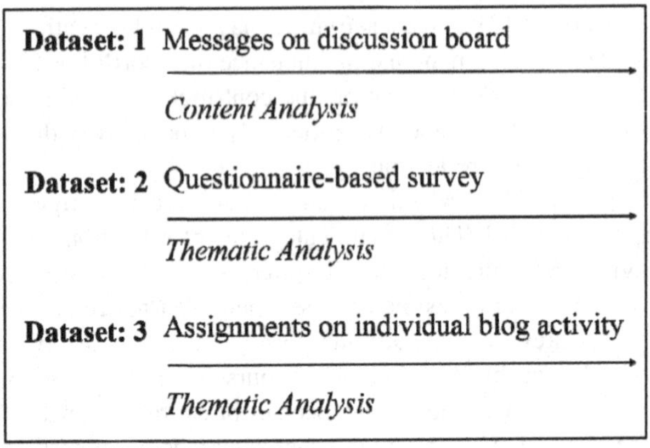

Dataset: 1 Messages on discussion board

Content Analysis

Dataset: 2 Questionnaire-based survey

Thematic Analysis

Dataset: 3 Assignments on individual blog activity

Thematic Analysis

Fig. 2. Data collection and analysis

5   Results

The findings showed that although the study participants followed educational blogs for both personal and professional purposes, they did not tend to comment on posts due to fear of exposure, even with their anonymity maintained. Corresponding the McAlpine et al.'s Model of Reflection [8], this would mean that their *goal* was not strong enough so as to be translated into decision. Being limited to reading the blog and not attempting to contribute to it, seemed to have a negative impact on the development of their reflective thinking.

Also, most of the participants acknowledged that blogging bore a learning curve for them at times. Yet they admitted often skipping posts and replies with unfamiliar concepts or terms instead of looking those up; this again discouraged any reflection process, while it may be inferred that their pursuit of *knowledge*, linking to the second component of the Model of Reflection reviewed earlier, was occasionally uninspired. Following the blog activity however, where participants had to follow an educational blog and purposefully challenge at least one post, was reported as a highly positive learning experience, corresponding to the *action* component of McAlpine et al's model [8].

As participants indicated, the assignment was valuable in encouraging them to gain not only new knowledge but new perspective also. It is important to note that all participants chose to follow educational blogs with professional responses usually authored by well-established figures in the international educational community, in an attempt to secure the source quality. In addition, it could be argued that, the pursuit of discussion quality is related to the *monitoring* component of the aforementioned model, according to which valuable feedback is key in the process. What seemed to be the case for all six participants was that, in view of the compulsory reply, their motivation to further explore the blog content increased with them becoming more interested in the subject matter, suggesting their *decision making* in continuing blogging (influenced action) even after the end of the activity.

Most of them even expressed their surprise how reflective thinking enabled their ideas and argumentation to flow naturally, despite their initial reservations about posting online. Overall, it was evident among participants that the reflective experience resulted in a perspective change. This last finding indicates the setup of a *corridor of tolerance,* linking students' present, past and future intentions towards blogging, which however we are not in position to evaluate since the study concluded following the end the blog-based activity. Yet, this is of key importance, especially within the context of education for adults, where participants consciously (and, as with the study sample, often on economic and family sacrifices) attend professional and academic programs, investing in the improvement of their learning curve.

6   Conclusion and Discussion

The study findings highlight the impact of blogging, not as a learning journal as it is often addressed in the literature, but as an educational activity for professionally interacting with and meaningfully challenging others' ideas and posted content, on the development of reflective thinking. Implications are, therefore, drawn for the integration of blogging activities in the design and implementation of programs for adult learners, so as for learner reflection to occur at all three spheres proposed by McApline et al. [8] (practice, strategic and epistemic), and not just the basic one (practice), as proved to be the case in this study. Future research avenues could include the repetition of the study involving a larger sample in order to strengthen the conclusions from this study and also generalize the findings to the broader adult learner population. Moreover, a similar but longitudinal study could be conducted so as to examine whether engagement with blog-based activities could impact on a more sustainable way on students' reflective attitude. Finally, it would be interesting to compare blogging and reflective thinking among young and older adults, taking into account that young adults are overall significantly more exposed to online messaging, discussion and reading.

References

1. Allen, I.E., Seaman, J.: Changing Course: Ten Years of Tracking Online Education in the United States. ERIC (2013)
2. Boling, E.C., et al.: Cutting the distance in distance education: Perspectives on what promotes positive, online learning experiences. The Internet and Higher Education 15(2), 118–126 (2012)
3. Bernard, R.M., et al.: How does distance education compare with classroom instruction? A meta-analysis of the empirical literature. Review of Educational Research 74(3), 379–439 (2004)
4. Rovai, A.P., Downey, J.R.: Why some distance education programs fail while others succeed in a global environment. The Internet and Higher Education 13(3), 141–147 (2010)
5. Zhang, P., Goel, L.: Is e-learning for everyone? An internal-external framework of e-learning initiative. Journal of Online Learning and Teaching 7(2), 193–206 (2011)

6. Dewey, J.: How we think. Courier Dover Publications (2012)
7. Baird, J.R., et al.: The importance of reflection in improving science teaching and learning. Journal of Research in Science Teaching 28(2), 163–182 (1991)
8. McAlpine, L., et al.: Building a metacognitive model of reflection. Higher Education 37(2), 105–131 (1999)
9. White, B.Y., Frederiksen, J.R.: Inquiry, modeling, and metacognition: Making science accessible to all students. Cognition and Instruction 16(1), 3–118 (1998)
10. Knowles, M.S., Holton III, E.F., Swanson, R.A.: The adult learner. Routledge (2012)
11. Williamson, A.: Reflection in adult learning with particular reference to learning-in-action (1997)
12. Wlodkowski, R.J.: Enhancing adult motivation to learn: A comprehensive guide for teaching all adults. John Wiley & Sons (2011)
13. Rodgers, C.: Defining reflection: Another look at John Dewey and reflective thinking. The Teachers College Record 104(4), 842–866 (2002)
14. Boud, D., Walker, D.: Promoting reflection in professional courses: The challenge of context. Studies in Higher Education 23(2), 191–206 (1998)
15. Garrison, D.R.: Critical thinking and adult education: a conceptual model for developing critical thinking in adult learners. International Journal of Lifelong Education 10(4), 287–303 (1991)
16. Kuhn, D.: A developmental model of critical thinking. Educational Researcher 28(2), 16–46 (1999)
17. Hung, H.-T., Yuen, S.C.-Y.: Educational use of social networking technology in higher education. Teaching in Higher Education 15(6), 703–714 (2010)
18. López-Pérez, M., Pérez-López, M.C., Rodríguez-Ariza, L.: Blended learning in higher education: Students' perceptions and their relation to outcomes. Computers & Education 56(3), 818–826 (2011)
19. Conole, G., Alevizou, P.: A literature review of the use of Web 2.0 tools in Higher Education. A report commissioned by the Higher Education Academy (2010)
20. Huang, H.M.: Toward constructivism for adult learners in online learning environments. British Journal of Educational Technology 33(1), 27–37 (2002)
21. Mason, R.: Learning technologies for adult continuing education. Studies in Continuing Education 28(2), 121–133 (2006)
22. McLoughlin, C., Lee, M., Chan, A.: Using student generated podcasts to foster reflection and metacognition. Australian Educational Computing 21(2), 34–40 (2006)
23. Stefani, L., Mason, R., Pegler, C.: The educational potential of e-portfolios: Supporting personal development and reflective learning. Routledge (2007)
24. Tétard, F., Patokorpi, E., Packalén, K.: Using wikis to support constructivist learning: A case study in university education settings. In: 42nd Hawaii International Conference on System Sciences, HICSS 2009. IEEE (2009)
25. Moreno-Ger, P., et al.: Educational game design for online education. Computers in Human Behavior 24(6), 2530–2540 (2008)
26. Halic, O., et al.: To blog or not to blog: Student perceptions of blog effectiveness for learning in a college-level course. The Internet and Higher Education 13(4), 206–213 (2010)
27. Li, K., et al.: Blogging for Teaching and Learning: An Examination of Experience, Attitudes, and Levels of Thinking. Contemporary Educational Technology 4(3) (2013)
28. Ahmad, R., Lutters, W.G.: Promoting reflective learning: The role of blogs in the classroom. In: Ozok, A.A., Zaphiris, P. (eds.) OCSC 2011. LNCS, vol. 6778, pp. 3–11. Springer, Heidelberg (2011)

Digital Identity of Researchers and Their Personal Learning Network

Nuno Ricardo Oliveira and Lina Morgado

Laboratório de Educação a Distância e eLearning,
Universidade Aberta, Lisboa, Portugal
nrloliveira@gmail.com, Lina.Morgado@uab.pt

Abstract. In a networked society, everyday experience is shared in networks at a personal, professional and academic level. Thus, there is a need to have digital literacy skills to obtain and produce contents in a collaborative way, sharing the knowledge acquired in the personal learning network.

This paper is a reflection of literature revision in the PhD project of Online Distance Education and e-learning, concerning themes such as digital identity and personal learning networks. In this way we aim to make a literature analysis about the necessity of digital literacy so that we may obtain competencies for a personal learning network.

Keywords: collaborative learning, Digital Identity, Digital literacy, personal learning network, skills.

1 Introduction

The appearance of emerging digital environments and pedagogies has enabled the introduction and adoption of new practices and behaviours of individuals in a university academic context. It is also in this context that the Web 2.0 has an increasing use by academic community – teachers, students and researchers - to create, stimulate and expand learning in an informal way, even when knowledge is acquired in a formal context. It is also in this background that we situate the importance of a digital literacy to improve the digital identity by members of academic communities, that enables, among other things, the creation of social connection networks (teachers, researchers, students or experts, etc.), which, in the perspective of Rodrigues & Beefun [1], are very important for an open and collaborative learning in the network.

The Web 2.0 encourages sharing, disclosure, collaboration and cooperation, making the web social and participatory whilst also an integrating part of a social platform and on a network, where each one can share their contents through the various applications, such as: blogs, forums, social networks, wikis, amongst others. They update and share information easily, creating personal learning networks, the user being the main mentor of the nodes of their personal network.

This article results in a literature review for the of a PhD thesis that looks at the questions related with the problematic area that presently constitutes in the Digital

P. Zaphiris and A. Ioannou (Eds.): LCT 2014, Part II, LNCS 8524, pp. 467–477, 2014.
© Springer International Publishing Switzerland 2014

Identity of an Online Distance Education and e-learning researcher, and their personal learning environment to study the genesis, management and dynamics of their Personal Learning Network (PLN). In this perspective, Digital Literacy is a patent parameter and important to analyze the reality of the community of researchers, studying on this project.

Therefore, the study looks to contribute to the comprehension that as of how a community of researchers construct, keep and make dynamic their Personal Learning Network (PLN) so as to make the most of collaborative and shared knowledge. By means of this process we understand the importance of the researcher to having digital literacy so as to promote a digital identity.

2   Emerging Digital Environments and Pedagogies

With the evolution of Internet, Web 2.0 is acknowledged as a platform of creation, sharing and constantly modifying contents, being user-centered, allowing both for interaction and communication as well as the creation of networks. According to some authors, among them Solomon and Schrum [2], this evolutionary phenomenon has altered some fundamental aspects on how individuals act and behave on the network: how they link within themselves, interact and share information, purchase, socialize, learn and work.

In this framework, the surging and growing of emerging digital environments is constant, defining new practices and behaviour of individuals. It is also in this context, that we note that the Web 2.0 is used more steadily by the academic community, teachers, students and researchers, to create and expand learning in an informal way, even when knowledge is acquired in a formal context.

The importance of a digital literacy and digital identity by the members of the community, allows among other actions, creations of very important social connection networks (teachers, researchers, students or specialists, etc.) in the perspective of Rodrigues & Beefun [1], for a collaborative learning on an open network.

Users make use of these networks and/or virtual learning communities in order to share information and knowledge in their area of interest, research or learning. According to Dias [3], the immersion of digital environments in an educational perspective can promote and sustain the development of open pedagogies, with evidence for interactions between the group members, those of collaborative nature standing out in a social network context [3], a digital literacy being necessary. Also Morgado [4] makes a perspective of the creation of virtual communities where personalization and openness are defining characteristics and in which, whether by the sharing of contents and experiences, or by the dynamics of interaction, follow the main open access allowing a collaborative open learning, designating a networked class. In turn, Keats & Schmidt [5] argue that, among the changes that have occurred in recent years with impact (both in technological, or educational terms), the greatest importance is attributed to the role of students as creators of shared knowledge, being that social networks play an important role in the process of collaborative open learning. The correct use of digital media is an asset for collaborative learning through a network of social connections [6].

Dias [3] states that the opening of formal learning spaces for social interaction of the web represents the possibility of members of traditional communities to participate in new cultural activities, using the potential of digital technologies to create networks of social interaction and collaborative learning. This then allows a new design and experience of learning scenarios and knowledge.

However, all these existing and emerging phenomena, as well as emerging pedagogies [7] lead us to convene for this discussion the issue of a digital literacy with the latest information which is fundamental while the facilitator is in the learning process, through social and collaborative interactions, not forgetting the critical insight needed to select what are important and meaningful contributions to the network.

Digital literacy is a concept of a recent and extensive diversity of views and interpretations. For Ala-Mutka, Punie & Redecker [8], Martin [9] and Goodfellow [10], digital literacy is the domain of tools and encourages the use of technology in the context of educational oriented digital skills promoting an awareness of criticism in the content created and used. On the other hand, it implies the effective use of technology in multiple digital formats, from a variety of sources and devices - computer, tablet or smartphone, etc., to obtain information or knowledge.

"Having digital literacy requires more than just the ability to use software or to operate a digital device it includes a large variety of complex skills(...) A conceptual model that was recently described by the authors suggests that digital literacy comprises five major digital skills: photo-visual skills ("reading" instructions from graphical displays), reproduction skills (utilizing digital reproduction to create new, meaningful materials from preexisting ones), branching skills (constructing knowledge from non-linear, hypertextual navigation), information skills (evaluating the quality and validity of information), and socio-emotional skills (understanding the "rules" that prevail in cyberspace and applying this understanding in online cyberspace communication)" [11].

Therefore, taking into account the specialized literature, digital literacy may include: (a) social practices - supported by skills, strategies and an attitude that encourages and supports the capacity of an individual to represent and understand the various ideas using digital tools [9],[12], (b) the use of technologies in a creative form - the use of tools to meet the personal and professional individual's needs [9],[13], (c) adequate knowledge to undertake the management of public and private digital spaces that enable the construction of an identity that reflects the profile and career of individuals in an academic, professional and personal level [4], [14], [15].

3   Digital Identity

The digital dimension of identity is understood as the total information about the individual, from credentials that allow access to the closed system, to the representation of the complex "I" in an open digital space [16]. In this sense, there is a tendency to optimize learning with the use of digital technologies available to the individual and through the network. With this development, there is an awareness of the need to promote new forms of learning, collaboration and dissemination of work as part of a digital brand, both at a personal and academic and professional level [14].

The digital presence of an individual is no longer a process that depends only on him, but also on the individuals who compose the network, whether they belong or simply have access to the information. Thus, the individual must know how to manage their presence in public and private online spaces [17], [18], being one more of the skills acquired by digital literacy.

For Williams, Fleming, & Parslow [19], the concept of Digital Identity (ID) is relatively recent and derives from the practices that individuals have been developing on the network. It is therefore an important element because it is the reflection of the personal, academic and professional life of the individual. According to research by Aresta [15] carried out in a case study with university students, two profiles of digital identity emerged: student awareness about their own digital identity and their reputation whilst a student and professional.

In turn, Costa & Torres [14] also highlight two major areas in which the ID is focused: presentation and reputation. At first the authors report that the ID deals with how individuals work online and how they engage and interact in shared spaces, i.e. their profile whilst online. The second focuses on the perspective that others have of the individual, i.e. what others think about your "I". To Warburton [16], the ID already allows the building of trust and also contributes to the reputation, and the persistence in maintaining credibility, a fundamental feature to obtain a relevant reputation.

White [20] refers to two perspectives of the representation of the "I" in the digital space – the visitor and resident. The visitor is one that will create different identities, so as not to bind to any in particular while the resident identity, however, feels the need and desire to build a strong and consistent identity, establishing through this the foundation for a network of "prestige contacts." Through this network, the individual reveals experiences, skills and capabilities on how to communicate, interact and share the online space.

Aresta [15] states that digital identity works in a sense better than a curriculum vitae, as it reveals to "friends" and/or to public in general, according to the notions of the privacy of the profile, a personal, educational and professional background.

Warburton [16], in turn, states that the ID reflects on the different aspects of the individual´s personality depending on the context, be it professional (researcher, lecturer, teacher, etc.) or private (personal relationships), the attitudes, behaviour and sharing made differently. Thus, our digital identity, as well as our own personality, is constantly changing and is mirrored in the environments in which we coexist online, be it on those in which we have permanent access, those that are irregular or even those that we simply created a profile to view and test its usefulness both on a private or professional level, i.e., a fragmented ID, consisting of various services and networks scattered around the Web in which we are present and/or in which we participate on a personal, academic or professional level. For some authors such as Margaryan, Nicol, Littlejohn, & Trinder [21] and Warburton [16], nowadays, with the evolution of the Internet and the importance given to the social web, the existence of an identity online on a network is an impossible phenomenon to contour. The knowledge and the capacity of researching, evaluating, creating, sharing information and synthesizing have become more and more important.

The social Web is characterized by media coverage and individual participation in various spaces and emerging environments through sharing, recording on databases (whether banking, institutional or social networking), blogs or discussion forums, allowing the construction of a digital identity network [16]. In an educational context, social software applications consist in providing the level of communication and interaction between individuals and/or groups, promoting the production of knowledge and sharing with the community [22]. This action enables a digital literacy, because the higher the share (of information), the more likely the individual will have to learn and acquire new knowledge.

4 Personal Learning Network

The technological evolution creates new challenges for education and research, as we nowadays live in a network. The network is comprised of individuals who are part of our everyday lives that share interests, resources, thoughts, links, insights and jokes, among many other things, but the key is that they enrich our professional and personal life [23].

In an interesting analysis of what he termed as digital scholarship, Weller [23] compares the use of the tools he used as a researcher and those he uses currently: the books - were accessed via library e-books and audiobook; magazines - through two online databases: Google Scholar and Mendeley; Delicious/social bookmarking, blogs, YouTube, Wikipedia, Slideshare, Scribd, Cloudworks, Twitter, personal networking, conferences and seminars. The individuals of an open digital world are defined less by the institutions to which they belong to and more through the network and digital identity they establish.

Therefore, the characteristics of Web 2.0, that motivate and facilitate the proliferation of tools that allow you to create, edit, simulate, comment, share, text, sound, image and video are great tools to give value to Personal Learning Environments (PLEs) and a motive for networked learning [24] allowing a collaborative and open social learning through Personal Learning Network (PLN).

Both the PLE and PLN are based conceptually on Siemens and Downes connectivism. The fundamental premise of connectivism is the binding of the individual through us (the connection points, which bring content or facilitate interaction) within a network, and that subsequently produce knowledge through the established connections [25], [26], [27]. Knowledge is, for these authors literally formed by the set of actions and experiences. This implies a pedagogy that (a) seeks to describe networks of success - identifying their properties, described by Downes [25] as diversity, autonomy, transparency and connectivity, and (b) seeks to describe the practices that lead to these networks, both in the individual as in the society - characterized as adapted practices of demonstration (by teacher), and practice and reflection (by student). According to connectivism a) learning occurs like a process in a distributed network, based on recognition and interpretation of patterns b) the learning process is influenced by the diversity of the network, i.e. the strength of the bonds c) the memory comprises of adapted patterns of connectivity of the actual state d) the transfer occurs through a process of connection and, e) the best for complex learning are learning domains in permanent change [25], [28].

In short, Connectivism presents a model of learning that acknowledges the great changes in society where learning is no longer seen as an individual activity. When new tools are used, people work and operate differently. In education, the recognition of these new learning tools has happened in a very slow manner. In this sense, connectivism provides insight into competencies and tasks required for students to grow and adapt to a digital age of knowledge [29].

Learning in this perspective, happens through practice, dialogue and interaction with others on networks that are themselves connected, interactive and open channeled, allowing each student to build their learning space, focusing on their interests and needs.

According to the first comprehensive review of the concept of PLE performed by Mota [24] there are several definitions given by various authors , some of which we refer to: Lubensky [30] defines PLE as centered on the ease for an individual to perform actions such as access and aggregation of digital artifacts in their learning experiences. Siemens [7] also refers to a collection of tools coupled through openness, interoperability and student control. Mota [24] highlights the vision of Anderson [31] on PLE, because such enhances and leverages the input of the learner; protects and values identity; respects academic property, is focused on the Internet, supports multiple levels of socialization, administration and learning; supports communities of inquiry between and within subjects, programs, institutions and individual learning contexts.

With the evolution of social software and conceptual discussion around PLEs, changes are found that intend to reflect on emerging pedagogies that result from digital environments and emerging technologies. For example, Schaffert & Hilzensauer [32] on reflecting this connection, identified seven aspects where there are changes in learning supported by PLE: 1) the role of the individual as active content creator, 2) personalization, with support from the community, 3) learning content as unlimited space, 4) the significant role of social participation; 5) ownership of individual data; 6) self-organized learning for the culture of schools and organizations, and finally 7) the use of social software tools and aggregating content from multiple sources.

For Castañeda & Adell [33], PLE consists of 3 dimensions and interoperable tools: 1) tools and strategies for reading, in that the sources that are accessed provide certain information in the form of object or artifact; 2) tools and strategies for reflection - this refers to space environments or services that can transform information (places to write, review, analyze, recreate and post); and finally, 3) tools and strategies regarding: the environments where there is a relationship with others and learning is made.

The third dimension- Personal Learning Network (PLN) - is a relatively recent concept, justifying thus that scientific production is still low. That is also why it is often confused with the concept of Personal Learning Environment (PLE).

The PLN is defined by the set of connections between individuals, with the objective of enhancing mutual learning through feedback, ideas, documentation, new contacts, in order to obtain a network of learning and acquiring new knowledge. It is a network of people with whom you are connected to in order to learn and that is created according to personal interests and needs, providing learning opportunities, providing answers to questions and contributing to mutual learning. Having defined its conceptual contours, it interests us at this moment to understand how to build a PLN. According to Digenti [34] firstly it is important to understand the role of individuals on the network, as a reciprocal relationship is created. In this perspective, each individual member of the network should be concerned with providing information representing an added value in the learning process of the other members.

In the era of experience in network, in which we are connected to the internet almost 24 hours a day, we have the opportunity and the challenge of being able to have a lump sum of human knowledge and billions of prospective teachers "with just one click," through informal learning. The PLNs of each individual allow us to have access to this reality, which, according to Richardson [35], is not difficult to build. This author proposes six steps to build a PLN and maintains that its value is the commitment and the maintenance of the interactions created.

From an analysis of learning networks, Downes [36] listed four properties that define a learning network:

1. Diversity - allows you to have multiple perspectives, enabling to "see things" from a different point of view, due to the heterogeneity of the elements that make up the network;
2. Autonomy - each individual acts independently with respect to their network and through social software and content creation tools (blogs, etc.);
3. Interactivity and connectivity - should be a reality in the individual links , in order to obtain knowledge produced from the activity performed in the network, in other words, through dialogue and interaction between members of the network;
4. Opening - each network entity should be able to contribute to and receive from the network. This openness is what allows interactivity between individuals and that allows students to have learning outside the classroom and share that learning with the world.

Although the web can itself be constituted as a learning platform in the sense given by Downes [36] and Mota [24], the learning environment is dependent on the relations established between individuals. The effectiveness of the web is on the opportunities it offers to individuals in forming themselves as creators of knowledge (rather than mere collectors). Despite web tools providing a space for interaction, its added value is the ability to leverage an environment of effective and interactive learning [37]. Flexibility and adaptability is the key to lifelong learning in a networked society, as well as opportunities for personalized learning [38].

Each individual, in an attempt to create connections with other people with similar interests, create their own PLN. The links grow by the dialectic of providing and acquiring relevant information and personal perspectives on topics that are important to the particular individual, but also to give something to others through Web 2.0 tools [39]. The practice of cultivating an online PLN contributes to the emancipation of the individual as well as to demonstrate their skills in digital literacy.

The PLN, in the opinion of Rajagopal et al. [40], is a network created by an individual specifically in the context of their professional activities through online platforms in order to support their needs in learning. So when a professional intentionally creates, maintains and activates their strong, weak and very weak links to contacts in your network, whether personal or professional contacts, the purpose is to improve their learning, using technology. Thus we are faced with creating a Personal Learning Network. In this perspective, the student at the network core organizes the whole environment, navigation, selects and chooses the most relevant sources of information [32], [41], [42], but this requires the student to have a high level of control over the tools used.

The technologies included in PLN allow students to use, modify and adapt their network to meet their learning needs [38]. But technology does not yet support the distinction of the degree of bonding (strong, weak or very weak), but provides a common platform where people can connect (social networks like LinkedIn, Facebook, Twitter, online conferences, workshops and Webinar platforms). It is yet important to stress that in face to face events, there is support for web-based technologies, thus allowing the possibility of creating valuable connections in the future.

According to Lalonde [43] building a PLN can be very personal and intimate, involving the negotiation of social relations with the goal of learning. In this sense, it is up to the individual to decide what to include in their PLN. Digenti [34] had already mentioned this fact when referring to collaborative learning, in which he stated that members should develop awareness on how to create strong networks among current and former members.

Rajagopal, Verjans, Costa, & Sloep [44] stress the importance of the issue of PLN in recent studies, due to the generalization of the theme itself, because the effective use of learning resources as PLNs depends on the knowledge of contacts that each individual is linked to. Students support their networking needs of informal learning through their links with other people and resources, often supported by information and communication technologies. These skills are related to the content, such as being able to engage in conversations and being able to communicate ideas, thoughts and opinions to a listener [45], [46] but also in relation to knowledge in building their own network and continuously maintaining and enabling PLN [47], in particular to be able to identify the experience and knowledge of the connections in PLN [40].

With the expertise to develop these skills, students will be able to build effective and valuable personal learning networks to support their learning needs in the present and future. Thus, it is important for individuals to realize that the experience and knowledge of individual contacts can benefit their learning [48].

In short, the main elements that characterize the relations developed between members of the network are reciprocity and trust, encouraging the exchange of information with the goal of learning. PLNs describe the habits of informal learning and create learning opportunities through relationships and interactions. They are not social networks, as the incentives to participate in them are learning. They are referred to as an environment of autonomous learning in social knowledge and contacts created on the network. Each individual in this whole network serves the personal learning needs, which is not limited by collective goals.

5   Conclusion

In the digital era in which individuals live in a social web and that Personal Learning Networks are constructed, it is fundamental to talk about the competencies for the construction of those networks. The proposal of this paper was to analyze how digital literacy allowed the creation, dynamics and maintenance of a Personal Learning Network of a community of researchers.

Throughout the article we analyzed and explored diverse authors that demonstrated the necessity of a digital literacy for the promotion and experience of a PLN, being that these competencies do not deplete in digital literacy.

To sum up, the Web 2.0 promotes the sharing, collaboration and cooperation, turning into a social platform and network, where each one shares their contents and acquires knowledge through sharing contacts that make up their PLN. Through this process we demonstrated the importance of researchers acquiring competencies of digital literacy in order to promote a digital identity of their PLN.

References

1. Rodrigues, M., Beefun, H.: A aprendizagem social, via web 2.0, na educação e formação. In: Actas do II Congresso Internacional TIC e Educação, Lisboa, December 2, pp. 1052–1058 (2012), http://ticeduca.ie.ul.pt/atas/pdf/221.pdf (retrieved November 01, 2013)
2. Solomon, G., Schrum, L.: Web 2.0 New Tools, New Schools. ISTE (Internet Soc. Tech. Educ.), Washington, DC (2007), http://books.google.pt/books?id=ZKKQMLir_mMC&printsec=frontcover&hl=pt-PT&source=gbs_ge_summary_r&cad=0#v=onepage&q&f=false (retrieved)
3. Dias, P.: Comunidades de educação e inovação na sociedade digital. Educação, Formação & Tecnologias 5(2), 3–9 (2012)
4. Morgado, L.: The networked class. In: Wankel, C. (ed.) Cutting-edge Technologies in Higher Education. Educating Educators with Social Media, vol. 1, pp. 135–152. Emerald Group Publishing, Bingley (2011)
5. Keats, D., Schmidt, J.P.: The genesis and emergence of Education 3.0 in higher education and its potential for Africa. First Monday 12(3) (2007)
6. Castells, M.: La galaxia Internet, p. 302. Areté, Barcelona (2001)
7. Siemens, G.: PLEs – I Acronym, Therefore I Exist. Elearnspace2 (2007) (retrieved September 30, 2013)
8. Ala-Mutka, K., Punie, Y, Redecker, C.: Digital Competence for Lifelong Learning. Institute for Prospective Technological Studies (IPTS), European Commission, Joint Research Centre, Seville (2008), http://ftp.jrc.es/EURdoc/JRC48708.TN.pdf (retrieved)
9. Martin, A.: Digital Literacy and the "Digital Society". In: Lankshear&, C., Knobel, M. (eds.) Digital Literacies: Concepts, Policies and Practices. Peter Lang, New York (2008)
10. Goodfellow, R.: Literacy, literacies, and the digital in higher education. Teaching in Higher Education 16(1), 131–144 (2011)
11. Eshet-Alkali, Y., Amichai-Hamburger, Y.: Experiments in digital literacy. Cyberpsychology & Behavior: The Impact of the Internet, Multimedia and Virtual Reality on Behavior and Society 7(4), 421–429 (2004)

12. McLoughlin, C.: What ICT-related skills and capabilities should be considered central to the definition of digital literacy? In: Bastiaens, T., Ebner, M. (eds.) World Conference on Educational Multimedia, Hypermedia and Telecommunications (EDMEDIA 2011), vol. 2011, pp. 471–475. EdITLib, the Digital Library for Education & Information Technology (2011)
13. Bawden, D.: Origins and Concepts of Digital Literacy. In: Lankshear, C., Knobel, M. (eds.) Digital Literacies: Concepts, Policies and Practices, pp. 17–32. Peter Lang, New York (2008)
14. Costa, C., Torres, R.: To be or not to be, the importance of Digital Identity in the networked society. Educação, Formação & Tecnologias, 47–53 (April 2011)
15. Aresta, M.S.L.: A construção da identidade em ambientes digitais: estudo de caso sobre a construção da identidade online no Sapo Campus e em ambientes informais. Dissertação de Doutoramento. Universidade de Aveiro, Portugal (2013)
16. Warburton, S.: Digital identity matters. Journal of the American Society for Information Science and Technology 56 (2010)
17. Cranor, L.F., Reagle, J., Ackerman, M.S.: Beyond Concern: Understanding Net Users' Attitudes About Online Privacy. Cornell University Library. Computers and Society; Human-Computer Interaction (April 18, 1999)
18. Alexander, B.: Web 2. 0 and Emergent Multiliteracies. Theory Into Practice 47(2), 150–160 (2008)
19. Williams, S., Fleming, S., Parslow, P.: This Is Me - Digital Identity for careers. CentAUR: Central Archive at the University of Reading. Lulu, Reading (2010)
20. White, D.: Not "Natives" & "Immigrants" but "Visitors" & "Residents." TALL blog. Online education with the University of Oxford (2008),
   http://tallblog.conted.ox.ac.uk/index.php/2008/07/23/not-natives-immigrants-but-visitors-residents/ (retrieved October 10, 2013)
21. Margaryan, A., Nicol, D., Littlejohn, A., Trinder, K.: Students' use of technologies to support formal and informal learning. In: Luca, J., Weippl, E. (eds.) Proceedings of World Conference on Educational Multimedia, Hypermedia and Telecommunications 2008, vol. 2008, pp. 4257–4266. AACE, Chesapeake (2008)
22. Jorge, N., Morgado, L.: Contextos de aprendizagem 2.0: a utilização de ferramentas Web 2.0 para uma aprendizagem em contexto. Revista Iberoamericana de Informática Educativa 12, 3–13 (2010)
23. Weller, M.: The Digital Scholar: How Technology Is Transforming Scholarly Practice. Bloomsbury Academic (2011), doi:
   http://dx.doi.org/10.5040/9781849666275
24. Mota, J.: Personal Learning Environments: Contributos para uma discussão do conceito. Educação, Formação & Tecnologias 2(2), 5–21 (2009)
25. Downes, S.: Connectivism and Connective Knowledge Essays on meaning and learning networks. National Research Council, Canada (2012)
26. Siemens, G.: Connectivism. Connectivism (2012),
   http://www.connectivism.ca/?cat=3 (retrieved October 01, 2013)
27. Morrison, D.: How to Create a Robust and Meaningful Personal Learning Network [PLN]. Online learning insights (2013), http://onlinelearninginsights.wordpress.com/2013/01/22/how-to-create-a-robust-and-meaningful-personal-learning-network-pln/ (retrieved September 25, 2013)
28. Siemens, G.: Connectivism: Learning as Network-Creation. eLearnspace everything elearning (2005a), http://www.elearnspace.org/Articles/networks.htm (retrieved October 01, 2013)

29. Siemens, G.: Connectivism: A Learning Theory for the Digital Age. International Journal of Instructional Technology and Distance Learning 2(1), 3–10 (2005b)
30. Lubensky, R.: The present and future of Personal Learning Environments (PLE). eLearning& Deliberative Moments, (2006), http://www.deliberations.com.au/2006/12/present-and-future-of-personal-learning.html (retrieved October 02, 2013)
31. Anderson, T.: On Groups, Networks and Collectives. Virtual Canuck (April 30, 2007), http://terrya.edublogs.org/2007/04/30/on-groups-networks-and-collectives/ (retrieved October 01, 2013)
32. Schaffert, S., Hilzensauer, W.: On the way towards Personal Learning Environments: Seven crucial aspects. eLearning Papers, pp. 1–11 (2008)
33. Castañeda, L., Adell, J. (eds.): Entornos Personales de Aprendizaje: claves para el ecosistema educativo enred. Marfil, Alcoy (2013)
34. Digenti, D.: Collaborative Learning: A Core Capability for Organizations in the New Economy. Reflections: The SoL Journal 1(2), 45–57 (1999)
35. Richardson, W.: Create Your PLN: 6 Easy Steps. Educational Leadership: Reflect, Refresh, Recharge 70, 20–22 (2013)
36. Downes, S.: Practice Learning Networks in Practice. Emerging Technologies for Learning 2 (2007)
37. Costa, C.: Lifelong learning in Web 2.0 environments. International Journal of Technology Enhanced Learning 2(3), 275–284 (2010), doi:10.1504/IJTEL.2010.033582
38. Costa, C., Keegan, H., Attwell, G.: Cartoon planet: Micro-reflection through digital cartoons - a case study on teaching and learning with young people. Romanian Journal of Pedagogy 7(9), 112–128 (2009)
39. Costa, C.: Educational Networking in the Digital Age. In: Thomas, M. (ed.) Digital Education: Opportunities for Social Collaboration, pp. 81–99. Palgrave Macmillan, UK (2011)
40. Rajagopal, K., Joosten-ten Brinke, D., Van Bruggen, J., Sloep, P.B.: Understanding personal learning networks: Their structure, content and the networking skills to optimally use them. First Monday 17(1), 1–12 (2012)
41. Wilson, S., Liber, O., Beauvoir, P., MIlligan, C., Johnson, M., Sharples, P.: Personal Learning Environments: Challenging the dominant design of educational systems (September 19, 2006), http://dspace.ou.nl/handle/1820/727 (retrieved)
42. Conole, G., Delaat, M., Dillon, T., Darby, J.: 'Disruptive technologies', 'pedagogical innovation': What's new? Findings from an in-depth study of students' use and perception of technology. Computers & Education 50(2), 511–524 (2008)
43. Lalonde, C.: How important is Twitter in your Personal Learning Network? eLearn Magazine. Education and Technology in Perspective (2012)
44. Rajagopal, K., Verjans, S., Costa, C., Sloep, P.: People in Personal Learning Networks: Analysing their Characteristics and Identifying Suitable Tools. In: Hodgson, V., Jones, C., de Laat, M., McConnell, D., Ryberg, T., Sloep, P. (eds.) Proceedings of the 8th International Conference on Networked Learning 2012, Maastricht, The Netherlands, pp. 252–259 (2012), http://dspace.ou.nl/handle/1820/4224 (retrieved)
45. Kintsch, W., van Dijk, T.A.: Toward a model of text comprehension and production. Psychological Review 85(5), 363 (1978)
46. Dillenbourg, P.: What do you mean by "collaborative learning"? In: Dillenbourg, P. (ed.) Collaborative-learning: Cognitive and Computational Approaches, vol. 1, pp. 1–15. Elsevier, Oxford (1999)
47. Nardi, B.A., Whittaker, S., Schwarz, H.: It's not what you know, it's who you know: Work in the information age. First Monday 5(5) (2000)
48. Cigognini, M.E., Pettenati, M.C., Edirisingha, P.: Personal knowledge management skills in web 2.0-based learning. In: Lee, M.J.W., McLoughlin, C. (eds.) Web 2.0-Based E-Learning: Applying Social Informatics for Tertiary Teaching, p. 109 (2011)

Blended Simulation Based Medical Education: A Complex Learning/Training Opportunity

Armineh Shahoumian[1], Murray Saunders[1], Maria Zenios[2],
Gale Parchoma[3], and Jacky Hanson[4]

[1] Lancaster University, Department of Educational Research, UK
{a.shahoumian,m.saunders}@lancaster.ac.uk
[2] Cyprus University of Technology, Cyprus
mkzenios@gmail.com
[3] University of Calgary, Werklund School of Education, Canada
gale.parchoma@ucalgary.ca
[4] Lancashire Teaching Hospitals, UK
jackie.hanson@lthtr.nhs.uk

Abstract. Simulation Based Medical Education (SBME) as an innovative approach in Medical and Professionals Allied to Medicine (PAM) education has received international attention in the past few years to support improvement of patient safety and providing better health care services within hospitals. Blended SBME (B-SBME) is a new instructional model recently introduced into the field, which blends on-line briefing sessions followed by a simulation session, and concluded with immediate face-to-face debriefing sessions. In this paper we discuss the complexity of learning in B-SBME and how individualistic learning theories do not support understanding of all these processes. A shift in theoretical lens to socio-cultural theories may develop our understanding of how we depict and theorise the learning that goes on in B-SBME and whether B-SBME can act as a "boundary crossing tool" and support expanding of learning into clinical setting.

Keywords: Simulation based medical education, blended learning, Social Practices Theory, boundary crossing tool.

1 Introduction

The use of Technology Enhanced Learning (TEL) in different educational and working environments has been increased significantly in the past few years to provide more educational opportunities for learners to catch up with the rapid changing world and the overload of new information, knowledge, and skills required for operating in different aspects of their career and life. Medical and healthcare organisations, among them English National Health Services (NHS) Trusts, are not exempt from these changes and there is a constant need to train and retrain the staff and refresh their employees' knowledge around new technologies, products, and services that are being introduced in their environment. "The need to meet the

P. Zaphiris and A. Ioannou (Eds.): LCT 2014, Part II, LNCS 8524, pp. 478–485, 2014.

Department of Health's Standards for Better Health and the NHS Litigation Authority's Risk Management Standards has been instrumental in increasing attention to, and appetite for, providing alternative methods of training using technology" [22] [page.4]. Simulation as an alternative educational approach has received significant international attention in the past few years within health care education and services. SBME is becoming popular for providing medical students and practitioners near real-life opportunities to practice and improve their clinical and non-clinical skills to "reduce the risk of complications for patients" [5] [page.5] and improve health care services as a result.

This paper focuses on B-SBME as a new instructional model introduced in the In Lancashire Simulation Centre, Lancashire Teaching Hospitals NHS Trust (LTHTR) training programme. The preliminary analysis of the data revealed that in B-SBME learning is very complex. Therefore, "standard learning theories have little to offer if one wants to understand [these] processes" [7][page, 66] and a shift in theoretical lens from individualistic learning theories to socio-cultural theories may provide a new perspective in understanding B-SBME in this particular context.

2   Simulations in Medical and PAM Education

Simulation Based Education (SBE) has been successfully integrated in the educational programmes of high-risk professional industries, such as aviation, astronomy, defence, and nuclear energy for decades [2, 8, 26]. The main two reasons for using SBE in these industries has been the cost and danger involved in training or testing a system in real life context [26] and the opportunity it provides for learners to practice rare events and prepare them to react quickly and efficiently in real-life events [6]. However, in medical professions only from the second half of the 20th century different types of low cost, low fidelity part task trainers started to be used and towards the end of the 20th century SBME received greater attention [2]. It is argued that simulations "in all its forms will be a vital part of building a safer healthcare system" in future [6] [page.55]. SBME has been introduced to health care services for the following reasons:

1. Medical Education shifted to more outcomes-based approach where demonstration of competence became important rather than how the competence was acquired. The need for training more effective junior doctors after undergraduate education [9] and "continuing education after higher specialist education" [2] [page.256] gained special attention. Moreover, the revalidation of doctors every five years was introduced to make sure doctors remain up-to-date [10].
2. Some of the changes in health care delivery such as shorter hospital stays and clinic visits, and greater numbers of patients with higher acuity of illnesses resulted in reduced number of patients available for learning purposes in hospitals (12). Moreover, reduction of working hours to 48 hour a week by introducing European Working Time Directive (EWTD) changed the working pattern and training opportunities [21] for clinical staff. Improving patients' safety and reduction of

medical errors [12] and ethical issues around using patients for educational purposes to avoid unnecessary risks [30] also gained greater attention.

3. Constant technological and scientific advancement for both diagnosis and treatment purposes [12] require clinical staff to learn new techniques and skills or upgrade their knowledge around the use of new medical technology more than before.

Simulation in medical and PAM education evolves and improves very quickly; new simulators are being introduced in the field therefore the boundaries of what can be simulated often change frequently [1]. It is important for educators to realise that the simulations and all the technology attached to it to simulate an event are tools in the hands of the educators and only skilful use of them can enhance educational practices and improve satisfaction among learners and educators, which may ultimately lead to sustainable use of technology for educational purposes. In other words, education should not be driven by technology but the educational agenda should adopt the type of technology that will support learning [18].

Although SBME has been shown to provide rich learning opportunities [11] it has remained educationally under-theorised and is being used as an alternative medical and PAM educational approach. "Simulations are often accepted uncritically, with undue emphasis being placed on technological sophistication at the expense of theory-based design" [15] [page.549]. Research into the conceptual framework of SBME is very limited and teaching and learning designs are mainly developed in practice. SBME is "a complex service intervention" [19] [page.50] with various learning opportunities that has to be theorised and managed carefully to provide meaningful learning environment for the learners.

3   Blended Simulation Based Medical Education

Blended Learning (BL) or sometimes called Hybrid Learning (HL) has gained considerable attention after realising that "single mode of instructional delivery may not provide sufficient choices, engagement, social contact, relevance, and context needed to facilitate successful learning and performance" [27] [page. 51]. BL offers "a real opportunity to create learning experiences that can provide the right learning at the right time and in the right place for each and every individual" [28][page.18]. BL, if designed carefully to provide a meaningful learning environment, may provide flexibility in learning that can support student-centred and self-initiated learning [14].

Blended SBME (B-SBME) has recently been introduced into the Lancashire Simulation Centre LTHTR training programme as an innovative instructional model. This instructional model blends on-line briefing sessions, which includes more theoretical aspects of clinical cases, an introduction to use of simulations, and some key points (both clinical and non-clinical) about management of acute situations. The online modules are followed by a simulation session, which includes hands on practice/experience in a near real life context. Sessions are concluded with immediate face-to-face debriefing sessions for reflection and feedback on experience. The introduction of the online modules as pre-session briefings provide learners with flexibility in preparing for sessions and allow facilitators and learners increased time for the hands-on sessions in the simulation centre.

4   Methodology

This work in progress is a qualitative case study which took place in LTHTR simulation centre over the course of two years. Ninety third year medical students and the simulation facilitators were the participants of this study. Data has been collected through participant observations of the practices taking place in the simulation centre and semi-structured interviews with fourteen medical students and four facilitators and medical educators. Data analysis was conducted in a five-phased cycle including compiling, disassembling, reassembling, interpreting, and concluding [29].

The aim of this study was to look at the activities taking place in B-SBME through the most discussed theoretical lenses in the field such as Situated Learning theory, and Experiential learning theory. It also aimed to explore how learning happens in this educationally rich environment where students have to interact with technology, texts and documents, medical instruments/drugs, other students, and facilitators.

5   Preliminary Results

The preliminary analysis of the data revealed that in B-SBME learning is very complex. From the moment the learners started the online modules, they reported thinking and reflecting on different aspects of the simulation and scenarios. These individual and collaborative reflections continued throughout the debriefing session and even afterwards. Data indicates learners are learning by getting engaged in cognitive activities, by doing/experiencing, by observing their peers, by reflecting on their own and their peers' performances, by collaborating with their peers, and by referring to documents and guidelines. Formal, informal, and non-formal learning may take place across activities, depending on the aims of a simulation session. There are opportunities to learn not only clinical skills but also non-clinical skills, i.e. communication skills required for providing safe practices in real life contexts.

The preliminary analysis of the data surfaced the complexity of learning in B-SBME and how individualistic learning theories are unable to capture the whole learning processes in this versatile learning environment. Activities taking place in B-SBME may be explored better if the theoretical lens shifts to socio-cultural theories.

5.1   Individualistic Learning Theories

Situated Learning Theory. Lave and Wenger argue that the important elements in situated learning are having an authentic context and social interactions and collaborations [16]. They also argue that learners' involvement in a "community of practice" starts as a beginner or novice and gradually moves from the periphery of a community to its centre and becomes more active and engaged within the culture and eventually becomes an expert contributor [17]. Although situated learning might be able to explain the role of context and social interactions and collaborations that are taking place in a simulated scenario, this learning theory could not capture the whole set of learning activities taking place in SBME. The context is near authentic and learners are role-playing, thus activities of SBME do not closely align with the requirements of situated learning. Collaborative learning is taking place but the learners are not categorised as novices and experts in this particular setting with this particular set of participants.

Experiential Learning Theory. In SBME learners are active and engaged from the beginning, all participating in a simulated scenario collaboratively experience a new practice, reflect on their learning, and possibly take away the newly learned practice into real clinical setting. However, Kolb's experiential learning, which presents a cyclical learning process: experiencing/practicing, observation/reflecting on the practice, forming abstract concepts, and planning new experiment/active experiment is not enough to describe these learning processes. Kolb describes Experiential Learning from a constructivist point of view [20] and to him learning, is transformation of experience into knowledge, skills, values and emotions [4]. One of the main criticisms that ELT has received is that experience cannot be shaped outside social relations [3]. Therefore, de-contextualising and individualising learning, and considering learning resulted from subjective experiences rather than "objective and rational process[es]" [13] [page.6] has little to say about contextually rich and social learning happening in B-SBME.

5.2   Social Practices Theory (SPT)

Considering a 'practice' as an opportunity for learning and extracting knowledge is a new approach which "turns to a consideration of the learning process but does so by figuring the locus of concern as learning in social or organizational contexts rather than individual cognitive process"[24] [page.15). Practices can include "the rooted identities and patterns of behaviour that characterise shape or constrain understanding of [that activity]" [25] [page.2].

In order to capture the dynamic learning environment in B-SBME 'social practices' might provide the right conceptual framework. Social practices are described as "recurrent, usually unconsidered, sets of practices or 'constellations' [clusters of activities] that together constitute the daily life" [25] [page.2]. Sometimes the clusters of practices "bound together by social groupings" [25] [page.3] and shape activity systems.

By applying SPT the clusters of practices taking place at universities and hospitals might be described differently. "If we depict educational organizations and the workplace as different activity systems, characterized by different communities of practice, then moving from one to another involves a form of social and cognitive 'brokerage' in which a variety of tools might aid and develop 'expansive' learning opportunities" [24] [page. 18). In this case B-SBME might act as a bridge between these two activity systems as a "boundary crossing tool" to prepare the learners for more productive and competent practices in the real context.

6   Conclusion

The demand for using Simulation Based Medical Education (SBME) has increased significantly in the past few years. However, SBME has remained as an alternative learning/training approach in medical and PAM education. Partially it can be related to the fact that SBME has been remained educationally under-theorised. Legislation mandates medical educators to provide evidence on the impact of SBME on patient safety and improvement of the services. However, evidence-based research in this complex learning environment may not be able to provide a comprehensive understanding of learning processes and how learning may be extended into the real clinical settings. Innovative research approaches need to be applied into the field to capture, analyse, and evaluate learning outcomes [23] and possibly integrate SBME in the core training programmes of medical and PAM education.

This work in progress may introduce a shift of understanding learning processes in SBME from individual to a social by using Social Practices Theory. By analysis of the social practices in B-SBME a new perspective may be introduced in using B-SBME as a "boundary crossing tool".

Acknowledgments. Partially supported a by KTP (Knowledge Transfer Partnership) project between Lancaster University and the UK NHS which was funded by ESRC and Technology Strategy Board, UK. Our special thanks go to Mike Dickinson, Mark Pimplett, Lorna Lee, and Sarah Lewis.

References

1. Bond, W.F., Lammers, R.L., Spillane, L.L., Smith-Coggins, R., Fernandez, R., Reznek, M.A., Vozenilek, J.A., Gordon, J.A.: The use of simulation in emergency medicine: A research agenda. Academic Emergency Medicine 14, 353–364 (2007)
2. Bradley, P.: The history of simulation in medical education and possible future directions. Medical Education 40, 254–262 (2006)
3. Brah, A., Hoy, J.: Experiential learning: A new orthodoxy. In: Weil, S.W., McGill, I. (eds.) Making Sense of Experiential Learning, pp. 70–77. Society for Research into Higher Education, Milton Keynes, Open University (1989)
4. Conole, G., Dyke, M.: What are the affordances of information and communication technologies? Journal of the Association for Learning Technology 12(2), 113–124 (2004)
5. Department of Health: A Framework for technology enhanced learning, http://www.dh.gov.uk/en/Publicationsandstatistics/Publicatio ns/PublicationsPolicyAndGuidance/DH_130924
6. Department of Health. 150 years of the annual report of the chief medical officer: On the state of public health (2008), http://www.dh.gov.uk/en/ Publicationsandstatistics/Publications/AnnualReports/DH_096206
7. Engeström, Y.: Developmental work research: Expanding activity theory in practice, vol. 12. Lehmanns Media (2005)
8. Gaba, D.M.: The future vision of simulation in health care. Quality Safety HealthCare 13(suppl. 1), i2–i10 (2004)

9. General Medical Council: Tomorrow's doctors: Outcomes and standards for undergraduate medical education, http://www.gmc-uk.org/education/undergraduate/tomorrows_doctors_2009.asp
10. General Medical Council, Department of Health, Healthier Scotland, Welsh Assembly Government. Department of Health, Social services and Public Safety: Revalidation a statement of intent, http://www.gmcuk.org/Revalidation_A_Statement_of_Intent_October_2010__Final_version_web_version_.pdf_35982397.pdf
11. Huang, G.C., Sacks, H., DeVita, M., Reynolds, R., Gammon, W., Saleh, M., Passiment, M.: Characteristics of simulation activities at North American medical schools and teaching hospitals. Simulation in Healthcare 7(6), 329–333 (2012)
12. Issenburg, S.B., Scales, R.J.: Simulation in health care education. Perspectives in Biology and Medicine 51(1), 31–46 (2008)
13. Kayes, D.C.: Experiential learning and its critics: Preserving the role of experience in management learning and education. Academy of Management Learning & Education 1(2), 137–149 (2002)
14. Khan, B.H.: Managing e-learning strategies: Design, delivery, implementation and evaluation. Information Science Publishing, London (2005)
15. Kneebone, R.: Evaluating clinical simulations for learning procedural skills: A theory-based approach. Academic Medicine 80, 549–553 (2005)
16. Lave, J., Wenger, E.: Situated Learning. Legitimate peripheral participation. University of Cambridge Press, Cambridge (1991)
17. Lave, J., Wenger, E.: Communities of practice: Learning, meaning, and identity. Cambridge University Press, Cambridge (1998)
18. Maran, N.J., Glavin, R.J.: Low- to high-fidelity simulation – A continuum of medical education? Medical Education 37(suppl. 1), 22–28 (2003)
19. McGaghie, W.C., Issenberg, S.B., Petrusa, E.R., Scalese, R.J.: A critical review of simulation-based medical education research: 2003–2009. Medical Education 44, 50–63 (2010)
20. Merriam, S.B., Caffarella, R.S., Baumgartner, L.M.: Learning in Adulthood: A comprehensive guide. John Wiley & Sons, San Fransisco (2007)
21. Modernising Medical Careers: Review of European Working Time Directive (EWTD) and its impact on the quality of training, http://www.mee.nhs.uk/our_work/work_priorities/review_of_ewtd__impact_on_tra.aspx
22. NHS Education South Central, http://www.dh.gov.uk/en/Publicationsandstatistics/Publications/PublicationsPolicyAndGuidance/DH_130924
23. Parchoma, G., Pimblett, M., Dickinson, M., Hanson, J.: Simulation based medical education: Constructing the patient's perspective. In: Parchoma, G., Hanson, J. (Chairs) A Networked Learning Approach to Introducing Blended Simulation Based Medical Education in a UK National Health Service (NHS) Trust. Proceedings of the E-Learn-World Conference on E-Learning in Corporate, Government, Healthcare, & Higher Education, Montreal, QB, October 9-12 (2012)
24. Saunders, M.: From 'organisms' to 'boundaries': the uneven development of theory narratives in education, learning and work connections. Journal of Education and Work 19(1), 1–27 (2006)

25. Saunders, M.: Setting the scene: the four domains of evaluative practice in higher education. In: Saunders, M., Trowler, P., Bamber, V. (eds.) Reconceptualising Evaluation in Higher Education: the Practice Turn, pp. 1–17. McGraw-Hill/Open University Press, Maidenhead (2011)

26. Scalese, R.J., Obeso, V.T., Issenberg, S.B.: Simulation technology for skills training and competency assessment in medical education. Journal of General Internal Medicine 23(suppl. 1), 46–49 (2007)

27. Singh, H.: Building effective blended learning programs. Educational Technology 43, 51–54 (2003)

28. Thorne, K.: Blended learning: How to integrate online and traditional learning. Kogan Page, London (2003)

29. Yin, R.K.: Qualitative research from start to finish. The Guildford Press, New York (2011)

30. Ziv, A., Wolpe, P., Small, S., Glick, S.: Simulation-based medical education: An ethical imperative. Simulation in Healthcare 1(4), 252–256 (2006)

Finding and Exploring Commonalities between Researchers Using the ResXplorer

Selver Softic[2], Laurens De Vocht[1],
Erik Mannens[1], Rik Van de Walle[1], and Martin Ebner[2]

[1] Ghent University - iMinds, Multimedialab
Sint-Pietersnieuwstraat 41, 9000 Ghent, Belgium
{laurens.devocht,erik.mannens,rik.vandewalle}@ugent.be
[2] Graz University of Technology, IICM - Institute for Information Systems
and Computer Media
Inffeldgasse 16c, 8010 Graz, Austria
{selver.softic,martin.ebner}@tugraz.at

Abstract. Researcher community produces a vast of content on the Web. We assume that every researcher interest oneself in events, persons and findings of other related community members who share the same interest. Although research related archives give access to their content most of them lack on analytic services and adequate visualizations for this data. This work resides on our previous achievements[1,2,3,4] we made on semantically and Linked Data driven search and user interfaces for Research 2.0. We show how researchers can find and visually explore commonalities between each other within their interest domain, by introducing for this matter the user interface of "ResXplorer", and underlying search infrastructure operating over Linked Data Knowledge Base of research resources. We discuss and test most important components of "ResXplorer" relevant for detecting commonalities between researchers, closing up with conclusions and outlook for future work.

1 Introduction

"ResXplorer"[1] is aggregated interface for search and exploration of the underlying Linked Data Knowledge Base. Data within originates from Linked Data repositories DBLP(L3S)[2] which is a bibliography of computer science conference proceedings, COLINDA[3] containing information about up to 15000 conferences in the time range from 2003 up to 2013, DBPedia[4] common knowledge encyclopedia and Open Linked Data repository with geographical information named GeoNames[5]. Schematic structure of Linked Data Knowledge Base contains graphs of different

---

[1] http://www.resxplorer.org
[2] http://dblp.l3s.de/
[3] http://colinda.org
[4] http://dbpedia.org
[5] http://geonames.org

P. Zaphiris and A. Ioannou (Eds.): LCT 2014, Part II, LNCS 8524, pp. 486–494, 2014.
© Springer International Publishing Switzerland 2014

semantic entities represented as RDF (Resource Description Framework)[6] data model instances indexed and searchable by Apache Solar[7] interface. Functionality for keyword based finding of commonalities between research related artifacts (persons, publications and conferences) is an extension consisting of our earlier work on module for path finding between resources in semantic entity graphs, which is a part of the "Everything is Connected" engine (EiCE) [3], and interface solutions for exploration of Linked Data research repositories [4] based on Web 2.0 technologies.

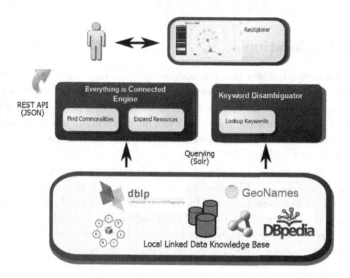

Fig. 1. ResXplorer concept for finding scholar artifacts necessary to reveal the commonalities

2   Finding Commonalities

As first step, a real-time keyword disambiguation via semantic entities from Linked Data Knowledge Base guides researchers by expressing their needs. Researcher select the desired meaning from a type-ahead drop down menu. Figure 2 shows the type-ahead expansion of results as disambiguation for "Laurens De Vocht" as "Agent" an entity which describes person or organisation in the Linked Data Knowledge Base. Expansion of results for entered terms happens in real-time. This feature is especially useful, during the early stages of the search as reported in [5].

Whole process around finding commonality is shown in figure 1. In behind the back-end (EiCE engine) connects the resources and ranks them according to the entered context. At the same time background modules also fetch neighbour links which match the selected suggestion. As result, choice of various resources is then presented to the researchers.

---

[6] http://www.w3.org/RDF/

[7] https://lucene.apache.org/solr/

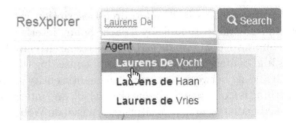

Fig. 2. Mapping of keywords

3   Visual Exploration

The visualization emphasizes commonalities by showing, on a radial map [6], how the current focused entity relates to the other found entities. It adopts the concept of affinity appropriately expressed in visual terms as a spatial relationship: proximity [7]. We additionally express the amount of unexpectedness as *novelty* of a resource in each particular search context. A typical example of such situation is in the Figure 3.

Features like color, shape and size of the items enhance user guidance during the exploration process [4]. The user expands the query space by clicking the results retrieved by the first keyword based search. Additional query expansion happens either through adding further keywords as well as through keyword combinations already entered where the back-end (EiCE engine) tries to deliver extra results based upon connection paths between the resources.

4   Evaluation of the Back-end

4.1   Setup

For evaluation of the module responsible to find commonalities, we defined a set of ten queries shown in table 1 consisting from the name pairs of authors of this paper knowing that they will deliver results, and that author profiles already exist in the DBLP bibliography archive. This set of queries is selected for reason to easier determinate relevance of results. Measurement of recall is left out intentionally because of the size of search space (hundreds of millions of potentially relevant resources).

4.2   Measures

Definition represented in equation (1) expresses precision as combination of *true positives* (TP), *false positives* results. Links discovered along traversing path of algorithm which lead to scientific resources (publications, persons and events) relevant for one of the both authors represent true positives. All other unresolvable or repeating links are false positives.

$$precision = \frac{TP}{TP + FP} \tag{1}$$

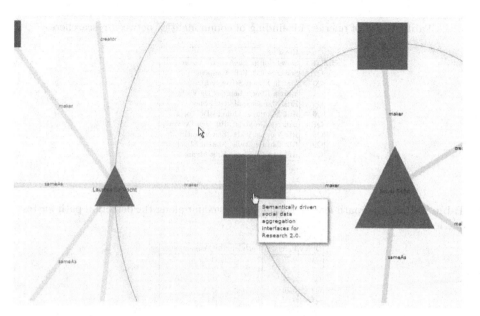

Fig. 3. Visual representation of commonality between *Laurens De Vocht* and *Selver Softic* based on common publications such as the highlighted *"Semantically...Research 2.0"*

4.3   Preliminary Results

Table 2 summarizes preliminary results of our tests. We measured precision of retrieved commonalities, path length between the two resources entered as terms of the query, and total count of discovered commonalities per query. The precision values range from **0.7** up to **0.95**. This precision rate is unexpectedly high even we knew that test queries represent authors who know and work with each other. These results are partly influenced by the well-connectedness of graph structures in the Linked Data Knowledge base. Path lengths are very short as expected and range from **2** up to **4** hops. Total count of detected commonalities ranges from **4** up to **11** except in query *Q10*. The explanation for this outlier is that relation in *Q10* is the strongest one because of the length of common period of collaboration between those two researchers and the number of together published works. They also have a bigger social network of collaborators which allows finding more alternative connection paths within semantic graphs than in the case of other queries. Evaluation of precision versus the path lengths in figure 4 reveals that; there is no linear dependency between the path lengths and precision. At least in our evaluation, results with shorter path lengths reach in average better precision then the ones with long paths.

Figure 6 shows that changes of total number of retrieved commonalities does not have any immediate significant impact on the precision score. This is not

Table 1. Set of queries, for finding of commonalities between researchers

Query	Keywords
Q1	Selver Softic, Laurens De Vocht
Q2	Selver Softic, Erik Mannens
Q3	Martin Ebner, Selver Softic
Q4	Martin Ebner, Laurens De Vocht
Q5	Erik Mannens, Martin Ebner
Q6	Erik Mannens, Laurens De Vocht
Q7	Laurens De Vocht, Rik Van De Walle
Q8	Rik Van De Walle, Selver Softic
Q9	Rik Van De Walle, Martin Ebner
Q10	Rik Van De Walle, Erik Mannens

Table 2. Precision, path length, commonalities count along the detection path for test queries

Query	Precision	Path length	Commonalities
Q1	0,75	2	4
Q2	0,86	4	7
Q3	0,78	2	9
Q4	0,75	2	4
Q5	0,82	4	11
Q6	0,83	2	6
Q7	0,83	2	6
Q8	0,7	4	10
Q9	0,7	4	10
Q10	0,95	3	37

surprising since the precision depends directly on the ratio of true positives and false positives.

For sure, most interesting finding reveals figure 6 where path lengths face the total counts of detected commonalities. The results depicted here discount the assumption that the length of a path traversed by algorithm within a graph structure which is well-connected implies inductively the increase of detected commonalities by each new hop. Even the outlier in the *Q10* proves this assumption wrong. This confirms once again the latter findings that solely quality of the detected commonality links determinate the precision and do not correlate strongly with changes of path lengths and total count of discovered commonalities. This finding is potentially influenced by the specific form of data graph structures in the Linked Data Knowledge Base, however this assumption is not confirm able with current results.

Quantitative reasons for the high precision are visible in figure 7 where total count of detected commonalities faces the count of true positives and false positives. The count of true positives almost correlates with the total count of commonalities which is a strong indicator for high precision.

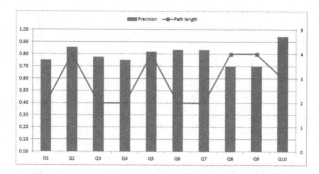

Fig. 4. Precision vs. Path lengths

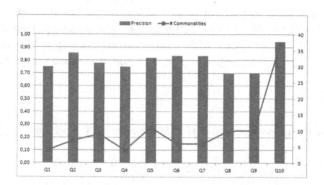

Fig. 5. Precision vs. total count of Commonalities

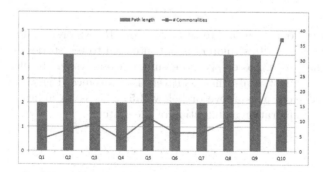

Fig. 6. Path lengths vs. total count of Commonalities

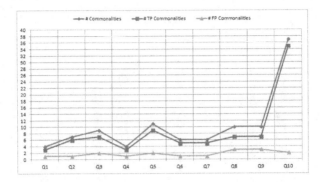

Fig. 7. Total count of Commonalities vs. TP Commonalities vs. FP Commonalities

5   Usability

We conducted a short survey on *percieved usefulness* based on the *Technology Acceptance Model (TAM)* [8] with 31 researches where users judged the usage of "ResXplorer" on a Likert-Scale with values (Strongly Disagree, Disagree, Undecided, Agree, Strongly Agree). The result of the evaluation shows the figure 8 and table 3.

Table 3. Preliminary results of the short survey on the *percieved usefulness*

ResXplorer			
What is the main goal of ResXplorer?	Goal	Score	Variance
1. [To explore]	**Explore**	**4.12**	1.61
2. [To discover]	Discover	3.88	1.86
3. [To search]	Search	3.71	1.10
4. [To analyse]	Analyse	3.18	1.78
5. [To clarify]	Clarify	3.12	1.74
6. [To tell stories]	**Tell stories**	2.47	1.70

The primary goal according to test-users for "ResXplorer" is to explore. According to the users, "ResXplorer" is not intended to tell stories. The users are unsure whether "ResXplorer" is more suited to analyse or to clarify. Highest score, at the moment it also has relatively low variance. Biggest variance and most averaged score goes above or below **2.5**. This is an indicator that users recognised the exploration as intention of the system.

Fig. 8. Results of the short survey on *usefulness*

6   Conclusion

The main contribution of our work is allowing researches to interactively explore relations between the resources and entities like events, places, publications or persons related to their work and discover commonalities between them. Preliminary tests on "ResXplorer" back-end show that module for finding commonalities reaches high precision which does not depend from the length of search path, and the count of found commonality links but only from their quality and relevance. We also observed that longer traversed paths does not necessary mean implicitly bigger amount of discovered commonalities. All these findings lead us to assumption that underlying data is well-prepared and well-connected as well, and offers a variety of potentially interesting and useful resources for researchers. Conducted short survey on the "precieved usefulness" approved the 'ResXplorer" as exploration interface. In the future we want to extend the usability survey with aspects about the *ease of use*. Further we are aiming to extend our precision measurement on bigger test set to verify initially achieved good results. Moreover, we also want to test the assumptions about the quality and well connectedness of data in used Linked Data Knowledge Base.

Acknowledgement. The research activities that have been described in this paper were funded by Ghent University, iMinds (Interdisciplinary institute for Technology) a research institute founded by the Flemish Government, Graz University of Technology, the Institute for the Promotion of Innovation by Science and Technology in Flanders (IWT), the Fund for Scientific Research-Flanders (FWO-Flanders), and the European Union.

References

1. Vocht, L.D., Softic, S., Ebner, M., Mühlburger, H.: Semantically driven social data aggregation interfaces for research 2.0. In: Proceedings of the 11th International Conference on Knowledge Management and Knowledge Technologies, i-KNOW 2011, pp. 43:1–43:9. ACM, New York (2011)
2. De Vocht, L., Van Deursen, D., Mannens, E., Van de Walle, R.: A semantic approach to cross-disciplinary research collaboration. International Journal of Emerging Technologies in Learning (iJET) 7(S2), 22–30 (2012)
3. De Vocht, L., Coppens, S., Verborgh, R., Van der Sande, M., Mannens, E., Van de Walle, R.: Discovering meaningful connections between resources in the web of data. In: Proceedings of the 6th Workshop on Linked Data on the Web, LDOW (2013)
4. Vocht, L.D., Mannens, E., de Walle, R.V., Softic, S., Ebner, M.: A search interface for researchers to explore affinities in a linked data knowledge base. In: International Semantic Web Conference (Posters & Demos), pp. 21–24 (2013)
5. White, R.W., Marchionini, G.: Examining the effectiveness of real-time query expansion. Information Processing & Management 43(3), 685–704 (2007)
6. Yee, K.-P., Fisher, D., Dhamija, R., Hearst, M.: Animated exploration of dynamic graphs with radial layout. In: Proceedings of the IEEE Symposium on Information Visualization, INFOVIS (2001)
7. Pintado, X.: The affinity browser. In: Object-oriented Software Composition, pp. 245–272. Prentice Hall (1995)
8. Davis, F.: A Technology Acceptance Model for Empirically Testing New End-user Information Systems: Theory and Results. Massachusetts Institute of Technology (1985)

Author Index